DIAGRAM FOR THE CLASSIFICATION OF WORLD LIFE ZONES OR PLANT FORMATIONS

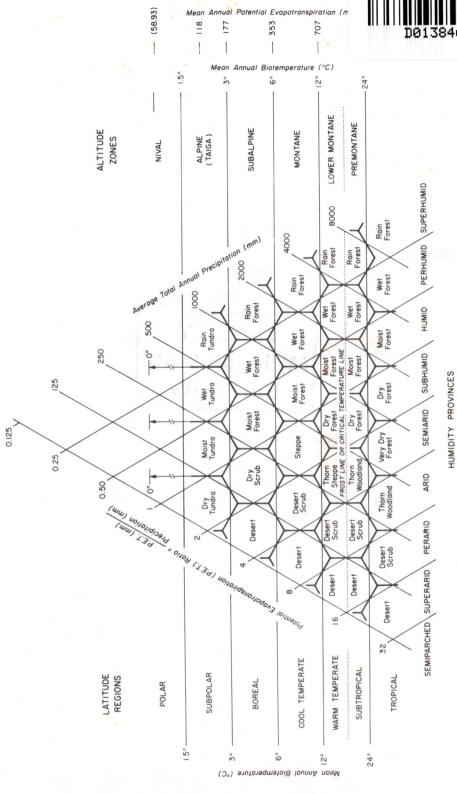

Redrawn from L. R. Holdridge, *Life Zone Ecology*, Tropical Science Center, San Jose, Costa Rica

INTRODUCTION TO
Forest Science

INTRODUCTION TO
Forest Science
SECOND EDITION

RAYMOND A. YOUNG
RONALD L. GIESE

Editors

University of Wisconsin–Madison

WILEY

JOHN WILEY & SONS

New York Chichester Brisbane Toronto Singapore

Cover Design by Laura Nicholls
Cover Photo by Peter Neumann
Mt. Moran; Grand Tetons, WY

Library of Congress Cataloging-in-Publication Data

Introduction to forest science / Raymond A. Young, editor, Ronald L.
  Giese, editor.—2nd ed.
     p.   cm.
  Includes bibliographical references and index.
  ISBN 0-471-85604-5
  1. Forests and forestry.   2. Forests and forestry—United States.
I. Young, Raymond Allen, 1945– . II. Giese, Ronald L.
SD373.I57   1990
634.9—dc20   89-34351

Printed in the United States of America

10 9 8 7 6 5 4 3 2 1

Dedicated to the senior editor's parents, Bill and Sylvia,
who lacked a college education
but not the foresight to ensure his

*To waste, to destroy, our natural resources, to skin
and exhaust the land instead of using it so as to
increase its usefulness, will result in undermining in
the days of our children the very prosperity which
we ought by right to hand down to them amplified
and developed.*

Theodore Roosevelt

Authors and Affiliations

John D. Aber
Department of Forest Resources and Institute for the Study of Earth, Oceans and Space
University of New Hampshire
Durham, New Hampshire

Robert H. Becker
Department of Recreation and Parks Administration
College of Forest and Recreation Resources
Clemson University
Clemson, South Carolina

John Bliss
Department of Forestry
University of Wisconsin–Madison
Madison, Wisconsin

James G. Bockheim
Departments of Soil Science and Forestry
University of Wisconsin–Madison
Madison, Wisconsin

Thomas M. Bonnicksen
Department of Parks and Recreation
Texas A & M University
College Station, Texas

Joseph Buongiorno
Department of Forestry
University of Wisconsin–Madison
Madison, Wisconsin

John W. Duffield
College of Forest Resources
University of Washington
Seattle, Washington

Alan R. Ek
College of Natural Resources
University of Minnesota
St. Paul, Minnesota

Robert D. Gale
Forest Service
U.S. Department of Agriculture
Washington, D.C.

Ronald L. Giese
Department of Forestry
University of Wisconsin–Madison
Madison, Wisconsin

James M. Guldin
Department of Forestry
University of Arkansas
Monticello, Arkansas

Gordon W. Gullion
Cloquet Forestry Center
University of Minnesota
Cloquet, Minnesota

Raymond P. Guries
Department of Forestry
University of Wisconsin–Madison
Madison, Wisconsin

Alan Jubenville
School of Agriculture and Land Resources Management
University of Alaska
Fairbanks, Alaska

Thomas W. Kimmerer
Department of Forestry
University of Kentucky
Lexington, Kentucky

W. David Klemperer
School of Forestry and Wildlife Resources
Virginia Polytechnic Institute and State University
Blacksburg, Virginia

Hans Kubler
Department of Forestry
University of Wisconsin–Madison
Madison, Wisconsin

Wayne C. Leininger
Department of Range Science
Colorado State University
Fort Collins, Colorado

William A. Leuschner
School of Forestry and Wildlife Resources
Virginia Polytechnic Institute and State University
Blacksburg, Virginia

Thomas M. Lillesand
Department of Forestry and Institute for
   Environmental Studies
University of Wisconsin
Madison, Wisconsin

Craig G. Lorimer
Department of Forestry
University of Wisconsin–Madison
Madison, Wisconsin

A. Jeff Martin
Department of Forestry
University of Wisconsin–Madison
Madison, Wisconsin

George L. Martin
Department of Forestry
University of Wisconsin–Madison
Madison, Wisconsin

John N. McGovern
Department of Forestry
University of Wisconsin–Madison
Madison, Wisconsin

Robert F. Patton
Departments of Plant Pathology and Forestry
University of Wisconsin–Madison
Madison, Wisconsin

F. Dale Robertson
Forest Service
U.S. Department of Agriculture
Washington, D.C.

Roger M. Rowell
Forest Products Laboratory
Forest Service
U.S. Department of Agriculture
Madison, Wisconsin

Robert M. Shaffer
School of Forestry and Wildlife Resources
Virginia Polytechnic Institute and State University
Blacksburg, Virginia

John D. Stednick
Department of Earth Resources
Colorado State University
Fort Collins, Colorado

Jeffrey C. Stier
Department of Forestry
University of Wisconsin–Madison
Madison, Wisconsin

Thomas A. Walbridge, Jr.
School of Forestry and Wildlife Resources
Virginia Polytechnic Institute and State University
Blacksburg, Virginia

Harold W. Wisdom
School of Forestry and Wildlife Resources
Virginia Polytechnic Institute and State University
Blacksburg, Virginia

Raymond A. Young
Department of Forestry
University of Wisconsin–Madison
Madison, Wisconsin

Preface

The science of forestry is a complex amalgamation of the biological, physical, managerial, social, and political sciences. Few, if any, forestry professionals are able to treat all aspects of forest science with complete authority. An edited book on forestry is thus the best alternate method for conveying the science of forestry in one text. *Introduction to Forest Science* is intended to provide beginning and intermediate students with a comprehensive introduction to important aspects of the field of forestry. The book represents a collective effort by a number of authors to present a broad view of the field. The authors give general coverage of their specialized fields within forestry and emphasize how decisions made by forest managers affect the forest ecosystem. References to other works that explore certain aspects of forest science are provided for the student interested in greater depth.

It seems that there are as many approaches to the organization of a book in forestry as there are professional foresters. In this book an attempt is made to maintain a flow from the basic cell and individual trees to the forest stand, followed by management of the forest stand, and finally the acquisition of goods and services from the forest. To this end, the book is arranged in four major parts. In the two chapters of the Introduction (Part 1), the development of American forest policy and the location and composition of forests around the world are described. Important events that have shaped forest policy, such as the environmental movement, are treated in the first chapter.

Part 2, Forest Biology, contains information on factors affecting individual tree growth through growth of the forest stand. Biotic and abiotic influences on forest growth are discussed in detail in this section, and the many agents affecting the complex forest ecosystem are analyzed in separate chapters on tree growth, soils, genetics, insects, and diseases.

The management of forest stands for multiple uses is treated in Part 3, Forest Management. Separate chapters are devoted to timber, rangeland, watershed, wildlife, recreation, and fire management. Forest measurements and biological aspects of managing forests (silviculture) are analyzed in depth. Views of the forest at the national level versus those of the private landowners can be compared in successive chapters in this section. The role of private nonindustrial forests, which make up almost 60 percent of commercial forestland, receives special treatment.

Part 4, Forest Products, deals with the conversion of forests to usable commodities. The structure and properties of wood are described, and the methods for conversion to lumber, reconstituted products such as particleboard, paper, chemicals, and energy are illustrated. The forest products economy is analyzed in a separate chapter, with special treatment given to the fuelwood crisis in underdeveloped countries.

In reality, the field of forestry cannot be separated into these four distinct sections because of the interdependence of the many factors affecting the forest. Therefore, the reader is encouraged to refer to other sections or chapters where appropriate. Cross references in the text designate when a specific subject is given more detailed treatment in another chapter. A glossary is also included to aid readers who are not familiar with the specialized terminology used in forestry.

A considerable number of changes have been incorporated into this second edition of *Introduction to Forest Science* in response to constructive criticism from students, colleagues and reviewers. New or totally revised chapters have been incorporated on structure and function of forest trees; forest soils; multiple-use management, planning, and administration; rangeland, watershed, and timber management; harvesting; nonindustrial private forests; measurement of the forest; remote sensing; properties and utilization of wood; wood for fiber, energy, and chemicals; and the forestry profession and career opportunities. Particular attention has been paid to the influence of computer technology and biotechnology in various aspects of forestry. The new edition gives greater deference to forestry in the broader context of natural resources.

As with the previous edition, the second edition of *Introduction to Forest Science* was designed to give students a broad overview of the field of forestry but with sufficient detail that they will be able to assess their specific role as practicing forestry professionals.

The book is intended to be the most advanced introductory text available. Indeed, current forestry professionals would find the text a convenient method for updating their own knowledge of forest science. Certainly the book conveys the broad scope of forestry and the great challenges that lie ahead.

Raymond A. Young
Ronald L. Giese
January 1990

Acknowledgments

The chapter authors and we have received many constructive comments on the chapters and the book from both our colleagues and outside reviewers. Craig Lorimer deserves special acknowledgment for help with several of the biology and management chapters. Appreciation is expressed to Norah Cashin and Benjamin Cashin for constructive comments on material throughout the book and for preparation of the glossary. We are grateful to the departmental secretaries, Pauline Miller, Janet Furrer, Janet Merlo, and Marian Jacobs, for many tedious hours of typing and other clerical assistance. The quotation by Theodore Roosevelt in the dedication was kindly located by Maureen Giese.

We are grateful to the following people for reviews or assistance. Chapter 1, Robert G. Lee, University of Washington; John A. Zivunska, University of California, Berkeley; and Susan L. Flader, University of Missouri. Chapter 4, Tim Ballard, University of British Columbia; David Grigal, University of Minnesota at St. Paul; and James Love, University of Wisconsin–Madison. Chapter 5, Reinhard Stettler, University of Washington; Nicholas Wheeler, Weyerhaeuser. Chapter 6, Jan Henderson, Forest Service. Chapter 7, Daniel Benjamin, University of Wisconsin–Madison. Chapter 8, John Berbee, and John Andrews, University of Wisconsin–Madison. Chapter 14, David Smith, Yale University; William Leak, Northeast Forest Experiment Station; and James Guldin, University of Arkansas. Chapter 17, Mary K. Witte-Ferguson (typing), Cloquet Forestry Center. Chapter 20, David Erickson, University of Kentucky. Chapter 21, Bruce M. Kilgore, National Park Service, Robert W. Mutch, Forest Service; Richard C. Rothermel, Northern Forest Fire Laboratory, Forest Service; and Ronald H. Wakimoto, University of California, Berkeley. Chapter 23, George Hajny, Forest Products Laboratory.

R.A.Y.
R.L.G.

Contents

PART 1

Introduction

Throughout history forests have been important to human beings. Forests provided shelter and protection, and trees provided many products such as food, medicine, fuel, and tools. For example, the bark of the willow tree, when chewed, was used as a painkiller in early Greece and was the precursor of the present-day aspirin; acorns from oak trees were an important food base to the American Indian. Wood served as the primary fuel in the United States until about the turn of the century; indeed, over one-half of the wood now harvested in the world is used for heating fuel. Today over 10,000 products are made from wood.

Forests provide many other benefits, such as control of erosion and flooding, and reduction of wind erosion. In addition to many utilitarian uses, the forest provides important aesthetic features to which quantitative values cannot be assigned. The amenities include forest wildlife such as songbirds, fall coloration, wildflowers, and beautiful landscapes (Figure P1.1). Urbanized society has placed increasing emphasis on preserving the natural qualities of the forest for recreational purposes, escape, and solace. This has led to the designation of "wilderness areas" intended to be unaltered by humans.

Obviously a conflict of interest has arisen over the use of the forest in modern American society. What a member of a preservationist group such as the Sierra Club defines as proper management of the forest will probably be in direct conflict with how a paper industry executive views the use of the forest. The forest manager, although recognizing this conflict, must understand both views and develop a management plan that reflects the values involved in both points of view.

We can now define forestry as the art, science, and practice of managing the natural resources that occur on and in association with forestland for human benefit. This definition necessitates that the forest manager consider not only the trees in the forest, but also such things as protecting wildlife and preserving water systems for drinking and for aquatic life. Foresters are often involved with the control of fire, insect pests, and diseases in the forest, and they can also assume the broad role of protecting the forest environment. The forester is a land manager responsible for all the goods, benefits, and services that flow from the forest (1).

The Multiple Use–Sustained Yield Act of 1960 recognized the many benefits derived from the forest: outdoor recreation, rangeland, timber, watershed protection, and wildlife and fish habitat. All need not be available at every location, but the value of each should be given equivalent recognition on a nationwide basis. Thus a clearcut for timber in a national forest should in some way, be balanced by opportunities for wilderness-type experience at another location. The importance of the legislative process in forestry is further discussed in the first chapter, "The Development of Forest Policy in the United States." In the 1970s we witnessed a dramatic increase in forestry legislation important to the future of forestry practices in the United States.

In conformation with legislation, managers of forests on public lands must strive to have a continual supply of the products, services, and amenities available from the forest. To do this they must have a solid knowledge of science and society. A broad background in physical, biological, and social sciences is a necessity. To this must be added administrative skills and an element of diplomacy for resolving conflicts. Clearly the task of the forest manager is a complex one requiring insight and many learned skills (2, 3).

1

Figure P1.1 A majestic, mature stand of western redcedar in western Washington State. Lichens clothing the dead branches attest to a humid climate. (Courtesy of U.S.D.A. Forest Service.)

The Forest

The forest is a biological community of plants and animals existing in a complex interaction with the nonliving environment, which includes such factors as the soil, climate, and physiography. A continuous canopy of large trees usually distinguishes forests from other types of communities. Forests are widespread, representing almost 30 percent of the earth's land surface, and typically have a predominant species composition; thus there are many *forest types*. The distribution of forest types around the world is discussed in Chapter 2, "Forest Regions of North America and the World." The remainder of the land surface of the earth is composed of desert (31 percent), grasslands (21 percent), polar ice caps and wasteland (11 percent), and croplands (9 percent) (1).

Although trees are the predominant woody vegetation in terms of *biomass,*[1] trees represent only a small proportion of the total *number* of species present in the forest. There are thousands, perhaps

---

[1]Terms that may be unfamiliar to the reader are defined in the Glossary.

millions, of different types of plants and animals in the forest. Shrubs, herbs, ferns, mosses, lichens, and fungi are present beneath the forest canopy and in the gaps of the forest cover. Large animals such as deer and bears coexist with smaller birds, insects, and tiny microorganisms. Each component makes a contribution to the flow of energy and materials through the system.

The forest is a dynamic ecosystem that is continually changing in structure and composition. Disturbances such as fire, windfall, and harvesting produce sites where new communities of trees, plants, and animals can exist and differ from the original forest. Fallen leaves and woody material that reach the forest floor decay and continue the cycling of energy and nutrients through the system. The forest community is a complex unit divided into many areas of study; these areas are treated in specific chapters in the text.

Tree Classification

Trees are generally classified into two categories as seed plants: *angiosperms* with encased seeds and *gymnosperms* with naked seeds (Figure P1.2). The angiosperms are the dominant plant life of this geological era. They are the products of a long line of evolutionary development that has culminated in the highly specialized organ of reproduction known as the flower. The seeds of angiosperms are enclosed in the matured ovary (fruit).

Two classes exist for the angiosperms, the Monocotyledones and the Dicotyledones (Table P1.1). Palms are classified as monocots, and the woody dicots are what we usually refer to as *broad-leaved* trees. Because the broad-leaved trees typically lose their leaves each fall, they are also often referred to as *deciduous* trees. However, a number of exceptions occur, such as southern magnolia or Pacific madrone, both of which retain their leaves all year. The broad-leaved or deciduous trees are also often referred to as *hardwood* trees, although this is a misnomer and does not refer to wood texture. Many broad-leaved trees such as basswood (linden) have soft-textured wood.

The other major class of trees is the gymnosperms, which bear their seeds in cones. The majority of the trees in this classification fall into the division Coniferophyta or *conifers*. A notable exception is the ginkgo tree, the only living species in the division Ginkgophyta. Some of the last living ginkgo

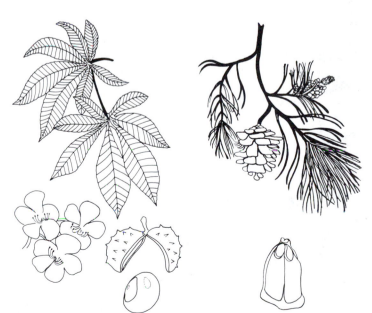

Figure P1.2 Depiction of angiosperms (encased seed) and gymnosperms (naked seed).

Table P1.1 Scientific and Common Terms for Trees

Angiosperms (Magnoliophyta; Encased Seeds)	Gymnosperms (Naked Seeds)
Liliopsida (monocots; parallel-veined leaves)	Cycadophyta
Palms and palmettos (Palmaceae)	Cycads
Yucca (Liliaceae)	Ginkgophyta
Magnoliopsida (dicots; net-veined leaves)	Ginkgo
Common terms for trees in this class[a]	Coniferophyta
Hardwoods	Common terms for trees in this class[a]
Deciduous trees	Softwoods
Broad-leaved trees	Evergreens
	Needle- (or scale-) leaved trees
	Conifers

[a]These terms are considered synonymous in common usage, but it is important to remember that many exceptions occur as described in the text.

Figure P1.3 The ancient ginkgo tree thrives in polluted urban environments and is planted as an ornamental worldwide. (Photograph by R. A. Young.)

trees were located by a botanical expedition in China in 1690. Subsequently seeds from the tree have been planted worldwide (Figure P1.3).

The conifers generally do not lose their needle-like leaves annually in the fall and therefore are termed *evergreens*. Again, there are exceptions such as larch and bald cypress, conifers that lose their needles each year like the broad-leaved trees. The conifers are also referred to as *softwoods*, but, like the hardwoods, the designation does not refer to the texture of the wood but to the *class* of tree. The terminology of hardwoods and softwoods probably originated in the early sawmills when most of the conifers used for timber were the soft-textured pines, whereas the broad-leaved trees were hard-textured maples and oaks. It is important to recognize the synonymous terms, since they are used interchangeably in both the literature and the common language.

References

1. R. D. NYLAND, C. C. LARSON, AND H. L. SHIRLEY, *Forestry and Its Career Opportunities,* Fourth Edition, McGraw–Hill, New York, 1983.

2. C. H. STODDARD, *Essentials of Forestry Practice,* Third Edition, John Wiley & Sons, New York, 1978.

3. G. W. SHARPE, C. W. HENDEE, AND W. F. SHARPE, *Introduction to Forestry,* Fifth Edition, McGraw–Hill, New York, 1986.

CHAPTER 1

The Development of Forest Policy in the United States

Thomas M. Bonnicksen

All residents of the United States derive benefits from forests either indirectly as consumers of forest products or directly as participants in outdoor activities within forest settings. Americans are also making increasingly varied and heavy demands on their forests. Although forest resources are renewable, there is only so much forestland from which to produce these resources, so as demand rises, competition for resources also rises. This competition for resources has led to the formation of interest groups that try to influence elected officials and government agencies on the allocation and management of forest resources. The policy-making process is the means by which these differences are resolved. Understanding this process and the forest policy it generates is the principal focus of this chapter.

According to Boulding, a policy "generally refers to the principles that govern action directed toward given ends" (1). But policies are more than this. They are also hypotheses concerning what is thought will happen in the future if certain actions are taken. Whether or not a policy will achieve the ends specified is always open to question until the results of implementing the policy are actually observed. If the policy does not perform as expected, the whole policy process might be reinitiated. Thus policy-making is a continuous process that is constantly attacking new problems as well as problems generated by past policies (2).

All of a society's history, philosophy, beliefs, attitudes, values, contemporary problems, and hopes are woven into the policy-making process. Furthermore, what is an acceptable forest policy to one society in a given physical setting may be inconceivable to another society in a different physical setting. Although U.S. forest policy incorporates many European forestry principles, it still represents a unique blend of approaches and goals tailored to American needs and circumstances. American forest policy is also continually developing to accommodate change. Thus the forest policies adopted in the late 1800s differ significantly from those adopted in the latter half of the 1900s. Which policies were better at one time cannot be judged using the standards of another time, just as forest policies appropriate to a given society cannot be judged according to the standards of another society.

Profile of Forest Policy Development

Throughout the remainder of this chapter the policy process will be used as the framework for visualizing the historical development of U.S. forest policy. We will look at the broad periods that characterize major shifts in our policies toward forests. In addition, we will describe the environmental context and goals of the policy process within each period, and we will evaluate the results of a policy in terms of those goals.

Because the topic of American forest policy is vast, it was necessary to limit the scope of this analysis. Therefore, we emphasize the federal government's role in forestry and the management of national forests. We also emphasize policies that are stated as legislative statutes, executive orders and decrees, administrative rules and regulations, and court opinions.

Native Americans and Forests (to 1607)

The relationship between American Indians and forests varied from place to place. In some situations the forest provided building materials, food, or both; in others it was an obstacle to cultivation. For instance, in the pre-Columbian period the heavily forested northwestern coast of North America was occupied by seafaring people who were highly skilled woodworkers (3, 4). Although many Indian tribes of the eastern deciduous forests also obtained raw materials from forests, the forest was principally an obstacle to the cultivation of maize, beans, and squash (5).

In some situations, American Indians made a conscious effort to favor certain species of trees over others. In California, for instance, the widespread and abundant oak trees produced acorns, which were the staff of life for the Indian. The Miwok Indians inhabiting Yosemite Valley burned the grass under the black oak trees in the fall to prevent the growth of other trees that could grow taller and shade out the black oak. They also burned to clear the ground so that acorns could be gathered more readily.

American Indians who resided in the forests of North America abided by certain rules while deriving their living from the land. These rules or guidelines were handed down from one generation to the next by word and action. Such an agreed pattern of behavior, which is designed to accomplish a specified goal, fits the definition of a policy. Consequently, although aboriginal peoples did not have forest policies that were explicitly recognized as such, they did have rules that governed their relationship to forests. Whether modern people agree or disagree with these rules is unimportant. What is important is that American Indians had the equivalent of forest policies that were successful in helping them survive.

Colonial Settlers and Forests (1607–1783)

Although the world known to Europe expanded to include North America in 1492, it was not until 1607 that Europeans successfully colonized what is now the United States. The site selected by the Virginia Company of London was Jamestown on the wooded banks of the James River in what is now Virginia.

Forests were the dominant feature of the colonial landscape and became one of its most valued resources. The forests surrounding Jamestown were used not only to construct the town but also as a source of fuel for a thriving glass industry. However, the thick forests made a good hiding place for unfriendly Indians, so the forests had to be cleared to make the area safe and to make room for farms and roads. Thus two attitudes toward forests developed that profoundly influenced forest policies for many generations. First, forests were a nuisance, and the citizen who made the greatest improvement in the land was the one who cut down the most trees. Second, the seemingly unending supply of trees led to an acceptance of waste and a view that forests were inexhaustible.

Wood was the primary fuel and energy source for colonial America and remained so until 1870 (see Figure 23.12). Because the colonists lacked transportation, wood for fuel and building material had to be cut near settlements. As the forest receded from the settlements it became increasingly difficult to haul wood. Although the forests as a whole seemed inexhaustible, local timber supplies were limited. As a result, the first American forest policy on record was established on March 29, 1626, by Plymouth Colony. The policy forbade the transport of any timber out of the colony without the consent of the governor and council. Similar policies were adopted by Rhode Island, New Hampshire, and New Jersey. In 1681 William Penn directed that in Pennsylvania ("Penn's woodland") 0.4 hectare (1 acre) be left forested for every 2 hectares (5 acres) cleared of forest.

Colonial policy-making included political rule by a distant monarchy. This meant that forest policies had to reflect the perceived needs of a distant society as well as the immediate needs of the colonists themselves. The tension between these two interests presented serious limitations for England's forest policies for the New World.

The abundance of large trees made it possible for the colonists to develop a shipbuilding industry. The *Blessing of the Bay,* launched at Medford, Massachusetts, in 1631, marked the beginning of both this industry (6) and a direct conflict with British interests in America's forests. As early as 1609 the first shipment of masts was sent from Virginia to England (6) (Figure 1.1). Trees of sufficient size for masts were scarce, and supply lines from northern and central Europe could be easily disrupted by hostile countries. Furthermore, Great Britain was competing with other countries for masts, so America became its principal source of supply. In order to protect its interests, Great Britain in 1691 granted a new charter to the Province of Massachusetts Bay that reserved for the crown all trees 61 centimeters (24 inches) or more in diameter growing on lands not in private ownership. This became known as the Broad Arrow policy because the reserved trees were marked with a broad arrow blaze—the symbol of the British Navy. By 1721 the Broad Arrow policy covered all colonial lands from Nova Scotia to New Jersey.

Although little is known about how well these policies worked during this period, it is probable that local wood supplies increased. Similarly, the British did obtain a relatively steady supply of masts and other naval timbers during the period. However, the Broad Arrow policy had to be enforced with large fines because it was vigorously opposed by the colonists. In 1772, for instance, in Weare, New Hampshire, Sheriff Benjamin Whiting arrested Ebenezer Mudgett for cutting the king's white pine. The colonists seized the sheriff in the night, beat him with rods, and forced him to ride out of town. This event was known as the "Pine Tree Riot" (6). The Broad Arrow policy was possibly one of the events that led to the American Revolution.

Building and Defending the Republic (1783–1830)

The British formally recognized the independence of the United States with the signing of the Treaty of Paris in 1783. This marked the beginning of America's control of her own forests, but it also served as the beginning of a set of new social and economic problems. The old belief that forests were inexhaustible remained unchanged, however.

The most significant change in the context of the forest policy process that occurred in the aftermath of the revolution was the development of a new government. The first government was based on the Articles of Confederation, a document designed to preserve the states as free and independent sover-

Figure 1.1 A sheer hulk stepping a mainmast. (Courtesy of Mr. Jack Coggins and Stackpole Books.)

eignties while granting Congress limited authority to act on behalf of all the states. The two most important powers denied to Congress were the authority to levy taxes and the authority to regulate commerce. Thus Congress under the confederation was purposely designed to be weak.

Approving the Articles of Confederation required the unanimous consent of all thirteen states. Six states were reluctant to sign because they did not have claims to large tracts of unsettled western lands. States with such lands had an advantage because they could sell them to defray debts incurred during the revolutionary war. Landless Mary-

land refused to sign the Articles of Confederation unless the other states abandoned their land claims. Maryland held out until March 1, 1781, when New York surrendered its western land claims to the federal government and Virginia appeared ready to do the same. Thus ratification of the confederation also marked the beginning of the public domain. (The public domain included all lands that were at any time owned by the United States and subject to sale or other transfer of ownership under the laws of the federal government.)

Congress pledged to dispose of the public domain for the "common benefit," partly to create new states and partly to make good on its promise to grant land to revolutionary soldiers and officers. Since Congress could not levy taxes, it had to use the public domain as a source of revenue to discharge the national debt and operate the government.

Although Congress was weak under the Articles of Confederation, it still managed to pass two major laws that have left their imprint on the landscape to this day. The first of these laws was the Land Ordinance of 1785. It provided that the Old Northwest, a territory lying between the Ohio and Mississippi rivers and the southern shores of the Great Lakes, should be sold to help defray the national debt. The land was also to be surveyed before sale using the now-familiar rectangular grid system of townships

and sections. Only the thirteen original states and Texas, whose admission to the union was contingent on state ownership of public lands, were not subjected to this survey system. The Northwest Ordinance of 1787 further provided that when a territory could claim 60,000 residents it might be admitted by Congress as a state. This scheme worked so well that it was ultimately carried over to other areas of the public domain (Figures 1.2, 1.3).

One of the problems facing the new Congress was the need to build and maintain a strong navy. Thus Congress authorized the construction of six frigates in 1794 and established a Department of the Navy in 1798 (6). Congress passed an act on February 25, 1799, that appropriated $200,000 for the

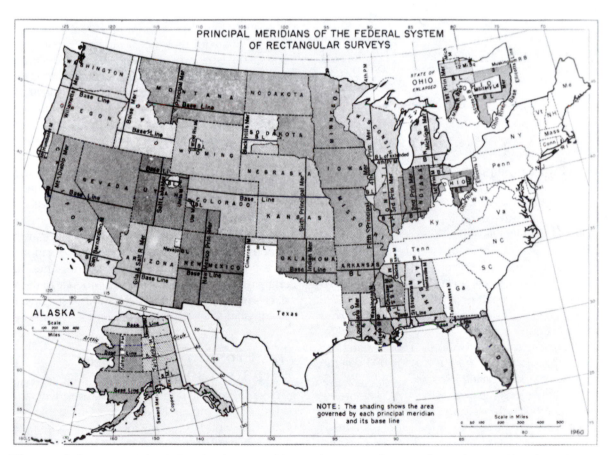

Figure 1.2 States subdivided under the U.S. Public Land Survey and principal meridians and baselines (U.S. Department of Interior).

Figure 1.3 An original witness tree marked by the Land Office in 1843, in Ouachita National Forest, Arkansas. The purpose of these witness trees was to indicate the location of lines in the land survey. (Courtesy of U.S.D.A. Forest Service.)

purchase of timber and lands growing timber suitable for naval construction. Two islands supporting live oak were promptly purchased off the coast of Georgia.

At the outbreak of the War of 1812, the United States had only sixteen ships in its entire navy to throw into battle against the 800 men-of-war in the British navy. By the end of the war the United States had only two or three ships left (7). Congress reacted by passing an act on March 1, 1817, authorizing the secretary of the navy to reserve from sale public-domain lands that supported live oak and red cedar to rebuild the navy. However, the president had to approve each reservation. An act on March 19, 1828, appropriated an additional $10,000 for the purchase of lands bearing live oak.

The timber reserves set aside by Congress received no more support from the public than did the earlier Broad Arrow policy of the British. Looting, or timber trespass, was common. In 1821 the commissioner of the General Land Office instructed his agents to stop illegal cutting on the reserves (6), but

the officials responsible for carrying out the order were political appointees with little interest in confronting thieves in the forest. Congress tried to help by passing an act on February 23, 1822, authorizing the president to use the army and the navy to prevent timber degradations in Florida, but there was little improvement.

Important Features of the Period 1783–1830 Forest policies adopted between 1783 and 1830 produced a mixed result. First, the revenues derived from the sale of public lands did not reach the expected amount. The Land Ordinance of 1785 provided that the lands should be sold in blocks of at least 640 acres (259 hectares) to the highest bidder, but at not less than $1 per acre. Unfortunately, land could be purchased elsewhere at lower prices, and the $640 required as a minimum purchase price proved difficult for most people to raise at the time. Subsequent laws providing for credit sales and a reduction in the minimum area did not improve the situation. As a result, people needing land "squatted" on the public domain in increasing numbers, and efforts to remove them met with little success.

The naval timber reserve policies had a similar result. Since forests were generally regarded as inexhaustible and the public domain was expanding, interest in the reserves gradually declined. Nevertheless, the policy of reserving forestlands as a source of timber set an important precedent for future forest policy decisions. The right of Congress to control the use of public lands in the national interest was also established during this period. Perhaps the most undesirable consequence of these policies was the failure to prevent timber stealing in sparsely settled areas of the frontier.

The Erosion of a Myth (1830–1891)

In 1830 Andrew Jackson was elected president, and control of government by the common people was securely established. Many people in the upper classes sneered at the "New Democracy," referring to "coonskin congressmen" and enfranchised "bipeds of the forest" (7). Nevertheless, politicians who could boast of birth in a log cabin had a real advantage in an election. The sturdy pioneer and settler of the forest was clearly in command.

By 1867, when Alaska was purchased, the public domain had grown an additional 405 million hectares. There was a great need to populate these lands with settlers who could protect them and make them productive. In fact, during this period more than any other, the nation's policy was to transfer the bulk of the land, including forestland, into private ownership and rely on market forces as a primary means for allocating natural resources.

Exploitation of the Forests With a seemingly inexhaustible supply of forests, and a government dominated by people sympathetic to the need for western settlement and economic expansion, a period of rapid exploitation of resources was inevitable. Furthermore, pressure on timberlands was increased by the demand for wood to build towns on the treeless Great Plains, for railroad construction, to fight the Civil War and repair what it destroyed, and to rebuild 10.4 square kilometers of the city of Chicago that burned in the Great Fire of 1871.

Settlers occupying lands on the Great Plains had to import most of their timber. Tree planting was thought to be a reasonable solution and might have the additional benefit of increasing rainfall. In 1866 Commissioner Joseph S. Wilson of the General Land Office supported the idea and recommended that homesteaders be required to plant trees in areas lacking timber (6). Congress responded in 1873 by enacting the Timber Culture Act. Under the law settlers could receive 65 hectares (160 acres) of public land by planting 16 hectares (40 acres) of it with trees.

With the exception of railroad land grants, most of the policies enacted during this period focused on the development of agriculture. However, by 1878 it became obvious that large areas of the public domain were more suitable for timber production than agriculture, and no provision had been made for the acquisition of these timberlands, or the timber, by the public. Congress tried to remedy the situation by passing two laws in 1878: the Free Timber Act and the Timber and Stone Act. The Free Timber Act stipulated that residents of nine western states could cut timber for building, mining, and other purposes without charge to aid in the development of their farms and mineral claims (Figure 1.4). Although this act was well intentioned, and undoubtedly provided substantial aid to deserving settlers, it was nevertheless widely abused. Enforcement of both the act and regulations issued by the secretary of the interior for its administration was nearly impossible.

The Timber and Stone Act provided that unoccupied, surveyed land that was principally valuable for timber production or stone, but not agriculture, could be purchased in 65-hectare (160-acre) tracts for $2.50 per acre in Washington, Oregon, California, and Nevada. The purchaser had to swear that the land was for personal use and not for speculation.

Throughout this period two major forest policy problems existed. First, speculation and fraud in the acquisition of public lands was rampant. Speculators and lumber executives interested in accumulating large holdings of timberland took advantage of almost every policy for the disposal of the public domain. Most of these policies were designed to encourage small owner–operator farms, but there was little control over what the owner did with the land after purchasing it. Military land bounties, for example, were granted to soldiers for their service and to encourage them to enlist. However, many soldiers were not interested in settling the frontier and sold their land to speculators and large companies. The volume of sales became so great that bounty warrants were quoted on the New York Stock Exchange (6).

Some timber operators made no pretense of purchasing timberlands but simply set up lumber mills on the public domain and began cutting trees. In other cases they purchased 40-acre (16-hectare) plots and proceeded to cut all the surrounding public timber on as much as a section of land. These were known as "round forties" or "rubber forties" because of the flexibility of the boundaries.

The beginning of the end of timber stealing occurred in 1877 with the appointment of Carl Schurz as secretary of the interior. Schurz immigrated to America from Germany where forest re-

Figure 1.4 Native Americans used wood under provisions of the Free Timber Act, Black Hills National Forest, South Dakota, in 1931. (Courtesy of U.S.D.A. Forest Service.)

sources were scarce and carefully husbanded. He advocated a similar approach to forest management in the United States. He also took exception to the popular belief that timber resources were inexhaustible. In his first annual report Schurz predicted that within 20 years the timber supply would not be capable of meeting national needs (8).

Schurz began vigorously to enforce laws against timber stealing (6). His authority was based primarily on an act of March 2, 1831, known as the Timber Trespass Law, which imposed both fines and imprisonment on those who cut timber from the public lands without authorization. In 1850 the U.S. Supreme Court upheld the act and extended it to include any trespass on public lands.

Conservation and Preservation of the Forests
The period from 1830 to 1891 was characterized primarily by rapid disposal and exploitation of the public domain. But the myth that timber and other resources were inexhaustible, though still widely held, was gradually eroding, and a concern for conservation and preservation was intensifying. As early as 1801 publications by Andre Michaux and his son, after their travels through the forests of the

United States, noted "an alarming destruction of the trees" and warned that an increasing population would make timber scarce (6). By 1849 the commissioner of patents was also warning of timber shortages (6); in 1864 George Perkins Marsh published his famous book *Man and Nature,* which pointed out the undesirable consequences of forest destruction. Beginning about 1866 annual reports from the secretary of the interior and the commissioner of the General Land Office regularly included an expression of concern about the exhaustion of forest resources.

In 1867 this concern was translated into action at the state level when the legislatures of both Michigan and Wisconsin appointed committees to investigate the potential long-term consequences of deforestation. The most dramatic state action was taken in 1885 by New York, when it created a "forest preserve" on state-owned lands in the Adirondack and Catskill mountains. In 1894 the new state constitution of New York forbade timber cutting on the preserve. Also in 1885, California established a State Board of Forestry and granted it police powers two years later.

Federal action aimed at forest conservation began

about this same time. In 1874 a committee of the American Association for the Advancement of Science (AAAS) prevailed on President Ulysses S. Grant to ask Congress to create a commission of forestry (6). Congress responded by attaching an amendment to the Sundry Civil Appropriations Bill of 1876, which provided $2000 to hire someone to study forest problems in the United States. This act also established a precedent by assigning the position to the Department of Agriculture. Henceforth, federal forest management would be primarily a responsibility of this department.

Franklin B. Hough, who had chaired the AAAS committee on forest preservation, was appointed to the job of studying America's forests. He discharged his duties by publishing three monumental reports containing most of what was known about forestry in the United States at that time. Later he became chief of the Division of Forestry, which was subsequently given statutory permanence in the Department of Agriculture by an act on June 30, 1886. This division was the precursor of the Forest Service. In that same year, Bernard E. Fernow, who had studied forestry in western Prussia, followed Hough as chief of the division.

The preservation movement, which was to have a profound effect on forest policy, also developed during this period. In 1832 George Catlin, a painter and explorer of the American West, called for establishment of "a nation's park" in the Great Plains, "containing man and beast, in all the wild and freshness of their nature's beauty!" (9). Catlin's plea for preservation was echoed by Henry David Thoreau in 1858, when he asked in an article in the *Atlantic Monthly,* "why should not we . . . have our national preserves . . . for inspiration and our true re-creation?" (10). Catlin and Thoreau were followed by other well-known preservationists such as Frederick Law Olmsted and John Muir. Together they helped to found our present system of national parks and monuments beginning with Yellowstone National Park, which was set aside in 1872 "as a public park or pleasuring-ground for the benefit and enjoyment of the people." Sequoia and General Grant (now Kings Canyon) national parks followed in 1890.

Important Features of the Period 1830– 1891 The period from 1830 to 1891 saw three separate movements. One, an exploitive movement, was to dispose of the public domain and cut forests intensively, but at the same time—and partly in response—two other movements encouraged scientific management of resources and preservation of natural scenery. One major success in meeting the goals of the period stands out clearly. About 405 million hectares, which was nearly the same amount of land as entered the public domain during this period, were sold to private owners (6). However, much of this land did not end up in the hands of small farmers but was added to large corporate holdings. Another major success was the encouragement of western expansion and settlement, but here, too, the benefits were mixed with problems. A quarter-section of land that was just the right size for the East, where water was plentiful, was completely inadequate for sustaining a farmer in the arid West. Thus many farms were abandoned and abused. Finally, prodigious amounts of timber products were produced, but a legacy of cutover and deteriorated land was handed to subsequent generations. Nevertheless, this period ended with a rapidly growing and prosperous nation that had already taken major steps toward improving the use of its forests.

Crystallizing a Philosophy (1891–1911)

The circumstances that affected forest policy in the United States between 1891 and 1911 were different from those of any previous period in American history. The shift from rural to urban life was accelerating. In 1790 only 2.8 percent of the population lived in cities with 10,000 or more people; by 1900 it was 31.8 percent (7). An urban population often perceives natural resources differently than a rural population, whose livelihood is directly and visibly dependent on the land. Thus this period clearly contains the conflict between urban residents of the Eastern Seaboard and their strong desire for preservation, and the rural residents of the West who wanted to expand their economy by developing resources.

This was the first period that began without a geographic frontier. In 1890 the superintendent of the census in Washington announced that a frontier line no longer existed (3). All of the United States and its territories contained settlements. Although the myth of inexhaustible resources had been eroding for decades, the loss of the frontier and the scalped land of the once heavily forested East made it obvious that something had to be done to conserve forests and other resources. A "timber famine" was seen as a real possibility.

Three general domestic goals of residents of the United States during this period strongly affected forest policies: defend the rights of the people, maintain a continuous supply of timber, and prevent waste in the exploitation of natural resources, particularly timber.

Creation of Forest Reserves Perhaps the single most important forest policy ever enacted in the United States was the General Revision Act of 1891. Important provisions of the act included the repeal of the Timber Culture Act of 1878 and the Preemption Act of 1841, as well as the imposition of restrictions on the Homestead Act of 1862 to discourage speculation and fraud. What made this act so important to forestry was Section 24, which provided that "the President of the United States may, from time to time, set apart and reserve any part of the public lands wholly or in part covered with timber or undergrowth, whether of commercial value or not." Thus the authority granted to the president by Section 24 (also known as the Forest Reserve Act) to set aside forest reserves from the public domain served as the basis for the U.S. system of national forests.

Less than a month after the Forest Reserve Act passed, on March 30, 1891, President Benjamin Harrison established the Yellowstone Park Forest Reservation. Over the next two years he proclaimed an additional fourteen forest reserves, bringing the total to over 5.3 million hectares. A storm of protests from western interests followed these proclamations, in part because the Forest Reserve Act did not include any provision for using the reserves. Consequently, the argument made by westerners that the

forest reserves were "locked up" and could not be used was absolutely correct. Logging, mining, or any other activity could not be legally conducted on the reserves. Nevertheless, there were too few agents and too little money to enforce the law, so timber stealing proceeded unobstructed.

Just a few months before the Forest Reserve Act passed Congress, Gifford Pinchot, the most famous person in the history of American forest policy, returned home from Europe where he had been studying foresty under Dr. Dietrich Brandis in France. Pinchot's motto, from the beginning of his career until the end, was "forestry is tree farming" (11). He did not believe in preserving forests but in using them "wisely."

Pinchot emerged on the national scene in forest policy when he joined a forest commission of the National Academy of Sciences, which was formed at the request of Secretary of the Interior Hoke Smith. The commission was charged with studying the question of forest reserves and their administration. In addition, it was supposed to make recommendations for new legislation that would help break the deadlock in Congress over the management of the reserves.

The commission submitted a list of proposed forest reserves to President Grover Cleveland without a plan for their management. Pinchot argued, without success, that such a plan should accompany the list so that western congressional representatives would know that the commission wanted to use the forests and not simply lock them up. Cleveland had only ten days left in office and was forced to act on the commission's recommendation. On February 22, 1897, he set aside an additional 8.6 million hectares of forest reserves.

Once again a storm of criticism arose in Congress, and legislation was introduced to nullify Cleveland's actions. Congress acted quickly to resolve the issue. On June 4, 1897, the Sundry Civil Appropriations Act was passed with an amendment (known as the Organic Administration Act) introduced by Senator Richard Pettigrew of South Dakota, providing that "no public forest reservation shall be established except to improve and protect the forest . . . for the purpose of securing favorable conditions of water flows, and to furnish a continuous supply of timber." The act excluded lands principally valuable for mining and agriculture, and it authorized the secretary of the interior to make rules for the reserves "to regulate their occupancy and use and to preserve the forests thereon from destruction."

The language in this act dated back as far as 1893 when Representative Thomas C. McRae introduced the first in a long series of bills for the management of the forest reserves. Early opposition to these bills came from western senators whose constituents were accustomed to obtaining their timber from the public lands without paying a fee. When a compromise was finally reached to handle western criticism, eastern senators continued to block passage of the bill because they feared that opening up the reserves would lead to more abuses by timber owners. Cleveland's bold action in setting aside reserves served as the catalyst to overcome the impasse in Congress. Enough votes were obtained to pass the bill, because even some eastern senators thought the new reserves created a hardship for people in the West.

The forest reserves were placed in the hands of the General Land Office, which was still, as Pinchot put it, governed by "paper work, politics, and patronage" (11). Reform seemed impossible, so when Pinchot became head of the Division of Forestry on July 1, 1898, he immediately set out to gain control of the reserves.

Pinchot was aided in his quest by his good friend Theodore Roosevelt, who became president in September 1901, after President William McKinley was assassinated. Roosevelt and Pinchot were both master politicians—persuasive, dedicated, and equipped with boundless energy (Figure 1.5). They were both driven by the same ideas about the meaning of conservation, epitomized by such words and phrases as *efficiency, wise use, for the public good,* and *the lasting good of men.* To them conservation was the "antithesis of monopoly" and, though wealthy themselves, they both abhorred "concentrated wealth," which they viewed as "freedom to use and abuse the common man" (11).

With the help of Roosevelt, Pinchot accomplished his goal to gain custody of the forest reserves. The

Figure 1.5 Chief forester Gifford Pinchot (right) with President Theodore Roosevelt on the riverboat *Mississippi* in 1907. (Courtesy of U.S.D.A. Forest Service.)

reserves were transferred from the Department of the Interior to the Department of Agriculture by the Transfer Act of 1905. One month later, on March 3, 1905, the name of Pinchot's agency was changed to the Forest Service. In 1907 the forest reserves were renamed the national forests.

Management of the forest reserves changed dramatically under the new regime. On the day the Transfer Act was signed, Secretary of Agriculture James Wilson sent a letter to Pinchot outlining the general policies he was to follow in managing the reserves. Actually, the letter was written by Pinchot (6). In keeping with the philosophy of the time, the letter required that the reserves be used "for the permanent good of the whole people, and not for the temporary benefit of individuals or companies." It also stipulated that "all the resources of the reserves are for use" and "where conflicting interests must be reconciled the question will always be decided from the standpoint of the greatest good of the greatest number in the long run" (6). These lofty, although somewhat ambiguous, goals still serve to guide Forest Service administration.

Many additional landmark policies affecting U.S. forests were enacted during this period. For example, the precedent set by the Forest Reserve Act was copied in the American Antiquities Act of 1906. This act authorized the president "to declare by proclamation . . . objects of historic or scientific interest" on the public lands "to be national monuments." This gave the lands protection against commercial utilization and opened them up for scientific, educational, and recreation purposes. By the end of his administration, Roosevelt had used the act to set aside eighteen national monuments, including what later became Grand Canyon, Lassen Volcanic, and Olympic national parks.

Roosevelt enlarged the area of the forest reserves more than any other president. At the beginning of his term there were 41 reserves totalling 18.8 million hectares, and by 1907 he had increased the number of reserves (now called national forests) to 159, bringing their total area up to 61 million hectares (12). Roosevelt's zealous expansion of the forest reserves moved Congress to pass an act on March 4, 1907, revoking his authority to establish reserves in six western states. Roosevelt left the act unsigned until after he had signed proclamations reserving an additional 30.4 million hectares of forestland (12).

The end of this period is marked by a controversy between Pinchot and Secretary of the Interior Richard A. Ballinger that led President William Howard Taft to fire Pinchot as chief of the Forest Service on January 7, 1910. Actually, Pinchot had decided several months earlier to "make the boss fire him" (12). He was upset by the policies of the Taft administration, which, in his view, did not carry on the traditions of Roosevelt and the philosophy of conservation.

Important Features of the Period 1891–1911. The period from 1891 to 1911 was undoubtedly one of the most colorful and active in the history of American forest policy. The goals that were formulated were clearly followed throughout the period. Nevertheless, eliminating waste and bringing the management of national forests up to the standard hoped for by Pinchot and Roosevelt constituted too great a task to be accomplished with meager funding and little time. The greatest forest policy accomplishments of the period were the creation of the Forest Service, the establishment of a system of national forests, and the crystallization of a utilitarian philosophy of conservation to guide their management.

Organization, Action, and Conflict (1911–1952)

The United States and most of the rest of the world faced enormous difficulties and hardships during the period from 1911 to 1952. The world went to war twice, taking a frightening toll in human lives and property, and underwent the agonies of the Great Depression. In the United States disastrous floods regularly ripped through some settled valleys, while large expanses of potentially good agricultural land in the West remained unused for lack of water. Intolerable working conditions and low wages drove urban laborers out into the streets to protest. At the same time, on the Great Plains, a lack of understanding of drought cycles and proper farming practices drove farmers off the land as the soil and their livelihood blew out of the region during the dust bowl era.

These were difficult years, but they were also relatively simple years in the sense that the problems faced were clearly understood by most people, and the goals, though always controversial, were also fairly clear. In forest policy, these goals included (1) keeping the watersheds of navigable streams and rivers covered with vegetation so that flooding and sedimentation could be reduced, (2) keeping sufficient wood flowing out of the forests to meet the nation's requirements for building its industries and successfully ending its wars, (3) protecting the nation's forests from overexploitation and losses due to insects, diseases, and fire, and (4) using the production of forest resources from public lands to aid in reducing unemployment during the Great Depression and in stabilizing the economies of communities dependent on local forests. In addition, a small but influential segment of society was also inspiring the public to preserve tangible parts of the United States' cultural and natural heritage.

Conservation versus Preservation Toward the end of Pinchot's term in the Forest Service, the conservation philosophy of people such as Catlin, Thoreau, and Muir was gaining ground. Private organizations were rapidly forming to represent this view. These "aesthetic conservationists," or preservationists, differed significantly from "Pinchot" or "utilitarian conservationists." Preservationists concentrated their efforts on protecting natural beauty and scenic attractions from the lumberjack's axe and miner's pick by placing them within national parks. On the other hand, the utilitarian conservationists' philosophy was rooted in the idea that resources must be "used." They referred to preservationists as "misinformed nature lovers" (12). This difference of opinion finally led preservationists to break away from the organized conservation movement because it was dominated by the utilitarian philosophy.

When conservationists and preservationists ceased to be allies, conflict over the disposition and management of the public lands was inevitable. This conflict has grown in intensity over the years. By the late 1960s and 1970s, it dominated American forest policy.

During the early 1900s the conflict between preservationists and conservationists centered on dividing up the public lands. At first, preservationists focused their efforts on creating a separate agency to manage the national parks. Pinchot countered this move by trying to consolidate the national parks with the national forests. Although the preservationists succeeded in gaining the support of Taft and Ballinger, Pinchot, arguing that such an agency was "no more needed than two tails to a cat" (12), carried enough influence in Congress to block the proposal. However, Secretary of the Interior Franklin K. Lane

came to the rescue of preservationists. He placed all national parks and monuments under the jurisdiction of an assistant to the secretary. He then filled the post with Steven T. Mather, a wealthy preservationist who helped usher the National Park Act of 1916 through Congress and was later selected as director of the Park Service. Thus preservationists obtained an administrative home in the Department of the Interior for their parks and monuments, and they gained a champion to expand and protect the national park system.

Pinchot was no longer chief of the Forest Service, but his successors during the early 1900s, Henry S. Graves (1910–1920) and William B. Greely (1920–1928), were utilitarian conservationists. Furthermore, Pinchot continued to be influential with Congress, both as an individual and through the National Conservation Association. Thus the adversaries were firmly entrenched in two separate agencies within two separate departments of the federal government, and each had its own constituency. Their first contest centered on the fact that the national forests contained most of the public land suitable for national parks, and the Park Service was anxious to take these lands away from the Forest Service.

The Forest Service was not really hostile toward national parks, but as Chief Forester Graves said, "the parks should comprise only areas which are not forested or areas covered only with protective forest which would not ordinarily be cut" (8). The problem was philosophical and, of course, territorial. The Forest Service, like any other government agency, did not want to give up land it was already managing. Therefore, the Forest Service countered Park Service advances by vigorously resisting the withdrawal of national forestland for park purposes. The Forest Service also continued its efforts to develop a recreation program that it hoped would make new national parks unnecessary.

Forest Recreation The formulation of a recreation program by the Forest Service also represented a response to a technological innovation—the automobile—and the expansion of roads pleasure-seekers could use to gain access to the national forests. In 1907 there were about 8000 kilometers (4971 miles) of roads in all the national forests. The need for roads increased with automobile use and, as a result, between 1916 and 1921 over $33 million was spent on roads in and near national forests (10). These roads brought in so many recreationists that rangers, concerned about fire hazards and other conflicts with commodity uses, sought to discourage them by concealing entrances to new trails and leaving roads unposted (10). The tide of recreationists could not be turned, however, and the Forest Service reluctantly began providing for their needs.

One of the most celebrated accomplishments in national forest recreation was the establishment of the nation's first designated wilderness area. In 1918 a road was proposed that would cut through the watershed of the Gila River in New Mexico. Aldo Leopold, an assistant district forester for the Forest Service, protested against building the road, claiming that "the Gila is the last typical wilderness in the southwestern mountains" (10). He then proposed designating the watershed a "wilderness" without roads or recreational developments. No action was taken on his proposal and, in 1921, when an appropriation of $13.9 million for developing forest roads and highways passed Congress, he publicly expressed his concern for wilderness protection. He defined wilderness as "a continuous stretch of country preserved in its natural state, open to lawful hunting and fishing, big enough to absorb a two weeks pack trip, and kept devoid of roads, artificial trails, cottages or the works of man" (10). This definition has remained relatively unchanged until the present.

It took nearly three more years for Leopold to convince the district forester of New Mexico and Arizona to approve the Gila Wilderness plan. This was only a local decision. However, with criticism of the Forest Service by preservationists mounting, and Park Service acquisition of national forestlands on the increase, Greely established a national wilderness system in 1926.

Although the Forest Service had to spend part of its time defending itself against incursions from the Park Service, it was still a popular and aggressive agency. The momentum of the Roosevelt–Pinchot era had slowed somewhat, but the Forest Service maintained a strong sense of mission. It advanced on four fronts: expanding national forests in the East, promoting forest research, developing the national forests, and regulating forest practices on private land.

Agitation from preservationists for adding lands to the national forest system in the East continued. As early as 1901 the Appalachian National Park Association joined with other private organizations to petition Congress for the preservation of southern Appalachian forests. By that time, however, most public lands in the East had already passed into private ownership. This meant that additional national forests would have to be purchased. Congress responded by authorizing studies of the question, but no purchases were made. A few years later the Society for the Protection of New Hampshire Forests joined forces with the Appalachian group, and together they succeeded in securing passage of the Weeks Act of 1911 (11).

The Weeks Act specified that the federal government could purchase lands on the headwaters of navigable streams and appropriated funds for their acquisition. This restrictive language reflected a congressional view that the federal government had the power to purchase national forests only if it appeared that the purchase would aid navigation. Naturally, the advocates of eastern forest reserves, including Pinchot, shifted their arguments from an emphasis on the forests themselves to the role of forests in preventing floods and reducing sedimentation. These arguments worked, and, influenced by the great Mississippi flood of 1927, Congress accelerated the acquisition of forestland when it passed the Woodruff–McNary Act of 1928 (13). By 1961 over 8.1 million hectares of forestland, mostly in the East, had been purchased under this act (8).

Forestry Research The second major task of the Forest Service was expanding its efforts in forest research. Documenting the relationship between forests and streamflow was part of the reason for the rise in forest research activity. However, reforesting cutover lands, increasing yields, and reducing waste through greater utilization of trees were also important goals of research.

Raphael Zon deserves much of the credit for the organization of research within the Forest Service. His emphasis was on applied research; he stated that "science . . . must serve mankind" (13). In 1908 he presented a plan to Pinchot for establishing forest experiment stations on key national forests. Pinchot, recalling his response, said that "I had seen forest experiment stations abroad and I knew their value. The plan, therefore, was approved at once" (11). When Pinchot left office in 1910, he had established two forest experiment stations and he had authorized the construction of the Forest Products Laboratory in Madison, Wisconsin.

Over the next fifteen years Congress was extremely tightfisted with research funding. A big boost came in 1925, when enough funds were appropriated to add six new experiment stations. Yet funding was haphazard at best, severely limiting research activities. With Greeley's enthusiastic support, the Forest Service obtained the assistance of private groups to campaign in Congress for long-

term research funding. Their efforts paid off in 1928 with passage of the McSweeney–McNary Act. This act raised research to the same level of importance as other Forest Service functions, such as timber and grazing. Furthermore, the act not only increased appropriations for forest research but also authorized a nationwide survey of timber resources in the United States.

Civilian Conservation Corps Development of the national forests received increased attention when President Franklin D. Roosevelt established the Civilian Conservation Corps (CCC) by executive order on April 5, 1933, as part of his New Deal. In a March 21, 1933, document asking Congress for its support of the CCC, Roosevelt detailed his goals as not only "unemployment relief" during the Great Depression but also advance work in "forestry, the prevention of soil erosion, flood control and similar projects." He also thought of the CCC's work as an investment "creating future national wealth" (9).

Between 1933 and 1942, when the CCC started to disband because of World War II, over two million people had worked in the program with as many as half a million enrolled at one time (Figure 1.6). The

Figure 1.6 Civilian Conservation Corps camp in the territory of Alaska. (Courtesy of U.S.D.A. Forest Service.)

Forest Service received nearly half the projects, but the Park Service and other federal agencies also received substantial aid from the program (8). Although the CCC was criticized for hiring enrollees from lists of Democrats (8), its accomplishments outweighed its problems. Young people built trails, thinned forests, fought fires, planted trees, and constructed campgrounds and other facilities. Their efforts substantially advanced the development of the national forests.

Regulation and Control of the Forests The final and most controversial action by the Forest Service during the period was its attempt to regulate private forest management. The agency had played an advisory role in private timber management until passage of the Transfer Act of 1905, when much of its attention shifted to managing the newly acquired national forests. This cooperation with private owners was generally accepted as beneficial by all concerned at the time. However, Pinchot later recalled that he had been "misled" into thinking that timber owners were interested in "practicing forestry" (11).

The regulation issue created a split in the ranks of professional foresters. Pinchot led the faction in favor of federal control, and Graves and Greely led the fight for state control. Pinchot argued that "forest devastation will not be stopped through persuasion" and his solution was "compulsory nation-wide legislation" (6). Pinchot firmly believed that state legislatures were too easily controlled by the lumber industry. Only the federal government, in his view, had the power to enforce regulations. The Forest Service argued that federal regulation was unconstitutional and that the federal role should be aimed more at cooperation than at direct intervention in private forest management.

The line was drawn and Congress became the battlefield. Bills were introduced favoring each position and both sides stood firm. Pinchot said it was "a question of National control or no control at all" (8). The two bills were stalemated in Congress. Greely then proposed to break the deadlock with a compromise measure that dropped regulation entirely and emphasized fire control. After all, he

contended, timber cutting was "insignificant" in comparison to wildfires as a cause of deforestation (8). Pinchot agreed (8), and Congress passed the Clarke–McNary Act of 1924.

Although the Weeks Act previously authorized state and federal cooperation in fire control, the Clarke–McNary Act expanded this cooperation and extended it into other areas as well. For example, it enabled the secretary of agriculture to assist states in growing and distributing planting stock, and in providing aid to private owners in forest management. These two acts stimulated the establishment of state forestry organizations throughout the country.

The Clarke–McNary Act also set a precedent by authorizing the purchase of land in the watersheds of navigable streams for timber production as well as streamflow protection. The purchase of timberland, particularly after it had been logged, was one approach to solving the deforestation problem on which most parties could agree. Overall, the Clarke–McNary Act is one of the most important pieces of legislation in the development of American forest policy.

World War II increased the nation's appetite for timber. Not only was it necessary to harvest great quantities of timber from both public and private lands, but certain important species were also in short supply. For example, Sitka spruce was needed for airplane construction, and at one point loggers were almost allowed to move into Olympic National Park to cut the necessary trees. Rapid cutting to satisfy wartime timber requirements intensified the public-regulation controversy. Timber executives mounted a major publicity campaign to thwart further attempts at federal regulation. They were particularly concerned that conditions might be attached to cooperative funds allocated under the Clarke–McNary Act.

The heightened pressure on forest resources induced by the war and by the regulation controversy, motivated passage of a number of pieces of forestry legislation. The continued threat of federal control helped lumber interests decide to support state laws as the least offensive alternative. By 1939 five states had enacted legislation to curtail destructive cutting practices, but they were generally ineffective. The Oregon Forest Conservation Act of 1941 set the precedent for more effective state action. This law was aimed primarily at securing and protecting tree reproduction, and it included several specific and even quantitative guidelines. Lumber owners could deviate from practices specified in the law only if they first obtained state approval for an alternative timber management plan. The state forester was also authorized to correct problems on timberlands caused by violating the law and to charge the cost to the owners. Similar acts were passed in Maryland (1943), Mississippi (1944), Washington (1945), California (1945), and Virginia (1948). Other states, such as Massachusetts (1943), Vermont (1945), New York (1946), and New Hampshire (1949), relied more on incentives and voluntary actions to control timber cutting on private land (6).

At the federal level, two major forest policies were enacted. In 1944 federal income tax laws were amended to allow any timber owner to declare net revenue from timber sales as capital gains instead of as ordinary income. This law reduced taxes for timber owners to encourage them to retain forestland in timber production. It was also supposed to discourage them from abandoning the land to avoid paying delinquent taxes. Roosevelt vetoed the bill, but his veto was overridden by Congress (8).

The second measure passed by Congress was the Sustained Yield Forest Management Act of 1944. Sustained yield, in a general sense, means that a particular area is managed to produce roughly equal annual, or regular periodic, yields of a resource such as timber. This concept can be traced back hundreds of years in Europe where timber resources were scarce, and predictable and steady yields were essential. The U.S. frontier economy made such an approach politically difficult to adopt until war-induced shortages helped to make the idea more acceptable.

The Sustained Yield Forest Management Act was not aimed at national needs. Instead, it focused on safeguarding the economies of forest-dependent communities from local timber shortages. The act authorized the secretaries of interior and agriculture to establish sustained-yield units composed of either federal timberland alone or, where ownerships intermingled, a mixture of private and public timberland. Thus the secretaries could enter into long-term agreements with private forest owners to pool their resources with the government to supply timber to local mills. Opposition from small companies and labor unions prevented the establishment of more than one cooperative sustained-yield unit. However, the Forest Service did manage to establish five federal sustained-yield units on national forests (8).

The rapid and destructive cutting practices associated with the need to pursue a war left millions of hectares that were not reproducing timber. Equally troubling was the fact that timber cutting during and immediately after the war exceeded forest growth. The Forest Service again laid the blame squarely on the shoulders of private timberland owners. The debate became more acrimonious as each side argued its position. Often technical arguments were set aside and the issue degenerated into an emotional debate. One timber industry spokesperson accused the Forest Service of leading the country into "totalitarian government and ultimately socialism" and even called the assistant chief of the Forest Service, Edward C. Crafts, a "dangerous man" because Crafts felt the public had the right to protect its interests in private land (8).

The debate was settled when Dwight D. Eisenhower let it be known during his presidential campaign that he was against "federal domination of the people through federal domination of their natural resources" (8). Eisenhower was elected president in 1952 and made Governor Sherman Adams of New Hampshire his presidential assistant. Adams had been a lumberman and had stated a year earlier that natural resources could be conserved and distributed "without succumbing either to dictatorship or national socialism" (8). The Forest Service, sensing that the election might bring a philosophical change, moved to have Richard E. McArdle appointed chief, in part because he was not identified with the regulation issue (14). The decision proved to be sound. McArdle dropped the Forest Service campaign for regulation and retained his position through the change of administrations.

Important Features of the Period 1911–1952 An evaluation of forest policies between 1911 and 1952 shows the usual mixture of successes and failures. The goal of preventing overexploitation of forest resources conflicted with furnishing the armed forces with the wood needed to help fight World Wars I and II. Maintaining a forest cover in the headwaters of navigable streams was only partially accomplished. All such watersheds could not be purchased, and cutover lands that were purchased were not always reforested. Similarly, technological constraints and shortages of money and workers during much of the period made it difficult to protect forests adequately from insects, diseases, and fire.

Nevertheless, at least four major accomplishments can be cited for this period, although none of them was considered a major societal goal when the period began in 1911. The national park system grew in size to include some of the nation's most scenic areas, and a new agency was established to coordinate their management. Next, a wilderness system was established by the Forest Service. Another important accomplishment was the development of cooperative arrangements in forest management among state, federal, and private timberland owners. Finally, the CCC converted the adversity of the Great Depression into one of the most positive contributions ever made to the development of U.S. forests.

Adjusting to Complexity (1952–present)

Although the forest policy problems of previous periods were never really simple, they still seem more comprehensible then the problems faced by contemporary society. Since World War II the United States has experienced unparalleled material affluence and technological advances; along with a burgeoning population, they have heightened competition for essential natural resources. After World War II came a rapid growth in demand for timber, particularly for housing construction. This demand resulted in a continuation of destructive logging practices. Timber needs were too great to be satisfied from private lands alone, so heavy logging also reached into the national forests.

At the same time, the prosperity that was supported by the rapid exploitation of natural resources also made it possible for people to spend more of their leisure time in the nation's forests. Extractive use and recreational use, other than hunting, generally conflict with each other. However, the issues were broader than those that produced the debates between preservationists and utilitarian conservationists. Preservation was only one of many environmental issues that society faced both then and now. All these issues influenced the development of U.S. forest policy.

Forest policies were also influenced by such global events as the cold war, the war in Vietnam, and Watergate. The government's lack of candor concerning these problems caused a large segment of society to become more suspicious of many public officials. Consequently, distrust of those in authority, including professional foresters, was widespread. Public demands for citizen participation in resource management decision making were largely a result of this lack of trust. Professional foresters were unprepared for this intense public scrutiny.

Most of the forest policy goals of the period between 1911 and 1952 were carried over into this period as well. The termination of Forest Service efforts to impose federal regulation of private forest management in 1952 was a major turning point for the forestry profession. Foresters were accustomed to strong public support for their aggressive actions to improve forest management. Now they were on the defensive. In addition, there was a great need to find ways to minimize conflicts over the allocation of resources, and to provide a growing nation with more raw materials and services from a fixed land base.

Achieving these goals had become more difficult because of the complexity of the period. This complexity, and the uncertainty it fosters, was exacerbated in 1981 when tax cuts and recession created a $200 billion annual federal deficit, followed by major budget reductions in forestry programs (15). Then in 1982 stumpage prices for timber fell 60 percent because housing construction had declined sharply. Consequently, the timber industry began selling timberland and cutting back on personnel and operations. It is too early to tell what these events will mean to the future development of forest policy.

Multiple Use of the Forests   Recreational use of the national forests grew steadily during the pre–World War II years, but it never reached parity with timber production as an objective of forest management. Recreation was formally recognized as an objective in 1935 when the Division of Recreation and Lands was created in the Forest Service. Nevertheless, the main reason for spending money on recreation was to build campgrounds and other facilities to keep recreationists confined and out of the way of commodity uses. Fire prevention was also an important reason for concentrating people in campgrounds (16), particularly in southern California.

The huge demand for timber products after the war dominated the attention of professional foresters, so they tended to overlook the implications of the equally enormous growth in recreation that was also taking place. For example, recreation visits to national forests climbed from fewer than 30 million in 1950 to about 233 million in 1982 (17, 18). The explosive increase in recreational use spurred competition between government agencies over the authority to administer this recreational use of public lands. Again, the two agencies principally involved in the dispute were the Park Service and the Forest Service. There was a revival of the idea prevalent in the 1930s that recreation should be administered by the Park Service, separately from other forest uses. For example, Oregon Dunes National Seashore and North Cascades National Park were both carved out of national forests.

Forest Service attempts to increase its recreation budget met with limited success. Part of the problem could be traced to a lack of statutory responsibility for providing recreational facilities on the national forests (16). The Forest Service had to find some way to increase its recreational budget and, at the same time, protect itself against what it viewed as unacceptable demands of the timber industry, the grazing industry, and the Park Service for exclusive use of certain national forestlands. The concept adopted for defending the agency was multiple use. In other words, the Forest Service felt that obtaining congressional endorsement to manage these lands for several uses, including grazing, wildlife, recreation, and timber, would both legitimate the agency's management of all these resources and enhance its position when asking Congress for funds. The vehicle for the concept was the Multiple Use–Sustained Yield Act of 1960. Through this act Congress directed that the national forests should be managed for outdoor recreation, range, timber, watershed, and wildlife and fish purposes.

Although, in Edward C. Craft's words, "the bill contained a little something for everyone" (19), it was nevertheless opposed by the timber industry, the Sierra Club (a preservationist group), and the Park Service. People in the lumber industry thought that timber had always been given the highest priority in national forest management and that the bill would eliminate this preferential treatment by placing all resources on an equal level. Their opposition to the bill was subsequently turned into mild support when the bill was amended to include the following phrase: "The purposes of this Act are declared to be supplemental to, but not in derogation of, the purposes for which the national forests were established as set forth in the Act of June 4, 1897" (10). In other words, they felt that since the Organic Administration Act of 1897 specified timber and water as the resources that forest reserves were meant to protect, these resources would be given a higher priority than other resources. However, today it is generally agreed that this ranking covers only the establishment of national forests and does not extend to their management (19, 20).

The Sierra Club opposed the multiple-use bill for two reasons. First, the members wanted wilderness added to the list of resources so that it would be considered equal to, but separate from recreation.

Second, they believed that the real purpose of the multiple-use bill was to stop the Park Service from taking lands out of national forests to make national parks. The former issue was partially resolved when the bill was amended at the request of the Wilderness Society to state that the wilderness was "consistent with the purposes and provisions" of the bill (21). However, the Sierra Club and the Park Service were blocked in their attempt to include an amendment stating that creation of new national parks would not be affected by the bill (19). The Sierra Club and the Park Service were never satisfied with the bill. Nevertheless, only four months after the administration's recommendation was sent to Congress, the Multiple Use–Sustained Yield Act of 1960 was passed and signed into law by Eisenhower.

The Multiple Use–Sustained Yield Act has been eminently successful in accomplishing the Forest Service's goals. The Forest Service preserved its broad constituency, its political flexibility, and its varied responsibilities. However, the boost in congressional funding for nontimber resources that was expected to follow passage of the act did not materialize. Only wildlife management received a significant average increase in funding relative to Forest Service requests (20) (Figure 1.7).

One of the unresolved issues in the multiple-use concept involves priorities for allocating land to various uses. The Multiple Use–Sustained Yield Act evades the issue of priorities entirely. What it mandates is that all the uses mentioned are appropriate for the administration of the national forests, that all

Figure 1.7 Bull moose in the Gallatin National Forest, Montana. (Courtesy of U.S.D.A. Forest Service.)

uses will be given equal consideration, that all uses will be managed according to sustained-yield principles, and that the productivity of the land will not be impaired.

The Wilderness System Forest Service problems with single-use advocates were not completely eliminated by the Multiple Use–Sustained Yield Act. There was still the matter of wilderness to be faced. The creation of a wilderness system may have aided the agency somewhat in defending its boundaries, but it also created a preservation-oriented constituency that wanted to protect scenic and roadless areas of the national forests against the commodity use programs of the Forest Service.

Over the years the Forest Service had been adding areas to its wilderness system and refining its administrative regulations. The agency also developed a classification scheme that included a continuum of levels of protection extending from primitive areas, where some roads and logging were permitted, to wild and wilderness areas where these activities were prohibited. However, in 1940 the Forest Service extended greater protection to primitive areas as well (10).

Wilderness enthusiasts watched as the Forest Service gradually reduced the size of wilderness, wild, and primitive areas. Logging roads advanced, and technology increased the feasibility of utilizing timber in remote areas, so pressures to open protected lands to harvesting also increased. Since the Forest Service could readily change the boundaries of protected lands, preservationists sought the increased security of congressional action for wilderness designation. In addition, they wanted to establish wilderness areas on other federal lands, particularly within national parks and monuments. After eight years of debate and eighteen public hearings the Wilderness Act of 1964 was passed by Congress (Figure 1.8).

The wilderness system created by the Wilderness Act began with setting aside 3.7 million hectares of land, within fifty-four areas, which the Forest Service originally identified as wilderness and wild areas. Bureau of Land Management (BLM) lands were not included under the Wilderness Act until passage of the Federal Land Policy and Management Act of 1976 (22). This act not only included wilderness among uses of the public domain, but also legislatively created the BLM and gave it land management responsibilities after more than 30 years had passed, since the bureau was established by executive reorganization (22).

One of the more interesting debates that emerged concerned whether or not wilderness was a renewable resource. The Forest Service stated that wilderness could not be renewed. In other words, the wilderness character of a piece of land could not be reestablished once it had been used for other purposes. On the other hand, preservation groups contended that "certain areas not wilderness . . . if given proper protection and management can be restored and regain wilderness qualities" (23). This was an important issue in the eastern United States, because much of the public land had been used for timber production and agriculture.

The Forest Service resisted attempts to classify wilderness areas in the East because it felt that most of these lands no longer retained their original character. Instead, it proposed a new eastern roadless area system that would be less restrictive and separate from the national wilderness preservation system. Preservationists refused to accept this alternative and succeeded in pressuring Congress to pass the Eastern Wilderness Act of 1975. The act added sixteen new areas to the wilderness system totaling nearly 83,772 hectares. An additional 50,587 hectares in seventeen areas were also set aside so that the secretary of agriculture could evaluate them for possible inclusion in the wilderness system. All these areas were within national forests.

The nearly insatiable appetite of wilderness advocates for land was, and continues to be, far from satisfied. They broadened their sights to include all national forest roadless areas as well as congressionally designed wilderness study areas. The Forest Service responded in 1967 by conducting a nationwide inventory of roadless lands within national forests. To evaluate these lands for wilderness suitability, the Forest Service devised a procedure known as RARE (Roadless Area Review and Evaluation). A total of 1449 sites, containing approximately

Figure 1.8 Packing into the Pecos Wilderness Area of the Santa Fe National Forest, New Mexico.

(Photograph by Harold Walter, courtesy of U.S.D.A. Forest Service.)

22.7 million hectares, were identified. In 1973 the chief of the Forest Service designated 235 of these sites for further study as possible wilderness areas.

Many criticisms of the RARE process were voiced by preservationists, so a new RARE II process was initiated in 1977. On January 4, 1979, Secretary of Agriculture Bob Bergland made public the results of RARE II. The department recommended to Congress that 6.1 million hectares of national forestlands be added to the wilderness system and that an additional 4.5 million hectares be held for "further planning" because of the need for more reliable information on mineral deposits. It was hoped that this recommendation would help to bring a rapid

resolution to the question of how much more land should be classified as wilderness. However, preservationists reacted with "acute disappointment" to the recommendation. Preservationists were concerned that the recommendations fell short of what was needed, but the timber industry argued that they were excessive (24).

As late as 1984 wilderness advocates were still winning. The Ninety-Eighth Congress added 2.8 million hectares of wilderness to the system, bringing the total to 13.1 million hectares. Unfortunately, the act led to a gradual decline in the standards used to judge wilderness quality. Today many groups use wilderness designation as a way to preserve areas that would not have qualified as wilderness under provisions of the Wilderness Act of 1964. In Wisconsin, for example, one new wilderness area contains a red pine plantation, and in new wilderness areas in Michigan there are pit toilets, private inholdings, and lakes used for motorboats. Thus wilderness is gradually losing its distinction as the repository of the last remnants of wild America. Clearly, wilderness issues will be around for some time.

The Clearcutting Issue The consumption of wood was increasing at the same time that environmental constraints, such as air and water pollution control standards and restrictions on the use of pesticides and herbicides, were limiting the amount of timber that could be produced and harvested. Furthermore, nationwide net losses of timberland in all ownerships to nontimber purposes was averaging about 2 million hectares per decade. Consequently, foresters believed that at some point in the future, wood shortages could develop. Although their apprehensions were not borne out, preservationists and professional land managers disagreed over which methods were best for producing timber.

The focal point of the debate over timber management practices centered on clearcutting. Clearcutting is a harvesting method in which all the trees on a certain area of land are cut and then the site is regenerated by natural seeding, seeding from aircraft, or planting. Preservationists claimed that clearcutting had "an enormously devastating environmental effect which includes soil destruction, stream siltation, and a stinging blow to the aesthetic sense" (25). Where properly applied clearcutting was not destructive, but little could be done to correct the unpleasant appearance of a recent clearcut.

Concern over management practices in the national forests erupted into a national debate on November 18, 1970, when the report *A University View of the Forest Service,* commonly known as the Bolle Report, was released by Senator Lee Metcalf of Montana and published in the *Congressional Record.* The report was prepared by a committee of scientists from the University of Montana at Metcalf's

request. The committee's final report not only was highly critical of Forest Service management practices, but also showed that a deep division existed within the ranks of professional foresters.

The problem began in 1968 when residents of the Bitterroot Valley in Montana complained that the national forest surrounding them was being abused because of large clearcuts. Most disturbing to local residents was the Forest Service practice of terracing steep mountain slopes to prevent erosion and improve reproduction where the timber had been removed. The Forest Service received a torrent of letters demanding that these practices be stopped.

The Forest Service responded by appointing a task force to conduct an impartial analysis of management practices in the Bitterroot National Forest. The task force was working on its study at about the same time that the Bolle committee was conducting its own investigation. However, the task force released its findings in April 1970, a full six months before the Bolle committee.

The task force report was remarkably candid relative to what would ordinarily be expected from a government agency that must evaluate its own actions. Task force members found, for example, that the attitude of many people on the national forest staff was "that resource production goals come first and that land management considerations take second place" (26). The Bolle committee concurred with many of the findings in the task force report, but it also found that "the Forest Service is primarily oriented toward timber harvest as the dominant use of national forests" (26). In short, the Forest Service had done an outstanding job of organizing itself to harvest timber, but it had failed to adjust to changing social values.

The Forest Service modified its forest management policies on the Bitterroot National Forest. However, the agency tended to disregard the national implications of public concerns over clearcutting. A few months after the Bolle committee report was released, the Subcommittee on Public Lands of the Senate Interior and Insular Affairs Committee, chaired by Senator Frank Church of Idaho, held hearings on management practices on the public lands. The Church subcommittee's attention was directed primarily at clearcutting in the national forests, especially in Montana, West Virginia, Wyoming, and Alaska. The subcommittee concluded that clearcutting had to be regulated. It also found that the Forest Service "had difficulty communicating effectively with its critics, and its image has suffered" (27). Although the Forest Service had taken some actions to adjust to public concerns over clearcutting, the subcommittee felt they "have made little impact" (27). The Forest Service lost the opportunity to make widespread and forward-looking revisions in its management policies. Instead, it found itself in the position of accepting the timber-harvesting guidelines recommended by the Church subcommittee.

The most important timber-harvesting policies adopted after 1952 were generated by the issue of clearcutting hardwood forests in the Monongahela National Forest in West Virginia (Figure 1.9). Clearcutting replaced selective cutting of the forest

in 1964, and the reaction was almost immediate. Concerned citizens rose up and pressured the West Virginia legislature to pass resolutions in 1964, 1967, and 1970, requesting investigations of Forest Service timber management practices. A Forest Service special review committee appointed to investigate the problem confirmed that some abuses had occurred (28). As a result, timber management policies were changed to encourage a wide variety of harvesting techniques. In addition, where clearcutting was necessary, the area cut was limited to 10 hectares or less, and the distances between clearcuts were regulated. Since many timber sales had already been contracted under the old 32-hectare limit, the reforms made by the Forest Service could not show immediate results on the ground (29).

Preservationists were not satisfied with these reforms. They wanted all clearcutting stopped immediately. On May 8, 1973, the Izaak Walton League of America and other preservation organizations

Figure 1.9 Clearcuts (background) on the Monongahela National Forest (Gauley District), West Virginia. (Photograph by R. L. Giese.)

filed suit alleging that clearcutting violated a provision in the Organic Administration Act of 1897 stating that only "dead, matured, or large growth of trees" could be cut and sold from the national forest. On December 3, 1973, Judge Robert Maxwell of the Northern District Federal Court of West Virginia accepted this interpretation of the act. His ruling had the effect of banning clearcutting on the national forests. The Fourth Circuit Court of Appeals unanimously upheld the lower court's decision in 1975, and the Forest Service halted all timber sales on national forests within the jurisdiction of the court. In 1976 the U.S. District Court of Alaska used the same reasoning to issue a permanent injunction against timber harvesting on a large area of Prince of Wales Island. These and similar lawsuits essentially halted timber sales on national forests in six states (30).

Numerous bills were introduced in Congress to overcome the bottleneck in timber production that resulted from the Monongahela decision. A key provision in the preservationist-sponsored bill would have substituted legislative prescriptions on timber harvesting for the judgment of professional foresters. Acting with unusual speed, Congress passed the National Forest Management Act (NFMA) on September 30, 1976, and it was signed into law on October 22, 1976.

This act contained many important provisions that have yet to be fully evaluated. For instance, the NFMA requires the Forest Service to prepare comprehensive interdisciplinary forest plans for 123 administrative units at ten-year intervals. By 1986 twenty-five national forest plans were in final form, but most of these plans are being challenged by various interest groups through administrative appeals and in the courts. Nevertheless, the act did repeal the section of the Organic Administration Act of 1897 that served as the basis for the lawsuits that stopped clearcutting within national forests, at least in situations in which it was found to be the "optimal" ("optimal" was left undefined in the act) silvicultural treatment. Clearcuts today are less extensive, and nontimber values, such as wildlife and recreation, are playing a greater role in timber-harvesting decisions. The NFMA did not completely resolve the clearcutting controversy; however, it did make foresters more alert and sensitive to public opinion. The act also brought forest management closer to the multiple-use ideal.

Judicial Involvement in Resource Policy-Making The Monongahela decision illustrated the growing importance of the courts in forest policy development. In 1978, for example, the U.S. Supreme Court further complicated management of the national forests by handing down what is commonly known as the Rio Mimbres decision. The Rio Mimbres flows through the Gila National Forest in New Mexico. The dispute centered on the legal right of the Forest Service to have enough water to manage the multiple uses of a national forest versus the rights of upstream water users who wanted to use it for irrigation and other purposes. Again, as in the Monongahela decision, the Organic Administration Act of 1897 was used against the Forest Service. The Court interpreted the act to mean that forest reserves were set aside to maintain timber supplies and favorable waterflows. The right to reserve water for other multiple-use purposes was not mentioned in the act. In essence, the Court ruled that the Forest Service had no legal right to Rio Mimbres water, and that it would have to satisfy its water needs through state water rights procedures (15). Thus the complexities and uncertainties of national forest management were dramatically increased.

Traditionally the courts have been restrained in both the number and scope of their reviews of administrative decisions. The judiciary gradually became more involved with administrative review as more and more preservationists, frustrated in their dealings with administrators, turned to the courts for relief. The number of suits was increased dramatically by the "Scenic Hudson" case of 1965, in which the court decided that an organization whose principal interest was scenic beauty could sue government agencies (31). This decision opened the door to the courts and ushered in the age of judicial involvement in resource policy-making, including the Monongahela case.

Lawsuits are expensive, time-consuming, and often embarrassing to the agency involved. Thus threats of a lawsuit also increased direct participation by citizens in formulating agency policy. However, lawsuits were used most frequently as a delaying tactic to permit government agencies to make more informed decisions. Preservationists were aided materially in their ability to delay decisions by passage of the National Environmental Policy Act of 1969 (NEPA) and similar legislation enacted by various states. The NEPA established a detailed procedure for assessing the environmental consequences of "federal actions significantly affecting the quality of the human environment." Legal challenges of noncompliance with these procedures had delayed decisions and, in many cases, brought about changes in forest policy. The large volume of environmental legislation passed by Congress and the states during the late 1960s and 1970s also provided increased opportunities for lawsuits.

Additional Legislation The Forest and Rangeland Renewable Resources Planning Act of 1974 (RPA) was perhaps the most far-reaching forest policy enacted during this period. The RPA was part of a congressional effort to gain greater control of the budgetary process. Congress was reacting to what it perceived as a decline in its authority relative to the executive branch (32). Furthermore, Congress had always shown greater support for resource programs than the executive branch, particularly the Office of Management and Budget (OMB), and RPA was one means of pressuring the president to raise budget requests for natural resources management.

The RPA initiated a procedure for setting goals and formulating forest policies. The act requires that the secretary of agriculture make periodic assessments of national needs for forest and rangeland resources. Then, at regular intervals, the secretary must make recommendations for long-range programs that the Forest Service is required to carry out in order to meet those needs. The assessment and program had to be transmitted to Congress in 1976 and again in 1980. A new assessment is required every ten years thereafter, and the program is to be revised every five years. In addition, the president is required to submit a statement to Congress with each annual budget explaining why the funding request differs from the program approved by Congress.

The Forest Service took advantage of the opportunity provided by RPA. In its first budget request under RPA, the agency asked for substantial increases in funds for managing all the resources in the national forests. Congress responded favorably, and President Jimmy Carter signed the appropriations bill for the 1978 fiscal year. The Forest Service budget was raised $275 million over the funding level of the previous fiscal year (33). Subsequent budgets, however, did not do as well. Massive federal deficits forced budget reductions that resulted in a 30 percent decline in national forest funding between 1978 and 1986 (34).

Although many important policies that dealt specifically with forest resources were developed during this period, a series of laws adopted for other purposes have also had a profound effect on forest management. These policies include enactment of the NEPA, the Clean Air Act of 1970, the Federal Water Pollution Control Act of 1972, the Federal Environmental Pesticide Control Act of 1972, the Endangered Species Act of 1973, the Toxic Substances Control Act of 1976, and the Clean Water Act of 1977. Two major attributes of these policies are particularly important. First, they rely on complex and detailed processes of federal and state regulation and the exercise of police powers. Second, they were adopted to achieve broad environmental goals not specifically focused on forestry, yet they influence forest policy development. For example, Section 208 of the Federal Water Quality Act amendments of 1972 required the establishment of "best management practices," which are enforceable, to control water pollution. These practices apply to timber harvesting and silvicultural treatments on public and private forestlands (35). Each of these policies has further complicated the forest policy process.

Important Features of the Period 1952 to the Present An evaluation of the development of American forest policy since 1952 shows a gradual transition to a more balanced and environmentally aware approach to resources management. The growing strength of groups with an interest in nontimber resources had helped to bring about this change, but timber production still remains paramount in the management of the nation's forests. Similarly, citizen participation in resource decision making has increased, yet no completely effective means, other than the traditional routes through the legislative and judicial processes, have been developed to reduce resource management conflicts. Much work remains to be done if equity is going to be achieved. In spite of the conflicts, however, nearly all groups have received substantially more forest resources, including timber products, than they obtained in any previous period. In addition, a legislative framework was provided for making even greater improvements in the years ahead. The current operations of the Forest Service are further discussed in Chapter 10, "Forestry at the National Level."

making be delegated entirely to scientists and professionals. Active citizen participation will remain an essential part of the forest policy process.

Second, both the lack of objective criteria for assessing policies and citizen participation ensure that debate and compromise will also continue to be the central means for making decisions in the forest policy process. Clearly, anyone ambitious to become a professional forester must be prepared not only to engage in these debates but also to compromise. The time has passed, if indeed it ever existed, when the judgment of a professional will be accepted without question.

Finally, the forest policy process is growing more complex. As demands for forest resources increase, and the diversity of interests widens, the problem of providing for these needs in an equitable manner becomes more difficult. Important strides have been made toward solving this problem, but its ultimate resolution remains the major challenge of American forest policy.

Conclusion

In this chapter we have traced the historical development of forest policy in the United States as seen through the policy process. This approach necessarily simplifies history by focusing on certain aspects that conform to stages in the policy process while ignoring other potentially important aspects of policy development. Nevertheless, from this analysis certain general principles about forest resource policy-making emerge, principles that can be expected to remain unaltered into the foreseeable future.

First, the forest policy process is inherently subjective. What is the preferred forest policy of some groups is considered disastrous by other groups. Thus far, at least, the search for objective measures to set goals and assess forest policies has proved futile. No single criterion of what is "best" exists that, if satisfied, can ensure agreement among all contending interests. Everyone uses different standards to judge forest policies. Therefore it is highly unlikely that the policy process will be converted to science, nor will the authority to practice policy-

References

1. K. E. Boulding, *Principles of Economic Policy,* Prentice–Hall, Englewood Cliffs, N.J., 1958.

2. J. E. Anderson, *Public Policy-Making,* Holt, Rinehart & Winston, New York, 1979.

3. G. F. Carter, *Man and the Land—A Cultural Geography,* Holt, Rinehart & Winston, New York, 1975.

4. H. E. Driver, *Indians of North America,* Univ. of Chicago Press, Chicago, 1961.

5. G. M. Day, *Ecology, 34,* 329 (1953).

6. S. T. Dana, *Forest and Range Policy: Its Development in the United States,* First Edition, McGraw–Hill, New York, 1956.

7. T. A. Bailey, *The American Pageant,* D. C. Heath, Boston, 1961.

8. H. K. Steen, *The U.S. Forest Service: A History,* Univ. of Washington Press, Seattle, 1976.

9. R. Nash, ed., *The American Environment,* Addison–Wesley, Reading, Mass., 1968.

10. J. P. Gilligan, "The development of policy and admin-

istration of Forest Service primitive and wilderness areas in the western United States," Vols. I and II, Ph.D. dissertation, Univ. of Michigan, 1953.

11. G. Pinchot, *Breaking New Ground,* Harcourt, Brace, New York, 1947.

12. S. P. Hays, *Conservation and the Gospel of Efficiency,* Atheneum, New York, 1975.

13. D. C. Swain, *Federal Conservation Policy 1921–1933,* Univ. of California Press, Berkeley, 1963.

14. E. C. Crafts, "Forest Service researcher and congressional liaison: An eye to multiple use," For. Hist. Soc. Publ., Santa Cruz, Calif., 1972.

15. J. Ramm and K. Bartolomi, *J. For., 83,* 363, 367, (1985).

16. F. W. Grover, "Multiple use in U.S. Forest Service land planning," For. Hist. Soc. Publ., Santa Cruz, Calif., 1972.

17. President's Advisory Panel on Timber and the Environment, Final Rept., U.S. Govt. Printing Office, 1973.

18. A. S. Mills, "Recreational use in national forests." In *Statistics on Outdoor Recreation,* Part II, C. S. Van Doren, ed., Resources for the Future, Washington, D.C., 1984.

19. E. C. Crafts, *Am. For., 76,* 13, 52 (1970).

20. R. M. Alston, "FOREST—goals and decision-making in the Forest Service." U.S.D.A. For. Serv., Intermountain For. Range Expt. Sta., Res. Pap. INT-128, 1972.

21. E. C. Crafts, *Am. For., 76,* 29 (1970).

22. S. T. Dana and S. K. Fairfax, *Forest and Range Policy: Its Development in the United States,* Second Edition, McGraw–Hill, New York, 1980.

23. T. M. Bonnicksen, *California Today, 2,* 1 (1974).

24. R. Pardo, *Am. For., 85,* 10 (1979).

25. N. Wood, *Sierra Club Bull., 56,* 14 (1971).

26. A. W. Bolle, "A university view of the Forest Service," U.S. Govt. Printing Office, Doc. 91-115, 1970.

27. U.S. Senate, "Clearcutting on federal timberlands," Rept., "Public Lands Sub-Committee, Committee on Interior and Insular Affairs, 1972.

28. G. O. Robinson, *The Forest Service,* Johns Hopkins Press, Baltimore, 1975.

29. L. Popovich, *J. For., 74,* 169, 176 (1976).

30. J. F. Hall and R. S. Wasserstrom, *Environ. Law, 8,* 523 (1978).

31. C. W. Brizee, *J. For., 73,* 424 (1975).

32. D. M. Harvey, "Change in congressional policy-making and a few trends in resource policy." In *Centers of Influence and U.S. Forest Policy,* F. J. Convery and J. E. Davis, eds., School of Forestry and Environmental Studies, Duke Univ., Durham, N.C., 1977.

33. L. Popovich, *J. For., 75,* 656, 660 (1977).

34. N. Sampson, *Am. For., 92,* 10, 58 (1986).

35. J. A. Zivnuska, *J. For., 76,* 467 (1978).

CHAPTER 2

Forest Regions of North America and the World

JOHN W. DUFFIELD

Forestry is practiced where forests exist or may be created. Thus forestry has a geographic dimension, and this chapter deals with a specialized area of the science of plant geography. The general characteristics of forest regions around the world are discussed, with special emphasis on the forests of North America.

Classification of Forest Areas

Forests are classified in several different ways. Perhaps the simplest is the division of forests into two broad categories: *commercial* and *noncommercial*. The U.S. Forest Service classifies forests as commercial if they are capable of yielding at least 1.4 cubic meters of wood per hectare per year and are suitable now or prospectively for timber harvesting. Obviously, people in regions where wood and other forest resources are scarce make economic use of forests and woodlands that would not be classified as commercial by this definition.

More detailed classifications consider whether the forests are available for economic use and their general composition—that is, whether coniferous or broad-leaved. Table 2.1 gives the forest areas of the world according to a broad classification scheme of this type.

Plant ecologists have developed other classifications of forests. A recent scheme recognizes four principal types of closed high forests.

33

Table 2.1 Forest Areas of the World[a]

Region	Total Land Area	Forest Area			Percentage of Total Forest
		Coniferous	Broad-Leaved	Total	
North America	18	4.0	2.6	6.6	18.2
Latin America	20	0.3	7.4	7.7	21.3
Europe (excl. Soviet Union)	5	0.9	0.6	1.5	4.1
Africa	30	0.1	6.9	7.0	19.1
Asia (excl. Soviet Union and Japan)	27	0.7	4.1	4.8	13.3
Japan	1	0.1	0.1	0.2	0.6
Soviet Union	21	6.0	1.7	7.7	21.3
Pacific area	8	0.1	0.8	0.9	2.2
World (excl. Antarctica)	130	12.2	24.2	36.4	100.0

Source: "Outlook for timber in the United States," U.S.D.A. For. Serv., Res. Rept. 20, 1973.
[a]Given in millions of square kilometers.

1. Mainly evergreen forests.
   a. Broad-leaved evergreen forests (mainly in warmer climates).
   b. Coniferous forests (mainly in cooler climates).
2. Mainly deciduous forests.
   a. Drought-deciduous forests (leaves shed in dry season).
   b. Cold-deciduous forests (leaves shed in winter).

The scheme outlined here is a great simplification of the system, which recognizes more than twenty kinds of high forest (1).

Trees grow in a wide range of climates and on a wide variety of soils, on all the continents except Antarctica. They will not grow in areas if the annual rainfall is less than about 300 millimeters, or if there is no soil, or where the soil is permanently frozen, or where animal and human activities prevent their reestablishment. Where trees grow closely together, and this happens only where the annual rainfall is 400 millimeters or more, they form the principal or dominant component of *forests*. Where trees occur in drier regions, they are more widely spaced, dominating plant communities known as *woodlands*.

Effect of Physiography and Climate on Forest Types

The amount of soil moisture available to trees depends first on the amount of annual rainfall, and second, but almost as important, on the seasonal distribution of this rainfall. The physical properties of the soil and the evaporative loss of soil moisture also determine availability of soil moisture to the roots of the trees. In very general terms, the availability of soil moisture determines both the height that trees attain (more moisture = taller trees) and the spacing between trees (more moisture = closer spacing), so that if we seek a simple general explanation for the distribution of forest and woodland on the earth's surface, we can find it by comparing maps of vegetation types with maps showing distribution of precipitation. We can find a somewhat closer relationship between forests and climate if we take into account temperature and wind movement as they affect the effectiveness of precipitation in supplying moisture to trees. Warm air, especially when it is in rapid motion, causes rapid water loss from vegetation and soil and thus increases trees' demands for water while at the same time decreasing the availability of soil moisture to the trees. But cold, dry winter winds, especially in areas such as the North American Great Plains, can also subject trees to severe drying.

The elements of climate that determine the existence and productivity of forests—namely, precipitation, temperature, and wind movement—are in turn largely influenced by geographic position, such as latitude and the relative placement of water and land masses, and by physiographic position including elevation, steepness of slope, and the direction in which the slope faces (aspect). These geographic and physiographic features interact and compensate. The climate and vegetation found at high elevations but low latitude (near the equator) resemble those found at lower elevations but higher latitude (Figure 2.1). Thus the forest vegetation at 2500 meters in the southern Appalachians at 35 degrees north latitude closely resembles that found near sea level at the mouth of the St. Lawrence River at 50 degrees north latitude. South-facing slopes in the Northern Hemisphere are generally warmer and

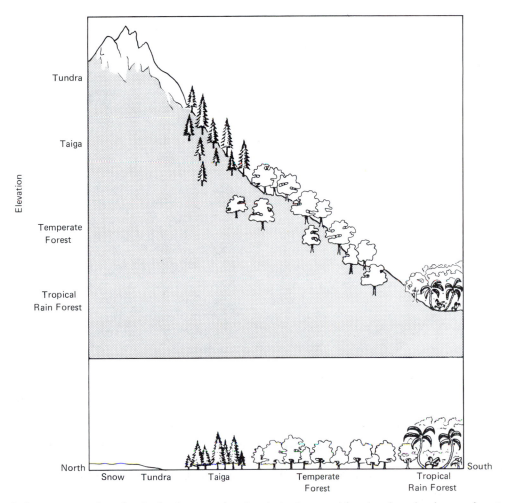

Figure 2.1 Vegetation found at high elevations but low latitude resembles that found at lower elevations but higher latitude.

drier than north-facing slopes, so that the elevational limits of a given vegetation type are higher on south-facing slopes. Finally, proximity to oceans and other large bodies of water lowers summer temperatures and raises winter temperatures, so that the vegetation of a mild maritime climatic region such as the Pacific Northwest is quite different from that of a harsher climatic region such as central Montana, at the same latitude. Moreover, temperature changes are generally smaller and less sudden in the coastal or maritime climates than in the continental climates, and we find that trees are generally less tolerant of sudden temperature change than grasses, herbs, and annual vegetation.

The present-day location, extent, and composition of forests represent only a brief episode in the long history of climatic change. We are beginning to discern evidences of past fluctuations in intensity and quality of solar radiation reaching the earth's surfaces, possibly associated with fluctuations in the composition of the atmosphere. One consequence of these fluctuations has been the advance and retreat of polar ice caps and continental glaciation, causing the migration and extinction of forests, including their animal components.

Since the last major glaciation, a new climatic element has emerged. Human populations and their domesticated animals are playing an increasing role in redrawing the boundaries of forest regions and changing the composition of the forests. Locally, and perhaps globally, burning fossil fuels and other industrial activities modify the composition of the atmosphere, with complex and often deleterious effects on plant and animal life. Diseases and insects have accompanied the intercontinental movement of crop plants, including forest trees, and of plant products, and have already caused the virtual extinction of once-widespread species of forest trees. Native animal populations have been similarly affected. Especially in subtropical and tropical forests, selective exploitation of tree species that produce woods of great value threaten to change forest composition irrevocably.

The overall effect of the new human climatic element is to accelerate the age-old process of extinction of species, a process slightly offset by deliberate breeding as well as the continuing evolutionary processes.

Effect of Soils on Forest Types

Trees, like most dryland vegetation, are rooted in soil. Soils, like the vegetation they support, vary from place to place, depending on (1) the parent material from which they are derived, (2) the local climate as it affects weathering of rock to form soil, (3) the manner in which soils are transported by wind, water, or volcanic action, (4) the effects of vegetation and soil-inhabiting animals, and (5) the length of time over which these factors have operated. In fact, distribution of vegetation types is both a cause and an effect of distribution of soil types. Vegetation type is influenced by soil texture (whether sandy or clay), by soil aeration, by chemical composition, and by various combinations of these and other soil properties. A striking effect of soil properties on forest vegetation type shows up in the distribution of loblolly, longleaf, and shortleaf pines, which are abundant east and west of the lower Mississippi River, but are absent from a wide zone of river-deposited soils in western Mississippi and northeastern Louisiana. Such soils are generally poorly aerated but of high fertility, often contain large amounts of calcium, and are favorable to the growth of grass and deciduous trees. In the forests of the Pacific slope of North America, soils derived from serpentine rocks support high proportions of such species as Jeffrey pine and incense cedar. In the southeastern United States, bald cypress grows in wet, poorly aerated soils that are unsuited to yellow-poplar. A more detailed description of soils and how they affect forest types is given in Chapter 4.

In the following descriptions of the forest regions, certain species of trees are listed as important. Some species, such as Douglas-fir, loblolly pine, or sugar maple, are important as timber producers. Others, such as giant sequoia or Montezuma cypress, are listed because of their large size, great age, or historical significance. Whitebark and limber pines make the lists because they provide scenic accents at high elevations.

Forest Regions of North America

Northern Coniferous Forest

Location and Extent Plant geographers refer to the northern coniferous forest as the boreal or northern forest, and in Eurasia by its Russian name, *taiga*. The northern coniferous forest is the largest forest region in North America; as shown in Figure 2.2, it stretches across Canada from eastern Quebec, its southern limit cutting across southern Quebec and Ontario, skirting along the north shore of Lake Superior, and then turning northwest across central Alberta and British Columbia. This forest reaches almost to the Bering Sea, and beyond this barrier continues westward across Siberia and the northern part of the Soviet Union, reaching almost to the Atlantic again in northern Sweden. North of this world-circling forest is the treeless tundra. The transition from forest to tundra is a woodland of scattered trees and shrubs, extending northward to Hudson Bay, and in western Canada almost to the Arctic Ocean. The northern coniferous forest clothes a region of relatively low elevation, with many rivers, lakes, and swamps (2).

Forest regions can be mapped in general outline simply, but only by overlooking some of the interesting details. The northern coniferous forest appears in many places south of its generally described southern limits, at higher elevations. Examples are the White Mountains of Maine and New Hampshire, the Adirondacks of New York, and the southern Appalachians as far south as North Carolina.

Principal Species Cold regions are notorious for having relatively few species of plants and animals, but large numbers of individuals represent each species. The northern coniferous forest is predominantly a spruce forest, with birches, poplars, and willows making up the broad-leaved component. In North America the white spruce essentially defines the region, but black spruce is almost as commonly found, occupying the colder and wetter sites (Figure

2.3). Paper birch, quaking aspen, and willows (many species of *Salix,* both trees and shrubs) provide color for the traveler and browse for wildlife. Tamarack, the north's only deciduous conifer, is found throughout most of the region, but balsam fir drops out of the northwestern section. Jack pine, like balsam fir, is limited to the eastern and central portions of the region.

Economic and Social Importance Until fairly recently, the chief economic importance of the boreal forest in North America was the population of mammals on which the fur trade was based. In the East, mineral resources and water power have been developed at the same time that the pulp and paper industry, based largely on spruce, but more recently on fir and jack pine, has been rising.

The vast extent of the northern coniferous forest makes it an important actual and potential source of wood and fiber, even though the growth rate of many of the forests in the region is severely limited by short growing seasons, thin and infertile soils, and poor soil drainage. Nevertheless, this region offers values greater than those of commodity production. To the extent that wilderness still exists on our planet, the greatest expanses of wilderness are here. Nowhere else in North America is wildlife, from large animals such as moose to the smallest insects, so near to the levels of abundance found by the first European invaders. A major portion of the wildlife of the region is an international resource, for the waterfowl and other migratory birds that winter in the United States and Mexico breed in the north woods and the tundra.

Northern Hardwoods

Location and Extent In eastern North America, the northern hardwoods region lies to the south of the northern coniferous forest. The northern hardwoods reach their strongest development in the northern Great Lakes states, southeastern Canada, and northern New York and New England, and reach down the northern Appalachians into Pennsylvania.

Northern Coniferous Forest
Northern Hardwoods Forest
Pacific Coast Forest
Rocky Mountain Forest
Central Broad-leaved Forest
Oak-Pine Forest (southern)
Bottomland Hardwoods Forest
Tropical Forest

Figure 2.2 Forest regions of North America.

Figure 2.3 Vast natural forests of white and black spruce occupy the southern part of the Alaska interior. (Photograph by Henrich Gohl, copyright Magnum Verlag AG, Basel, Switzerland.)

A more descriptive name for this region is the hemlock–white pine–northern hardwoods region (Figure 2.2).

Principal Species In the northern hardwoods region, all the principal species of the northern coniferous forest are found, plus a good many more. Table 2.2 lists the principal species of the northern hardwoods region, omitting those found in the northern coniferous forest. The species are listed in the table more or less in the order of their abundance throughout the region. The first four give one of the commonly used names for the region—"beech, birch, maple, hemlock" (Figure 2.4). All the species listed in the table are important timber producers, except possibly red maple and northern white-cedar. Red maple is important because it is both widely distributed and abundant throughout the region. White-cedar is included for its wildlife and horticultural values.

White pine was found by the European explorers and settlers throughout the northern hardwoods region, but most abundantly in areas that had been cleared of hardwoods by ancient fires or blowdowns and on areas of sandier soils. It was particularly abundant on sites in Maine and the western Great Lakes states. In New England it came in as an old-field "pioneer" following land abandonment in the last third of the nineteenth century. Many present-day hardwood or spruce–fir forests in the

Table 2.2 Some Important Species of the Northern Hardwoods Region

Scientific Name	Common Name
Fagus grandifolia	American beech
Betula allegheniensis	Yellow birch
Acer saccharum	Sugar maple
Tsuga canadensis	Eastern hemlock
Pinus strobus	Eastern white pine
Acer rubrum	Red maple
Pinus resinosa	Red pine
Populus tremuloides	Quaking aspen
Populus grandidentata	Bigtooth aspen
Quercus rubra	Northern red oak
Fraxinus americana	White ash
Ulmus americana	American elm
Thuja occidentalis	Northern white-cedar
Tilia americana	American basswood
Prunus serotina	Black cherry
Picea rubens	Red spruce
Pinus banksiana	Jack pine

region stand on land once occupied by white pine (3).

Economic and Social Importance White pine was the first economic prize that European explorers, who would have preferred gold, found on the north Atlantic Coast. White pine became a strategic material, vital for providing masts for the ships of England's navy and merchant fleets, especially during the frequent wars that cut off supplies of Scotch pine from the Baltic regions. Another early contribution of the northern hardwoods forest to Europe was northern white-cedar, first brought to the attention of Jacques Cartier as a cure for scurvy (because of the vitamin C extracted by boiling the foliage) in the winter of 1535–1536 on the lower St. Lawrence River, and one of the first North American trees imported to the gardens of the Old World.

Until about 1900, white pine was North America's most important producer of timber, particularly along the southern and eastern edge of the northern coniferous forest. It was gradually replaced either by farms (some of which reverted to white pine as farmers moved west) or by spruce, fir, birch, and

other broad-leaved species. The importance of white pine as a timber species diminished partly through the fires and land clearing that followed the logging, partly because of the competition with southern pines and later with Douglas-fir, and partly because of the damage caused by a native insect, the white pine weevil, and a disease, white pine blister rust. The development of the pulp and paper industry extended into the northern hardwoods region, taking advantage of the older spruce–fir forests in the region and of the younger ones that in places followed the white pine.

The recent development of waferboard and oriented-strand board has increased the commercial importance of the aspens in the Lake States portion of this region. A unique forest-based industry of the northern hardwoods region is based on the sap extracted in late winter from sugar maple trees and processed to produce maple sugar and syrup.

Red pine is not as widely distributed as white pine or as useful for such a range of products; it has had a similar history but remains an important source of saw timber. Jack pine, once regarded as a sort of forest weed by timber owners interested only in white and red pine, has now become an important source of pulpwood. Red and jack pines are especially important in the western part of the region.

Although historically the northern hardwoods region was once one of the world's most important timber producers, its forests are of much greater importance today as places for people to enjoy outdoor recreation of all types and at all seasons. The northern hardwoods forest contains many of the animal species found in the northern coniferous forest—though less abundantly, to be sure. Moreover, the region is accessible to North America's greatest concentration of human population; it seems that recreation and water supply will be the dominant values of these forests, which will, however, remain important suppliers of wood and fiber.

Pacific Coast Forests

Location and Extent West of the Great Plains, the forests follow the mountain ranges of the Cordillera until they reach the northern coniferous forest

Figure 2.4 Mature sugar maple in the Nicolet National Forest, Wisconsin. (Courtesy of U.S.D.A. Forest Service.)

in northwestern Canada. In general, the more westerly of these mountain ranges catch more rain and snow and have less extreme winters. These climatic differences account for denser, taller forests nearer the Pacific and are a cause of some contrasts in species composition between the Pacific slope and the Rocky Mountain forests.

The Pacific Coast forests extend from southeast Alaska along the coast ranges to Baja California and in a parallel chain farther inland include the Cascade–Sierra range in Washington, Oregon, and California and the mountains of southern California. In the north these forests extend upward from sea level; the most southerly sea-level forests are found in the vicinity of Monterey, California (Figure 2.2).

Principal Species Conifers predominate in the Pacific Coast forests, but there are several important broad-leaved species, particularly in the southern portion of the region. At lower elevations in the foothills surrounding the Sacramento and San Joaquin valleys in California and the Willamette Valley in Oregon, the forest grades into woodland in which oaks and other broadleafs are intermixed with conifers (4).

Table 2.3 lists important trees of this region according to their occurrence in four subregions: the Coast Ranges, the Cascades, the Sierra Nevada, and the Sierra de San Pedro Martir in Baja California. From the table it is evident that the number of species decreases in the more inland and southerly

Table 2.3 Some Important Species of Pacific Coast Forests

Scientific Name	Common Name	Coast Ranges	Cascades	Sierra Nevada	Baja California
Abies amabilis	Pacific silver fir	+[a]	+		
Abies concolor	White fir		+	+	
Abies grandis	Grand fir	+	+		
Abies lasiocarpa	Subalpine fir	+	+		
Abies magnifica	California red fir	×[b]	+	+	
Abies procera	Noble fir	+	+		
Acer macrophyllum	Bigleaf maple	+	+	+	
Alnus rubra	Red alder	+	+		
Arbutus menziesii	Pacific madrone	+	+	+	
Chamaecyparis nootkatensis	Alaska cedar	+	+		
Juniperus occidentalis	Western juniper	×	+	+	
Libocedrus decurrens	Incense cedar	+	+	+	×
Picea sitchensis	Sitka spruce	+	×		
Pinus contorta	Lodgepole pine	+	+	+	×
Pinus jeffreyi	Jeffrey pine	×	+	+	×
Pinus lambertiana	Sugar pine	×	+	+	×
Pinus monticola	Western white pine	+	+	+	
Pinus ponderosa	Ponderosa pine	×	+	+	
Pinus radiata	Monterey pine	×			
Populus trichocarpa	Black cottonwood	+	+	+	×
Pseudotsuga menziesii	Douglas-fir	+	+	+	
Quercus kelloggii	California black oak	+	+	+	
Sequoia sempervirens	Redwood	+			
Sequoiadendron giganteum	Giant sequoia			×	
Thuja plicata	Western redcedar	+	+		
Tsuga heterophylla	Western hemlock	+	+		

[a] + indicates widespread occurrence.
[b] × indicates localized occurrence.

subregions. It is also true that, in general, the height of the trees decreases inland and southward. (The northern coastal forests have been called oceanic or giant evergreen forests by some plant geographers.) The forests of the Coast Ranges include the coast redwoods, some of which reach more than 110 meters in height. Other "giants" in the coastal forests are Sitka spruce, Douglas-fir, and western redcedar. The only other forests in the world where trees taller than 90 meters may be found are the stands of eucalyptus in the well-watered mountains of Tasmania and Victoria in Australia (5).

Monterey pine has been listed as important, despite its restricted occurrence in California, because it has been so widely planted in mild climates of Mediterranean type, particularly in the Southern Hemisphere.

Economic and Social Importance The forests of the Pacific Coast are among the most important in the world. The climate of this region favors extremely high rates of production of wood, and proximity to the Pacific Ocean facilitates water shipment of logs and finished products overseas and to East Coast U.S. markets. Douglas-fir is rivaled only by loblolly pine of the southeastern United States as a timber producer (Figure 2.5). The forest products industry is one of the leading employers in British Columbia, Washington, and Oregon.

Forest watersheds supply the region with some of the least costly hydroelectric power in North America as well as major irrigation projects in the Colum-bia Basin and the Central Valley of California. Sports and commercial fisheries and aquaculture also depend on the flow and quality of water from these watersheds. Recreation, wildlife, and scenic resources are available to the public in a chain of four provincial parks in British Columbia and nine national parks, three national monuments, and innumerable state parks and national forest campgrounds in the Pacific Coast states. Big-game hunting and sport fishing are major uses of public and industrial forests throughout the region. Puget Sound and the Strait of Georgia, with their many

Figure 2.5 (*a*) Old-growth Douglas-fir in western Washington with an understory of mostly western hemlock. (*b*) A 79-year-old second-growth Douglas-fir stand in western Washington. (Courtesy of U.S.D.A. Forest Service.)

forested islands and shores, float large fleets of boats for fishing and sailing all year.

Rocky Mountain Forests

Location and Extent South of the Canada–United States border, the Cordillera is divided by the Columbia Basin and plateau and farther south by the Great Basin. To the east of this dry region with few forests lie the Rocky Mountains, which extend southward into Mexico as the Sierra Madre, divided into the eastern and western ranges in the drier north of Mexico.

The forests of the Rocky Mountain region do not form the continuous cover found in some of the other forest regions; however, many of the individual forest stands, particularly of such species as lodgepole pine and Engelmann spruce, often become quite dense (Figure 2.6). The patchy nature of the Rocky Mountain forest is a consequence of the uneven distribution of precipitation in this region, the generally rough topography lying to the leeward, and the coastal ranges, which catch a large share of the moisture drawn from the Pacific Ocean.

Principal Species In the Rocky Mountain forests, even to a greater extent than in those to the west, conifers predominate. Quaking aspen nevertheless forms extensive stands in the forests of the northern and central Rockies and in a number of the forests at higher elevations in the southern Rocky Mountains.

Figure 2.6 Stand of 200-year-old lodgepole pine in the Targhee National Forest, Idaho. (Courtesy of U.S.D.A. Forest Service.)

As the forests thin out at lower elevations, the woodlands in the southern Rockies are dominated by piñons and junipers.

Table 2.4 lists the important trees of the region according to their occurrence in three subregions: the northern Rockies in western Canada, eastern Washington, northeastern Oregon, Idaho, Montana, and Wyoming; the central Rockies in Wyoming, Utah, and Colorado; and the southern Rockies in Arizona and New Mexico and the northern states of Mexico.

Perhaps the most striking feature of the forest composition of the region as a whole is the large number of pine species. The forests of the Rocky Mountains provide a good illustration of the difficulty of mapping forest regions in a simple manner, for in this region the compensating effects of altitude, latitude, and aspect are most evident. For example, the high mountains of Arizona have forests that, if not in detailed species composition, at least in general appearance closely resemble those of the northern Rockies.

In the discussion of the Pacific Coast forests, it was pointed out that the diversity of species decreases from west to east. This trend continues, as indicated by the comparison of the number of species listed for the northern Rockies subregion in Table 2.4 with the number listed for the three Canadian and U.S. subregions listed in Table 2.3.

Economic and Social Importance Throughout the region, the chief importance of forests is the protection of water resources. This is true even in the relatively well-watered northern Rockies, where

Table 2.4 Some Important Species of the Rocky Mountain Forests

Scientific Name	Common Name	Northern Rockies	Central Rockies	Southern Rockies
Abies concolor	White fir		+[a]	+
Abies lasiocarpa	Subalpine fir	+	+	X[b]
Larix occidentalis	Western larch	+		
Picea engelmannii	Engelmann spruce	+	+	+
Picea glauca	White spruce	+		
Picea pungens	Blue spruce		+	+
Pinus albicaulis	Whitebark pine	+		
Pinus contorta	Lodgepole pine	+	+	
Pinus engelmannii	Apache pine			X
Pinus flexilis	Limber pine	+	+	
Pinus leiophylla	Chihuahua pine			X
Pinus monticola	Western white pine	+		
Pinus ponderosa	Ponderosa pine	+	+	+
Pinus strobiformis	Southwestern white pine			+
Populus tremuloides	Quaking aspen	+	+	X
Prunus serotina	Black cherry			X
Pseudotsuga menziesii	Douglas-fir	+	+	+
Thuja plicata	Western redcedar	+		
Tsuga heterophylla	Western hemlock	+		

[a] + indicates widespread occurrence.
[b] X indicates localized occurrence.

an important forest products industry exists. Farther south, the importance of the forests for watershed protection increases. Forest grazing of cattle and sheep is also important in this region, particularly in the more open stands of ponderosa pine. No other forest region in North America can equal the Rocky Mountains in diversity of wildlife, including big game. Some of the best bird-watching areas of the continent are located here. The recreational importance of the region is very important, as exemplified by the chain of more than two dozen national parks in Canada and the United States, in addition to a large number of provincial parks, state parks, winter sports developments, and dude ranches.

Central Broad-Leaved Forests

To a much greater extent than is true of the forests of northern and western North America, the forests of the eastern United States have been modified in various ways by human activities. The most obvious of these changes has been clearing for farming, which converted some of the finest hardwood forests to the present-day corn belt. In many areas such as New England and the Piedmont, the soils cleared early eventually proved unprofitable for farming and were naturally reforested by pines and other pioneer tree species. Moreover, many mixed forests were selectively logged for white pine and hemlock and were thus converted to broad-leaved forests with little or no coniferous component. Finally, artificial reforestation has played a large role in the constitution of the forests in many parts of this large area.

The most detailed classification of the eastern deciduous forests of North America recognizes eight distinct regions south of the northern hardwoods. For the purposes of this brief chapter, six of these will be dealt with as the central broad-leaved forests, a regional grouping recognized also in the somewhat similar climates of western Europe and eastern Asia.

Location and Extent The central broad-leaved forests are found in twenty-four of the states east of the Great Plains and south of the northern hardwood forests. The region does not include the pine–oak (southern) and bottomland forests of the south Atlantic and Gulf coasts or the lower Mississippi Valley. Although the region at present includes much nonforested land, it is by far the largest forest region in the United States. Forest ownerships in the region are generally small in comparison with those in other forest regions, and there are comparatively few large federal forest areas such as national forests and national parks.

Principal Species More than 100 species of native trees are found in the central broad-leaved forests (Figure 2.7). In terms of both number of species and economic value, the oaks are the most important group. During this century the most important change in the species composition of this forest is the extinction (for practical purposes) of the American chestnut in the aftermath of chestnut blight, and its replacement by oaks and yellow-poplar. Table 2.5 lists some of the more important species of this forest.

Economic and Social Importance With the exception of the Pacific Coast, eastern Canada, and central Mexico, most of the concentrations of population and industry in North America are located within the central broad-leaved forest region. Thus these forests are much more directly influenced by the needs and desires of urban centers than are the forests of any other region on the continent. Production of industrial raw materials by the central broad-leaved forests is by no means trivial, although it is not as intensive in any particular locality as in, for example, the Pacific Coast region. The hardwoods of the central broad-leaved region supply a large furniture industry and, particularly in recent years, a growing demand for pallets for mechanized handling and storage of materials. In some portions of this region, hardwoods stands on poorer soils are being replaced by pine plantations for the production of pulpwood. Increasingly, the importance of these forests lies in their role in protecting water supplies, providing wildlife habitat, and affording opportunities for outdoor recreation. State, county, and municipal parks provide the major share of

Figure 2.7 Beech growing with eastern hemlock in Pennsylvania. (Courtesy of U.S.D.A. Forest Service.)

recreational facilities, but the Park Service, the Forest Service, and the Corps of Engineers have numerous recreational areas throughout the region. Freshwater fishing and boating are among the most popular recreational activities.

Oak–Pine (Southern) Forests

Location and Extent The oak–pine region lies along the south Atlantic and Gulf coasts, extending westward into eastern Texas and Oklahoma. It includes the Piedmont region and the sandhills region of the Carolinas. Along the coasts it is penetrated by the bottomland hardwoods forests, which lie along the river courses, most notably along the lower Mississippi River (Figure 2.2).

Principal Species There has been a major shift in the species composition of the forests of the oak-–pine region since the invasion by Europeans. The first change was occasioned by clearing mixed pine–hardwoods forests and planting clean-cultivated row crops, a type of agriculture that proved destructive to the soils of the Piedmont region, which are highly erodible and are subjected to rainstorms of tropical intensity. Widespread farm abandonment was followed by natural reforestation

Table 2.5 Some Important Species of the Central Broad-Leaved Forest

Scientific Name	Common Name
Acer rubrum	Red maple
Acer saccharum	Sugar maple
Aesculus octandra	Yellow buckeye
Betula alleghaniensis	Yellow birch
Carya cordiformis	Bitternut hickory
Carya ovata	Shagbark hickory
Carya tomentosa	Mockernut hickory
Cornus florida	Flowering dogwood
Diospyros virginiana	Common persimmon
Fagus grandifolia	American beech
Fraxinus americana	White ash
Juglans nigra	Black walnut
Liquidambar styraciflua	Sweetgum
Liriodendron tulipifera	Yellow-poplar
Magnolia acuminata	Cucumber magnolia
Nyssa sylvatica	Black tupelo
Pinus strobus	Eastern white pine
Quercus alba	White oak
Quercus macrocarpa	Bur oak
Quercus marilandica	Blackjack oak
Quercus prinus	Chestnut oak
Quercus rubra	Northern red oak
Quercus stellata	Post oak
Quercus velutina	Black oak
Robinia pseudoacacia	Black locust
Tilia americana	American basswood
Tilia heterophylla	White basswood
Tsuga canadensis	Eastern hemlock
Ulmus americana	American elm

of the worn-out lands, first by the light-seeded pines, with rapid invasion of these pine stands by oaks and other hardwoods such as sweetgum. In many areas on the poorer upland soils, intensive forest management took the form of selective elimination of the low-value hardwoods from pine–hardwoods stands by girdling, the use of herbicides, or prescribed burning. Finally, the harvesting of "old-field" pine (Figure 2.8) or of pine–hardwoods stands has been followed by large-scale planting of pines. The major share of the pines being planted in the region at present are grown from seed produced in seed

orchards made up of selected superior trees. Table 2.6 lists some of the more important species of this forest region.

Economic and Social Importance The oak–pine region has the most intensively managed forests in North America, and is one of the leading producers of pulp and paper in the world. To a large extent, the pulp and paper industry has been based on the pine stands that followed agricultural failures, but more recently pine plantations have become an important source of raw materials. A current development in the industry is an increasing use of various hardwood species for pulpwood production. Loblolly pine is the leading species throughout most of the region, but in the Deep South slash pine is a major timber resource. The wildlife resources of the region are quite diverse. Two of the major game species—quail and deer—can be managed compatibly with intensive timber production. Wild turkey has been successfully reestablished in many parts of the region. The numerous water impoundments are heavily used for boating and fishing.

Bottomland Hardwoods Forests

Location and Extent The bottomland hardwoods forests are scattered along the central and south Atlantic and Gulf coasts and in the lower Mississippi Valley. Although many types of bottomland forests are recognized in this region, depending on soil type and drainage pattern, they may be grouped in two broad categories: swamps such as the Great Dismal and the Okefenokee, and floodplains, of which the Mississippi delta is the most extensive.

Principal Species Three conifers are found in these otherwise hardwood forests. Bald cypress, often associated with water tupelo, is found in swamps and frequently flooded bottoms. Atlantic white-cedar and pond pine occur, often in pure stands, on peat soils in swamps. Table 2.7 lists some of the important species of this region.

Figure 2.8 Stand of 80- to 90-year-old loblolly pine that colonized an abandoned field in North Carolina. (Courtesy of U.S.D.A. Forest Service.)

Economic and Social Importance Hardwood lumber and veneer logs for the furniture industry and for paneling are leading products of the bottomland hardwoods forests. Along the lower Mississippi the "batture" lands between levee and river are planted with cottonwoods for the production of pulpwood. In recent years pulpwood plantations of sycamore have been installed on bottomland soils.

The bottomland forests are particularly rich in wildlife, including such large animals as the black bear. The region has a large number of wildlife refuges and public recreation areas. Recreational resources are largely water-based.

Tropical Forests

Location and Extent The tropical forests of North America are located in Mexico and southern Florida. In Mexico there are three characteristic types of tropical forests, the distinctions coming from differences in topography and seasonal distribution of rainfall. The tropical rain forest is located principally near the Gulf of Mexico in the south, where ample rainfall occurs every month. A winter dry season characterizes the second type, the tropical deciduous forest that extends mostly along the Pacific Coast, but with representatives in the North-

Table 2.6 Some Important Species of the Oak–Pine (Southern) Forest

Scientific Name	Common Name
Acer rubrum	Red maple
Carya cordiformis	Bitternut hickory
Carya ovata	Shagbark hickory
Carya tomentosa	Mockernut hickory
Cornus florida	Flowering dogwood
Juniperus virginiana	Eastern redcedar
Liquidambar styraciflua	Sweetgum
Liriodendron tulipifera	Yellow-poplar
Nyssa sylvatica	Black tupelo
Pinus clausa	Sand pine
Pinus echinata	Shortleaf pine
Pinus elliottii	Slash pine
Pinus palustris	Longleaf pine
Pinus taeda	Loblolly pine
Pinus virginiana	Virginia pine
Quercus alba	White oak
Quercus coccinea	Scarlet oak
Quercus falcata	Southern red oak
Quercus marilandica	Blackjack oak
Quercus nigra	Water oak
Quercus phellos	Willow oak
Quercus rubra	Northern red oak
Quercus velutina	Black oak

Table 2.7 Some Important Species of the Bottomland Hardwoods Forests

Scientific Name	Common Name
Acer negundo	Box elder
Acer rubrum	Red maple
Acer saccharinum	Silver maple
Betula nigra	River birch
Carya cordiformis	Bitternut hickory
Carya illinoensis	Pecan
Celtis laevigata	Sugarberry
Chamaecyparis thyoides	Atlantic white-cedar
Fraxinus pennsylvanica	Green ash
Gleditsia triacanthos	Honey locust
Liquidambar styraciflua	Sweetgum
Magnolia grandiflora	Southern magnolia
Nyssa aquatica	Water tupelo
Nyssa sylvatica biflora	Swamp tupelo
Pinus serotina	Pond pine
Platanus occidentalis	American sycamore
Populus deltoides	Eastern cottonwood
Populus heterophylla	Swamp cottonwood
Quercus falcata pagodaefolia	Cherrybark oak
Quercus lyrata	Overcup oak
Quercus michauxii	Swamp chestnut oak
Quercus palustris	Pin oak
Quercus virginiana	Live oak
Taxodium distichum	Bald cypress

east. The third type, the oak and pine forests, with a winter dry season, occur at higher elevations in the Sierra Madre (oriental and occidental) and in the south. The tropical forests of Florida are restricted to the extreme southern tip of the peninsula and to the keys and have well-distributed rainfall (Figure 2.9).

Principal Species To an even greater extent than in the account of the central hardwoods forest, the listing in Table 2.8 of the principal species of the tropical forests is a very small sample of the great diversity of species present in these forests. Eastern white pine is one of the several species of Mexico's tropical forests that are of major importance in the eastern United States, two others being black cherry and sweet gum.

Economic and Social Importance The pines of the mountainous oak and pine forests are an important source of lumber and pulpwood. Charcoal

Figure 2.9 Mangrove trees with arching prop roots (adventitious roots) in the Florida Keys. As sand, mud, and debris are lodged in the maze of prop roots, the shallows eventually become dry land and an islet is formed. (Photograph courtesy of Michael and N. J. Berrill.)

Table 2.8 Some Important Species of the Tropical Forests

Scientific Name	Common Name	Rain Forests	Deciduous Forests	Oak–Pine Forests	Southern Florida
Abies religiosa	Oyamel			+[a]	
Acacia farnesiana	Huisache		+		
Alnus jorullensis	Aliso			+	
Avicennia nitida	Black mangrove				+
Alvaradoa amorphoides	Camaron		+		
Bumelia celastrina	Rompezapato		+		
Bursera simaruba	Gumbo-limbo	+	+		+
Ceiba pentandra	Silk-cotton tree	+	+		
Cecropia mexicana	Trumpet wood	+	+		
Coccoloba diversifolia	Doveplum				+
Dialium guianense	Ironwood	+			
Eugenia confusa	Redberry eugenia				+
Ficus aurea	Florida strangler fig				+
Gilbertia arborea	Hoja fresca	+			
Guaiacum sanctum	Lignum vitae				+
Krugiodendron ferreum	Leadwood				+
Lysiloma bahamensis	Wild tamarind				+
Pinus ayacahuite	Pinabete			+	
Pinus leiophylla	Piño chino			+	
Pinus montezumae	Piño de Montezuma			+	
Pinus oocarpa	Piño prieto			+	
Pinus strobus	Eastern white pine			+	
Pinus teocote	Piño colorado			+	
Piscidia piscipula	Florida fish poison tree				+
Pistacia mexicana	Achin		+		
Poulsenia armata	—	+			
Rhizophora mangle	Red mangrove				+
Roystonea elata	Florida royal palm				+
Sapindus saponaria	Wingleaf soapberry				+
Sideroxylon foetidissimum	False mastic				+
Sterculia mexicana	Castano bellota	+			
Swietenia humilis	Caoba		+		
Swietenia mahagoni	West Indies mahogany				+
Taxodium mucronatum	Montezuma cypress		+		
Zanthoxylon fagara	Lime prickly ash		+		

[a] + indicates widespread occurrence.

produced locally from the oaks is used as a cooking fuel in many rural areas. With the rapid urbanization of the population, water has become the dominant resource of Mexico's forests. The principal—and very great—value of the tropical forest of south Florida is as a unique ecosystem in the continental United States, most of it within the Everglades National Park.

Forest Regions of the World

Climate and soil determine the general appearance of a forest—whether it is open or closed; tall or short; evergreen or deciduous; coniferous, broad-leaved, or mixed. These various broad forest types may be found in all continents, but the species that constitute the forests of a given broad type usually differ from place to place. On the other hand, genera often are common to widely separated forests of the same general type. This is particularly true of the cooler, more northerly forest regions. Southern Hemisphere forests, however, differ markedly in their composition from Northern Hemisphere forests.

Because it is possible to recognize these broad general types of forests, we can make a comprehensive survey of world forest regions in a relatively short account (Figure 2.10).

Northern Coniferous Forest

Location and Extent In Eurasia, as in North America, the northern coniferous forest or *taiga* is the most extensive forest region, stretching from Sakhalin and Hokkaido in the Pacific across Siberia and European Russia to the Scandinavian peninsula.

Principal Species The Eurasian *taiga* resembles its North American counterpart in the general composition of its forests, but differs in two important respects. In Eurasia, particularly in Scandinavia, Finland, and European Russia, the *taiga* extends, in the form of low open woodland, north of the Arctic

Circle, whereas in North America the conifer woodland barely reaches the Arctic in the west. Moreover, the Eurasian *taiga* is somewhat richer in number of species of larch, spruce, and fir and is especially notable for the northern extension of Scotch pine, the world's most widely distributed pine, and for the occurrence in the far north of several small white pines. As in North America, the Eurasian *taiga* has numerous species of birch, poplar, and willow.

Economic and Social Importance As indicated in Table 2.1, the Eurasian *taiga,* most of which is within the borders of the Soviet Union, is the world's largest native coniferous forest region (Figure 2.11). It is an important producer of lumber and pulpwood, particularly in its western sections, where Scotch pine is the leading commercial species. The rivers and lakes of the region are important in the transportation of sawlogs and pulpwood.

The region has abundant wildlife—from mosquitoes to moose—and, like the North American northern forest, continues to be important in the fur trade. In Scandinavia recreational use of the northern forest is important.

Pacific Coniferous Forest

Location and Extent The Pacific coniferous forest region is relatively small in extent and is scattered in Japan, Korea, and southern coastal Siberia.

Principal Species The region is mountainous, with a relatively mild coastal climate, and therefore provides a variety of habitats that are occupied by a large number of coniferous and broad-leaved species. The conifers include most of the genera found in western North America, the species of fir, larch, spruce, pine, and hemlock being especially numerous. Douglas-fir is also represented. *Cryptomeria* (sugi), the principal native conifer of Japan, is intensively cultivated.

Economic and Social Importance Heavy pressure for agricultural production limits commercial forests to steeper and higher lands. Despite inten-

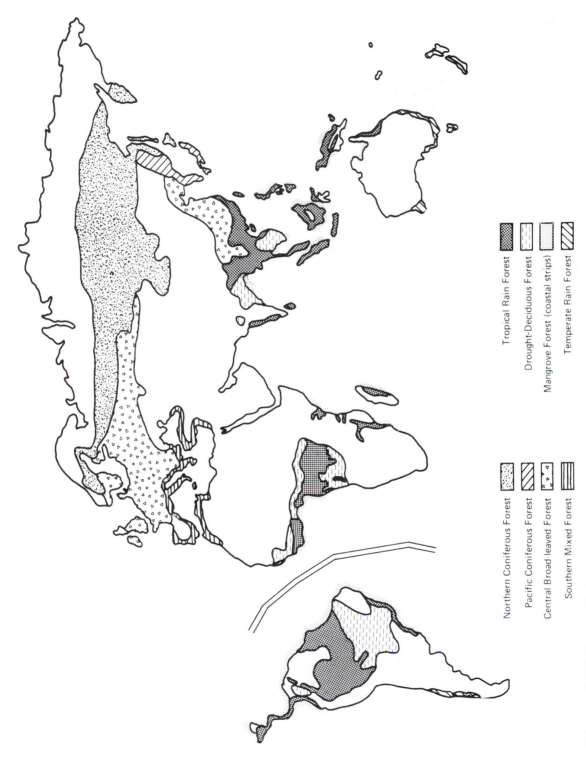

Figure 2.10 The world's forests.

Tropical Rain Forest

Drought-Deciduous Forest

Mangrove Forest (coastal strips)

Temperate Rain Forest

Northern Coniferous Forest

Pacific Coniferous Forest

Central Broad-leaved Forest

Southern Mixed Forest

Figure 2.11 Timber floating on the Mana River, Krasnozarsk region, Soviet Union. (Photograph courtesy of Novosti Press Agency, Soviet Union.)

farming and for urban and industrial development (Figure 2.10).

Principal Species Most of the principal species of the central broad-leaved forest of Britain and Europe have closely related counterparts in the forests of eastern North America and have, moreover, been commonly planted as ornamentals in the United States. In Table 2.9, which lists the principal forest tree species of the broad-leaved forests of Europe and Britain, species well known in eastern North America are marked with an asterisk. Three of the conifers (Scotch pine, Norway spruce, and European larch) have been planted for timber production fairly extensively in parts of the northeastern United States, whereas Scotch pine is commonly planted for the production of Christmas trees.

The central broad-leaved forests of western Europe have conspicuously fewer species than those of eastern Asia and eastern North America. More than two dozen genera of trees and shrubs that are found

sive cultivation of commercial forests in Japan, these are insufficient to supply the demands for lumber and paper, which are increasingly met by importation from the forest regions surrounding the Pacific. The forests of Japan and Korea are important for watershed protection and for recreational use. Japanese horticulturists have developed many interesting and beautiful varieties of their native trees, which are now found in gardens throughout the world.

Central Broad-Leaved Forest

Location and Extent The central broad-leaved forest of Eurasia is divided into two quite distinct regions by the immense steppe and desert areas of central Asia and eastern Europe. The western broad-leaved forest originally covered western Europe and Britain, and the eastern region constitutes much of eastern China. As in North America, the broad-leaved forest of western Europe and Britain has been substantially reduced in extent by clearing for

Table 2.9 Some Important Species of the Central Broad-Leaved Forest of Europe and Britain

Scientific Name	Common Name
Abies alba	Silver fir
Larix decidua[*][a]	European larch
*Picea abies**	Norway spruce
*Pinus sylvestris**	Scotch pine
*Taxus baccata**	Common yew
*Acer platanoides**	Norway maple
*Acer pseudoplatanus**	Sycamore maple
Alnus glutinosa	Common alder
*Betula verrucosa**	Silver birch
Carpinus betulus	Hornbeam
*Fagus sylvatica**	Common beech
Fraxinus excelsior	Common ash
Populus tremula	Aspen
Quercus petraea	Durmast oak
*Quercus robur**	English oak
*Tilia cordata**	Small-leaved linden
*Ulmus procera**	English elm

[a]Trees well known in eastern North America are marked with an asterisk.

in the North American and east Asian forests are absent from the western European forests, which were seriously depleted of species as a consequence of the last glaciation.

In strong contrast to those of western Europe, the central broad-leaved forests of eastern Asia contain a fascinating array of species. Indeed in recent times Chinese botanists have discovered in China two hitherto-unknown genera of conifers: *Cathaya* and *Metasequoia*. Table 2.10 lists a few of the more commonly planted trees introduced into North America from China, but a more complete list of trees and shrubs introduced into Europe and North America from east Asia numbers more than 100 species.

Economic and Social Importance After hundreds of years and several drastic deforestations, the central broad-leaved forest of western Europe continues to play an important role in the production of solid wood and fiber, as well as providing habitat for large populations of game and other wildlife. With a large urban population distributed throughout the region, the recreational use of the forest is heavy.

The science and practice of forest management and silviculture were born in the broad-leaved forests of western and central Europe, and forest managers in all parts of the world continue to look on European forestry as a model (Figure 2.12).

Much of the broad-leaved forest in east Asia has, so far, played a comparatively small part as a source of industrial raw materials because of inaccessibility, although local populations make extensive use of

Table 2.10 Some Species Introduced into North America from China

Scientific Name	Common Name
Ailanthus altissima	Tree of heaven
Albizzia julibrissin	Silktree
Ginkgo biloba	Ginkgo
Koelreuteria paniculata	Goldenrain tree
Lagerstroemia indica	Crape myrtle
Melia azedarach	China tree
Metasequoia glyptostroboides	Metasequoia
Paulownia tomentosa	Paulownia

the forests. Areas of China long ago deforested are currently being restored to forest productivity by massive tree-planting programs.

Southern Mixed Forest

The general designation of southern mixed forest covers a number of forest and woodland formations in the warmer but subtropical regions of both Northern and Southern Hemispheres. The principal forest regions in this category are the Mediterranean forest, small areas in coastal California and Chile, and several coastal areas in Australia. What these forest regions have in common are mild maritime climates in which snowfall is infrequent, temperatures seldom fall below −10°C, and precipitation is moderate to slight and occurs mostly in winter. Such a climate is often referred to as Mediterranean.

Mediterranean Forest When the French essayist Chateaubriand wrote, "Forests precede people; deserts follow them," he could well have had the Mediterranean Basin in view (Figure 2.13). This region, with its relatively mild climate, is adjacent to early centers of agricultural production in the Fertile Crescent and the Nile Valley. It became a cradle for civilizations that engaged in breeding livestock and shipbuilding—activities that made heavy inroads into the forests. The effect was particularly severe in the summer-dry Mediterranean climate, where soil moisture is barely sufficient to sustain closed forests even when they are not subjected to the added stresses of grazing, burning, and heavy cutting.

Location and extent The Mediterranean forest extends around the Mediterranean littoral, with the exception of the coasts of Libya and Egypt, which are essentially desert or steppe. It extends also to portions of the south and east coasts of the Black Sea and along the Atlantic coasts of Morocco and of southern Portugal and Spain. At lower elevations the Mediterranean forest (or rather its remains) is often in fact woodland and scrub, termed variously *maquis, macchia, shikara,* and *chaparral.* At higher elevations (with heavier precipitation) closed forests resembling the central hardwoods forest are found.

Figure 2.12 Selective cutting in a spruce–fir forest in the mountains near Zalusina, Yugoslavia. (Photograph by R. A. Young.)

Principal species In Table 2.11, which lists some of the important species of the region, evergreen broad-leaved species are marked with an asterisk. Evergreen broad-leaved trees are generally prevalent in warm climates.

Figure 2.13 Typical Mediterranean vegetation near Delphi, Greece. (Photograph by R. L. Giese.)

Economic and social importance The Mediterranean forest, except for certain stands at the higher elevations, is no longer an important source of timber. Nevertheless, these forests and woodlands are heavily exploited for various products. Most of the species listed are utilized for fuel, but this is especially true of the oaks, which are the raw material for local charcoal producers. Many of the species are important as food plants, most notably the olive, which also yields a wood outstandingly suited to fine wood carving. Other food plants are the chestnut, cornelian cherry, hazel or filbert, carob or St. John's bread, and stone pine. Cork oak is the basis for a large and active cork industry, situated mostly in the western Mediterranean and in Portugal, and maritime and black pines are tapped to produce rosin, tar, and turpentine. Grazing by sheep and goats is increasingly recognized as an abuse of these forests and woodlands. At present the amenity values of these forests eclipse all others as the

Table 2.11 Some Important Trees and Large Shrubs of the Mediterranean Forest

Scientific Name	Common Name
*Arbutus unedo**a*	Strawberry tree
Carpinus orientalis	Eastern hornbeam
Castanea sativa	Spanish chestnut
Celtis australis	European nettle tree
*Ceratonia siliqua**	Carob tree
Cercis siliquastrum	Judas tree
Cornus mas	Cornelian cherry
Corylus avellana	European hazel
Fraxinus ornus	Flowering ash
Juniperus oxycedrus	Prickly juniper
*Laurus nobilis**	Laurel
*Olea europaea**	Olive
Ostrya carpinifolia	Hophornbeam
Pinus halepensis	Aleppo pine
Pinus nigra	Black pine
Pinus pinaster	Maritime pine
Pinus pinea	Stone pine
Platanus orientalis	Oriental plane
Quercus cerris	Turkey oak
Quercus frainetto	Hungarian oak
*Quercus ilex**	Holm oak
Quercus pubescens	Pubescent oak
*Quercus suber**	Cork oak

a Evergreen broad-leaved species are marked with an asterisk.

region's tourist industry attracts visitors to Europe's sun belt (1).

Coastal Forests of California and Chile The mild summer-dry, winter-wet Mediterranean climate occurs also along the central California coast and a short stretch of the coast of Chile, at about the same distance from the equator.

In both areas the dominant vegetation consists of hard-leaved (sclerophyllous) shrubs with patches of open woodland in situations with adequate soil moisture and shelter from the wind. The forest in California is notable as a scenic and recreational area, in part because of the rugged beauty of two tree species, Monterey pine and Monterey cypress, which are restricted in their natural distribution to this area. Coast live oak is the dominant large broadleaf in this forest. Monterey pine has attained

worldwide renown as a highly productive timber species in various areas of Mediterranean climate, and has been particularly successful in the region south of Santiago and Valparaiso in Chile.

Coastal Forests of Australia The summer-dry forests of Australia are restricted to a fairly narrow zone that extends from approximately the Tropic of Capricorn in Queensland southward and around the coasts of New South Wales and Victoria to eastern South Australia. Between Adelaide in South Australia and the southern tip of Western Australia, the coastal zone is treeless or open woodland. About half of the island state of Tasmania is in the summer-dry high forest zone. Two genera, *Eucalyptus* and *Acacia,* dominate these forests, and both include many species. About 600 species of *Eucalyptus* have been described. Many of these are shrubs or small trees, as are most of the species of *Acacia.* Nevertheless, some of the world's tallest trees are eucalyptus. *Eucalyptus diversicolor* (karri) in Western Australia attains 75 meters, and trees of *E. regnans* (mountain ash) of 100 meters have been measured in Victoria (Figure 2.14). These heights are attained only in forests at higher elevations where the rainfall is higher than occurs in a strictly Mediterranean climate. The eucalpyts are the principal producers of

Figure 2.14 Virgin karri (*Eucalyptus diversicolor*) in Western Australia. (Courtesy of Forests Department of Western Australia.)

timber and fiber in Australia, but in the drier portions of the coastal forests, eucalypts are being replaced by highly productive plantations of Monterey pine and, in Western Australia, of maritime pine. The Australian coastal forests are not only importers of these exotic pines; they also have exported hundreds of species of eucalypts, acacias, and other trees and shrubs to the forest plantations and gardens of the parts of the world that have similar climates (5).

Tropical Rain Forest

The tropical rain forest is restricted to a belt within 22 degrees north and south of the equator and is found at low to moderate elevations. Rainfall varies from 2000 to 4000 millimeters, evenly distributed throughout the year. Amount and seasonal distribution of rainfall distinguish the tropical rain forest from the drought-deciduous tropical forest and the arid tropical regions.

The most extensive area of tropical rain forest is found in the Amazon Basin of northern Brazil and adjacent portions of Ecuador, Venezuela, and the Guianas (presently called Guyana, Surinam, and French Guiana). Other areas of tropical rain forest in the Western Hemisphere are in south coastal Brazil, the Central American countries, some of the islands of the Caribbean, and the southern tip and keys of Florida. In Africa the tropical rain forest is restricted to the Congo Basin of the western equatorial region and to the eastern side of Madagascar. Southeast Asia, Indonesia, New Guinea, the Philippines, and the northeast coast of Australia constitute the largest extent of tropical rain forest in the Eastern Hemisphere (Figure 2.10).

The outstanding characteristic of the tropical rain forest is extreme diversity of all life-forms. Among the plants, diversity is evident not only in number of species but also in growth forms, resulting in a many-layered high forest, the evergreen leaves of which so efficiently trap radiation that even at noon on a sunny day the forest floor is in much deeper shade than one experiences in the densest temperate-region forest (Figure 2.15). This forest is therefore the earth's most productive terrestrial ecosys-

Figure 2.15 Layering of tropical vegetation in the Amazon region of Brazil. (Photograph by R. A. Young.)

tem in terms of fixation of carbon as biomass. Approximately 2500 tree species have been described in the Amazon rain forests, but there may be as many as 4000 tree species in this region. A major effort is under way in Brazil to identify these undescribed species and assess their properties.

At present there is widely expressed concern about the future of the tropical rain forests of the world, and at the same time the importance of these forests for the world's climate and biological endowment is becoming more clearly recognized. Heretofore the industrialized world has exerted relatively little impact on these forests, the indigenous people have subsisted essentially as hunter–gatherers in equilibrium with the ecosystems of which they are a part. Early exploitation of these forests by the industrialized world was relatively benign, consisting mainly of extracting from the complex forests by manual and animal logging single species such as mahogany and rosewood. In the late twentieth century a combination of population increases in the tropics as well as in the temperate regions, along with the development of more effective road-building and logging equipment (Figure 2.16), has made it possible and profitable to intensify the harvesting of rain forest timber and to clear whole forests for replacement with plantations of subtropical pines or exotic broadleafs such as *Gmelina* or to convert the forests to agricultural croplands or pastures (Figure 2.17).

To focus exclusively on the timber-producing (or agronomic or pastoral) potential of these highly diverse forests is to pass up opportunities of which we are just becoming aware. As an economic botanist has written, "Nature's storehouse has hardly been touched. We should begin exploring it and sampling its offerings. This is especially so because we may be losing species and genotypes through the rapid loss of native habitats in the tropics and deserts" (6).

There are two principal reservations to the application of temperate-region industrial forestry techniques to tropical rain forests. In the first place, it is unlikely that in the long run replacement of these complex forests will prove biologically sound and economically rewarding. At stake in particular is the supply of mineral nutrients needed to support the whole ecosystem. In temperate ecosystems a substantial share of the mineral nutrient stock (chiefly nitrogen, phosphorus, potassium, and calcium) is held in the soil (see Chapter 4), whereas in tropical rain forests this nutrient stock is held largely in the aboveground living and rapidly decaying vegetation. Thus removing the trees from a tropical rain forest takes away a major share of the nutrient capital of the ecosystem.

Second, the loss of these complex ecosystems could have much wider implications than the displacement and destruction of the indigenous human, animal, and plant populations. There is substantial reason to believe that the tropical rain forests are of worldwide climatic importance in fixing carbon as biomass and hence in slowing the buildup of carbon dioxide in the atmosphere. The current rise in world temperatures could be attributable to the "greenhouse effect" of carbon dioxide as a constituent of the atmosphere. Moreover, intensive logging and replacement of tropical rain forests will inevitably cause many plant and animal species to become extinct, a process increasingly less acceptable in many nations of the temperate world. It seems unlikely that world opinion, as it becomes more clearly articulated, will continue to tolerate this process in the tropics.

Drought-Deciduous Forest

Adjacent to several of the areas of tropical rain forest are regions that have a heavy rainfall during the summer and extreme drought in winter and spring. In these climates various so-called drought-deciduous forests have developed. Examples are regions along the central western coast of Mexico and in outliers of the northern Andes, regions adjacent to the extensive rain forests of Brazil, and forests north and south of the rain forest of western Africa. The extreme development of this climate is in India, Burma, and Thailand, where the name *mon-*

Figure 2.16 New logging road in Papua, New Guinea. (UN photograph.)

Figure 2.17 Agroforestry development in Amazonia. (UN–FAO photograph.)

soon is applied to the heavy seasonal rains that break the winter drought. The forests within this region have long been of great commercial importance as sources of teak, sal, and bamboo.

Mangrove Forest

The mangrove swamp forest, though restricted to coastal saltwater areas and brackish streams in the humid tropics, is in the aggregate a large and important forest formation. A number of genera of saltwater-adapted trees and shrubs compose these low forests. The most common are *Rhizophora,* with stilt roots, and *Avicennia.* Human populations are heavy in the areas adjacent to the mangrove forests, which are important sources of fuel and shelter for varied wildlife populations.

Temperate Rain Forest

The temperate rain forest, growing in a temperate climate with abundant, well-distributed precipitation, is found largely in New Zealand, southern Chile, and a few coastal areas in Australia. The native species are a number of gymnosperms including members of the families Podocarpaceae and Araucariaceae as well as the angiosperm genus *Nothofagus* (southern beech). These have been producers of valuable timber, but have so far not proved adaptable to conventional modes of forest management, with the possible exception of some of the araucarias and eucalypts in Australia. In consequence, this forest region, particularly in New Zealand and Chile, has undergone large-scale conversion to plantations of Northern Hemisphere conifers such as Monterey pine and Douglas-fir, and in the warmer parts of the region in Australia, to plantations of slash pine, loblolly pine, and Caribbean pine.

"New" Forests

Portions of southern Africa, South America, and New Zealand, previously unforested or with woodland of low productivity, have over the past few decades been forested with nonindigenous species of trees.

The objective is to provide raw materials for local industries. The species used include Monterey pine, slash pine, loblolly pine, Caibbean pine, the tropical Asian *Pinus merkusii* (Merkus pine) and *kesiya* (Khasia pine), and species of *Acacia* and *Eucalyptus*.

References

1. H. WALTER, *Vegetation of the Earth,* Springer-Verlag, New York/Berlin, 1973.

2. J. S. ROWE, "Forest regions of Canada," Dept. of Northern Affairs and National Resources, Can. For. Br. Bull. 123, 1959.

3. E. L. BRAUN, *Deciduous Forests of Eastern North America,* Hafner, New York, 1950.

4. J. F. FRANKLIN AND C. T. DYRNESS, "Natural vegetation of Oregon and Washington," U.S.D.A. For. Ser., Gen. Tech. Rept. PNW-8, 1973.

5. A. RULE, *Forests of Australia,* Angus & Robertson, Sydney, 1967.

6. N. D. VIETMEYER, *Science, 232,* 1379 (1986).

Additional Reading

M. G. BARBOUR AND W. D. BILLINGS, EDS., *North American Terrestrial Vegetation,* Cambridge Univ. Press, Cambridge, England, 1988.

H. A. GLEASON AND A. CRONQUIST, *The Natural Geography of Plants,* Columbia Univ. Press, New York, 1964.

H.-L. LI, *The Origin and Cultivation of Shade and Ornamental Trees,* Univ. of Pennsylvania Press, Philadelphia, 1974.

E. L. LITTLE, JR., "Atlas of United States trees, Vol. I. Conifers and important hardwoods," U.S.D.A. For. Ser., Misc. Publ. 1146, 1971.

V. E. SHELFORD, *The Ecology of North America,* Univ. of Illinois Press, Urbana, 1963.

Forest Biology

PART 2

Trees are the largest and oldest of the known living plant species in the world today (Figure P2.1). Starting as a minute seed, they can grow to heights over 120 meters and accumulate as much as 1500 cubic meters of wood in the process. In addition, trees possess a water-transporting system so powerful that it can raise water about a hundred times as efficiently as the best suction pump ever made by human beings (1). Trees are truly remarkable mechanisms of nature.

Like all other plants, trees are constructed solely of cells, the basic units of life. However, the cells in a leaf, for example, are quite different from those in the trunk and different again from those in the root. Each kind of cell is usually found in association with similar cells; groups of similar cells make up tissue, and tissues combine into even more complex groups known as organs (1). Clearly the specialized organs serve different purposes in the tree. The complex functions of the tree and its component parts are treated in detail in Chapter 3, "Structure and Function of Forest Trees."

The growth and vigor of trees are a function of many factors. Certainly the bountiful diversity in form and style of trees is related to their genetic constitution. Chapter 5, "Forest Genetics and Forest Tree Breeding," discusses the heritable variation of trees and the application of genetic principles to the

Figure P2.1 One of the oldest known living plants in the world: a 3000-year-old bristlecone pine sculptured by the wind, sand, and ice of the White Mountains in eastern California. (Courtesy of U.S.D.A. Forest Service.)

development of lines of trees of increased value to humankind.

Environmental factors can have a profound influence on tree growth. Minerals in the soil, water shortages, wind and climate, the availability of sunlight, and attack by insects and disease all affect the patterns of tree growth (Figure P2.2). The impact of these influences and human interaction for control of tree growth and vigor are treated in the following chapters. Integration of the many factors that affect tree and stand growth is discussed in Chapter 6, "Forest Ecology and the Forest Ecosystem." New methodologies for studies on the forest ecosystem through computer-modeling techniques are also described in this chapter.

A forest community must be considered as a dynamic structure that responds to the laws of cause and effect, one in which all organisms intertwine to form a harmonic ecosystem (2). The forest has evolved through *plant succession,* the orderly replacement of one plant community or forest stand with another. Generally a temporary plant community is replaced by a relatively more stable community until a dynamic equilibrium is attained between the plants and the environment. The factors affecting succession of forests and the characteristics of the successional stages are further described in Chapter 6.

Disturbances in the forest can be either natural (wind, fire, insect and disease outbreaks) or caused by human beings (forest harvesting and fire) and can result in destruction of small or large segments of the forest. The effect of disturbance is to produce sites where new communities of the trees, plants, and animals can exist. These new communities may differ from those of the native forest (Figure P2.3). Thus disturbances can alter the biological succession of the forests. These and other effects are considered in the following chapters on forest biology.

Figure P2.2 Twisted aspens on the Grand Canyon's northern rim in Arizona are called "The Crooked Forest." The resilient trees were bent as saplings by winter winds and deep snowdrifts. (Courtesy of Life Picture Service.)

References

1. P. Farb, *The Forest,* Time–Life Books, New York, 1969.

2. H. W. Hocker, Jr., *Introduction to Forest Biology,* John Wiley & Sons, New York, 1979.

Figure P2.3 The blast from the eruption of Mount Saint Helens in the state of Washington flattened previously lush, green forests. Ecologists are closely monitoring the return of plant and animal life. (Photograph by R. L. Giese.)

CHAPTER 3

Structure and Function of Forest Trees

THOMAS W. KIMMERER

Trees and other woody plants are the largest and longest-lived organisms on earth. Bristlecone pines live in excess of 4000 years, and many other species are capable of attaining ages in excess of 1000 years (Figure P2.1). Trees can attain heights of 100 meters and diameters greater than 10 meters. This potential for great longevity and size imposes many physiological constraints on trees. Trees must transport water from the soil to great heights, and carbohydrates synthesized in the leaves during photosynthesis must travel great distances to nourish the roots. Trees must also withstand the extremes in weather that can occur in the course of a liftime. To us, with our brief life span of 80 years or so, a severe drought occurring on average every 50 years seems a rare event, but to an organism that lives for 1000 years it is a common event. Gravity and wind also exert significant stress on a tree.

Despite the special problems of trees, they do not differ fundamentally from other plants in their anatomy, physiology, and biochemistry. Trees differ from other plants mainly in how they allocate energy and substrates for growth. Trees allocate a great deal more energy and substrates to diameter growth than do other plants; in contrast, tomato plants allocate more of their energy and substrates to fruit growth than to diameter growth. In this chapter we will review basic aspects of plant growth, emphasizing how trees differ from other plants.

Our understanding of the physiology and biochemistry of tree growth is still rather limited. Tree physiology is a young science, and progress in understanding how trees grow has been slow. Nevertheless, tree physiology and biochemistry have important applications in forestry today, ranging from improvements in seed germination and in establishing plantations to the new technologies of tissue culture and genetic engineering. As the pioneer tree physiologist Paul Kramer said, "We will know how to grow trees when we know how trees grow."

Primary Growth

Primary growth originates from *apical meristems* and brings about the ·formation of shoots, roots, leaves, and reproductive parts. The results of primary growth in trees is increased height of the shoot and increased length of the root system. Primary growth produces all the organs in the plant body. Secondary growth originates in the *vascular cambium;* it increases the diameter of stems and roots but does not produce new organs.

Organs and Tissues

A tree consists of three major types of organs: stem, leaves, and roots. Other organs can be viewed as modifications of these basic organs. A flower, for example, is a modified stem bearing modified leaves. Each of these organs is composed of three basic tissue systems, the *ground, vascular,* and *dermal* (Table 3.1). The ground tissue consists mostly of parenchyma cells, forms a continuous system of living cells throughout the plant body, and functions largely in metabolism; parenchyma cells carry on photosynthesis, respiration, storage, and conduction. Unlike many other cells in the plant body, parenchyma cells retain the ability to divide and differentiate to form new cells; they are thus responsible for all growth in a plant, including meristematic growth and wound closure. In addition to parenchyma cells, the ground tissue includes *collenchyma* and *sclerenchyma,* which serve primarily for support in the primary plant body.

The vascular tissue system comprises two tissues responsible for conduction and support, *xylem* and *phloem.* Produced by the apical meristem, primary vascular tissue occurs in discrete vascular bundles. The vascular cambium produces secondary vascular tissue, which includes the entire *bole* of a tree except for the outer bark. Trees contain far more secondary vascular tissue, by weight or volume, than any other tissue. The xylem transports water and mineral nutrients from the soil to the leaves in specialized conducting tissues, called tracheids in conifers and vessels in hardwoods. In addition, the xylem plays important roles in support of the plant body and in storage of carbohydrates, especially starch, in living parenchyma cells. The structure of this complex tissue is described in more detail in Chapter 22.

Table 3.1 Tissue Systems, Tissues, and Cells in the Plant Body

Tissue System	Tissue	Major Function
Ground	Parenchyma	Metabolism, storage
	Collenchyma	Support
	Sclerenchyma	Support
Vascular	Xylem	Conduction of water and minerals
		Support
		Storage
	Phloem	Conduction of carbohydrates
		Storage
Dermal	Epidermis	Protection
	Periderm (bark)	Protection

Phloem, the other vascular tissue in plants, is responsible primarily for transport of carbohydrates and other organic chemicals. Phloem also plays a role in support and storage.

The dermal tissue system forms the "skin" of the tree; it consists of the *epidermis,* a primary tissue, and *periderm* (the outer bark), a secondary tissue. Dermal tissue covers most of the plant body and protects the plant against desiccation and the invasion of microorganisms and insects.

Most plant organs contain all three tissue systems. For example, a leaf (Figure 3.1) is covered with a layer of epidermal cells (dermal tissue system), which protect several layers of green parenchyma cells (ground tissue system) responsible for photosynthesis. Vascular bundles of xylem and phloem (vascular tissue system) carry water to the leaf and carbohydrates away from it.

Shoot Growth

Primary growth in shoots occurs by the division of cells in the apical meristem followed by elongation and differentiation. As cells in the meristem divide, they produce longitudinal files of cells behind them. As these daughter cells elongate, the shoot grows in length. During or after elongation, the daughter cells differentiate to form new dermal, vascular, and ground tissues. In addition, the apical meristem produces leaf *primordia,* which develop into leaves, and bud primordia, which remain meristematic,

forming lateral buds that may later develop into branches (Figure 3.2).

Since all shoot growth is by the division, elongation, and differentiation of cells that originate in the apical meristem, shoot growth should be viewed as occurring from the tip. As a shoot grows, the end of the shoot, including the meristem, moves upward, and no further elongation occurs in the rest of the shoot. If we put a nail into the stem of a tree 1 meter above the ground, it will remain at that height as the tree grows, since all growth in length is from the tips of the shoots.

The mature shoot of a tree (Figure 3.2) is divided into *nodes* and *internodes.* Each node bears one or more leaves (or leaf scars, after leaves are shed), in the *axils* of which are lateral buds. Each lateral bud is, in turn, a telescoped shoot, bearing leaves or leaf primordia and lateral-bud primorida. Generally, the growth of the terminal bud of a shoot inhibits the development of the lateral buds, in a process known as *apical dominance.* If the terminal bud is damaged, one or more lateral buds are released from inhibition and may form a new shoot. Apical dominance generally decreases as the distance from the terminal bud increases, so that lateral buds lower on the stem may be released from inhibition even in the absence of damage to the terminal bud. These lower lateral buds form branches when released from inhibition. The control of apical buds over lower lateral buds is more complex in woody plants than in herbaceous plants, and it has been suggested that

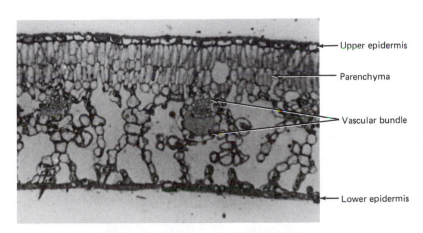

Upper epidermis

Parenchyma

Vascular bundle

Lower epidermis

Figure 3.1 Cross section of a leaf of American holly. The vascular bundle contains xylem and phloem and in holly is stiffened by fibers. The lower epidermis contains stomata, but the upper epidermis does not.

Figure 3.2 Primary shoot of eastern cottonwood. (*a*) A young cottonwood stem. The apical meristem is enclosed by the youngest, developing leaves at the top. All leaves above the asterisk are immature; all leaves below the asterisk are mature and fully grown. The cambium is beginning to form in the stem just below the asterisk. (*b*) Closeup of a cottonwood stem. The petioles, which bear the leaves, are inserted at nodes, and the space between two petioles is an internode. A lateral bud is in the axil of each petiole. The lenticels make the epidermis of the stem more permeable to gases.

the term "apical control" is more apt than "apical dominance" when referring to woody plants.

Patterns of Shoot Growth

At the beginning of the growing season, the apical meristem is enclosed in a bud, which also contains leaf primordia, young leaves, and lateral buds. Terminal buds, like lateral buds, may be thought of as telescoped shoots. Spring growth is initiated by elongation of the shoot and expansion of the leaves that were formed inside the developing bud late in

the previous growing season. There are three basic patterns of shoot growth in trees: *fixed, free,* and *recurrent flushing* (1,2). Fixed growth is the expansion of a bud containing a preformed shoot. Fixed shoot growth consists simply of the expansion of the leaves and internodes that were already present in the overwintering bud. New leaves for the following season then develop inside a new bud and overwinter before expansion. Fixed shoot growth occurs rapidly in the early part of the growing season and is often complete, and a new bud formed, before the middle of the annual growing season. For example, shoot elongation in flowering dogwood is complete within 15 to 20 days following budbreak in Kentucky (Figure 3.3).

Free shoot growth consists of the expansion of the preformed leaves, termed *early leaves,* and internodes in the overwintering bud, followed immediately by the production of new leaves, termed *late leaves,* through the continuous formation and expansion of new leaf primordia on the apical meristem. The early leaves expand at the beginning of the growing season, but late leaf growth continues over a much longer portion of the growing season than does fixed growth. Free growth in eastern cottonwood may continue for more than 120 days after budbreak (Figure 3.3).

The third pattern of shoot growth, recurrent flushing, is a variation of fixed growth. Shoots with recurrent flushing grow by expansion of a preformed shoot, and all leaves are formed inside a resting bud, as in fixed growth. However, growth occurs by several sequential flushes within one growing season, each flush ending in bud set. Vigorous young trees may produce from three to seven flushes of growth each year (2). Young white oaks in Kentucky exhibit two flushes of growth, each lasting 20 to 25 days (Figure 3.3).

The pattern of shoot growth in a given tree is a function of age, vigor, and species. Fixed growth is a characteristic of many temperate-zone hardwoods and conifers, including white pine, northern oaks, beech, and sugar maple. However, young and vigorous trees of these species may exhibit free or recurrently flushing growth. Free growth is characteristic of many fast-growing temperate hardwoods, including yellow-poplar, willows, cottonwood, and sweetgum. Old or low-vigor trees of these species may have a high proportion of shoots with fixed growth. For example, young and vigorous cottonwoods may exhibit only free growth, but very old trees may have few or no free-growing shoots. Fixed growth is more common in the temperate zone than free growth. Recurrent flushing is characteristic of many fast-growing conifers, such as southern pine, and of some hardwoods, such as southern oaks.

These patterns of shoot growth occur in temperate-zone trees and may serve to minimize exposure of delicate apical meristems and leaf primordia to frost. In the tropics, where frost is not an important influence on natural selection, growth is nevertheless usually episodic (1). The most common growth patterns, *intermittent* and *manifold,* resemble recurrent flushing in temperate trees (3). Intermittent growth is recurrent flushing in which the entire tree is synchronized, so that all branches flush and set buds at the same time. There may be from one to five flushes a year, and flushing is often correlated with slight changes in weather, especially rainfall. The manifold pattern is recurrent flushing with no synchrony: individual branches flush and set bud independent of the other branches. This pattern is especially common in older trees.

Terminal buds and some lateral buds go through an annual cycle of growth in temperate and tropical trees, but this is not true of the vast majority of lateral buds, most of which remain dormant as a result of apical dominance or control (4). These *trace buds* may remain permanently suppressed and become buried in the bark as a result of secondary growth. When a tree is stressed or wounded, these trace buds may be released, forming epicormic branches on the bole of the tree. Epicormic branching severely degrades the quality of a tree for timber production and is a major problem in hardwood silviculture.

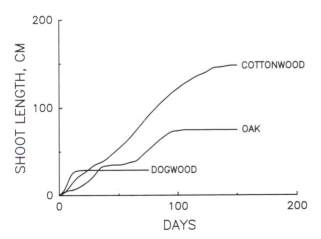

Figure 3.3 Duration of shoot growth in three trees in central Kentucky.

Root Growth

Roots, like shoots, grow as cells in apical meristems divide and then expand and differentiate. However, the basic plan of primary root growth is simpler than that of shoots. The first root formed during germination is a *taproot,* which grows directly downward, giving rise to branch roots; in many trees, however, the taproot does not persist. The root systems of trees are much more plastic than the shoot, and the morphology of the root system depends as much on soil factors as on the physiology and genetics of the tree. For example, red maples on dry upland sites may be strongly taprooted, whereas on poorly drained soils the same species may produce only a shallow, fibrous root system (5).

The root system of a tree consists of a framework of large perennial roots and huge numbers of small, more or less ephemeral roots. The small roots, sometimes called *fine roots,* are often differentiated into *long roots* and *short roots.* Most growth in length occurs in long roots, but short roots comprise most of the surface area of the root system. These short roots, often called *feeder roots,* are responsible for nearly all the water and nutrient uptake in a tree. The larger roots mainly provide a conduction pathway, mechanical support, and a reservoir for carbohydrate storage.

The fine roots of trees are not entirely the products of the tree. Rather, most fine roots are *mycorrhizae* (literally, "fungus–root"), a specialized organ formed of tissues of both the host tree and a fungus (6). Mycorrhizae benefit the host plant in several ways. By increasing the surface area of the root, through extension of hyphae into the soil, they increase uptake of water and limiting nutrients, particularly nitrogen and phosphorus (7). Mycorrhizae also increase the resistance of roots to pathogens and nematodes. The fungal partner receives most or all of its carbohydrate supply from the host plant. Mycorrhizae are crucial to the survival of trees, and all trees are mycorrhizal. Trees planted in soils lacking in appropriate mycorrhizal fungi are usually stunted and may not survive. Inoculation of nursery soils with appropriate mycorrhizal fungi can improve the growth and survival of trees, espe-cially when the trees are planted on poor sites (Figure 3.4).

Flowering and Reproduction

A flower develops through the orderly transition of a vegetative shoot apical meristem to a reproductive meristem. Unlike the vegetative meristem, which remains permanently meristematic, the floral meristem eventually disappears as the flower differentiates. Flowering shoots are thus termed "determinate," as opposed to the indeterminate growth of vegetative shoots.

In gymnosperms such as pines, male and female cones are borne separately on the same tree. The male cones are usually borne lower on the tree than are the female cones; this minimizes self-pollination. The male cones are usually small (1 to 2 centimeters), and the pollen is produced on small scalelike microsporangia. The female, or ovulate, cones are much larger and consist of scales bearing megasporangia, which in turn bear two ovules. Pollen is released in the spring, one year after the cones form, and all pollination is by wind. Most conifers shed their seeds two years after pollination, when the cone scales separate, releasing the seeds into the wind. In some fire-tolerant conifers such as jack pine, cone scales may not separate until a fire occurs.

Reproduction in angiosperm trees is much more diverse. Pollination may be by wind, insects, birds, or bats. Flower and seed development may occur in the space of a few weeks, as in poplars, or several years, as in some oaks. Some angiosperm trees bear male and female reproductive parts in the same flower (perfect flowers) or in separate, imperfect flowers on the same tree. Such trees are termed *monoecious* ("one house"). In other species, male and female flowers occur on separate individuals. These species are termed *dioecious* ("two houses").

Seeds dispersed in the spring in temperate forests are generally capable of germination immediately, provided adequate light and moisture are available. Many temperate trees disperse seeds in fall and winter. These seeds are usually dormant and

Figure 3.4 Virginia pine seedlings two years after planting, (*a*) without and (*b*) with inoculation with mycorrhizal fungi.

will remain in the soil or on the parent tree until spring. For example, silver maple and red maple drop seeds in the late spring, and these germinate immediately; sugar maple seeds are dispersed in the fall and germinate the following spring. Seeds may also remain in the soil for many years without germinating, usually because light conditions are not favorable. When light conditions become favorable, such as following a harvest of the overstory trees, these seeds may germinate, regenerating the forest rapidly.

Secondary Growth

Perhaps no single feature differentiates trees from other plants as much as their tremendous diameter growth. Even the great height trees can attain is largely the result of the mechanical support and conduction system provided by the thick stem (8). A tree grows in height through the activity of apical meristems, whereas, as we have seen, it acquires diameter through the activity of a lateral meristem, the vascular cambium (Figure 3.5).

The Vascular Cambium

The apical meristem is only a small bundle of cells in the shoot or root apex, but the vascular cambium is a vastly larger sheet of cells lying below the bark. The cambium forms in continuity with the shoot and root apical meristem. It begins as a small group of cells within vascular bundles of the primary shoot, and develops until it ensheaths the plant body, with xylem to the inside and phloem to the outside. All growth below this point is said to be secondary. Thus primary growth occurs by division, elongation,

Bark
Phloem
Sapwood
Heartwood

Figure 3.5 Cross section of a stem of red oak. The heartwood is darkly colored. The light lines radiating from the center are rays, and the darker, concentric lines are annual rings.

and maturation of cells derived from the shoot or root apical meristem, whereas secondary growth occurs by division, elongation, and maturation of cells derived from the vascular cambium (or from the cork cambium, as we shall see).

During the growing season, the cambium divides tangentially to produce xylem to the inside and phloem to the outside; these divisions are termed additive divisions, since they add new xylem and phloem to the tree. Two cell types occur in the cambium: the *fusiform initials* give rise to the axially oriented elements of the xylem and phloem, the *ray initials* to rays. The cambium must increase in diameter, since it is a cylinder ensheathing the growing xylem. This occurs by multiplicative divisions, which increase the number of cambial cells.

Xylem Formation and Function

The vascular cambium is only a single layer of cells, yet from it comes the enormous mass of wood found in a tree. The cambial cells divide tangentially to produce new cells to the inside. These cells differentiate to give rise to all the cells in the xylem. Cambial activity is greater in the spring than in the summer, so that wood cells have larger diameters and thinner walls in earlywood than in latewood. This gives rise to the characteristic pattern of *annual rings* in trees; in temperate-zone trees one ring per year is usually produced.

In years when there is abnormal weather such as drought, or when insects defoliate trees, ring formation may be abnormal. Often an extra ring termed a "false" ring will form, especially if an early-season drought causes ring formation to cease early, and later rainfall causes the cambium to be reactivated. Injury to the stem may cause incomplete rings to form, and frost injury to the cambium may produce characteristic "frost rings." Severe drought or defoliation, especially of low-vigor trees, may allow no wood production in a given season, which means that rings are missing. Counting the annual rings in a felled tree will give an approximation of the age of the tree, but precise numbers should be interpreted with caution because of the possibility of false or missing rings (8).

The amount of xylem produced by the cambium varies from year to year, often as a result of rainfall variation. Ring width also varies depending on canopy position: a dominant tree, with much of its crown above the canopy, will produce more xylem than will a suppressed, shaded tree. Xylem increment within the tree also varies; the annual ring is usually widest at the base of the crown.

Once formed, the annual increment of xylem plays three important roles: conduction, support, and storage. All the water transpired by the crown of the tree is transported through the xylem. In most conifers the first two functions are fulfilled by the same cell type, *tracheids*. These elongated cells, dead at maturity, form vertical files through which water can pass. In angiosperm trees the functions of conduction and support are undertaken by separate cell types. Water is transported through specialized cells stacked end-on-end to form long tubes, called *vessels*. There is less resistance to water movement through vessels than through tracheids, so that angiosperm stems are hydraulically more efficient than conifer stems. In *diffuse-porous* angiosperms such as sugar maple, small-diameter, short vessels are scattered throughout the annual increment. In *ring-porous* angiosperms such as oak, a few very large, very long vessels are formed in the earlywood, with small vessels in the latewood. The large vessels are visible to the naked eye. In both types of angiosperms, the vessels are more or less surrounded by thick-walled cells which provide mechanical support.

In both gymnosperms and angiosperms, parenchyma cells in the xylem are responsible for storage and translocation of carbohydrates. These cells may be in rays (Figure 3.5) or in axial strands. In the sapwood these cells remain alive, and living cells as old as 300 years have been reported in wood.

Eventually most parenchyma cells die, and the vessels or tracheids lose their conductive capacity. Wood in which the parenchyma cells are dead is termed *heartwood* (Figure 3.5); it is often colored by the deposition of chemical compounds, which serve to deter fungal growth. All trees form heartwood, though in some, such as poplars, it may not be colored (9).

Phloem Formation and Function

Just as the cambium produces xylem cells to the inside, it produces phloem cells to the outside. These cells divide, elongate, and differentiate to become secondary phloem. In angiosperm trees, secondary phloem consists of *sieve tubes* along with a large amount of parenchyma. Sieve tubes are vertically arranged files of living cells in which the end walls of each cell are quite porous. Sieve tubes transport organic substances, primarily in the form of sugars, from the crown of the tree to the roots, although they can also carry materials in the opposite direction. In conifers sieve cells form vertical files, but they are not arranged in distinct tubes. The phloem is connected via parenchyma cells to the ray cells of the xylem, allowing carbohydrates and other compounds to move from the crown, where they are produced, to the rays, where they may be stored (10). Xylem elements, whether vessels or tracheids, are dead at maturity, and waterflow is through the lumens of dead cells, whereas phloem transport requires that sieve elements be alive. Unlike secondary xylem, which persists throughout the life of the tree, secondary phloem remains functional for only one or a few years. As diameter growth continues, most of the sieve elements and parenchyma cells become crushed.

The Cork Cambium and Bark Formation

As the stem of a tree grows, the *epidermis,* a primary tissue, is replaced by the *periderm,* or outer bark, a secondary tissue. The periderm is formed from a specialized lateral meristem, the *cork cambium,* which originates in the epidermis or in cortical parenchyma cells beneath the epidermis. The cork cambium produces cells to the outside, which are heavily invested with a thick layer of a waxy substance called *suberin.* The bark is thus very water-repellent and impermeable to bacteria and fungi. Cork cells are dead at maturity. New periderms continuously form in the cortical parenchyma and give rise to very characteristic bark patterns. For example, periderms that form in overlapping layers produce scaly or platy bark. These characteristic patterns are so regular that most tree species can be recognized by their bark. The cork oak produces extremely thick outer bark, which is harvested to produce commercial cork (11).

Biochemistry of Tree Growth

Plants use the energy of the sun to transform the inorganic to the organic. All the nutritional requirements of a plant can be met by the provision of carbon dioxide, oxygen, water, minerals, and light. From these, plants can synthesize an enormous number of complex organic compounds, many of which are used in growth, and an even larger number of which have no known role. The rate of growth of a tree, its form, longevity, and resistance to insects and disease depend on the amounts of organic compounds produced and the ways in which they are used. In this section we will briefly review the biochemistry of tree growth, particularly as it relates to the synthesis and movement of carbohydrates.

Carbohydrates

Carbohydrates can be considered to be the main currency of plant growth. Proteins, nucleic acids, lipids, growth substances, and other metabolites are all essential to plant function, but plants are predominantly constructed of carbohydrates. Over 70 percent of the dry weight of a tree consists of sugars and sugar polymers (2). The most abundant of these is *cellulose;* the main *structural* material of the cell wall, cellulose is a polymer of glucose (see Figure 23.2, 23.3, and 23.4). The major storage form of carbohydrate in most trees is *starch,* which is also a glucose polymer. Cellulose cannot be reused once it has been synthesized by the plant, since plants lack the enzymes necessary to depolymerize cellulose. Starch, on the other hand, is readily degraded by several enzymes; it can thus be stored in parenchyma cells and later be depolyermized, translocated, and metabolized. Carbohydrates are also the

first product of photosynthesis and are the basic building block for all other compounds, including proteins and lipids.

Photosynthesis

Photosynthesis is arguably the most important chemical reaction on earth, since without it there would be no life. In photosynthesis solar energy is used to transform carbon dioxide from the atmosphere into simple sugars. The basic equation for photosynthesis is

$$6\,CO_2 + 6\,H_2O \xrightarrow{\text{light}} (CH_2O)_6 + 6\,O_2$$

Or as this equation is stated in words: six carbon dioxide molecules and six water molecules combine, using light energy, to form a carbohydrate molecule and six oxygen molecules. The source of the oxygen is not intuitively obvious: although it was long assumed that the oxygen was obtained from CO_2, we now know that it actually comes from the water. Our present atmosphere contains 21 percent oxygen, nearly all of which comes from photosynthesis. The amount of CO_2 in the atmosphere places limits on the growth of trees, which evolved when the atmosphere was much richer in CO_2 and lower in oxygen. However, the amount of CO_2 in the present-day atmosphere is slowly increasing as a result of the activities of human beings, particularly the burning of fossil fuels and the clearing of tropical forests. The CO_2 concentration has increased from about 300 parts per million to 350 parts per million in the last 50 years, and some atmospheric scientists predict that it could go as high as 600 parts per million in the next century (12). It is uncertain what effect this will have on tree growth: although it is true that the photosynthesis rate of trees is limited by the availability of CO_2, tree growth is probably more limited by the availability of nitrogen in the soil. Forests may thus be unable to take advantage of an increase in CO_2 in the air.

Photosynthesis in trees occurs primarily in the mesophyll cells of the leaves (Figure 3.1). Carbon dioxide diffuses into the leaves through the stomata (Figure 3.6), and thence to the chloroplasts. In the chloroplasts light energy is converted to chemical

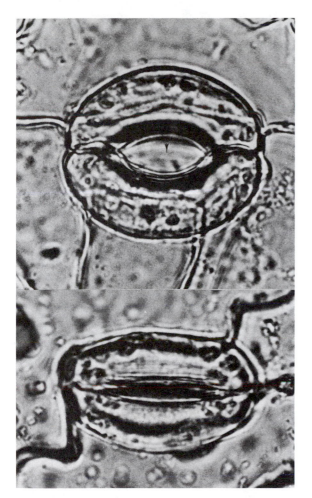

Figure 3.6 Light micrograph of two stomata. The balloon-shaped objects are guard cells. The upper stoma is open, the lower one closed. (Micrograph courtesy of James Pallas.)

energy by chlorophyll, and this energy is used to reduce CO_2 to simple organic compounds, including sugars. Any environmental factor that reduces the availability of light or closes the stomata will reduce or stop photosynthesis. Drought, for example, reduces photosynthesis by causing stomatal closure. Photosynthesizing leaves are the source of nearly all the carbohydrate in a tree, but some photosynthesis occurs in bark, fruits, and flowers as well. The sugars produced in photosynthesis may be stored in the leaf in the form of starch or translocated in the phloem to other parts of the plant.

Transport and Utilization of Carbohydrates

Many sugars can be transported in the phloem, but sucrose is by far the most common. Produced in the cytoplasm of the mesophyll cells, sucrose diffuses to cells near the phloem. Parenchyma cells take up sugars and load them into the phloem, where they move by mass flow out of the leaf to any part of the plant, down a concentration gradient. Carbohydrates that arrive in an organ via the phloem may be used in respiration, transformed into other compounds such as new cell walls, or stored.

Large amounts of carbohydrates are consumed in *respiration,* providing energy for growth, the construction of new cells, and for maintenance, the repair and upkeep of existing cells (13). Whereas photosynthesis is the reduction of CO_2 to sugars, respiration is precisely the opposite: the oxidation of sugars (or other molecules) to CO_2 and water, releasing usable chemical energy. The chemical equation for respiration is

$$(CH_2O)_6 + 6\,O_2 \longrightarrow 6\,CO_2 + 6\,H_2O$$

or, in words, a carbohydrate molecule combines with six oxygen molecules to produce six carbon dioxide molecules and six water molecules. Note that, unlike photosynthesis, this process does not require light.

Respiration uses very large amounts of carbohydrates, consuming about 60 percent of the carbohydrates fixed in photosynthesis in large, temperate-zone trees, and a much larger fraction of photosynthate in the warmer forests of the tropics (2). Whereas photosynthesis is carried on primarily in leaves, respiration occurs in all living cells. Since the total number of respiring cells increases throughout the life of a tree, and the total number of photosynthetic cells is more or less fixed in a mature tree, the ratio of photosynthesis to respiration declines throughout the life of a tree after maturity.

Carbohydrates are also transformed into compounds needed for growth, such as cellulose for cell walls, lignin for walls of xylem cells, lipids for cell membranes, and proteins and nucleic acids. Carbohydrates that are not immediately consumed for respiration or synthesis are stored, usually in the form of starch. Starch forms in parenchyma cells, especially in the xylem parenchyma, including ray cells and axial parenchyma. Starch also accumulates in the phloem parenchyma and in other parenchyma cells. This starch represents an enormously important reserve, which can be mobilized in the spring of the year for the construction of new leaves, flowers, xylem, and phloem. However, not all the starch is used every year: trees tend to maintain a large excess reserve capacity. In white oak, for example, it has been estimated that there is enough reserve starch to refoliate the canopy three times (14). This reserve allows the tree to recover from the loss of tissues—particularly leaves and fine roots—caused by adverse weather, insects, and disease. Trees defoliated by insects, for example, commonly refoliate and usually show little or no long-term adverse effects.

Lipids, Proteins, and Nucleic Acids

Although trees consist primarily of carbohydrate polymers, other biochemicals are crucial to metabolism. Lipids, synthesized from carbohydrates, are more highly reduced (i.e., contain less oxygen) than sugars. A gram of lipid contains many more calories than a gram of sugar. Lipids thus represent an extremely important form of energy storage; many trees, particularly conifers, store large amounts of lipid. Many tree seeds contain as much lipid as carbohydrate. Lipids also play important metabolic roles aside from storage. Cell membranes are constructed of lipid and protein, and the waxy cuticle of leaves and the suberin in cork are usually synthesized from lipids.

Nucleic acids—deoxyribonucleic acid (DNA) and ribonucleic acid (RNA)—and proteins regulate all processes in trees. The genetic code is embodied in DNA; the central dogma of biology is that "DNA makes RNA makes protein." That is, the genes, composed of DNA, are the template for RNA, which

in turn constructs proteins. Proteins may be *enzymes* or *structural proteins*. Among the structural proteins are storage proteins, which, like lipids and starch, are important reserves—particularly for the development of seeds.

Growth Substances

Trees do not simply grow. They also differentiate, change in form, reproduce, and undergo other changes, all of which require the continuous construction of a wide variety of different cells and tissues. How do these processes occur, and what regulates them? We still know relatively little about what governs growth and development in trees, but it is clear that growth substances, simple chemical compounds active at very low concentrations, are the main regulators of growth and development. Growth regulators, sometimes called plant "hormones" (by analogy with animal hormones), can promote or inhibit growth. They often exert their action from a distance, having been produced in one organ or tissue and then acting on another after translocation. Although animal hormones are largely peptides (small proteins), no peptide plant growth substances have been discovered.

The first plant growth regulator discovered was *auxin,* or indoleacetic acid. Auxin promotes the elongation of cells; it is also responsible for *phototropism,* the growth of a shoot toward light, and for apical dominance. We often see understory trees bending toward light gaps in the canopy. This is a result of auxin-directed phototropism. Auxin has important applications in nursery production of trees, since it can promote rooting of cuttings. Perhaps no other single growth substance is so important in determining the form of a tree.

Cytokinins are a class of growth substances that promote cell division, delay senescence, and may be responsible for determining root–shoot ratios. Cytokinins are also involved in apical dominance. *Ethylene* is a very unusual growth substance, because it is a gas. Ethylene is produced by plant tissues during critical stages of development, such as fruit ripening, leaf senescence and abscission, and during stress. Ethylene can even change the sex of flowers on monoecious plants. *Gibberellins* promote stem elongation by stimulating both cell division and elongation, and can promote germination of dormant seeds and flowering of some plants. *Abscisic acid,* a growth inhibitor, maintains dormancy in buds and seeds and promotes stomatal closure during stress.

The effects of growth substances are extraordinarily complex; these effects depend on interactions among several growth substances, the sensitivity of the target tissue, and environmental influences. Although we do not yet understand the mechanism of action of any of these substances, they are of great practical use. Many herbicides are synthetic auxins. Gibberellins can be used to overcome seed dormancy and to promote early flowering. Ethylene can be used to promote fruit ripening. In tissue cultures the amounts of auxin, gibberellin, and cytokinin are carefully manipulated to promote the formation of shoots and roots. Forest tree breeding and production will depend increasingly on the use of growth substances as we learn more about their roles and effects.

Secondary Compounds

Plants are the most prolific organic chemists on earth. They produce many thousands of chemical compounds, most of which do not play a role in primary metabolism—such as in photosynthesis or respiration. These compounds, which have come to be called secondary compounds, include many that have no known function. Some of these compounds are known to play a defensive role. For example, *tannins* occur in the majority of tree species, and they are known to deter some herbivores and inhibit the growth of bacteria and fungi. Other herbivores and pathogens, however, seem unaffected by tannins. *Terpenoids* are important in deterring herbivory in pines; these compounds are familiar as pine pitch. Most herbivores are deterred by terpenoids, but some insects have evolved elaborate strategies to overcome the defenses, and some even use the odor of terpenoids to locate their preferred host plants. *Alkaloids,* which are nitrogen-containing toxins, occur in only a few tree species, such as yellow-poplar, and act as a highly effective deterrent to many insects. It should not be concluded, however, that all secondary compounds are defensive in nature. Many—perhaps most—secondary compounds seem neither to be highly toxic nor to act as effective deterrents to herbivores and pathogens. Many of the secondary compounds, also referred to as *"extractives,"* have commercial value and are further described in Chapter 23.

Environmental Physiology of Tree Growth

The environment in which a tree grows is constantly changing, in ways both predictable and unpredictable. Trees must respond to these changes in order to survive and grow. Predictable changes include diurnal (daily) changes in light, and seasonal changes in daylength, temperature, and moisture availability. Unpredictable factors include drought, floods, and windstorms. Trees in general have a very high degree of phenotypic plasticity—that is, the ability to change in response to changing environmental conditions. In addition to acclimating to changes in the environment, trees must obtain adequate supplies of water and nutrients, which are often in limited supply. The major responses to changes or deficiencies in the environment are (1) growth changes to increase acquisition of a limiting nutrient and (2) physiological adjustments to ameliorate stress. As an example of the first response, some tree species respond to a deficiency in available light by a tremendous increase in the rate of shoot elongation and by positive phototropism. This growth adjustment will cause the tree to grow rapidly toward a light source, such as a canopy gap, until the crown of the tree is in the gap and receiving adquate light, at which point height growth will slow down. As an example of the second response, trees stressed by a lack of available soil moisture may close their stomata during part of the day, which will reduce the rate of water loss from the leaves and prevent desiccation.

Water

The availability of water is probably the single most important determinant of a tree's ability to grow and survive. Trees rarely exist where water supplies are extremely limiting, such as in deserts and prairies. Water is necessary as a reagent in biochemical reactions, such as in photosynthesis, where it is the source of oxygen. Water is the principal constituent of living cells, making up at least 80 percent of the mass of a parenchyma cell, and is the medium in which substances are transported in the xylem and phloem. Maintenance of cell turgor is essential for plant growth, because it supplies the force for cell elongation.

The vast majority of the water taken up by a tree, however, is lost to *transpiration*. Trees support a tremendous leaf area, which is necessary for adequate photosynthesis. The stomata in the leaves must be open for CO_2 to be taken up and thus for photosynthesis to occur (Figure 3.6). Since the relative humidity of the air is rarely 100 percent, water from within each leaf inevitably evaporates when the stomata are open. This water must be replaced if the leaf is not to lose turgor and become desiccated. A tree contains a continuous column of liquid water— from the wet surfaces of mesophyll cells, to the xylem in leaf vascular bundles, down to the xylem within the stem and roots. This water column, continuing across the root and out into the soil, has come to be called the *soil–plant–atmosphere continuum*. It closely couples the evaporation of water from the leaves with uptake of water from the soil (15). The evaporation of water from the leaf exerts a force on the soil–plant–atmosphere continuum, pulling water upward through the plant. A tree's ability to maintain turgor, and thus growth, depends on the balance between water loss from the leaves and water availability in the soil. A tree can become water-stressed when there is inadequate water in the soil; however, even when the soil contains adequate water, high rates of water loss from the leaves can result in water deficits within the crown. This can happen when the relative humidity of the air is low and the temperature is high, and water cannot be taken up from the soil as rapidly as it is lost from the leaves.

The effect of a drought depends on its severity. Even mild water deficits can cause severe retardation of growth if turgor is not adequate for growth. Most trees undergo some degree of water deficit almost daily, as the rate of water uptake from the soil lags behind the rate of loss from the canopy. Such deficits are usually corrected by continued water uptake at night. When rainfall is inadequate, making soil moisture less available, deficits may be more severe. Ultimately, leaves will wilt as a drought continues and then they may abscise. Fine roots may also die during prolonged or severe drought.

The effects of drought can be mitigated by physiological responses of the tree. When turgor in the leaves is reduced, the stomata usually close. Since most water loss is through the stomata rather than through the rather impermeable cuticle, stomatal closure will drastically reduce the rate of transpiration and allow the leaf to recover at least some turgor (Figure 3.6). Obviously, however, stomatal closure will also reduce the rate of CO_2 uptake, and photosynthesis will cease. The stomata can sense the intracellular CO_2 concentration, the leaf turgor, and probably the air relative humidity (15). Stomatal opening is therefore regulated both by the rate of photosynthesis and by water loss; and stomatal regulation tends to optimize the ratio of photosynthesis to water loss. Stomatal closure is not a perfect barrier to water loss, some of which continues through the cuticle even if the stomata are closed. During severe drought wilting will occur even if guard cells are closed. There are other mechanisms by which trees can acclimate to drought stress. One of these, osmoregulation, is a process that maintains turgor through the accumulation of solutes and water within leaf parenchyma cells (15). In addition, large trees contain a substantial amount of water in the stem, and this can act as a reservoir during drought. Shrinkage of tree stems can be measured during a drought, indicating that this reservoir is drawn down by transpiration (5).

Despite these mechanisms for coping with water deficits, drought may cause leaves and fine roots to die. But drought rarely kills trees outright. As discussed previously, trees maintain immense reserves of starch. If drought causes the loss of leaves and fine roots through wilting and abscission, these can usually be replaced using reserves to construct new leaves and roots. However, drought often increases the susceptibility of trees to insects and disease, and the mortality in forest stands is commonly substantial for several years after a drought. Seedlings have few reserves and cannot replace leaves and fine roots lost to drought. They are often killed outright. Even modest droughts can be a major cause of mortality for young tree seedlings.

Mineral Nutrients

Although they do not require any externally supplied organic compounds for their growth, trees do require a number of essential mineral nutrients, which they acquire from the soil. These elements and their functions are listed in Table 3.2. A nutrient is considered essential if its absence prevents the completion of a plant's life cycle, if no other nutrient can be substituted for it, and if it has a demonstrated biochemical or metabolic role (16). The list is not necessarily complete, since it is not entirely certain that all the essential elements have been discovered.

The elements nitrogen, phosphorus, potassium, calcium, magnesium, and sulfur are termed *macronutrients,* and they are required in much larger amounts than are the remaining elements, which are called *micronutrients* (see Chapter 4). Of the macronutrients, nitrogen and phosphorus are most commonly found to be limiting to the growth of forest trees. Deficiencies in the other nutrients are uncommon, except in certain soils. Nursery soils may become deficient in many nutrients as they are

Table 3.2 Essential Mineral Nutrients for Tree Growth

Element	Symbol	Functions	Ionic Form Taken Up by Tree
Macronutrients			
Nitrogen	N	Component of amino acids, proteins, nucleic acids, chlorophyll	NH_4^+, NO_3^-
Phosphorus	P	Component of high-energy compounds (e.g., ATP), nucleic acids, phospholipids	HPO_4^{2-}, $H_2PO_4^-$
Potassium	K	Enzyme activator, counterion for osmoregulation, stomatal function	K^+
Calcium	Ca	Cell wall stabilizer, enzyme activator, regulator of cell membrane functions	Ca^{2+}
Magnesium	Mg	Enzyme activator, component of chlorophyll	Mg^{2+}
Sulfur	S	Component of some amino acids and proteins	SO_4^{2-}
Micronutrients			
Iron	Fe	Electron transport protein component	Fe^{2+}, Fe^{3+}
Chlorine	Cl	Osmoregulation and ion balance	Cl^-
Copper	Cu	Enzyme activator	Cu^{2+}
Manganese	Mn	Enzyme activator	Mn^{2+}
Zinc	Zn	Enzyme activator	Zn^{2+}
Molybdenum	Mo	Nitrate reduction, nitrogen fixation	MoO_4^{2-}
Boron	B	Phloem transport activator?	BO_3^{3-}
Cobalt	Co	Required by nitrogen-fixing symbionts of legumes	CO^{2+}

Source: Data from references 2 and 16.

removed by the rapidly growing tree seedlings, and these soils commonly require the addition of fertilizers.

Nitrogen is widely recognized as a limiting factor in the growth of trees throughout the world. Although there are huge amounts of inorganic N_2 in the atmosphere, and very large amounts of organically bound N in soils, these are not available to plants, which generally can take up only nitrate and ammonia. Nitrogen cycling is discussed in more detail in Chapters 4 and 6. A few trees are able to convert atmospheric nitrogen into organic nitrogen, a process known as *nitrogen fixation*. This is done not by the tree but by symbiotic microorganisms growing on the roots. Trees in the Leguminosae, including black locust, have the bacterial symbiont *Rhizobium* in nodules on the roots; these organisms convert N_2 into amino acids, which are then taken up by the plant. The symbiont in some nonleguminous trees, such as alders, is an actinomycete rather than a bacterium. Nitrogen fixation is not without cost to the plant, which must provide carbohydrates to the symbiont. Many nitrogen-fixing trees are early-successional plants, which grow where soil nitrogen is extremely limiting.

Light

Three attributes of light are relevant to our discussion of tree physiology: *quantity, quality,* and *duration*. The quantity of sunlight received by the crown of a tree is determined by time of day, latitude, cloud cover, and canopy structure. Although higher light intensities generally increase photosynthetic rates in trees, this is not always the case. Photosynthesis in a tree leaf saturates at about one-third of full sunlight intensity. That is, as the light intensity on a leaf increases, photosynthesis increases to about one-third of full sunlight, and continued increases in light intensity produce no increased photosynthesis. At very high light intensities, photosynthesis may be reduced because of bleaching of chlorophyll. In a tree canopy, however, many lower leaves do not receive adequate light for maximal photosynthesis, so that increased light intensity may saturate photosynthesis of upper canopy leaves, but not that of

lower canopy leaves. *Canopy structure* is one of the principal determinants of how much light penetrates the canopy at various intensities. For example, southern pine forests have very open canopies, with substantial light penetrance to the forest floor, whereas spruce stands in the boreal forest allow almost no light to pass all the way through the canopy (17). The ability of a tree to grow in the shade of other trees, its *shade tolerance*, is important in determining where individual tree species occur. Intolerant trees like trembling aspen cannot survive in even moderate shade, but tolerant trees like eastern hemlock thrive in deep shade. One of the major adaptations that allows shade-tolerant trees to survive at low levels of light is the maintenance of low respiration rates, which reduces the consumption of carbohydrate and allows the trees to maintain a positive carbon balance.

Light quality is determined by the relative intensity of various wavelengths of light. There is surprisingly little variation in the quality of sunlight, even on cloudy days. Late-afternoon and early-morning light is often enriched in red wavelengths. Shade-light, the light that penetrates the canopy, is enriched in far-red light. This far-red enrichment appears to be one of the promoters of rapid stem elongation in trees that "seek out" canopy gaps. Light quality is of critical importance in the design of greenhouses and other facilities for propagation of forest tree seedlings.

Light duration, or *photoperiod,* has profound effects on the growth and development of trees. This can be demonstrated by experiments with artificial manipulation of the photoperiod. Short days tend to promote bud set in trees with free growth, and conversely, long days will either maintain shoots in free growth or promote recurrent flushing. Leaf senescence and abscission are also promoted by short days. In many trees flowering is promoted by long days. Plants are able to detect the length of the day because of the action of a compound called *phytochrome,* which seems to mediate all daylength-associated phenomena in plants.

Why should plants have such precise mechanisms for measuring photoperiod? Daylength by itself is not of critical importance to the growth of a tree.

Rather, daylength changes provide signals to the plant that enable it to escape adverse conditions, particularly cold. The shortening days of later summer cause buds to set and leaves to begin abscission well before killing frosts occur. By these means the exposure of delicate meristems to frost is minimized, and nutrients are retranslocated from the leaves back into the stem before the leaves are killed.

Temperature

Temperatures over the forested regions of the earth fluctuate widely. Despite these fluctuations, the growth of trees occurs only within a fairly narrow temperature range. Below freezing (0°C), tissues will be killed by formation of ice crystals within cells, rupturing cell membranes. Above about 40°C some enzymes become denatured, and biochemical pathways no longer operate efficiently. Between these extremes, trees are able to function and grow, and the rate of growth is generally proportional to temperature.

As just indicated, meristematic tissues and leaves are particularly susceptible to damage by freezing temperatures. Trees become dormant in fall, and in this dormant condition they are able to tolerate extremely low temperatures without damage to apical meristems or to the cambium. Following bud set and leaf fall, which are induced primarily by short days combined with cooling weather, buds become dormant and are not capable of growth, even if temperatures become favorable. Subsequent growth of buds in spring depends on prolonged exposure to low temperatures, followed by higher temperatures in the spring. This necessary sequence prevents growth from resuming on warm fall or early-winter days.

As with buds, seeds that overwinter in the soil before germination in the spring also exhibit dormancy. For example, sugar maple seeds collected in the fall cannot be made to grow simply by sowing them in moist, warm soil. Instead, the seeds need to be exposed to a long period of chilling to overcome dormancy and will then grow upon warming. This process of chilling seeds to overcome dormancy,

known as *stratification,* is of great practical importance to the nursery industry.

Other environmental factors such as air pollutants and wind are of importance to tree growth, but water, mineral nutrients, light, and temperature are more often limiting to tree growth than any other environmental influence.

Coordination of Tree Growth

The growth of a tree is regulated by environmental and genetic factors acting together on the physiology and biochemistry of the tree. The mechanism by which growth is coordinated is one of the major unsolved problems of tree physiology. Although we are beginning to understand how the functions of growth substances affect growth of particular organs or tissues, we know relatively little about regulation at the whole-plant level.

Primary Growth Regulation of Secondary Growth

One of the few areas in which we have some understanding of coordination at the whole-plant level is in the relationship between shoot growth and cambial growth. During the dormant season, in temperate-zone trees, both the apical meristems in the buds and the vascular cambium are quiescent and no growth occurs. When weather conditions become favorable, buds begin to swell. At this time auxin flows downward from the buds, which reactivates the cambium. In diffuse-porous trees such as maple, and in conifers, a downward wave of cambial reactivation occurs, beginning just below the buds and reaching ground level days to weeks later. In ring-porous trees such as oak, the entire cambium becomes reactivated simultaneously. If buds are removed prior to expansion, there is no cambial growth. Cambial activity ceases when buds again become dormant and the downward flow of auxin stops.

Periodicity

Many periodic phenomena that occur in trees have already been discussed. Shoot growth is periodic, and cambial growth follows shoot growth. Root growth is much less predictable than shoot growth, in part because it is more difficult to observe. In general, roots grow any time soil temperature and moisture conditions are favorable. However, there appears to be competition between the shoot and the root for carbohydrates. During the middle of the growing season, when shoot growth is maximal, relatively little carbohydrate reaches the roots via the phloem. As a result the production of fine roots is often out of synchrony with shoot growth, occurring in the early spring before bud opening or sometimes in the fall after shoot growth ceases. In fact, many processes that occur in trees can be considered to result from competition between various growing and respiring tissues for substrate, mainly carbohydrates, and for growth substances. In mast-fruiting trees such as oak, which produce large fruit crops at irregular intervals, heavy-mast years are associated with reduced annual growth increment. Evidently, the developing fruits are able to outcompete the cambium for substrates and growth substances.

Form

Form is one of the most characteristic attributes of trees. Many tree species can easily be recognized on the basis of their form. However, form is often heavily modified by environmental factors, age, competition, and vigor. Trees with very strong apical control and with a single terminal leader are termed *excurrent* (Figure 3.7*a*). Most pines, for example, are strongly excurrent. Trees with very weak apical control often lack a recognizable central leader and have a round crown or bushy appearance; these are termed *decurrent* (Figure 3.7*b*). An extreme example of decurrency is the weeping habit, such as in weeping willow. These forms are not genetically fixed, although they are under strong genetic control. Age is an important factor in modifying these forms. Decurrent trees generally begin life with an excurrent habit, reverting to a more decurrent habit at an age that varies with species. Excurrent trees often become decurrent when very old, so that old

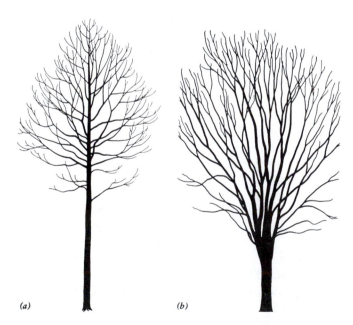

(a)   *(b)*

Figure 3.7 (*a*) Excurrent growth in yellow-poplar. Notice the single main stem. (*b*) Decurrent growth in American elm. There is no single main stem within the crown.

pines, for example, have a flat-topped appearance. Stress—particularly chronic drought—tends to make trees more decurrent (1).

Longevity and Aging

Trees show distinctive aging patterns. During early development, trees are nonreproductive and produce no flowers. Growth rates are generally high in such juvenile trees, and juvenile trees are usually excurrent. Cuttings from juvenile plants often root easily. Leaves are often retained after frost, without complete abscission. At a particular age, which varies enormously with species, trees undergo a more or less abrupt transition to maturity. Mature trees flower and bear fruit by definition, but many other changes occur as well. Growth rates of mature trees decline; they may become more decurrent, cuttings usually do not root, and leaves are completely abscissed. Frequently, however, a juvenile zone remains on a mature tree, in the lower crown near the bole. This portion of the tree bears no flowers or fruits, and cuttings from it can often be rooted. This juvenile zone is easily recognized in beech and oak in winter, because leaves do not abscisse completely.

The life span of trees varies enormously, from 40 years for gray birch to more than 4000 years for bristlecone pine, redwood, and giant sequoia. Almost nothing is known about the factors that contribute to longevity in trees, except that there is generally an inverse relation between growth rate and longevity (although this is not true for redwood, a fast-growing species). The longest-lived trees are mostly conifers. Trees that reproduce clonally by root sprouting, such as aspen and creosote bush, can have extraordinarily long life spans, although the longevity of an individual shoot is not great.

Eventually all trees die. Trees almost always die as a result of specific insults, such as disease, insect attack, and windthrow. As a tree ages and its growth rate slows, it becomes less able to resist pests and pathogens. As with so much of tree physiology, the processes that contribute to longevity and eventually lead to mortality are poorly understood. Many of the answers to questions about what regulates the growth of trees will require a great deal more research.

References

1. M. H. ZIMMERMANN AND C. L. BROWN, *Trees, Structure and Function,* Springer-Verlag, New York/Berlin, 1971.

2. P. J. KRAMER AND T. T. KOZLOWSKI, *Physiology of Woody Plants,* Academic Press, New York, 1979.

3. F. HALLÉ, R. A. A. OLDEMAN, AND P. B. TOMLINSON, *Tropical Trees and Forests, An Architectural Analysis.* Springer-Verlag, Berlin/New York, 1978.

4. J. A. ROMBERGER, "Meristems, growth and development in woody plants," U.S.D.A. For. Serv. Tech. Bull. 1293, 1963.

5. T. T. KOZLOWSKI, *Growth and Development of Trees,* Academic Press, New York, 1971.

6. J. L. HARLEY AND S. E. SMITH, *Mycorrhizal Symbiosis,* Academic Press, New York, 1983.

7. R. FOGEL, *New Phytologist, 86,* 199 (1980).

8. H. C. FRITTS, *Tree Rings and Climate,* Academic Press, New York, 1976.

9. W. E. HILLIS, *Heartwood and Tree Exudates,* Springer-Verlag, Berlin/New York, 1978.

10. W. HÖLL, "Radial transport in rays." In *Transport in Plants I,* Vol. 1. *Encyclopedia of Plant Physiology, New Series,* M. H. Zimmermann and J. A. Milburn, eds., Springer-Verlag, Berlin/New York, 1975.

11. W. H. HARLOW, E. S. HARRAR, AND F. M. WHITE, *Textbook of Dendrology,* Sixth Edition, McGraw–Hill, New York, 1976.

12. J. R. TRABALKA AND D. E. REICHLE, EDS., *The Changing Carbon Cycle, A Global Analysis,* Springer-Verlag, Berlin/New York, 1986.

13. D. D. DAVIES, *Metabolism and Respiration,* Vol. 2, *Biochemistry of Plants,* Academic Press, New York, 1980.

14. S. B. MCLAUGHLIN, R. K. MCCONATHY, R. L. BARNES, AND N. T. EDWARDS, *Can. J. For. Res., 10,* 379 (1980).

15. P. J. KRAMER, *Water Relations of Plants,* Academic Press, New York, 1983.

16. F. B. SALISBURY AND C. W. ROSS, *Plant Physiology,* Third Edition, Wadsworth, Belmont, Calif., 1985.

17. W. LARCHER, *Physiological Plant Ecology,* Second Edition, Springer-Verlag, Berlin/New York, 1980.

CHAPTER 4

Forest Soils

JAMES G. BOCKHEIM

The science of forest soils is a broad field involving chemistry, physics, geology, forestry, and other disciplines. Because soils have a profound influence on both the composition and productivity of a forest, it is important for persons dealing with the forest ecosystem to understand the basic character of soils.

Concept of Forest Soil

There are at least four concepts of the forest soil (1). The forest soil may be viewed as a medium for plant growth. Indeed, soils are important to trees because they offer mechanical support and supply moisture and nutrients. The forest soil differs from the agricultural soil or soils under natural grassland or desert vegetation in that it contains a forest floor, tree roots, and specific organisms whose existence depends solely on the presence of forest vegetation. Soil also has been defined as a natural body with

physical, chemical, and biological properties governed by the interaction of five soil-forming factors: initial material (geologic substratum), climate, organisms, and topography, all acting over a period of time. A third view holds that the forest soil is a vegetated, water-transmitting mantle. This hydrologic view of the soil is based on the ability of the soil to store and transmit water. Finally, the soil may be considered as a component of the forest ecosystem where materials are added, transformed, translocated, and lost because of natural cycling mechanisms.

Properties of Forest Soils

Forest soils may be characterized in terms of their morphological and physical properties, their organic matter and moisture contents, their populations of organisms, and their chemical properties.

Soil Morphology

A *soil profile* is a two-dimensional section or lateral view of a soil excavation. The soil profile is divided into a number of sections termed *soil horizons*, which are distinct, more or less parallel, genetic layers in the soil.

The capital letters O, A, E, B, C, and R represent the master horizons and layers of soils. The forest floor (*O horizon*) is a layer of relatively fresh and partially decomposed organic matter that overlies a series of mineral horizons. The forest floor is important as a "slow-release" source of nutrients, as an energy source for organisms, and as a covering for protecting the soil against runoff, erosion, and temperature extremes. *A horizons* are mineral horizons

formed at the surface or below an O horizon that contain humified organic matter intimately mixed with the mineral fraction or have properties resulting from cultivation or similar kinds of disturbance. *E horizons* are mineral horizons that have lost silicate clay, iron, and aluminum, leaving a concentration of sand and silt particles of quartz or other resistant minerals. *B horizons* contain weathering products, such as silicate clay, iron, aluminum, and humus, that have either been translocated from A, E, or O horizons above or have developed in situ. A key property of the B horizon is that all or much of any original rock structure has been obliterated by soil-forming processes. *C horizons* are horizons or layers, excluding hard bedrock, that are little affected by soil-forming processes and lack properties of horizons already described. *R layers* represent hard bedrock that can only be investigated with heavy power equipment.

Lowercase letters are used as suffixes to designate specific kinds of master horizons and layers. For example, Figure 4.1 shows two contrasting soil profiles, along with their horizons, beneath northern hardwoods and red pine in northern Wisconsin. The soil under northern hardwoods is derived from wind-blown, silty sediments (*loess*) over an unsorted, medium-textured glacial till. The soil beneath red pine is derived from stratified sandy glacial outwash. The profiles differ in at least two respects.

1. The profile featuring northern hardwoods contains a thick A horizon, which reflects mixing of organic matter by earthworms, and the profile supporting red pine has a distinct O horizon and no A horizon.

2. The soil beneath northern hardwoods has a clay-enriched B horizon, designated as Bt (t = clay accumulation), and the soil under red pine has an iron-enriched B horizon, designated as Bs (s = accumulation of translocated iron and aluminum oxides and hydroxides and organic matter).

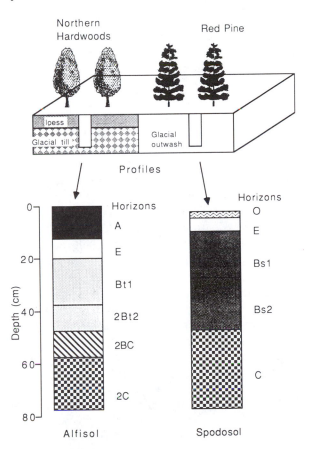

Figure 4.1 Contrasting soil profiles beneath northern hardwoods and red pine in northern Wisconsin.

In the soil taxonomic system for the United States, these soils beneath northern hardwoods and red pine are designated as an Alfisol and a Spodosol,

Figure 4.2 A soil profile occurring beneath a northern hardwoods forest near L'Anse, Michigan. The profile contains a thin forest floor and above it an organic-enriched A horizon, a bleached E horizon, an iron-enriched Bs horizon (being pointed out by the observer), and a relatively unaltered sandy C horizon. (Photograph by J. Bockheim.)

respectively (see the section on "Soil Survey and Classification" in this chapter).

An example of a soil profile occurring beneath a northern hardwoods forest in Upper Michigan is shown in Figure 4.2. This soil contains a thin O horizon, followed by a dark-colored, organic-enriched A horizon, a bleached E horizon, an iron-enriched Bs horizon (being pointed out by the observer), and a relatively unaltered sandy C horizon.

Physical Soil Properties

Soils can be differentiated according to a range of physical properties. These properties are discussed fully in textbooks on forest soils (2); therefore, only three such properties will be discussed here: soil color, texture, and structure.

Soil Color Soils display a wide array of colors. This has been recognized by landscape artists who have depicted soil profiles in their paintings. Soil color is dependent on mineral composition, organic matter content, and drainage class, among other factors. For example, red colors are due to the presence of iron oxides; Native Americans have used red soils to

prepare paints. Black or dark-brown colors are typical of soils enriched in organic matter. Blue and green colors may exist in poorly aerated soils. Soil color may be measured in the field by comparing samples of the soil to standardized soil color charts.

Soil Texture Soil texture refers to the relative proportion of the various mineral particles, such as sand, silt, and clay in the soil. The U.S. Department of Agriculture developed a classification system in which the diameter of sand particles ranges between 2 millimeters and 0.05 millimeter, that of silt particles ranges between 0.05 and 0.002 millimeter, and clay particles are less than 0.002 millimeter in diameter. Trained people can estimate soil texture in the field by simply feeling the soil in moist and dry states. However, soil texture is measured in the laboratory using sedimentation, centrifugation, and sieving techniques. After such analyses are completed, particle-size data are plotted on a soil-textural triangle, as shown in Figure 4.3. Thus, for example, a soil that contains 60 percent sand, 30 percent silt, and 10 percent clay by weight is termed a sandy loam. Texture is important because it influences other soil properties such as structure and aeration, water retention and drainage, ability of the soil to supply nutrients, root penetrability, and seedling emergence.

Sandy forest soils often support pines, hemlocks, scrub oaks, and other trees with low moisture and nutrient requirements. In contrast, silt- and clay-enriched soils usually support trees requiring large amounts of moisture and nutrients, including Douglas-fir, maple, hickory, ash, basswood, oak, elm, spruce, fir, tulip poplar, and black walnut. Soil texture is thus an important consideration in reforestation, in the selection of silvicultural treatment and system (Chapter 14), and in establishment of forest nurseries.

Soil Structure Soil structure refers to the arrangement of primary soil particles into secondary units called *peds*. Peds are characterized on the basis of size, shape, and degree of distinction. Common ped shapes include prisms, columns, angular or subangular blocks, plates, and granules (Figure 4.4).

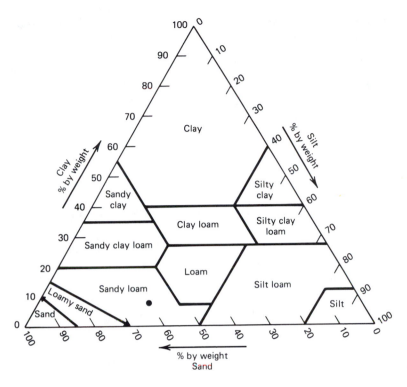

Figure 4.3 A soil-textural triangle using the classification scheme of the U.S. Department of Agriculture. A soil with 60 percent sand, 30 percent silt, and 10 percent clay (designated by the point within the triangle) is classified as a sandy loam. (Courtesy of U.S. Department of Agriculture.)

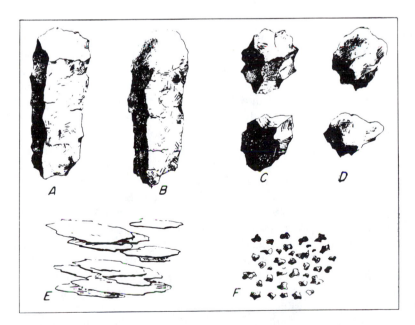

Figure 4.4 Examples of common types of soil structure: (*A*) prismatic; (*B*) columnar; (*C*) angular blocky; (*D*) subangular blocky; (*E*) platy; (*F*) granular. (From U.S. Soil Survey Staff, 1951.)

The major causes for such differences in soil structure are chemical reactions, the presence of organic matter and organisms, and wetting and drying or freezing and thawing cycles.

Organic Matter

Organic matter in the forest soil serves several important functions. It improves soil structure by binding mineral grains, and it increases soil porosity and aeration. In addition, organic matter moderates soil temperature fluctuations, serves as a source of energy for soil microbes, and increases the moisture-holding capacity of forest soils. Upon decomposition, soil organic matter is an important source of plant nutrients.

Most organic matter is added to the forest soil and in the form of *litter,* which includes freshly fallen leaves, twigs, stems, bark, cones, and flowers. Many factors influence litter production. Annual production in temperate latitudes is 1000 to 4000 kilograms per hectare. Litter is composed predominantly of cellulose and hemicellulose (which are carbohydrates), lignins, proteins, and tannins, the characteristics of which are treated in more detail in Chapter 23. Many nutrient elements are supplied by litter, including calcium, nitrogen, potassium, and magnesium, in descending order of abundance.

Once litter reaches the forest floor, a host of macroorganisms and microorganisms act on it. As litter is decomposed, carbon dioxide, water, and energy are released. A by-product of litter decomposition is *humus,* which is a dark mass of complex amorphous organic matter. Organic matter may be produced below ground by the annual turnover of small roots. The organic-matter content of an undisturbed, mature forest soil represents the equilibrium between agencies supplying fresh organic debris and those leading to its decomposition. The ratio of carbon to nitrogen is stable in soils where this equilibrium exists. Whereas the carbon–nitrogen ratio of agricultural soils commonly ranges from 8 : 1 to 15 : 1, the ratio is wider in the surface mineral horizon of forest soils, usually 15 : 1 to 30 : 1.

Organic matter may be regulated in the forest soil by careful selection of a silvicultural system—either shelterwood or clearcutting—and by deciding whether only the merchantable stem or the entire aboveground portion of the tree is to be harvested. Slash may or may not be left on the ground following pruning or thinning (see Chapters 14 and 16). Burning may be prescribed in some areas to release nutrients from thick, undecomposed humus and slash.

Soil Water

Moisture supplies in the forest soil are rarely at optimum levels during the growing season, as described in Chapter 3. Studies with forest trees invariably have shown growth responses to changes in soil moisture. Not only does soil water influence the distribution and growth of forest vegetation, but it also acts as a solvent for transporting nutrients to the tree root. The content of soil water influences *soil consistency* (i.e., resistance to deformation or rupture), soil aeration, soil temperature, the degree of microbial activity, the concentration of toxic substances, and the amount of soil erosion.

The ability of the soil to retain water is influenced by adhesive and cohesive forces associated with the soil matrix and by attraction of water molecules for ions produced by soluble salts in the soil. Often soil scientists speak of "available" water, that is, the proportion of water in a soil that can be readily absorbed by tree roots. Many factors influence the amount of available water in soils, including the amount and frequency of precipitation, runoff, soil storage and leaching, and the demand placed on water by the vegetation.

Water moves in forest soils under saturated and unsaturated conditions and as water vapor. Saturated flow occurs predominantly in old root channels, along living roots, in animal burrows, and in other macropores of the subsoil. Saturated flow also occurs in smaller soil pores in the surface soil during and immediately following heavy rainstorms. Unsaturated flow occurs by capillarity at the upper fringe of the water table, from the soil matrix to the tree root, and in small to medium pores in the soil matrix whenever moisture gradients exist in the available-water range.

A mode of water loss from the soil is through

transpiration, as described in Chapter 3. In a humid, temperate environment, trees transpire nearly as much water as will be evaporated from an open body of water. Agricultural crops transpire less than a forest because of lower leaf area indexes and a shorter growing period. However, during the peak period of growth, agricultural crops may consume more water than a forest. A measure of the efficiency of water consumption is the *transpiration ratio,* which is the number of grams of transpired water required to produce 1 gram of dry matter. Whereas the transpiration ratio of trees commonly ranges between 150 and 350, the transpiration ratio of agricultural crops generally ranges between 400 and 800. Therefore, trees, particularly conifers, are more efficient in their use of water than are agricultural crops.

Excessive amounts of soil water may be controlled by ditching, ridging, or bedding, mechanical breakup of barriers such as a hardpan, and underplanting with species requiring large amounts of moisture. Wilde (3) described a situation in which Trappist monks were able to reduce standing water and the incidence of malaria by planting eucalyptus trees. Flooding and irrigation have been used on a limited scale in areas where water deficiencies exist. Silvicultural treatments, such as thinning and herbicide application to control weed growth, may be an economical way to increase the amount of moisture available to trees in some areas.

Soil Organisms

Soil organisms play an important role in forest soils and tree growth. They decompose organic matter and release nutrients for consumption by trees. By incorporating organic matter into the soil, they improve soil physical properties, soil moisture, temperature, and aeration. Soil organisms also influence soil profile development, particularly the nature of the forest floor.

Perhaps the most important organisms in the forest soil are the roots of higher plants. These roots do the following: (1) add organic matter to the soil, (2) stimulate microorganisms via root exudates, (3) produce organic acids that solubilize certain compounds that are relatively insoluble in pure water,

(4) hold and exchange nutrients within the soil, (5) give off toxic compounds that inhibit the establishment and growth of other plants (Figure 6.9), (6) act as an important soil-forming agent, and (7) protect against soil creep and erosion.

The mycorrhizae are another group of important soil organisms. As indicated in Chapter 3, mycorrhizae increase the absorbing surface area of tree roots; moreover, roots infected with mycorrhizal fungi usually live longer than uninfected roots. Mycorrhizae may also increase the ability of trees to take up nutrients, particularly nitrogen, phosphorus, potassium, calcium, and magnesium (see Figure 3.4). Other types of fungi also are important in forest soils; for example, saprophytic-type fungi decompose forest litter, and parasitic fungi may cause "damping off" or may kill young seedlings by decay of the stem or roots. The influence of certain fungi on growth of forest trees is discussed further in Chapter 8.

Bacteria, microscopic unicellular organisms of different forms, are also important soil organisms. Some types of bacteria break down organic matter, and others utilize nitrogen directly from the atmosphere or mutually with higher plants. A variety of other organisms occur in forest soils, such as protozoa, algae, nematodes, earthworms, insects, and small invertebrates. In terms of soil organisms, forest soils tend to contain an abundance of fungi, agricultural soils a greater number of bacteria. This is mainly because fungi are favored by the more acidic forest soils, whereas bacteria respond more favorably to the mildly acidic or neutral agricultural soils (see later section on "Soil Reaction").

Chemical Soil Properties

As in the case of physical properties, soils can be differentiated according to a range of chemical properties. Since detailed discussions are provided in forest soils textbooks (2), only three chemical properties will be discussed here: soil reaction, cation exchange capacity, and essential chemical elements.

Soil Reaction (pH) The acidity or alkalinity of a soil solution is often measured according to the pH;

a pH of less than 7 indicates an acidic solution, a pH between 7 and 14 an alkaline solution. The pH of forest soils is extremely important, because it influences the microbial population of the soil, the availability of phosphorus, calcium, magnesium, and trace elements, and the rate of nitrification—that is, biological oxidation of ammonium to nitrate. Because tree litter is commonly acidic and releases hydrogen ions upon decomposition, forest soils are often more acidic than grassland or agricultural soils. In addition, trees may naturally acidify the soil by taking up calcium, magnesium, and other elements that tend to form bases in the soil. Atmospheric deposition in the form of "acid rain" may also acidify soils. Liming, replacing hydrogen with calcium or magnesium, is a common method of raising the pH in agricultural ecosystems, but cost limitations make it impractical for forest ecosystems, with the exception of forest nurseries. Soil pH may decrease following fertilizer application and increase following burning of litter and slash.

Cation Exchange Capacity Cation exchange is the ability of the soil to hold and exchange positively charged forms of plant nutrients. These positively charged ions, or cations, are held on "exchange sites" on the surfaces of clay particles and humus. Dominant cations in most forest soils are hydrogen ion (H^+), aluminum (Al^{3+}), calcium (Ca^{2+}), magnesium (Mg^{2+}), potassium (K^+), ammonium (NH_4^+), and sodium (Na^+), in descending order of abundance. Cation exchange capacity (CEC) is dependent on the amount of organic matter, the amount and types of clays, and pH. Low in sandy soils, cation exchange capacity is higher in finer-textured soils.

Essential Chemical Elements In addition to carbon, hydrogen, and oxygen, which constitute the bulk of the dry matter of plants, thirteen chemical elements are considered essential for normal growth and development of trees. The macronutrients nitrogen, phosphorus, potassium, calcium, magnesium, and sulfur are absorbed in relatively large amounts by trees. Iron, manganese, boron, copper, molybdenum, zinc, and chlorine are called trace elements or micronutrients, because they are taken up in comparatively small but important quan-

tities. Macronutrients and micronutrients must be present in the necessary forms, in sufficient quantities, and in the proper balance for normal tree growth.

The sources and available forms of the macronutrients and micronutrients are shown in Table 3.2. Nitrogen is present largely in the organic form in forest soils. Trees utilize nitrogen in inorganic forms, as ammonium (NH_4^+) or as nitrate (NO_3^-). Bacteria are able to convert organic nitrogen to ammonium and nitrate, a series of processes called *nitrogen mineralization.*

Phosphorus is present in organic forms and also as secondary inorganic phosphate compounds in combination with calcium, iron, and aluminum; $H_2PO_4^-$ and HPO_4^{2-} are soluble forms taken up by trees. Phosphorus is most available under near-neutral pH conditions.

Potassium, calcium, and magnesium are contributed mainly by weathering of soil minerals. Potassium is present largely in minerals such as micas and orthoclase feldspar. Calcium and magnesium exist in dolomite, olivines, pyroxenes, and amphibole minerals. These chemical elements are available to trees as exchangeable and as water-soluble monovalent and divalent cations.

Sulfur is present in organic and mineral forms and can be taken up by trees as exchangeable and as water-soluble sulfate, SO_4^{2-}. In addition, sulfur dioxide (SO_2) gas may be taken up directly by trees through their stomata (see Figure 3.6).

Micronutrients are present in mineral forms and as complexes with organic matter. Acid sandy soils, organic soils, and intensively cropped soils, such as those in forest nurseries, may be depleted in micronutrients.

Forest Soils and Tree Nutrition

Soil–Site Factors Related to Tree Growth

In soil–site evaluation foresters use soil properties (as discussed earlier in the chapter) and other site factors, such as topographic and climatic features, to predict tree growth. The ability to predict tree growth is of great value to the forester and for planning in the forest products industry. The forester begins by locating plots in stands representing the range of sites and soils found within a particular region. Measurements of tree growth and soil properties taken in these plots can then be correlated using statistical methods. The resulting equations can be used to predict site quality of stands that are heavily cut or too young for traditional site index measurements. Measurement of site quality is discussed further in Chapter 12.

Soil features important in soil–tree growth studies usually include depth, texture, and drainage (4). Site factors other than soils that are important to tree growth include slope position, orientation (aspect), and steepness (see Figure 2.1). These factors influence soil moisture and temperature relations and the degree of erosion. Elevation and rainfall vary considerably in western North America and influence the productivity of western conifers.

Diagnosis and Correction of Nutrient Deficiencies

Three methods are commonly used to diagnose nutrient deficiencies in forest ecosystems: visual tree symptoms, soil analysis, and plant tissue analysis (2, 5). Nutrient deficiency symptoms that are visible include chlorosis and necrosis of foliage, unusual leaf structure, deformation or rosetting of branches, and tree stunting. Although many of these symptoms are relatively easy to recognize, nutrient deficiency symptoms of trees may be difficult to isolate from those caused by disease, insects, or other site limitations, such as a moisture deficiency. Thus it is important to combine a visual technique with soil or plant analysis.

Soil testing involves determining the "available" nutrient content of the soil and relating it to productivity of a particular tree species. Two problems with this technique include (1) selecting a chemical that will extract that portion of the nutrients available to the plant, and (2) establishing optimum levels of soil nutrients for the various tree species.

The third method for identifying nutrient deficiencies is tissue analysis, which is the determination of the nutrient content of a particular plant tissue, usually the foliage, and relating it to visible deficiency symptoms and tree growth.

Nutrient deficiencies may be corrected through the use of fertilizers. Forest fertilization is becoming more widely practiced in North America than a decade ago. Forest fertilization may increase not only fiber yield but also resistance to insects and disease and the aesthetic quality of the vegetation. However, use of fertilizers in the forest constitutes use of a nonrenewable resource for perpetuating a renewable resource. Fertilization is also expensive and may contribute to environmental pollution when not applied judiciously.

Rate of fertilizer application depends on initial soil fertility level, tree species, age of stand, and type of fertilizer. The nutrient most commonly applied to forests is nitrogen, given at rates of 100 to 400 kilograms per hectare to stands of Douglas-fir in the Pacific Northwest and at rates of 5 to 100 kilograms per hectare to pines in southeastern United States. Phosphorus is applied to pines in the Southeast at rates of 30 to 100 kilograms per hectare. Fertilizer is generally applied to open land or young plantations using mechanical spreaders. In established stands and those occupying large land areas, application may be aerial. Municipal and industrial effluents and sludges may be applied as a fertilizer substitute in some forested areas.

Soil Survey and Classification

In a *soil survey* foresters systematically examine, describe, classify, and map soils in a particular area. Mapping of soils requires a knowledge of the interaction of the five soil-forming factors: initial material, climate, organisms, topography, and time.

A soil survey report contains soil maps at scales commonly ranging from 1 : 10,000 to 1 : 60,000 and the following information: descriptions, use and management, formation and classification of soils, laboratory data, and general information pertaining to the area. The resulting soil surveys provide the forester with valuable information for planning forest activities. For example, soil surveys can be used to locate roads and landing areas, to match harvesting systems with soil conditions for minimizing site degradation, and to match tree species with soil type during reforestation for increasing yield. These soil surveys also enable the forester to plan silvicultural treatments such as thinning and fertilization more efficiently. Finally, soil surveys are useful for planning recreational facilities, for evaluating potential impacts of mining, grazing, and waste disposal, and for predicting water yield and quality in forested areas.

Numerous schemes have been used to classify forestland and to predict site quality. *Multiple-factor systems* have been used extensively in western North America (6). These systems differentiate and classify ecologically significant segments of the landscape using landform, soil initial material, forest cover type, and soil taxonomic unit.

Single-factor systems are used to map and classify individual components of the ecosystem, such as vegetation or soils. The *habitat system* is an example of a single-factor system and is based on climax plant associations that can be used to predict site–succession relationships and site quality (7).

The U.S. soil taxonomy method (8) is an example of a single-factor (soil) system used to classify forestland. There are seven levels of soil classification in the system, listed here from the broadest to the most specific: order, suborder, great group, subgroup, family, series, and type.

The following discussion describes each of ten soil orders and the associated forest cover types. Three soil orders of particular importance to North American forestry are Ultisols, Alfisols, and Spodosols. *Ultisols* are forest soils with less than 35 percent of the exchange sites containing calcium, magnesium, potassium, and sodium. These soils occur in areas with moist, warm to tropical climates, with an average annual temperature of more than 8°C. Ultisols contain a yellow E horizon and a reddish, iron- and clay-enriched B horizon. These soils support loblolly and shortleaf pine in the southeastern United States and oak–hickory and oak–pine in the south-central United States.

Alfisols are forest soils with greater than 35 percent of the exchange sites containing calcium, magnesium, potassium, and sodium. They contain a gray E horizon and a brown, clay-enriched B horizon. These soils feature oak–hickory in the central United States, northern hardwoods in northern New York, aspen–birch in the northern Great Lakes states, and ponderosa and lodgepole pines in western North America.

Spodosols contain a grayish E horizon and dark reddish-brown B horizons that are enriched in organic matter or iron and aluminum oxides, or both (Figure 4.2). These soils develop from coarse-textured, acid initial materials under cold humid climates. Major forest cover types are spruce–fir, eastern white pine, and northern hardwoods in New England and eastern Canada, and northern hardwoods and aspen–birch in the Great Lakes region. In southwest Alaska, Spodosols support western hemlock–Sitka spruce, and in Florida poorly drained Spodosols support longleaf and slash pines.

Entisols are mineral soils with weakly expressed B horizons. They occur predominantly on floodplains, steep slopes, or shifting sands. Entisols occur on excessively drained sands supporting jack pine and scrub oaks in the Great Lakes region and on poorly drained sands supporting slash pine in Florida. *Inceptisols* are also poorly developed but contain a weak B horizon. Inceptisols support oak–pine in the Appalachian Mountains, oak–gum–cypress in the southern Mississippi River valley, ponderosa pine, western white pine, and larch in the northern Rocky Mountains, spruce–hardwoods in interior Alaska, and western hemlock–Sitka spruce in the Pacific Northwest and western Canada.

Aridisols are desert soils and do not feature commercial forest vegetation in North America. *Mollisols* contain a deep, dark-colored surface horizon with strong granular structure and an abundance (50 percent or more) of potassium, calcium, and magnesium on the exchange sites. They occur predominantly under grassland. However, some Mollisols, such as brown forest soils, have developed under forests that contain ponderosa pine in western North America. *Vertisols* have been subjected to excessive shrinking, cracking, and shearing because they have an abundance of swelling clays. These soils are of limited extent in North America and do not support commercial forest vegetation. *Histosols* are organic soils that support spruce–fir, aspen, and swamp conifers primarily in the northern Great Lakes region and in the coastal plain of southeastern United States. *Oxisols* are intensively weathered soils enriched in iron oxides and depleted in weatherable minerals. They occur in tropical areas and therefore are absent in North America. Large areas of Oxisols occur in South America and central Africa.

Forest Soils and Environmental Quality

As the demand for forest products continues to increase, forest soils will be more intensively used. The following forest management practices may have profound effects on soil and water quality: shortened rotations, close utilization, use of fast-growing hybrid species, and mechanical and chemical site preparation. The first three practices make added demands on soil nutrients. *Nutrient balance sheets* may be used to assess whether or not sufficient nutrients will be available to sustain these practices. Table 4.1 is a nitrogen balance sheet on good loblolly pine sites with alternative harvests of

products and rotation lengths. A complete-tree harvest (total aboveground biomass) would remove from two and a half to four times as much nitrogen as a conventional stem harvest (see Table 4.1, depletion—total per rotation). The annual depletion would be less over a 32-year rotation than for a 16-year rotation (complete-tree harvest only), because young loblolly pine trees take up greater amounts of nutrients than older trees. Comparing the total inputs and total outputs (depletion) reveals that a complete-tree harvest, whether at 16 or 32 years, would remove more nitrogen than is supplied by precipitation and nitrogen fixation.

Industrial foresters have expressed interest in *short-rotation intensive culture* (SRIC), which has also been called fiber farming or "puckerbushing." This practice utilizes fast-growing hybrid cuttings that are grown at close spacings and are harvested every few years. Generally fertilization is required to supply an adequate amount of nutrients.

Site preparation refers to soil manipulation techniques designed to rid areas of logging slash or other debris, reduce weed competition, prepare a mineral seedbed, reduce compaction or improve drainage, create more favorable microsites for tree planting, and control diseases (9). Site preparation

Table 4.1 Nitrogen Balance Sheet on Good Loblolly Pine Sites with Alternate Harvests of Products and Rotation Lengths

	16-Year Rotation		32-Year Rotation	
	Complete Tree	Stem Only	Complete Tree	Stem Only
Demands				
Erosion and leaching	89	67	156	134
Harvest	282	115	428	233
Total	371	182	584	367
Inputs				
N fixation	36	36	52	52
Precipitation	86	86	172	172
Total	122	122	224	224
Depletion				
Total per rotation	249	60	360	143
Total per year	16	4	11	4

Source: C. G. Wells and J. R. Jorgensen, *Tappi J., 61,* 31 (1978).

Figure 4.5 Skidding during logging operation. (Photograph courtesy of U.S.D.A. Forest Service.)

techniques include prescribed burning, chemical applications, mechanical techniques, and combinations of these practices (described further in Chapter 14 and 21). Where injudiciously applied, these practices may increase erosion and runoff and cause an overall decline in site quality.

Improper road-building practices are often cited as a major cause of sedimentation in forest environments, particularly in steep mountainous areas. Timber removal may also contribute to sedimentation of streams, lakes, and reservoirs by exposing the surface soil, particularly during skidding and yarding operations (see Chapter 16 for methods of timber harvesting). Skidding of logs with tractors and rubber-wheeled vehicles is more likely to cause soil erosion and mass-wasting than when high-lead cable, skyline cable, balloon, or helicopter systems are employed. Wet-weather logging is especially detrimental to soils and should be avoided if at all possible (Figure 4.5).

A major concern in recent years has been the potential effects of widespread deforestation in tropical regions on carbon dioxide accumulation in the atmosphere. The accumulation of CO_2 in the atmosphere could be related to climate warming—that is, to the "greenhouse effect". However, more research is necessary to establish definite correlations.

References

1. E. L. STONE, "Soil and man's use of forest land." In *Proc. 4th. N.A. For. Soils Conf.,* B. Bernier and C. H. Winget, eds., Laval Univ. Press, Quebec, 1975.

2. W. L. PRITCHETT, *Properties and Management of Forest Soils,* John Wiley & Sons, New York, 1987.

3. S. A. WILDE, *Forest Soils: Their Properties and Relation to Silviculture,* Ronald Press, New York, 1958.

4. W. H. CARMEAN, *Adv. Agron., 29,* 209 (1975).

5. K. A. ARMSON, *Forest Soils: Properties and Processes,* Univ. of Toronto Press, Toronto, 1977.

6. J. BOCKHEIM, ED., *Proc. Symp. on Forest Land Classification: Experiences, Problems, Perspectives,* Dept. of Soil Science, Univ. of Wisconsin, Madison, 1985.

7. M. S. COFFMAN, E. ALYANAK, J. KOTAR, AND J. E. FERRIS, *Field Guide Habitat Classification System,* Michigan Technical Univ., Houghton, 1984.

8. U.S. SOIL SURVEY STAFF, *Soil Taxonomy: A Basic System of Soil Classification for Making and Interpreting Soil Surveys,* U.S.D.A. Agr. Handbook 436, 1975.

9. R. C. STEWART, "Site preparation." In *Regenerating Oregon's Forests,* B. D. Cleary, R. D. Greaves, and R. K. Hermann, eds., Oregon State Univ. and U.S.D.A. For. Serv., Pac. Northwest For. Range Expt. Sta., Portland, Ore.

CHAPTER 5

Forest Genetics and Forest Tree Breeding

RAYMOND P. GURIES

Forest genetics is the study of the *heritable variation* in forest trees. Like other fields of genetics, it is grounded in the dogma of classical genetics and molecular biology. Thus, at the level of the gene, what is true for garden peas and fruit flies is true for forest trees. The exact details of origin and evolution vary from organism to organism, but the mechanics of inheritance transcend species lines, providing a common denominator for the study of life. Research in forest genetics provides information on the genetic properties of trees, both as individuals and as populations. Such information is needed for the wise utilization of forest resources.

Forest tree breeding is the application of genetics principles to the development of lines of trees that will have increased value for humans. It is primarily a domestication process that involves the selection, propagation, and testing of trees possessing desirable characteristics. Specific details of the process vary depending on whether the primary goal is increased wood production, pest resistance, amenity values, or some combination of such traits.

It might be possible to infer from the definitions just given that there is relatively little overlap between these "basic" and "applied" lines of research. Nothing could be farther from the truth. In fact, much of the basic forest genetics research being conducted today was initiated in response to problems encountered in applied breeding programs. The flow of information and ideas is very definitely bidirectional.

Some Problems Unique to Forest Genetics

The use of trees as research organisms poses a number of problems. For example, their *large size* makes them poor objects for most studies in laboratory settings. Because the basic cellular processes and the mechanics of inheritance are remarkably similar among most plants and animals, many questions pertaining to metabolic functions, the mutation process, and other topics requiring precise experimental control are best investigated with organisms other than trees.

The large size of most trees poses additional problems for forest geneticists. Seed or cone collection, or the need to make controlled pollinations, frequently requires spending long hours in the crown of a tree, thereby limiting the number of trees from which seeds and cones can be collected or the number that can be worked with in any one season (Figure 5.1).

The *long life cycle* of many trees poses the problem of long intervals between generations in a research program. Many species do not commonly attain sexual maturity for fifteen, twenty, or more years. This slows the progress of a breeding program to a pace commensurate with the life cycle of the species, so that the possibility of breeding more than a few generations of trees during an individual researcher's lifetime is remote.

An associated feature of this size–longevity problem is the *large land area* needed to complete many genetics experiments. Once established, such experiments are impossible to relocate and are subject

Figure 5.1 Making control pollinations in the crown of a Norway spruce tree. The steel pole with guy wires permits the worker to reach the top of the tree. (Courtesy of Hans Nienstaedt, U.S.D.A. Forest Service, Rhinelander, Wisconsin.)

to destruction by natural catastrophes such as drought, storm, or pest epidemic. Highway construction, fire, and vandalism also take a toll. In addition, much valuable information may be lost following personnel changes because plantings frequently outlive their originator.

All these problems combine to reduce the pace at which reliable genetics information becomes available on forest trees. Although human knowledge of crop plant genetics is encyclopedic, knowledge of forest tree genetics is still extremely limited. The tremendous gains achieved by many grain and vegetable crop breeders in the last few generations is due largely to an increased understanding of the genetics of these crops as well as to their having relatively short life cycles. Such gains in plant breeding are both important and impressive, but research in forest genetics does offer certain advantages that few agronomic crops can match. One of the most important is the opportunity to work with an enormous and as yet relatively unexploited genetic resource.

Finally, it should be noted that trees possess other unique features, including the capacity for wood production and the facility for long-distance transfer of photosynthate, water, and nutrients between roots and branches. Despite the obvious importance of such features to tree growth, very little is known concerning their genetic control or evolution. But it is recognized that such subjects can be studied only in trees despite the technical difficulties involved.

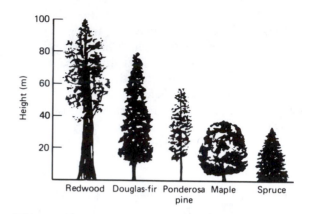

Figure 5.2 Tree characteristics such as height and shape are inherited, but environmental factors also play a significant role in the growth and development of a tree.

Forest Genetics

Natural Variation in Forest Tree Populations

The existence of considerable stores of natural genetic variation in forest tree populations is one of the major findings of forest genetics research during the last century. Numerous studies of such variation have provided evidence for the operation of evolutionary processes and adaptation in trees. Although the evidence is usually indirect, there is little doubt that this variation is a key to long-term species survival and continued evolution. Natural genetic variation provides the "buffer" that has permitted trees to adapt to variable and changing environments and thereby dominate the landscape (Figure 5.2).

From the standpoint of tree breeding, the presence of considerable variation is a particularly pleasing circumstance because it enhances the prospect of locating individual trees that are well above average in economically important traits. Whether selection is imposed by nature, or artificially by human beings, variation must be present if the domesticated populations are to be different from

the wild ones, and this variation must be genetically based. In the absence of such variation, no selection is possible, by either human beings or nature.

Continuous versus Discontinuous Variation
During the formative years of plant genetics, considerable attention was paid to characters that appeared to be inherited as discrete units in discontinuous fashion. Characters such as flower or seed color of the type studied by Gregor Mendel in peas during the nineteenth century could be shown to be controlled by a single "factor," or *gene*. During the early twentieth century it became increasingly obvious that many, perhaps most, plant characters did not display this *discontinuous* either–or pattern of variation. Characters such as plant weight, leaf length, fruit weight, numbers of veins in leaves, and numerous others displayed a *continuous* pattern of variation. Such patterns typically approximate a "normal distribution" when the frequency of occurrence is plotted against a range of performance or size classes (Figure 5.3).

Most of the individual measurements are clustered about the mean with smaller numbers of observations falling into classes farther removed from the mean. Geneticists now recognize that these metrical (or quantitative) characters are controlled by a large but unknown number of genes. Most

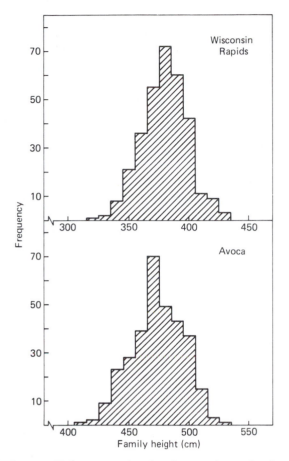

Figure 5.3 Average height of 310 red pine families raised at two locations in Wisconsin. The exact shape of the distribution is different at each location, but both approximate a normal distribution.

characters of interest to tree breeders are of this metrical type.

The inability to identify precisely the genes responsible for producing a particular character in many instances led to the origination of the terms *genotype* and *phenotype*. The term *genotype* refers to the genetic constitution of an individual. It is the sum total of all the genetic information that an individual possesses. The term *phenotype* refers to the external appearance of an individual. The stature, girth, and various other qualities are the end product of the interaction of the individual genotype and the environment in which it develops. The

phenotype of an individual can be seen and measured, but this is almost never possible for an individual's genotype. A useful concept may be to consider a genotype as a potential phenotype. At the start of development, an enormous array of possible phenotypes may be produced, but the one that ultimately develops is the product of a genotype developing in a certain environment.

A great deal of effort has gone into attempts to separate "nature from nurture" during the course of development. For traits of economic interest such as growth rate, geneticists would like to know the extent to which a particular character is inherited. If the variation observed has little or no heritable basis, efforts to improve it will be unfruitful, or at least very inefficient. In contrast, characters under strong genetic control are generally more amenable to rapid improvement because a good phenotype is more likely to reflect a good genotype.

Extent and Patterning of Variation Most information on the amount and distribution of natural genetic variation in forest trees has come from *provenance studies*. In such studies seeds from a number of geographic origins or stands are collected and grown together in one or more locations under conditions that make it possible to compare the relative performance of each seed source with all others (Figure 5.4). The original aim of provenance testing was to identify superior seed sources for reforestation needs, but in the process a great deal has been learned about the *evolution* of many tree species.

The first tests to establish that *seed origin* was an important factor in determining the ultimate form of a tree were initiated by Phillipe-André de Vilmorin in France. Between 1820 and 1850 de Vilmorin set out plantations of Scotch pine on his estate using seeds collected from a number of stands throughout Europe. Although poorly designed by today's standards, these tests documented that Scotch pine from different geographic origins varied considerably in height and diameter growth, needle length, stem form, and other characters. Because all the trees were grown at the same location, de Vilmorin concluded that the differences among seed sources

Figure 5.4 An indication of the magnitude of differences in the growth rates of two provenances of lodgepole pine in the nursery at Redrock, British Columbia. Both rows of trees are six years old. (Courtesy of Nicholas Wheeler, British Columbia Forest Service.)

were due to factors inherent in the trees. De Vilmorin's work was repeated and confirmed with Scotch pine and other species by a number of foresters in Europe and the United States from 1885 to 1920.

Provenance studies demonstrated that many tree species were genetically quite variable, but the patterning of variation was not considered until Olof Langlet's analysis of Scotch pine during the 1930s. Langlet collected seeds from 582 populations throughout Sweden and raised them under carefully controlled conditions. His studies showed that certain patterns of variation were closely related to climate, because the characters he studied changed *systematically* with increasing altitude and latitude

of origin. Such patterns of variation appeared to be established and maintained in response to environmental factors such as the length of the growing season or minimum winter temperature.

The *adaptation* of tree populations to climate is well documented, especially for coniferous species. Pines and spruces have been studied especially well because of their economic importance. Results for a number of species indicate that patterns of continuous variation (*clinal variation*) are quite common for survival and growth-related traits, as well as certain wood quality traits such as specific gravity. Such patterns are generally correlated with length of growing season, date at which spring temperature exceeds a certain level, or other environmental features that have a dramatic influence on physiology and that also exhibit clinal variation. Such geographic patterns of variation are most easily explained as optimal (or near-optimal) growth strategies that develop in response to selection imposed by the environment (1).

Some very complex adaptations have evolved in tree species as a result of *competitive interactions* for light, for moisture, and even for pollinators such as bees and small mammals. Even within the crown of a single tree, morphological differences in leaves are apparent and greatly affect the overall "capture" of light energy. Botanists have recognized two different leaf forms, "sun leaves" and "shade leaves," each with a characteristic size, thickness, and chlorophyll content. Sun leaves, those on the outer shell of branches, tend to be smaller and thicker and tend to have a higher concentration of chlorophyll on a leaf weight basis than shade leaves. This adaptation permits plants to take best advantage of the filtering effect that leaf canopies have on light quantity and quality.

Plants have many adaptations to special soil conditions, to fire, to heavy snow and ice conditions, to insect and disease attack that allow pollination, seed dispersal, and other functions to proceed. These have been described and form part of a rich botanical literature on the subject. Today, adaptations are recognized as features that reflect the interactions occurring between organisms and their environment. Patterns of variation may be quite local, as could be expected if they arose in response to some physical or biological feature of the environment that changed rapidly over short distances. Some patterns are more regional in nature, perhaps reflecting gradual changes in one or more climatic variables such as temperature or moisture variation. Some patterns are quite obvious; others can be more cryptic or complex, requiring careful analysis before they become apparent. But to understand the nature of adaptation and its control, the mechanisms responsible for bringing about evolutionary change must be considered.

Origin and Modification of Natural Variation

Almost all evolutionary change can be attributed to certain causal factors or mechanisms that are responsible for changing the frequencies of different genes in populations. These factors can be assigned to one of two classes: those that create or release natural variation, and those that subsequently modify this variation. Much of the work of population genetics has involved an elaboration of evolutionary mechanisms from a theoretical standpoint, followed by laboratory field studies to support their operation. At times certain concepts have to be modified or refined to bring them into agreement with observations made in the natural world. But there is no doubt concerning the general validity of these mechanisms and their importance in bringing about evolutionary change. A number of excellent introductory texts on population genetics and evolution are available for those desiring a more complete treatment (2–4).

Mutations as a Source of Variation Mutations are the ultimate source of all genetic variation. Although most mutations are generally harmful, they are still a vital part of the evolutionary process because they provide the "raw material" upon which natural and artificial selection may act. Mutations may consist of the alteration of a single gene by way of the addition, deletion, or substitution of one of the "building blocks" of the DNA molecules. The end result may be completely undetectable, or it

may lead to a gross change in the morphology or development of an organism. Mutations affecting cotyledon and leaf pigments, tree stature, branching habit, and other traits that appear to be controlled by one or a few genes have been observed in a number of tree species.

Mutations may also involve a major alteration in the genetic material, such as the loss or addition of a whole chromosome or a set of chromosomes. Such changes in chromosome number or patterning are rarer than single-gene mutations, but they have occurred in many plant species at one time or another. Just as in the case of single-gene mutations, these changes are sudden and irreversible. Naturally occurring and artificially produced triploid aspen is a good example of such a mutation.

Forest trees are relatively poor organisms for studying the mutation process, however, because of their large size and long life cycle. Mutation rates for most well-studied organisms range from 1×10^{-4} to 1×10^{-6} per gamete per generation, and this is probably correct for trees as well. Mutation rates vary depending on the site of the change in the DNA molecule, the organism involved, and the specific environment in which the organism is placed. Radiation and certain chemicals are known *mutagens* and can greatly increase the rate of mutation. However, human beings have essentially no control over the exact kinds of mutations produced. *Mutation breeding,* a practice seldom employed in forest genetics, can be used to create new variation by increasing the frequency of new mutations. The vast bulk of these mutations are still harmful, but a small number may be useful. Although the thought of somehow directing the mutation process has considerable appeal, especially to breeders of agronomic crops, this subject is fraught with moral and ethical issues concerning possible extensions to other organisms, especially humans. However, genetic engineering at this level still eludes even the most ingenious scientist, although enormous progress has been made in this field in recent years.

Recombination as a Source of Variation Whereas mutations provide the intial source of genetic variation, genetic recombination appears to be a more immediate source of variation in sexually reproducing populations. In trees, as in most other sexual organisms, new combinations of genes are created in each generation by the segregation, assortment, and recombination of genes and chromosomes during *meiosis*. The pollen and eggs produced during meiosis can then reunite at fertilization and eventually develop into seed. The vast array of new genotypes produced in this way provides the successors to the parent generation and contains the variation required for coping with a potentially new or changing environment. Because virtually all tree species are capable of sexual reproduction, it is probable that recombination is an extremely important evolutionary mechanism in forest tree populations.

Migration or Gene Flow as a Source of Variation The migration of genes from one population to another via seed and pollen dispersal is another way in which variation can be introduced into populations over a period of time. Unlike mutation, however, the genes in question already exist in some populations. It follows that if migration is to have a significant effect, these genes should be absent, or present at a low frequency, in the population into which they are introduced. Seed and pollen dispersal are the obvious modes of migration for forest trees.

Seed dispersal distances of most forest tree species are rather small, but occasional propagules may travel considerable distances. Long-distance dispersal has been reported for seed such as coconuts, which have sometimes been carried by ocean currents. Such dispersal is obviously quite important in colonization events, especially when suitable habitats are widely dispersed. In general, though, it appears that gene migration via seed dispersal is slow in most forest trees.

Gene flow via *pollen dispersal* is a somewhat more difficult process to measure, at least in part because some estimates of the distance pollen is dispersed may be biologically irrelevant. That is, simply knowing that pollen grains of a particular species can be detected many kilometers from their point of release does not mean that they are capable

of or likely to effect a fertilization. This question is particularly important from the seed orchard perspective, because orchard managers are concerned that pollen contamination from outside the orchard may seriously hinder the production of improved seed.

As with seed, when a single tree serves as a point source, the vast bulk of any pollen released falls within a short distance of the tree. When a forest is considered as the pollen source, however, the relatively small, widely dispersed contribution from each tree is summed over a large number of trees. This total volume may be considerable inasmuch as the pollen production of a forest of large trees must total billions or trillions of grains. Pollen dispersal is probably more effective than seed dispersal as a migration mechanism, especially in insect-pollinated species, but few data are actually available on forest trees to confirm this point. However, theoretical calculations indicate that the rate of gene migration required to prevent populations from becoming sharply differentiated is very low, so even limited gene flow may be important.

Random Processes That Modify Variation Random processes as well as directional ones can produce changes in gene frequencies from one generation to the next. Random genetic drift occasioned by a restriction of population sizes or isolation of populations by distance could play a major role in the evolution of many tree species.

The seed produced in any year carries only a sample of the genes available in the parental population, so small population size can lead to large and unpredictable changes in gene frequencies. As population sizes become very small, the operation of such chance factors may assume considerable importance in the evolution of these populations. It seems likely, then, that species such as bristlecone pine, knobcone pine, or others with small, patchy distributions have been considerably influenced by such random processes.

The "founder effect," or the establishment of a population from one or a few individuals, is another example of the operation of chance influences in tree populations. It is quite easy to envision how natural catastrophes such as fire may decimate a forest, leaving only a scattered few individuals to reproduce and create the next generation. An analogous situation would be the long-distance dispersal of a few seeds to a new habitat. As a sample, these seeds may not represent accurately the distribution of gene frequencies that existed in the original population. Because of chance alone, some genes present in the original population may be absent from this new population.

Although the likelihood that such events will occur can be predicted, the direction and magnitude of change in any one instance is indeterminate. In the absence of any directional forces, the net effect of such chance occurrences over a long period of time would be to create a mosaic of populations, each with a gene frequency distribution quite different from any other. It is more likely, though, that some combination of directional and random factors operates together to establish patterns of variation in natural populations.

Selection: The Directional Modification of Variation

The power of Selection, whether exercised by man, or brought into play under nature through the struggle for existence and the consequent survival of the fittest, absolutely depends on the variability of organic beings. . . . The importance of the great principle of Selection mainly lies in this power of selecting scarcely appreciable differences, which nevertheless are found to be transmissible, and which can be accumulated until the result is made manifest to the eyes of the beholder (5).

Charles Darwin clearly recognized the importance of heritable variation to selection in his studies of wild and domesticated plants and animals. Darwin saw natural selection as a process that could account for the enormous diversity of adaptations he observed in natural populations. He also realized that the development of domesticated plants and animals was an analogous process wherein humans, not natural processes, exercised control over survival and reproduction via *artificial selection*. But

the role of heritable variation was clearly central to both natural and artificial (or "methodical") selection.

Darwin's theory is still central to the understanding of evolutionary processes and the origin of adaptations, but it has undergone much refinement since its conception a century ago. One source of refinement was the work of Gregor Mendel, which blossomed into the science of genetics during the twentieth century and provided the mechanism of inheritance that Darwin's theory needed. This merger of Darwinism and Mendelism forms the basis for the present understanding of organic evolution.

Despite its obvious importance, *natural selection* has proved to be a difficult phenomenon to study. Indeed, a great deal of evidence for the existence of natural selection is indirect. Lerner addressed this problem when he noted that

Natural selection is not an *a priori* cause of any phenomenon observed in nature, in the laboratory, or on the farm. Natural selection is a term serving to say that some genotypes leave more offspring than others. Natural selection has no purpose. It can be deduced to have existed and its intensity can be measured only *ex post facto*. For any given generation, natural selection is a consequence of the differences between individuals with respect to their capacity to produce progeny (6).

Viewing natural selection as a consequence instead of a cause of differences—and one that can be studied only after the fact—we can appreciate the problem potential researchers face in studying it.

Artificial selection is somewhat easier to approach, at least from the standpoint of choosing traits of human value; moreover, the hundreds of lines of domesticated plants and animals serve as testimony to the effectiveness of such selection. Human beings are the selective agents here, and within the bounds established by natural variation, artificial selection can proceed toward the development of lines of increased value. However, it is important not to lose sight of the fact that natural selection still operates whether we practice artificial selection or not. Human desires may be counter to those that have guided evolution over a long period of time, and compromises may have to be struck between the intensity of our breeding activities and biological factors that work to ensure the long-term survival of the species.

Forest Tree Breeding

"It is therefore very desirable, before any man commences to breed either cattle or sheep, that he should make up his mind to the shape and qualities he wishes to obtain, and steadily pursue this object" (5). This remark, attributed to Lord Spencer in 1840, is obviously true for trees as well. Tree-breeding programs are long-term, expensive propositions which require a great deal of commitment. The development of appropriate guidelines at the formative stages is essential if the program is to be successful. Major concerns include the selection of a suitable species and characters to be improved, an assessment of the biological, technical, and financial resources available to support the program, and the formulation of a working plan to guide program development. In what follows, some of the various approaches to tree improvement in use today are described. More detailed accounts are provided in the excellent textbooks of Wright (7), and Zobel and Talbert (8).

Some Economic Concerns

Most tree improvement programs have developed around a species that was historically the mainstay of the forest industry in that region. The loblolly pine program in the southeastern United States, as described by Zobel (9), is a good example of such an effort. Such an approach can be advantageous, especially if a good deal is already known about the amount and patterning of genetic variation within the species. This information is very useful in directing our selection strategies toward particular characters or toward particular regions. This early phase of a tree improvement program, where large numbers of stands or individual trees are being examined, is one of the most expensive because of time and travel costs. Some prior knowledge of the native

variability permits a more efficient use of funds in exploiting this variation.

The concerns of the wood-using industries also must be addressed at the formative stage. These industries are generally familiar with the properties of the wood of most species but may have particular interests in only a few species. Although more wood volume per unit land area is certainly one of their concerns, different industries may have a preference for wood with high or low specific gravity, wood with long or short fibers or tracheids, wood with more or fewer extractives, and other properties depending on their products. The ability to accommodate their specific interests could have a significant impact on the products industry and make the improvement program economically viable.

A major concern, particularly with regard to financing, is how much improved material is needed and at what date, depending, of course, on the areas to be reforested and the reproductive biology of the species. Neither of these can be considered a constant when a number of years must pass between initiation of the program and the time at which improved planting stock becomes available. Typically, an agency will develop seed orchards of a size to satisfy just its own needs, unless the market price of improved seed is attractive. Estimates of the number of seeds produced per seed orchard tree per year, together with estimates of the number of seedlings needed per acre per year, permit one to equate supply with demand, but the vagaries of local climate, insect attack, and numerous other problems that affect seed production make such estimates far from perfect. Like other factions in agriculture, breeders are reduced at present to stockpiling seed during the good years to provide for the lean years that inevitably follow. Good seed orchard management practices should provide the stimulating environment needed for adequate, predictable seed crops. Many major problems in seed orchard management remain to be solved at this time.

Finally, it should be obvious that tree-breeding activities can abbreviate but not circumvent the long rotation period needed to produce a crop of trees. Money invested now will not be recovered for decades. If growing trees is not a profitable operation for a particular set of circumstances, the substitution of improved material may not alter this situation. Tree improvement is not a "cure-all" for forestry's ailments. Sound management practices are still required, and careful examination will show that in certain instances good silvicultural practices will be more beneficial than conversion to improved planting stock.

Approaches to Forest Tree Domestication

Several alternative avenues can be followed in developing improved lines of trees. At the start of an improvement program, there may be little or no information available on the genetic biology of a species. Some rather questionable assumptions (or outright guesses) may have to be made concerning

the extent and patterning of heritable variation within a species. In addition, improvement strategies may have to vary considerably depending on the characters to be improved. For example, in some early attempts at developing elms in the United States that were truly resistant to Dutch elm disease, forest geneticists searched for resistance within the American elm. Unfortunately, levels of resistance to Dutch elm disease were limited within the American elm, with the result that several elm improvement programs now are based on breeding exotic elms (Figure 5.5). Similar examples could be cited for the American chestnut, a number of poplars (especially in Europe), and other species of forest trees.

Figure 5.5 (*a*) An urban American elm with Dutch elm disease (notice the dying, defoliated branches at top). (*b*) A Dutch elm disease-resistant hybrid, "Regal Elm," developed at the University of Wisconsin-Madison. [Photographs (*a*) by R. A. Young and (*b*) by R. P. Guries.]

Provenance Selection As discussed earlier, the practical side of provenance testing involves the identification of suitable seed sources for reforestation needs. Once such provenances have been identified, the seed needed for reforestation can be collected from specific stands or areas. In some species such as Scotch pine, which has a large natural range covering much of Eurasia, and which also has been studied well, differences in growth rate of the fastest- and slowest-growing provenances when planted in a given locale vary by as much as 400 percent. Sizable differences also exist among provenances for foliage color (of importance to Christmas tree growers), cold-hardiness, resistance to various insect defoliators, and other biochemical and morphological characters (7). For many tree species, the simple movement of seed a few hundred kilometers has resulted in the improvement of growth rate or other traits by 5 to 10 percent or more. Because the differences between stands or provenances may be several times as large as differences between trees within a stand, the results of provenance tests are usually quite useful to an agency planning a more intensive improvement program. It is almost always more efficient to select the best stands before selecting the best trees within a stand. An especially good account of provenance selection is given by Wright (7).

Exotic Introduction The term exotic might conjure up images of bizarre or wondrous plants, but for breeding purposes it refers only to a plant growing outside of its native range. Sugar maple trees planted in California are exotic by this definition. The use of exotic plants becomes a more comfortable notion when it is realized that almost all the domesticated crops raised in the United States—corn, wheat, oats, barley, rice, potatoes, tomatoes, and beans, to name just a few—are exotics introduced for satisfying human food needs. North America is blessed with an abundance of valuable forest tree species, but many other countries are not so fortunate. For biological or historical reasons, many countries have had to rely on exotics to enrich otherwise limited forest resources. South Africa, like many Southern Hemisphere regions, lacks good softwood species and has relied on exotic introductions of conifers from North America to satisfy its softwood and fiber needs.

Other countries may have only one or a few species suitable for their wood needs, and introduce exotics that grow faster or produce high-quality wood. For this reason, several European countries have developed large-scale testing and breeding programs using conifers from the western United States and Canada, especially Douglas-fir, Sitka spruce, and lodgepole pine (Figure 5.6).

Finally, as noted earlier, exotics may be introduced in the search for disease or pest resistance. An important or wide-ranging species may be virtually destroyed when a new or exotic pest is suddenly introduced. This was the case with American elm when Dutch elm disease was introduced from Eurasia. Although little or no natural resistance to the disease existed in American elm, a number of Eurasian elms are moderately to highly resistant, presumably because they evolved together with the pathogen for millennia. The development of disease-resistant elms will certainly be based on this naturally occurring resistance.

In the introduction of exotics, provenance testing is a logical starting point. However, a number of factors that govern successful introductions permit us to select species with a high probability of success. Perhaps the most important indication of usefulness elsewhere is performance in the native range. A tree that is slow-growing, has very poor form, and produces poor-quality wood is not likely to improve markedly in new surroundings.

Environmental similarity is an important consideration for successful introductions. Species adapted to warm, dry summers and cool, wet winters will probably perform poorly, or fail to survive, if moved to a region with wet summers and dry winters. Minimum winter temperature, soil types, amount of annual rainfall, and other climatic and *edaphic* factors should be checked to obtain an approximate match between environment and species adaptability. Although some latitude can be tolerated for variation between environmental fea-

Figure 5.6 Douglas-fir seedlings grown for industrial plantation development in Banja Luka, Yugoslavia. (Photograph by R. A. Young.)

tures in the native and exotic locations, the more the two regions differ in this regard, the greater the probability of disappointing performance.

Interspecific Hybridization Hybrid breeding has a special appeal in most areas of applied plant science that is akin to the alchemist's changing base metal into gold. Most people think only of "hybrid vigor" whenever they see the word *hybrid*. However, increased vigor (or "heterosis," as it is sometimes called) may or may not result from crossing two different species. In most hybrid-breeding programs involving agronomic crops, different lines of the same species are crossed, instead of different species. In such crops, uniformity of performance or disease resistance may be the objective, rather than increased vigor.

Some hybridization programs have been quite successful in plant breeding, but the number of documented successful hybrids in forestry is actually quite small. In fact, certain hybrids such as black × red spruce, once considered superior to

either parental species, are actually inferior in growth rate to either parental species (10). The rate of growth syndrome that fascinated many early tree breeders has slowly given way to the belief that hybridization will find its greatest use in the development of trees resistant to pests and pathogens, or tolerant to adverse environmental conditions.

One example of a currently successful hybridization program involves the production of the pitch pine × loblolly pine hybrid in Korea. Pitch pine possesses a relatively poor form with large branches but is quite hardy in northern climates. Loblolly pine has a much better form and is faster-growing than pitch pine, but it is not especially cold-hardy. The hybrid performs quite well in Korea, apparently because it combines some of the cold-hardiness of pitch pine with the better form and growth rate of loblolly pine (11).

Plus-Tree Selection Perhaps the most common approach to tree improvement involves the selection of trees from wild populations based on their

Figure 5.7 A superior selection of lodgepole pine near Babine Lake, British Columbia. The trees have excellent stem forms and crown characteristics. (Courtesy of Nicholas Wheeler, British Columbia Forest Service.)

apparent superiority in one or more traits of interest. Either seeds or cuttings (scions) are collected from these trees and propagated in one or more locations to serve eventually as seed orchards (Figure 5.7). Genetically improved seed will be obtained from such orchards to satisfy reforestation needs.

No one selection method is suitable for all species under all conditions. For example, a method known as "comparison-tree selection" has been widely employed in the southern pine region with apparent success. In this system, a "candidate" tree is compared to a number of neighboring trees and is included in the selections only if it exceeds these neighbors by an arbitrary amount in the characters

examined. The fact that most stands of southern pine tend to be even-aged, and that such stands occur in large blocks on relatively homogeneous sites, operates in favor of this selection method.

A number of species, especially hardwoods, tend to occur in uneven-aged or uneven-sized stands, and individual trees may be widely separated, making direct comparison with neighbors impossible. In such cases researchers may employ a system known as "baseline selection," selecting a "candidate" and comparing it to a regional average (or baseline) for the species calculated from a composite of measurements taken on a number of trees within the region. To be selected, the candidate must exceed this regional average by some arbitrary amount.

At the outset, the researcher must decide on the optimal size of breeding population that will secure genetic gains for economically important traits and maintain a reserve of variation for future selection and breeding. Available resources—especially time and money—are important considerations, but the levels of genetic variation in wild populations are also important determinants of population sizes needed for breeding. In essence, a balance must be achieved between the desire to include only the most exceptional trees to obtain substantial genetic gains quickly, and the need to develop an adequate genetic base for long-term breeding.

Once a selection approach has been chosen, it generally proves convenient to collect and assemble the selected materials in one or a few places so that further evaluation and breeding can proceed efficiently. *Scions* can be propagated in an orchard by grafting or rooting so that the original parent genotype is retained intact. In some instances it may be easier or more desirable to collect seed instead of (or in addition to) scions and raise the seed in a plantation or orchard setting. In this method the genes of the selected tree are preserved, but the original genotype is no longer intact. Each seedling contains a different sample of the genes of the selected tree, the other genes coming from whichever tree provided pollen for fertilization.

The decision to use clones versus seedlings can have some effect on the level of improvement obtained during the first generation, with clonal orchards generally providing greater opportunities for improvement. Many tree breeders would prefer not to be concerned with the propagation effort, considering it the domain of the horticulturist. But the success of many applied tree improvement programs depends on the successful propagation of selected materials for seed orchards. This is one area in which an applied program has been the catalyst for renewed research in propagation techniques, especially hormone physiology.

Eventually the propagation effort culminates in the development of seed orchards (Figure 5.8). Now the geneticist must be concerned with problems involving flowering, cone or fruit protection, harvesting, processing, and storing seed. In many instances, tree nurseries are located at or near the orchard site, so raising the improved seedlings is an attendant responsibility. Obviously, the more seed produced, or the earlier seed production begins, the

more profitable the orchard becomes. Cooperation with soil scientists, plant physiologists, entomologists, and others is necessary if the expected level of improvement is to be realized.

Evaluation of Select Trees Our initial selection procedure is somewhat limited, as we noted earlier, by our inability to equate phenotype with genotype. Wild-tree selection serves as a first approximation of an individual tree's genetic worth to a breeding program. Subsequent observations on the performance of the candidate tree or its relatives are needed to refine our original evaluation.

Many tree-breeding programs have relied on a separate testing phase during which the offspring of selected parents are raised and compared. The practice of evaluating a parent's genetic worth on the basis of progeny performance is termed *progeny testing*. This test is used to rank selected trees so that

Figure 5.8 A portion of the seed orchard–provenance test complex of the U.S. Forest Service and the Wisconsin Department of Natural Resources in northern Wisconsin. (Courtesy of Hans Nienstaedt, U.S.D.A. Forest Service.)

undesirable genotypes may be eliminated from the seed orchard, and also to serve as a check on the level of genetic gains achieved to date. Progeny tests may serve other functions as well, such as a political demonstration to management that its investment has been well spent, but alternative procedures for this and other functions are usually more desirable. In recent years the use of large, expensive plantings that serve the primary purpose of ranking candidate trees has diminished. In their place, breeding designs that mate selected parents have led to the creation of new populations in which further selection can be practiced.

Genetic Gain The term *genetic gain* is an apt synonym for the term *improvement* in the breeder's language; both have the connotation of economic benefit to the producer in particular and society in general.

Symbolically, the expression for genetic gain is

$$G = S \times h^2$$

where G is *gain*, S is *selection differential,* and h^2 is *heritability*. Because they are based on estimates that vary from species to species and population to population, neither term on the right side of the equation is fixed, and it is possible to alter the level of gain obtained by manipulating these terms. Selection differential is a measure of the average difference between the selected population and the wild population. Its magnitude depends not only on how many (or few) individuals we select, but also on how much variation exists within the wild population. Thus it is possible to change the selection differential for a character by selecting a smaller fraction of the original population. If this reduced fraction represents a significant shift from the population mean, the process will be successful. In practice, there are limits to just how small a fraction can be included, and *inbreeding depression,* or loss of vigor caused by matings among closely related individuals, could become a serious problem if the breeding population is severely reduced. A viable alternative, at least with forest trees, is to expand the number of stands in which selections are made. This serves the purpose of expanding the base population.

One of several alternative ways to increase the expected gain is to increase the *heritability estimate.* Heritability is a measure of the proportion of variation in the population that is attributable to genetic differences among individuals. Thus the larger the estimate, the greater is the expected tendency for parents to pass their characteristics on to their offspring. For a given population the heritability estimate could be increased by providing very uniform growing conditions. By minimizing differences caused by environmental variation, we can maximize our estimate of variation caused by genetic differences. However, it is important to remember that heritability estimates are not fixed and may change over time as the trees mature. Naturally, different populations possessing different genes could be expected to yield very different heritability estimates.

Any or all of the methods described can lead to increased gains in tree improvement programs. Current estimates of genetic gain based on the selection of wild trees are on the order of 10 to 20 percent, depending on the species and trait in question (7, 8). It is likely that subsequent generations of breeding and selection will lead to additional gains of at least this magnitude.

Advanced-Generation Breeding There will be a continuing need for breeding and further selection and evaluation activities beyond this first generation. Certainly the gains produced by this first generation are important, but continued progress will require that appropriate mating and evaluation designs become a part of all tree improvement programs. This will be essential for continuing advances via artificial selection, as well as the maintenance of a broad genetic base for future generations.

Many tree improvement programs are now at the point where advanced-generation breeding can begin. The formidable prospects and problems associated with this phase have been given considerable thought (8). We are essentially at the point of creating new, synthetic populations that will be tailored to meet growing needs for fiber and energy. The lines developed to this end will stem largely from the new genotypes generated by crossing among our select trees. To be sure, new variability will have to enter the breeding program from time to time, either from additional wild-tree selections or from lines developed in other programs or geographic regions. But the bulk of the materials finding their way into production seed orchards will be one to several generations removed from the wild.

In recent years, as the need for creating advanced-generation populations from original selections became evident, considerable attention has also been devoted to a comparison of *mating designs*. In general, a large number of possible crossing schemes could be employed to produce progeny of known and related parentage. The problem is primarily one of determining precisely what information can be obtained from these populations and then which designs are most efficient at providing this information. Like most other tree improvement problems, some sort of compromise is generally struck between adoption of a complex, elegant design and the cost and likelihood of actually completing such a design in the field. Fortunately, the large number of mating design variations available virtually ensures that the creation of populations needed for advanced-generation breeding will be accomplished.

Domestication of the Forest

Plantation Forests—Pro and Con

Forests that originated by natural processes are rapidly being replaced. In some instances they are being harvested and replanted with native or exotic trees. In many more instances they are yielding to the crush of humanity, as it expands its urban and agricultural activities on an ever-widening scale. Although the need for food and shelter is very real, many environmental groups are alarmed at the rapid replacement of natural forests with *monocultures*. Certainly the process has shortcomings. In the case of agriculture there appear to be no easy choices for increasing food production, but many people view forest plantations with a suspicious eye. At times their fears are well placed, and breeders

should attempt to minimize potential problems before they arise.

Natural populations are generally well adapted to their sites because their ancestors evolved on or near the same site. Replacement with trees originating from a distant source may produce a poorly adapted population with resultant low survival and inferior growth. However, these new forests may be very productive if care is taken to use seed from local sources or from provenances that evolved under very similar ecological conditions. This is the basis for the establishment of seed zones to control the movement of seed and planting stock into areas where performance will be acceptable. Large tree improvement programs with species such as Douglas-fir also control the movement of improved planting stock by developing seed orchards for specific regions within the species range.

Many people perceive *plantation forests* to be ecologically unstable monoculture systems tottering on the brink of disaster. In this regard, it is worth noting that many tree species such as jack pine, lodgepole pine, and Douglas-fir form naturally occurring monocultures (Figure 5.9). Pest epidemics occur here and in other forest types as well. The real cause for concern here should not be species monocultures *per se,* but rather the genetic uniformity that often accompanies monocultures. Almost all documented examples of devastated monoculture systems involve clones (for example, the nineteenth-century destruction of the French wine industry which used clonal varieties of rootstock). Almost all forest tree plantations are produced from seed arising from large numbers of parents. Even in seed orchards producing improved seed, the numbers of parents are considerable, thereby ensuring a broad array of genotypes. In those few species, such as some poplars, for which clonal propagation is used, steps can be taken to mix cuttings from a number of clones into the planting, thereby minimizing this monoculture hazard.

Perhaps a more objectionable feature of plantation forests is their *visual uniformity*. Such forests are even-aged and established at a regular spacing. Mechanized planting equipment and ease of maintenance during the early life of the stand necessitate the regular spacing, and it seems unlikely that cur-

Figure 5.9 Many natural forests such as this virgin stand of Douglas-fir in California (Siskiyou Mountains) consist of a single species—like many planted monocultures. (Photograph by C. G. Lorimer.)

rent procedures will change in the near future. An irregular thinning process could mitigate this problem, but not before the stand is ten to twenty or more years old. A more permanent solution to this aesthetics problem could be the development of techniques for raising *mixed-species plantings.* Mixtures of species, either by rows or by plots, was once common practice in forestry, but has generally been abandoned. Species or provenance selections were usually such that one species overtopped and eliminated the other before any merchantable harvest was possible. Perhaps if more were learned about mixed-species culture and how to select compatible species, the variety that such mixed plantings could create would make plantation culture more attractive. Opponents of monoculture would feel that such plantings also were "more stable" ecologically.

The advantages of plantation forests can be enormous if the breeding process has progressed to the point that significant improvement in growth rate, pest resistance, wood quality, or other traits has been achieved. For example, an adequate level of pest resistance may represent the difference between a crop of wood and nothing at all. Breeding progress in many areas can increase yields of forest products in a shorter period of time from forests occupying a diminishing land base. The concept of forest plantations as sources for energy is further developed in Chapter 23.

Preserving Natural Variation—The Case for Genetic-Resource Conservation

The need for genetic-resource conservation is widely recognized by plant and animal breeders. The original wild populations from which most important crops and breeds of animals were developed were lost centuries ago. These *progenitor populations* could be of great value today as sources of variation for breeding, especially in the area of pest resistance. Vulnerability to pests is a real danger in crops that are planted widely but have a narrow genetic base.

Most forest tree species still occupy large ranges and appear to be genetically quite variable. Many people, then, would conclude that concern for genetic-resource conservation in tree species is unnecessary. However, a species need not be pushed to the brink of extinction before a serious reduction of the genetic resource has occurred. Either directly or indirectly, many human activities have depleted the genetic base of forest tree populations. Harvesting practices that systematically remove the best trees in a forest (high-grading) and the replacement of natural stands with plantations of a single species both operate to reduce genetic variability. The inadvertent introduction of pests, which caused the chestnut blight and Dutch elm disease in North America, has also lost us genetic resources that can never be recovered. These and similar events that occur during a relatively short period of time can have enormous long-term consequences.

The problem of preserving genetic resources can be approached in several ways. Certain measures could provide for the preservation of "*gene pools*" using existing natural populations or populations created to serve this specific role. Created populations may be far removed from their native range. Alternatively, we can preserve genes via the *storage* of seed, pollen, or other plant parts in special collection facilities such as those already established for agronomic crops.

Natural scientific or preservation areas offer some promise as genetic-resource conservation sites, especially those containing large populations of trees occurring in a number of different habitats. Appropriate management practices could ensure that even pioneer species that require occasional disturbances to perpetuate themselves are maintained on such areas. Fortunately, the national forests and parks in many countries also serve a genetic-resource conservation function to some degree,

even though management practices on such areas must meet other priorities. Whether such areas are plentiful enough or large enough to isolate natural stands effectively from gene migration effects is an open question. Certainly they are a start, but they are inadequate to satisfy the entire conservation need.

The breeding orchards, clone banks, provenance and test plantings, and other collections of trees brought together during the conduction of tree improvement activities also serve a conservation function. Although the size of such populations is small relative to those in national parks and forests, these plantings represent some of the most valuable genetic materials for breeding purposes. Selections included in such plantings were obtained in many instances following an intensive examination of millions of trees in thousands of stands. Such collections may also contain representative samples of many populations to enhance further their usefulness as genetic reserves. Finally, it might be pointed out that many such collections are located outside their native range and therefore may be free from pollen or seed migration emanating from domesticated forests.

Future Directions for Forest Genetics and Forest Tree Breeding

Anticipating Tomorrow's Needs

History provides countless examples of human failure to anticipate accurately the long-term consequences of our actions. National and international strife, recessions and depressions, and overpopulation with all its attendant problems are among the more conspicuous examples of such shortsighted behavior. Given the potential for disaster, it will be of paramount importance that forest geneticists avoid possible blind alleys in *tree domestication programs*. Tree breeders will generally need to adopt conservative yet creative approaches in programs of selection, testing, and breeding. The time and effort required may occasionally be considerable, but the eventual impact of a wrong decision at a central point may be disastrous.

The problems of forecasting anticipated needs and demands one, two, or more generations into the future are difficult, even when accurate information on past trends is available. The forest products industry fluctuates wildly in its demands for raw materials. In addition, there are continuing changes in the quality of the raw materials available and in the nature of goods being produced. All these factors impinge on tree improvement activities.

Presettlement forests of large, long-boled trees are a thing of the past. They have been replaced by regrowth forests established by natural and artificial means. As demand for forest products increases, trees will be harvested at an increasingly smaller size and younger age. The principal change in wood quality will be the relatively high proportion of less desirable juvenile wood contained in small-sized trees. Although it may prove possible to manipulate juvenile wood volume and characteristics genetically, it is obvious that the products industry will also have to adapt its technology to a changing resource.

The kinds of products being manufactured have also changed since colonial times. Veneer and particleboard panels have replaced sawed lumber in many uses for a variety of economic and technological reasons. The development of new and better products, some of which cannot be foreseen even one generation ahead, requires that the forest resource not be modified to the point that new technologies cannot be accommodated. This does not mean that a status quo situation must exist, only that wood characteristics suitable for a variety of uses be selected. "Specialty" strains of trees can occasionally be developed to satisfy particular needs as long as a broad genetic base is maintained.

Fortunately, many of the directed changes advocated by forest geneticists, such as increased volume per unit time or area, or increased disease or pest resistance, need not inadvertently alter other characters. However difficult it is to envision circumstances in which seemingly well-advised manipulations of growth rate or other characters of economic importance could ultimately prove to be liabilities,

the possibility cannot be ruled out. The possibility provides one strong argument for "gene banks" and the maintenance of natural populations. However, fail-safe mechanisms are no substitute for clear insights and a job done well the first time.

Prospects for Continued Improvement

Present tree improvement programs are only the beginning of efforts to provide more and better products from our forests. The genetic gains being obtained today are the result of only one generation of selection. Theoretical arguments, as well as early results from second-generation tests, indicate that additional gains will be possible for a number of generations in the future. These gains will not come effortlessly, however, and it will be imperative that breeders exercise good judgment in planning and conducting future research.

In addition to the steady pace of improvement resulting from the selection, propagation, and testing of candidate trees, forest genetics research has provided a number of important and exciting developments. The finding that flowering can be induced in juvenile trees, either directly by application of plant growth hormones or indirectly by manipulating photoperiod and temperature, will permit a reduction in the length of time between flowering in successive generations. Breeders who once had to wait ten to fifteen years for young trees to begin flowering, can now induce such flowering in trees only one or two years old. This will permit greatly accelerated breeding and testing programs when the characters of interest, such as disease resistance, can be evaluated in young plants.

Biotechnology and Forest Productivity

The 1980s have witnessed a rapid expansion of biotechnology research efforts in medicine, agriculture, food processing, and other industries. The most spectacular progress has come in areas such as

Figure 5.10 The node of a greenhouse-grown eastern cottonwood develops an axillary shoot and callus tissue in vitro. Such cultures supply starting tissues for research in the genetic engineering of specific traits, such as herbicide stress resistance. (Courtesy of U.S.D.A. Forest Service.)

human health care that engender strong support for basic research and have a large market guaranteeing that successful research and development efforts will be profitable. Crops that are economically important and that have been well characterized genetically and biochemically have also received increasing attention. Genes that regulate photosynthetic efficiency, confer herbicide resistance, or control protein, cellulose, or lignin production have been identified and studied in a number of crops. In a few instances genes from one organism have been successfully introduced into a second, thereby heightening prospects for the creation of novel plants via genetic engineering.

Predictably, biotechnology efforts with forest trees have lagged behind, in large part because trees are recalcitrant organisms whose genetic properties are only partially understood. In addition, the economic "payoff" is necessarily slower with a crop of trees as compared with agronomic crops. Nevertheless, biotechnology methods are being applied in forestry and the forest products industry, and it seems only a matter of time before the remaining barriers to full utilization of these new technologies fall (12) (Figure 5.10).

Like most rapidly developing research areas, biotechnology studies can appear to be too esoteric to many field practitioners. Initially, the prospects for translating forest biotechnology efforts into practical applications may appear remote, especially if these efforts are viewed as isolated activities operating outside of mainstream forestry. In fact, biotechnology is not an end in itself, but instead represents a collection of techniques that will in time become integrated into tree breeding, silviculture, pulp and paper manufacturing, and other forestry disciplines. The biotechnology techniques related to genetics will become part of, rather than replace, traditional breeding programs.

Forest genetics has been and continues to be a stimulating area for research and development directed toward increasing forest yields. Agriculture has provided the precedent for domestication programs; if the breeder keeps an eye to the past and its painful lessons, as well as an eye to the future, the prospects for continued improvement are enormous.

References

1. K. STERN AND L. ROCHE, *Genetics of Forest Ecosystems,* Springer-Verlag, New York/Berlin, 1974.

2. D. BRIGGS AND S. M. WALTERS, *Plant Variation and Evolution.* McGraw–Hill, New York, 1969.

3. L. E. METTLER AND T. G. GREGG, *Population Genetics and Evolution,* Prentice–Hall, Englewood Cliffs, N.J., 1969.

4. D. L. HARTL, *A Primer of Population Genetics,* Sinauer, Sunderland, Mass., 1981.

5. C. DARWIN, *The Variation of Animals and Plants under Domestication,* Vol. 2, Second Edition, D. Appleton & Co., New York, 1900.

6. I. M. LERNER, *The Genetic Basis of Selection,* John Wiley & Sons, New York, 1958.

7. J. WRIGHT, *Introduction to Forest Genetics,* Academic Press, New York, 1976.

8. B. ZOBEL AND J. TALBERT, *Applied Forest Tree Improvement,* John Wiley & Sons, New York, 1984.

9. B. ZOBEL, *So. J. Appl. For., 1,* 3 (1977).

10. S. M. MANLEY AND F. T. LEDIG, *Can. J. Bot., 57,* 305 (1979).

11. S. K. HYUN, *Silvae Genetica, 25,* 188 (1976).

12. P. C. TROTTER, *Tappi J., 69,* 22 (1986).

CHAPTER 6

Forest Ecology and the Forest Ecosystem

JOHN D. ABER

Ecology is the study of the interactions between organisms and their environment. Such interactions are understandably varied and complex. However, the application of the results of ecological studies has helped to change forestry from an exploitive business to a sophisticated profession. Depending on one's perspective, ecology focuses on the individual and its relationship to the environment (*autecology*) or on a community of organisms and the interaction between the community and the environment (*synecology*). For many problems in forestry, it is necessary to understand how the forest ecosystem works through the interactions between the community and the environment (1,2).

Other perspectives have given rise to different areas of ecology. Foresters and forest ecologists have a patent interest in the structure and function of forest ecosystems. The structure of the ecosystem is the organizational pattern of a community. As a simple example, a forest of many small trees packed closely together would represent quite a different structure from one with a few large trees widely spaced. The function of the forest ecosystem relates to biological activities or processes associated with the community. For example, the addition of wood to stems by tree growth is a process that changes the structure of the forest.

Some also distinguish between theoretical and applied ecology. *Theoretical ecology* is the development of ecological principles such as succession, nutrient cycling, and energy exchange, all of which will be subsequently described. *Applied ecology* uses ecological principles to solve particular land management problems. Studies of fertilization of forest stands, for example, are done with the express purpose of trying to find a way to grow timber or other forest crops bigger, better, or faster. Such studies rely on the ecological principles developed by the theoretical ecologist but represent ecology applied to solve a particular problem.

Forest Community Development

Forest ecosystems have long developmental periods. The time required to produce a mature forest varies from as few as 35 years in the Southeast to over 100 years in the Rocky Mountains. The developmental process is not only long but also complex. Under natural conditions, it consists of the establishment of young individuals of pioneer species,[1] growth, and then replacement by other species through a complex set of interactions that form the basis of the science of ecology. This ecological development is called *succession.*

Through the practices of silviculture (Chapter 14), foresters may affect the succession of a forest. Their treatments may be designed to maintain the status quo, speed succession (i.e., move the stand ahead to a later successional stage), or set it back to an earlier stage. The ecological development of a forest ecosystem, however, implies much more than the establishment and growth of the trees that dominate it. Many other organisms are involved, and many emergent properties may only be indirectly tied to the trees. Understory plants make up an important part of any forest ecosystem. Insects and fungi play an important role by consuming or infecting vascular plants. Birds and mammals nest, mate, and obtain their food and shelter from the resources of the forest and in turn affect many of the functional aspects of the ecosystem such as energy flow and nutrient cycling. Bacteria, insects, and fungi in the soil may fix nitrogen or contribute to the cycling of all the nutrients through decomposition.

The forester can affect succession by every treatment made to the forest. A planting may speed succession by establishing a species that is characteristic of later stages in the successional sequence. An improvement cut will either speed or set back succession, depending on whether earlier or later successional species are favored. Selective harvest of

scattered trees will maintain a mature stand's structure and composition without allowing succession to proceed to an overmature or climax situation.

Intelligent management of a forest demands that decisions be based on knowledge and understanding of the ecosystem. Under these conditions, we can predict the probable outcomes of a treatment with a large degree of certainty. If a prescribed fire is the treatment, what will be the outcome? How will the forest be affected? We should try to know the answers to these questions before deciding to implement such a treatment. In order to do this we need to understand quite fully the ecological development of the forest.

Forest Tree Growth and Distribution

A question raised in the study of forest ecology is "Why are there so many species of trees in a forest region and why do certain species tend to occur on sites with certain characteristics?" The earliest settlers in the New World recognized that certain species in the primeval forest, such as sugar maple, tended to grow on the richest soils, so that crops planted on these soils grew best. Other species, for example, hemlock, were associated with poor soils and poor crops and were to be avoided. The relationship between the distribution and abundance of tree species and the characteristics of sites on which they grow will be described in this section.

Tolerance, Competition, and Succession

What determines the distribution of tree species? We have seen in earlier chapters that different species have different physiological responses to the availability of a given growth-promoting resource. For example, Figure 6.1 shows the relative rates of growth for three different species at various levels of light intensity (3). The curves in this figure express the concept of shade tolerance, which has traditionally been a key to forest ecology and management. A

---

[1]Pioneer species are those present in the first stage of the ecological development of a community—that is, the pioneer stage.

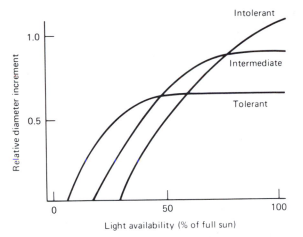

Figure 6.1 Relative rates of growth as a function of light availability for tolerant, intermediate, and intolerant species. [Adapted from Larcher (3).]

tolerant species is one that can grow comparatively well when little light is available but does not show large increases in growth with increasing light levels. An *intolerant species* shows the opposite trends: very poor growth at low levels of light, but faster growth rates than those of tolerant species at light levels approaching full sun exposure. Trees of different tolerance levels are expected to grow under different conditions in natural forests. The relative tolerances to shade of some North American tree species are given in Table 6.1 (4).

Imagine a mature forest with tall trees whose crowns completely occupy the upper canopy levels. In deciduous forests of this type, only 2 to 5 percent of the light striking the top of the canopy will reach the forest floor. From Figure 6.1 it can be seen that trees of intolerant or intermediate species growing below the canopy will not be able to have a positive growth rate, because light levels are below the *compensation point,* or the level at which a net positive energy gain is possible. Only tolerant species will be able to grow in this dense shade. The tolerant species will be the only ones represented in the understory and the only species in a position to grow up into the canopy later (see Figure 6.2*a*). Thus, unless some sort of disturbance occurs, this stand will continue to be dominated by the same

tolerant species and will not change much in species composition.

Imagine that a hurricane, tornado, or fires sweeps through this stand, felling large numbers of the old tolerant trees and flooding the forest floor with light. Conditions are now much better for intolerant species; if a source of seed is available and ground surface conditions are suitable, intolerant species will germinate and grow at a much faster rate than the established seedlings (called "*advance regeneration*"). The intolerant trees will soon overtop the tolerant species because of their faster rate of growth in full sun and will soon dominate the stand (Figure 6.2*b*). However, they will not cast shade that is darker than their compensation point. This leaves light levels below their crowns sufficient for the growth of intermediate species and in turn for tolerant species. Thus a stratified canopy may develop with intolerant species at the highest level, intermediate species below them, and tolerant species lower still (Figure 6.2*c*). Eventually, as the tolerant trees slowly grow taller and the intermediate and intolerant trees die, a stand dominated by tolerant trees will be reestablished (Figure 6.2*d*).

The process of *succession,* which has just been described by means of our example, is a central concept in the field of ecology. Succession can now be more specifically defined as the orderly replacement of species through time in a given location, leading eventually to a generally stable plant community. This end point has been called the "*climax community*"; however, some scientists feel that even late-successional communities will change in composition through time. The type of succession described is called *secondary* succession. In secondary succession an established plant community has been destroyed without severe disturbance of the site, mainly the soil in which the new plants will grow. *Primary* succession occurs when plants invade an area in which no plants have grown before, such as bare rocks or new lakes created by the retreat of glaciers. In primary succession on land, the plants must build the soil; a much longer time is required for the process—hundreds to thousands of years. Secondary succession usually takes only decades to perhaps hundreds of years (5). Before we

Table 6.1 Relative Tolerance to Shade of Some North American Species[a]

Eastern Conifers	Eastern Deciduous	Western Conifers	Western Deciduous
Very Tolerant			
Balsam fir	American beech	Western redcedar	
Eastern hemlock	American hornbeam	Silver fir	
	Flowering dogwood	Western hemlock	
	American holly	California torreya	
	Eastern hophornbeam	Pacific yew	
	Sugar maple		
Tolerant			
Northern white-cedar	Rock elm	Alaska yellow-cedar	California laurel
Red spruce	Blackgum	Incense-cedar	Canyon live oak
White spruce	Sourwood	Port-Orford-cedar	Tanoak
	Red maple	Grand fir	
	Hickory spp.	Subalpine fir	
		California red fir	
		White fir	
		Mountain hemlock	
		Redwood	
		Englemann spruce	
		Sitka spruce	
Intermediate			
Eastern white pine	Ash spp.	Douglas-fir	Red alder
Black spruce	Basswood	Monterey pine	
	Sweet birch	Sugar pine	
	Yellow birch	Western white pine	
	Buckeye	Blue spruce	
	American elm	Giant sequoia	
	Sweetgum	Noble fir	
	Hackberry		
	Cucumber magnolia		
	Silver maple		
	Black oak		
	Northern red oak		
	Southern red oak		
	White oak		
Intolerant			
Baldcypress	Paper birch	Bigcone Douglas-fir	Madrone
Loblolly pine	Butternut	Juniper spp.	Bigleaf maple
Pitch pine	Catalpa spp.	Bishop pine	Oregon ash
Pond pine	Black cherry	Coulter pine	California white oak
Red pine	Chokeberry	Jeffrey pine	Oregon white oak
Shortleaf pine	Kentucky coffeetree	Knobcone pine	Golden chinkapin
Slash pine	Honeylocust	Limber pine	
Virginia pine	Pin oak	Lodgepole pine	

Table 6.1 Relative Tolerance to Shade of Some North American Species[a] *(continued)*

Eastern Conifers	Eastern Deciduous	Western Conifers	Western Deciduous
	Scarlet oak	Piñon pine	
	Pecan	Ponderosa pine	
	Persimmon		
	Yellow-poplar		
	Sycamore		
Very Intolerant			
Jack pine	Aspen spp.	Alpine larch	Quaking aspen
Longleaf pine	Gray birch	Western larch	Cottonwood spp.
Sand pine	River birch	Bristlecone pine	Willow spp.
Eastern redcedar	Black locust	Digger pine	
Tamarack	Post oak	Foxtail pine	
	Turkey oak	Whitebark pine	
	Blackjack oak		
	Willow spp.		

Source: Adapted from H. W. Hocker, Jr., *Introduction to Forest Biology,* John Wiley & Sons, New York, 1979.
[a]Arranged in order of tolerance among groups but not within groups.

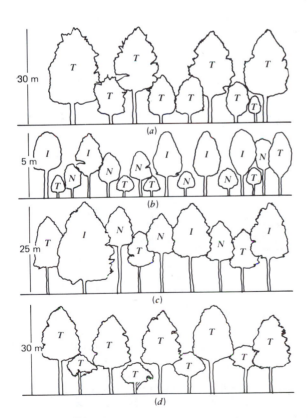

Figure 6.2 Schematic view of the distribution of tree crowns by tolerance class and height for four stages of succession initiated by severe disturbance. (*a*) Before disturbance; (*b*) immediately after disturbance (5 years); (*c*) midpoint of succession (50–75 years); (*d*) full recovery and return to predisturbance conditions. (*T* = tree of tolerant species; *N* = tree of intermediate species; *I* = tree of intolerant species.)

continue with the treatment of secondary succession, we will describe the basic principles and classification schemes for primary succession.

Primary Succession Three basic types of primary succession correspond to the character of the substrate on which succession is initiated: xerarch, mesarch, and hydrarch succession. It is important to recognize that these types represent only nodes or reference points along a gradient of site conditions from dry to wet, including many intermediate situations. *Xerarch* succession is illustrated by the bare rock to juniper shrub sequence (6). In this successional sequence, called a *sere,* invading plants, lichens, and mosses, together with the strong influence of weathering forces of the climate, modify the substrate so that the other plants can develop. This sere is characterized by dry conditions and a lack of soil, even though the site may be in an area of ample rainfall. The substrate has little water-holding capacity, and therefore water is available only intermittently as precipitation falls and shortly thereafter. The successional sequence in this type of site is very closely tied to the development of the soil. The time it takes for ultimate development of the mature community is too long to be of much consequence to the forestland manager.

Mesarch succession is illustrated by community development following glacial retreat in southeast Alaska (6–8). The climate of the area is cool and moist. The parent material of the soil is glacial rubble deposited at different times, and therefore a series of plant communities with different ages have become established. The soil material itself is raw and unweathered as it is laid down by the retreating glacier.

Pioneer species in this sere possess specialized mechanisms for transport of seeds, such as feathery plumes or wings that catch the wind, or barbs or burrs that stick to animals. These include such species as Drummond's dryas, Sitka alder, dwarf fireweed, willows, and cottonwood. It is notable that two of these pioneers, dryas and alder, are also nitrogen fixers, which means they can obtain nitrogen from the atmosphere and compensate for a lack of this essential nutrient in the young soil. A lichen–

moss stage is essentially absent here, being swamped out by the much more rapidly growing vascular plants.

Some vascular plants do not appear to enter the sere until these pioneers have improved the nutrient and organic matter status of the soil. The mature pioneer stage, dominated by alder and willow, gives way to cottonwoods, hemlocks, and spruces, which eventually overtop and replace the earlier species. The conifers will assume dominance of the site after about 170 years following glacial retreat.

Beneath the new overstory of hemlock and spruce, regeneration of the species is going on, seeming to ensure the replacement of this type of climax forest. However, mosses and litter are building up under the conifer canopy, and eventually sphagnum will dominate, as it does inland in white spruce forests (9); sphagnum may slowly eliminate the hemlock and spruce, creating a muskeg. What happens after the muskeg forms is uncertain, but there are some indications that an alder–willow community might eventually be reestablished, possibly allowing this whole cycle to occur again. This sere is illustrated in Figure 6.3.

Hydrarch succession is illustrated by community development in cold, freestanding water, the kind of site frequently found in the Great Lakes region. In this sere floating vegetation such as water lilies and

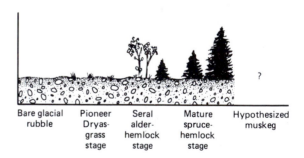

| Bare glacial rubble | Pioneer Dryas-grass stage | Seral alder-hemlock stage | Mature spruce-hemlock stage | Hypothesized muskeg |

Figure 6.3 Sequence illustrating a mesarch succession from Alaska. Pioneer stages rapidly invade freshly exposed glacial rubble. Shrubs including alder and tree seedlings of hemlock and spruce invade the pioneer community. The mature conifer forest develops after the spruce and hemlock grow through and replace the shrub stage.

pondweed and mat-forming sedges or other grass-like plants initiate the sequence. These species invade a bog, often from around the edges, and by means of vegetative reproduction creep out farther into the freestanding water. Sphagnum moss often invades after the sedge mat has been formed, which helps bind the vegetation together. At this point the vegetation is floating on what may be several meters of water. Later in the sere, shrubs such as bog rosemary, labrador tea, or cranberries invade the area, and tall shrubs such as willow, birch, or alder will eventually replace the low shrubs. Last, conifer trees such as tamarack or black spruce will become established. While all this is going on, the sedge mat or floating pond-lily type of vegetation pushes farther out into the bog. What one often sees, therefore, is a sequence stretching over space from the pioneer sedges and pond lilies near the center of a bog to the shrubs and trees dominating around the edges of the bog (Figure 6.4). This sequence in space is interpreted as a sequence in the ecological development of a community over time (i.e., it is a sere). Such a succession from sedge mat to conifer bog appears to be a reasonable interpretation of the sequence; however, the statement that this sere will ultimately yield a closed conifer forest similar to those that develop on adjacent glacial soils is probably misleading. The organic soil formed in the bog will never resemble the inorganic soil of a well-developed spruce forest, which is usually derived from glacial rubble in the area.

Examples of primary succession per se are infrequently encountered in forestry. However, all places on earth have yielded a primary succession at some time in history, and some, such as places that have been repeatedly glaciated and deglaciated, have yielded several. Events that disrupt successional development and set the sere back to an earlier stage, thus initiating a secondary succession, are called *perturbations*.

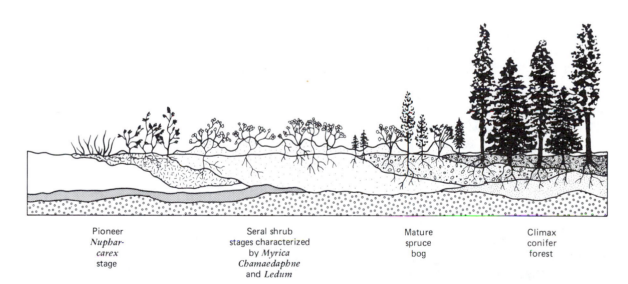

Pioneer
*Nuphar-
carex*
stage

Seral shrub
stages characterized
by *Myrica
Chamaedaphne*
and *Ledum*

Mature
spruce
bog

Climax
conifer
forest

Figure 6.4 Successional stages of a hydrarch sere from the Great Lakes region. In pioneer stages floating plants invade open water, followed by shrubs that invade the floating mat. Water-tolerant conifers (black spruce and tamarack) come next and characterize the mature spruce bog. The mature spruce–fir forest that develops on inorganic soil substrate is shown to the right to complete the transect from the pond (left) to terra firma (right). [Reproduced with permission of the National Research Council of Canada from the *Canadian Journal of Botany, 30,* 4390–520 (1952).]

Secondary Succession Secondary succession can be considered as a modification of the longer-lasting primary succession. One way of viewing succession is that for any place on earth, a primary succession began during the last period of time in which the place was completely cleared of plants and soil. Secondary successions complicate the series by "setting back" parts of the system to an earlier or less-developed stage. When the disturbance is over, succession begins again, and the community develops toward some theoretical end point called the climax. A secondary succession reaches its climax much more rapidly than a primary succession.

Clearing a natural forest and farming the land for several years is an example of a severe forest disturbance, leading to a distinct secondary succession. The plowing and lack of plant cover cause substantial changes in the soil, particularly the loss of organic matter and nutrients. If the field is then abandoned, the succession that follows is quite different from one that develops after a natural disturbance. Such an *old-field succession* usually begins with herbaceous instead of tree species and takes longer to reach the climax state. Because most forestry practices deal with some form of secondary succession, the emphasis in the rest this section will be on this phase of plant community development.

Small-scale disturbance or gap-phase regeneration

Disturbance in the forest is not always on the large scale previously described for tornados or fires that clear large tracts of land. Lesser storms or the natural death of older trees that fall and crush smaller trees in their path may create small gaps on the order of tens to hundreds of square meters (Figure 6.5*a*). Light levels in these gaps are not as high as in the open because of partial shading by the remaining trees surrounding the gap. Frequently these gaps are filled by intermediate species that grow well at moderate light levels (Figure 6.5*b*). Species of intermediate tolerance, such as tulip poplar and yellow birch, are often called gap-phase reproducers for this reason. *Gap-phase succession* is a form of secondary succession, but few if any intolerant trees will be present and the size of the area is smaller. Because this type of small-scale

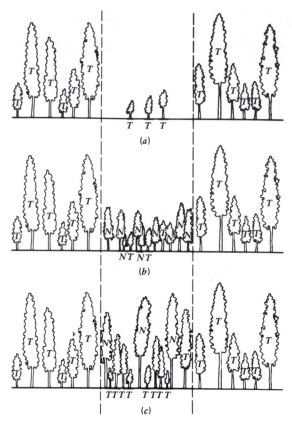

Figure 6.5 Schematic view of the distribution of tree crowns by tolerance class and height during succession in canopy gaps (gap-phase regeneration). (*a*) Immediately following the creation of gap; (*b*) after the initial regeneration of gap-phase intermediate species; (*c*) at the end of gap succession with few remaining intermediate species. (T = tolerant tree species; N = intermediate tree species; I = intolerant tree species.)

disturbance (usually attributed to natural mortality) is very common in otherwise undisturbed forests, species of intermediate tolerance can become established and will often be present in old, mature, or "climax" stands (Figure 6.5*c*).

Relationship between tolerance and life history phenomena

In addition to light responses, natural selection has acted on many other aspects of plant growth to allow adaptation for different sizes, frequencies, or intensities of disturbance. Selection may produce quite different results in different forest regions; therefore, it is very difficult to make general conclusions for all forest ecosystems. The following discussion emphasizes relationships that occur in the *eastern deciduous forest region.*

We have mentioned the need for a seed source if intolerant species are going to grow in a newly disturbed area. If this area is surrounded for any distance by mature forests without intolerant species, how will the seeds get to the area? Two principal methods have evolved. As mentioned previously, many of the earliest successional species (such as cottonwood and aspen) produce large quantities of light seeds, often with large networks of filaments, that can be dispersed for miles by air movements. This has been called the *"fugitive strategy."* A species must maintain only a small number of stems over a fairly large area to be able to reach any disturbed site with fresh seed. A second method of having seeds available in an area where no trees of the same species are currently growing is the *"buried-seed"* strategy. Some species (such as pin cherry and many of the blackberries) produce heavy seeds in large numbers, most of which fall directly beneath the parent plant. These seeds can remain dormant but alive in the forest floor for 100 years or more. Succession can occur on the site, eventually eliminating all trees of the intolerant buried-seed species. But if there is a disturbance again while the seeds are still viable, new trees of this species will appear, even though no parent tree exists for miles around.

Species having this method of reproduction often produce fleshy fruits surrounding the seeds, so that birds will consume them and carry some of each seed crop into new areas (10).

At the other extreme, tolerant species are most likely to reproduce successfully within the stands occupied by the parent tree where little or no change will occur. Many of these species (such as beech and sugar maple) tend to have heavier seeds that are not transported any great distance by either wind or animals.

Intermediate species tend to have either seeds of intermediate weight or some means of catching a wind to assist in dispersal. The dispersal distances are intermediate between those of the fugitive species and those of the tolerant trees.

A number of other characteristics tend to coincide with the tolerance of eastern deciduous forest tree species (see Table 6.2). All these characteristics reflect the need for intolerant trees to reach disturbed areas, grow quickly, and reproduce prolifically at a young age. Tolerant species occupy the other extreme; they live longer, grow more slowly and to greater size, reproduce at a later age, and have fewer, larger seeds. Intermediate species lie between these extremes in their seed characteristics and rate of growth, but they tend to be fairly long-lived because this is their method of maintaining a seed source in an undisturbed area. In a mature stand they consist of a few large stems among the many stems of the tolerant species (see Figure 6.5c).

Life history characteristics (rate of growth, size at

Table 6.2 Tolerance versus Relative Life History Characteristics for the Eastern Deciduous Forest[a]

Characteristic	Intolerant	Tolerant
Maximum size	Small	Large
Longevity	Short	Long
Growth rate	Fast	Slow
Age at first reproduction	Young	Old
Seed weight	Light or fleshy fruits	Heavy
Number of seeds per year	Many	Few

Source: Data from reference 5.
[a]Western conifers show a distinctly different relationship.

maturity, etc.) are important not only in understanding the function of plant communities and ecosystems but also for the management of forests. Different characteristics make different species more or less attractive as crop trees. For example, fast growth is very important for high yields, which would indicate that managers should favor intolerant species. The managers would therefore want to create the type of environment favorable to reproduction and growth of intolerant trees, usually by clearcutting practices (see Chapters 14 and 16). However, some intolerant species do not grow large enough to be harvestable for timber. If dominant intolerant trees die before harvest, the energy captured by the leaves during their lifetime is lost as the wood decomposes. In the more controlled conditions of *plantation forestry,* the need for faster growth and the possibility of early harvests, by shortening the periods of rotations and thinnings, often means that the most intolerant species—red pine, aspen (as hybrid poplars), loblolly pine, which grow to harvestable size—will be used. Other characteristics such as wood strength and fiber length are also important. The manipulation of forest stands to achieve specified objectives is treated in more detail in Chapter 14.

Competition for resources other than light —the niche concept So far most of our attention has been given to the effects of light on growth rates and the related implications for natural succession and forest management. However, plants have other requirements for growth; the ability of different sites to provide them influences tree growth rates. Chief among these are water and nutrients, as discussed in Chapters 3 and 4 on tree physiology and forest soils.

The availability of the *macronutrients* (nitrogen, phosphorus, potassium, calcium, magnesium, and sulfur), in forest soils was described in Chapter 4. Extensive tests with various types of fertilizers that increase the availability of different combinations of nutrients have shown that forests are almost always limited when little nitrogen or phosphorus is available. A lack of nitrogen is by far the more common.

Interestingly, species responses to nitrogen avail-

ability can be described in much the same way as their response to light. In a classic study in the 1930s (11), it was determined, through response to fertilizer trials, that tree species could be grouped as tolerant, intermediate, or intolerant of low nitrogen availability. The response curves looked almost identical to those in Figure 6.1, with the x-axis labeled as nitrogen availability instead of light availability. However, species that are tolerant of low light levels are not necessarily also tolerant of low nitrogen availability. Figure 6.6 lists the species examined in this classic study with their tolerance ratings for both low amounts of nitrogen and low levels of light. The data in this table indicate where each species might be dominant within a large forested area containing young, disturbed and old, undisturbed stands. For example, white ash is intermediate for low levels of light and intolerant for a lack of nitrogen and it tends to occur in small (gap-phase) disturbances on rich sites. The type of site where each species group would be found is also listed in Figure 6.6.

It may now be apparent why there are so many species of trees in a given forest region. Nine distinct types of environments are delineated by their light and nitrogen availability. Through competition and natural selection, each species tends to specialize for a certain type of environment where it can outcompete other species, dominate the stand, and reproduce successfully. This is the basic concept of the *ecological niche.* A species niche is the set of environmental conditions in which the species can survive, compete, and reproduce. The niche of white ash, for example, is defined as high nitrogen and moderate light availability. Many ecologists believe that no two species can occupy the same niche, so no two species in a region should be identical in their responses to environmental conditions. In Figure 6.6 there are still some boxes with more than one species, which indicates that more than one species occupies the same niche with regard to light and nitrogen. However, there are other growth-limiting resources to which species may respond differently.

Water is crucial to plant life, and forest trees frequently undergo moisture stress and suffer growth reductions as a result. Species responses to

Tolerance class for shade

Tolerant	Intermediate	Intolerant
Closed canopies-poor sites Hickory	Gaps-poor sites White oak Chestnut oak	Open-poor sites Bigtooth aspen
Closed canopies-moderate sites Beech Red maple	Gaps-moderate sites Basswood	Open-moderate sites Trembling aspen
Closed canopies-rich sites Sugar maple Black gum	Gaps-rich sites White ash Northern red oak	Open-rich sites Tulip poplar

Intolerant   Intermediate   Tolerant

Tolerance class for
low nitrogen availability

Figure 6.6 Separation of several deciduous tree species in the northeastern United States by tolerance classes for shade and low nitrogen availability. [Adapted from Mitchell and Chandler (11).]

129

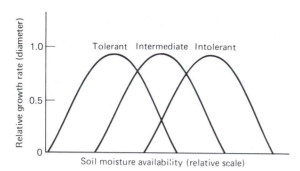

Figure 6.7 Relative rates of growth (to maximum potential for each species) as a function of moisture availability. (*Tolerant species* in this figure refers to tolerance for low moisture levels.) The curve may be bell-shaped because oxygen is lacking in the rooting zone when moisture content is high (12). Absolute growth rates may vary.

water availability usually follow a bell-shaped curve (Figure 6.7), with growth fastest at some point between the wettest and driest conditions. Figure 6.7 shows that this optimal point can be at different levels for different species (12). This water gradient could separate red maple and beech in Figure 6.6, because the maple tends to occur on wetter sites, even into swampy conditions.

Length of growing season and average temperature during the growing season also affect tree growth differently for different species. The growth of species exhibits a bell-shaped response to temperature (Figure 6.8). Species with optimal growth at levels closer to the origin (species A), such as yellow birch, would be expected to occur either farther north or at higher elevations than species with optimal growth farther along the *x*-axis (species B and C), such as white ash (12).

By combining species responses to all four of these growth-limiting resources and expanding Figure 6.6 into three (and then four!) dimensions, we can divide species until each box in the figure contains only one species. This would represent the species niche as defined by these four growth-limiting resources. If we had three classes of responses (tolerant, intermediate, and intolerant) to each resource, with four resources (light, nitrogen,

water, temperature), there would be 3^4 or eighty-one boxes allowing eighty-one separate species to coexist, each with its own niche description.

In a complete niche analysis, reproductive strategies (fugitive strategy versus buried-seed strategy) and life history characteristics (life expectancy, age at reproduction, etc.) would be considered as well, increasing still further the number of potential niches. We can begin to understand the occurrence of several hundred species of trees in the eastern deciduous forest region. A chemical factor that may affect associations or keep certain species from inhabiting a particular site will be discussed in the next section.

Competition through chemical alteration of the soil environment—allelopathy Certain associations of trees and other plant species have been noted in the forest throughout history. In 1832 de Candolle (13) suggested that some plants may excrete from their roots chemicals that are harmful to other plants. This effect, known as *allelopathy,* is more generally defined as the inhibition of germination, growth, or metabolism of one plant by another through the production of chemical compounds

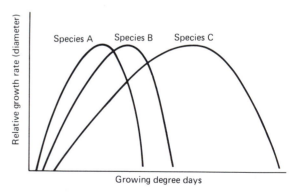

Figure 6.8 Relative rates of growth (to maximum potential for each species) for three species as a function of the number of growing degree days: summation of the total number of days with mean temperature above 40°F (4.5°C) times the difference between mean temperature and 40°F; a measure of length and average temperature of the growing season (12). Absolute growth rates may vary.

Figure 6.9 Growth inhibition of shrubs under a black walnut tree, possibly caused by the allelopathic substance juglone. (Photograph by R. A. Young.)

that escape into the environment (14). This form of inhibition is distinct from competition, which acts through the depletion of resources. The importance of allelopathy lies in its capacity to alter the structure, function, and diversity of plant communities.

Through allelopathy a dominant species may speed its invasion of a previous community and delay its replacement by other species. Chemical effects of a species on the soil may limit the number and kinds of species able to coexist with it. In mixed-species stands, a mosaic of differing chemical effects may form on the soil and contribute to the patterning and species diversity of the forest stand (15).

Probably the most well-documented allelopathic effect of trees is the suppression of plant growth exhibited by established black walnut trees (Figure 6.9). As early as 1881, Stickney and Hoy (16) observed very sparse vegetation under black walnut trees and pointed out that no crop would grow under or near the trees. Later reports verified that neither alfalfa nor tomatoes could grow near black

walnut; the growth of red pine, yellow birch, and apple trees was inhibited by this tree species (14,15).

An active substance, *juglone,* was isolated and identified as the major inhibitory chemical compound responsible for the allelopathic effects. Juglone is present in the roots, leaves, and fruit hulls of the tree. Thus the chemical can accumulate in the soil in a variety of ways—for example, through rain washing the compound from the leaves to the forest floor or by leaf and hull litter accumulating on the ground (14).

The occurrence of allelopathy is apparently widespread in forest communities. The growth of yellow birch is reportedly restricted by the presence of sugar maple, and some observers have reported a pattern in which yellow birch grows in the presence of beech but not of sugar maple (17, 18). The abundance of each of these species in the beech–birch–maple climax association may therefore depend on the abundance of the other two species. Additional tree species suspected of exhibiting allelopathic effects include black cherry, sassafras, ailanthus, eucalyptus, white pine, lodgepole pine, Scotch pine, European larch, and winged sumac (19).

Although the potential for allelopathic effects has been demonstrated, there is still much uncertainty about their importance in forests. Aside from the clear effects of a few species such as black walnut, it has been difficult to separate allelopathic interactions from the competitive effects of shading, water use, and other forms of site modification by trees.

Species–site interactions So far the effect of light, water, nutrients, and chemicals on the succession of forest stands has been discussed. It was noted that deficiencies or excesses in any of these important factors can dramatically alter tree growth and species composition of a site. However, availability of these factors is not constant over time. In the example of the old-field succession previously described, severe disruption of the forest soil for agriculture reduced soil organic matter and nitrogen availability. Less severe disturbances such as harvesting or changes in species composition can also change nutrient availability. A constant interaction between the species and the site determines the overall rate of movement of nutrients, water, and energy between plants and the soil and between the plant–soil system and the surrounding atmosphere, groundwater, streams, and lakes. This brings us into the realm of forest ecosystem studies, the subject of the next section of this chapter.

Ecosystem Studies and Forest Management

The focus of ecosystem studies is on the movement of energy, water, and chemicals, including plant nutrients and pollutants, into, out of, and within units of the landscape called ecosystems. It has become an important part of forestry research and management in the last twenty years because so many of the services we expect from forests depend on these processes.

For example, stemwood is produced when carbon is fixed by photosynthesis. A considerable amount of water is required during photosynthesis to replace water lost by evaporation from the internal leaf surfaces (transpiration). Nutrients such as nitrogen are also required in certain amounts to produce the leaf tissues that carry out photosynthesis. Thus we need to know something about the interactions between the movements of water, nitrogen, and carbon if we are to understand the production of wood in forests.

We also rely on forest ecosystems for supplies of clean water for urban and industrial uses. Although we generally think of streamwater draining from a natural forest as clean and pure, current loadings of air pollutants may exceed the retention capacities of forest ecosystems, with reduced water quality an important result. Again, understanding the movement of nutrients and pollutants through ecosystems becomes important for protection of this vital service of forests.

The study of ecosystems is integrative or *holistic,* in that it requires expertise from many different disciplines. Subjects such as plant physiology, soil science, microbiology, hydrology, and geology all contribute to the understanding of the operation of these whole-landscape units called ecosystems. Integrating all these diverse kinds of information into a form useful for forest management often involves computer modeling. In this part of the chapter we will present two examples of ecosystem-level studies in forests, discuss the cycle of nitrogen, an important element that often limits forest growth, and examine both the process of computer modeling and an application to a specific set of forest management questions.

What Is an Ecosystem?

The emphasis on inputs and outputs makes the boundaries of the system crucial. An ecosystem can be as large or as small as fits the purposes of the study. Some have used a single leaf as the system under study and looked at the inputs and outputs of energy (3). At the other extreme, one of the first and now classic studies in environmental science centered on the movements of the pesticide DDT through food chains around the world. Finding traces of this chemical in animals far removed from areas where DDT had been applied demonstrated that the entire globe can be seen as a single interconnected ecosystem (20).

The definition of the extent of an ecosystem is determined by the nature of the study and the type of information desired. For forest ecosystems one of two definitions is generally used: the watershed or the stand. A *watershed* is a topographically defined unit of land all of whose precipitation falling into it flows out in a single stream. Watersheds can range in size from a few hectares near ridgetops in mountainous area with extreme topography to thousands of square kilometers, as in the Mississippi River watershed, which drains nearly one-third of the United States. The advantage of using a watershed is that, as presented previously, most of the movement of nutrients in and out of forests occurs in water, and a watershed simplifies the measurement of the water budget or the quantities of water that enter and leave the system.

A *stand* is any area of forest vegetation whose site conditions, past history, and current species composition are sufficiently uniform to be managed as a unit. This definition indicates the importance of both current vegetation and past human or natural disturbance on processes within the system, as discussed in the next section.

Examples of Ecosystem Studies

Perhaps the best example of an ecosystem-level study of a forested watershed is the one carried out at the Hubbard Brook Experimental Forest in New Hampshire (5, 21, 22). The Hubbard Brook valley contains six small watersheds (those studied range from 12 to 43 hectares) with very similar soils, vegetation, and geology (Figure 6.10). Each watershed represents a separate ecosystem, but all are so similar that they are considered replicates for the

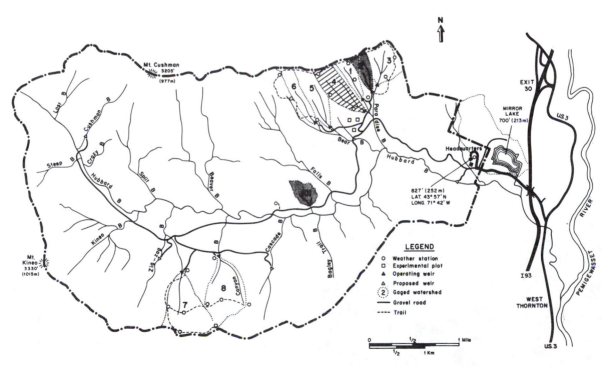

Figure 6.10 The Hubbard Brook Valley. The map shows the Hubbard Brook Experimental Forest (HBEF) with its gauged watersheds, weirs, weather stations, roads, experimental treatments, and drainage streams tributary to Hubbard Brook. (Reproduced with permission of Springer-Verlag from *Biogeochemistry of a Forested Ecosystem*, G. E. Likens et al., 1977.)

purposes of comparing results. These replicate watersheds offered a unique opportunity to test the effects of different experimental management treatments at the ecosystem level. Because the six watersheds were essentially identical to begin with, any differences between watersheds could only be attributed to the treatment.

Another important characteristic of the Hubbard Brook watershed ecosystems is that they all have shallow soils over watertight bedrock. This meant that all the water entering as precipitation either evaporated to the air or appeared in the stream that drained the watershed. Losses to groundwater by deep seepage were found to be negligible, which was crucial because the first characteristics examined in the watersheds were the chemical and hydrological balances over the study area. Precipitation gauges were installed throughout the watershed (see Figure 6.10), and a V-notch weir (Figure 6.11) was put in the stream. The difference between precipitation and streamflow was assumed to be equal to evaporation from soil and plants (i.e., evapotranspiration). By measuring the concentration of chemical elements in precipitation and streamflow and multiplying by the amount of water, the investigators obtained the total input and output for each element.

The results of these studies provided fresh insights into the function of forested ecosystems that were essentially unavailable from studies of the individual parts of the system (e.g., soils, trees, etc.). Figure 6.12 shows seasonal and annual patterns of variation for water and for the essential nutrient nitrogen. These data demonstrate a number of important characteristics of many undisturbed ecosystems. First, Figure 6.12*a* shows that the yield of water from the forest ecosystem in streamflow is highly predictable from the amount of precipitation coming into the system. Such predictability can be important in managing urban or agricultural water supplies downstream. The ecosystem also exhibits a large degree of control over the nitrogen balance. It was found that the nitrate (NO_3^-) concentration in the precipitation exhibited no definite pattern through time; however, Figure 6.12*b* shows very marked seasonal changes in nitrate concentrations in the streamwater. Again, this demonstrates that the forest ecosystem dramatically influences the water and nutrient balances. An additional characteristic of this system is that it is gaining more nitrogen from precipitation than it is losing in streamflow. Most undisturbed forests gain nitrogen in this way (5, 21).

Comparisons of results between the six replicate watershed ecosystems showed very similar patterns, indicating that they were indeed nearly identical with respect to hydrology and the nitrogen balance. The next step was to carry out an experiment at the ecosystems level. In one watershed (number 2) all

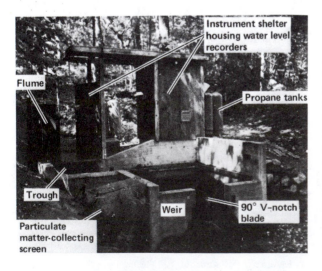

Figure 6.11 Stream-gauging weir. The metal flume on the left measures high streamflows; the 90-degree sharp-edged, V-notch weir on the right measures low streamflows. The gauging station is built on bedrock so that all streamflow is channeled first through the flume and then into the weir. Recording instruments for both flume and weir monitor streamflow continuously. Propane burners are used during the winter to prevent freezing. Large particulate matter transported by the stream during high flows is caught either in the screen as the flow cascades from the flume over the trough, bypassing the V-notch, or in the ponding basin behind the V-notch. (Reproduced with permission of Springer-Verlag from *Biogeochemistry of a Forested Ecosystem,* G. E. Likens et al., 1977.)

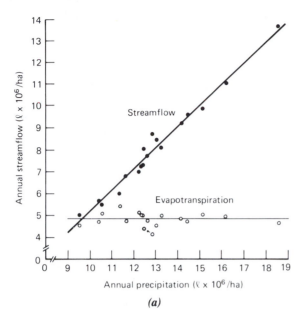

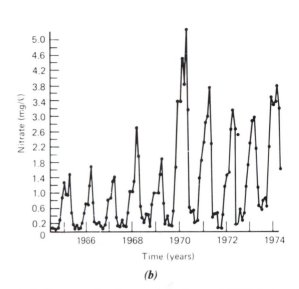

(a) | *(b)*

Figure 6.12 (*a*) Relationship between precipitation and streamflow for the Hubbard Brook Experimental Forest (HBEF) during the period 1956 to 1974. (*b*) Nitrate levels in stream flow at HBEF during the period 1965 to 1974. (Reproduced with permission of Springer-Verlag from *Biogeochemistry of a Forested Ecosystem,* G. E. Likens et al., 1977.)

the vegetation was cut down, and herbicides were used to suppress regrowth for three years (starting in 1965). The purpose of this experiment was to determine the effect of the biological activity of trees and shrubs on the hydrologic and chemical patterns of watersheds. With the plant material removed, any differences between watershed 2 and a control (undisturbed) watershed (number 6) could be related mainly to the suppression of plants. The differences were extreme, as shown in Figure 6.13. The increase in streamflow (Figure 6.13*b*) was somewhat predictable because transpiration by plants was removed, but the increased nitrogen output (6.13*d*) was many times higher than the increase in streamflow and indicated strong biological control over the accumulation and loss of this element. Nitrate concentration in the stream actually exceeded U.S. public-health standards for drinking water during parts of this experiment. However, the nitrate level did return to normal after revegetation of the watershed (22).

The initial results of this study were very timely, because they coincided with the national debate on

clearcutting as a means of harvesting national forestlands. It was argued by some that the complete devegetation on watershed 2 was similar to clearcutting and that therefore this practice would reduce water quality substantially. Others argued that the total suppression of all plant growth was an extreme treatment and that in commercial clearcutting with immediate regrowth nitrogen losses would be lower. Still others said that clearcutting might be even more severe than on watershed 2 because in the experiment the cut trees were left on the site and no roads were built into the watershed, as would be the case in an actual logging operation.

To settle this controversy, investigators carried out stream chemistry studies on a number of other watersheds with different harvesting histories (23, 24). Increases in nitrogen losses were measured under all conditions, but the amounts were less than on watershed 2 and were directly related to how much of the watershed was harvested. This information begins to allow prediction of the effects of different harvesting practices on local and regional water quality.

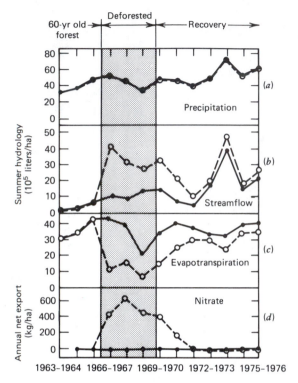

Figure 6.13 Effects of deforestation on hydrology and nitrate concentrations in an experimentally deforested northern hardwoods forest ecosystem (HBEF) (o---o, watershed 2) compared with a forested reference ecosystem (•——•, watershed 6). The 60-year-old forest was devegetated during the autumn of 1965, maintained bare for three growing seasons, and then allowed to revegetate during the growing season of 1969. [Adapted from reference 22 (*Science*) with permission of the American Association for the Advancement of Science.]

During the clearcutting debate results from similar experiments in other forest types began to show that not all forests exhibited the large nitrogen losses seen at Hubbard Brook. For example, studies in the Douglas-fir forests of Washington demonstrated a negligibly larger nitrogen loss after clearcutting (25). Other studies showed intermediate results. Unfortunately, the different investigators used different methods to measure nitrogen losses, and therefore the results were not always directly comparable.

These different results led to a comparative study carried out by six researchers from around the United States (26). In this study a standardized disturbance was applied to nineteen forest types in the six regions, and all stands were analyzed for nitrogen losses. A complete range from high to essentially no losses was found spread across forest types and regions (Table 6.3). The only general conclusion was that "rich" sites with relatively fertile soils tended to lose nitrogen more rapidly.

As a result of these kinds of ecosystem-level studies, and also because it is known that reduced

Table 6.3 Nitrogen Losses Caused by Disturbance in Nineteen Forest Ecosystems Throughout the United States

Site	Nitrogen Losses
Indiana	
Maple, beech	Very high
Oak, hickory	High
Shortleaf pine	Low
Massachusetts	
Oak, pine	Medium
Red pine	Low
Oak, red maple	Low
New Hampshire	
Maple, beech	High
Balsam fir	Medium
New Mexico	
Ponderosa pine	Very low
Mixed conifer	Medium
Aspen	Medium
Spruce, fir	Very low
North Carolina	
Mixed oak	Low
White pine	Medium
Oregon	
Western hemlock	Medium
Washington	
Alder	Very high
Douglas-fir (low site quality)	Low
Douglas-fir (high site quality)	Medium
Pacific silver fir	Very low

Source: Adapted from P. M. Vitousek et al., *Science, 204,* 469 (1979).

availability of nitrogen to plants limits growth in many forest types, a considerable amount of research effort has been expended to determine what factors control the rate of nitrogen loss from forest ecosystems and the rate at which nitrogen cycles within the system.

The Nitrogen Cycle

Figure 6.14 outlines the important components of the *nitrogen cycle* in two very different forest ecosystems. In the previous section we were concerned with only the nitrogen introduced into the ecosystem in precipitation and that moving out with streamflow. The streamflow losses depend not just on inputs of nitrogen in precipitation but also on the processes that control the cycling of nitrogen within the system (27–30).

Each step in the nitrogen cycle has a specific name. When rainfall hits the forest canopy and then drips through, it is called *throughfall.* Thus, the nitrogen content of precipitation changes as a result of contact with the leaf and stem surfaces. This nitrogen then enters into the soil and is available for *uptake* by plants. Uptake rates are very different in the two forest types, and this difference is fairly characteristic of deciduous compared to coniferous forests. The coniferous forest is not less productive in terms of weight of material synthesized from sunlight in a year, but it has lower nitrogen concentrations in leaves, needles, and wood and therefore apparently needs less nitrogen to produce the same amount of material.

Much of the nitrogen taken up is returned in the same year to the *forest floor* through *litter fall,* which is the shedding of leaves or needles, roots, and branches plus toppling of whole live or dead trees. Some additional nitrogen is returned in the throughfall in instances in which throughfall nitrogen content is greater than nitrogen content in precipitation. However, some of the nitrogen may be retained in the growing vegetation. This is true for the hardwood stand in Figure 6.14, which is younger and still increasing in total biomass (live weight of trees), but not for the conifer stand, which

in this example is losing more live biomass through tree mortality and litter fall than it is producing each year.

Aboveground litter falls on top of and becomes part of the forest floor, the mostly organic uppermost soil horizon. A considerable amount of root litter also occurs in the forest floor. Input to the mineral soil is mostly through root litter. This nitrogen is not immediately available to plants, because it is still bound up in organic materials. Plants require nitrogen in simple ionic compounds such as nitrate (NO_3^-) and ammonia (NH_4^+). Decomposition of the organic material in the litter and soil releases the nitrogen in ionic form, which the plants can then utilize. This process is called *mineralization* and occurs much more rapidly in the hardwood stand (see Chapter 4). In both stands the total nitrogen content of the forest floor is increasing while the amount in the mineral soil is decreasing.

The total amount of nitrogen in the available pool at any one time is very small. Once it is in the simple ionic forms, it is either taken up very quickly or washed away (leached) below the rooting zone and into the stream.

Two additional processes make the nitrogen cycle even more complex. *Nitrogen fixation* is the uptake of N_2 gas from the atmosphere by certain microorganisms living either free in the soil and litter, a nonsymbiotic relationship, or in a mutually beneficial or symbiotic relationship with plant roots. The opposite process, the release of nitrogen-containing gases to the atmosphere, can occur simultaneously and is called *denitrification.* These processes have not been studied as extensively as other transfers within forest ecosystems, but the quantities appear to be fairly small and nearly equal in most undisturbed forests.

Systems Analysis

The simple diagrams shown in Figure 6.14 represent "models" of the nitrogen cycles in the two forest types and can be put into computer form. However, the data from these diagrams can also be utilized for simple calculations to determine how fast nitrogen is moving through each part of the system and

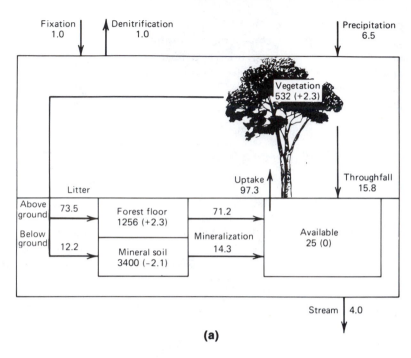

(a)

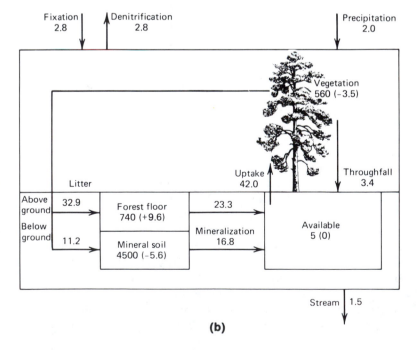

Figure 6.14 (*a*) Nitrogen cycle for a typical deciduous forest in the northeastern United States (*b*) Nitrogen cycle for a typical coniferous forest of the Pacific Northwest. Values next to the arrows are transfers between compartment in kilograms per hectare per year. Values within boxes are amounts stored in each compartment in kilograms per hectare. Values in parentheses are changes in the amount of nitrogen stored, also in kilograms per hectare per year. [(*a*) Adapted from references 25, 26; (*b*) adapted from references 27, 28.]

(b)

possibly which factors limit the overall rate of nitrogen cycling. This is a very important bit of information because total tree growth is often limited by the amount of nitrogen available; any management practice that speeds nitrogen's rate of movement through the whole system would increase the amount passing through the available pool.

This approach to the analysis of ecosystems is part of a relatively new science called *systems analysis,* which deals with many kinds of complex sets of interacting parts or systems. These can be production systems such as factories, information systems such as telephones and computers, or biological systems such as forests. In general, systems analysis deals with the movement or transfer of energy or materials to different parts of the system. In our forest ecosystems shown in Figure 6.14, the compartments are vegetation, forest floor, mineral soil, and available nitrogen. The transfers are precipitation, throughfall, leaching, litter fall, mineralization, fixation, and denitrification. Systems analysis is a complex and highly mathematical field, but we can use two simple measurements from this discipline to compare the nitrogen cycles in the two forest types: turnover rate and residence time. Both relate to how much nitrogen passes through a compartment versus how much is in the compartment at any one time.

Residence time is calculated as the sum of all the inputs to a compartment divided into the total in the compartment. For example, the residence time for nitrogen in the forest floor of the hardwood stand is 1256/73.5 kilograms per hectare per year or 17.1 years. We could calculate a resident time for the whole ecosystem by dividing all the nitrogen in all the compartments (5213 kilograms per hectare) by precipitation and fixation inputs (7.5 kilograms per hectare per year), which gives 695.1 years. Residence time is the average retention time of nitrogen in a particular compartment.

Turnover rate is just 1 divided by the residence time. For the hardwood forest floor, turnover rate is $1/17.1 = 0.058$ or 5.8 percent. This is the fraction of the nitrogen in the compartment to enter in that year.

Table 6.4 Turnover Rates for Nitrogen in Different Compartments of Two Contrasting Forest Ecosystems

Compartment	Deciduous		Coniferous	
Vegetation	$\frac{103.8}{532}$	0.195	$\frac{44.0}{560}$	0.079
Forest floor	$\frac{73.5}{1256}$	0.058	$\frac{32.9}{740}$	0.044
Mineral soil	$\frac{12.2}{3400}$	0.0036	$\frac{11.2}{4500}$	0.0025
Available	$\frac{101.3}{25}$	4.05	$\frac{43.5}{5}$	8.70

Source: Prepared from data in references 27–30 and Figure 6.14.

Table 6.4 lists the turnover rates for all the compartments in both forest types. The results are very different for the different compartments and indicate where nitrogen cycles quickly and where it cycles slowly. In both stands the fastest turnover is in the *available pool* and the slowest is in the *mineral soil.* Turnover is intermediate in the vegetation and forest floor. These numbers express quantitatively what was stated previously in this chapter—that nitrogen is made available relatively slowly from the soil and is either taken up or leached quickly from the available pool. We might conclude that the decomposition rates limit the total rate of nitrogen cycling in both stands, but to a greater extent in the conifer forests.

Looking at these models also gives some clues as to why Hubbard Brook watershed 2, with a nitrogen cycle similar to that in Figure 6.14*a* before devegetation, exhibited such large losses of nitrogen after devegetation. Uptake was completely cut off, and therefore all the nitrogen made available by mineralization either remained in the available pool or leached to the stream. In addition, removing the forest canopy raises temperatures in the soil and increases soil moisture because transpiration is reduced. This in turn leads to faster decomposition rates, greater mineralization, and more total available nitrogen for leaching. On the other hand, the coniferous forest may lose less nitrogen after harvesting because of the generally slower cycling of this element and additional differences in the effect of the species on turnover rates for nitrogen (27,28).

Computer Models and Management of Forest Ecosystems

The complexity of forest ecosystems is such that building computer models is nearly the only way to predict quantitatively the effects of different management practices. The kind of information presented in Figure 6.14 is complicated in itself, but for management decisions we must also know how all these transfers change with different species at different ages, under different soil conditions, as a result of disturbance, and so on. Thus we need to know not only how fast nitrogen moves through the system but also what controls the rate. The results of different studies on rates of litter decomposition as a function of the type of material, on growth rates of different species for different mineralization rates, and on other important interactions within the system are combined in the computer model, which represents a synthesis and summary of everything quantitatively known about the system.

Construction of an Ecosystem Model

The construction of a model of forest ecosystem dynamics follows four basic steps.

1. **Model Structure.** The general outline of the data and information available is translated into a series of computer language statements. This is like drawing the boxes and arrows in Figure 6.14.

2. **Parameterization.** The specific data are entered in the general structure of the program. The difference between these first two steps is that the outline or structure of the model may be identical for different forests, but the specific data or parameters will be different. For example, the structures of the models in Figure 6.14 are identical but the data are different.

3. **Validation.** The model is used to predict the results of an experiment that was not used in building the model. This tests the accuracy of the completed model.

4. **Prediction.** The model can now be used to predict the effects of experiments not yet carried out in the field or the effects of potential management practices.

Forest Ecosystem Models

Several models of forest ecosystems have been developed, and some have been used to predict the effects of different management practices. An example is the model developed from the Hubbard Brook study (12, 31, 32), which predicts the movement of organic matter and nitrogen through these northern hardwoods forest ecosystems.

The structure of this model is similar to that presented in Figure 6.14, but with greater detail included regarding types of litter and types of species in the system. The *parameters* for the model are too lengthy to present here, but they come from many different studies of this forest type.

Validation is a key process because it allows us to appraise the accuracy of the model. If it cannot predict the results of past experiments, it cannot be relied on to predict effects of new management practices. Two examples of validation are shown in Figure 6.15, where the model predictions are matched with data measured in the field but not used in building the model. These data are for changes in the weight of organic matter in the forest floor and in the basal area of all living trees.

Once the accuracy of the model has been assessed through validation, it can be used for *predictive purposes.* For example, recent increases in demand for wood yields from a shrinking forestland base have in some stands led to more intensive harvesting—removing more of each cut tree from the site and harvesting more frequently. Because these are new practices, no field trials are available to test their long-term consequences. An accurate model can predict these consequences and avoid costly mistakes.

The Hubbard Brook models have been used to

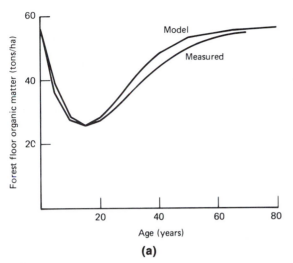

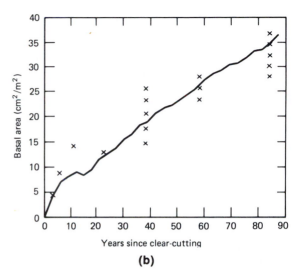

(a)

(b)

Figure 6.15 (*a*) Model predictions for changes in weight of organic matter in the forest following clearcutting and the measured values. (*b*) Model predictions (solid line) for changes in basal area over time following clearcutting, with the measured values (×). [Reproduced by permission of the National Research Council of Canada from the *Canadian Journal of Forest Research, 8,* 306–315 (1978).]

make these predictions for the northern hardwoods forest type. Different intensities of harvesting, such as stem only or clearcutting, whole tree including branches and leaves, and different frequencies of cutting, were simulated with the models. Table 6.5 shows projected results of more frequent and intensive harvests on total productivity and total harvestable yield. Under the conditions in the model, the more intensive harvesting (whole tree and complete

forest), especially on short rotations, actually *reduces* the yield of wood instead of increasing it (31, 32). Such projections are only as accurate as the model itself, and a critical assessment of the outline and parameters of the model is an absolute necessity before projections based on the model can be accepted.

Models such as this can also predict the impacts of pollution on forest ecosystems. One pollution prob-

Table 6.5 Estimates of Total Net Production and Total Yield (Harvested) Obtained from the Forest Floor–Forest Growth Model for Seven Harvesting Regimes over a 90-Year Period

Type of Cutting	Length and Number of Rotations	Total Net Productivity (tons/ha/90 years) and Rank	Total Yield (tons/ha/90 years) and Rank	Percentage of Total Productivity Harvested
Clearcutting	90 (1)	1090 (2)	154 (4)	14
Whole tree	90 (1)	1120 (1)	197 (2)	18
Whole tree	45 (2)	853 (4)	108 (6)	13
Whole tree	30 (3)	478 (6)	93 (7)	19
Complete forest	90 (1)	1055 (3)	252 (1)	24
Complete forest	45 (2)	841 (5)	171 (3)	20
Complete forest	30 (3)	476 (7)	150 (5)	32

Source: J. D. Aber, D. B. Botkin, and J. M. Melillo, *Can. J For. Res., 9,* 10 (1979).

lem of current interest is the incidence of "acid rain" caused by the burning of fossil fuels, which creates sulfuric and nitric acids in the atmosphere. Acid rain of this form can cause numerous problems in the forest, including direct damage to plants and a decrease in mineralization rate. However, the acid rain can also act as fertilizer, in that nitrogen is a component of acid rain. Again, a computer model can combine all these effects and predict which might be the greater, growth reduction or growth enhancement. But again, the accuracy of the model relies entirely on the accuracy of the information that goes into it.

In summary, the study of forests as ecosystems is an attempt to place all the major processes in the system—for example, production of plant parts or decomposition of litter and soil—in a single unified framework, to show how they all interact and how the entire system will respond to different disturbances, pollution impacts, and management practices. It has been called a "holistic" science in that the emphasis is on the cumulative response of the entire system instead of on any single component. As such, it draws from many traditional disciplines and places them in the framework of the ecosystem.

References

1. E. P. ODUM, *Fundamentals of Ecology,* W. B. Saunders, Philadelphia, 1971.

2. S. H. SPURR AND B. V. BARNES, *Forest Ecology,* Third Edition, John Wiley & Sons, New York, 1980.

3. W. LARCHER, *Physiological Plant Ecology,* Springer-Verlag, New York/Berlin, 1979.

4. H. W. HOCKER, JR., *Introduction to Forest Biology,* John Wiley & Sons, New York, 1979.

5. F. H. BORMANN AND G. E. LIKENS, *Pattern and Process in a Forested Ecosystem,* Springer-Verlag, New York/Berlin, 1979.

6. H. J. OOSTING AND L. E. ANDERSON, *Bot. Gaz., 100,* 750 (1939).

7. W. S. COOPER, *Ecology, 20,* 130 (1939).

8. R. L. CROCKER AND J. MAJOR, *J. Ecol., 43,* 427 (1955).

9. P. E. HEILMAN, *Ecology, 47,* 825 (1966).

10. F. B SALISBURY AND C. W. ROSS, *Plant Physiology,* Wadsworth, Belmont, Calif., 1978.

11. H. L. MITCHELL AND R. F. CHANDLER, "The nitrogen nutrition and growth of certain deciduous trees of northeastern United States," *Black Rock For. Bull. 11,* 1939.

12. D. B. BOTKIN, J. F. JANAK, AND J. R. WALLIS, *J. Ecol., 60,* 849 (1972).

13. A.-P. DE CANDOLLE, *Physiologie Vegetale,* Bechet Jerene, Lib. Fac. Med., Paris, 1832.

14. E. L. RICE, *Allelopathy,* Academic Press, New York, 1974.

15. R. H. WHITTAKER AND P. D. FEENEY, *Science, 171,* 757 (1971).

16. J. S. STICKNEY AND P. R. HOY, "Timber culture," *Trans. Wis. State Hort. Soc., 11,* 156 (1881).

17. L. K. FORCIER, *Science, 189,* 808 (1973).

18. C. H. TUBBS, "Effect of sugar maple exudate on seedlings of northern conifer species," U.S.D.A. For. Serv., Res. Note NC-213, Washington, D.C., 1976.

19. M. A. K. LODHI, *Am. J. Bot., 64,* 260 (1976).

20. G. M. WOODWELL, *Sci. Am., 216,* 24 (1967).

21. G. E. LIKENS, F. H. BORMANN, R. S. PIERCE, J. S. EATON, AND N. M. JOHNSON, *Biogeochemistry of a Forested Ecosystem,* Springer-Verlag, New York/Berlin, 1977.

22. G. E. LIKENS, F. H. BORMANN, R. S. PIERCE, AND W. A. REINERS, *Science, 199,* 492 (1978).

23. R. S. PIERCE, C. W. MARTIN, C. C. REEVES, G. E. LIKENS, and F. H. BORMANN, "Nutrient loss from clearcutting in New Hampshire." In *Proc. Symp. Watersheds in Transition,* Ft. Collins, Colo., 1972.

24. J. W. HORNBECK, G. E. LIKENS, R. S. PIERCE, AND F. H. BORMANN, "Strip cutting as a means of protecting site and streamflow quality when clearcutting northern hardwoods," In *Proc. 4th N.A. For. Soils Conf.,* B. Bernier and C. H. Winget, eds., Laval Univ. Press, Quebec, 1975.

25. D. W. COLE AND S. P. GESSEL, "Movement of elements through a forest soil as influenced by tree removal and fertilizer additions." In *Forest–Soil Relationships in North America,* C. T. Youngberg, ed., John Wiley & Sons, New York, 1965.

26. P. M. VITOUSEK, J. R. GOSZ, C. C. GRIER, J. M. MELILLO, W. A. REINERS, AND R. L. TODD, *Science, 204,* 469 (1979).

27. J. M. MELILLO, "Nitrogen cycling in deciduous forests." In *Nitrogen Cycling in Terrestrial Ecosystems. Ecol. Bull., 33,* 427, Stockholm, 1981.

28. F. H. Bormann, G. E. Likens, and J. M. Melillo, *Science, 196,* 981 (1977).

29. G. S. Henderson, W. T. Swank, J. B. Waide, and C. C. Grier, *For. Sci., 24,* 385 (1978).

30. P. Sollins, C. C. Grier, F. M. McCorison, K. Cromack, Jr., and R. Fogel, "The internal element cycles of an old-growth Douglas-fir stand in western Oregon," *Ecol. Monogr., 50,* 261 (1980).

31. J. D. Aber, D. B. Botkin, and J. M. Melillo, *Can. J. For. Res., 8,* 306 (1978).

32. J. D. Aber, D. B. Botkin, and J. M. Melillo, *Can. J. For. Res., 9,* 10 (1979).

CHAPTER 7

Interaction of Insects and Forest Trees

RONALD L. GIESE

Insects and trees have complex interactions in forest habitats; insects create impacts on forest trees, and, conversely, forests have important influences on insects. Thus *forest entomology* is concerned with the influences of insects on forests and their products. It is a biological discipline that deals with insects and their associates, and their effects on trees, forests, and forest products. It also provides a means of quantification and management of insects and insect damage within the forest ecosystem.

Introduction

Attention to forest insects is an ancient phenomenon; ravages have been noted for centuries. Linnaeus, in the mid-eighteenth century, formally named and described many insects we know as forest pests today. Just as forestry had its roots in Europe, modern forest entomology found its beginnings there in the last century. A classical treatise on forest insects was published by the German J. T. C. Ratzeburg; in France, A. de La Rue wrote on the natural history of forest insects in the mid-nineteenth century. Modern forest entomology literature is very extensive, and current American reference books usually emphasize either principles (1, 2) or taxonomic–life history approaches to forest entomology (3, 4).

Beneficial Effects of Insects in Forest Ecosystems

Although the destructive activities of forest insects are well known and are sometimes dramatic, it is best to realize that many insects play a beneficial role in forest ecosystems. Were it not for parasitic and predacious insects, outbreaks of pest species would be even more common. We will see how elimination of these advantageous species, or disruption of the predator–prey relationships, can have massive biological consequences. Insects are also primary pollinators of some tree species (e.g., maples and willows). They play a key role in the decomposition of dead trees and leaves and consequently aid in nutrient cycling. Insects help to thin dense forest stands by eliminating overmature trees; this thinning promotes the growth of young seedlings and the regeneration of an "old" forest. Insects aid in the development of mixed stands, thereby prompting succession toward more climax states.

Importance and Mode of Action of Destructive Agents

Accidental fire damage extracts a large toll on forest resources, yet insects remove even larger volumes of timber. Such destructive events can be assigned to any of three categories depending on duration, extent, and predictability. When the destruction is a widespread, unpredictable event of dramatic proportions, it is classified as a *catastrophe.* Examples include massive windstorms, fires, extensive damage caused by insects, and contagious diseases of trees. During this century over 123 million cubic meters of timber were destroyed during forest insect catastrophes.

Perhaps more important, though less spectacular than catastrophic phenomena, is *growth impact,* which is a pervasive, ongoing feature in forests. Growth impact is the sum of *growth loss* and *mortality,* which are the second and third categories of destructive events. Growth loss is the cumulative and continuous absence or reduction of normal growth caused by destructive agents, such as insects. Tissue may not achieve its potential dimensions in terminal length and diameter. Insects are present in every forest ecosystem, whether they be wood borers or bark beetles, and their toll, no matter how subtle, proceeds at all times. The other element of growth impact is mortality, the removal of trees from growing stock or sawtimber through death from natural causes. Table 7.1, which gives a comparison of the losses attributable to the major destructive agents, shows just how momentous is the effect of these destructive yet quite natural forces. Although updated information is needed in a resource-short society, the table suggests the immense importance of insects in terms of the relative losses incurred, as well as the total volume consumed by these small organisms.

Regional tree mortality estimates for the United States were provided for 1962 and 1970 (Table 7.2). For 1970 the mortality loss was calculated to be 130.2 million cubic meters of growing stock and 36.3 million cubic meters of sawtimber; about one-fifth of all annual growth was nullified by mortality. (For these data, catastrophic losses were included with other forms of mortality.) Unfortunately, of the total volume of dead timber, only about 7 percent of the softwood and 3 percent of hardwood were salvaged. The following indicates the importance of protecting our forests against destructive agents: "The annual mortality and growth reduction attributable to only three pests . . . —western dwarf mistletoes, western bark beetles, and southern pine beetles — . . . are estimated to equal about 13 percent of the current timber harvest" (6).

Table 7.1 Estimated Losses to Forests Caused by Destructive Agents

Loss Factor	Total Volume Reduction[a]	Percentage of Total Volume Loss Resulting from Various Agents			
		Insects	Diseases	Fire	All Other[b]
Mortality					
Growing stock	99.4	28	22	7	43
Sawtimber	29.9	40	18	6	36
Growth loss					
Growing stock	217.7	10	56	19	15
Sawtimber	73.5	11	57	21	11
Catastrophe[c]					
Volume	286.8	43	15	26	16

Source: "Timber resources for America's future," U.S.D.A. For. Serv., Res. Rept. 14, 1958.
[a]Million cubic meters.
[b]Includes weather, animals, suppression, logging damage.
[c]Cumulative for first half of century.

Geographic Origin of Forest Insects

Although most insects affecting North American trees are native to the continent, a number of significant pests are exotics; that is, they were introduced from foreign countries. For example, of thirty-seven major North American pests (7), over one-fifth were inadvertently imported; among these were the European pine shoot moth, gypsy moth, larch casebearer, European pine sawfly, and the smaller European elm bark beetle, which is the principal vector of the Dutch elm disease pathogen. Six of the eight introduced pests on this partial list arrived in North America during the twentieth century.

Table 7.2 Recent Estimates of Volume Losses from Mortality

Region	Softwoods		Hardwoods	
	1962	1970	1962	1970
Growing Stock Volume Loss (million m³)				
East	19.8	25.5	39.6	45.3
West	56.6	56.6	2.8	2.8
Total	76.4	82.1	42.4	48.1
Sawtimber Volume Loss (million m³)				
East	3.8	4.7	8.0	8.5
West	23.8	22.2	.7	.9
Total	27.6	26.9	8.7	9.4

Source: "The outlook for timber in the U.S.," U.S.D.A. For. Serv., Res. Rept. 20, 1973.

Ecological Considerations

Theoretical Numerical Increase

We can consider forest pests outside of their environmental context and examine their inherent capability to expand their numbers. In its simplest form, the equation is

$$N = I(EF)^n$$

where N is the final number of individuals, I the initial number of insects, E the number of eggs produced per female, F the decimal fraction of females in the population, and n the number of annual generations. For example, if an initial population consists of six female and four male European pine sawflies on a pine tree, and if each female produces eighty eggs, there will be $10(80 \times 0.6) = 480 = N$ individuals at the end of a single generation, and 23,040 in two generations. By the fifth year there would be 2.55×10^9 sawflies. This concept, termed *reproductive potential,* provides an estimate of the pest's ability to multiply in the absence of countervailing forces.

Population Fluctuations

In natural situations, however, numerous factors reduce an insect population's innate capacity to increase *ad infinitum.* Collectively called *environmental resistance,* these factors are both physical and biological. The balance between reproductive potential and environmental resistance is an extraordinarily important and dynamic interaction that determines the distribution of forest insects and whether populations will rise or fall.

If insect numbers were represented over time, the resulting graph would probably be a series of peaks and valleys indicating periods of population growth and decline (Figure 7.1). We can broadly classify the condition of a population with respect to the amplitude and frequency of these peaks. Populations maintained at low levels are termed *endemic* or latent; this is the normal situation for most insects in forest ecosystems. In some areas abnormal forest

conditions (e.g., tree plantations) may permit insect numbers to stabilize at high densities, resulting in serious—though not necessarily fatal—injury to trees. The white pine weevil and European pine shoot moth are two pests whose populations are balanced at high densities.

When the amplitude of a population exceeds its general equilibrium position and produces economic losses above some minimum threshold, the population is considered to be in an outbreak or epidemic phase. Outbreaks may be either *sporadic* or *periodic* depending, as the terms imply, on whether they can be anticipated. Pests that persist at economically insignificant numbers for years, then suddenly explode to outbreak proportions because of lowered environmental resistance, cause sporadic outbreaks.

Periodic outbreaks constitute some of the most difficult and challenging problems of contemporary forest entomology. They are the result of the interactions of several factors, including favorable weather conditions over a period long enough to launch the outbreak, and an insect population whose cycles of increase and decline occur at fairly regular intervals. Periodic outbreaks are most common in monotypic stands and tend to produce their most significant effects in mature stands.

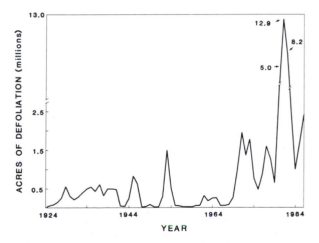

Figure 7.1 Population fluctuations of the gypsy moth. When actual numbers of insects are impossible to measure, the degree of damage inflicted may be used as an index of population levels.

Physical Factors of the Environment

Temperature Because forest insects are exposed to the atmosphere during some of their life stages, they are greatly influenced by elements of the physical environment. Although other environmental factors may ameliorate the effects of temperature, or modify them through interaction, temperature itself is regarded as the single most important physical environmental factor. Insects as a class have no mechanisms for controlling their internal body temperature as do higher animals; that is, they are cold-blooded. Since body temperatures of insects vary with ambient conditions, metabolism and developmental processes are directly related to "outside" temperature; consequently, successful development is dependent on favorable temperatures. Each forest insect species has a thermal preferendum. This is a temperature continuum that includes an optimum temperature range for the insect's life activities, and upper and lower thresholds beyond which development ceases. These developmental thresholds are bounded by lethal thresholds, or limits, that cause mortality when exceeded. When the temperature limits of an insect species are known, zones of potential population levels can be illustrated on a map as irregular contour lines. If based on climatic history, and on both empirical and experimental knowledge of the insect's behavior, these zones can be useful for predicting the distribution and population levels possible in different geographic areas.

An example of contoured zones of abundance was revealed by a study of the European pine shoot moth at a time when Wisconsin was being newly invaded by this pest (Figure 7.2). To assess potential problem areas, investigators determined for points throughout the state the frequencies of occurrence of the lower lethal threshold for the overwintering stage ($-28°C$). Although the moth's hosts are distributed throughout Wisconsin, it was predicted that about half of the state would remain free of serious infestation. In the thirty years since its original publication, the map has been proved correct: one known outbreak occurred in zone III, with all remaining major infestations in zone II.

Most north-temperate forest insects are endowed with a fail-safe mechanism that prevents continued development into periods of extreme temperatures. Termed *diapause,* this mechanism is a physiological state of arrested development resembling hibernation. Insects in diapause, however, do not respond immediately to temporary changes in the physical environment. The advantages of diapause include resistance to severe weather, synchronization of the insect's life cycle with that of its food supply, and synchrony with seasonal temperatures favorable for its rapid development and reproduction.

Generally, springtime insect activities are later as they proceed north, east, and upward; the opposite is true for fall activities. It is often useful to combine the physical environmental factors affecting devel-

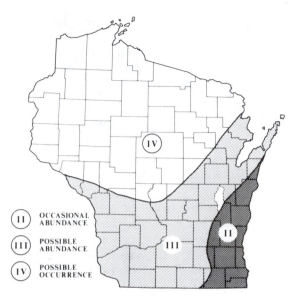

Figure 7.2 Zones of abundance for Wisconsin populations of European pine shoot moth based on the probability of low lethal temperatures. The normal zone of abundance (I) would appear to the southeast of the map. [Adapted from Benjamin, D. M., P . W. Smith, and R. L. Bachman. 1959. The European pine shoot moth and its relation to pines in Wisconsin. Wisconsin Conservation Dept. Tech. Bull. No. 19:7–23.]

opment of a particular population of animals or plants. This is most efficiently done by measuring the result of all these interacting factors—namely, the *phenological* development of individuals in the population. When this information is transferred to a map, contour lines can be drawn to denote areas where environmental conditions have combined to produce similar results—that is, the same stage of plant–animal development at the same point in time (Figure 7.3). If the average of several years of data is mapped, the resulting contours are a reliable indication of areas of equal development, and of the annual developmental lag time between areas. The study of the relation of a periodic biological phenomenon to climate is called phenology. These phenological maps are of practical value in forestry, especially when a temperature-dependent event is to be managed on a regional level. Using one phenological event to predict a second event is

Figure 7.3 Isophenes (contours based on phenology) showing locations of equal biological development. Isophenes pass through an area 5, 10, 15, and 20 days later in spring phenology than the 0 line. [Adapted from Benjamin, D. M. and D. W. Renlund. 1961. A phenological survey of red pine in Wisconsin. Wisconsin Academy Review, pp. 26–28.]

another tool of forest managers; for example, shoot elongation of balsam fir closely corresponds with development of the larval stages of the spruce budworm and is often used to schedule surveys and the initiation of aerial spray programs against this pest.

Moisture Though secondary to temperature as a predominant, driving force, moisture levels are nevertheless crucial outside a rather narrow zone of acceptability. Insects can tolerate only small fluctuations in the amount of water maintained in their bodies. These fluctuations are controlled by balancing moisture intake and loss. Larvae typically regulate evaporation by seeking favorable moisture levels—for example, by moving into or out of the direct rays of the sun.

Just as insects have a thermal preferendum, they also exhibit a preference for a particular range of moisture levels, or evaporation rates, during each developmental stage. Representing these ranges graphically produces curves that are often helpful in classifying insects according to their adaptations for dry, mesic, or wet conditions; adults of the white pine weevil are most active in dry habitats (20 percent relative humidity), whereas nymphs of the Saratoga spittlebug live only in a nearly saturated atmosphere.

Insects cannot always choose their accommodations, however; weather events with inadvertent, indirect effects often transpire. Driving rain, for instance, can dislodge insects from their feeding sites. Long periods of rainfall can coincidentally lower temperatures below the level favorable for feeding or development. Higher than normal relative humidity can promote fungus diseases, which act as insect pathogens or competitors for food.

Light The response of insects to light is well known, although it is generally of less importance than temperature and moisture. Natural light (daylength) often acts as a *token stimulus* to insects; that is, it indicates the parallel occurrence of biological events important to the insects' survival, such as the "readiness" of host plants for feeding. Daylength is a consistent and reliable indicator of seasonal changes in temperature and food availability. It is also the stimulus for other important events. An insect's "biological clock" is a physiological mechanism that, when stimulated by changes in photoperiod, triggers a biological response such as the spring termination, or fall initiation, of diapause.

Some insects have a particular attraction for discrete light sources; the most typical examples are moths. The attraction of many flying insects to light is the principle behind the scientific use of light traps. These traps are employed to assess the presence of certain species, to estimate population levels, or to indicate proper timing of control measures.

Wind The movement of air significantly influences the behavior and location of forest insects. Wind affects insects in three general ways. Depending on its speed, wind can act as a deterrent or as a positive stimulus to active, directed flight of adult forms. It also serves as a carrier for olfactory stimulants, enabling insects to find suitable host material or, in the case of pheromones, a mate. Sometimes wind causes the passive mass displacement of insects. This displacement might be only a short distance—such as dislodging larvae from their feeding sites—but nevertheless could cause mortality by starvation or increased vulnerability to predators. Displacement over long distances—sometimes hundreds of miles —can occur when a cold front passes over an area, picks up insects, and deposits them at other locations. This phenomenon is known as *convective transport*. In the "new area" more individuals are present than the resident population could have produced and, hence, there is the possibility of an "instant outbreak." This phenomenon suggests that even careful quarantine enforcements cannot always confine pests to rigid geographic boundaries.

Bioclimatology The integrated workings of all these factors of the physical environment over a period of years at a given locale constitute *climate*. Relating climate to living organisms is the study of bioclimatology. Recent technology, especially in the areas of synoptic meteorology and the movements of large air masses, has helped elucidate many of the ecological relationships of forest insects. By concomitantly studying the population trends and climatic patterns of a region backward in time, investigators may be able to build a methodology for predicting population trends forward in time.

Two forest pests of the Great Lakes states serve as an interesting example: the spruce budworm and the forest tent caterpillar. Both species are residents of the same region, but their populations never reach outbreak proportions at the same time. In fact, because of differing physiological requirements and behavioral attributes, the two pests respond to quite different climatic patterns: spruce budworm populations are nurtured by prolonged sunny, dry weather, forest tent caterpillars develop better under partly cloudy, warm, humid conditions (8). If polar air masses predominate for several years in succession, conditions become increasingly favorable for a surge of spruce budworm numbers. If, however, tropical air masses of maritime origin prevail for successive years, the potential for an

outbreak of forest tent caterpillars greatly increases. Conditions favorable to one species are actually detrimental to the other; hence, only one of these pests will be a threat to forests at a given time.

Studies of this nature led to the formation of the theory of *climatic release* (8): no initial increase of indigenous populations occurs until seasonal climatic control is relaxed, and favorable weather recurs for several years in succession. The population's reproductive potential is then realized, and its growth proceeds so rapidly that even adverse physical and biotic factors cannot bring it under control immediately. Understanding such climatic influences enables practicing foresters to monitor ecological conditions in view of their entomological consequences, and to initiate preventive, ameliorative, or salvage operations before potential consequences become history.

Biological Factors of the Environment

We have discussed some of the physical environmental factors that influence population levels of insects. Equally important, however, are the biological mechanisms affecting insect numbers. These may be internal, such as intraspecific competition, or external, such as biological control factors.

Intraspecific Competition Intraspecific competition (i.e., within the species) acts as a function of density or crowding and operates within the biological life processes of each individual in a population. Competition for food or space is a key element in determining population levels of the mountain pine beetle. Studies of this pest on lodgepole pine in the western United States have revealed that numbers of new adult beetles are drastically reduced when density increases. Similarly, the Douglas-fir beetle of the Pacific Northwest produces the greatest number of progeny when its population density is low; as crowding increases, fewer eggs are laid and mortality among those that are produced is higher. In general, when food supplies or space diminish, the size of adult insects declines, as well as the number of eggs produced per female; the sex ratio may be strongly influenced, and migration could be provoked. This form of self-regulation is well known among defoliating insects such as the gypsy moth, and it is one of the factors contributing to density fluctuations, or cycles.

With respect to spatial competition, many insects must feed and develop singly. Even with sufficient food, group rearing is deleterious to these species because of mutual interference. Examples of two such pests are the elm spanworm and the walkingstick. Other insects, like the pine sawflies, must feed in colonies to complete larval development successfully (Figure 7.4).

Biotic Control Mechanisms External factors such as parasites, predators, disease organisms, and

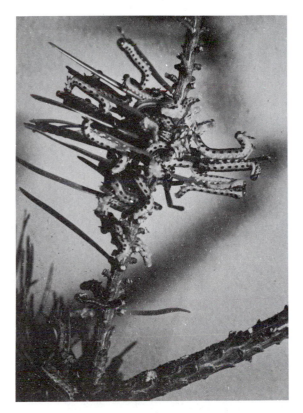

Figure 7.4 Red pine sawfly larvae are defoliators that must feed gregariously if they are to grow and develop normally.

natural host resistance are natural means of controlling insect populations. Although they may act individually, these factors exert their greatest influence when they act in concert, or in sequence, with each other. They are primarily responsible for maintaining forest insects at their normal, endemic levels.

A parasite typically requires one host to serve as its food supply while it completes its development. It normally lives on or in the host for its entire larval stage; the death of the host insect follows some time after the initial attack. Many species of flies and wasps, for example, deposit their eggs in or on other insect species. After hatching, the developing larvae feed on their host until they are ready to pupate; eventually the host dies. Most parasites are members of the orders Diptera (flies) and Hymenoptera (wasps); others are found among the Coleoptera, Lepidoptera, and Strepsiptera.

Predators (as opposed to parasites) are free-living and require numerous prey for food, killing each host at the time of encounter. Ants and ladybug beetles are common predacious insects. A wide variety of birds and small animals, such as mice and shrews, also function as entomophagous organisms. In particular, woodpeckers, nuthatches, and chickadees have been known to reduce populations of larch casebearers, bark beetles, cankerworms, and sawflies. Moles, mice, and shrews feed voraciously on insects that must spend a portion of their lives on or in the soil.

Forest insects are subject to infection by many pathogenic microorganisms, some of which can produce widespread insect diseases that result in the population collapse of the host species. Viruses, bacteria, rickettsia, protozoa, and fungi are typical "micro" control agents. Among the many insect species that are particularly susceptible to viruses are the eastern tent and forest tent caterpillars, Douglas-fir tussock moth, European pine sawfly, red-headed pine sawfly, linden looper, and the white-marked tussock moth. A virus (nuclear polyhedrosis) sometimes plays a major role in controlling gypsy moth numbers in the northeastern United States and Europe. An outbreak of the European spruce sawfly in eastern Canada and the United States was halted by a similar virus in the 1930s.

Naturally occurring bacteria infect several species of forest insect pests. The "milky disease" of larvae of the Japanese and June beetles is so effective at reducing beetle populations that once the soil is infected, no further beetle outbreaks can occur. Several varieties of the *Bacillus thuringiensis* bacterium appear to be efficient in controlling insect numbers, and these are currently being cultured for use in microbial control strategies.

Fungi (entomophagous) take a continuing, modest toll among forest insects, but mortality attributable to fungi rarely rises above a few percent. Exceptions are noteworthy, however. In 1958 fungus disease caused 97 percent mortality in a population of European elm bark beetles in Connecticut (9); in Ontario, between 1949 and 1952, fungi were responsible for a high degree of control of a forest tent caterpillar outbreak.

Another type of biotic control agent is the *nematode* (roundworm), which infests the gut and hemocoel of an insect host. Grasshoppers, bark beetles, and wood wasps often succumb to nematode attacks; other insects may not die as a result of roundworm infestation, but they may become sterile or produce fewer eggs. Nematodes have also been influential in reducing the effects of insect outbreaks, but their importance has generally been less than the previously mentioned organisms. The sirex wood wasp in New Zealand and the fir engraver in New Mexico are pests whose upward population trends have been reversed primarily by nematode infestations.

Deliberate manipulation of insect parasites, predators, and microorganisms is called *biological control* or biocontrol. A form of biological control using microorganisms is microbial control. Sometimes referred to as biological pest suppression, biocontrol is usually a long-term preventive endeavor to maintain pest populations at low levels.

Biocontrol has distinct advantages over the use of chemical pesticides. Once established, biotic agents may be self-perpetuating, relatively permanent, and more economical in the long run. If properly chosen, they are not hazardous to use and do not create harmful pollution or persistent toxic side effects. Experience with synthetic organic insecticides has

shown that we must use great caution when infusing potent toxicants into the complicated communities that make up forest ecosystems.

Interactive Considerations

We have discussed a few of the environmental and biological aspects of insect populations in a forest community. We should remember that the forest ecosystem is composed of a complex mixture of interacting factors. The position of a beetle on a leaf or in a tree is not due simply to any one factor in the mixture. Although temperature, light, predators, and other influences have been treated individually, it is the interplay of these and all the other known and unknown elements that creates a "dynamic stability" in the forest—a condition that nurtures both continuity and change. The intricacies of the ecosystem necessitate the study of elemental parts as an entree to understanding, but it should be remembered that the simple addition of parts bears no semblance to the whole. With this in mind, we will consider some of the parts implicated in the kinds of damage forest insects do, individually and collectively, on trees.

Impact of Insects on Forest Trees

Defoliators Defoliators are insects that eat needles and leaves; they include caterpillars, cankerworms, tussock moths, webworms, sawflies, leaf beetles, walkingsticks, skeletonizers, and leafminers (Figures 7.4 and 7.5). Understanding the impact of defoliation on forest trees is a prerequisite to the intelligent management of these pests. In some instances complete defoliation may cause tree death in a single season; in another situation trees might withstand complete foliage destruction without dying.

As a general rule, partial defoliation (50 to 90 percent) of both broad-leaved and coniferous trees reduces terminal and radial growth. Tree branches rarely die until after several seasons of severe defo-

Figure 7.6 Jack pine mortality resulting from defoliation by the pine tussock moth.

Figure 7.5 The walkingstick belongs to the group of pests known as defoliators.

liation. Tree response to complete destruction of its needles or leaves varies greatly, depending on the individual characteristics of the species. In the case of the Pinaceae[1] with persistent leaves, complete defoliation in one growing season can cause immediate tree death (Figure 7.6). Two major exceptions to this generally exist: several southern pines (shortleaf and longleaf pines) can be completely defoliated and refoliate with only rare mortality; the annually deciduous larch and bald cypress can also withstand complete defoliation for several years with little or no mortality.

Complete defoliation rarely causes mortality among the broad-leaved trees. Exceptions are hard maple and yellow birch, which may die if completely defoliated during mid-July to mid-August (10).

Insect defoliators vary greatly in their seasonal histories, biologies, and methods of feeding. Some species are *polyphagous* and include many tree species in their host list. The red-headed pine sawfly, for example, feeds on over twenty species of conifers. The gypsy moth, too, has a long host list. Other defoliators are *oligophagous* and feed only on a few hosts; examples are the European pine sawfly, which

prefers to feed on about half a dozen pine species, and the red pine sawfly, which will feed on three hard pine species. Defoliators that seek out a single host species are *monophagous;* some, like the Swaine jack pine sawfly, further restrict their feeding to needles only one or more seasons old.

Some defoliators consume entire needles or leaves; others mine tunnels between the epidermal layers of the tree's foliage. One group, the skeletonizers, feed on leaf tissue between the veins and produce "skeleton" leaves with an almost lacy appearance.

Defoliators often cause indirect destruction by weakening their hosts and rendering them susceptible to invasions by other insects such as bark beetles and borers, which can cause severe or fatal damage. For example, defoliation by budworms may predispose spruces and pines to the attacks of *Ips* and *Dendroctonus* bark beetles; cankerworms have so weakened oaks that the two-lined chestnut borer can often successfully colonize these otherwise-resistant trees. The hemlock looper begins the collapse of mature–overmature hemlock forests of eastern North America by defoliating and weakening its host, and making it vulnerable to subsequent attacks by the hemlock borer, which then delivers the coup de grace.

Defoliator outbreaks are often spectacular and may cover thousands of hectares of forest. The larch sawfly outbreak of 1920–1930 involved the entire

---

[1]The Pinaceae includes the pines, spruces, firs, hemlocks, sequoias, cedars, cypresses, junipers, and larches.

Figure 7.7 Tree mortality on a Colorado mountainside resulting from tunneling activity of the Douglas-fir beetle. (Courtesy of W. E. Waters.)

Figure 7.8 Galleries excavated by larvae of the smaller European elm bark beetle. Not only does this beetle inflict damage by its feeding activities, but it is also a major vector of the Dutch elm disease fungus.

tamarack type of eastern North America; the 1956–1957 outbreak of the forest tent caterpillar encompassed most of the aspen type of north-central North America; and budworm outbreaks on spruce–fir types have covered the North American continent. Because of the vastness of these outbreaks, emergency controls could be applied only to high-value forests.

Bark Beetles Bark beetles are among the most devastating forest insects in the world; they have been responsible for the stunting and killing of vast areas of forests (Figure 7.7). Although many species attack and kill trees in overmature forests, or those under environmental stress, other bark beetle species are capable of successfully infesting healthy, vigorously growing forests, where they often inflict serious damage.

Bark beetle adults may be attracted to their hosts, or they may arrive by random dispersal. Adult beetles bore through the bark; after mating, females lay their eggs either along their boring tunnels or in special galleries cut in the region between the bark and the wood (Figure 7.8).

After hatching, the larvae feed in the phloem and xylem, eventually girdling the trunk or branch with their tunnels. This girdling interrupts the translocation of nutrients and moisture, and the tree may soon wilt and die. Trees that are growing vigorously

often "pitch out" or drown the adult bark beetles in resin or sap; however, overmature trees and those weakened by drought or insect defoliators may not be able to repel the mining adults or larvae.

Some beetle species also act as the carriers or vectors of a variety of lethal tree pathogens. The pine bark beetle, for example, frequently carries the spores of a blue-stain fungus and inadvertently inoculates its host tree as it tunnels beneath the bark. Spores of blue-stain fungi produce mycelia that block the conducting (xylem) tissue and kill the tree. The pine engraver, the western pine beetle, and the mountain pine beetle are also vectors of blue-stain fungi. (The wood is stained blue by the fungus, but its structural strength is not impaired).

Another group of bark beetles are vectors for pathogens of the deadly Dutch elm disease, which was responsible for killing most of the American elms in cities and villages of the entire eastern half of North America in the last thirty to fifty years.

Ambrosia beetles (Figure 7.9) are classed as bark beetles, even though many species bore directly through the bark and into the solid wood of their host. Ambrosia adults carry with them ambrosia fungi that infest their galleries and serve as food for the young larvae. The larvae and fungus inflict little direct physiological damage to the tree; however, the galleries may become stained dark gray, brown, or black, and reduce the economic value of the tree.

Figure 7.9 Adult stage of the ambrosia beetle, *Xyloterinus politus.* These individuals have recently emerged from their pupal cases and will soon disperse to infest other trees.

In higher-value species such as mahogany the stained pinhole galleries enhance the value. Still another group of bark beetle species infests cones and seeds of pines and can cause nearly complete destruction of seed crops.

Sucking Insects Both coniferous and deciduous trees are subject to assaults from sucking insects, such as aphids, scales, and spittlebugs (Figure 7.10). These pests have modified mouthparts that enable them to pierce the foliage, tender twigs, or roots of trees and to suck the sap or resin as food. These pests create a continuous drain on the vitality of healthy trees, and, if their numbers are great enough, they may cause serious stunting or death of their hosts.

Aphids or plant lice usually attack a tree's tender new foliage or twigs, withdrawing sap and secreting honeydew, which then becomes infected with sooty mold. Sooty mold is a diagnostic to foresters, indicating the presence of sucking insects.

Wood Borers Wood borers are found in a variety of insect groups, including beetles, moths, and wasps. Most wood borers attack trees that are overmature, dying, or suffering from environmental stress. They may also invade cut pulpwood, logs, and fire-scarred trees. Borers are among the most seri-

Figure 7.10 Spittle masses formed by immature stages (nymphs) of the pine spittlebug help the insect maintain a high-humidity environment while feeding on sap extracted from the tree. This feeding results in necrotic areas on the stem or branch and causes stunting or death of many coniferous species in the eastern United States.

ous enemies of forests under stress. A few species even attack healthy, vigorous trees.

Two major groups of wood-destroying beetles are the *long-horned* or *round-headed borers* (Figure 7.11), and the *short-horned* or *flat-headed borers.* These latter insects are often called metallic borers. As their name implies, the long-horned–round-headed borers have long filamentous antennae, and they emerge from deep in the wood through a circular hole. The short-horned borers are generally flat and metallic in appearance, with short antennae; they emerge through an oval or lens-shaped hole. Females of both groups lay eggs in notches cut into the bark, and the new larvae mine for a period in the phloem. They then turn inward to feed in the wood, where they construct large and damaging tunnels. The whitespotted sawyer, a transcontinental enemy of pines, spruce, and fir, is a

Figure 7.11 Larval (left) and pupal (right) stages of the poplar borer.

typical long-horned borer; the bronze birch borer is a short-horned borer that seriously infests birches throughout the continent.

Shoot and Bud Insects The growing meristem—the buds and shoots of trees—is often seriously infested by insect pests. Although the tree rarely dies, stunting, distortion, and forking of its main bole are common. The pine tip moths, the best known of these pests, occur throughout the world. They are especially damaging in even-aged forests, in plantations, and in ornamental beautification plantings. One species, the European pine shoot moth, has spread across eastern North America and into Washington, Oregon, and British Columbia since its introduction in New York in 1914.

The white pine weevil is the most injurious pest of the white pine in northeastern North America (Figure 7.12). Damage is of two types: first, infestation may cause permanent forking of the main bole and render the tree unmarketable; second, the recoverable volume often is of low quality. Severe stunting occurs also in plantations of jack and Scotch pines and in Norway spruce.

Root Weevils The root weevils constitute an insidious group of insects that infest the roots and root collar regions of planted conifers. Habits of these pests vary greatly, depending on the host species,

age, and mode of attack, but tree stunting and killing often occur.

Adult pales weevils are attracted to areas in eastern and southern North America were pines are being harvested. Females lay their eggs in stumps of the harvested trees, and the emerging adults debark newly replanted seedlings; mortality of entire plantations is common. In the same parts of the country, a second species, the pine root collar weevil, infests the trunks of hard pines from 3 to 20 years old between the soil surface and the root system. Feeding by the larvae causes stunting, and severely injured trees often break off at the soil surface or die suddenly during windy periods.

White grubs, the larvae of May and June beetles, pose serious problems to forest nurseries and new plantings. The adults feed mainly on broad-leaved trees nearby and lay eggs in areas of heavy grass and sod. Larvae feed on the roots and stunt or kill seedlings.

Impact of Insects on Forest Stands

Insects are an essential component in the continuing ecological succession of the forest from its pioneer status to maturity, and they are intimately involved in the recycling of nutrients within the forest ecosystem. The dense growth of seedlings and saplings occupying recently burned or harvested pine stands often are naturally thinned by root weevils, scales, and defoliating sawflies. As competition intensifies among the young trees for nutrients and sunlight, defoliators and scales enter the picture to reduce stand density further. As the monotypic pioneer forest reaches maturity, then begins to decline in vigor, bark beetles, borers, and defoliators complete its destruction and set the stage for the entry of more tolerant and aggressive forest trees. This cycle may be repeated sequentially, each time with a slightly different mix of tree species, or it may be interrupted and repeat itself innumerable times with the same species. Ultimately the climax forest is developed; but this too, succumbs, with insects often providing the major impetus for this marvel of natural succession.

 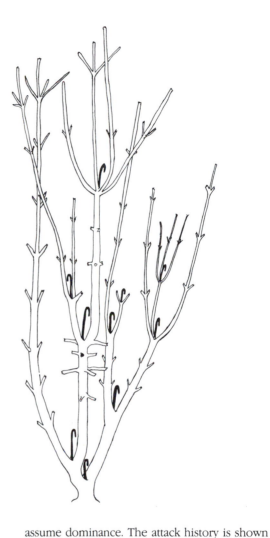

Figure 7.12 A 13-year-old spruce tree with evidence of numerous white pine weevil attacks. The weevil kills the terminal shoot, causing lateral shoots to assume dominance. The attack history is shown schematically on the right. Dead leaders appear as black crooks.

An example of the influence of insects on forest stands is found in the pioneer jack pine monotype following catastrophic fires. Mineral soil is exposed, the serotinous cones have opened, and seedlings rapidly cover the area. Not uncommonly, 40,000 to 100,000 saplings per hectare survive the first few years. Then the onslaught of insects and competition begins. During the first ten years, insects that reduce the stand may include pine tortoise scale, red-headed pine sawfly, Swaine jack pine sawfly, pine anomela beetle, pine shoot borer, white pine weevil, and the pitch nodule maker.

In the subsequent 10 to 30 years, other insect species are dominant: pine tortoise scale, jack pine sawfly, red pine sawfly, and the pine tussock moth.

In the last phase of the succession, from 40 years onward, the following insect species will be instrumental in the ultimate collapse of the jack pine monotypic forest: pine engraver, jack pine budworm, pine sawyer, and the Swaine jack pine sawfly.

With the demise of the dominant jack pine, the more tolerant pines and firs surviving, but suppressed, in the understory can begin to occupy the area as ecological succession proceeds.

The walkingstick, a defoliator of deciduous hardwoods in east-central North America (Figure 7.5), is another insect often associated with altering the composition of forest species. It prefers black oaks, basswood, elm, and wild cherry, but the walkingstick will also feed on white oak, aspen, ash, paper birch, and hickory. Walkingstick outbreaks frequently develop in mixed-hardwoods forests of the Great Lakes states, and the resulting defoliation of oaks may cover large areas. The insect's inherent preference for black oaks benefits the less-preferred white oak, which gradually gains greater dominance in the forest canopy. This process has not gone unnoticed by forest managers, for white oaks are generally more valued than black oaks for lumber. In fact, the walkingstick has been suggested as a management tool to encourage the predominance of white oak over black oak in mixed-hardwoods forests.

As will be discussed later, stand structure may be manipulated in order to control damage by particular insects, but sometimes this can result in species compositions different than originally intended. For example, as a defensive strategy against the white pine weevil, red, white, and jack pine can be interplanted beneath a light hardwood overstory. Although these conditions reduce damage caused by the weevil, they create a favorable environment for the red-headed pine sawfly. The sawfly exhibits a feeding preference for jack pine and, during outbreaks, may completely eliminate this tree species from the understory, leaving only red and white pines beneath the hardwood canopy.

Besides changes in species composition, the age class distribution of forest trees may also be altered by insect activity. The selective feeding of insects on trees of specific ages in the mixed forest is the usual mechanism.

The Eastern Spruce Budworm Situation —An Overview As a practical illustration of many of the topics discussed in this chapter, a synopsis of the spruce budworm situation in the northeastern United States and southeastern Canada is included. The intensity and duration of problems directly and indirectly related to this pest merit special attention.

The spruce budworm exhibits both species-specific and age-specific feeding preferences. Under natural conditions the spruce budworm usually remains at endemic levels in spruce–fir forests, and erupts to outbreak levels roughly every 40 years if weather and food conditions are favorable. This pest has a distinct preference for balsam fir trees, or spruce 50 to 75 years old. When fir trees account for approximately 50 percent of the forest stand, or when young spruces have matured to a palatable age, food conditions are favorable for budworm outbreaks.

Before the advent of pesticides, and before the harvesting of forest resources became an economic necessity, spruce budworm populations were natural "thinners" of spruce–fir forests, promoting the vitality of the forest as a whole by eliminating the mature spruces in the overstory and releasing young trees from conditions that restricted their sunlight and nutrients. When the supply of fir or mature spruce was exhausted, or when weather conditions became unfavorable, the inflated insect populations collapsed, and numbers of budworms returned to endemic levels.

Whereas the density of an endemic budworm population is extremely low (it is often difficult to trap even a single specimen), budworm densities in some areas of southeastern Canada have been maintained at artificially high levels for many years by attempts to control the insect's damage chemically. Spray operations have largely been aimed at protecting trees instead of controlling or eradicating budworms. Indeed, spraying has been effective at maintaining defoliation at about one-third of the total foliage. This condition, however, provides more than ample food for the budworm larvae that survive the chemical treatments. "Although chemical control has the ability to prolong the life of trees and prevent loss, it may also prolong the duration of the outbreaks" (11). Spray operations aimed at reducing budworm numbers to endemic levels were attempted in the western United States in the mid-1950s; however, the amount of pesticide required, the vast areas needing spraying, the ecological consequences on other forest life, and the lack of funds combined to make this goal unfeasible.

The spruce budworm problem is further complicated by the mobility of the moths. The passage of a cold front over an infested area in the late evening hours has been known to carry massive numbers of moths as far as 70 miles in a single night, and adults may fly on more than one night. In particular, the behavior of female moths predisposes them for extensive dispersal and propagation. Females usually deposit only a portion of their full egg complement in the evening before they are drawn to the airstreams above the forest canopy by phototropic responses and favorable weather conditions (12).

There is some evidence that "More recent outbreaks have apparently been more severe than those prior to 1900" (13), possibly because the balsam fir predominates in previously clearcut areas. There is also some indication in New Brunswick that the intervals between outbreaks may be decreasing, the last two being 37 and 22 years apart (outbreaks in 1912, 1949, and 1971) (14). (Aerial spraying of DDT first began in 1951.) If this seeming trend toward increasing frequency and severity of outbreaks is valid, it is clear that much more foresight and caution are needed in selecting harvest methods and control strategies than have been exercised in the past.

It becomes obvious that the control measure for a given region must take into account the measures adopted by adjacent regions, especially those "upwind." The immediate alternatives for dealing with outbreak or potential outbreak conditions are to spray, or not to spray and let the outbreak take its course (15). Salvaging dead or dying trees, especially when the outbreak is allowed to take its course, would help mitigate the economic loss in the short run, but it could do nothing to sustain the pulp and timber industries in the long run should an outbreak become severe or extensive. These industries have declared their inability to recover from the economic consequences of a do-nothing policy and, hence, have devoted much time and money to protecting trees via pesticide applications. However, as mentioned earlier, this spraying has sustained artificially high budworm populations, which, in turn, have necessitated more spraying. At present, some areas of New Brunswick have become locked indefinitely into extensive annual programs of aerially applied chemical controls. Ironically, the reduction in growth rate of budworm-stressed trees could eventually create another economic crisis for the forest industry within the next twenty to thirty years because of an overall decrease in the volume of harvestable timber.

As we can see, there is neither a simple statement of, nor a simple solution to, the spruce budworm situation. Many aspects have not even been mentioned in this brief section. In recognition of the complexities, controversies, and lack of adequate knowledge in many areas surrounding the spruce budworm problem in both the United States and Canada, a six-year international program (CANUSA) was established in 1978 to coordinate and focus research in both countries toward the cooperative development of a workable, integrated approach to pest management. As explained in a later section, this approach to insect control is based on sound ecological principles and makes use of a variety of control strategies as needed.

Western Spruce Budworm The western spruce budworm (16) is recognized as a separate species. Like its counterpart in the east, it is a defoliating pest. This budworm annually infests 2 million hectares in western North America. The principal host trees include Douglas-fir, grand fir, white fir, western larch, and Engelmann spruce. Chronically high population densities are common in Idaho and Montana. In one stand, for example, defoliation persisted for 29 straight years. The more general pattern is that outbreaks last for one to two years.

Defoliation varies inversely with site index. The effects of defoliation in infested areas relate both to species composition and to structure of the stands. A much higher proportion of suppressed trees are killed by severe defoliation, causing the crown class structure of infested stands to shift to a larger fraction of dominant and codominant trees. In mixed stands, because of differential mortality, there may also be a change in species composition in favor of Douglas-fir or other species. The western budworm exerts "a regulatory influence on tree stress and forest succession, in part replacing the functional role of natural fire" (16).

Southern Pine Beetle This bark beetle (17) is the most destructive insect of pine forests in the southeastern United States. It is known to attack and kill all pine species in its range, but loblolly and shortleaf pine are the preferred hosts. Under endemic conditions the southern pine beetle is confined to weakened trees, but in an epidemic situation it will attack and kill vigorous trees as well. In addition to causing direct economic loss of timber from widely distributed outbreaks, this pest also has an impact on recreation, the aesthetic appeal of the forest, and water supplies. Infestations vary from year to year. The South is never completely free of outbreaks, and at epidemic levels the southern pine beetle can occur in over 6 million hectares. The life cycle is short and the number of beetles can increase tenfold in each generation. With as many as seven overlapping generations per year, a small population can turn into an outbreak within a single growing season. Infestations are usually found in patches of various size, and under epidemic conditions trees of all ages are killed. The result is canopy openings and high concentrations of fuel susceptible to fire.

Impact of Forest Trees and Stands on Insect Populations

Stand Attributes A primary determinant of insect population levels is the availability and condition of food; that is, the species composition and stand structure of the forest are influential in the population growth of insects. As a general rule, forests with the greatest diversity of tree species are more resistant to outbreaks of forest insects.

Uniform age distribution functions much like species composition, in that even-aged stands are more vulnerable to insect assaults than those com-

posed of a mixture of ages. Trees are subject to attack from different insects at different stages of their growth, as well as to pests that attack host trees by species. It follows, then, that the greater the mix of tree species and ages, the more varied the mixture of insect species that can be supported—but the fewer individuals of each species. It is an accepted ecological premise that stability is proportional to diversity.

Biotic catastrophes were unknown in the climax forests of upland northern hardwoods in Wisconsin until maple blight appeared several decades ago. Researchers were at first surprised to observe damage of major consequences in these "climax" stands, but later they discovered that previous selective cutting had created almost pure stands of maple. Consequently, through the interactions of trees, insects, disease organisms, and human beings, the ecological groundwork had been laid for increasing vulnerability to insect outbreaks (18).

Tree Attributes Individual host trees exhibit varying degrees of pest susceptibility depending largely on their size. Small trees, particularly those that are suppressed (i.e., have strong competitors for sunlight and nutrients), and the very large, overmature trees are most likely to succumb to insect attacks. This ***bimodal mortality*** distribution occurred in the maple blight situation (Figure 7.13). When measured against a tree diameter gradient, the highest death rates were found at the high and low ends of the continuum, with mortality lowest in the middle range.

Certainly other elements, such as genetic and morphological factors, affect a tree's resistance to damage; but growth rate, indirectly measured by tree size or age, is of primary importance. The dominant and codominant individuals undergoing vigorous growth will be most able to offset major pest damage.

Many of a tree's physiological processes interact with insect pests. The ***oleoresin phenomenon*** of softwood trees is an excellent example of a physiological defense mechanism. Oleoresin is widely recognized as a major factor in the resistance of conifers to bark beetle damage. Oleoresin, or

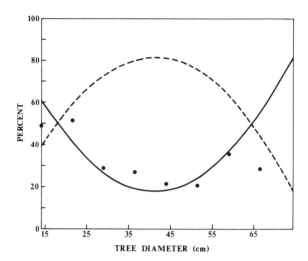

Figure 7.13 The relative mortality of different-sized sugar maple trees in defoliated stands of northern hardwoods. The solid mortality curve may be equated with susceptibility in order to show its complement, resistance (dashed curve).

Task and Scope of Forest Entomology

Qualitative Methods

Among the responsibilities of the forest entomologist is the development of techniques and procedures for conducting surveys to detect harmful species and populations of insects in the forest and to predict future population levels of pest species. Surveys have many designs depending on the kind and degree of information that is sought. Qualitative survey methods are used to detect tree injury and determine its cause—that is, identify the pest responsible. First-line defenses also include detecting the presence of new insect species or of a change in numbers of a particular resident pest species. These observations may be casual and unscheduled, as in the case of a backpacker reporting dead or dying trees to a ranger, or they may be part of a regular, planned survey to keep track of changes in the forest's condition.

Where forests are extensive, periodic surveillance is often conducted by airplane. Aerial surveillance can vary from simple visual inspection to the use of color-infrared photography or computer-enhanced satellite images. Aerial photographs are used to detect and map defoliation; this technique, along with satellite imagery, is being developed in conjunction with control measures for the gypsy moth, spruce budworm, forest tent caterpillar, larch sawfly, and the Douglas-fir tussock moth.

On the ground, many sampling and survey techniques are designed to provide qualitative and quantitative information. Qualitative information is often obtained from insect surveys at semipermanent sample stations in various forest types. Survey and measurement techniques utilized in forestry are also discussed in Chapter 12.

Quantitative Methods

When qualitative surveys indicate a disturbance in the population level of a pest species, more refined and definitive surveys are undertaken to produce

"pitch," is stored in canals in the sapwood and serves to seal wounds that penetrate the phloem layer. When a boring beetle ruptures a resin canal, the reduced pressure causes the pitch to flow into the tunnel created by the insect, often pushing the intruder completely back out of the tree. The rate and duration of resin flow vary among conifer species, and even among individuals of the same species, making it difficult to anticipate which trees are most vulnerable to beetle attack. Recent experimental work, however, has demonstrated that oleoresin exudation pressure (OEP) varies with the season, time of day, weather conditions, and age of the tree. By measuring OEP, researchers discovered a close correlation between it and water balance in the tree. In fact, OEP is now recognized as a criterion of a tree's physiological condition and is an effective quantitative measure of tree resistance to bark beetles. Trees with low OEP may succumb to persistent attack by bark beetles; trees with high OEP are more resistant. Large infestations of the pest are usually associated with older conifers or stands subjected to drought or defoliation.

numerical descriptions of the changes. *Numerical surveys* follow a regimen specifying the locations, number, and frequency of samples to be taken. In some areas these numerical assessments are made on a regular basis in order to keep close surveillance on pest species with potentially explosive populations. During one such survey in Wisconsin, which monitored overwintering stages of the jack pine budworm, it was discovered that the percentage of parasitization by *Apanteles* was very high. This indicated that defoliation in late spring and summer would be greatly reduced. Consequently, an aerial spray operation scheduled to cover 81,000 hectares was reduced by 85 percent. The monetary savings were significant, and in addition continued parasitization by beneficial insects was encouraged.

The methods and techniques used to measure insect populations depend on the biological and ecological characteristics of the species, the proposed use of the information, the size of the area to be surveyed, the nature of the terrain, the availability of skilled personnel and funding, and the value and intended use of the threatened resources. If the survey is in response to a newly discovered infestation or outbreak, sampling may be intensive and extend well past estimated boundaries in order to determine borders accurately and to calculate intensity.

Survey procedures have been standardized for most major forest insect pests. The life stage that provides the criterion for estimating population levels depends on the species being measured. For many species eggs serve as a population indicator (eggs are particularly useful because of their immobility); in other species larvae are counted. Symptoms and signs provide indirect population information; for example, the number of exit holes of bark beetles or wood borers in a standardized area of bark surface implies internal beetle densities and tree damage. Whatever the survey technique used for the life stage sampled, the goal of quantitative surveys is to provide an estimate of the pest's population or tree damage on a per-unit-area or per-tree basis—that is, its *density*. The survey information is later used in conjunction with biological and ecological knowledge to predict future population levels

or damage impact. Hence, if we know how many insects are present in a given stand via a quantitative survey, and have prior knowledge of the density of insects that will cause stand mortality (i.e., economic damage levels), we can make management decisions regarding the necessity of future pest control measures.

Specific survey techniques are too numerous to detail here, but we will focus on two innovations that have increased efficiency and reduced survey costs. Traditionally, surveys have been employed using a fixed sample size; for example, 10 percent of the trees in a plantation may be examined to determine the number of sawfly colonies per tree. A modern variation of this approach uses a flexible sample size based on the principle of *sequential sampling*. Sequential techniques require extensive prior knowledge and are based on sophisticated statistical methods. In its simplest form the sequential survey is conducted in conjunction with a table or graph. For example, a graph (Figure 7.14) used for classifying population levels of the Douglas-fir tussock moth is employed in an egg-counting survey. To begin, twig samples are taken from four trees and the number of eggs is counted: a total of 50 eggs is found (point A, Figure 7.14). The numbers of eggs found on twig

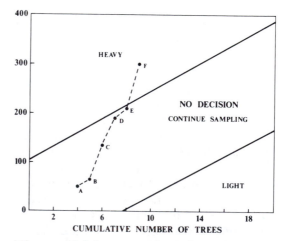

Figure 7.14 Sequential-sampling graph for classifying Douglas-fir tussock moth populations. (Modified from Mason (19), U.S.D.A. Forest Service.)

samples from five more trees are 15, 70, 55, 20, and 90. The points given by using the successive, cumulative numbers of trees as the *x*-coordinates, and the corresponding cumulative numbers of eggs as the *y*-coordinates (points B through F), are plotted on the graph. The area in which a point falls determines whether more samples must be taken. Whereas it took nine samples to denote a "heavy" classification in our example, it might take twenty samples to determine a light population level. Similarly, if the first twig sampled contained 200 eggs, no further sampling would be necessary. As long as the point resulting from the coordinates for cumulative trees and eggs falls in the "no decision" band, surveying must be continued (up to a predetermined maximum number of samples), because it is not statistically possible to classify the level with certainty. Depending on the particular objectives, the terms *heavy* and *light* on the graph might be replaced with *control* and *no control,* or with other decision paradigms.

A second innovative approach to damage–insect surveys concerns managing white pine plantations in eastern North America to control the white pine weevil. This weevil kills the terminal shoot of sapling- and pole-sized white, red, jack, and Scotch pines, and causes a permanent crook or fork to develop in the main bole of the tree. These forked trees often are of limited value, for they rarely produce high-quality lumber when they reach the marketable age of 75 to 150 years. Obviously, the objective of a sound forest management plan is to grow white pines that produce straight and clear lumber. White pine plantations generally are planted at a mean density of about 3000 trees per hectare; harvest of sawlog-sized trees is aimed at 250 to 370 trees per hectare. The final crop trees are selected early in the life of the plantation according to criteria of rapid growth and good form. Slow-growing, stunted, and weevil-injured trees are gradually removed during intermediate harvesting and thinning.

Under this procedure, white pine plantations are scheduled for control only if they are approaching the limit of tolerable injury by the weevil. This requires assessing the annual decrease in the num-

ber of unweeviled trees and charting the information, as shown in Figure 7.15. When the decreasing number of healthy, well-formed, unweeviled trees approaches the critical level of 300, controls will be applied to protect these final crop trees. The investment required for weevil control is based on affording protection to the final crop trees; control of weevil injury to trees producing less valuable products is not accepted as good managment.

Control of Forest Insects

The decision to control insects infesting natural forests and plantations must be based on a comprehensive review of all factors bearing on the management and culture of these multiple-use, renewable, natural resources. Ecological, sociological, and economic implications must be weighed carefully. The perpetuation of forests requires long-term management of insects that are a natural force in the

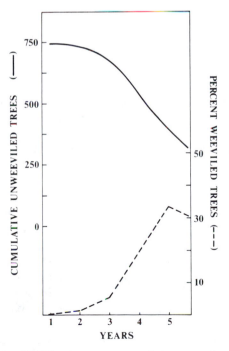

Figure 7.15 White pine weevil damage indexes, used as criteria for decisions about control. [Modified from Waters (20), U.S.D.A. Forest Service.]

ecological succession of living biological systems. It is inevitable that periodically the forest environment may become favorable to some species of pest insects. The forest entomologist has the responsibility to acquire sufficient basic information concerning the pest species in the region to be able to recommend sound practices that will temper the effects of these population eruptions. The tools available for this task, as well as their effectiveness, are being steadily improved and expanded.

Silvicultural Control The objective of silvicultural control is to reduce the adverse impact of pest insects through the implementation of various forest management practices. (Silvicultural practices are discussed in more detail in Chapter 14.) To be effective, methodologies must be based on a fundamental understanding of the biology and ecology surrounding the pest species and the ecological requirements of the forest type being managed.

The use of silvicultural methods for controlling insect pests is *preventive* instead of corrective, and the effect may be reflected some years beyond the time the practice is initiated. For example, delaying the replanting or reseeding of an eastern North American coniferous forest immediately after a clearcut harvest will avoid a devastating outbreak of the pales weevil among the new seedlings one to two years later. Adult weevils, drawn to the odor of pitch from the harvested trees, feed on bark of the newly established seedlings. Successive generations of weevils, hatching from eggs laid in the cut stumps, may destroy the entire crop of young pines.

Many silvicultural techniques are the result of careful study and experience. For example, in eastern North America it was found that planting hard pines too deeply makes the distances between tree roots and the soil surface abnormally long. This condition predisposes the trees to serious injury by the pine root collar weevil 5 to 20 years after planting. The solution to the problem has been simply to plant less deeply.

In the Great Lakes region, the adult Saratoga spittlebug causes substantial tree mortality of hard pines by sucking the sap from twigs. The spittlebug requires an alternate host during the nymphal stage.

Sweetfern, brambles, and broad-leaved weeds serve as alternate hosts. This information has been put to use in the three options currently employed to alleviate the problem: (1) avoid establishing hard pines in areas of dense alternate hosts; (2) reduce the density of alternate hosts with herbicides before planting; (3) establish plantations at a minimum density of 3000 stems per hectare to effect early crown closure and thereby shade out alternate hosts.

Similarly, the ravages of bark beetles may be curtailed in a variety of ways. The pine engraver and pine sawyer can be controlled in cutting sites by "hot logging"—that is, removal of cut logs and pulp within 30 days during spring and summer and removal of all winter-cut wood from the forest by May 15. The western pine beetle, a problem among more mature trees and those of less vigor, is controlled by thinning. Low-vigor, thin-crowned, and overmature ponderosa pines that are likely to succumb to the beetle before the next scheduled thinning are removed during a special cut.

Chemical Control The application of chemical insecticides for insect control in the forest is an emergency undertaking, designed to avoid or reduce damage immediately. Except for rare instances, the objective is not to eradicate the pest. If properly planned and carefully executed, application of the pesticide should have a negligible effect on the environment or natural control factors such as parasites and predators. Natural control factors are subsequently expected to exert sufficient influence to hold the pest population at endemic levels.

Most insect control programs involving forest insects are directed against defoliators like the spruce and pine budworms, tussock moths, tent caterpillars, cankerworms, gypsy moths, and sawflies. Among the sucking insects, controls have been applied for scales, spittlebugs, and balsam woolly aphids. Bark beetles have also been subject to controls, the major targets being the western pine beetle, the spruce weevil, the southern pine beetle, and the pine engravers. Shoot moths, seedeaters, and conefeeders, and the white pine weevil have also received special attention.

The habits of the pest species, the area involved, the proximity to water, and the potential for adverse impacts on area wildlife all must be taken into account when considering if, which, when, how, and how much pesticide is to be applied. These decisions are among the most serious facing the forest manager, for their consequences are often felt for many years afterward.

Pesticides can act on an insect in a variety of ways, and they are therefore often classified according to how the poison enters the insect's body.

1. **Stomach Poison.** Taken in by mouthparts (includes poison baits, systemics).
2. **Contact Poison.** Absorbed through the body wall.
3. **Fumigant.** Taken in through respiration.

Pesticides can also be classified according to their chemical makeup: (1) inorganic poisons, (2) chlorinated hydrocarbons, (3) carbamates, (4) organophosphates, and (5) natural plant products.

Methods of pesticide application in the forest depend on the vulnerability or exposure of the pest and the magnitude of the area. Most defoliators are exposed while feeding, and stomach poisons applied to the foliage will be taken into the body along with their food. On individual trees or small forest areas (1 to 10 hectares), pesticides are usually applied by hydraulic sprays or mist blowers. For large areas (more than 10 hectares) airplanes or helicopters are more efficient. Trees infested by bark beetles and wood borers are often treated with insecticide by hand or machine spraying of the tree trunk. The same technique has been used successfully to treat pulpwood and log piles that must be left in the forest for long periods.

For insects feeding inside buds, shoots, seeds, and foliage that are not exposed to external sprays, systemic pesticides are employed. Application is either externally to the foliage, whence they are absorbed and translocated throughout the tree, or on the soil around the tree as granules, which are subsequently dissolved and washed into the root zone. The pesticide is then absorbed by the roots and translocated to all parts of the tree.

A large number of pesticides are available for forest insect control. It should be emphasized that the user of pesticides must very carefully read and follow the instructions on the package label, because almost all pesticides are poisonous to human beings as well as insects. The label specifies the target insects of the pesticide, the dosage rate, best method of application, and the major safety precautions required. A casual attitude toward pesticide handling and use not only may be a violation of state or national regulations for pesticide use but could also endanger the health and lives of all who come in contact with the chemical. Pesticides can be used safely and effectively if the required precautions are heeded.

Novel Chemical Approaches   Among the chemicals available for forest pest control are several that exploit an insect's particular biological characteristics. Most insect species require mating before the female is able to lay fertile eggs. In some species like the gypsy moth, males find females by following the particular identifying "odor" of a chemical substance secreted by the females, called a *pheromone.* Chemists have synthesized this pheromone, and it is now used as a lure to detect male moths in areas of low density and in areas beyond the species' normal range. Forests infested with gypsy moths might also be sprayed with this sex attractant to confuse the males and prevent their finding and fertilizing females.

In a similar biological exploitation, a large number of males are raised in the laboratory, sterilized, and then released in the infested area. These males mate with virgin females but, because there is no fertilization, only infertile eggs are produced.

A recent innovation in insect control employs a chemical that inhibits chitin formation and deposition. (Chitin is a major component of the insect's exoskeleton.) This chemical is not toxic to insects, but it causes the body wall to become weak during molting. The exoskeleton does not develop properly, and the insect fails to complete its life cycle or dies when its exoskeleton ruptures.

Other chemicals, called feeding inhibitors, are not poisons but are used to inhibit or stop an insect's feeding. Eventually the target pests starve themselves.

Novel chemicals and methods are rapidly being developed, and each must be carefully examined for its impact on target insects and on the flora and fauna of the entire forest ecosystem.

Biological Control As mentioned earlier, biological control is the planned use of living organisms and their products to abate noxious insects. Even though organisms of many types have been studied as potential control agents, the vast number of insect species, viruses, fungi, and other organisms makes it evident that research in this area is still in its infancy. Current research focuses on control agents that are naturally associated with a pest species (or closely related species), especially when the pest has been introduced from another area or country. In such instances the natural enemies of the introduced species are also imported, and the possibilities of their establishment are evaluated for the new area. This process requires great care, however, because the introduction of exotic new species into an established ecosystem—or the attempted extermination of a longtime resident species—can have unanticipated, dramatic consequences.

Control agents for a variety of pest insects have been successfully imported and established. Following are several examples of the use of imported controls in the management of insect pests.

1. The *larch casebearer,* a tiny moth whose larvae feed on larch needles, is an exotic pest from Europe. Two of its European parasites were introduced to combat the pest in this country, and they are now considered responsible for reducing larch defoliation to a nominal level.

2. Both native and exotic *sawflies* defoliate conifers throughout North America. The European parasite *Dahlbominus fuscipennis* (Zett.) was introduced to bolster the control exerted by native beneficial insects. The parasite was successfully established in many parts of Canada and the United States where it has contributed to the control of the red-headed pine and European pine sawflies.

3. A nematode is being tested as a control agent for the *Sirex wasp* in New Zealand and Australia. The *Sirex* wasp is a threat to Monterey pine, and during outbreaks the pest kills large numbers of these trees. Female wasps infected by the nematode become sterile. Infected males transmit the nematode to their offspring when they mate with an uninfected female.

4. *Calasoma sycophanta,* a large, iridescent, green beetle, was imported from Europe to control gypsy moths in the northeastern United States. Both the larval and adult stages of the beetle prey on moth populations.

Introductions of parasites and predators are not always successful. One of the most extensive biological control projects in the United States has been in operation against the gypsy moth since the early 1900s. Large-scale importation of natural enemies from Europe and Japan was carried on for almost 30 years, with over 100 million individuals, constituting 40 species of parasites and predators, released in this country. Of these, only 11 species have become established.

Integrated Pest Management Control of forest pests, like protection of agricultural crops, has a history of environmental abuses brought about by ignorance. Whatever the vagaries of the past, the maturity of experience now demands establishment of a new system for dealing with pests of all types. A new concept called *integrated pest management* (IPM) is at hand, and great international efforts are being orchestrated to bring it to a practical reality. A pest control strategy based on ecological principles, IPM integrates methodologies from several disciplines in a management plan designed to be effective, practical, economical, and protective of human health and the environment. Refinements in IPM will enhance efforts regarding sustainable forest production.

Historically, scientists in different disciplines —entomology, pathology, soils, forestry, and chemistry—approached a pest problem with minimal communication with their colleagues in the other fields. Occasionally controls imposed for one pest conflicted with those used against another or had undesirable effects on the pest population and on the beneficial species. It was finally realized not only that is it feasible to integrate pest control methods, but also that this integration must consider simultaneously the effects on a multitude of other factors, including other organisms, other forest management activities, and other uses of the ecosystem.

Two relatively new fields of study providing information important to the construction of viable IPM programs are *population dynamics* and *forest ecology*. Research in population dynamics has led to a better understanding of how a myriad of factors affect population fluctuations. Forest ecology has expanded its traditional limits to encompass investigations in the interdependency of various organisms, and the quantification of stand dynamics. Modern economic theory and systems analysis are being utilized in IPM. The progression of computer technology and the parallel development of systems concepts were timely events in the human quest for modern pest management strategies.

By definition, IPM brings together old knowledge, new ideas, policy considerations, treatment techniques, prediction, monitoring, and decision making in a way only recently possible. The environmental and biological factors discussed in this chapter are used as tools for evaluating pest management needs: thresholds, tree species composition, climatological concepts, damage impact, and so on. The function of IPM is to employ the various elements of silvicultural, biological, and chemical control as needed, so that they work in concert, not in conflict, with one another.

A major national effort for IPM was recently sponsored by the federal government in cooperation with universities, states, and private industry. This multimillion-dollar research project focused on the gypsy moth, the tussock moth, and the southern pine beetle. Although some problems remain unsolved, major progress was made toward understanding. This program must rank as one of the most intensive national efforts of any country to resolve important forest pest problems.

The science of IPM is in its infancy; there is still much to learn in many areas. Existing knowledge and creative research can produce a pest management system that integrates two seemingly incompatible conditions: the economic need to control pest damage and the ecological necessity of preserving, as nearly as possible, the natural vitality and beauty of forested land.

References

1. K. Graham, *Concepts of Forest Entomology,* Reinhold, New York, 1963.

2. A. A. Berryman, *Forest Insects: Principles and Practice of Population Management,* Plenum Press, New York, 1986.

3. A. T. Drooz, "Insects of eastern forests," U.S.D.A. For. Serv., Misc. Publ. 1426, 1985.

4. R. L. Furniss and V. M. Carolin, "Western forest insects," U.S.D.A. For. Serv., Misc. Publ. 1339, 1977.

5. Anon., "Timber resources for America's future" U.S.D.A. For. Serv., Res. Rept. 14, 1958.

6. Anon., "The outlook for timber in the United States," U.S.D.A. For. Serv., Res. Rept. 20, 1973.

7. A. G. Davidson and R. M. Prentice, eds., "Important forest insects and diseases of mutual concern to Canada, the United States and Mexico," Dept. For. Rural Dev. —Canada, Publ. 1180, 1967.

8. W. G. Wellington, *Meteor. Monogr., 2,* 11 (1954).

9. C. C. Doane, *Ann. Entomol. Soc. Amer., 52,* 109 (1959).

10. R. L. Giese, J. E. Kapler, and D. M. Benjamin, "Studies of mapleblight. IV. Defoliation and the genesis of maple blight," *Univ. Wisc. Agr. Expt. Sta. Res. Bull. 250,* 81 (1964).

11. D. O. Vandenburg, "Protection of selected forest resources (crop protection) as a management strategy," *Proc. Symp. Spruce Budworm,* U.S.D.A. For. Serv., Misc. Publ. 1327, 1976.

12. G. A. Simmons, "Influence of spruce budworm moth dispersal on suppression decisions," *Proc. Symp. Spruce Budworm,* U.S.D.A. For. Serv., Misc. Pub. 1327, 1976.

13. J. R. Blais, *For. Sci. 11,* 13 (1965).

14. D. O. Greenbank, "The dynamics of epidemic spruce budworm populations." In *Memoirs of the Entomol. Soc. Canada,* 31, R. F. Morris, ed., 1963.

15. L. C. IRLAND, "Notes on the economics of spruce bud-worm control," Univ. of Maine, School of Forest Resources, Tech. Notes 67, 1977.

16. M. H. BROOKES, R. W. CAMPBELL, J. J. COLBERT, R. G. MITCHELL, AND R. W. STARK, TECH. COORD., "Western spruce bud-worm," U.S.D.A. For. Serv., Tech. Bull. 1694, 1987.

17. R. C. THATCHER, J. L. SEARCY, J. E. COSTER, AND G. D. HERTEL, EDS., "The southern pine beetle," U.S.D.A. For. Serv., Tech. Bull. 1631, 1982.

18. R. L. GIESE, D. R. HOUSTON, D. M. BENJAMIN, AND J. E. KUNTZ, "Studies of maple blight. I. A new condition of sugar maple," *Univ. Wisc. Agr. Expt. Sta. Res. Bull., 250,* 1 (1964).

19. R. R. MASON, "Sequential sampling of Douglas-fir tussock moth populations," U.S.D.A. For. Serv., Res. Note PNW-102, 1969.

20. W. E. WATERS, "Uninjured trees—a meaningful guide to white pine-weevil control decisions," U.S.D.A. For. Serv., Res. Note 129, 1969.

CHAPTER 8

Diseases of Forest Trees

ROBERT F. PATTON

Like all other organisms, forest trees are subject to injury and disease caused either by adverse environmental influences or by a variety of destructive biotic agents. They may be affected at all stages in their life cycle, from seed to mature tree, and even afterward as the wood product. These agents have a variety of effects on the forest and cause losses in both quality and yield.

The losses we are concerned with in this chapter are those caused by *disease,* as opposed to losses from fire, insects, animals, and weather. Disease can be defined as a malfunction of a metabolic process, or as a disturbance of normal structure, that is caused by continuous irritation by some abiotic or biotic agent. These activities of the suscept and the pathogenic agent produce symptoms and signs, respectively, and these evidences of disease are used to characterize and diagnose the disease. *Injury,* as opposed to disease, also may impair vital functions or disrupt the normal structure, but it is caused by an agent such as fire, insects, or animals that affects the plant only once or intermittently, and the irritation is discontinuous, temporary, or transient. *Damage* is sometimes used as a synonym for injury, but it usually connotes a decrease in quantity or quality of a product that decreases its economic value.

The study of forest disease is called *forest pathology* and is one of about forty scientific disciplines that make up forestry (1). In its broadest sense it includes the study of diseases that cause damage or loss to the forest as an economic unit, diseases of shade and ornamental trees, and microbiological deterioration of forest products after harvest (2). In forest pathology we are interested in the influence of diseases on forest management practices, but also in the influence of management practices on the occurrence and development of diseases.

Significance of Forest Disease Losses

The total loss, including all the various effects, resulting from tree diseases is referred to as *growth impact*. This loss includes both *mortality* and *growth loss;* growth loss includes a reduced growth rate, losses of accumulated growth (e.g., by decay), losses of efficiency in utilizing a site, and losses in quality.

Our knowledge of the loss caused by forest tree diseases is grossly inadequate, and for lack of better figures, we continue to quote the estimates made at the time the concept of growth impact was derived in 1952, as shown in Table 7.1 (3). Losses caused by disease amounted to about 35 percent of the gross annual timber growth (2). This loss of about 300 million cubic meters (11 billion cubic feet) was equal to about 92 percent of net sawtimber growth and 90 percent of the sawtimber cut in 1952. Thus losses from disease are indeed enormous. Reductions in such losses would go far toward increasing the timber supply necessary to meet future demand.

Although there are differences in the magnitude of increases, all recent projections indicate substantially larger demands on domestic forests in the future than at present (4). The amount of available timber has increased (through tree growth) faster than total wood consumption, but increased costs of stumpage, processing, and marketing are reducing the economic supply even as the timber inventory grows. Beyond about the year 2000, however, increased forestry effort will be necessary if timber supply is to meet demand. Opportunities for increasing timber supplies develop through intensified forest management. One aspect of more intensive forest management is reduction of the great impact on growth caused by disease. Because of adverse economic and environmental impacts caused by the increasing use of wood substitutes, programs to increase timber crops are important,

and the reduction of losses through the management of disease in our forests represents a challenge and an opportunity for foresters.

One of the principles in plant disease management is the establishment of economic thresholds (1). The term threshold connotes a time for taking action to control disease, but economic thresholds have been defined variously. In the original and simplest concept, a particular control strategy is initiated at the size or level of pest infestation at which the cost of potential damage—a decrease in yield or economic loss—to be avoided by such control equals the cost of the treatment. The economic situation may determine the real significance of the impact of disease losses, and values vary with the ultimate management objective—how the forest crop is used. Thus, there is an increasing need for better and more complete estimates of forest disease losses. They should always be stated in terms of how the timber is to be utilized to meet the particular demands of society.

The Causes of Forest Diseases

The health of forest trees is affected by a number of factors that subject them to *stress*. At any point in time, several stress factors may be operating concurrently, so that the general state of health of a tree may be determined by the total effect of all stresses (5). For convenience in study and understanding, however, we separate the treatment of these factors into various disciplines, such as pathology and entomology. In forest pathology the diseases caused by these factors may be classified in several ways, for example, according to the causal agent, the portion of the tree affected, the process or function disrupted, or the stage of development of the tree.

Agents That Cause Disease

Agents or factors inducing diseases in plants, including forest trees, are classed as abiotic or biotic. Abiotic agents are noninfectious and nonparasitic, biotic agents infectious or parasitic. A specific biotic agent causing a disease is designated as a *pathogen.*

Abiotic or Noninfectious Agents A number of abiotic agents cause disease in trees, including extremes of moisture and temperature, nutrient excess or deficiency, and toxic substances in the air or soil. Mechanical injury may be inflicted by hail, ice, snow, and windstorms; lightning damage may kill individual trees or even trees in groups. Diseases caused by abiotic agents are often difficult to diagnose because the causal agent is no longer present or active, or because the cause–effect relationship is difficult to establish.

Some of the most complex forest disease problems are those induced by adverse variations in the environment. An episode of pole blight, which is characterized by severe root and crown decline, attacked second-growth pole-sized western white pine for twenty years, beginning in the 1930s. It was brought on by an abnormally long period of drought superimposed on certain sites in the Inland Empire region of Washington, Idaho, and Montana that had little capacity to store moisture. A number of hardwood declines, "blights," or diebacks appeared in the 1950s; again drought was implicated as the primary inciting factor. Oak decline, ash dieback, and sweet gum blight are among diseases for which the causal relations are extremely complicated, consisting of an interaction of various factors. Indeed, insect defoliation is one of the causes of oak decline.

Temperature or moisture extremes may cause direct damage to trees or so weaken them that they are predisposed to attack by microorganisms. Sunscald canker of thin-barked trees often follows upon a sudden exposure to direct summer sun, for example, after thinning. Days and nights of high and low temperatures during late winter or early spring may cause a similar injury to bark, exposing it to sun and then freezing it again by a rapid drop in temperature at night. When warm winds in winter cause excessive transpiration, and roots in frozen ground cannot replace the water, the foliage of conifers may suffer winter injury or winter drying.

Soil conditions in which nutrients or other chemicals are deficient or in excess may be encountered in local areas, especially in nurseries and forest plantations. Pine and eucalyptus plantations have failed in Africa because of boron deficiency. In Scotland plantations of Sitka spruce suffering from phosphate deficiency were immediately improved by aerial fertilization with phosphate. As forest management becomes more intensive, forest fertilization may become almost routine, but there is also likelihood of damage from a variety of chemicals such as fertilizers, fungicides, insecticides, and herbicides, if they are applied at excessive rates or under improper conditions.

In recent decades air pollution has reached such high levels that both forests and urban trees in most of the industrialized regions of the world have been damaged, arousing grave concern (Figure 8.1). Many chemicals highly toxic to trees and other plants are introduced into the atmosphere, especially by transportation vehicles, industrial processes, and power plants. Sulfur dioxide, produced in coal combustion and other industrial processes, and the photochemical pollutants ozone and peroxyacetyl nitrate, the main components of urban smog, are major causes of damage to conifers in particular. In the East white pine has suffered considerable damage from sulfur dioxide and ozone, and the chlorotic-decline disease of ponderosa pine in Southern California is attributed to prolonged exposure to aerial oxidants, mainly ozone. Fluorides

Figure 8.1 Symptoms of sulfur dioxide injury to aspen. (Courtesy of U.S. Department of Agriculture.)

have caused local damage to forest and orchard trees when released into the atmosphere from ore reduction, fertilizer, and ceramics installations. The role of acid precipitation, including both wet and dry deposition of acidic substances, in influencing plant growth and especially that of forests, is also attracting considerable attention. At present, however, the effects of acid precipitation on forest productivity remain unknown, and most statements about "acid rain" are largely speculative. There are no research results indicating that acid precipitation has a direct damaging effect on forest vegetation, but the complexity of forest ecosystems makes it difficult to document such effects conclusively. The possibility of significant changes in species composition and forest productivity is currently under investigation (6).

Recent dieback and decline of forests in Scandinavia, Germany, northeastern United States, and of the red spruce and Fraser fir at high elevations in the southern Appalachians has been discussed in terms of acidic precipitation, but it is still not possible to determine the relation between reduction in tree growth, decline, and dieback on the one hand, and acid deposition on the other. In several countries of central and western Europe, a large-scale regional decline of many different forest ecosystems, collectively called *Waldsterben,* has occurred largely since about 1979. It has been widely assumed that atmospheric deposition of toxic, nutrient, acidifying, and growth-altering substances is involved. Several hypotheses have been advanced, and it is agreed at present that this decline is caused by a complex of several predisposing and stress-inducing factors, followed by a number of secondary effects of abiotic and biological origin (7).

Biotic or Infectious Agents Most diseases of forest trees are caused by various biotic agents. These include viruses, mycoplasmas, bacteria, fungi, parasitic higher plants, and nematodes. Of these the *fungi* cause the largest number of diseases as well as the greatest total loss. Examples of diseases caused by these agents are described in the following sections.

Diseases Caused by Viruses, Mycoplasmas, Bacteria, and Nematodes

Viruses are extremely small infectious agents visible only in the electron microscope. Although plant viruses cause many major diseases of important agricultural crops, known virus diseases of forest trees such as elm mosaic, birch line pattern, or black locust witches'-broom are apparently of minor importance (8). As their incidence becomes better known through future research, perhaps they will be considered of greater significance. Moreover, because vegetative propagation perpetuates viruses, the trend to plantation forestry—and in some species (e.g., poplars) an emphasis on vegetative propagation—will tend to increase the threat and extent of virus diseases in commercial forest plantings throughout the world.

A few tree diseases, formerly thought to be caused by viruses, are now known to result from infection by the smallest of free-living organisms, commonly referred to as *mycoplasmas*. They lack a cell wall but possess a distinct flexible membrane and are often smaller than bacteria. None is known to cause any diseases of major importance in American forestry, although one tree disease caused by a mycoplasma, phloem necrosis of American elm and winged elm, has killed many elms in the central United States. Mortality from this disease alone was considerable, but its presence in the area in which Dutch elm disease was introduced has made efforts to control the introduced disease, including attempts at breeding for resistance, more difficult than they would have been otherwise.

Bacteria cause diseases in species of all the important families of higher plants, but few are direct causes of disease in forest and shade trees. The bacterial canker of poplar is a serious disease in Europe but so far is unknown in North America. The United States prohibits all imports of poplar from Europe, largely because of this disease. No new clones for poplar culture are released in European countries without intensive selection and testing for resistance to this disease. With the objective of developing disease-free plants for international exchange, projects have been instituted in the United States and Europe to produce disease-free trees from tissue cultures. Successful trials should eventually open the way for safe transport of poplars and other tree species.

In many species of trees a water-soaked condition of the heartwood, called "wetwood," along with discoloration and production of gas (principally methane), is associated with bacteria, apparently as direct causes of the malady. If the wetwood core is punctured by wounds, stem breaks at branch crotches, or cracks or holes made to inject systemic fungicides, liquid is forced out of the tree by the abnormally high gas pressure, which is usually associated with wetwood. After the exudate is colonized by secondary miroorganisms, it is called "slime flux." Such bleeding or fluxing from injection wounds has become conspicuous now that stem injection is used to control Dutch elm disease in American elms in urban areas (9). The maintenance of an anaerobic situation and the presence of anaerobic bacteria, especially *Clostridum* spp. and *Methanobacterium* spp., are key factors in the production of wetwood rather than normal heartwood (10). Ring shake, a crack formed in the tree along an annual ring, lumber checking, and the abnormally long time required to dry lumber are problems associated with products from trees with wetwood. On the plus side, however, is another aspect of wetwood. *Abies* spp. commonly contain wetwood, and in such affected trees wood decay fungi were inhibited (11). Bacteria are also significant in the successional processes, causing discoloration and decay in the wood of trees. They are among the principal pioneer microorganisms that invade wounds and initiate the succession of changes that ultimately ends in decay of wood by fungi (12–14).

Plant-parasitic *nematodes* are microscopic eelworms of great importance as pests of agricultural and ornamental crops, yet we have little knowledge about nematode diseases of forest trees. This situation may be due partly to difficulties in measuring the loss of tree growth that is caused by damage to

feeder roots (15). Nematode attacks on roots that lead to dieback and abnormalities of roots, stunting of the plant, and even mortality have inflicted economic loss in tree nurseries (Figure 8.2). Most of the available information is on associations of nematodes with forest trees in plantations or natural stands, but evidence of pathogenicity (proof of parasitism) is usually lacking. Symptoms may include galling, devitalized root tips, and browning and shriveling of feeder roots, but such symptoms can also be produced by other organisms or soil conditions. Typical damage caused by nematodes gradually decreases the water-absorbing and nutrient-absorbing area of feeder roots; the afflicted trees slowly decline. In the southern United States high

Figure 8.2 Healthy sand pine on left and seedling injured by lance nemotodes on right. (Courtesy of U.S.D.A. Forest Service.)

densities of nematodes often occur in forest plantations that have been established on abandoned
farmlands, causing significant root damage and
stunting.

In sharp contrast to these reports on the indefi-
nite nature of nematode damage to forests are the
effects of the pine wood nematode, *Bursaphelen-
chus xylophilus*. In Japan this nematode causes a
lethal disease of Japanese red pine and black pine
and has been epidemic in the country for more than
thirty years. Since its identification in the United
States in 1979, the pine wood nematode has attracted much attention and concern that it could be a
serious menace to our pines. At present local epidemics have appeared in Illinois, largely on two
exotic pines, Austrian pine and Scots pine, but the
nematode may be considered endemic in numerous
other areas of the United States. In the United States,
however, the pine wood nematode does not seem to
be associated with the severe disease afflicting forests in Japan and at present appears not to pose a
threat to the coniferous forests of North America. It
may, however, continue to be damaging in areas
where the more susceptible species of pine are
planted, such as the large numbers of Scots pines in
landscape, windbreak, and Christmas tree plantings
in the central United States. The pine wood nematode disease has been termed the most destructive
of all pine diseases in Illinois (16), but it is likely to
cause major damage only to trees that have been
stressed or severely weakened by other biotic agents
or by unfavorable environmental influences (17).

In 1984 the pine wood nematode was discovered
in wood chips exported from the southern United
States. By 1986 all the Scandinavian countries, which
were the prime importers of chips from the United
States, had placed permanent embargos on all raw-
softwood shipments from the United States, Canada,
Japan, and other infested regions. This curtailment
in the export of southern pine chips to Nordic
countries was estimated to represent a loss of $20
million to the forest industry in the southern United
States. Although the risk of establishing the nematode in forests of foreign countries through importation of wood chips is deemed low, the embargoes
have had an impact on international trade.

Diseases Caused by Fungi

The most destructive agents causing disease in forest
trees are the fungi. These organisms are usually
classified as plants without chlorophyll and with a
very simple structure undifferentiated into stem,
leaves, and roots. The basic structural unit of most
fungi is a microscopic threadlike filament or tube
which contains the cytoplasm. These filaments or
hyphae in aggregate make up the mycelium or
vegetative body of the fungus. It is seen in the fuzzy
growth of the common bread mold or the white
mycelial fans beneath the bark of a tree root attacked
by the shoestring root rot fungus *Armillaria mellea*.
Fungi reproduce by spores produced on fruiting
structures that vary in complexity from a simple
hypha to complex bodies, such as the mushroom
that emerges from the soil or the bracket or "conk"
on the trunk of a tree with heartrot. Most fungus
spores are disseminated by wind, but there is also
chance distribution by agents such as splashing rain,
surface water and groundwater, insects, birds and
other animals, and even human beings. On a suitable substrate the spore germinates to form a simple
hypha or germ tube, which then elongates and
branches to form another mycelium (Figure 8.3).
Fungi live on organic material, either as *saprophytes*
on dead material or as *parasites* on living plants or
animals.

Most fungi are saprophytes, and the degradation
and consumption of dead organic material by saprophytic fungi is often designated as rot or decay. The
decay of heartwood in living forest trees is brought
about by a succession of activities by saprophytic
organisms and is responsible for over 70 percent of
the loss in forests attributed to diseases. The conversion of dead plant and animal remains on the forest
floor into humus is a beneficial act of saprophytic
fungi.

Some fungi are parasites and obtain their food
from living plants or animals. The activities of such
fungi disrupt the life processes of their hosts, and
disease results, as in the girdling of a stem by the
white pine blister rust fungus or the spotting and
death of longleaf pine needles by the brown spot
needle blight pathogen.

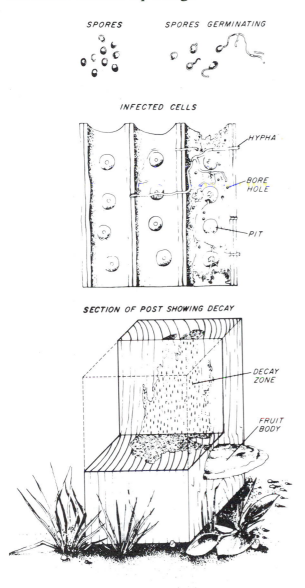

Figure 8.3 Cycle of decay. (Courtesy of U.S.D.A. Forest Products Laboratory.)

The activities of fungi cause both a loss of growth and mortality. The most numerous and most important diseases of forest trees are incited by fungi. These diseases vary enormously in the species and parts of tree affected, in symptoms, and in the type of damage they cause. Consequently, their effects on forest yield and their significance to forest management are also variable; some may be inconsequential, but others may be limiting factors in growth and management of a species.

A major objective in forestry is wood production. When wood of the tree trunk is utilized as food by fungi, the cell walls are degraded, altering the color and texture as well as physical and chemical properties of the wood. This process is known as *decay* or *rot*. The term "rot" is also applied to the result of the decay process; a wood rot is the type of decay caused by a particular species of fungus. Decay is caused primarily by fungi.

Heartrot

Most decay occurs in the central core of dead wood, or "heartwood," of the tree and is often termed *heartrot* (Figure 8.4). The sapwood is relatively resistant to decay in the living tree and protects the underlying heartwood against invasion by most decay fungi. Under some circumstances, however,

Figure 8.4 Typical brown cubical heartrot in a log of Douglas-fir. (Courtesy of Canadian Forestry Service, Pacific Forest Research Center, Victoria, B. C.)

some fungi may decay both sapwood and heart-wood.

The wood rots are commonly grouped into two main types, *brown* and *white rots*. These are classi-fied according to the type of decay process that ensues, but the predominant color changes are really incidental accompaniments of the decay pro-cess. Brown-rot fungi decompose wood by utilizing primarily the carbohydrates (cellulose) of the cell walls, whereas white-rot fungi utilize both the carbo-hydrate and lignin components of the cell wall. These differences are important in that they can affect the utilization of decayed wood. The wood is weakened by both types of decay, and rotted wood is of no use for construction. Pulp yields from white-rotted wood may be relatively high and of fairly good quality, whereas brown-rotted wood cannot be used. Chapter 23 contains further discussion of the chemical nature of wood.

Heartwood decay, which may make wood vol-ume unmarketable or lower its quality, has the greatest impact on the growth of forest trees of all destructive agents and accounts for over 70 percent of the total loss attributed to diseases of forest trees. Destruction of accumulated wood volume is the most significant factor in this loss, and the activities of decay fungi, since their effects are largely on dead wood cells, figure little in reducing vigor or in mortality. Of course, structural weakness can lead to increased storm damage.

Many different species of fungi cause heartrot, but each has its own particular manner of behavior and distinctive characteristics. Some attack many differ-ent tree species. The shoestring root rot fungus, *Armillaria mellea,* which may cause both root rot and heartrot of forest trees, has a host range extend-ing to both woody and nonwoody plants. The most important single decay of forest trees, red ring rot caused by *Phellinus (Fomes) pini,* occurs only in conifers. Others, such as the important white trunk rot fungus of aspen, *Phellinus (Fomes) tremulae,* are restricted to certain hardwood species. In some species such as trembling aspen, one or a very few species of decay fungi account for most of the volume loss from decay. In other species such as the

oaks and maples, many different fungi contribute significantly to the total decay loss. Interestingly, susceptibility or resistance to decay of wood in the living tree is no indication of durability of that wood in service.

Decay fungi have many different pathways of entry into the wood of a tree, and these *infection courts* are formed for the most part when protective barriers, such as the bark and sapwood of the tree, are wounded or damaged. Infection courts may include broken stems or branches, dead branch stubs, dead branches, and wounds of all kinds, including logging wounds and, in particular, fire scars.

In recent years *discoloration* and *decay* in the wood of forest trees have come to be recognized as complex processes involving typical successions of many organisms. A variety of organisms including bacteria, non-wood-rotting fungi, and true wood-rotting fungi all seem to be important in the pro-cesses that lead to discoloration and decay, even though the ultimate rotting of the wood may be due only to a certain species of fungus present in a given situation. During these processes the tree itself responds to this invasion; the response may be to compartmentalize or confine the decay to a certain limited portion of the tree trunk (12–14).

The amount of decay in forest stands is extremely variable. Generally the number of trees decayed and the total volume of decay increases as trees age. Events in the history of the stand influence its decay situation, for example, past fires, severe sleet and ice storms, and past silvicultural practices. Determining the amount of decay in given forest stands is impor-tant for the preparation of accurate inventories of present and potential growing stock; these invento-ries are basic to proper forest management. Forest-ers can estimate the amount of decay in a stand with information from sample plot measurements and by examining trees for external indicators of decay, such as fruiting bodies or "conks," swollen knots, and branch stubs (Figure 8.5). Gross volume esti-mates are corrected to net volumes by applying these decay estimates, expressed as cull factors or percentages of gross volume. Accurate determina-

Figure 8.5 Fruiting body of *Fomes fraxinophilus* on a stem of white ash. (Courtesy of U.S.D.A. Forest Service.)

tions of yields, allowable cuts, sales costs, and other factors necessary in timber management can then be made (see Chapter 12).

Decay in the forest is controlled for the most part by applying *preventive measures*. There is no "cure" for decay once it develops in the individual tree. Feasible control methods are aimed at (1) securing the greatest return in the harvesting of present merchantable (mostly virgin) stands, and (2) minimizing losses from decay in future stands.

Information on both qualitative and quantitative decay losses allow closer utilization, and thus greater yields, from diseased trees. The size and

other characteristics of the rot column can influence how the tree is utilized and thus the profit in logging. Decay losses can be reduced by refining technological and economic utilization practices; decayed material, especially white rots, can be used in pulp or in various specialty products such as veneer and plywood.

To reduce decay losses in our future stands, foresters must apply silvicultural practices, as described in Chapter 14. One such measure is the adjustment of rotation age and cutting cycles—for example, a rotation age of 70 years for balsam fir with cutting cycles of about 20 years, and cutting ages for aspen of about 50 years or less in the Great Lakes states and between 80 and 100 years in the West. Foresters now make considerable effort not to inflict logging and other operational injuries to trees in the residual stand, such as in selectively logged stands of northern hardwoods. In second-growth stands of ponderosa pine in the Southwest, future losses from red rot can be reduced by controlling the size of branches, by maintaining proper stand density, and by pruning. Other silvicultural practices that could help reduce decay are sanitation or timber stand improvement cuts to remove cull trees and early selective thinning of hardwood stump sprouts. Protecting trees against basal wounding from fire is particularly important because basal fire scars serve as infection courts for decay fungi. In the future, as forest management becomes more intensive and as trees are grown on shorter rotations, losses from decay may become less a factor than at present.

Root Rots

A substantial portion of a tree exists in the soil, and in this very complex belowground environment trees develop root diseases that are among the most telling causes of loss and among the most difficult to control. *Fungi* are the most important agents of root disease. Some may attack only young, succulent roots such as the feeder roots, essentially causing the tree to decline through starvation. Others, acting as wood-destroying fungi, kill the roots by parasitic attack and then decay the killed roots, causing a *root rot* of all or of a portion of the root system.

Root diseases may kill the tree, and they can interfere with the vigor of growth, density, form, and composition of a forest stand, all the way from the seedling stage to the rotation age. They may kill even dominant and codominant trees that would otherwise form part of the final crop. Some root diseases cause *butt rot*—decay of the basal stem portion—causing a loss of growth and reduction in both volume and quality. Decay of the root system makes trees especially subject to windthrow. Underground spread of the causal fungus from a focal point of infection frequently causes disease to appear in patches.

Root disease may have an important effect on the silviculture and management of forests. Conversely, one of the important problems facing many forest managers is the effect that various forestry practices have on the subsequent incidence and development of root disease. Forest plantations are particularly liable to damage from root rots. The forest manager must often take special preventive measures to avoid root rots in such stands.

One of the most important root rots in forests throughout the world is caused by the honey mushroom, or the shoestring root rot fungus, heretofore known as *Armillaria mellea* (Figure 8.6). The role of the fungus as a pathogen has been controversial over the years. The fungus has sometimes been described as an aggressive killer of healthy trees, sometimes as only a secondary pathogen of trees of reduced vigor. *Armillaria mellea* is known also as a saprophyte and in this role causes dead residual roots in the soil to decay and heartrot of standing trees. Recent taxonomic and genetic studies have delineated the *A. mellea* complex into several different species in Europe, North America, and Australia and New Zealand (18). This more detailed classification has helped to explain some of the variations in pathogenicity, symptom expression, and host preferences that were observed in the past in disease situations ascribed to the fungus traditionally classified as *A. mellea*.

For all species the infection cycle is similar. After colonization of a food base such as a tree stump or a

Figure 8.6 Clump of mushroom fruiting bodies produced by the shoestring root rot fungus, *Armillaria mellea,* at the base of a white pine sapling killed by the fungus. Notice the white mycelial fan on the stem and the characteristic resin-infiltrated mass of soil around the root collar.

root system, the fungus spreads through the soil by black, shoestringlike strands of mycelium. Called *rhizomorphs,* these strands can penetrate the healthy bark of living roots and initiate infection and colonization of new substrate as far as several meters from the original food base. Spread by direct root-to-root contact is also possible. The fungus attacks the living tissue of the roots as a parasite and continues activity as a saprophyte in rotting the dead woods of roots and the butt of the tree. Damage resulting from *Armillaria* root rot varies greatly, but it is of concern to forest managers in most of the temperate regions of the world. As research to determine the identity of the *Armillaria* species causing individual disease situations continues, the interactions between pathogen and suscept will become clarified. We shall better understand the role of the pathogen complex as a cause of root disease in the forest.

Root and butt rot caused by *Heterobasidion annosum (Fomes annosus)* is one of the most important forest tree diseases in Europe, especially in coniferous plantations. In the United States it is present in many forest regions, but it is a special problem in pine plantations in the South, after they have been thinned; and in second-growth stands, of western hemlock in particular, in the Pacific Northwest. Infection commonly begins with germination of the wind-borne spores on freshly cut stump surfaces. The fungus colonizes the stump and grows down into the root system, from which through root contact it can infect the roots of healthy adjacent trees. Colonization of new root systems causes root rot along with subsequent butt rot and sometimes mortality of the formerly healthy trees to which the fungus has spread. Stump infection can often be prevented in the South by treating stumps with borax immediately after trees are cut. On hemlock in the Pacific Northwest borax has not been as effective as on southern pines, and other chemicals such as zinc chloride are being tried. Another preventive measure successful on pines, both in the South and in England, is applying to the stump surface a spore suspension of a competitive fungus, *Phlebia (Peniophora) gigantea*. This fungus colonizes the stump and prevents *Heterobasidion annosum* from becoming established, but it does not itself cause disease in the residual trees. This technique is an excellent example of *biological control* applied to forest disease management.

The reduction of root disease losses is a formidable task because of the difficulties in diagnosing root disease and in determining the complex relationships among root pathogens, the tree host, and the soil environment. As information accumulates, it is integrated with our knowledge of silviculture to formulate the best possible management practices. For example, *Phellinus (Poria) weirii* root rot is the most destructive disease of young-growth Douglas-fir in the Pacific Northwest of the United States and in British Columbia (Figure 8.7). Because of the inten-

Figure 8.7 Wind-thrown trees in a *Phellinus weirii* infection center of a 50-year-old stand of Douglas-fir. (Courtesy of G. W. Wallis and Canadian Forestry Service, Pacific Forest Research Center, Victoria, B. C.)

sity and extensive distribution of the disease, foresters have considered various proposals for managing it on infested sites. The usual management strategies available to the forest, such as shortened rotation and intensive salvage, may keep some of the trees from dying, but inoculum is still present on the site and the effects of the disease in the next stand are the same. New strategies for managing laminated root rot are under investigation in long-term field tests. Control strategies being tried include land clearing and removing stumps where this is topographically and economically feasible, fertilizing an infested site with large amounts of nitrogen before reforestation, reducing inoculum by treating stumps or trees with chemicals that kill *P. weirii,* introducing into infested stumps naturally occurring antagonistic microorganisms, and changing to less susceptible species for the site. A major objective of such investigations is to give the land manager some measure of flexibility in dealing with this disease (19).

Deterioration of Killed or Injured Timber

When trees are killed by various agencies such as fire, windthrow, or insects, the dead sapwood deteriorates so rapidly that within a few years salvage may not be economically possible. Sapwood in living trees is relatively resistant to decay, but after trees are killed sapwood is readily susceptible to invasion by microorganisms and insects. The first invaders are stain fungi and wood-boring insects, and damage occurs through seasoning checks as the sapwood dries. Next, the wood-destroying fungi attack, and later the same or different fungi invade the heartwood. The younger the timber, the more rapidly it deteriorates, because of its smaller size and greater proportion of sapwood to heartwood. Fortunately, much of the wood in stands of overmature, large-sized timber—particularly of species with relatively decay-resistant heartwood such as Douglas-fir—may be salvageable for many years after the trees have died. The cause of death, whether insects, fire, or whatever, figures in the rate of deterioration and the succession of organisms, both of which in turn ordain what time is available for salvage to reduce the loss from the catastrophe.

One of the beneficial aspects of decay in the forest is the breakdown and decay of *logging slash*. The economical disposal of logging slash remains a problem in fire protection and stand improvement. The rate of breakdown and decay varies widely in major forest types. Our accumulated knowledge of slash decay has important implications for forest protection and management, since the amount of slash is closely related to the fire hazard and may affect the nature of the seedbed available for natural reproduction.

Stain and Decay of Forest Products

Just as stains and decay can develop in standing trees in the forest, they can develop in wood after the tree is felled, during storage and seasoning, and in wood that is in service. Extensive losses are produced by such deterioration, costing hundreds of millions of dollars annually. Most of such deterioration can be controlled by applying relatively simple preventive techniques when handling and using the product. The control methods are derived from knowledge about the causes of wood deterioration and about what factors favor the causal agents.

Wood stains are confined largely to sapwood and cause unsightly discolorations that make the wood unacceptable for many uses such as furniture, paneling, food containers, and similar products whose appearance is important. Fungus stains appear for the most part in freshly cut logs during the period they are held and in green lumber and veneer. The most common sap stain is called "blue stain" because of the blue-gray to black color imparted to the wood penetrated by the hyphae of the causal fungi. Surface molds impart various colors to lumber and veneer by their masses of spores; these can be brushed or planed off lumber but cannot be removed as easily from veneer. Less important are stains caused by enzymatic reactions, by excessive heating during processing, and by weathering. Fungus stains and molds develop under favorable moisture and temperature conditions and occur most commonly during warm, humid weather. Prevention is the only means of controlling fungus stains, and rapid drying by air seasoning or in a kiln is the most effective method. Fungicide dips for lumber and chemical treatments of log ends may help prevent staining when drying is ineffective.

Wood-destroying fungi can cause decay in wood products when conditions foster their growth. Such conditions are the presence of oxygen, temperatures generally in the range from above freezing to about 35°C (95°F), and a moisture content of the wood above the fiber saturation point, approximately 25 to 32 percent of the dry weight of the wood. Excluding oxygen by storing logs and pulpwood in water or under sprinkling systems is one method of preventing decay. For most wood products the key to controlling decay is to dry wood quickly to a moisture content of 20 percent or less, and to keep it dry. When wood is used in places with little risk of decay, proper construction practices will minimize losses to decay (Figure 8.8). Durability of wood varies with the species, and some protection against decay is offered through proper selection of species for particular uses. When the risk of decay is high, as it is for wood placed in contact with soil, *preservation* of wood by chemical toxicants can control decay. A variety of both water-soluble and oil-soluble preservatives are available, and applications vary from brushing or dipping to high-pressure treatment.

Canker Diseases

A number of causal agents, but mostly a variety of fungi, can cause relatively localized areas of bark and cambium tissues on trunks, branches, and even twigs of trees to die. These lesions are termed "cankers," and even though they may be caused by unrelated incitants, including nonliving agents, many of the more important canker diseases have important similarities. Cankers may be annual or perennial. Perennial cankers continue activity over a period of years. Some may be a diffuse type, whereby the pathogen grows rapidly through the host bark with little or no callus development. Such cankers eventually girdle the stem and kill the tree. Others are long-standing and more limited in extent with continual production of callus tissue, often in concentric ridges or layers. These are called "target" cankers. The progress of the pathogen is slow as it gradually enlarges the lesion. Some canker fungi also extend into the wood beneath the face of the

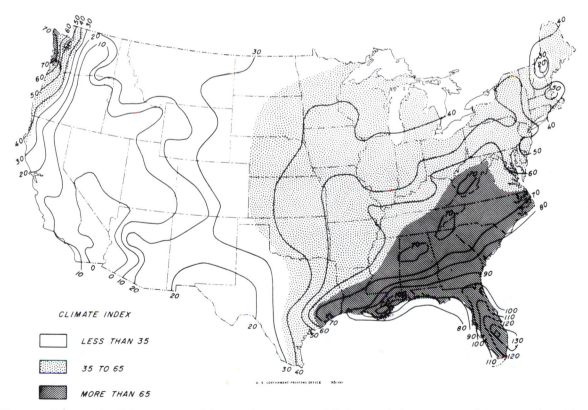

CLIMATE INDEX

☐ LESS THAN 35

▒ 35 TO 65

▓ MORE THAN 65

U. S. GOVERNMENT PRINTING OFFICE   R5-141

Figure 8.8 Levels of decay potential for wood in aboveground service, exposed to weather, based on a climate index derived from standard temperature and rainfall data. In darker areas wood is more vulnerable to decay. (Courtesy of U.S.D.A. Forest Products Laboratory.)

canker and cause the stem to decay, making it susceptible to wind breakage at the canker. The *Hypoxylon* canker of aspen and the *Eutypella* canker of maple cause such damage (Figure 8.9). Canker diseases occur in both gymnosperms and angiosperms, but they are most numerous and of greatest significance in deciduous hardwoods. The *Hypoxylon* canker of aspen, the most important disease in the Great Lakes area, can decimate entire young stands. Unfortunately, no suitable control methods are known.

Most of the persistent perennial cankers do not kill the host tree, but they do cause malformation of the stem and discolor the wood. They reduce quality and may reduce volume, often of the lowest, most valuable log of the tree. The characteristics of such canker diseases as *Nectria* canker of many important hardwoods and *Eutypella* canker of sugar maple have implications for the control of these diseases. Stands under intensive management can be handled so that cankers are recognized in their incipient state and young infected trees are removed from the stand early.

Perhaps the most notorious of all forest diseases, *chestnut blight,* caused by the fungus *Cryphonectria (Endothia) parasitica,* is a canker disease of the diffuse, rapidly developing type. Apparently introduced on nursery stock imported from the Orient, this fungus was first noticed in 1904 in the New York Zoological Park. In less than fifty years it had spread throughout the natural range of the American chestnut and destroyed it as a commercial species. Chestnut blight caused the most spectacular devastation ever wrought by a known forest tree disease. Today sprouts from persisting stumps and root systems continue to appear but eventually are killed by the disease before they mature. Scientists have attempted to breed disease-resistant chestnuts by hybridizing resistant Asian species. Their considerable efforts to obtain a resistant tree of good timber type have been only partially successful, however. Since the mid-1960s chestnut blight has again attracted considerable attention. Researchers have demonstrated that inoculating certain strains of the pathogen that have limited virulence (hypovirulent) in trees can heal cankers and protect against infection by the virulent strain. After the first report of chestnut blight in Italy in 1938, an epidemic ensued, but then slowed, presumably because hypovirulent strains spread naturally. Today there is little killing of the Italian chestnut by blight cankers.

Although in the United States there seems to be little natural spread of such controlling agents, on commercial plantations in France artificial inoculations with mixtures of hypovirulent strains have had some success. Continuing research on the transmissible and competitive nature of the genes controlling this hypovirulent expression is in progress with the hope that we will gain practical biological control of this disease in the United States (20, 21).

Vascular Wilt Diseases

The vascular *wilt* diseases are caused by fungi that grow principally in the xylem vessels. Their activity reduces or inhibits normal water conduction in the stem, so that the tree wilts and dies. Wilt diseases are of primary significance in angiosperms, and some of the most publicized tree diseases are in this group, including *Verticillium* wilt, Dutch elm disease, and oak wilt. With some, such as *Verticillium* wilt, roots are directly infected from soil, but with others the fungi move underground from tree to tree through root grafts and above ground by insect vectors. One approach to control has been by breaking the root

Figure 8.9 Stem breakage and cankering (arrows) in a stand of aspen trees severely affected by *Hypoxylon* canker.

connections between trees either mechanically or with soil fumigants. Other efforts have been directed toward the insect vectors, in particular the elm bark beetles for control of Dutch elm disease.

Dutch elm disease has killed many elm trees in the forest, but its greatest impact has been on the most susceptible species, shade and ornamental American elms in urban environments. Introduced into the United States from Europe, the disease was discovered first in Ohio and some east-central states in the early 1930s, but it has since spread westward to the Pacific Coast states.

Dutch elm disease is the most destructive shade tree disease in the United States today, and the cost of control, or even of merely removing the killed trees because of the hazard they pose, amounts to millions of dollars annually. The causal fungus is transmitted overland by the European elm bark beetle and the native elm bark beetle. Local spread from a diseased to a healthy tree through root grafts is also very prevalent and is responsible for much of the mortality that has occurred in rows of street trees.

Control efforts have been considered successful when losses in a community are kept under about 2 percent annually. The organized program for control may encompass strict sanitation, spraying to control insect vectors, attempts at preventing root graft spread, good tree maintenance, and prompt replacement of killed trees with nonsusceptible species. Programs to develop resistant elms have released several selections both here and in Europe (see Figure 5.5). The treatment of individual elms by injecting trunk or roots with systemic fungicides is also showing promise.

Oak wilt, caused by a fungus closely related to the Dutch elm disease pathogen, is a native disease and perhaps the most serious disease of oaks in the north-central United States. All oak species are susceptible, but symptoms and severity vary, depending on whether the affected tree is a member of the red oak group, in which killing is relatively rapid, or of the white oak group, in which wilt symptoms develop more slowly, over a period of several years. Local spread through root grafts may allow the fungus to kill large pockets of trees in a forest (Figure 8.10).

Oak wilt may be spread overland by sap-feeding

Figure 8.10 Large oak wilt "pocket" in an oak forest stand continues to enlarge by marginal spread through root grafts.

beetles in the family Nitidulidae and possibly by some other insect vectors that are, however, much less efficient than are the vectors for the Dutch elm disease pathogen. Control of local spread through root grafts is expensive but effective. Roots are cut by mechanical trenching or root sections are killed by injecting the soil with chemical fumigants, especially Vapam (sodium N-methyldithiocarbamate). Overland spread is difficult to control, and the major objectives of such efforts have been to reduce the abundance of inoculum by girdling and removing diseased trees and by preventing unnecessary wounding.

Oak wilt is not known to be present in Europe, but the Commission of European Communities (CEC) has expressed concern that the pathogen may be introduced to the forests of that continent. Restrictions have been placed recently by the CEC on the importation of oak logs and lumber from the United States. The forest industry and government agencies are now conducting research to determine whether standards can be less restrictive and still ensure the safety of oak exports.

Rust Fungi

The *rust fungi,* so called because of the rusty orange color of so many of their spore forms, constitute a group of highly specialized parasitic fungi. Species in this group attack cones of certain conifers, leaves of both hardwoods and conifers, and stems of conifers (Figure 8.11). Many of the fungi in this group are unique in that they require two different and widely unrelated host plants to complete their life cycle. Moreover, most of the rusts produce five different spore stages appearing in a definite sequence, although some species have as few as one. Thus *Cronartium ribicola,* the cause of the *white pine blister rust* disease, produces pycniospores (spermatia) and aeciospores on white pines, and three other spore forms (urediniospores, teliospores, and basidiospores) on the alternate host plants, which are currants and gooseberries in the genus *Ribes*. Stem rusts of conifers, especially white pine blister rust and fusiform rust of southern pines, are diseases of major impact in natural forests and plantations.

Figure 8.11 Aecial pustules or "blisters" containing orange masses of aeciospores on a branch canker of white pine blister rust.

White pine blister rust, like chestnut blight and Dutch elm disease, is an introduced foreign disease. This fungus, a native of Asia, spread to Europe and from there was introduced to North America on imported white pine planting stock in about 1900. On this continent it found a number of highly susceptible hosts in the white (five-needle) pines, and it has spread to become their most serious disease and one of the limiting factors in growth and management of our commercially important white pines. The fungus produces branch and stem cankers that girdle and may kill trees of all ages and sizes, although the disease is most important as a cause of death of seedlings and trees of the younger age classes up to pole-sized trees.

For many years, and at a cost of millions of dollars, foresters attempted to control the fungus in both the

East and the West by large-scale eradication of currants and gooseberries. Theoretically this approach seemed possible, as explained later in the section on influences on disease occurrence and development. But after many years of trial it proved not to be feasible, especially in the West. It was impracticable because of the high susceptibility of western white and sugar pines, climatic conditions which are extremely favorable for spread and infection, and the impossibility of completely eliminating the alternate host plants. Sufficient spores were still produced on remaining plants to cause highly damaging levels of infection in the pine stands. By about 1970 ribes eradication had been abandoned in the West, and in the East ribes "suppression" is being used only to protect eastern white pine in some forest nurseries and forest stands in a few restricted areas.

The most promising hope for control of white pine blister rust lies in selecting and breeding resistant trees (22). Programs for developing resistant planting stock of eastern white pine for the East and of western white and sugar pines for the West are making good progress, and some seed orchards already have been established (see Chapter 5). Of course, the tree breeder recognizes the great biological variability that exists not only in trees but in pathogens as well, and breeders and pathologists work with this knowledge as a basis for their tree improvement operations. For a long period there was no information on the occurrence of "races" or forms of white pine blister rust fungus with differing degrees of virulence, or with different pathogenic capabilities; however, in recent years evidence of pathogenic variation in the rust fungus has accumulated. The Champion Mine strain, which appeared first in 1970 in the Cascade Range of central Oregon, has the best documentation for being a new virulent strain of *Cronartium ribicola* (23).

Research must continue to determine what implications this, and perhaps other pathogenic strains that may appear in the future, have for rust resistance breeding and development programs. Clearly, breeders must incorporate the widest possible genetic diversity in their programs, and the forest manager must use resistance only where necessary and as only one component of a program for integrated management of white pine blister rust. For the management of present natural stands of western white pine, researchers have recommended selecting "leave trees" with a high probability of producing progeny for the next generation that will exhibit increased resistance to blister rust.

The *fusiform rust* of southern pines is a good example of a disease that has been widely spread through human activities in the forest. Loblolly and slash pine, the main pine hosts, are killed by the development of fusiform-shaped galls or "cankers," whereas longleaf pine is relatively resistant and shortleaf pine essentially immune (Figure 8.12). Oaks are the alternate hosts on which the spores that infect the pines are produced. Unlike the introduced white pine blister rust, this fungus had developed through the ages as a part of the natural forest ecosystems in the southern United States. Prior to 1900 it was rare and little more than a curiosity. After clearcutting and logging of the virgin forest, distribution of the pine hosts was markedly altered. The original stands of longleaf pine were replaced by the highly susceptible slash and loblolly pines, which were favored by the introduction of fire protection and the artificial restocking of the site by planting. Such extensive cutting also favored the release of oaks, which increased in abundance. This combination of circumstances favored buildup of the rust to a level that now constitutes a major epidemic. In the United States the disease has been estimated to be increasing at the rate of 2 to 3 percent per year and causes approximately $75 million worth of damage annually (24).

The management of fusiform rust in southern pine forests is a major component of southern pine forest management and represents a synthesis of available knowledge about the disease and practical methods of forest management. The principal strategies are prevention of the disease in pine nurseries and young stands and minimization of losses in diseased stands. Seedlings in nurseries can be protected by applying fungicides, especially newly developed systemic fungicides such as triadimefon.

Various silvicultural procedures are recommended to minimize losses in rust-infected stands.

Figure 8.12 Spindle-shaped gall on the main stem of a loblolly pine, induced by *Cronartium fusiforme* (Courtesy of U.S.D.A. Forest Service.)

The primary effort to keep rust from attacking young stands is to develop and use resistant planting stock both from natural sources and from tree improvement programs. A South-wide seed source study had demonstrated that seed from specific geographic areas around the periphery of the natural range of loblolly pine produced seedlings with relatively high levels of resistance to fusiform rust. Bulk collection of seed from these areas yields seedlings with enough resistance to reduce rust incidence by at least one-third. By 1972 seeds from these areas were commercially available. One of the sources of seed most heavily used for subsequent plantings is Livingston Parish, Louisiana.

A cooperative Rust Resistance Testing Center was established near Asheville, North Carolina, to improve the efficiency of the widespread tree improvement operations in the South (25). The center evaluates resistance in progenies, originally from slash and loblolly pine selections, and more recently from longleaf pine. Clonal selections identified through such progeny testing are now being incorporated in rust-resistant seed orchards, and seedlings derived from the seed produced by these orchards are being planted on a large scale throughout the South. A further measure to improve control is the development of a seedling seed orchard, which may increase the percentage and quality of resistance as well as broaden the genetic base of the trees in the rust-resistant seed orchard, thus ensuring a greater diversity of genetic material in the outplantings (26, 27). Eventually hybrids between various species of pine to obtain fusiform rust resistance may be incorporated in the disease management program, and it is anticipated that the loblolly pine × shortleaf pine hybrid in particular will prove valuable in certain areas at high risk for rust.

Numerous other stem rusts occur on conifers, some of which may cause extensive damage in local areas. One of these, the pine–pine gall rust (western gall rust) caused by *Endocronartium harknessii,* has a high probability of limiting improvements in lodgepole pine and ponderosa pine. When large-scale breeding programs with these species get under way, selection for resistance to this disease, as well as for the other characteristics that are economically valuable, should have a high priority. Of somewhat less importance are many foliage rusts both of conifers and hardwoods. The *Melampsora* rusts of poplars have received increased attention because losses from premature defoliation have become a greater threat with the increasing emphasis on plantations of hybrid poplars or cottonwood, particularly in the South.

Foliage Diseases

The foliage of hardwoods have numerous diseases, but most of these are seldom considered serious. Leaf diseases that cause major defoliation or that attack and damage most of the leaves so that their normal functioning is impaired have the greatest impact. Growth and vigor may be reduced, but the time of year of the attack and shoot and foliage characteristics of the tree greatly influence the amount of damage caused. Sometimes leaf diseases can become limiting factors in growth of a species. Since about 1960 the *Marssonina leaf blight* has become of considerable significance in the culture of hybrid poplars in Europe. The *Melampsora leaf rust* has also been of major concern in hybrid poplar culture. Systems for evaluating the resistance of clones to both these diseases have been developed. In the United States *Melampsora* leaf rust has been the most damaging to hybrid poplars. As more and more hybrid poplars and cottonwood are grown in this country, there is evidence that both diseases represent potential threats. Hybrid poplars and cottonwood should be bred for disease resistance, as discussed in Chapter 5 (28).

Extensive foliage injury to conifers may result in severe damage or death. Generally defoliation reduces increment growth in proportion to the degree of defoliation, and there is usually an accompanying reduction in vigor. Quality reduction is also important in ornamentals, especially in Christmas trees; a single year of attack may completely destroy the marketability of the crop. The *needle cast fungi,* as exemplified by *Lophodermium,* often cause rather spectacular epidemics, especially in nurseries and plantations. There are fungicidal sprays to control *Lophodermium* needle cast. Attempts to protect nursery seedlings, and in the north-central states, Scots pine trees in Christmas tree plantations, by applying these sprays, have been relatively successful.

In the West a related fungus, *Elytroderma deformans,* causes the most serious needle disease of

pines, particularly ponderosa, Jeffrey, and lodgepole pines. The fungus is prevalent in western forests at a low, endemic level, but occasionally in some areas it builds up to epidemic proportions. The fungus initially infects needles of pines but eventually grows into branch tissues and there within the phloem region. After an outbreak the fungus persists in infected trees for years, reducing vigor and growth, and eventually killing the trees. Conditions that lead to the buildup of epidemic outbreaks are not well understood, and in high-risk sites there is still a potential for a loss of growth and periodic heavy mortality from *Elytroderma* disease (29).

The brown spot needle blight, caused by *Scirrhia acicola* (recently reclassified as *Mycosphaerella dearnessii*) (Figure 8.13), has also produced extensive damage in Christmas tree plantations of Scots pine, especially in the Great Lakes regions. Furthermore, it has proved to be a major obstacle to

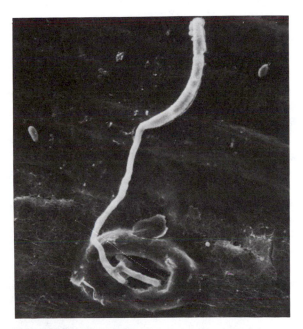

Figure 8.13 Growth of a germ tube of a conidiospore of the brown spot fungus, *Scirrhia acicola,* on a needle of Scots pine, and development in the stomatal antechamber as seen with the scanning electron microscope.

production of longleaf pine in the South, where it defoliates seedlings and kills young trees or greatly delays their growth, keeping them in the "grass stage" for unacceptably long periods. Because longleaf pine possesses a fire-resistant terminal bud, prescribed burning in young established plantations during the dormant season will often control brown spot needle blight.

In New Zealand another needle disease, caused by a fungus usually known by the name for its imperfect state, *Dothistroma septospora* (or *D. pini*), once threatened the forest industry. Plantings of exotic pine species, especially two American species that are highly susceptible to this fungus, Monterey and ponderosa pine, were the culprits. This was one instance in forestry in which control by protective chemical sprays proved feasible. Aerial sprays of copper fungicide on a large scale have been both effective and economical in controlling a disease that might otherwise have had disastrous consequences.

Insect–Fungus Complexes

Insects and fungi interact in many interesting and unique relationships in the forest ecosystem. Some of these bear on our consideration of losses in timber productivity from forest insects and diseases. Fungus–insect associations may result in diseases that can be considered to have multiple causal agents, such as the beech bark disease discussed later in the chapter, in the section on disease complexes. Moreover, insects have important roles in the incidence of some vascular wilt diseases, as noted for Dutch elm disease and oak wilt.

A significant relationship between insects and fungi that is commonly encountered by the forester is the association of *blue-stain fungi* with *bark beetles* (see Chapter 7). Bark beetles have a special repository in which spores of blue-stain fungi are carried. The spores are inoculated into trees when the beetles tunnel beneath the bark; after spore germination the mycelium grows in cells of both phloem and xylem. Eventually large sectors of sapwood are colonized. Cells are killed, the wood is stained blue, the trunk is girdled by nonfunctional

sapwood, and eventually the tree declines and dies. Thus, not only are trees killed quickly through the disastrously successful interaction of the symbiotic insect–fungus complex, but the wood is also degraded by stain. Efforts to control bark beetle epidemics by chemical sprays, salvage logging, and other techniques have temporary effects only, but these may complement preventive management practices aimed at reducing stand susceptibility, as discussed in Chapter 7.

Another example is a similar association between *Sirex* wood wasps and their *Amylostereum* fungal symbionts, which cause damage or death of trees in the genus *Pinus*. In all species of *Sirex* investigated, adult females carry a symbiotic fungus, either *Amylostereum areolatum* or *A. chailletii,* in a pair of intersegmental sacs. When eggs are deposited the spores of the fungus are placed in the wood; there the fungus grows around the resulting holes and larval tunnels. The *Sirex* wood wasp larvae obtain some nutrition from the fungus, and the fungus is dispersed and inoculated into its host. Activities of both organisms combine to damage and even kill the tree. Although *Sirex* wood wasps are known in many parts of the world, the *Sirex–Amylostereum* association has caused major damage only in New Zealand and Australia to plantations of Monterey pine. Attacks by *Sirex noctilio* in these countries were mostly on trees under stress from either environmental or biological factors.

Mistletoes

Mistletoes are true seed plants, perennial evergreens that are parasitic on stems or branches of trees or shrubs. The leafy, or so-called true, mistletoes are really semiparasites and are well known largely for their ornamental and sentimental uses at Christmastime. They occur chiefly on hardwoods, but some grow on a few conifer species, especially juniper, cypress, and incense cedar. They are most abundant in warmer regions and especially in the arid Southwest. In general, the true mistletoes have not caused major economic damage in forest stands of the United States.

The numerous *dwarf mistletoe* species, however, in the genus *Arceuthobium,* have come to be recognized as the single most important disease problem in conifer forests of the western United States; damage ranks second to that caused by heartrot (Figure 8.14). Once remaining virgin stands are cut, losses from the effects of dwarf mistletoe will exceed those from decay. Management of affected stands is a major silvicultural problem (30). In the East only one species occurs, causing problems in management of black spruce, especially in Minnesota.

The parasitic growth of these tiny plants stunts growth of the host to an extreme extent. Often abnormal branches known as *witches'-broom* grow in the crown, the leader and branches die back, and eventually the tree dies. The parasite spreads in the stand by forcible ejection of sticky seeds for distances of 12 meters or more. Isolated new infection centers may be established when seeds are carried by birds.

Management of affected stands to reduce losses consists mostly of direct control measures: physical removal of infected trees or their parts by pruning, poisoning, burning, or cutting entire trees. Treat-

Figure 8.14 Shoots of dwarf mistletoe emerging from an infected branch of ponderosa pine. (Courtesy of U.S.D.A. Forest Service.)

ments of sawtimber or pole-sized stands are designed to eradicate dwarf mistletoe through silvicultural practices. The objective is to obtain and retain stands free of dwarf mistletoe after the harvest cutting. For some areas there are computer simulation programs that enable foresters to examine a number of alternatives for managing dwarf mistletoe-infected stands and decide on the best treatment to meet management objectives.

Influences on Disease Occurrence and Development

The forest is a dynamic community of plants and animals interacting in a constantly changing environment. It follows a successional development governed by the interactions of all the living organisms and the site. Moreover, the site will also change with the successional development of the forest, as discussed in Chapter 6.

During the course of a forest's development, there is also a succession of diseases. These may affect not only whether individual trees survive early in their development but also the later development of the forest (31). This principle of dynamic interaction between the forest and its environment emphasizes a major concept relating to disease. A disease does not necessarily result from the mere juxtaposition of a *susceptible host* and a *virulent pathogen;* there must also be a *favorable environment.* Furthermore, these must interact in relation to *time.* The disease triangle of host–pathogen–environment is given a three-dimensional aspect when these components are related to time to form a disease *pyramid* (1).

This concept of the disease pyramid is well illustrated by the environmental influences on the white pine blister rust disease. The causal fungus, *Cronartium ribicola,* requires two different types of host plants for completion of its life cycle: the white pines and the currants and gooseberries in the genus *Ribes.* Spores produced on leaves of ribes plants infect the pine through the needles, and the fungus grows into branches and stems where it forms girdling lesions or cankers (see Figure 8.11). The spores produced in the blisters that erupt from stem cankers cannot reinfect pines but can only infect the leaves of ribes plants, thus completing the cycle. The fungus is delicately adjusted to seasonal changes and weather conditions, so that unfavorable conditions at one period may prevent any significant number of new pine infections for that year. In general, moist growing seasons favor intensification and spread of blister rust, and dry seasons hold it in check. The most critical periods are those influencing germination of the spores that infect pine and ribes. The formation and germination of basidiospores, which infect the pine needle, require a period of at least 18 hours of high-moisture conditions, either relative humidities above 96 percent or contact with a film of free water, and temperatures within reasonable limits, above freezing but below about 20°C (68°F). A period of hot, dry weather preceding this time of germination unfavorably affects development of the fungus on the ribes leaves, and chances for pine to escape infection are increased.

One method of control has been to remove the alternate host from the vicinity of pines and thereby protect them from infection. Establishing protection zones from which ribes have been eradicated is based on the extreme susceptibility of basidiospores to drying and on evidence that infection of pines decreases rapidly with increasing distance from the ribes bushes that harbor the spores. Accumulated knowledge about the microclimatic relations of blister rust has made it possible to predict the blister rust potential of various sites and to delineate infection hazard zones in the Great Lakes states. Control of the disease by ribes eradication and by silvicultural procedures, including pruning a portion of the lower crowns of crop trees, can be modified for each zone. Pruning protects trees from infection in the high-hazard zone by removing needles likely to be infected within about 6 to 10 feet of the ground; the great majority of infections occur in this area on young trees. Thus consideration of the interrelated components of a particular disease helps the pathologist and the forest manager to determine the major factors governing its occurrence and development and to plan an appropriate disease management strategy that will minimize losses.

Our continuing efforts to make timber supply meet timber demand inevitably encourage more intensive forest management practices. Intensive practices bring both dangers and benefits. The risk of disease may increase because residual trees receive more wounds or because stumps in thinned stands serve as infection courts for root rot fungi. On the other hand, in short-rotation management, salvage or disease-preventive measures may give better protection and reduce losses. Silvicultural operations may change the interrelations of the components of the disease pyramid so that the probability of disease and consequent loss is either fostered or lessened.

Disease Complexes

The concept that the forest is a dynamic community in which organisms interact under the influence of a constantly changing environment has been well established. Often the trees are affected by a number of stress factors acting in concert or in succession, so that it is sometimes difficult to assign priority to one rather than another as a disease-producing agent. Thus diseases may result from the action of joint causal agents. Moreover, the activity of, or the result of activity by, a specific causal agent may be so modified by environmental influences that a disease may or may not be initiated and develop.

The influence of environmental stresses on the incidence and development of disease is sometimes called *predisposition*. Two of the most common "predisposing" factors to disease are water stresses or drought and freezing. Although these and other similar factors can directly damage plants, they can also seriously weaken plants. Many nonaggressive pathogens, often thought of as "secondary" organisms, may then act in combination with stress to attack weakened (or predisposed) trees and cause disease, producing a syndrome that often encompasses cankers, dieback, and general decline (32).

Among such diseases are several declines and die-backs of sugar maple and also oak decline and the mortality in the Northeast initiated by the stress of gypsy moth defoliation.

The *beech bark disease* is an example of a disease that has more than one causal agent. It is caused by fungi that infect minute feeding wounds made by scale insects in the bark of beech. The principal fungus is *Nectria coccinea* var. *faginata,* although other species of *Nectria* may also be involved. The fungus may infect large areas on the trunks of some trees, completely girdling and killing them, whereas on other trees narrow strips of bark are infected, parts of the crown become chlorotic and die, and the tree survives in a weakened state for many years. Little injury is caused by each organism attacking separately.

Beech bark disease has transformed beech in the Maritime provinces of Canada to a poorly formed, low-grade weed species and rendered it an unimportant component of the hardwood forests of that area. The disease spread through New England and is now in western New York and Pennsylvania. The aftermath zone in Maine and New Hampshire, where the disease has been present for the longest time, now comprises a forest of beech sprout thickets of diseased and highly defective trees. These arose after the severe mortality from the front that passed through the original forest many years earlier.

A different type of disease complex is illustrated by the *little-leaf disease* of shortleaf and loblolly pines in the southeastern states. In this disease the fungus *Phytophthora cinnamomi* attacks feeder rootlets, causing chlorosis and decline of the crown, and eventually death of the tree. But the disease develops only in heavy and wet soils with poor aeration and low fertility. On such sites trees are of low vigor, and their poor root regeneration potential following repeated attacks by the fungus prevents recuperation of the root system. As a result, intake of nutrients is hindered, and little-leaf disease follows. On good sites the fungus may be present and may even attack the rootlets, but lost rootlets are quickly replaced and little damage is sustained because of the greater tree vigor and different environmental conditions.

Disease Problems in Forest Nurseries

Seedlings are subject to a wide range of both noninfectious and infectious diseases. Little is known about diseases of seedlings under forest conditions, but seedling diseases in forest nurseries are known to cause extensive losses at all stages from seed in storage to sowing to outplanting. Nursery diseases also pose a threat to forests when infected seedlings are planted in forested areas where the pathogen has not previously existed. The most notorious example of this was the introduction of *white pine blister rust* into North America. Among the most important seedling diseases are the damping-off diseases, root rots, stem and foliage blights, and stem rusts (33).

Damping-off is the most important disease problem in nurseries and is one of the chief obstacles in raising coniferous seedlings, although a number of hardwood species are also susceptible. Damping-off is really a group of similar diseases caused by many fungi, but most commonly by species of *Pythium, Rhizocotonia, Fusarium,* and *Phytophtora.* Early attacks, or preemergence damping-off, may kill the seedling before it emerges from the soil. Postemergence infection generally occurs at or just below the groundline; stem tissues collapse and the seedling topples over. Root rot in either early or late stages of seedling development is another aspect of the disease, and seedlings may be killed but remain standing. Control is sometimes achieved by cultural practices, but chemical control either by applying seed-protectant fungicides or by fumigating the soil is often necessary.

Mycorrhizae

The emphasis given in this chapter to pathogenic fungi as causal agents of diseases of forest trees might give the mistaken impression that all fungi are harmful. Fortunately this is not the case, and one major *beneficial* aspect of saprophytic fungi is their role in the conversion of dead plant and animal remains to the essential humus of the forest soil. Another important beneficial role of fungi is one already mentioned, the formation of *mycorrhizae* (34), the vital symbiotic association of mycelium of a fungus with the feeder roots of a higher plant in which a distinctive morphological structure develops.

Mycorrhizae result from infection of cortical cells of short roots by a fungal symbiont; when this occurs, a physiologically balanced reciprocal parasitism that is mutually beneficial to the host and the fungal symbiont is established. So prevalent throughout the plant world is this association that nonmycorrhizal plants are proving to be the exception. Without mycorrhizae most plants, including our important forest and horticultural species, could not survive in the highly competitive biological communities in natural soil habitats.

As we have seen, mycorrhizae are of great benefit to the host plant. They increase the solubility of soil minerals, improve uptake of mineral nutrients, facilitate movement of carbohydrates from one plant to another, and even protect feeder roots against infection by certain root pathogens. In turn, the host provides the fungal symbiont with carbohydrates, vitamins, and growth factors.

Mycorrhizal development is influenced by the previous history of the site. Most forest soils seem to have sufficient populations of mycorrhizal symbionts, but there are some sites devoid of mycorrhizae. Trees will not grow on them until the soils have been inoculated with mycorrhizal fungi. Such sites include, for example, prairie-type soils, surface material left after strip mining, and the artificial "soils" often used for growing containerized seedlings. The great potential benefits of selecting specific symbionts for specific sites have stimulated much research aimed at developing techniques for inoculating growing seedlings with fungi adapted to selected sites or types of environments. Successful techniques for commercial production of pure-cul-

ture inoculum have been developed for one mycorrhizal symbiont, *Pisolithus tinctorius,* but consistent results from inoculations with such inoculum have not been obtained as yet in field trials.

Principles of Forest Disease Management

The "products" provided by the forest depend on the objectives of the managers and users of the land. The various objectives may be included under the broad concept of *multiple use,* which embraces use of forests for many purposes, including timber, wildlife, watershed protection, recreation, and others. On this basis the control of forest pests might be undertaken only when the activity of a pest can be shown to interfere significantly with the management objectives of the particular forest. The goal of forestry is to obtain optimum production from the forest, which means paying attention to the efficiency of the management system. Disease must more often be treated as part of the broader field of forest management.

More and more we are substituting the term *"disease management"* for "disease control." Use of the term *management* conveys the concept of a continuous process and implies that diseases are inherent components of the forest ecosystem and that they must be dealt with on a continuing basis. The goal of disease management is reducing disease damage or loss to economically acceptable levels. Another facet of this view is increasing emphasis on the concept of *integrated pest management* (IPM), whereby all aspects of a pest–host system are examined to provide the resource manager with an information base on which to make a decision, as discussed in Chapter 7. The ecological and economic principles involved are integrated through the use of systems analysis, which brings together many skills and products of sciences that underlie forestry to meet the protection needs of the resource manager (35).

Most forest disease control methods, rather than being concerned with cure of diseased individuals, are preventive and are directed toward protection of the future crop. Moreover, most forest disease control is indirect in that it is effected through adjustments in forest management practices. In contrast, *direct-control* measures expend efforts and money specifically and solely for the control of a given disease and operate separately from normal silvicultural operations, such as the ribes eradication program that was formerly in effect for control of white pine blister rust.

Since *prevention* is the most important principle in forest disease control, most control strategies are *cultural measures,* such as selecting site and species, choosing the proper rotation age, and employing a variety of operations to improve the timber stand, including thinning, burning, pruning, and others.

The ultimate objective of forest disease management might be the development of predictive models for forest ecosystems (Chapter 6), through which the management decisions can be made, evaluated, and implemented to give the maximum benefits to the producer, the consumer, and the public at large. There are now several computer programs that list management recommendations for insects and diseases of trees in various regions, and these are continuing to be developed and improved. The present version of FIDMREC, for example, covers twelve tree species of the Pacific Northwest and has recommendations for more than twenty-five insects and diseases. A similar program called *Integrated Pest Management—Decision Key* has been available for several years in the southeastern United States. These programs are mainly computerized means of disseminating pest management information to forest managers. More sophisticated computer-assisted forest management information systems are being developed; one such project in the process of development at this writing is called the *Integrated Pest Impact Assessment System* (IPIAS). The scheme is designed to provide forest managers with a method for efficiently and effectively evaluating the implications of alternative management actions. With such modeling techniques all pertinent components of an interdisciplinary approach to forest planning and management can be incorporated, and "disease management" can routinely become an integral part of forest management.

References

1. J. G. HORSFALL AND E. B. COWLING, EDS., *Plant Disease—An Advanced Treatise,* Vol. 1, *How Disease Is Managed,* Academic Press, New York, 1977.

2. G. H. HEPTING AND E. B. COWLING, *Annu. Rev. Phytopathol., 12,* 431 (1977).

3. G. H. HEPTING AND G. M. JEMISON, "Forest protection." In *Timber Resources for America's Future,* U.S.D.A. For. Serv., Res. Rept. 14, 1958.

4. ANON., "An analysis of the timber situation in the United States 1952–2030," U.S.D.A. For. Serv., Res. Rept. 23, 1982.

5. W. H. SMITH, *Tree Pathology: A Short Introduction,* Academic Press, New York, 1970.

6. ANON., "Acid precipitation in relation to agriculture, forestry and aquatic biology," Council for Agricultural Science and Technology, Rept. 100, Ames, Iowa, 1984.

7. P. SCHUTT AND E. B. COWLING, *Plant Dis., 69,* 548 (1985).

8. C. E. SELISKAR, "Virus and virus-like disorders of forest trees." In *Documents, FAO/IUFRO Symp. on Internationally Dangerous Forest Disease Insects,* Vol. 1, Oxford, FAO/UN, July 20–29, 1964.

9. C. W. MURDOCH AND R. J. CAMPANA, *Plant Dis., 68,* 890 (1984).

10. J. G. ZEIKUS AND J. C. WARD, *Science, 184* (4142), 1181 (1974).

11. J. J. WORRAL AND J. R. PARMETER, JR., *Phytopathology, 73,* 1140 (1983).

12. A. L. SHIGO, "Tree decay. An expanded concept," U.S.D.A. For. Serv., Agr. Info. Bull. 419, Washington, D.C., 1979.

13. A. L. SHIGO, *Annu. Rev. Phytopathol., 22,* 189 (1984).

14. A. L. SHIGO AND W. E. HILLIS, *Annu. Rev. Phytopathol., 11,* 197 (1973).

15. J. L. RUEHLE, *Annu. Rev. Phytopathol., 11,* 99 (1973).

16. R. B. MALEK AND J. E. APPLEBY, *Plant Dis., 68,* 180 (1984).

17. M. J. WINGFIELD, R. A. BLANCHETTE, T. H. NICHOLLS, AND K. ROBBINS, *Can. J. For. Res., 12,* 71 (1982).

18. P. M. WARGO AND C. G. SHAW, III, *Plant Dis., 69,* 826 (1985).

19. W. G. Thies, *J. For., 82,* 345 (1984).

20. S. L. Anagnostakis, *Science, 215,* 466 (1982).

21. N. K. Van Alfen, *Annu. Rev. Phytopathol., 20,* 349 (1982).

22. R. T. Bingham, R. J. Hoff, and G. I. McDonald, eds., "Biology of rust resistance in forest trees," *Proc. NATO–IUFRO Adv. Study Inst.,* U.S.D.A. For. Serv., Misc. Publ. 1221, 1972.

23. G. I. McDonald, E. M. Hansen, C. A. Osterhaus, and S. Samman, *Plant Dis., 68,* 800 (1984).

24. H. R. Powers, Jr., R. A. Schmidt, and G. A. Snow, *Annu. Rev. Phytopathol., 19,* 353 (1981).

25. R. J. Dinus and R. A. Schmidt, eds., *Proc. Symp. Management of Fusiform Rust in Southern Pines,* Univ. of Florida, Gainseville, 1977.

26. H. R. Powers, Jr., *Eur. J. For. Pathol., 14,* 426 (1984).

27. H. R. Powers, Jr., and J. F. Kraus, *Plant Dis., 67,* 187 (1983).

28. K. D. Widin and A. L. Schipper, Jr., *Can. J. For. Res., 10,* 257 (1980).

29. R. F. Scharpf and R. V. Bega, "*Elytroderma* disease reduces growth and vigor, increases mortality of Jeffrey pines at Lake Tahoe Basin, California," U.S.D.A. Pac. Southwest For. Range Expt. Sta., Res. Pap. PSW-155, 1981.

30. R. F. Scharpf and J. R. Parmeter, Jr., tech. coord., *Proc. Symp. Dwarf Mistletoe Control through Forest Management,* U.S.D.A. For. Serv., Pac. Southwest For. Range Expt. Sta., Gen. Tech. Rept. PSW-31, 1978.

31. D. V. Baxter, "Development and succession of forest fungi and diseases in forest plantations," Univ. Mich., School of For. and Conserv. Circ. 1, Univ. of Michigan Press, Ann Arbor, 1937.

32. D. F. Schoeneweiss, *Plant Dis., 65,* 308 (1981).

33. G. W. Peterson and R. S. Smith, Jr., tech. coord., "Forest nursery diseases in the United States," U.S.D.A. For. Serv., Agr. Handbook 470, 1975.

34. E. Hacskaylo, ed., "Mycorrhizae," *Proc. 1st N.A. Conf. Mycorrhizae,* U.S.D.A. For. Serv., Misc. Publ. 1189, 1971.

35. R. W. Stark, *J. For., 75,* 251 (1977).

PART 3
Forest Management

The forests make up one of the earth's greatest reservoirs of renewable natural resources. Managed properly, they can provide us with essential products indefinitely and at the same time can remain a home for wildlife and a vital source of water supplies (Figure P3.1). However, the management of the forests for each of the many products, services, and benefits presents a complex problem. This section presents the methods and practices by which the successful forest manager obtains these benefits from the forest without adversely affecting the environment.

In the opening Chapter 9 an overview of "Multiple-Use Management, Planning, and Administration" in forestry is given; the approaches to management of public and private organizations, the interests of ownership, and the planning of operations are discussed. In the next two chapters views and policies for "Forestry at the National Level" can be compared with the attitudes of small "Nonindustrial Private Forests" landowners. The nonindustrial private forests may hold the future for forest-derived benefits; almost 60 percent of commercial forestland is owned by the private nonindustrial sector.

Specific procedures for assessment of forest and timber resources are provided in Chapters 12 and 13, "Measurement of the Forest" and "Remote Sensing." The various methods available for determining individual tree sizes and volumes and those for estimating the volume of timber in forest stands are presented. The chapter on remote sensing describes methods for evaluating stand composition, density, and the health of forests from aerial photographs and satellite data.

Chapter 14, on "Silviculture," then describes the biological management of the forest—how forest regeneration, species composition, and growth are regulated by biological means. The use of silvicultural and other techniques for timber management is described in Chapter 15, followed by a description of harvesting methods in Chapter 16.

Forests are used for timber, wildlife, rangeland, watersheds, and recreation. Their management for each of these uses is treated in successive Chapters 15 through 20. Methods of integrating management decisions for protection of all the natural resources provided by the forest are proposed in these chapters. Extraction of timber from forests does not necessarily diminish the other benefits derived from them. A moderate-sized clearcut, for example, provides additional habitats for wildlife, and selection cutting in the forest creates areas more suitable for aesthetics and recreational activities.

Although human beings cause most forest fires today, fires have probably always occurred in the forest, for as long as there have been forests, there have been lightning storms. The importance of fires in shaping the forest landscape is discussed in the final chapter in this section, "Behavior and Management of Forest Fires." The use of fire as a management tool (i.e., "prescribed burns") is also described in Chapter 21.

Figure P3.1 Our forests make up one of the earth's great reservoirs of renewable resources. Properly managed, they can provide us with essential products indefinitely and at the same time remain a home for wildlife and a vital source of water supplies. (Courtesy of U.S.D.A. Forest Service.)

CHAPTER 9

Multiple-Use Management, Planning, and Administration

JAMES M. GULDIN

Forest Management
Multiple Uses
Multiple-Use Interactions

Forest Owners and Ownership
Land Ownership and Distribution

Forest Planning and Administration
Public Forest Management Agencies
Industrial Forests

Summary and Conclusions

References

Forests existed long before the dawn of humankind, and if managed properly they should outlast our society's brief evolutionary occupancy of the planet. For eons, trees have efficiently converted water and atmospheric carbon dioxide with sunlight and a handful of mineral resources into the sugars and metabolic by-products required for growth, and they have done so in a way that collectively confers productivity at the ecosystem level as described in Part 2, "Forest Biology." Thus it is perhaps arrogant to discuss the value of forest resources under human administration; forest ecosystems will be rich in natural resources even if human beings do not tamper with them.

There is, however, a great deal of variability and complexity in the productivity and distribution of resources in any given forest ecosystem. Some natural resources, such as wood fiber in a riverfront cottonwood stand, are produced in abundance and extremely rapidly. Other natural resources are produced in very small quantities over longer periods of time; for example, the endangered red-cockaded woodpecker in southern pine forests constructs its nest only in the decayed heartwood of pine trees that are generally over 100 years old. Some natural resources require such an extended period of devel-

opment that they might be considered essentially nonrenewable; the aesthetic inspiration that we all feel when we look upon a grove of stately redwood trees is heightened when we realize that the trees are over a thousand years old.

A forest in the management sense is simply a collection of individual forest ecosystems or stands. Forest management is the process of organizing these stands so that they produce a continuous stream of whatever resources are desired from that forest—whether they be timber, wildlife, awe-inspiring aesthetic experiences, or any conceivable combination of the resources of the forest presented in this and the other chapters of Part 3. The forester's task, then, is to facilitate the production of resources from the forest in a manner that ensures that they will be forever available. The management techniques for accomplishing these purposes vary from the extraordinarily simple to the exceedingly complex, as will be seen in Chapters 14 through 21.

Forest Management

Forests consist of many different species of flora and fauna, each with a unique set of physical and biological properties. The community of organisms, or the ecosystem, also has certain physical and biological attributes. Thus a given forest can be defined both in terms of its component species and as an entity in itself.

Forest resources are made valuable by their desirability to society. Fundamental economic concepts such as supply and demand, and noneconomic considerations such as concern for the preservation of endangered species and for maintaining environmental quality, play roles in determining their value. A century ago timber was unquestionably the most valuable resource in the forest. Although we as a society still ascribe high monetary value to timber resources, today we increasingly find important intangible values in nontimber forest resources.

For example, a stand of black walnut trees growing along a stream has value on many levels. It can serve not only as a source of beautiful cabinet lumber or as a prime squirrel habitat, but also in a protective capacity by promoting water quality and providing a buffer against soil erosion. It is easy to ascribe a monetary value to the timber; it is more difficult to place a dollar value on each squirrel, on each cubic foot of uneroded soil, and on each unit of clarity in the streamwater. Yet, all these resources are desired by society, and no one can dispute that it would be difficult to maintain a constant level of squirrel habitat and water quality if all the black walnut trees were harvested for lumber.

If a given resource were readily renewable and capable of being used without affecting other resources in the forest, forest management would be a simple task. However, there is often a fine line between careless exploitation of a resource and a conservation-based use that ensures resource renewability. In addition, nearly every practice that a forester uses to manage a particular resource also affects the other resources in the forest; the more resources that are desired from a given forest area, the greater is the likelihood that the management and use of one desirable resource will affect another.

Forest resource management optimizes the supply of ecosystem-based resources relative to the demand for them, and it concurrently ensures a perpetual supply of resources with minimal conflict in using one or another of them. Management is typically implemented by means of a *forest management plan* that identifies the objectives of the landowner, outlines the treatments and timetables required to manage the resources in each stand over the entire forest, and describes a program of resource evaluation to ensure that the ownership objectives for the forest property are being attained.

Generally, the greater the number of resources that are desired from a particular forest, the more comprehensive will be the plan. In addition, plans are usually more complicated for resources that have high intrinsic or monetary value. Finally, the greater the number of owners of a particular forest, the more difficult it will be both to identify ownership objectives and to express these objectives in terms of the many resources found in the forest.

Multiple Uses

In the abstract sense, there are an infinite variety of resources in a forest that can be used in either a consumptive or a nonconsumptive fashion. Trees can be used for lumber; for split-bark hickory chairs, for maple syrup, or as supports for a hammock; an outdoor enthusiast can enjoy forest fauna by hunting deer with a rifle, rainbow trout with a fly rod, or butterflies with a camera. This multiplicity of resources available in a forest and their multiplicity of uses reveal the challenge to modern forest management both in choosing which resources should be used and in giving society access to them.

In the practical sense, however, the forestry profession recognizes a standard broad categorization of the infinite variety of resources. Easy, convenient, and commonly accepted categories are those given in the Multiple Use–Sustained Yield Act of 1960.

> **The national forests are established and shall be administered for outdoor recreation, range, timber, watershed, and wildlife and fish purposes.**

Accordingly, these five categories have come to be known as *multiple uses*. The degree to which forestlands are managed for any one of these multiple uses depends on the goals of ownership. However, because federal lands are collectively owned by the American people, this law was essentially a statement of the ownership objectives of the national forests. Each national forest must expressly provide an adequate supply of each of these multiple uses over a fifty-year period of management.

The single dominant objective of forest ownership has been the management of the *timber* component (Figure 9.1). Timber management is often used to finance forest ownership and to support other uses for which a financial value is more difficult either to assess or to administer. In most

Figure 9.1 A 38-year-old loblolly pine plantation in Ashley County, Arkansas, that has been intensively managed for the production of sawtimber. (Photograph by J. M. Guldin.)

regions of the country, trees of sawlog size bring a fairly high monetary return. Markets for smaller trees are more variable and usually depend on the species being managed as well as their proximity to processing facilities such as paper mills. Such markets, if they exist, provide timber management with another avenue of activity, the opportunity to conduct economical operations in young stands. Finally, since trees are the dominant ecological component of a forest ecosystem, the value of nontimber resources can often be enhanced by a judicious manipulation of the timber component.

In certain situations, of course, the values of other resources far outweigh the value of timber; for example, the gate receipts at a 100-unit campground over a year's period undoubtedly exceed the value of the annual growth of the timber within the campground. There are many other sites on which the pursuit of timber production is not an economical proposition; it is difficult to justify capital investment in sites with low productivity such as ridgetops or swamps, especially since such sites also tend to be relatively inaccessible. At still other sites the management of timber is at odds with uses that derive from an undisturbed or unharvested ecosystem, such as wilderness areas or scenic trail corridors.

Forest ecosystems provide an important *watershed* value by serving as a living filter for precipitation. Many cities and towns throughout the United States rely on forested watersheds to enhance both the quantity and quality of the consumable-water resource (Figure 9.2). In many arid western states the yield of water from high-altitude forests is increased by creative patterns of harvest that gather more snow in the winter and prolong the snowmelt period into early summer.

Organizations that manage forestlands are required to control *nonpoint sources of water pollution* (i.e., dispersed), such as nutrient discharges and sedimentation associated with forest management.[1] The most likely source of water pollution in forestry is erosion from access roads, which can

---

[1]Dispersed sources of pollution can be compared to *point pollution* from a single source, such as a factory drainspout.

Figure 9.2 Watershed uses of the forest. (*a*) View of the Quabbin Reservoir in central Massachusetts, which provides fresh water for the city of Boston. (*b*) Sign explaining the use of the reservoir at a scenic overlook. (Photographs by J. M. Guldin.)

be minimized by proper engineering practices. To a lesser extent, erosion from the forest itself is exacerbated by exposing fragile streambanks to operations such as skidding, harvesting, and site preparation. This pollution can be effectively eliminated by retaining a buffer strip of trees within a streamside management zone and excluding forest operations from this zone (see Chapter 19).

Forests and *wildlife and fish* have such an intimate interrelationship that almost all timber management practices affect the forest fauna. Wildlife species tend to be associated with certain successional stages in the forest, and practices that promote a given stage of forest succession are likely to promote the species of wildlife adapted to that particular stage (Figure 9.3). The general tendency of the forest industry to manage early-successional forest ecosystems is favorable to wildlife species for which the brushy-habitat mosaic is home. Popular game species such as white-tailed deer, ruffed grouse, and bobwhite quail all find early-successional forests to be an excellent habitat. As a result, the popularity of hunting on privately held lands has increased tremendously in certain areas of the country. For example, the hunting leases held by some forest industries in the bottomland hardwood stands

Figure 9.3 Elk grazing in an opening within a lodgepole pine forest, Banff National Park, Alberta. (Photograph by J. M. Guldin.)

along the Mississippi River provide annual monetary returns per acre that are comparable to that of timber. Other industries lease their land to hunters for a nominal fee that provides significant nontimber income from the forest property. Game management has always been a by-product of timber management, but these recent trends epitomize the increasingly lucrative nontimber uses of industrial forestlands.

A productive fish resource is generally achieved by promoting good water quality. Many of the practices that prevent turbidity, siltation, and excessive eutrophication of a stream will obviously benefit fish. An aquatic habitat can be quickly degraded by sudden changes in stream temperature. If the protective streamside vegetation is removed, direct solar radiation upon the water surface will increase stream temperature by a biologically significant amount which may be detrimental to fish. For this reason the practice of retaining streamside buffer strips of trees is beneficial for fish populations.

Good forest management includes management not only of the popular game species but also of nongame species. It is common practice on industry and government forestlands to leave dead standing trees called snags on a harvested site. In addition to the nesting habitat provided by these old hollow trees, their insect fauna provide forage for nongame bird species. Furthermore, the primary emphasis is increasingly on preservation of the habitats of wildlife on the federal list of endangered species. For example, the endangered red-cockaded woodpecker mentioned earlier thrives in a habitat of mature southern pine over 100 years old (1). As can be imagined, this bird has not prospered under modern timber management regimes, with sawtimber rotation targets commonly at ages 35 to 50. It is obvious that responsible forest management in southern pine stands must include some concession of timber and game production in order to ensure the survival of this endangered woodpecker. Wildlife management is discussed further in Chapter 17.

Range resources consist of the grasses commonly found within forest ecosystems. The primary use of rangeland resources is to allow domesticated livestock such as cattle to roam the forest, foraging on the grass resource (Figure 9.4). This activity is by far most common in western forests. For example, ponderosa pine forests in the southwestern United States are sufficiently open for sunlight to reach the forest floor, which promotes development of the grassy component of the ecosystem. In modern forest management rangeland allotments allowing a certain number of animals on specific areas of the forest are established. The goal of range management is to balance the quality and quantity of forage with the grazing intensity, both for a given area and forestwide.

A dramatically increasing use of forestland in the United States is for *outdoor recreation*. Participation in outdoor recreation on national forestland increased by 37 percent during the 1970s, highlighted by activities relating to snow, ice, and water-based resources (2). Recreational use of forest resources ranges through a progression requiring varying amounts of facility organization and development, from organized bus tours of our national parks to solo backpacking trips in the Alaskan wilderness, or from a three-week transcontinental journey to a fifteen-minute stroll in the woods. Forest recreation typically centers on the ecosystem-based resources of the forest. The challenge to the manager is

Figure 9.4 Handling stock on the Bull Mountain Allotment, Deerlodge National Forest, Montana. (Photograph by G. R. Walstad, U.S.D.A. Forest Service.)

simultaneously to enhance the quality of the resource and to promote conditions that satisfy the expectations of the resource user. Management of recreation resources is discussed further in Chapter 20.

Multiple-Use Interactions

The concept of multiple use implies that on any given acre of forestland, the opportunity exists to utilize more than one forest resource. Forest management would be a simple task were the owner of the forest interested in a single resource such as timber or recreation. Multiple use is the philosophy that each acre can support the socially desirable utilization of many different resources. This is an easy philosophy to espouse, but it can be difficult to carry out.

A given pair of uses can interact in one of three ways. The interaction can be *neutral*, in that one use does not particularly affect another; a wildflower enthusiast is not likely to be affected by a nearby fisherman. The interaction may be *compatible*, such as the beneficial effects of small clearcuts on wildlife species that inhabit early-successional ecosystems. Finally, the interaction may be *incompatible*: a genuine wilderness experience is impossible in an area under intensive timber management. Clawson (3) derived a qualitative model in which the degree of compatibility of a variety of uses was assessed; the trade-offs can only be quantitatively assessed by carefully specifying exactly which resources are being used, in what fashion, and within which specific forest ecosystem constraints.

When multiple uses of the forest are incompatible, there may be conflicts. The conflict may be between the resources themselves, as between solid pine trees and red-cockaded woodpeckers. In this instance, it is necessary to separate directly conflicting resources either in space, allocating each resource to different areas, or in time, allocating each resource to a given area in different seasons, years, or decades. The concept of *dominant use* (4), in which one particular use of the forest is given relative priority over others, can be implemented with techniques such as zoning specific areas (5) and instituting seasonal controls over resources and users.

Because there are usually precise guidelines for management of individual resources, the conflict may be between the techniques used to manage the resources. For example, a hiker who detests the visual impact of a two-year-old clearcut may not even notice a recent timber harvest in an uneven-aged stand. Under these conditions the conflict may be resolved by evaluating the range of alternative practices that can be used for the management of each resource. The forest manager may choose to refine or modify practices to create compatibility, such as converting all trailside forests to an uneven-age condition. Should this fail, it may be necessary to partition resource uses either spatially or temporally: rerouting the trail or withdrawing the area from timber management.

According to projections from the U.S. Department of Agriculture Forest Service, the demand for each of the multiple-use resources available from the forest is increasing (Figure 9.5). The challenge to forest management is to provide a supply of forest resources that meets these projected demands and that increasingly implements the multiple-use concept on lands not restricted to a dominant or single use. Management in each of the three major ownership categories—the public forests, industry forests, and forests of the nonindustrial private landowner—must broaden its base.

Forest Owners and Ownership

It is a fundamental tenet in the practice of forestry that the landowner, not the forester, determines the objectives of ownership. The task of the forester is to implement the landowner's objectives by developing and administrating a forest management plan. Foresters can and should use their professional expertise to suggest management alternatives to the landowner, but the ultimate decision-making authority about resource management objectives is generally retained by the landowner.

By no means does every forest landowner seek to emplace every multiple use on his or her land. For example, owners of forest industry lands will acquiesce to nontimber uses such as hunting as long as these uses have no worse than a neutral effect on timber production. Conversely, the nonindustrial private landowner, discussed in Chapter 11, has objectives that may or may not be well defined, and that may be oriented either to a precise single use or to a veritable panoply of multiple uses. Lands managed by the U.S.D.A. Forest Service within the National Forest System are generally required to provide for multiple use at the district level through planning within each national forest. An investigation of ownership patterns will suggest the kinds of uses of the forest in different regions of the country.

Land Ownership and Distribution

About one-third of the land area of the United States is classified as forestland (Table 9.1); the rest is either rangeland or other land, which includes farmland and urban and suburban areas. Forestland is subdivided into three categories. *Commerical forestland* is defined as forestland that is capable of

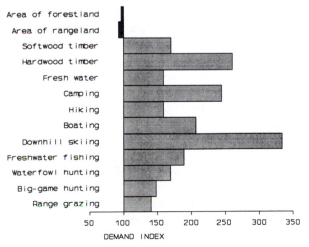

Figure 9.5 Projected changes in forest area and demand increases for selected resources to the year 2030 (2).

Table 9.1 Land Area of the United States, by Major Class of Land and Region

| Region | Total Land Area[b] | Forestland[a] | | | | Rangeland | Other Land |
		Total Forest	Commercial Forest	Productive Deferred Forest	Other Forest		
North	252.4	71.9	67.2	2.5	2.1	29.7	150.8
South	205.2	83.7	76.1	0.9	6.7	42.1	79.4
Pacific Coast	230.8	86.7	28.5	2.2	56.0	123.7	20.4
Rocky Mountains	224.1	55.7	23.4	4.7	27.7	136.3	32.1
U.S. total	912.5	298.1	195.3	10.2	92.6	331.8	282.6

Source: Anon., "An analysis of the timber situation in the United States, 1952–2030," U.S.D.A. For. Serv., For. Res. Rep. 23, 1982.

[a] Defined as land at least 10 percent stocked by forest trees of any size, including land that formerly had such cover and will be regenerated.

[b] Given in millions of hectares.

producing more than 1.4 cubic meters per hectare per year (20 cubic feet or 0.25 cord per acre per year) of industrial wood under natural-stand conditions, and that is not allocated to nontimber single uses. The land may or may not be under any program of forest management, but would exceed the indicated volume if it were. The northern and southern regions contain about 69 percent of the total forestland, and about 75 percent of the commercial forestland, in the United States. Within these regions commercial forestland constitutes more than 90 percent of the total forestland base. *Productive deferred land* is sufficiently productive to be commercial forestland, but it has been deferred expressly for nontimber uses such as wilderness areas, wildlife sanctuaries, and national parks. This category represents a small (3.4 percent) but significant resource legacy to future generations. *Other forestlands* consist of slow-growing forests on poor sites that fall below the standard for commercial timber production. More than 31 percent of the nation's forests fall in this category. However, more than 90 percent of this area is found in the western regions, where almost 59 percent of the total forestland base is in nonproductive types of timber ranging from arid lowland pinyon–juniper forests to high-altitude, slow-growing coniferous forests. Although these forests are not productive for timber, they possess other resource values that are often of far greater importance to society.

Approximately 18 percent of the nation's commercial forestland is in the national forest system, of which 75 percent is located in the western regions of the country (Table 9.2). Only 14 percent of the country's commercial forests are owned by the forest industry, but 53 percent of these are located in the South, an important region in the timber economy of the nation. The majority of the commercial forestland in the United States—almost 60 percent—is owned by private individuals whose major source of income is not from their forestland. These nonindustrial private forest owners, to whom special attention is given in Chapter 11, own 71 percent of the commercial forestland in both the heavily populated North and the timber-dependent Southern regions. They are a critical population as society's demand for forest resources carries into the next century.

Almost two-thirds of the growing stock on commercial forestland in the United States consists of coniferous softwoods (Figure 9.6). Of this coniferous component, 69 percent is found in western forests, where conifers constitute more than 90 percent of the growing stock. Three-quarters of these western coniferous forests are found on federal lands. A large proportion of these are old-growth forests in the national forests and are the last virgin forests in North America. In contrast, more than 90 percent of the hardwood growing stock in the United States is found in the northern and

Table 9.2 Commercial Forestland in the United States, by Ownership and Region

Ownership Category	Total, United States[a]	North	South	Pacific Coast	Rocky Mountain
Commercial forestland	195.3	67.2	76.1	28.5	23.4
Total public forestland	54.9	12.4	7.2	17.9	17.5
National forests	35.9	4.0	4.4	17.8	14.8
Other federal	4.3	0.5	1.4	1.8	0.7
State, Native American, county, and municipal	14.7	7.9	1.4	3.4	2.0
Total private forestland	140.3	54.9	68.9	10.6	5.9
Forest industry[b]	27.8	7.3	14.7	5.1	0.9
Nonindustrial private[c]	112.5	47.6	54.3	5.5	5.1

Source: Anon., "An analysis of the timber situation in the United States, 1952–2030," U.S.D.A. For. Serv., For. Res. Rept. 23, 1982.

[a]Given in millions of hectares.

[b]Defined as companies or individuals operating wood-using plants.

[c]Includes all private ownerships except forest industry.

southern regions. Most of this volume is on nonindustrial private land, and is produced in greatly variable quantity, quality, and efficiency.

These statistics illustrate the challenge to forest management over the next several decades. A virgin forest storehouse of western coniferous growing stock and an equally large underutilized area supporting hardwood growing stock in the eastern regions are under ownership patterns that render both of only marginal accessibility as a timber resource to the forest industry. Yet, projections indicate that the forest resources desired by society, including timber, will surely increase as our country's population grows. The pressures for access to these lands for timber production are increasingly in conflict with the pressure to derive satisfactions from the forests that depend on their ecosystems remaining unharvested. These conflicts will be resolved through improvements in forest resource planning and administration.

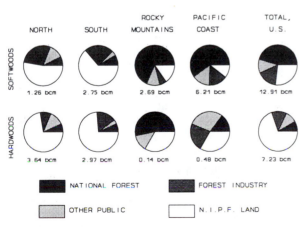

Figure 9.6 Volume of softwood and hardwood growing stock on commercial forestland in the United States by region and major ownership class (billion cubic meters, bcm) (8).

Forest Planning and Administration

The organizations that manage forestlands exist in a diversity that parallels the diversity of forest ownership. Large land management entities such as federal agencies and forest industry companies have a complicated internal organization that reflects their many products, the complicated nature of ownership, or both. Small entities such as a specialized wood products plant, a cross-country ski resort, or a woodlot owned by a farmer have a correspondingly smaller management infrastructure. Regardless of size, the implementation of management generally consists of two stages, each of varying complexity: planning and administering the plans.

In *planning* the managing organization first assesses both the ownership objectives and the resources of the forest that can satisfy these objectives. Using this assessment as a basis, management usually draws up a written plan. This plan details the methodology and treatment schedules whereby each stand in the forest will be managed, so that when the resource flows from all the stands in the forest are combined, the objectives of the owner are satisfied. *Administration,* then, is simply the organization of management tasks in order to implement the plan. Administration includes all manner of personal supervision, development and monitoring of operational budgets, and monitoring of both resource supply and satisfaction of resource demand. In combination, planning and administration can be as informal as a loose collection of ideas formulated by an industry forester to provide assistance to a farm woodlot owner, or a formal, publicly approved plan to meet the provisions of federal law governing the management of public forestlands.

Public Forest Management Agencies

The forests of the public sector are managed by a variety of agencies. At the federal level, forest management lies mostly with the Forest Service of the U.S. Department of Agriculture, which administers both the National Forest System and the extensive research-oriented network of forest experiment stations. The Department of the Interior is responsible for the management of diverse forest resources through the Bureau of Land Management, the U.S. Fish and Wildlife Service, the National Park Service, and the Bureau of Indian Affairs. The Department of Defense also coordinates forest management on the larger military bases throughout the country. Forest management on state lands is generally coordinated through an appropriate department or commission and is supplemented by county commissions or

municipal authorities, which manage forests such as those affiliated with public schools.

The U.S.D.A. Forest Service has the most advanced system of planning and administration of virtually any public or private forest management agency in the United States. This is not surprising given the federal mandate for multiple use and the varied clientele inherent in public ownership. Guidance for current management of the National Forest System emanates directly from the Multiple Use--Sustained Yield Act of 1960, the Renewable Resources Planning Act (RPA) of 1974, and the National Forest Management Act (NFMA) of 1976, all discussed in Chapter 1. The RPA charges the Forest Service to conduct an economically based assessment that essentially allocates scarce forest resources among their many conflicting uses (6), and the NFMA ensures that there is ample opportunity for both scientific and public input into the planning process (7).

Planning within the Forest Service occurs at national, regional, and local levels. The chief of the Forest Service develops the long-term national goals, programs, and production levels for management of the national forests based on data generated by the RPA assessment. The national goals established for each region are based on regional supply of and demand for resources. Within each region, the regional standards and guidelines are formulated on the basis of regional RPA assessments; these standards and guidelines are expressed as long-range program objectives and production levels for individual national forests within the region. At the national forest level, the planning team summarizes the management situation, establishes long-term goals and objectives, specifies in detail the activities that will be conducted throughout the planning horizon for each of a variety of alternatives, selects the desired alternative through public input and consideration of associated environmental impacts, and establishes a program to monitor the implementation of the plan. The management plan for a national forest typically provides general directions for forestwide management and specific directions for implementing the plan. A further description of forestry at the national level is given in Chapter 10.

The organization of the state agencies that exist to manage forestlands depends largely on the amount of forestland and the importance of forestry within the state. Some states, such as California, Oregon, and Washington, have large forestry agencies and comprehensive procedures for planning and administrating state lands. In other states activities center on the control of wildfires, which is a major responsibility of state forestry commissions through the South, and the coordination of assistance to private landowners.

Industrial Forests

Management of lands owned by forest industries differs greatly from that of public lands. Forest industry lands are those lands owned by companies or individuals operating wood-using plants (8). The size of such companies may range from a small open sawmill with a few thousand hectares of land to multinational, multiproduct conglomerates operating several dozen mills, employing thousands of people, and owning millions of hectares of productive forestland.

The organization of forest management activities within the forest industries relates more closely to the satisfaction of company goals than it does to the efficient management of forests. A major goal of forest industries is to provide an uninterrupted flow of wood and wood products to the mill or manufacturing facility, and a great deal of planning and administrative ability is required to ensure the optimal regulation of a forested property for continual timber production. However, a superseding objective is to optimize profits for the firm. The concern of industry foresters with the flow of timber to the mill—in part related to the professional ideal of theoretical forest regulation—is pointedly aimed at avoiding the huge costs of shutting down a manufacturing facility for want of raw material. The same concerns, driven by the competition that thrives in the markets of our society, brook little interference with the efficient and intricate conduct of forest management operations. In the western states forest industries own a disproportionate number of the more productive forests found at lower elevations (8).

By and large, timber is generally managed by forest industries with admirable efficiency and intricate complexity. With increasing regularity, however, forest industries are promoting the management of multiple-use resources from several perspectives. The opportunity to profit from management of resources such as wildlife, fish, or recreational facilities is often advantageously pursued by industry. Nontimber resource specialists increasingly find employment with forest products firms, and their responsibilities range from encouraging hunting strategies that effectively reduce browsing damage on seedlings to providing an internal corporate advocate to ensure compliance with nonpoint pollution standards. In addition, the good public relations that attend the flow of desirable nontimber resources are not lost on industrial forest managers. Such benefits extend beyond genuine corporate altruism to the enhancement of local ecosystems and the preservation of endangered species and their habitats.

The organization of administrative efforts varies for the different forest products industries. Some firms operate with a chief forester and a staff of assistants with regional responsibilities for implementing production quotas and forest management programs. Others are organized within a timberlands division, generally headed by a corporate vice-president and subdivided into districts of approximately 20,000 hectares, the administrative responsibilities for which reside with two foresters and a crew of technicians. Within the firm the woodlands division may exist as a profit center, required to show acceptable returns from all its forestry investments, from the establishment of stands through harvest. Or the woodlands division may be one element of a vertically integrated profit center, in which case the division might even operate at a financial loss if such operation promotes an efficiency that maximizes the profits of the firm or otherwise contributes to corporate goals.

Because of the size, complexity, and increasing importance of private nonindustrial forestlands, their discussion is reserved for Chapter 11.

Summary and Conclusions

From the resource perspective, a forest ecosystem can be viewed either as a valuable whole or as a sum of valuable parts. Multiple-use forestry is a philosophy of resource utilization that provides a theoretical basis for developing qualitative and quantitative predictions of resource interrelationships. In some instances the valuable whole receives priority, such as in the preservation of wilderness areas and of the ecological habitats for rare or endangered species. In other instances the valuable components of a forest ecosystem, such as timber or wildlife species, receive management emphasis. However, contemporary forestry on both public and private lands increasingly appreciates and provides for the multiple-resource values that characterize forest ecosystems.

The choice between dominant-use or multiple-use management depends on many factors. First and foremost are the unique attributes of the ecosystem itself, which determine both the availability of specific resources and the degree to which management can develop the resources for economical use. The methods by which management is planned and administered affect the economic efficiency of resource utilization, which may or may not be important in bringing forest products into the marketplace. The objectives of the owner of the forestland, whether an individual or society, are another critical factor. It is the owner who has ultimate decision-making authority regarding the patterns of resource management, if any, that are implemented by the forest manager. As populations grow, demands for a diverse array of forest resources increase; but the area of commercial forestland will decline into the next century. The centennial of forestry in North America will be characterized by both redoubtable management challenges and gratifying professional rewards.

References

1. ANON., "Red-cockaded woodpecker." In *Wildlife Habitat Management Handbook,* Chap. 420, U.S.D.A. For. Serv. Handbook, Region 8, Amendment 6, December, 1980.

2. ANON., "An assessment of the forest and range land situation in the United States," U.S.D.A. For. Serv., Res. Rept. 22, 1981.

3. M. CLAWSON, *Environ. Law, 8*(2), 287 (1978).

4. W. A. DUERR, D. E. TEEGUARDEN, N. B. CHRISTIANSEN, AND S. GUTTENBERG, *Forest Resource Management: Decision-Making Principles and Cases,* W. B. Saunders, Philadelphia, 1979.

5. C. F. BROCKMAN AND L. C. MERRIAM, JR., *Recreational Use of Wild Lands,* Third Edition, McGraw–Hill, New York, 1979.

6. J. V. KRUTILLA, M. D. BOWES, AND E. A. WILMAN, "National forest system planning and management: An analytical review and suggested approach." In *Government Interventions, Social Needs, and the Management of U.S. Forests,* R. A. Sedjo, ed., Resources for the Future, Washington, D.C., 1981.

7. S. T. DANA AND S. K. FAIRFAX, *Forest and Range Policy: Its Development in the United States,* Second Edition, McGraw–Hill, New York, 1980.

8. ANON., "An analysis of the timber situation in the United States, 1952–2030," U.S.D.A. For. Serv., Res. Rept. 23, 1982.

CHAPTER 10

Forestry at the National Level

F. Dale Robertson
Robert D. Gale

The question is often asked, "What do all those bureaucrats and lobbyists do in Washington?" Although many other chapters in this text cover technical forestry, this one will attempt to answer this question by highlighting another aspect of forestry —forestry at the national level. The national and the technical focuses are equally important aspects of forest management.

This chapter examines national forestry in two ways. First, a general overview is presented. Diverse groups and agencies with interests in forestry issues and policies are examined. Second, specific examples of national activities are discussed, using the U.S. Department of Agriculture *Forest Service* as an example to explain national policy-making and the dynamics of interaction between groups and agencies (Figure 10.1).

Much of what distinguishes forestry at the national level is its political and administrative context. This is the focus of the chapter. Laws, executive orders, and histories of forestry policy are touched on where relevant. Others chapters, such as Chapter 1, provide a more in-depth legal and historical overview of forestry in the United States.

Defining Forestry from a National Perspective

Applied technical forestry concentrates on a forest's potential to produce resources and the relationships of these resources. Forestry at the national level concentrates on the relations between forestry and other public policy issues, such as inflation, unemployment, environmental quality, and international trade, and the opportunities that forest resources provide to address these national issues.

It is often thought that forestry policy is established only at the national level; this is not really true. Forestry at the national level sets the goals and overall direction for practicing forestry, but this must be done with full recognition of the physical, biological, and social constraints facing forestry at

209

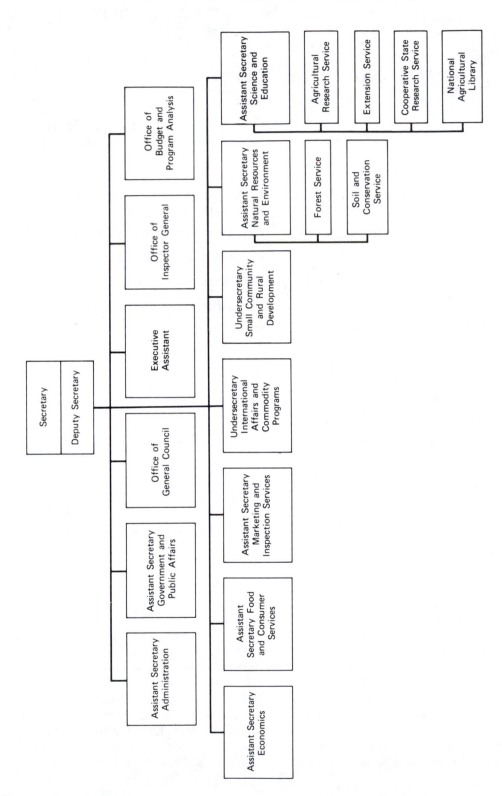

Figure 10.1 Abbreviated organization chart of the U.S. Department of Agriculture.

the field level; the two aspects are interdependent. To a degree, forest policy is actually set at all levels of management—national, regional, state, and local.

What distinguishes forestry at the national level is the context within which its is practiced, especially with regard to federal forestry. Foresters must view the needs and opportunities for forest resource management in terms of their relationships to national issues, while not losing sight of local situations. The Forest Service, like other agencies, develops a general program that it feels will best protect, improve, and utilize forest resources, while also attempting to serve local, regional, and national needs. The Department of Agriculture, working with the president's Office of Management and Budget (OMB), must mesh this program with other resource and nonresource programs, and this must be done within the framework of a national budget that meets the goals and objectives of the administration. This requires almost continuous interaction with other agencies, special-interest groups, Congress, and foresters in the field. Forestry becomes a job of balancing the goals of an administration with the professional aspects of resource management's existing laws.

National policy often depends on the political climate in our nation's capital. To illustrate this, we will examine the role of the Forest Service in the activities of the president's antiinflation task force. In a speech to the nation in June 1979, President Jimmy Carter outlined four steps to try to curb inflation. One directed the Forest Service to explore opportunities to increase the supply of timber from the nation's forests.

Sharp escalation of prices for new houses and increasing lumber and plywood prices led the president's Council on Wage and Price Stability (in 1979) to see timber inventories in national forests as a nationally controlled asset that could be used to help the nation's inflation problems. At the same time, the Council on Environmental Quality and the Environmental Protection Agency expressed their concerns about the loss of nontimber values that would result from increased timber production. The OMB was concerned with the budgetary implications of increasing timber production. The Washington office

of the Forest Service, in consultation with its field units, contributed technical expertise by outlining what the options were and the consequences of alternative policy directions. The president's Domestic Policy Council was assigned responsibility to work with the president's economic advisors and the concerned agencies to try to arrive at a reasonable solution to the issue.

After several months of analysis, discussion, and negotiation, a decision was reached by the president.

> **I hereby direct the Departments of Agriculture and Interior, consistent with existing legal requirements, to use maximum speed in updating land management plans on selected National Forests with the objective of increasing the harvest of mature timber through departure from the current nondeclining even-flow policy. In updating land management plans, all relevant economic and environmental implications must be taken into account. A schedule for rapid completion of this process on those forests with substantial inventories of mature timber should be developed with regular progress reports to me. (A memorandum for the secretary of agriculture.)**

It was a *compromise* that provided for an increase in timber production from public lands by permitting a short-term departure from even-flow timber management practices, but within the context of the existing laws and planning process.

Three important points should be noted about forestry at the national level: (1) there is no single, fixed, overall forestry policy; (2) national responsibility for providing forestry leadership and technical information is charged to the Forest Service; (3) there are important international dimensions of forestry as practiced in the United States.

There are several reasons why the United States has no single, overall *forestry policy.* Despite several generations of exploitation and use, in our country there are still large expanses of forests for which management is significantly less intense than for other forests. In addition, forestry policy in a national perspective is dynamic and ever-changing. People use forests in many ways. Forestry policy must be flexible enough to respond to society's changing needs and demands, even when the demands conflict with each other. Many people and interest groups focus their demands on forestry at the national level—individual citizens, resource professionals, politicians, and citizens' groups representing common and vastly different interests. These interests must all be taken into account. This does not mean that there is any lack of national policy, only that policy must be *dynamic* and capable of accommodating many interests and changes. Currently, Forest Service policies are best articulated in the Forest and Rangeland Renewable Resources Planning Act of 1974 (discussed later) and related policy statements.

Demands and new opportunities for forest resources are continually changing as society changes. Newly emerging needs for protecting wild ecosystems (Figure 10.2), for promoting wood as a structural and energy resource, and for managing forestry in urban environments—to name but a few—have been incorporated into national forestry policy for the 1980s. By the 1990s there will be new needs, many as yet unforeseen. Many of the needs that persist throughout the decade will change in scope and focus. Forestry at the technical level changes with advances in knowledge about how to manage resources. Forestry at the national level changes with changing societal needs.

The fact that our system of government was designed to spread authority across separate but equal branches is another reason for a *diversified national policy*. Both Congress and the executive branch have active roles in forestry, and the judicial branch is often employed to seek a balance between various aspects of forestry and differing interests. (The relationship between these branches of government are discussed more completely later in the chapter.) The diversity of both resources and social interests means that national forest policy is actually a collection of policies addressing many concerns. Although this arrangement is possibly cumbersome,

Figure 10.2 Old-growth redwood on a ridgetop site in Del Norte County, California. (Courtesy of U.S.D.A. Forest Service.)

its multifaceted nature is more flexible than a single policy could be in meeting the range of social demands that forestry faces.

The Forest Service has an expanded national role in forestry. The agency, as directed by laws and regulations of the secretary of agriculture, is a national *source of information* about forestry. The Forest Service has two major programs that deal directly with the development and transfer of technical information: a research program and a second major program of activities for cooperating with state and private forest owners. The national promotion of both research and state and private forestry activities is discussed in greater detail later in the chapter. These two programs, along with a third that deals with management of the national forests and human resource programs, make up the activities of the Forest Service. Drawing on expertise from these programs, the Forest Service provides technical advice on forestry matters to the Congress and the executive branch. The Fish and Wildlife Service of

the U.S. Department of the Interior has a similar advisory role specific to migratory and endangered fish and wildlife aspects of forest management.

Forestry at the national level also has *international implications*. Many of the forests in developing nations are publicly managed (Figure 10.3). The manner in which our public and private forests are managed and influenced by a nationally guided agency is often used as an example of how to structure forest management in other countries. In addition, the United States provides technical knowledge for increasing the utilization and productivity of the natural resources of developing nations.

In summary, forestry at the national level is characterized by the comprehensive context within which it is practiced. Forestry becomes a component of important national and international policies and issues. Forestry policy is shaped by the overall executive program, Congress, the courts, and the opportunities that exist at the technical level where

Figure 10.3 Plantation of *Pinus patula* in the Stapleford Forest near Umtali, Zimbabwe. The stand is about 17 years old and was thinned at 8 and 14 years and pruned to 22 feet with crop trees to 36 feet. (Courtesy of M. Wotton.)

it is to be applied. National forestry also includes providing technical assistance to Congress and developing nations.

Agencies and Organizations with National Interest in Forestry

Agencies

The nation's forestlands total about 300 million hectares. Approximately 70 percent of the commercial forestland is controlled by nonfederal owners. Several agencies directly administer forestlands and rangelands for various purposes, depending on the agency's particular responsibilities. Approximately 10 percent of the forestland and rangeland is administered by federal agencies for which forestry functions are generally minor or incidental to their major responsibilities. The Department of Defense, for example, manages forestland on military reservations. Although activities such as grazing, timber production, and wildlife management are permitted on some of these lands, they are primarily managed for defense purposes.

Four federal agencies have land management as their primary responsibility: the Forest Service of the Department of Agriculture, the Bureau of Land Management, the Fish and Wildlife Service, and the National Park Service of the Department of the Interior. Of these four agencies, the Forest Service manages 25 percent of the federally controlled forest and rangeland and the Bureau of Land Management (BLM) 62 percent. However, the Forest Service is responsible for approximately 80 percent of the federal *commercial* timberland, whereas the BLM manages fewer than 25 million hectares of these forests. All the BLM lands are located in the thirteen western states, mostly in the two states of Alaska and Oregon.

Federal agencies such as the Soil Conservation Service, the Agricultural Stabilization and Conservation Service, the Forest Service, and the Extension Service of the U.S. Department of Agriculture provide assistance to private forest owners in the form of funds, technical assistance, educational instruction, and published information.[1]

The Forest Service was established in 1905 to protect and manage forestlands and rangelands and to ensure a continuous flow of natural-resource benefits for the growing nation (Figure 10.4). The term *conservation* was used to characterize the management that was intended to be practiced on forested lands. It was defined as wise use and has since been clarified to mean the production of *multiple products* to ensure a sustained flow of goods and services to the public.

National park management is probably the oldest federal forestland management program. In 1872 Congress established Yellowstone National Park by withdrawing it from public-domain lands open to entry for homesteading. The early parks were under the protection and administration of the Department of the Army. In 1916 Congress created the National Park Service within the Department of the Interior to manage the growing system of national parks. The mission of the National Park Service is to preserve unique American cultural and landscape heritages. These resources are managed primarily for recreation use and enjoyment, while maintaining their existing natural quality.

The *Fish and Wildlife Service* of the Department of the Interior manages approximately 400 wildlife refuges. The management of these refuges aids in the conservation of migratory birds, certain mammals, and sport fish.

The *Bureau of Land Management* of the Department of the Interior manages the largest segment of the nation's public lands. Its management goals are similar to those of the Forest Service. However, the vast majority of its lands are rangelands instead of forests.

Most land management agencies have other responsibilities as part of their mission. These include informing the public in their field of resource management and assisting and encouraging good man-

---

[1]Extension here means providing educational opportunities and other resources, by means of special programs and methods, to persons without other access.

Figure 10.4 Oldest ranger station in the United States, Bitterroot National Forest, Montana. (Courtesy of U.S.D.A. Forest Service.)

agement practices on private lands with characteristics similar to those of the public lands they manage. In addition to the land-managing agencies, there are a host of departments and agencies with responsibilities that have an impact on forestry activities. They include the Departments of Commerce and Treasury, the State Department, the Environmental Protection Agency, the U.S. Agency for International Development, the Agriculture Research Service, the Soil Conservation Service, and the Extension Service. Because of the national importance of the Forest Service to forest management, the organization of this federal agency is discussed further.

Forest Service

As outlined previously, the Forest Service is divided into three main parts: the national forest system, forestry research, and state and private forestry (Figures 10.5 and 10.6). The *national forest system,* the dominant part of the agency, is the part responsible for managing the national forests. *Forestry research* provides support for basic and applied research on all aspects of forest management. *State and private forestry* covers a variety of services to the

state and private forestry sectors, such as technical and financial assistance in forest fire and pest control, tree planting, and timber stand improvement (1, 2).

The *field organization* of the Forest Service has four main levels. At the top is the Washington, D.C., office, headed by the chief of the Forest Service. Although general policy-making and planning takes place in the Washington office, most Forest Service operations—including substantial policy-making authority—are delegated to Forest Service field offices.

The national forest system field offices are divided into nine regions at the second level. Each *regional office* is headed by a regional forester, who exercises broad authority over all activities in the region. Immediately below the regional office at the third level is the *national forest,* headed by a forest supervisor. Except for Alaska, with only two—albeit large—national forests, there are from thirteen to thirty-three national forests within a region. In addition to the national forests, there are nineteen national grasslands in the prairie states, administered by national forest supervisors.

The lowest administrative unit within the Forest

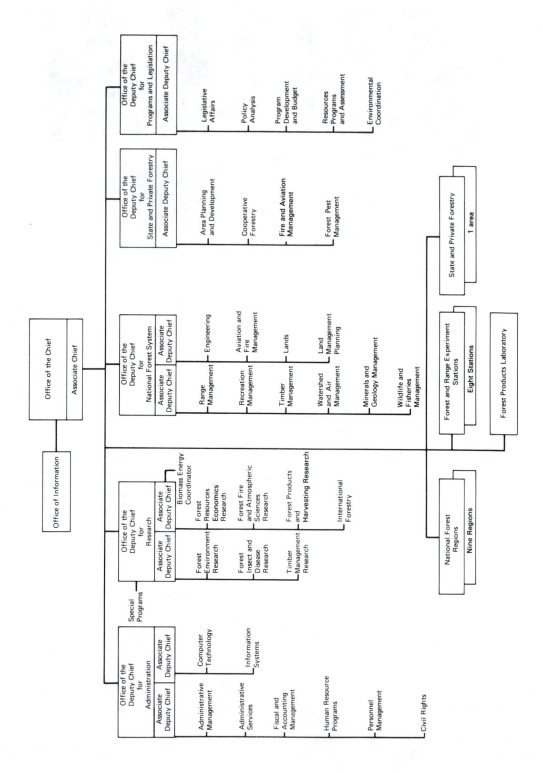

Figure 10.5 Flowchart of management responsibility within the Forest Service.

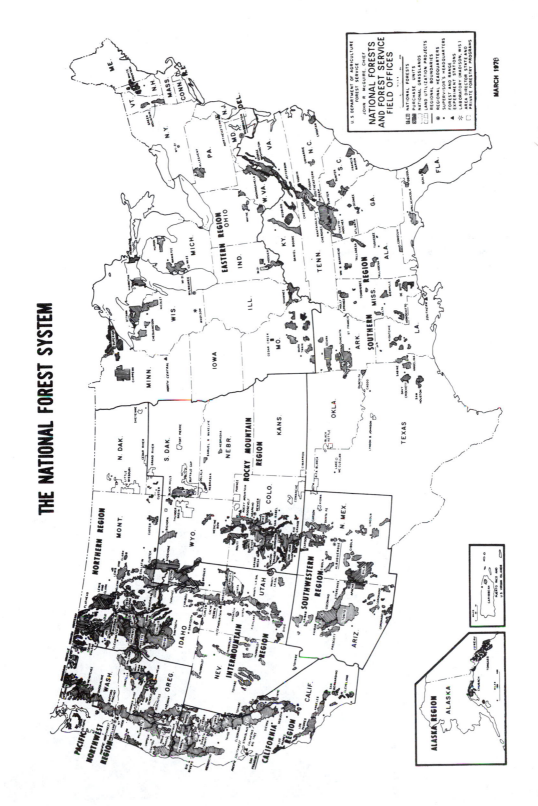

Figure 10.6 National Forest System and related-data map. (Courtesy of U.S.D.A. Forest Service.)

217

Service is the *ranger district,* headed by a forest ranger who directly supervises forest management activities within the district. The district ranger is the primary line officer of the Forest Service—an operating officer, not a policymaker.

The *research field organization* has eight experiment stations and a separate forest products laboratory (Figure 10.7). Each of these has a director and several assistant directors. Research is carried out through approximately 200 research work units, each having a specific mission. Units consist of a unit leader and one or more scientists who conduct studies within the overall mission. State and private forestry consists of one area office that covers activities in the Northeastern States. It reports directly to the chief. In other parts of the country, state and private forestry is organized as a division within the regional offices.

National Interest Groups

So far we have spoken only of formal government at the national level. Of equal importance is the vast array of national interest groups. They are often referred to as the "lobby," although many would not consider lobbying as their primary objective. These

groups can be classified into four general categories: (1) the commodity user group, (2) the noncommodity user group, (3) the professional group, and (4) the special-issue group. It is important to recognize that specific organizations may have activities in more than one group. However, one overriding interest usually tends to be reflected.

The commodity and noncommodity groups are both forest users. Both groups try to promote forest policies and budgets that favor their interests. The *commodity group* is composed of the organizations associated with an industry that produces a marketed product such as paper, lumber, or beef. Examples are the American Plywood Association and the National Forest Products Association.

The *noncommodity group* is also a user of the forest, but the use does not involve the production of a forest product. The organizations use the forest primarily for enjoyment. Examples of the organizations in the noncommodity group are the National Wildlife Federation, the Sierra Club, Forests Unlimited, and the All-Terrain Vehicle Association.

The third group, referred to as the *professional group,* consist of organizations that exist primarily to maintain and advance the technical and scientific level of the forestry profession. This group includes

Figure 10.7 Forest Products Laboratory, Madison, Wisconsin. (Courtesy of U.S.D.A. Forest Service.)

such organizations as the Society of American Foresters, Resources for the Future, and the Society for Range Management.

The final category has been called the *special-issue group*. These are organizations that formally support or oppose a single issue. Their existence is usually limited to the duration of the issue. However, on occasion, they take on new issues and evolve into organizations with broader interests. Examples of special-issue groups are Citizens Against Toxic Substances and Friends of the Boundary Waters Wilderness.

All these national interest groups contribute to formulation of national policy. However, the Society of American Foresters (SAF) plays an additional significant role in the development of the forestry profession.

The SAF was founded in 1900 with the objectives of advancing the science, technology, education, and practice of professional forestry in America and of using the knowledge and skill of the profession to benefit society. The SAF publishes the monthly *Journal of Forestry* and *Forest Science,* a quarterly research journal.

The functions of the agency also include formulating a code of professional ethics for foresters, promoting international forestry relations, preparing descriptions of forest cover types, putting together cutting practice guides for different regions of the country, and classifying forestry literature, to name a few.

The Functioning of Federal Agencies and Forestry

In order to appreciate forestry in a national frame of reference, we must understand how the groups discussed in the previous section function and interrelate with the three branches of government to help formulate forestry policy. As discussed previously, there are several departments and agencies in the *executive branch* with direct interest in forestry matters. They develop procedures and establish direction for managing forest resources under their jurisdiction. In the process they must interact with and seek approval from the president's staff, the Office of Management and Budget, and the Congress. This section will examine the "give and take" within government necessary to develop a forest management program.

Within an agency there are staff units, each sometimes having different concepts about what forestry policy should be. Informal discussions, staff meetings, and other means are employed to hammer out policy direction. Constraints are set by the limitations of the resources to be managed, laws, regulations, tradition, and executive orders from the president. This process goes on within a legal framework established by Congress in a single charter act or by a series of acts for different components of the agency's program.

The management program of an agency such as the Forest Service is part of an overall *executive program.* It is also part of one finite budget. Forestry programs must be balanced with other programs such as health care, transportation systems, and defense matters. The central issue is how much should be allocated to forestry programs in relation to other programs to serve the American public most effectively.

The unenviable task of recommending to the president how to slice the pie falls to the president's *Office of Management and Budget.* The OMB must take all the agency and department budget proposals and fit them into one or more cohesive packages. This office operates under the president's overall direction and with no allegiance to any one agency or department. Generally, staff members at OMB referred to as "examiners" are assigned responsibility for one agency (at most three or four). The examiner analyzes the agency's budget proposal, for use in program-balancing deliberations. The agency must provide full information and justification to its examiner. Analyses and assessments must accompany each program request. If support is not deemed adequate, the OMB representative may challenge or even recommend dropping a specific program. Effective interaction with the examiner and support by the secretary and departmental staff are critical to an agency in maintaining its position within an administration budget.

The OMB not only plans the budget but also monitors the agency's programs. Programs, policies, and activities are watched for results within the context of the president's overall program. The agency faces detailed scrutiny at budget time if OMB questions have not been resolved during the year. The role of OMB in this sense is not punitive.

Forestry issues and policy are then incorporated into several parts of the president's annual program budget proposal. Implementation of any part of this plan must await *congressional action* to approve the activity and its funding. Congress can of course increase, decrease, or otherwise change the president's budget proposal. Congressional interest in forestry issues is evidenced both by individual members of Congress and by committee or subcommittee members. No single committee or subcommittee has overall jurisdiction over forestry matters; for example, committees on foreign trade consider log exports, and committees on energy issues may consider wood fiber as an alternative energy source.

A representative or staff member may have expertise in forestry matters or may rely on an agency for specific knowledge. Congressional committee staffs have recently increased their forestry expertise. Although most members of Congress have little background in forestry, they still may take a strong interest in particular forestry issues. The Forest Service manages land in many states and congressional districts. As a result, it is not unusual for legislators to represent the interests of their constituents in specific forestry matters during the annual congressional budget review process.

The overall role of Congress in forestry issues is somewhat similar to that of a local forest manager. Congress tries to resolve disputes over conflicting uses, but on a broader scale—that of forestry in a national context. The role of Congress is threefold. First, Congress reviews and revises the president's program budget requests. It often provides direction in the annual appropriation act and the appropriation committee reports. The budget review process provides an overview of an agency's plans and policies; here congressional direction is restricted to existing laws. The direction usually alters funding or alters the manner in which funds may be used.

Congress performs another role in national pol-

icy matters by *passing legislation*. Laws define, redefine, or clarify the context within which agencies administer policy. Congress tends to legislate infrequently regarding forestry, although the 1970s were an exception to this rule. The legislature has generally set broad guidelines or frameworks but prefers that the agencies develop and carry out specific forestry policy for three reasons. First, as discussed previously, forests in the United States are very diverse and must respond to many often-changing needs. Second, Congress is not a very appropriate forum to produce specific direction because of its size and diverse membership. Third, many members of Congress consider it unwise to legislate on professional forestry matters. The position of Congress on forestry also leads to support for, and strong reliance on, the agencies that are heavily staffed and run by professional resource managers.

A final but important role performed by Congress is monitoring and reviewing the day-to-day activities and occasional crises that occur during agency operations. These tasks are performed by the *General Accounting Office* and the *Congressional Budget Office,* both arms of Congress, and also through congressional oversight hearings. The results of these activities take the form of reports to or from Congress.

The executive and legislative branches sometimes employ subtle methods of reaching an agreement when establishing programs and setting program direction. The executive branch may omit from its budget recommendation programs that are enthusiastically supported by members of Congress, because they are considered of lower priority. Then, in return for congressional compromise on another issue, the executive branch will include a portion or all of the omitted program. This process may also work in reverse. It must be remembered that the key national issues of compromise often are not forestry matters, but other matters of domestic or foreign policy. Professional foresters generally participate at the fringes of this process. They provide factual information on forestry opportunities and the consequences of various actions to the forest resources and to the public who rely on these resources.

The *judicial branch* of the federal government is concerned with forestry issues only at the request of an interested party. Its role is to interpret and clarify actions and policies in terms of existing law and to offer redress to petitioners. The courts can either approve or prohibit specific activities and policies according to legal interpretation. They cannot initiate new direction unless an existing basis can be shown to support it. However, if this base exists, an agency's operating policies may need to be changed in order to comply with the court's decision. In areas where the law is overly broad or unclear or controversy touches on constitutional matters, the courts may, in fact, provide considerable directions that the agency must follow. Each time a law is tested in court, new case law or precedent is established. If the law or action being tested is confirmed as being appropriate, the law or action takes on new support or strength for similar future actions.

This section has stressed the *functional roles* of the three branches of the federal government and the way they *interact* to produce and interpret laws and policies. An example may help to provide a clearer picture of the processes. In very general terms, we will follow public interest and government action in the evolution of forestry management policy for the Forest Service. A key point is that forestry policy has changed with social needs and demands over the past nine decades. These processes and relationships are summarized in Table 10.1 and are discussed here.

In the 1860s and 1870s, public opinion grew to

Table 10.1 Major Events and Participants in the Evolution of Forest Policy

Date	Public Interest	Legislative	Executive	Judicial
1879	AFA and AAAS petition Congress to reserve forest/lands[a]			
1891		Reservation Act		
1891			President establishes reserves	
1896	NAS reserve management report to president[b]			
1897		Organic Act		
1897			Establishment of reserves continued; forestry management concepts stated	
1905			Establishment of Forest Service	
1960		Multiple Use–Sustained Yield Act		
1973	Public petition of courts to review compliance			Court rules noncompliance
1974	with Organic Act	Renewable Resources Planning Act (RPA)		
1976		National Forest Management Act	Forest Service produces first national inventory and long-ranged programs based on RPA	

[a]AFA: American Forestry Association; AAAS: American Association for the Advancement of Science.
[b]NAS: National Academy of Sciences.

favor federal management of forests. In 1879 the American Forestry Association (AFA) and the American Association for the Advancement of Science (AAAS) both petitioned Congress to reserve or set aside forested lands from public entry. Then in 1891 Congress passed a bill for general revision of the public land laws. When the bill emerged from House–Senate conference, Section 24 had been added. It provided authority for a president to reserve forestlands from public entry. One month later, President Harrison set aside the Yellowstone Park Forest Reserve, south of Yellowstone Park. He proclaimed executive reserves but gave no specific direction on how or for what purpose they were to be managed.

In 1896 the president asked the National Academy of Sciences to study what had become known as the forest reserves. Congress incorporated the concepts of forestry management resulting from the study into an amendment to an appropriation bill. This 1897 action, called the Organic Act, laid the groundwork for how the reserved federal forestland would be managed and used.

In 1905 the president, with congressional approval, transferred the Bureau of Forestry from the Department of the Interior to the Department of Agriculture and changed its name to the Forest Service. Two years later, the former forest reserves became known as national forests. Throughout the 1900s the Forest Service managed the national forests and set specific policy based primarily on the Organic Act and the annual budget review. In 1960 Congress stepped back into center stage by passing a new law to ensure that national forests would be managed for multiple uses at levels providing a sustained yield for the future (Figure 10.8). This was a codification of policies already followed by the Forest Service.

In the early 1970s several groups of people became concerned about how forestry was being practiced in some national forests. These groups petitioned the courts in 1973. The courts ruled that forestry practices were not in accordance with the law of 1897. Congress reentered the scene in 1974 with the Renewable Resources Planning Act (RPA). This bill requires the secretary of agriculture to

Figure 10.8 Properly managed forest stands can offer a multiplicity of uses to both people and animals. Shown in Minnesota is a mature stand of eastern white pine with an understory of hardwood saplings. (Courtesy of U.S.D.A. Forest Service.)

assess natural resources periodically and to submit a five-year renewable-resources program to Congress, based on this assessment of future supplies and demands.

In 1976 Congress amended the RPA legislation and enacted the National Forest Management Act (NFMA), also in response to the 1973 court action. This bill provides general guidelines for the agency by establishing the general content and process to be followed in developing national forest plans.

Over the century from 1879 to 1979, forestry policy has moved into the spotlight several times and has been scrutinized and reshaped by public interest, the executive branch, the legislature, and the judiciary. Reviewing this long time span from a national perspective will clarify how the policy for managing our national forests was forged.

Incorporating Public Interests into Forestry at the National Level

Forestry at the national level, as we have seen, is concerned with the public interest in forest resources. This section of the chapter considers how people express their common interests and how those interests become input for forestry policy. There are many ways by which people can make themselves heard by policymakers. Individuals and groups can contact management agencies and their congressional representatives, or they can resort to some form of public expression. Concern with the public interests and the integration of diverse interests into the formulation of public policy are not new to our political scene.

In 1789, James Madison discussed in the *Federalist Papers* the role and importance of what we call *public-interest* or *pressure groups*. Madison indicated that a major function of the governmental process was to integrate opposing interests and reconcile conflicting views. Almost fifty years later, Alexis de Tocqueville, the eminent French publicist, in his classic assessment of American culture and government entitled *Democracy in America,* commented on the tendency of Americans to form and join organizations, which in turn often had agendas for political action.

In more recent times political scientists have suggested the "group basis of politics" as one fundamental characteristic of American government. Economists have recognized "countervailing power" and interactive forces as important elements in public-policy decision making. Matters of the environment, natural resources, and forestry are taken into consideration by interest groups in developing public policy.

Two related developments in recent years have intensifed both individual and group involvement in questions of forestry policy and management. One of these is the widespread and growing interest in issues concerning the environment. The issuing of statutory requirements governing forestry practices, their reinforcement by court decisions, and agency responses to public views and comments are the other development.

Numerous court challenges to government agency actions have occurred. A preliminary step to such action is often the formation of an ad hoc group, should there be no permanent group. In this context, the National Environmental Policy Act (NEPA) of 1969, as discussed in Chapters 1 and 15, has had major significance in providing the basis for legal challenges to government agencies (and thus has indirectly contributed to group formation and growth). Among other things, the NEPA requires federal agencies to prepare impact statements assessing the consequences of alternative ways of carrying out major federal actions affecting the environment. Citizens dissatisfied with the content and rationale of such statements have filed suits challenging findings and other aspects of agency decisions.

Citizen surveillance of the courts has considerably sharpened the awareness of decision makers to consequences and alternatives of action and has stopped or delayed actions as well. In many instances these delays have contributed to wiser decisions. Most observers would agree that this emphasis on impact analysis has been materially advanced by the willingness of the federal courts to give "standing to sue" to a variety of interest groups. One result has been that federal agencies have taken the requirements of the NEPA and other statutes more seriously than they might otherwise have done. A few law professors have, in fact, asserted that this access to the courts is crucial to democratic government in this technocratic age. In any case, these developments have undoubtedly contributed to the growth and expansion of group activities with respect to environmental policy and administration.

It has also been pointed out, however, that on any issue or set of issues, neither the involved groups nor the individual participants are likely to represent all people and all possible interest configurations. In part, the problem is one of span of attention. People cannot possibly get involved in all the issues that will affect them and their interests, nor is it clear that the decision to become involved is always rational or deliberate. Such variables as personality, friendship, and presence—as well as preferences—may determine both the fact and the degree of involvement. Failure to be involved with issues that affect one's interests may mirror a lack of commitment, time, money, or understanding. As a result, it is crucial to recognize that less vocal citizens must also be considered and might not remain silent if a wrong decision is reached. By exercising informed judgments on what they perceive are the interests of the expressed and the silent publics, professionals and their agencies must begin to approximate the overall *public interest*.

In forest management, as in many resource and environmental decisions, the articulation of the public interest is often complicated by the fact that decisions made today have very *long-term* consequences. The responsible professional public servant must attempt to address the future. To be sure, the crystal ball is always clouded, and there is a tendency to address the immediate crisis. Hence, analysis must substitute for prophecy and foreknowledge. If public agencies respond only to current public outcry, the real potential public interest may be overlooked.

It should be recognized that the very multiplicity of interests in forestry at the national level ensures a high level of conflict and controversy. In many situations one set of interests will run counter to another. A major task of Congress and agencies is conflict resolution, that is, seeking to reconcile and choose the appropriate solution from a wide range of possible outcomes.

Cooperative Forestry Activities

Millions of hectares of forestlands are not administered by federal agencies. Nonfederal owners include forest industries, states, local governments, and small landowners. There are several formal programs to facilitate forest management on these various ownerships. Some programs provide forestry assistance to landowners, primarily nonindustrial owners of small parcels of land. Other programs coordinate the activities of managers of large land parcels, primarily public agencies and forest industries. The term *cooperative forestry* is often used in referring to these types of programs.

The Forest Service has a major program (state and private forestry) specifically dedicated to cooperative forestry activities. A major effort is made to work with state forestry agencies to strengthen their programs and provide coordination between states and other organizations. Both financial and technical assistance is provided.

In recent years state agencies have become stronger and federal funds have dwindled. This situation has spawned a national effort to focus federal assistance on activities that require a federal role, have multistate implications, and will provide for long-term improvements (3). An example of a large national coordination effort can be found in what is referred to as the "urban-wildland fire protection initiative." Following the severe 1985 fire season, during which some 1400 structures were lost, it was decided to focus national attention on the growing fire problem brought about by the urbanization of wildlands. A group consisting of the National Fire Protection Association, the Forest Service, the National Fire Administration, and others was formed to draw attention and seek a solution to the problem. Cooperative agreements were worked out for pooling personnel and financial resources. A series of workshops were designed to seek solutions that range from restructuring building codes and insurance rates, to improving fire suppression plans.

Private nonindustrial forestlands have always been a concern to professional foresters. Their current contribution is considerable, but they have an even greater potential to contribute to future forest resource production in the United States. Nearly 60 percent of the commercial forestland in the United States is in farm and other private nonindustrial ownership. These owners also hold millions of acres of noncommercial forest. Private nonindustrial lands produce a significant share of the nation's timber, support livestock herds, and provide recreational opportunities for many people. The majority of these forest ownerships are small parcels of fewer than 400 hectares (1000 acres), and for some little thought is given to management of their natural resources.

Much is known about the extent of private nonindustrial forest ownership and about the resource production capabilities of these lands. However, not enough is known about the landowners themselves. Their motivations for retaining forest tracts are quite diverse, and forest management may not be a major consideration. Returns from the forest often take the form of selling stumpage prior to selling the land itself.

Controversy now surrounds private nonindustrial forestry at the national level—just as it did forestry on public lands 100 years ago. Policies for small-woodlot owners will from the national perspective be in a state of flux during the 1990s. The first area of discussion is whether or not these lands are a matter of significant national forestry concern. Should private nonindustrial lands be part of the national effort to intensify forest management, or are they outside that effort? How can forestry management be encouraged on these lands? Work is under way to determine how forest management objectives might coincide with ownership objectives for small private forest parcels. Not only the Forest Service, but also state forestry agencies, the forest industry, forestry consultants, and universities are currently discussing these issues and examining the alternatives. There is a close parallel between this process for nonindustrial private lands and the one that went on 100 years ago and resulted in a program of conservation for public forestlands. A further discussion of private nonindustrial forests is given in Chapter 11.

International Forestry

Washington, D.C., is not only a hub for national forest policy; it is also one of the world's major centers for international forestry. Headquartered in Washington are a number of U.S. government agencies, international organizations, and nongovernmental entities with international programs in forestry or natural resources.

Among the U.S. agencies, the largest international forestry program is managed by the *U.S. Agency for International Development* (USAID). Currently USAID contributes to forestry projects in some thirty-six tropical countries at an annual cost of about $135 million. Assistance projects include training, disaster relief, and private-sector development efforts. The largest U.S. employer of foresters overseas, however, is the Peace Corps, which now has 550 foresters in forty-six countries. The U.S.D.A. Forest Service also manages an active international program. It represents the U.S. government on major world forestry issues, promotes scientific exchange and cooperative research among countries, works directly with various countries on mutually beneficial technical programs, and provides technical support to USAID. Other government agencies with international forestry or natural-resource programs include the State Department, National Park Service, Fish and Wildlife Service, U.S. Geological Survey, and the Smithsonian Institute. On tropical matters, informal coordination of activities is achieved through the Interagency Task Force on Tropical Forestry.

International organizations with home offices in Washington are the *World Bank, Inter-American Development Bank,* and the *Organization of American States* (OAS). Each is active in international forestry and natural resources, and the World Bank is the largest with annual forestry disbursements of about $150 million in seven countries. Over the past fifteen years it has invested approximately $1.5 billion in forestry development in fifty-five countries. The World Bank's policy and lending strategy on forestry emphasizes a balanced program of small-scale tree farming, institution building, and industrial projects. Activities include village forestry, environmental protection, and rural development. The Inter-American Development Bank has a growing forestry portfolio, which is limited to the Western Hemisphere. The OAS supports forestry, agricultural research, information exchange, and training in tropical America. Though headquartered in Rome, Italy, the *Food and Agricultural Organization* (FAO) of the United Nations also maintains a Liaison Office for North America in Washington.

Since its creation in the early 1940s, the FAO has directed the world's leading international forestry program. Through technical meetings and publications, it facilitates the worldwide exchange of technical information and provides technical assistance to developing countries. Its office in Washington manages policy and administrative concerns, not technical programs, with North America. Coordination among the world's major forestry donor agencies is achieved on an ad hoc basis through periodic donors' meetings.

Nongovernmental organizations are playing an increasingly important role in international forestry. Many are located in Washington, D.C., such as *World Resources Institute,* the *International Institute for Environment and Development,* and the *Pan American Development Foundation.* The World Resources Institute recently demonstrated leadership in tropical forestry by developing a major report entitled "Tropical Forestry: A Call for Action," which outlines problems, successful experiences, and financial resources needed to stem the rampant deforestation of tropical forests. The International Institute for Environment and Development emphasizes natural-resources policy and planning, and often works closely with USAID on development projects.

Two major professional societies concerned with international forestry issues, the *Society of American Foresters* (SAF) and the *International Society of Tropical Foresters* (ISTF), are also headquartered in Washington. Through its International Forestry Working Group and Committee on World Forestry, the SAF keeps its members abreast of international forestry concerns. It also sponsored a major policy report called "International Forestry: The Role of the Society of American Foresters." The report explores opportunities for an expanded SAF role in international forestry. Communication among the world's tropical foresters is facilitated by the ISTF, especially through issuance of its quarterly newsletter.

As can be seen, international forestry is a growth area for the profession. As we continue to become more aware of world forestry problems, opportunities and the essential need for the professional forester become more apparent.

Forestry Research

Advocacy for research has long been a part of the national concern for forest resource management. Currently forestry management is a blend of basic and applied research investigations. Research projects are initiated to examine particular management questions, often at the request of resource administrators.

The need for research is not a recent phenomenon. Before 1890 reports and recommendations on the nation's forests specifically called for national research initiatives. The Reverend Frederick Starr, Jr., called for "extensive, protracted, and scientific experiments in the propagation and cultivation of forest trees" in 1865. The "Report on Forestry" by Franklin B. Hough in 1882 called for research on the effect of forests on climate and for the establishment of experiment stations.

Forestry research at the national level has three functions: (1) to assist in identifying *areas of major concern* that require research, (2) to establish and *maintain continuity* between research and evolving management policy, and (3) to provide *coordination* and *management* of the nation's research programs.

As previously discussed, national forestry policy and direction change with fluctuating social conditions and needs. Quite often, management policy options depend on new ways of monitoring uses and impacts, new methods of doing old jobs, new means of incorporating and balancing resource needs, and the like. National forestry policy and the national research agenda are closely related. National forestry policies must be based on sound scientific information. In addition, research findings may indicate a need to change national policy.

The research staff at the national level maintains the links between needed research and current policy. The link to policy helps determine which areas of study have high priority. High-priority research is not simply a matter of which forest problem is the greatest. The national staff encourages research that has applicability beyond a particular problem in a particular area. The other area of national responsibility for research is coordination.

Figure 10.9 Wildlife such as the majestic moose are carefully managed in Yellowstone National Park, Wyoming. (Photograph by R. A. Young.)

The national staffs seek to coordinate regional research to avoid duplication and research voids.

Many agencies and groups have national interests in forestry research. These programs vary considerably in size and diversity. The Fish and Wildlife Service studies the protection and management of animal resources (Figure 10.9). The National Park Service studies how to protect and manage park resources. The Environmental Protection Agency sponsors research on environmental protection and the consequences of forest activities on air and water quality. Forest Service research covers a wide spectrum of biological, economic, engineering, and social problems related to forest and rangeland management. They emphasize opportunities for taking products from the forest; how to protect and enhance noncommodity values; and how to improve forest products.

Several special-interest groups also support research. They often do not have a national program of study but concentrate on the interests of the organization. The National Wildlife Federation has a program of grants to sponsor research by university students. The National Forest Products Association

sponsors research of interest to its members. Organizations such as these study forest technology, the resource base, changing social needs, and interactions between social demands and renewable resources.

Several national organizations seek to focus and direct research to current and future areas of concern and, when appropriate, to develop a greater understanding of the present state of the art. Examples of these groups are Resources for the Future and the Society of American Foresters.

University studies often depend on an individual investigator's interests and funding sources, whether or not there are overall department programs. Studies may investigate social demands and needs on ways to improve product utilization (Figure 10.10). National research coordination is much more difficult to achieve between agencies, organizations, and universities than within an agency or organization. Some umbrella-type organizations formally link federal and state research bodies. These linkages facilitate communication and help set national priorities. For example, at the national level, the Joint Council on Food and Agriculture Sciences fosters planning and coordination of research, extension, and higher education between U.S.D.A. agencies and the private sector. A related U.S.D.A. organization, the User's Advisory Board for National Agriculture Research and Extension, provides input into policy and program development by identifying research and extension priorities from the view of the citizen user. Where formal connections do not provide a national network between scientists, coordination may frequently be initiated by individual scientists.

The Forest and Rangeland Renewable Resources Planning Act of 1974 requires that forestry research planning be a continual process with ample opportunity for public participation. In compliance with this act, there have been several recent efforts to enhance coordination of national research planning. One such effort, "1980–1990 National Program of Research for Forests and Associated Rangelands," was developed as a joint effort by the U.S.D.A. Forest Service, the U.S.D.A. Cooperative State Research Service, and the National Association of State Univer-

Figure 10.10 A large part of university research is government-sponsored. Academic research involves work (*a*) in the greenhouse and (*b*) at the "bench," as well as fieldwork. (Photographs by R. A. Young.)

sities and Land Grant Colleges (4). This document describes current and projected research programs of the U.S.D.A. Forest Service and sixty-one forestry schools.

The program was designed to satisfy several needs. First, it provides an updated guide for long-range planning in the U.S.D.A. Cooperative State Research Service and the participating forestry schools as required by Title XIV of the Food and Agriculture Act. Second, it fulfills the requirement of the RPA of 1974 and complements the current RPA document titled "A Recommended Renewable Resources Program—1980 Update" (5). Third, it is a guide for coordinated annual program development among the Forest Service, Cooperative State Research Service, the university community, and others.

The need for certain policy changes to strengthen the overall forestry research effort was recognized. Some recommendations were to expand or intensify research already under way, whereas others pointed to new directions. Future research goals are described for four broad geographic regions of the country and for the U.S.D.A. Forest Service, Forest Products Laboratory in Madison, Wisconsin.

People use forest environments in many ways. New knowledge is continually needed to manage the complex and changing relationships between people and forests. Research provides this knowledge.

Summary and a Look Ahead

Forestry at the national level is different from that practiced at the field or technical level. It focuses on forestry issues as components of many diverse national policies. Many groups, agencies, and individuals are involved in shaping national policy—some solely to carry out or influence certain aspects of forestry. However, for most individuals concerned with national activities, forestry is only a small part of their mission. By necessity, forestry from a national perspective must be viewed in a context of larger,

national concerns such as employment, housing, energy, and international relations. Much effort goes into identifying how forestry can address these major national concerns.

It might be helpful in concluding this chapter to look ahead to the future of forestry from a national perspective. Forest resources—both commodity and noncommodity—are renewable. This should increase their importance as nonrenewable resources continue to dwindle. The ways in which forestry issues are important to national policies will become even more complex and diverse in the coming decades as we increase our knowledge of forest ecosystems.

The complexity of issues and opportunities will require agencies and other organizations to work more closely together. Such important subjects as acid rain, global warming and the UN Decade for Natural Disaster Reduction are helping to form new and exciting partnerships.

Increasing public interest in and access to forestry issues will lead to questions about the roles of both resource professionals and interested citizens. Forestry professionals will need to develop better ways of analyzing alternative actions and giving the public access to the decision-making process. People with little forestry background whose interests may be narrowly defined must be able to understand these processes. An increased awareness of international forestry will create new demands and will result in a broader range of issues and problems for foresters to address.

People will increasingly employ available means of influence, through all branches of government—executive, legislative, and judicial—as they become more involved with national forestry issues. Competing interests and uses for forest resources will require new approaches to balance social needs and resource capabilities. This is the future realm of forestry at the national level. The possibilities are challenging and intriguing. To serve the public in this future scenario foresters will need to

Grow more trees.

Use more reconstituted wood products.

Improve public understanding and management of the ecosystem.

Compensate private landowners for providing public values.

Learn to accommodate additional segments of society in managing forests.

The future of forestry issues in national and international policies promises to be active and controversial. The coming decades will be perplexing and frustrating to those professionals who continue to see forestry solely in terms of applying technical forestry principles. On the other hand, the coming decades can be a time of challenge and excitement for the professional who understands the national perspective of forestry. For this professional, the times ahead will provide the opportunity to make valuable contributions to forestry in the tradition of Bernhard Fernow, Franklin Hough, and Gifford Pinchot.

References

1. G. O. ROBINSON, *The Forest Service,* Resources for the Future, Washington, D.C., 1975.

2. M. FROME, *The Forest Service,* Praeger, New York, 1971.

3. ALLAN J. WEST, "Letter to Regional Foresters and Area Directors," U.S.D.A. For. Serv., June 1986.

4. ANON., "1980–1990 national program of research for forests and associated rangelands," U.S.D.A. For. Serv., Gen. Tech. Rept. WO 32, 1982.

5. ANON., "A recommended renewable resources program," U.S.D.A. For. Serv., Publ. FS 346, 1980.

CHAPTER 11

Nonindustrial Private Forests

A. Jeff Martin
John Bliss

Almost 60 percent of the land designated by the U.S. Forest Service as timberland (commercial forestland) is owned by nonindustrial private forest (NIPF) owners (Figure 11.1). Private owners of timberland other than forest products industries are classified as NIPF owners. A considerable portion of this timberland may not actually be available for timber production at any given time because of population density, ownership size and objectives, and site quality. Nonindustrial private forestlands are of enormous importance to the U.S. timber supply today, and their importance will be even greater in the future. By the year 2030 removals of both softwoods and hardwoods from industrial and other private forests are projected to exceed growth (1). In addition, these lands are under increasing pressure to provide environmental and recreational amenities.

The projected wood shortfall is at the heart of one of the most discussed topics in U.S. forestry, the "small-woodland problem." For several decades forestry observers have claimed that private forests have not been managed effectively and thus have not met their productive potential. Although this claim had long gone unquestioned, some analyses now suggest that NIPF lands have been at least as productive as public and industrial forests (2). Furthermore, one observer commented that the NIPF

231

Figure 11.1 Nonindustrial private forests provide timber, recreation, wildlife habitat, and scenic beauty throughout the eastern half of the United States.

"problem" is not the landowners' problem at all: it is the forest industry's problem: "Private timberland owners have something industry wants and needs; productive timber resources and growing stock" (2). He could have added that these landowners have other things that people want, too: green forests of great aesthetic and recreational value.

Management of NIPF lands is a unique challenge to the forestry profession, both because the resource is important and because the task is inherently difficult. Unlike industrial forests, which are managed primarily for timber production, and publicly owned forests, which are managed for multiple uses including timber production (as described in Chapters 9 and 10), NIPF lands are controlled by an estimated 7.8 million owners, each of whom has unique objectives and management capabilities. The challenge of the forestry profession is to motivate these owners to practice good stewardship of their forestlands. To meet this challenge, foresters must be as well versed in psychology and sociology as they are in silviculture and forest measurements.

Another aspect of the NIPF challenge is the political dimension. Public forestry agencies at the local, state, and federal levels have not always agreed on who should be responsible for NIPF programs, or on what form these programs should take. Furthermore, forest industries have not always seen eye to eye with government NIPF policymakers on the necessity for public involvement in NIPF affairs. Furthermore, NIPF owners themselves have not until recently participated to any great extent in formulating policies that affect management of their forests.

This chapter introduces the reader to the key elements of nonindustrial private forest management in the United States. First, it outlines the dimensions of the NIPF resource. Next, the NIPF owners are discussed. Third, the historical development and present form of federal, state, industrial, and private programs that encourage NIPF management are described. Finally, recent issues in NIPF management policy and future NIPF trends are discussed.

The NIPF Resource

Size and Distribution

There are NIPF landowners in every state, but many are concentrated in the eastern half of the United States. Lands in this category comprise some 112.5 million hectares of U. S. timberland. These lands support about 42 percent of the total U. S. growing-stock volume of timber. This share of the total forest resource has not changed much over the past thirty years (3).

A 1978 U.S. Forest Service survey of 11,076 owners of private forestland has provided new insight into various dimensions of NIPF ownership (4). Although the basic study focused on all forms of private forest ownership, Fedkiw (1) provided additional information on the NIPF sector. The results of this study indicate that the distribution of NIPF landowners by the size of their forests is highly skewed. The average size of an NIPF holding is 14.6 hectares, which is rather misleading (Table 11.1).

Most NIPF holdings are smaller than 40 hectares, and 71 percent of the private forest owners own fewer than 4 hectares of forest. However, these small tracts make up only 4 percent of the NIPF land (1). Only 8 percent of the NIPF landowners own 40 or more hectares of timberland, but this 8 percent controls about 74 percent of the total NIPF land (Table 11.1)! Almost 40 percent of NIPF land is held by less than one percent of NIPF owners in tracts of at least 200 hectares, and an additional 40 percent of the NIPF lands are owned by another 7 percent of the owners in tracts of between 40 and 200 hectares.

The geographic distribution of NIPF lands is important because of their concentration in the eastern United States. In 1977, 91 percent of all NIPF timberland was east of Montana, Wyoming, Colorado, and New Mexico. These forests represent about 70 percent of the timberland in the eastern states. In the western states NIPF lands account for only 20 percent of the timberland.

Forest Productivity, Growth, and Removal

The NIPF lands contain somewhat more hardwood volume (59 percent of the NIPF growing-stock inventory) than softwood and in fact constitute 70 percent of the nation's hardwood inventory. When sawtimber volumes are considered, NIPF lands contain 49 percent hardwood, and 51 percent softwood, a nearly equal split.

Net growth on these NIPF lands is sometimes criticized as being quite low compared to growth on holdings under other forms of ownership. However,

Table 11.1 Distribution of NIPF Lands in the United States by Size of Tracts and Number of Owners, 1978

Size Class (ha)	Owners		Land Owned	
	(1000s)	(percent)	(million ha)	(percent)
Less than 4	5,528	71	4.5	4
4–19	1,164	15	11.3	10
20–39	464	6	13.4	12
40–199	538	7	41.3	37
200–404	40	1	10.9	10
405–4050	21	—	19.4	17
Over 4050	2	—	11.7	10
Total	7757	100	112.5	100

Source: J. Fedkiw, "Background paper on non-industrial private forest lands, their management, and related public and private assistance," U.S.D.A. For. Serv., Off. Budget Prog. Anal., Off. of the Secretary, Washington, D.C., 1983.

the figures do not support this criticism. The NIPF share of net annual growth in 1976 was equal to their proportion of forestland (58 percent), and somewhat greater than their proportion of growing-stock volume.

Nationally, current net annual growth on NIPF lands ranks between that obtained from all public lands and growth on industrial lands. However, this ranking does not hold for all regions. In the North and the Rocky Mountains the productivity on NIPF lands falls below that of the public sector. According to Forest Service projections (3), the current NIPF productivity is only about 62 percent of its potential on a national basis. This productivity is only slightly below that for industrial lands, but it is about 15 percent higher than the figure for national forestlands. The comparison of current growth to potential growth is not uniform throughout all regions, ranging from 50 percent in the North to 73 percent in the South.

Total NIPF timberland declined about 6 percent between 1952 and 1977. Forest Service projections indicate that this declining trend will continue into the future at approximately the same rate, so that by 2030 we can expect about 100.4 million hectares of NIPF land. This was the largest change in all classes of ownership during the 1952–1977 period, as well as being the largest expected change for the future.

In the period between 1976 and 2030 the major increase in timber supplies—the amount of timber harvested—is expected to be from NIPF lands. This forecast reflects both the extent of NIPF ownership and the responsiveness of NIPF owners to price and inventory increases.

Indications are that NIPF lands will supply a greater share of softwood supplies in the future. The majority of this increase is expected on lands in the South, whereas supplies from Pacific Coast industrial lands are expected to decline. The projections call for the largest shift to occur in softwood sawtimber supplies. The NIPF share of sawtimber production is expected to increase from 29 percent in 1976 to 41 percent in 2030. Minor changes are expected from public lands, and the major decline will occur on industrial lands. Owners of NIPF land are expected to continue to supply about 75 percent of the nation's hardwood roundwood and sawtimber (Figure 11.2). The proportions contributed by other

Figure 11.2 Nonindustrial private forest owners supply about 75 percent of the nation's hardwood roundwood and sawtimber.

ownerships are also projected to remain about the same between 1976 and 2030.

The growth of timber volume on NIPF lands is not expected to be as favorable. Net annual growth of softwood is projected to increase on all lands except NIPF lands, where a decline is forecast. The major causes for this decline are slow growth rates brought about by overstocking in the North and reversion of softwood stands to hardwoods in the South. The expected trend for hardwoods shows a drop in net annual growth for all lands. However, since most of the hardwood supplies grow on NIPF lands, the decline in growth will have its biggest effect on this segment of our timberland. Again, overstocking, particularly in the East, is a significant factor.

Softwood volumes on NIPF lands are projected to increase from 21.5 percent of the total softwood inventory in 1977 to 33.5 percent in 2030. Lands in other ownership categories are expected to see only slight increases at best in softwood inventories. Hardwood inventories are expected to increase on land of all ownerships through 2010, with the largest increase on NIPF lands. Some decline in NIPF hardwood inventory levels is anticipated between 2010 and 2030.

The NIPF Owners

The 1978 survey (4) classified private forest owners by race, sex, education, residence, method and date of acquisition of forestland, and tract size. The survey indicates that most individual forest owners are white, male, over 50 years of age, and own forestland in the same county in which they live or work. Women and racial minorities tend to own smaller tracts of timber than white males. People with less than an eighth-grade education own as much forestland as college graduates, but the average size of holdings increases with increasing education.

Farmers own more forestland than any other group of individual owners. Furthermore, the average size of forest tract owned by farmers is over 40.5 hectares; this is considerably larger than the average size of tract for other individual owner groups. The next largest category of NIPF land is that owned by

white-collar workers, followed by land owned by retirees and blue-collar workers (4).

Over half of the private forestland (including corporately owned lands) was acquired after 1950; three-quarters of the owners acquired their land during this time. Almost 16 percent of the private forestland has been in the same ownership for over 40 years.

Many researchers have analyzed characteristics of NIPF owners and their forestlands to determine which owner and ownership variables are the most useful in predicting forest management activity (Figure 11.3). Several regional studies indicate that owners of large tracts of timber are more likely to harvest timber than owners of small tracts (5, 6). O'Leary and others (7) found that owners of tracts larger than 12.1 hectares were more knowledgeable about forestry and appeared to be more amenable to forest management than owners of smaller tracts. The authors were able to predict landowners' views of how land should be managed using size of tract, education and age of the owner, size of the community in which the owner lives, and membership in farm and conservation organizations. A number of studies have demonstrated that the intensity of forest management is positively correlated to the size of forest holding and the landowner's financial position. Some studies have found that farmers are more likely than nonfarmers to harvest timber. Fesco and others (8) discovered that 84 percent of the harvested land in the South was on tracts of at least 40.5 hectares. An additional 9 percent of the harvested land was on tracts of 20.2 to 40.4 hectares. If this same relationship of tract size to harvest activity were to hold throughout the country, 93 percent of all NIPF timber harvest activity would occur on only 14 percent of the tracts. This conclusion strongly suggests that efforts to increase timber production from NIPF lands will be most effective if concentrated on large tracts.

Several studies have asked the question, "Why do people own forestland?" (Figure 11.4). In a study of New Hampshire and Vermont NIPF owners, Kingsley and Birch (5) found that 45 percent of the owners owned their forestland because it was part of their residence. These owners' tracts averaged only 8.5

Figure 11.3 Nonindustrial private forest owners have many different reasons for owning forestland. Because management objectives change over time, and lands change hands, timber production from NIPF lands is difficult to predict.

hectares in size. They cited anticipated appreciation in land value, aesthetic enjoyment, and "green space" as important benefits provided by their forestlands. Fully half of all respondents said that the aesthetic enjoyment obtained from their land would be the most important benefit of ownership in the future. Recreation was the main reason for owning forestland for 21 percent, and 10 percent said they owned forestland primarily as an investment. For 8 percent of respondents farm and domestic use was

Figure 11.4 Most NIPF properties are managed for multiple purposes. This Wisconsin farm raises dairy cows, corn, tobacco, and oak.

the primary reason for ownership. Finally, 6 percent of the owners indicated that timber production was their primary reason for owning forestland. However, this 6 percent of the private owners controlled 21 percent of the timberland in the two states.

Several studies have classified NIPF owners into behavioral groups using such criteria as tract size, ownership objectives, and attitudes toward forest management. Yoho (9) suggested classifying NIPF owners by investment strategy. He recognized five classes of NIPF owners.

1. **Custodial Investors.** These owners acquired forestland without any direct action on their part. They have no investment strategy.

2. **Sideline Forest Investors.** These owners acquired forestlands as an incidental part of desired lands. The properties are often small, and forest management gets limited attention.

3. **Speculators.** The objective of this group is to hold forestland in anticipation of an increase in market value. Speculators try to minimize holding costs and therefore do not generally invest in forest management.

4. **Hobby Investors.** The typical hobby investor is a tree farmer who follows a forest management plan, invests in forest productivity, and is motivated by a sense of land stewardship.

5. **True Investors.** Members of this group have a high degree of economic awareness and behave like "economic man." True investors respond to investment incentives and market conditions. Their primary objective is estate building.

Such classifications of NIPF owners are useful, but they do not account for an owner's behavior completely. There is frequently a discrepancy between what NIPF owners say they intend to do with their forests, and what actually occurs on these lands. Opinions regarding forest management change over time, and lands change hands. Both shifts affect the management of NIPF forests. According to Clawson (10),

> While many present owners will say, with complete honesty, that they will not sell timber from their forests, the probability is very

great that over the life of the timber stand, during which its ownership will often change several times, some owner will accept a good offer, if one is made, for merchantable volumes of timber when these have developed. Over the long run, very little really merchantable timber will go unharvested.

A recent study by Carpenter (11), which was a continuation of two older studies, provides some interesting documentation of Clawson's statement. Carpenter surveyed properties in 1979 that had previously been surveyed in 1960 and in 1967. This 19-year time span provides some much-needed insight into the changes in ownership, behavior, and management practices affecting the same units of land. One conclusion of this work is that a proportion of the holdings, whose owners in 1960 or 1967 had no desire to harvest timber, had in fact received one or more harvests during the period between successive surveys. Carpenter found that "Different owners are an overwhelming factor as timber cutting prospects. At one time or another, most timber on these ownerships will be available, and the portion unavailable over a long time period is much smaller than many believe it to be." Carpenter found that 15 percent of the tracts whose 1967 owners were opposed to, or were not planning, a timber harvest had in fact been harvested only 12 years later. Owners of 12 percent of these tracts were new owners; 3 percent of these tracts were still held by the 1967 owners.

History of Government Assistance to NIPF Owners

Since the turn of the century, NIPF owners have received forest management assistance from public agencies. Recognizing the crucial contribution NIPF lands make to U.S. timber production, the U.S. Forest Service early in its existence assigned a high priority to improving management of these lands. Government programs in this area have always been controversial. From the inception of public forestry assistance programs in 1898 to the present, proponents of increased government involvement in private forest management have felt that regulation of harvesting on private lands is necessary to protect the public interest, and that subsidies and tax incentives are needed to assure effective management. Critics on the other side decry governmental interference in private-land management. They argue that the working of the free marketplace will ensure responsible forest management in the long run.

There have been three key players in the development of private-forestry assistance programs: the *federal government,* particularly the Forest Service, *state governments,* and *forest industries.* Until quite recently private forest owners themselves have played only a minor role in shaping NIPF policies and programs.

One historian of the Forest Service, William G. Robbins (12), stresses the importance of forest industries in shaping public policy toward private forestlands.

> **For most of the twentieth century important natural resource industries like lumber have enjoyed congenial relations with the federal government. Forest products leaders have been largely successful in convincing legislators that federal support for private policy would serve the national (and public) interest. Federal foresters, with a few conspicuous exceptions, have concurred in this belief. Congressional legislation in the twentieth century has slowly and steadily integrated this relationship into the national polity.**

Robbins concludes that "Industrial conditions have determined the kind and quality of federal resource programs."

The U.S. Forest Service role in private forestland management began with the 1898 publication by Gifford Pinchot of Circular 21. Pinchot believed that proper management of private forests was in the public interest. Circular 21 offered free forest management advice to farmers and other owners of large tracts of forestland. Forest Service foresters were so swamped with requests for services that by 1904 program costs were shifted to the landowners.

The *Weeks Law* of 1911, though primarily concerned with fire protection on private forests, paved the way for federal–state cooperation in private forestry programs. The *Smith–Lever Act* of 1914 permitted federal–state cooperation in agricultural extension work, including farm forestry.

The 1924 *Clarke–McNary Act* provided the foundation for all subsequent federal assistance to the states for private forest management. The act became a focal point for debate on the federal role in private forestry. Forest industry leaders lobbied vigorously against government regulation of harvesting practices on private land. The forestry community, as represented by a Society of American Foresters committee chaired by Pinchot, argued that regulation was needed to protect the public interest. The committee's report, "Forest Devastation: A National Danger and How to Meet It," concluded that "National legislation to prevent forest devastation should [provide] such control over private forestlands . . . as may be necessary to insure the continuous production of forest crops . . . and to place forest industries on a stable basis in harmony with public interest. . ." Pinchot added some personal comments to those of the committee.

> **Forest devastation will not be stopped through persuasion, a method which has been thoroughly tried out for the past twenty years and has failed utterly. Since otherwise they will not do so, private owners of forest land must now be compelled to manage their properties in harmony with the public good. The field is cleared for action and the lines are plainly drawn. He who is not for forestry is against it. The choice lies between the convenience of the lumbermen and the public good (13).**

Congress ultimately shied away from regulation and opted for cooperation between the federal government and the states in a number of programs designed to encourage proper forest management. Cooperation has been the central theme of private-forestry assistance programs ever since.

The Clarke–McNary Act extended fire protection assistance to the states, provided matching funds for the establishment of tree nurseries, and authorized a comprehensive study of state forest tax policy. The study was expected to reveal means of counteracting the "cut-and-get-out" pattern of forest exploitation

Figure 11.5 Following the uncontrolled cutting and burning in the North at the turn of the century, settlers found much of the cutover land unsuitable for agriculture. Thus rehabilitation of northern forests became a major interest of state governments in the region.

and land abandonment, which had left behind vast areas of tax-delinquent land (Figure 11.5).

Depression Era Programs

In the 1930s *Civilian Conservation Corps* (CCC) projects furthered forestry objectives for private forest owners through demonstration projects and the establishment of windbreaks and small plantations (Figure 11.6). In 1936 the *Soil Conservation and Domestic Allotment Act* established the *Agricultural Conservation Program* (ACP), which provided funding for many conservation practices, including tree planting.

The *Norris–Doxey Cooperative Farm Forestry Act* of 1937 strengthened the role of extension in forestry and provided low-cost planting stock and marketing assistance to private forest owners (Figure 11.7). By 1947, when the Norris–Doxey program was transferred from the federal government to the states, most states had developed their own private-forestry assistance programs, and many had passed legislation regulating forest practices (13).

Early State Forest Taxation Programs

Since the early nineteenth century states have recognized that traditional property taxes are a disincentive to forestry investments. The *ad valorem* tax taxes land on the basis of its present market value; thus it discriminates against slow-growing crops such as trees, which produce income only once every decade or longer. Several alternatives to the *ad valorem* system have been adopted. The first forest property tax exemption became law in the Nebraska Territory in 1861. Wisconsin's *Forest Tax Law* of 1868 exempted "tree belts" of at least 2 hectares from taxation until the trees reached 3.6 meters in height, and thereafter paid owners a tax rebate of $5 per hectare. In 1911 Michigan adopted the first *forest yield tax.* Under this arrangement landowners pay annual property taxes based on the value of the bare land, and then pay a severance tax on the value of the timber when it is harvested. In this way premature or excessive harvesting is discouraged. Several other eastern states adopted similar measures in the 1920s and 1930s. Washington passed a *mandatory yield tax* in 1931.

Year 1950 to the Present

The 1950s and 1960s were decades of tremendous growth in federal and state cooperative forestry assistance programs. The *Cooperative Forest Management (CFM) Act* of 1950 provides for direct technical forestry services to all classes of private forest ownership, including small, nonfarm tracts. This law was resisted by industrial and consulting foresters who were concerned about increasing government intervention in the marketplace and the future possibility of glutted timber markets. These groups also lobbied against the *Conservation Reserve* or "soil bank" program of the late 1950s. This program made planting stock available for forestation of marginal cropland and was partly responsible for a great expansion in tree planting (Figure 11.8).

The John F. Kennedy Administration attached a high priority to alleviation of rural poverty. The *Rural Areas Development (RAD) program,* begun in

Figure 11.6 A 1930 farm forestry education panel. (National Agricultural Library, Forest Service Photo Collection.)

Figure 11.7 This 1943 tree-planting machine was designed to reforest lands cut over at the turn of the century.

1961, gave new impetus to the already mushrooming CFM program. In 1973 The *Federal Incentives Program* (FIP) made federal cost sharing available to landowners not covered by ACP.

During the "Environmental Era" of the late 1960s and early 1970s, several states passed legislation to protect environmental quality from poor timber-harvesting practices. California's 1973 *Forest Practice Act* included the most comprehensive harvest regulations. The act required that a harvesting plan prepared by a registered professional forester be approved by the state before logging could commence. Prior regulations required that all logging companies be registered. The act prescribed limits on the size of clearcuts, harvest procedures near streams, and other measures designed to protect water quality and other environmental values, while enhancing forest productivity. A 1976 California yield tax provision subjects all forestlands within certain "timberland preserve zones" to a tax on harvested timber (13).

As federal and state programs grew in number and complexity, so too did interagency rivalry over program administration and funding, particularly as budgets began to shrink. By the 1980s responsibility for private-forestry assistance programs was increasingly being shifted from the federal level to the states.

The *Resources Planning Act* (RPA) of 1974 and the *Cooperative Forestry Assistance Act* (CFA) of 1978 reinforced federal objectives of strengthening state resource management capabilities and ensuring that federal guidelines were followed despite decreasing federal involvement. The RPA mandated

Figure 11.8 Land conservation measures on the farm include planting row crops in the valleys and trees on slopes too steep to plow. This pine plantation was part of a 1954 flood prevention project in Mississippi. (National Agricultural Library, Forest Service Photo Collection.)

long-range resource planning by the states. The CFA enabled the secretary of agriculture to establish requirements for state forest resource programs. As a result of this and other legislation, the role of the federal government in private-forestry assistance has been largely reduced to an administrative one. In contrast to the intensive federal involvement in Depression era programs, primary responsibility for private-forestry assistance is now on state shoulders (12). The role of government in forestry programs is discussed further in Chapters 1 and 10.

NIPF Assistance Programs

Present NIPF programs reflect both the legacy of Depression era programs and the budgetary constraints of the 1980s. The primary federally supported programs are the Cooperative Forest Management (CFM) program, the Agricultural Conservation Program (ACP), the Forestry Incentives Program (FIP), and the Conservation Reserve Program (CRP).

Cooperative Forest Management

The CFM program annually serves between 130,000 and 180,000 landowners nationwide, providing technical information, management advice, and on-site assistance in all aspects of forestry. Under the program the federal government provides a percentage of program costs, and the states provide the remainder. The field implementers of the program are state-employed service foresters (Figure 11.9).

A 1980 case study of cooperative forestry assistance summarized the activities of service foresters in the twenty northeastern states (14). The study found that, in a typical year, a service forester in the region gives 1370 hours of technical assistance to 133 forest owners, covering 2266 hectares of forestland. Fifty-three percent of the landowners have been previously assisted. The forester prepares or revises fifty-four management plans covering 1297 hectares of forest, examines 372 hectares, and assists

40 owners in marketing timber on 457 hectares. This timber sale assistance generates forest products worth $185,000. The forester assists 52 landowners with improving timber stands on 398 hectares. Thirty-four owners receive tree-planting help on 119 hectares, and site preparation assistance is given on 54 hectares. An additional 80 people are advised or assisted with wildlife protection and development, recreation and aesthetic improvement, erosion and streambank protection, pest and disease control, establishment of natural regeneration, access road and fire break development, Christmas tree culture, fencing, maple syrup production, and use of forest tax laws. Six landowners are referred to consultant foresters for further help.

From 1950 to 1977 the CMF program grew at an average rate of 6.4 percent per year. Federal funding peaked in 1966 and has since declined. States have responded both by making up for lost federal monies and by reducing staffs. In 1983 many states were considering reducing their service forestry staffs, and 13 percent of the states were considering eliminating their service forestry staffs altogether (1).

Federal Cost-Sharing Programs

The Agricultural Conservation Program (ACP) and the Forestry Incentives Program (FIP) provide incentives to landowners to manage their forests wisely and increase their productivity. The ACP is designed for smaller forestlands, the FIP for forestlands of up to 405 hectares. Under both programs, which are administered by the Agricultural Stabilization and Conservation Service (ASCS), eligible landowners receive a percentage of the average cost of implementing forestry practices such as site preparation for natural regeneration, tree planting, and timber stand improvement. Service foresters, upon request by the landowner, evaluate the need for management practices and make appropriate recommendations to the county ASCS committee. If the practice is approved by the committee and completed by the landowner, the forester inspects the treated area and recommends for or against payment of the cost share amount.

Figure 11.9 Service foresters are the primary source of forest management information and assistance for many landowners.

Conservation Reserve Program

In December 1985 Congress passed and the president signed a farm bill that contained a Conservation Reserve Program (CRP). Though similar to the CRP within the old Soil Bank Program, the latest version has some major differences as well. The program is administered by the ASCS with technical assistance from the Soil Conservation Service, Forest Service, and state agencies.

The goal of the current CRP is to remove highly erodible farmland from crop production and place it in other cover such as trees, grass, and shrubs. Although about 28 million hectares of land meet the criteria of the CRP, the goal is to withdraw approximately 16 to 18 million hectares over a five-year period starting in 1986. The expectation is that about 1.4 to 2.0 million hectares will be planted to trees over the five-year period. If this expectation materializes, the CRP will become the largest single tree-planting effort in our nation's history, exceeding the peak years of the CCC, Soil Bank, ACP–FIP, and Forest Service planting programs. The program is open to farmers who submit a bid reflecting the value of the crops that will no longer be produced on the land. Bids are ranked, and the lowest ones are accepted first.

Though not available to all NIPF landowners, the CRP does represent an opportunity to increase greatly our acreage of timberland for future needs. Concurrently it should provide a substantial measure of soil and water conservation, which is greatly needed on these lands. However, some question the affect this planting will have on future markets for species that may already be in oversupply locally.

There was also some pressure from Congress to discontinue the program after 1986, or to reduce the funding appropriation. The program was inaugurated during a period when considerable budget-cutting efforts were under way by both the executive and congressional branches of government. Initial interest in the CRP, after the first two sign-up periods in 1986, resulted in about 1.54 million hectares of land being tentatively accepted, with about 8.4 percent of these lands to be planted in trees.

Federal Reforestation Tax Incentive

As of 1980, timber growers have been able to take advantage of two tax incentives for planting trees for use in the commercial production of timber products. Under *Public Law 96-451* persons who plant one or more acres (0.4 hectare) of trees are eligible for a 10 percent investment tax credit on capitalized reforestation costs up to a maximum of $10,000 annually. Furthermore, tree planters can deduct from annual earnings up to $10,000 over a seven-year period.

For example, if a landowner spends $10,000 for such tree-planting costs as site preparation, seeds, seedlings, and labor, $1000 can be subtracted from the amount of federal income tax otherwise owed for that year. Moreover, over a seven-year period the entire $10,000 can be deducted from the landowner's taxable income.

Current State Forest Taxation Programs

Several states administer special property tax programs designed to protect forestlands from conversion to other uses and to encourage timber production. These programs have developed in response to the traditional property tax, which bases taxation on "highest and best use" of the land and assumes production of an annual income. Because forestlands do not generally produce annual income, collection of property taxes from such lands is often considered to be inequitable and to encourage overexploitation of timber resources.

Current alternatives to the property tax for forestlands fall into three categories: exemptions and rebates, yield taxes, and modified property taxes. Eleven states have forest tax laws of the *exemption and rebate* variety. Exemption laws remove forestland or timber from property tax rolls. They may remove all standing timber, or only specified species, planted trees, or special-purpose plantings such as windbreaks. Rebate laws refund a portion of paid property taxes to landowners who complete certain approved forest practices such as tree planting.

Yield taxes on timber products partially or wholly replace property taxes on forestland in sixteen states. Under this type of arrangement, the land may be taxed annually, but the timber is not taxed until it is harvested. Alternatively, some portion of the tax on land and timber may be deferred until harvest.

The trend in forest taxation in the past decade has been toward establishing *modified property taxes* for forestland. Thirty-eight states currently follow this approach, by which forestland is either assessed like any other property but taxed at a lower rate, or assessed differently from other property. Most commonly, it is assessed at its current-use value, rather than for its "highest and best use." Some states require that all forestland meeting certain requirements be subject to special taxation provisions. In other states participation in forest tax programs is optional.

None of the alternatives just outlined is perfect. Several questions are legitimately related about each approach. How effective is it in protecting forestland from development that is incompatible with forest management? How equitable is the program? How economically efficient is it? What is the program's effect on the ability of units of government to raise needed revenue?

Cooperative Extension Service

The Cooperative Extension Service (CES) is a three-way partnership between the Federal Extension Service, cooperating state universities, and county administrations. The primary forestry mission of CES is to provide educational programs and materials to NIPF landowners, professional resource managers, forest products industry personnel, loggers, policymakers, and the general public (Figure 11.10).

Sometimes the educational service is one-on-one, but more often the process engages a group of individuals. Workshops, conferences, field days, TV and radio programs, "how-to" publications, videotapes, marketing bulletins, newspaper stories, and computer programs are some of the most common modes for distributing the educational information (Figure 11.11).

Forestry extension in some states is an active part of the forestry community and is a major source of information on all aspects of forestry. In other states the program has either few people or few dollars, or both, and the effort is spread rather thin.

The NIPF landowners seeking specific answers about forestry have only to contact a county exten-

Figure 11.10 Forestry demonstration days have introduced landowners to the "latest" technological innovations for many years. Here an early power crosscut saw is being demonstrated at a mid-1940s field day.

Figure 11.11 Since the 1914 Smith–Lever Act established a role for the Federal Extension Service in private-forest management, thousands of woodland owners have participated in forestry demonstration days.

sion office for free information. If county-level personnel do not have the needed information, landowners can turn to state specialists who either provide answers directly or route the request to experts who can. Thus the CES is an informational network available at no charge to the NIPF landowner.

Private-Sector Initiatives

Tree Farm Program of the AFC

Another program available to the NIPF landowner is the Tree Farm Program sponsored by the *American Forest Council* (replacing the American Forest Institute). The AFC is an association supported by the forest products industry, and the Tree Farm Program is only one of its functions (Figure 11.12).

Any NIPF landowner with a minimum of 4 hectares of woodland and a commitment to forest management can become a tree farm member. The

Figure 11.12 The Tree Farm Program provides recognition and technical assistance to NIPF owners who wish to manage their woodlands.

landowner receives free assistance in developing a management plan, and in turn agrees to manage the woodland for the production of periodic timber crops and to harvest the timber according to guidelines within the plan. Although timber production is the primary goal, the owner is encouraged to enhance other values such as wildlife and recreational opportunities in the process.

Every year the AFC, through a selection process involving state committees, chooses a state, a regional, and a national *Tree Farmer of the Year.* Such recognition provides some very beneficial publicity to the practice of forestry and the importance of the NIPF landowner.

Like many assistance efforts, the Tree Farm Program is reorienting its approach to working with the NIPF landowner. Recent proposals, if adopted, would focus more attention on the landowner who owns 40.5 hectares or more of timberland, and would also target and direct growth in the number of tree farms. Uncontrolled growth in numbers may, it is felt, be counterproductive to the goals of the Tree Farm Program.

Industrial Tree Farm Families

Many forest products firms throughout the country have instituted individual tree farm programs of their own. Although each program is unique, they normally offer management-planning assistance; direct assistance in management activities such as planting, herbicide release, and tree marking; and marketing assistance. In return for this assistance, many firms develop written agreements with landowners that guarantee the firm first option on the timber crops as they become available for market. Some arrangements are less formal. Generally these programs offer a good opportunity for the NIPF landowner to manage and market timber, particularly in times or regions with limited markets. Many companies hold at least one annual event for their tree farm family members: a picnic, tour, or field day.

Landowner Associations

A number of states have active associations of NIPF landowners that provide a range of services to their members. As of 1985 there were fourteen states with one or more NIPF landowner associations having memberships ranging from fewer than 100 to over 6000. A total of twenty-one states have associations that involve both NIPF landowners and the forest products industry; memberships range from about 250 to over 4000.

Activities include (1) sponsorship of conferences, tours, workshops, and field days, (2) publication of newsletters, magazines, informational hotlines, management guides, and the like, (3) promotional activities, (4) legislative liaison and advocacy, (5) cooperation with other segments of the forestry community, (6) environmental education, (7) policy development, and (8) marketing services.

The *National Woodland Owners Association* (NWOA), with headquarters in Washington, D.C., was formed to serve as a national voice for NIPF landowners. Currently a number of state associations are affiliate members of the NWOA, which participates actively in national organizations and committees that deal with many forestry and NIPF concerns. The NWOA is actively providing organized lobby representation for NIPF landowners on Capitol Hill in Washington, D.C.

Forest Cooperatives

Another form of organization that has been employed to assist NIPF landowners is the forest cooperative. Although the success of these organizations has been mixed, it is a concept that has potential. A forest cooperative is a group of landowners who combine forces for timber management, harvesting, and marketing activities. The association may be quite formal or rather informal. The premise is that if enough small landowners cooperate by pooling resources and land holdings, economies of scale can be achieved. Collectively, cooperative members may be able to afford the services of a consulting forester, and perhaps to place sufficient volume of timber on the market that they attract competing buyers and thereby obtain a better price.

The concept seems logical, yet many cooperatives have failed because markets are scattered, informa-

tion about them is meager, land holdings are small and harvest periods lengthy, and there is a lack of equipment, transportation facilities, and managerial expertise. The limited progress of forestry cooperatives contrasts with the massive success of agricultural cooperatives in the United States.

Importance of the Professional Forester

One piece of advice frequently offered to NIPF landowners by government agencies and private organizations alike is to use the services of a professional forester in forest management planning and activities. The value of this advice was not fully known until a recent Georgia study quantified the impact. Cubbage (15) studied the affect of professional technical advice on a group of landowners in the Georgia Piedmont. His findings indicate that (1) NIPF landowners who used the assistance of professional foresters generally left more seed and crop trees for future stand development and harvests; and (2) these landowners received a greater average price per unit of volume than owners who did not obtain technical advice.

Thus it appears that assumptions concerning the importance of professional assistance have been correct. The effectiveness of technical advice can be measured, and indications are that NIPF landowners can benefit greatly if they seek out such assistance.

Consulting Foresters

If the present trends to diminish budgets for public-assistance programs continue, the role of the consultant will surely grow. Management services will always be needed, and if they are not available from the public sector, the private sector will undoubtedly be called on to fill the void.

In 1983 there were about 1900 consulting foresters in the United States (16). This represented an increase of about 700 over the previous seven years—an average increase of slightly over 8 percent per year. Consultants often work with clientele other than NIPF owners; however, the NIPF group is a very important segment of the consultant's business. About 28 percent of the average consultant's income from NIPF landowners comes from those who own between 40.5 and 202 hectares of timberland.

Not all woodland owners can benefit from the services of a consultant, but those with sufficient land or timber may find the investment very worthwhile. Consultants offer a wide range of services including appraisals, taking inventories, improving timber stands, planting trees, applying herbicides, marketing timber, administering timber sales, and managing wildlife (Figure 11.13).

Forestry consultation is not a free service; the consultant is in business and thus must charge for the services rendered. Some charge by the job, others by the hour or by the day; still others may charge a percentage of the sale value when timber is marketed. Many consultants belong to the *Association of Consulting Foresters* (ACF), and several states have their own consulting foresters' associations as well.

Current NIPF Issues

Policymakers have always been interested in improving management of NIPF forests, because NIPF lands represent such a large share of the nation's timberland. However, the focus of this interest has shifted over time. Initially these lands were referred to simply as "farm woodlots"; later they became "small private ownerships," and finally nonindustrial private forestlands. Research into the NIPF sector has evolved from the descriptive reports of the 1950s and 1960s to a more analytical approach in the 1980s. Policy debate over what to do with the NIPF "problem" has begun to swing from an *educational imperative* ("if they were only educated they would manage their lands wisely") to a *motivational science*.

We are starting to realize that NIPF landowners do not have a "problem" as we have always inferred; rather, as Ticknor (2) said, "We in forestry and resource management have the problem." This realization has helped forestry professionals to see new

approaches and bring new philosophies to the NIPF issue.

A 1980 symposium addressed the issue of what data and information were needed for formulating NIPF policy. One of the editors of the proceedings introduced the subject by saying, "In short, we can find near unanimity on the importance of goods and services from nonindustrial private lands, but we can rarely find agreement on the actions deemed necessary and appropriate to ensure the production of those goods and services" (17). Other speakers at the symposium pointed out that, although many surveys have described the general characteristics of NIPF owners, what motivates landowner behavior remains incompletely understood. An official from the National Forest Products Association summed up the dearth of appropriate information: "We cannot relate programs to people because we do not know anything about the people . . . even with all these [landowner] studies, we do not have much information about the private landowner which can be used to predict behavior patterns" (18).

Participants at this symposium identified some of the specific information needed for formulating effective NIPF policy.

Information on owner characteristics, goals, and trends.

More penetrating analyses of owners' behavior and of linkages between owners.

More insightful analyses of forms of organizations that can be used to join forest owners together.

In-depth owner profiles and suggested incentive–assistance packages.

Community social factors that affect public programs for private forest management.

One major change is emerging (still slowly in some quarters) in our thinking about NIPF owners. We recognize that these landowners have *widely varying interests* in owning forestland. Although most foresters who have dealt with private landowners have recognized this diversity of interests, it has not been a part of our policy-making efforts until recent years. As we have already learned from the study of New Hampshire and Vermont NIPF owners,

Figure 11.13 Government and consulting foresters help NIPF landowners plan forest management strategies.

some own forestland for recreational pursuits such as hunting, fishing, hiking, and skiing. Some people simply enjoy the view and appreciate the aesthetics of forested areas. Other owners have an economic interest in holding forestland: they may invest in growing timber and hope to market forest products, or they may hold the land for speculative investment purposes.

Targeting of NIPF Programs

Because of these diverse ownership objectives, we are starting to see an interest in programs that are targeted to specific audiences, rather than applied broadly to the entire NIPF population. For example, because of the skewed size distribution of NIPF ownerships discussed earlier, it has been suggested that assistance programs and educational efforts designed to enhance timber production be targeted to those who own 40.5 hectares or more of timberland (6, 19). In other words, when dealing with timber management on NIPF lands, let us focus on those 600,000 owners who own 74 percent of the land rather than on the entire population of 7.8 million owners.

Although this approach makes sense to many people, others do not accept it. Those who disagree with the concept argue that targeting public programs to larger tracts would subject to unfair competition the consulting forester, whose livelihood depends mainly on the larger holdings. They also suggest that it would be difficult to identify target groups of landowners and allocate funding accordingly. Some critics also charge that such targeting would alienate portions of the voting, tax-paying public, thus jeopardizing support for the entire forestry program. There is also concern that ethnic minority landowners, whose holdings are typically smaller than the average, would be discriminated against with the targeting-by-size approach.

A report prepared by a group of state foresters from the twenty northeastern states viewed the targeting issue as "a conscious choice to favor effectiveness over equity" (19). Proponents of targeting claim that economic efficiency dictates the approach as a means of allocating tax dollars wisely. Studies have shown that management costs per hectare are lower and returns per hectare are higher from the large NIPF tracts (20, 21). There is also concern, particularly among those who administer public programs, that projects on small tracts have a low probability of being followed up with additional management in future years. A 2-hectare plantation is at greater risk of abandonment than a 16-hectare stand (21); moreover, as mentioned previously, owners of larger tracts are more likely to manage and harvest crops of timber.

Furthermore, indiscriminate application of NIPF assistance programs may have detrimental effects on local wood markets. Resource economist Robert Marty (6) pointed out to Michigan forest policymakers that "Little purpose is served by directing program effort toward practices which provide additional quantities of timber already in oversupply." He advised directing efforts to practices that increase the local availability of species in high demand and low supply.

Thus it would appear that there should be a *multifaceted* targeting approach for NIPF programs. Fostering better land management for timber production may require that we target our assistance and educational programs to the larger ownerships and the demanded products. However, to provide equity among all landowners and thus retain political support for forestry programs, we must also provide other services that help the owners of small holdings achieve their objectives. The availability of adequate funding will ultimately determine how successful we are in meeting the needs of all NIPF owners.

The St. Louis Forum

Most projections of future trends indicate that an increasing share of our timber supply will have to come from NIPF lands. More and more constraints are being placed on public lands that impinge on the efficient production of timber. Because of this trend, a major national forum on NIPF lands was held in St. Louis during the fall of 1983. Called by then Assistant Secretary of Agriculture John Crowell, the highly structured forum was aimed at exploring how this increasing need for NIPF timber supplies can be met while providing landowners an opportunity to manage for their varied objectives. Twenty-one active participants examined a list of twenty-five issue

questions and developed options and solutions in a group dynamics format. Various small working groups were also formed to deal with specific issues such as targeting, assistance programs, and tax incentives.

The conference produced unanimous agreement that there is a need to *increase sustained productivity* on NIPF lands to meet future domestic and potential export opportunities. There was also strong agreement that maintaining current programs would not achieve the desired increases in productivity. The participants concluded that there is a real need for *national leadership* to provide policy direction, coordination, and national focus, and state and local action groups to coordinate on-site activities. The forum produced a list of recommended responsibilities for the federal government, the Federal Extension Service, the states, private consultants, and the forest products industries.

A direct result of the St. Louis form was the founding of the *National Council on Private Forestry* to spearhead the overall coordination of NIPF efforts, and the Federal Extension Service produced a report on suggested directions for NIPF educational programs. However, during these same years federal and state budget cutting and "reprioritizing" have generally spelled less for NIPF programs and not more.

Regulation of Management Practices

Regulations restricting forest management and timber harvesting on private lands have become a fact of life for NIPF landowners and the forest products industry. Some consider these regulations necessary to protect environmental quality, and others find them a threat to or a revocation of individual rights (Figure 11.14).

Under the tradition of common law and established legal doctrine, the rights of individual landowners are constrained in two ways. *First,* they may not use their property in such a way that it becomes a nuisance to neighboring landowners or to the public at large. *Second,* they may not damage or

Figure 11.14 In some parts of the country, foresters consider woodland grazing to be the most serious deterrent to successful forest management.

destroy their property to the extent that its renewable natural resources are made unavailable to future generations of landowners. On the basis of these legally tested and upheld principles, eighteen states and numerous local units of government have passed regulations restricting the forest management practices of private forest owners. These regulations clearly favor the general public welfare over individual property rights.

Early forest practice laws were concerned primarily with ensuring the future availability of timber and hence stressed *erosion control* and *regeneration standards*. More recent laws are directed mainly at ensuring that forest management activities do not adversely affect *environmental quality*. Thus they typically put restrictions on timber-harvesting methods, road construction and location, and the use of herbicides and pesticides.

Recent years have witnessed an increasing number of forest practice laws enacted by counties and local units of government, many of them more restrictive than state statutes dealing with similar issues. When these laws have been enacted without

input from landowners, industry, or public foresters, they have created confusion for all parties. For example, loggers may be confronted with differing requirements as they move from one location to a nearby tract.

This trend of *increasing regulation* is almost certain to grow. Therefore, NIPF landowners will likely be faced with additional constraints in the management of their lands. Regulation of forest practices may actually improve our land management, or it may dissuade NIPF landowners from managing intensively. The active involvement of concerned forestry professionals and forest landowners will be needed to ensure that regulatory changes do in fact benefit the resource.

The Role of Public Assistance

The recent past has witnessed a rather intense political battle over the pros and cons of public-assistance programs for NIPF owners. One side argues that these programs are essential to achieving sound management on NIPF lands, and the other side argues just as intently that such efforts should be provided by the private sector if, in fact, they are needed at all.

One issue that has polarized the camps is that of *tax relief or incentives*. Should we subsidize a landowner for growing and marketing forest crops? Should the landowner get a property tax break, receive capital gains treatment of timber sale income, and be allowed to capitalize reforestation costs? Federal tax reforms in 1986 reduced or modified certain income tax incentives for the woodland owner.

At the same time the current budget proposals are also continuing the trend to eliminate or reduce such NIPF assistance as the Cooperative Forest Management program with the states, the ACP–FIP activities, the U.S.D.A. Forest Service's State and Private Forestry Program, and the Federal Extension Service. Where all this debate will lead is still unknown. One thing is fairly certain, however: as long as the national debt remains a central political issue, NIPF assistance programs and management incentives will continue to be debated as well.

The Future

In summary, it appears that *five major trends* will affect future management of nonindustrial private forestland: (1) increasing demand for forest products and amenities from NIPF lands; (2) decreasing ability of these lands to produce demanded products owing to parceling, nonforestry development, and insufficient management; (3) decreasing federal financial support for NIPF assistance programs; (4) increasing legal constraints on forest management practices on NIPF lands; and (5) continuing debate on appropriate and effective measures for influencing management of NIPF lands.

Increasing demands for NIPF products and amenities may well provide the key to improving the management of these lands, for where markets exist, management is drawn to the land. While intensifying the pressures on resource use, heightened demand also creates greater opportunities for land manage-

ment activities relating to all the diverse NIPF landowner interests. By improving and diversifying the markets for forest products, we will enhance our ability to manage overstocked NIFP timberlands and thereby achieve the growth rates necessary to provide adequate resources for future generations.

These trends present immense challenges to the forestry profession. The challenges can be met only by individuals who understand the social as well as the biological dimension of resource management.

References

1. J. Fedkiw, "Background paper on non-industrial private forest lands, their management, and related public and private assistance," U.S.D.A. For. Serv., Off. Budget Progr. Anal., Off. of the Secretary, Washington, D.C., 1983.

2. W. D. Ticknor, "Gloria reminiscences." Unpublished remarks to American Forestry Association Conference, Traverse City, Mich., October 1985.

3. Anon., "An analysis of the timber situation in the U.S. 1952–2030," U.S.D.A. For. Serv., Res. Rept. 23, 1982.

4. T. W. Birch, D. G. Lewis, and H. F. Kaiser, "The private forest-land owners of the United States," U.S.D.A. For. Serv., Res. Bull. WO-1, Broomall, Pa., 1982.

5. N. P. Kingsley and T. W. Birch, "The forestland owners of New Hampshire and Vermont," U.S.D.A. For. Serv., Bull NE-51, 1977.

6. R. Marty, "Retargeting public forestry assistance programs in the North." In *Proc. Symp., Nonindustrial Private Forests: A Review of Economic and Policy Studies,* J. P. Royer and C. D. Risbrudt, eds., Duke University, Durham, N.C., 1983.

7. J. T. O'Leary, D. C. Zumeta, and R. M. Pace, "Differential targeting in policy development for nonindustrial private forestlands." In *Proc. Symp., Nonindustrial Private Forests: A Review of Economic and Policy Studies,* J. P. Royer and C. D. Risbrudt, eds., Duke University, Durham, N.C., 1983.

8. R. S. Fesco, H. F. Kaiser, J. P. Royer, and M. Weidenhamer, "Management practices and reforestation decisions for harvested southern pinelands," U.S.D.A. Stat. Rept. Serv., Staff Rept. AGES 821230, 1982.

9. J. G. Yoho, "Continuing investments in forestry: Private investment strategies." In *Investments in Forestry: Resources, Land Use, and Public Policy,* R. A. Sedjo, ed., Westview Press, Boulder, Colo., 1985.

10. M. Clawson, "Nonindustrial Private Forest Lands: Myths and Realities," *Proc. 1978 Joint Convention of Society of American Foresters and Canadian Institute of Forestry,* Soc. Am. For., Washington, D.C., 1979.

11. E. M. Carpenter, "Ownership change and timber supply on nonindustrial private forestland," U.S.D.A. For. Serv., North Cent. For. Expt. Sta., Res. Pap. NC-265, St. Paul, Minn., 1985.

12. W. G. Robbins, *American Forestry: A History of National, State, and Private Cooperation,* Univ. of Nebraska Press, Lincoln, 1985.

13. S. T. Dana and S. K. Fairfax, *Forest and Range Policy: Its Development in the United States,* Second Edition, McGraw–Hill, New York, 1980.

14. D. A. Ganser and O. W. Herrick, "Cooperative forestry assistance in the Northeast," U.S.D.A. For. Serv., Res. Pap. NE-464, 1980.

15. F. W. Cubbage, "Measuring the physical effects of technical advice from service foresters." In *Proc. Symp., Nonindustrial Private Forests: A Review of Economic and Policy Studies,* J. P. Royer and C. D. Risbrudt, eds., Duke University, Durham, N.C., April 1983.

16. D. B. Field, *J. For., 84*(2), 25 (1986).

17. P. J. Royer, "Introduction." In *Proc. Conf., Nonindustrial Private Forests: Data and Information Needs,* P. J. Royer and F. J. Convery, eds., Duke University, Durham, N.C., 1981.

18. M. E. Conkin, "A forest industry view on data needs for policy decisions." In *Proc. Conf., Nonindustrial Private Forests: Data and Information Needs,* P. J. Royer and F. J. Convery, eds., Duke University, Durham, N.C., April 1981.

19. Anon., "Forest resources in the Northeast: Contributing to economic development and social well being," prepared by the State Foresters of the 20 Northeastern States, 1984.

20. F. W. Cubbage, "Economies of forest tract size: Theory and literature," U.S.D.A. For. Serv., South. For. Expt. Sta., Gen. Tech. Rept. SO-41, 1983.

21. J. Dirkman, T. Rumpf, and L. C. Irland, "Treatment size, administrative cost relationships and 'washout' in forestry incentive programs in Maine," In *Proc. Symp., Nonindustrial Private Forests: A Review of Economic and Policy Studies,* J. P. Royer and C. D. Risbrudt, eds., Duke University, Durham, N.C., April 1983.

CHAPTER 12

Measurement of the Forest

GEORGE L. MARTIN
ALAN R. EK

There are as many reasons to measure forests as there are uses of forests, and each use has its own specific needs for information. A forest landowner may want to sell some timber, and the determination of a fair price will require information about the species, size, quality, and number of trees to be sold. Forest managers need to make long-range plans concerning planting, thinning, harvesting, and other treatments in their forests. These plans must be based on detailed information about the type, size, density, and growth rates of the existing timber stands, together with information about the location, accessibility, and quality of the forest sites. Forest scientists also want to understand how forests grow and interact with their environment. This understanding requires precise measurement of trees and forests under carefully controlled conditions.

The many needs for information about forests encouraged the founding of a specialized branch of forestry, *forest mensuration* (also *forest biometrics*), which consists of techniques for the efficient measurement of forests, including their growth and response to management practices. The word *efficient* means that the measurement techniques strive to provide the most accurate information possible, and to obtain this required information at a minimum cost.

This chapter presents an overview of some of the measurement techniques used in forestry. Both English and metric units of measurement are in use today, so both systems are described in this chapter. To help the reader become familiar with both systems, measurements in some tables and examples are in English units, and measurements in others are in metric units. The emphasis is on timber resources, but the measurement of some nontimber resources is also briefly described. Textbooks (1, 2) are available for readers who want to learn more about forest mensuration.

Measurement of Primary Forest Products

To get an idea of how forests are measured, we first need to understand how we measure the primary products derived from forests. These primary products include *sawlogs, bolts,* and *chips.* Sawlogs are logs of sufficient size and quality to produce lumber or veneer. They must be 8 feet or more in length with a minimum small-end diameter of 6 to 8 inches. Bolts are short logs, less than 8 feet in length, and used primarily for manufacture into pulp and paper. Chips are small pieces of wood obtained by cutting up logs and sawmill wastes. They are used as a raw material for manufacturing a variety of forest products and as a source of fuel.

Product Scaling

The process of measuring the physical quantity of forest products is called *scaling.* During the nineteenth century the practice became established in the United States to scale sawlogs in terms of their board foot contents. Actually, the *board foot* is a unit of sawn lumber equivalent to a plank 1 foot long, 1 foot wide, and 1 inch thick. Estimates of the board foot contents of a log must take into account the portions of a log lost to saw kerf, the saw cuts between the boards, and to slabs, the rounded edges of the log. By 1910 over forty *log rules* had been devised to estimate the volume of logs in board feet, based on measurements of the diameter inside bark on the small end of the log (Figure 12.1), and the length of the log. Most of these log rules were very inaccurate and are no longer in use; but a few managed to achieve widespread acceptance and continue to be used today, notably the Doyle, Scribner, and International log rules.

The *Doyle log rule* was first published in 1825 by

Figure 12.1 First step in scaling: determining the diameter inside the bark on the small end of the log.

Edward Doyle of Rochester, New York. This rule is based on the simple formula

$$V = (D - 4)^2 L/16$$

where V is the volume of the log in board feet, D is the small-end scaling diameter in inches, and L is the length of the log in feet (after allowing 3 to 4 inches for trim). The Doyle log rule grossly underestimates the volumes of logs less than 20 inches in diameter, but it continues to be used because of its simplicity and because it encourages the delivery of large-diameter logs to mills.

The *Scribner log rule* was published in 1846 by John Marston Scribner, an ordained clergyman and teacher of mathematics in a girls' school. Scribner got the idea of how to estimate log volumes from diagrams of boards drawn on circles of various sizes corresponding to the small ends of logs. Boards were drawn with a $\frac{1}{4}$-inch allowance for saw kerf and with the assumptions that boards would be 1 inch thick and not less than 8 inches wide. He further assumed that the logs were cylinders, so no adjustments were made for log taper. Scribner published his log rule in the form of a table, but the following formula has since been developed to describe his rule:

$$V = (0.79D^2 - 2D - 4)L/16$$

A variation of the Scribner rule is the *Scribner decimal C rule,* obtained by rounding the former rule to the nearest 10 board feet and then dropping the rightmost zero. For example, a 16-foot log with an 18-inch scale diameter would have 216 board feet according to the Scribner rule and would scale as 22 by the Scribner decimal C rule.

The most accurate log rule in use today is the *International log rule* developed by Judson Clark in 1906. Clark was a professional forester who had been bothered by the inconsistent and radically different estimates that he obtained from the Doyle, Scribner, and other log rules. He concluded that these rules grossly underestimated the volume of long logs because they did not take into account the increased board foot yield caused by log taper. In its basic form this rule assumes a $\frac{1}{8}$-inch saw kerf and estimates the volume of a 4-foot section. The volume of the entire log is estimated by adding the volumes of each 4-foot section and assuming a $\frac{1}{2}$-inch increase

in diameter for each section. In this way the International rule allows for an increase in log volume owing to taper. The basic formula for the volume of a 4-foot section is

$$V = 0.22D^2 - 0.71D$$

For a $\frac{1}{4}$-inch saw kerf this formula is multiplied by 0.905.

Table 12.1 shows that there are substantial differences between the estimates obtained with the log rules just described, especially for smaller log sizes. A wise buyer or seller will study the differences before completing any agreements.

Sawlogs can be scaled more consistently by simply estimating the volume of solid wood in the log. *Smalian's formula* is often used for this purpose,

$$V = (A_1 + A_2)L/2$$

Table 12.1 Board Foot Volume of 16-Foot Logs for International Rule and Other Rules in Percentage of the International Rule[a]

Scaling Diameter (in.)	International[b] (bd ft)	Scribner (percent)	Scribner Decimal C (percent)	Doyle (percent)
6	20	90	100	20
8	40	80	75	40
10	65	83	92	55
12	95	83	84	67
14	135	84	81	74
16	180	88	89	80
18	230	93	91	85
20	290	97	97	88
22	355	94	93	91
24	425	95	94	94
26	500	100	100	97
28	585	99	99	98
30	675	97	98	100
32	770	96	96	102
34	875	91	91	103
36	980	94	94	104
38	1095	98	98	106
40	1220	99	98	106

Source: D. L. Williams and W. C. Hopkins, "Converting factors for southern pine products," U.S.D.A. For. Serv., Tech. Bull. 626, South. For. Expt. Sta., New Orleans, 1969.

[a]Terms used in this table are defined in the text.

[b]Quarter-inch kerf (cut made by saw).

Figure 12.2 Examples of stacked-wood units, from left to right: standard cord, face cord (pieces 16 inches long), split face cord, and a split face cord piled in a small truck.

where V is the volume of solid wood (in cubic feet or cubic meters), A_1 and A_2 are the cross-sectional areas inside bark on the two ends of the log (in square feet or square meters), and L is the length of the log (in feet or meters). Despite numerous attempts to promote cubic-volume scaling in the United States, board foot scaling still prevails.

The sawlog volume obtained with a log rule or cubic-volume formula is called the *gross scale*. A *net scale* must then be calculated by deducting for *scale defects* that will reduce the usable volume of wood in the log. Scale defects include rot, wormholes, ring shake (separation of wood along annual rings), and splits. In addition, if the log is not sufficiently straight, a scale deduction is made according to the amount of sweep or crook in the log.

Pulpwood and firewood are usually scaled by measuring the dimensions of a stack rather than measuring individual bolts. A *standard cord* of wood is a stack 4 by 4 by 8 feet and contains 128 cubic feet of wood, air, and bark. The number of standard cords in any size stack can be calculated by dividing the product of the stack's width, height, and length (in feet) by 128. Variations of the standard cord include the *short cord* or *face cord,* a stack 4 feet high and 8 feet wide with individual pieces cut

to a length less than 4 feet. The dimensions of various types of cords are illustrated in Figure 12.2.

The amount of solid wood in a standard cord may range from 64 to 96 cubic feet, depending on several factors. Solid-wood content is reduced by thick bark, small-diameter bolts, crooked bolts, and loose piling, so these variables must be assessed when estimating the actual amount of wood in a given stack.

In recent years much of the pulp and paper industry has adopted weight scaling for stacked pulpwood and wood chips. With this method, a truck carrying a full load of wood is weighed before and after it is unloaded. The difference is the weight of the wood, which can then be converted to volume or dry weight by taking into account the specific gravity and moisture content of the wood. Weight scaling is favored because it is fast and objective, and it encourages delivery of freshly cut wood to the mill.

Product Grading

The value of forest products, particularly sawlogs, can be greatly reduced by *grade defects* that lower their strength, take away from their appearance, or otherwise limit their utility. Defects that lower the grade of sawlogs include knots, spiral grain, and stain.

Rules for grading hardwood logs emphasize defects, such as knots, that affect the amount of clear lumber that can be sawn from the log. Four classes of log use have been defined for the grading of hardwood logs (3).

1. **Veneer Class.** Logs of very high value as well as some relatively low-value logs that can be utilized for veneer. Many logs that qualify for factory lumber grades 1, 2, and 3 can be utilized as veneer logs.

2. **Factory Class.** Boards that later can be remanufactured to remove most defects and obtain the best yields of clear face and sound cuttings.

3. **Construction Class.** Logs suitable for sawing into ties, timbers, and other items to be used in one piece for structural purposes.

4. **Local-Use Class.** In general, wood suitable for products not usually covered by standard specifications. High strength, great durability, and fine appearance are not required for the following types of products: crating, pallet parts, mine timbers, industrial blocking, and so on.

The majority of softwood logs fall into the *veneer class* or the *sawmill class,* which includes logs suited to the production of yard and structural lumber. The number, location, and size of grade defects determine the grade of softwood logs in these two classes.

Land Surveying and Mapping

Land-surveying and land-mapping techniques are used in forestry to locate the boundaries of forest properties and stands of timber, to measure the land areas enclosed within these boundaries, and to locate roads, streams, and other features of importance within the forest. Surveying techniques are also used for locating sample plots as described later in this chapter.

Forestland surveys in the United States are usually done with the English system of units. Distance is measured in *feet, chains* (1 chain = 66 feet), and *miles* (1 mile = 80 chains); land area is measured in *acres* (1 acre = 10 square chains) and *square miles* (1 square mile = 640 acres). In the metric system, distance is measured in *meters* (1 meter = 3.28084 feet) and *kilometers* (1 kilometer = 1000 meters), and land area is measured in *hectares* (1 hectare = 10,000 square meters) and *square kilometers* (1 square kilometer = 100 hectares). Acres and hectares are both used to describe land areas in the United States, so it is useful to remember that 1 hectare is equal to 2.471 acres or about 2.5 acres. Additional converting factors for units of distance and area can be found in Appendix III.

Distance

There are several methods for measuring distance in forest surveys, and the choice depends on the accuracy required. *Pacing* is often used for locating sample plots and in reconnaissance work where great accuracy is not required. Foresters must first calibrate their individual pace by walking a known distance, say 10 chains, and counting the number of paces. In forestry a pace is considered two steps, using a natural walking gait, and should be calibrated for each type of terrain encountered. Having determined the average number of paces per chain, the forester can then measure and keep track of distances by counting paces while walking through the forest. An experienced pacer can achieve an accuracy of 1 part in 80; that is, for every 80 chains traversed the error should be no more than 1 chain.

When greater accuracy is required, steel tapes are used in a technique known as *chaining.* The steel tapes may be 2 chains, 100 feet, or 30 meters in length, depending on the units desired. Chaining requires a minimum of two people to hold each end of the tape. The head chainer usually uses a magnetic compass to determine the direction of the course line while the rear chainer keeps a record of the number of tape lengths traversed. Careful chaining can achieve an accuracy of 1 part in 1000.

There are also a variety of *electronic* and *optical instruments* for measuring distances. These instruments require a line of sight free of obstacles such as trees and shrubs. For this reason they are not well suited for timber surveys in densely wooded areas, but they are used for road and boundary surveys.

Direction

Many of the instruments available are more accurate for measuring direction, but the *magnetic compass* is favored by foresters because of its speed, economy, and simplicity. With a magnetic compass, directions are measured in degrees (0 to 360) clockwise from magnetic north, the direction pointed by the compass needle. These direction angles are called *magnetic azimuths* and must be converted to *true azimuths* by correcting for *magnetic declination,* that is, the angle between true north and magnetic north. Many compasses allow this correction to be made automatically by the instrument.

Land Surveys

Much of the land subdivision in the world is based on the *metes and bounds* system. Under this system property lines and corners are based on physical features such as streams, ridges, fences, and roads. Locating such legal boundaries is often difficult, especially when descriptions are vague, corners that were once marked have been lost, and lines such as streams have moved over the years. However, most of the United States west of the Mississippi River and north of the Ohio River, plus Alabama, Mississippi, and portions of Florida, have been subdivided according to a *rectangular survey system.* This system was conceived by Thomas Jefferson at the close of the Revolutionary War, and enacted as the Land Ordinance of 1785 "to survey and sell these public lands in the Northwest Territory" (see Figure 1.2).

The rectangular survey system uses carefully established *baselines* and *principal meridians* as references for land location. The baselines run east–west, and the principal meridians run north–south. The intersection of a baseline and principal meridian is called an *initial point* and serves as the origin of a survey system. Over thirty of these systems were established as land was acquired and development progressed westward in the United States.

Figure 12.3 shows how land is subdivided under the rectangular survey system. At intervals of 24 miles north and south of the baseline, *standard parallels* are established in east–west directions. At 24-mile intervals along the baseline and each of the standard parallels, *guide meridians* are run north to the next standard parallel. Because of the earth's curvature, guide meridians converge to the north and the resulting *24-mile tracts* are actually less than 24 miles wide at their northern boundaries.

The 24-mile tracts are then subdivided into sixteen *townships,* each approximately 6 miles square. Townships are numbered consecutively north and south of the baseline. Township locations east and west of the principal meridian are called *ranges* and are also numbered consecutively. For example, in Figure 12.3a the township labeled T3N, R2W denotes a township that is three townships north of the baseline and two ranges west of the principal meridian.

Townships are subdivided into thirty-six *sections,* each approximately 1 mile square and 640 acres in area. Figure 12.3b illustrates how the sections are numbered within a township. Each section is subdivided into *quarter-sections* of approximately 160 acres, which are further subdivided into 40-acre parcels known as *"forties."* Figure 12.3c illustrates how the subdivisions of a section are identified.

A legal description for a parcel of land begins with the smallest subdivision and progresses to the township designation. For example, the forty in the northwest corner of section 14 (Figure 12.3c) would be described as NW 1/4 NW 1/4 S14, T3N, R2W.

Forest Type Mapping and Area Measurement

Forest type maps are very useful to forest managers because they show the locations and boundaries of individual forest stands, that is, areas with similar species, size, and density of trees. These maps also show nonforested areas such as lakes, rivers, and fields. Vertical aerial photographs are extremely useful for preparing forest type maps because they can be viewed with a stereoscope (Figure 12.4) to provide a three-dimensional picture of the forest.

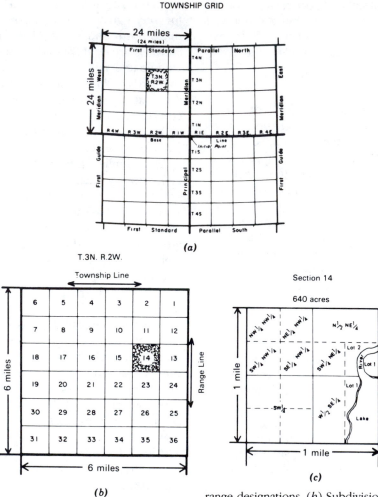

Figure 12.3 Diagram of the U.S. rectangular survey system. (*a*) Township grid showing initial point, baseline, principal meridian, standard parallels, and guide meridians, along with examples of township and range designations. (*b*) Subdivision of township into sections and the system of numbering sections from 1 to 36. (*c*) Subdivision of a section into quarter-sections and forties. (Adapted from the Bureau of Land Management, U.S. Department of Interior.)

Trained interpreters are able to identify forest stands on the photographs and outline their boundaries (Figure 12.5). Chapter 13 describes the use of aerial photographs and other forms of remote sensing in forestry.

After the forest type maps have been prepared, it is usually necessary to measure the land area within each of the stand boundaries. Forest stands normally

have irregular boundaries, so their areas are often measured with a *dot grid,* a sheet of clear plastic covered with uniformly spaced dots. The grid is laid over the map and all the dots falling within the stand boundary are counted. Multiplying this dot count by an appropriate converting factor gives the land area of the stand. For example, the converting factor for a dot grid with sixty-four dots per square inch and a

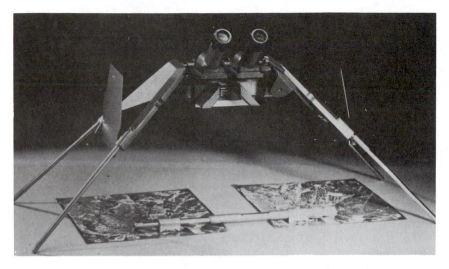

Figure 12.4 Parallax bar oriented over overlapping vertical aerial photographs under a mirror stereoscope. The stereoscope facilitates three-dimensional study of the photographed scene. The parallax bar is used to determine approximate tree heights and terrain elevations. (Courtesy of Wild Herrbrugg, Inc.)

map scale of 1 : 20,000 is 0.996 acre per dot. Suppose the number of dots falling within a given stand boundary is forty-seven; then the estimated area of the stand is

$$47 \times 0.996 = 46.8 \text{ acres}$$

For more precise estimates, an average of several dot counts can be used.

Measurement of Timber Resources

There are many different types of timber surveys ranging from the precise measurement of individual trees on a woodlot while marking them for a timber sale, to the assessment of the timber supply in the United States, including its rate of growth and con-

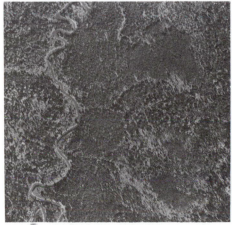 

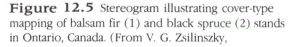

Figure 12.5 Stereogram illustrating cover-type mapping of balsam fir (1) and black spruce (2) stands in Ontario, Canada. (From V. G. Zsilinszky,

"Photographic interpretation of tree species in Ontario," Ontario Department of Lands and Forests, 1966.)

sumption. The major types of surveys are periodic *national surveys* used primarily for setting forest policies, *state inventories* for developing management plans for state and county forests, *local inventories* designed to aid forest managers by providing details on the quantity and location of timber, and *timber appraisals* to determine the value of a timber or land sale. The objectives of these surveys differ considerably, as do the measurement procedures they employ. The following discussions provide an overview of some of the more common tools and techniques used in these timber surveys.

Standing Trees

Most timber surveys require the measurement of individual trees. Standing-tree measurements may be required to estimate the volume or mass (weight) of various products obtainable from the trees, or they may be used to assess the relative sizes of trees to aid in the development of management prescriptions for the forest.

Diameter at Breast Height One of the most useful tree measurements is the diameter at breast height (dbh). This is the diameter, outside bark, of the tree stem at a height of 4.5 feet (or 1.3 meters when the metric system is used), above ground on the uphill side of the tree. The *tree caliper* (Figure 12.6) is one of the most accurate instruments for obtaining this measurement. Another instrument, the *tree diameter tape,* is a steel tape with special calibrations that convert the circumference of the tree to its corresponding diameter, assuming the cross section of the tree is a perfect circle. Since trees are not usually circular, the diameter tape tends to overestimate tree diameters and, hence, is somewhat less accurate than the caliper. Even less accurate, but very quick and easy to use, is the *Biltmore stick* (Figure 12.7). Invented in 1898 by Carl Schenck for use on the Biltmore Forest in North Carolina, this stick is held horizontally against the tree at arm's length (25 inches), with the left edge in line with the left side of the tree. The diameter is then sighted on the stick in line with the right side of the tree. The Biltmore stick is specially calibrated according to the principle of similar triangles.

Figure 12.6 Forester using a caliper to measure a tree diameter at breast height (dbh).

Figure 12.7 Field crew in the process of observing and recording species and tree diameters on a plot. Diameters are being measured with a Biltmore stick held at a fixed distance from the eye. Observations with this instrument are based on the geometric principle of similar triangles.

Basal Area The dbh measurement is frequently converted to basal area, that is, the area (in square feet or square meters) of the cross section of a tree at breast height. The formula for the area of a circle (pi times radius squared), together with appropriate unit-converting factors, is used to calculate tree basal area. If dbh is measured in inches, tree basal area, b, in square feet is given by

$$b = 0.005454 \, dbh^2$$

If dbh is measured in centimeters, tree basal area in square meters is given by

$$b = 0.00007854 \, dbh^2$$

The basal area of a forest stand is expressed as the sum of the tree basal areas divided by the area of the stand, and is expressed in square feet per acre or square meters per hectare. Stand basal area is used by forest managers as a measure of the degree of crowding of trees in a stand (see later under "Stocking and Density").

Height There are a number of different instruments for measuring tree height, and the required level of accuracy dictates the instrument of choice. *Height poles* provide very accurate measurements for trees that are not too high. A variety of sectioned, folding, and telescoping poles are available, and they are best suited to trees with branches that allow the poles to pass readily between them but also give the poles lateral support. Height poles become too cumbersome for trees taller than 60 feet, and their use is primarily restricted to research plots for which great accuracy is required.

Tree heights can be measured indirectly with instruments called *hypsometers.* Many types of hypsometers have been devised over the years, but they all work on either trigonometric or geometric principles. Figure 12.8 illustrates the trigonometric principle, which requires knowledge of the horizontal distance between the observer and the tree, and an instrument to measure the angles between this horizontal and the top and base of the tree. Most hypsometers employing the trigonometric principle are calibrated in terms of the tangents of the angles, so the observer can read tree heights directly on the

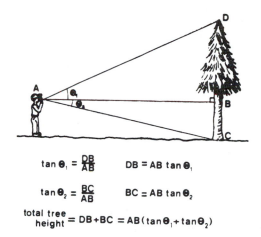

$$\tan \Theta_1 = \frac{DB}{AB} \qquad DB = AB \tan \Theta_1$$

$$\tan \Theta_2 = \frac{BC}{AB} \qquad BC = AB \tan \Theta_2$$

$$\text{total tree height} = DB + BC = AB(\tan \Theta_1 + \tan \Theta_2)$$

Figure 12.8 Three measurements are required to determine the total height of a tree using *trigonometric* principles: the angle Θ_1 from horizontal to the top of the tree, the angle Θ_2 from horizontal to the base of the tree, and the horizontal distance *AB* from the observer to the tree.

instrument's scale. Hypsometers employing the geometric principle must be used at a fixed horizontal distance from the tree and, in addition, must be held a fixed distance from the observer's eye (Figure 12.9).

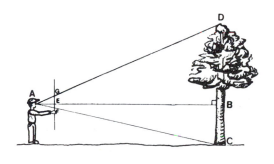

$$GF : DC = AE : AB$$

$$\text{total tree height} = DC = \frac{AB \times GF}{AE}$$

Figure 12.9 Measurement of total tree height using *geometric* principles: ratios of distances are constructed using the principle of similar triangles.

When trees are measured to assess the volume or weight of merchantable products in the tree, the *merchantable height* or *length* is often measured instead of the total height (Figure 12.10). Merchantable length is a measure of the usable portion of the tree above stump height (usually 1 foot) to a point on the stem where the diameter becomes too small or too irregular to be used.

Volume and Mass There are at present no instruments that allow the direct measurement of the volume or mass (weight) of a standing tree. Instead, volume and mass must be estimated from other tree dimensions. Tree height and dbh are most frequently used for this purpose, and many *tree volume*

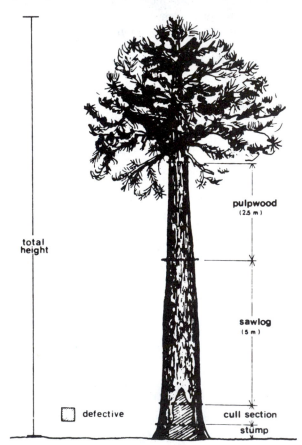

Figure 12.10 Diagram of a tree stem showing the total height of the tree and the length of merchantable sections.

tables giving the average volume or mass for trees of different diameters and heights have been developed (Table 12.2).

More accurate estimates of tree volume can be obtained by measuring upper-stem diameters with instruments called *optical dendrometers* (Figure 12.11). With diameter measurements taken at various heights on the tree, volumes may be calculated for individual stem sections (see earlier section, "Product Scaling") and then summed.

Age and Radial Increment Many tree species in the northern temperate region produce annual rings of wood corresponding to light-colored earlywood and darker latewood. This property makes it possible to measure tree age by using an *increment borer* to extract a core of wood and then counting the number of annual rings (Figure 12.12). Increment borers are also used to determine the rate of tree growth by measuring the length of the last several rings in the core. This measurement is called a *radial increment* and can be multiplied by 2 to estimate the diameter growth during the period.

Forest Sampling

It is seldom necessary or desirable to measure every tree on a forest property. Sufficiently accurate estimates can be obtained from measurements of a subset or sample of the trees in the forest. The process of selecting a representative sample of trees and obtaining the required estimates is called *forest sampling*.

Sampling Units Sample trees are usually selected in groups at different locations throughout the forest. Each group of trees is called a sampling unit and may be selected in a variety of ways. One approach is to tally (count and measure) all the trees on a plot of fixed area at each location. *Sample plots* may be square, rectangular, or circular and are usually between 0.01 and 0.20 acre in area. All trees (or all trees of merchantable size) with a midpoint at breast height lying within the plot boundary are tallied (Figure 12.13).

Table 12.3 presents an example of a forest sample

Table 12.2 Portion of a Tree Volume Table for Approximating Merchantable Volume of Commercial Species in the Great Lakes States[a]

Diameter at Breast Height (cm)	Volume[b] (m³) for Total height (m)					
	10	15	20	25	30	35
10	0.021	0.024				
20	0.126	0.186	0.247	0.311		
30	0.292	0.429	0.570	0.718	0.853	
40	0.524	0.767	1.017	1.281	1.523	
50		1.200	1.592	2.005	2.384	2.783
60		1.728	2.294	2.887	3.436	4.010

Source: Adapted from S. R. Gevorkiantz and L. P. Olsen, "Composite volume tables for timber and their application in the Lake States," U.S.D.A. For. Serv., Tech. Bull. 1104, 1955.

[a]As an example of usage, a tree with a measured diameter of 30 centimeters at breast height and a total height of 25 meters would have an estimated usable volume of 0.718 cubic meter)

[b]Volume inside bark from 0.3-meter stump height to limit of merchantability—that is, to a point on the stem where the diameter inside the bark is just equal to 8 centimeters.

obtained from 0.10-acre plots at fifteen different locations within a forest stand. Each sample tree was measured to determine its dbh to the nearest inch and its merchantable volume in cubic feet. Columns 1, 2, and 3 in Table 12.3 summarize the number of trees tallied and the total volume tallied for each dbh class. These data can be used to calculate estimates of the average number of trees, basal area, and

Figure 12.11 Observation of the upper-stem diameter with a Wheeler optical caliper.

Figure 12.12 Tree age determination with an increment borer.

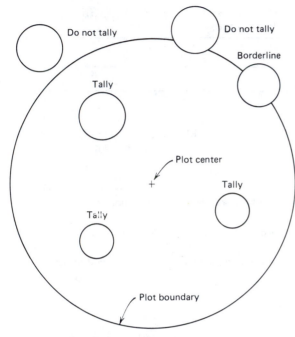

Figure 12.13 In fixed-area plot sampling, field crews tally all trees with a midpoint at breast height lying within the plot boundary.

volume per acre. The average number of trees per acre (column 5) for each dbh class is given by

$$\text{average number of trees per acre} = \frac{\text{number of trees tallied}}{nA}$$

where n is the number of sample plots (fifteen in this example) and A is the area of each sample plot (0.10 acre in this example). The average basal area per acre (column 6) for each dbh class is given by

$$\text{average basal area} = \frac{(\text{number of trees tallied})b}{nA}$$

where b is the basal area per tree, given in column 4 of the table (see earlier section, "Basal Area," for formulas). The average volume per acre (column 7) for each dbh class is given by

$$\text{average volume} = \frac{\text{total volume tallied}}{nA}$$

Another very useful type of forest-sampling unit was devised in 1948 by Walter Bitterlich, a German forester. With Bitterlich's method, also known as *horizontal point sampling,* observers tally all trees

Table 12.3 Example of a Tree Tally and Averages for a Sample of Fifteen 0.1-Acre Plots

1 Diameter at Breast Height (in.)	2 Number of Trees Tallied	3 Total Volume Tallied (ft^3)	4 Basal Area per Tree (ft^2)	5 Average[a] Number of Trees per Acre	6 Average Basal Area (ft^2/acre)	7 Average Volume (ft^3/acre)
6	89	223	0.1963	59.3	11.6	149
7	54	216	0.2672	36.0	9.6	144
8	34	204	0.3491	22.7	7.9	136
9	21	195	0.4418	14.0	6.2	130
10	15	195	0.5454	10.0	5.5	130
11	12	204	0.6599	8.0	5.3	136
12	8	160	0.7854	5.3	4.2	107
13	6	162	0.9217	4.0	3.7	108
14	3	96	1.0690	2.0	2.1	64
Total	242			161.3	56.1	1104

[a]A procedure for calculating the averages in columns 5, 6, and 7 is explained in the text.

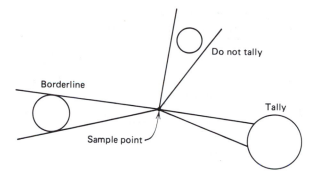

Figure 12.14 In Bitterlich horizontal point sampling, field crews tally all trees with a dbh larger than the angle projected by a gauge.

with a dbh larger than the angle projected by a gauge viewed from each sample point (Figure 12.14). A variety of *angle gauges* are available for use with Bitterlich's method. Figure 12.15 illustrates the use of a stick-type angle gauge; the observer's eye corresponds to the sample point, and the stick is rotated

through a complete circle while the observer views each tree at breast height to determine whether it is "in" or "out."

Instead of tallying every tree on a fixed-area plot, Bitterlich's method is equivalent to tallying each tree on a circular plot with an area proportional to the basal area of the tree. Hence, large-diameter trees are tallied on large plots and small-diameter trees are tallied on small plots. One advantage of this approach lies in the fact that large-diameter trees contribute more to stand basal area and volume than do small-diameter trees; so, by including more of the large trees in the sample and fewer of the small trees, more precise estimates of stand basal area and volume can usually be obtained with less effort. The geometry of Bitterlich's method gives it another advantage. If the basal area of a tree is divided by the area of its corresponding sample plot, the result is a constant, F, called the *basal-area factor*, and depends only on the angle projected by the gauge. Hence, each tree tallied represents the same basal

MEASUREMENT OF THE FOREST

Figure 12.15 Use of a stick-type angle gauge to tally trees on a Bitterlich horizontal sample point.

Borderline trees are checked with distance tapes and careful measurement of the diameter to determine whether they are "in" or "out."

Table 12.4 Example of a Tree Tally and Averages for a Sample of Fifteen Bitterlich Points with a Basal-Area Factor (*F*) of 10 Square Feet per Acre

1 Diameter at Breast Height (in.)	2 Number of Trees Tallied	3 Total Volume Tallied (ft³)	4 Basal Area per Tree (ft²)	5 Average[a] Number of Trees per Acre	6 Average Basal Area (ft²/acre)	7 Average Volume (ft³/acre)
6	17	43	0.1963	57.7	11.3	146
7	14	56	0.2672	34.9	9.3	140
8	12	72	0.3491	22.9	8.0	137
9	10	93	0.4418	15.1	6.7	140
10	9	117	0.5454	11.0	6.0	143
11	8	136	0.6599	8.1	5.3	137
12	6	120	0.7854	5.1	4.0	102
13	6	162	0.9217	4.3	4.0	117
14	3	96	1.0690	1.9	2.0	60
Total	85			161.0	56.6	1122

[a]A procedure for calculating the averages in columns 5, 6, and 7 is explained in the text.

area per acre regardless of the tree's size, and stand basal area can be estimated by simply multiplying the average number of trees tallied per point by the basal-area factor. This result is illustrated in the following example.

Table 12.4 gives an example of a forest sample obtained from Bitterlich points with a basal-area factor of 10 square feet per acre, at fifteen different locations within a forest stand. Each sample tree was measured as in the previous example. Columns 1, 2, and 3 in Table 12.4 summarize the number of trees tallied and the total volume tallied for each dbh class. Again, these data can be used to calculate stand averages, but the formulas are different from those used for fixed-area plots. The average number of trees per acre (column 5) for each dbh class is given by

$$\frac{\text{average number of trees}}{\text{per acre}} = \frac{F(\text{number of trees tallied})}{nb}$$

where *F* is the basal-area factor of the angle gauge (10 square feet per acre in this example), *n* is the number of sample points (fifteen in this example), and *b* is the basal area per tree, given in column 4 of the table (see earlier section, "Basal Area," for for-

mulas). The average basal area per acre (column 6) for each dbh class is given by

$$\text{average basal area} = \frac{F(\text{number of trees tallied})}{n}$$

Notice that this formula can be used even if trees are not tallied by dbh class. For example, if only the total number of trees tallied is known (eighty-five in this example), we can use the formula just given to calculate the total basal area per acre:

$$\text{total basal area} = \frac{F(\text{total number of trees tallied})}{n}$$

$$= \frac{10 \times 85}{15}$$

$$= 56.7 \text{ ft}^2/\text{acre}$$

This result is in agreement with the total basal area at the bottom of column 6 in the table (the slight difference is due to rounding error). So it can be seen that Bitterlich's method provides a very quick and easy way to obtain basal-area estimates. All one has to do is count the number of "in" trees.

The average volume per acre (column 7) for each dbh class is given by

$$\text{average volume} = \frac{F(\text{total volume tallied})}{nb}$$

One of the important decisions in a forest-sampling design is the size of plot to use, or the basal-area factor of the angle gauge when using Bitterlich's method. Larger plots will include more trees, will be less variable, and will yield more precise estimates. However, if there are too many trees on the plot, the time and cost of tallying them may be excessive and there is a good chance that some trees may be overlooked. A rule of thumb that seems to work well is to use a plot size that gives an average of 15 to 20 trees per plot. For example, a large sawtimber stand may have 75 to 100 trees per acre, so a good plot size to use in this stand is ⅕ acre. A poletimber stand with 150 to 200 trees per acre would be sampled with a ¹⁄₁₀-acre plot.

Bitterlich's method works best if an average of 6 to 12 trees are "in" at each sample point. The important thing to remember here is that the larger the basal-area factor of the angle gauge, the fewer the number of trees tallied at each point. If the average basal area of the stand is divided by 10, the result is a good basal-area factor to use. For example, if a large sawtimber stand has a basal area of 200 square feet per acre, a good basal-area factor to use is 20. A poletimber or small sawtimber stand with 100 square feet per acre of basal area would be sampled with a 10-factor angle gauge.

Sampling Methods Once appropriate sampling units have been selected, it is necessary to decide how many units to measure and how they will be located in the forest. The total number of sample units is called the *sample size,* and the manner in which they are located is called the *sampling method.*

Random sampling is a method in which sample units are located completely at random within each stand (Figure 12.16*a*). Random sampling ensures

SURVEY DESIGN CONSIDERATIONS FOR TIMBER RESOURCES

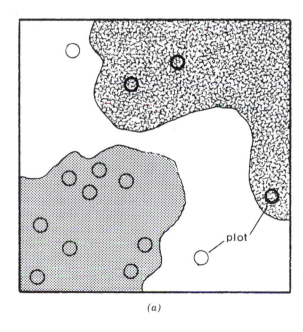

(*a*)

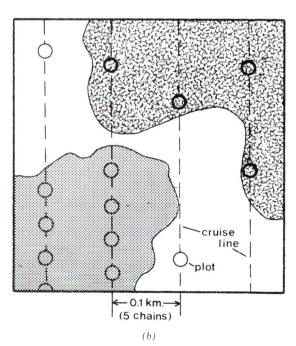

(*b*)

Figure 12.16 Portion of a forest tract illustrating (*a*) random and (*b*) systematic allocation of sample plots for three cover types. Sampling intensity (number of plots per unit area) varies by cover type.

that estimates obtained from the sample will be *unbiased;* that is, on the average they will tend toward the true stand values. *Systematic sampling* (Figure 12.16*b*) is often preferred because it is easier to implement, the time it takes to walk between plots is usually less, and sketching field maps and adjusting type lines on aerial photographs is more easily done while *cruising.*[1] In systematic sampling, also called *line-plot cruising,* sample units are located at specific intervals along straight cruise lines running across the forest property. If appropriate precautions are observed, systematic sampling will not introduce undue bias. In particular, it is important to ensure that cruise lines do not force plots along a line to be in some atypical forest condition. One way to prevent this type of bias is to run cruise lines up and down slopes, since timber conditions tend to vary with changes in elevation.

The number of sample units located in a given stand is usually determined by the maximum allowable error that can be tolerated in the final estimates. The more sample units measured, the smaller the errors will be, on the average, in estimates obtained from the sample. Sampling errors are usually expressed as a percentage of the timber volumes or values being estimated. For example, if the objective of sampling is to determine a fair price for a large, valuable stand of sawtimber, the maximum allowable error may be set at 3 to 5 percent. If, however, estimates are desired for the purpose of making long-range management plans, less accuracy is required and allowable errors may be set at 10 to 20 percent.

Foresters can use statistical formulas to determine the minimum number of plots required to achieve a specified sampling error. The actual formula depends on the sampling method. For example, the following formula gives the number, n, of sample units required when using random sampling in a single stand of timber,

$$n = \left(\frac{t\text{CV}}{E}\right)^2$$

where E is the allowable percentage of error, CV is the coefficient of variation in the stand, and t is a value obtained from a table of Student's t distribution.[2] The CV is a measure of how variable the size and density of timber are from place to place in the stand. A very uniform stand, like a plantation (Figure 12.17*a*), will have a relatively low CV. With clustering (Figure 12.17*b*), which can occur to varying degrees in naturally regenerated stands, CV values are higher.

The CV plays a major role in determining the required number of sample units in a given stand. Suppose the CV in a relatively uniform stand is 20 percent, the maximum allowable error for the timber cruise is set at 5 percent, and the value of t is approximately 2. In this stand our formula gives a required sample size of

$$n = \left(\frac{2 \times 20}{5}\right)^2 = 8^2 = 64 \text{ units}$$

If the trees in the stand were clustered and the CV were, say, 40 percent, the required sample size would be

$$n = \left(\frac{2 \times 40}{5}\right)^2 = 16^2 = 256 \text{ units}$$

Because the required sample size varies with the square of the CV, a doubling of the CV (as happened in this example) means that four times as many sample units are required to achieve the same sampling error. Careful selection of efficient types and sizes of sampling units helps reduce the CVs in forest sampling designs, and can considerably reduce the required sample size and cost of a forest inventory.

Forest sampling is generally carried out by survey crews of two people each. The crew chief is responsible for locating sample units and recording data. The second crew member is responsible for tree measurements such as dbh, height, and age. Data are

---

[1]To cruise a holding of forestland is to examine and estimate its yield of forest products.

[2]Procedures for calculating CV and determining t are explained in forest mensuration textbooks (1, 2).

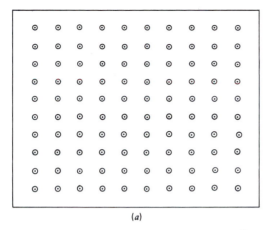 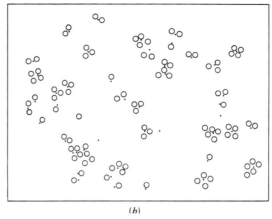

(a) (b)

Figure 12.17 The circles in these diagrams illustrate the locations of tree stems in (a) uniform and (b) clustered forest stands.

often recorded on tally sheets and then entered into an office computer for statistical processing. However, with the advances made in computers and electronics, data may now be entered directly into small battery-operated computers, which are taken into the forest (Figure 12.18). These devices help reduce the chance of data entry errors and speed subsequent data handling and compilation.

Statistics Estimates obtained from forest sampling are called statistics, and they will vary in detail according to the type of timber survey. In general, the most detailed statistics are required for timber appraisals and for scientific research. This level of detail may include stand and stock tables (Table 12.5) for each timber stand in the forest, together with maps showing the boundaries, area, and topography of each stand. Stand and stock tables show a breakdown of the trees and volume of timber in a stand by dbh class and species. They may also tabulate the volume of sawtimber by tree or log grades. These important factors affect the value of timber, together with accessibility and distance to mills.

Management-planning inventories usually do not require as much detail. They are more concerned with estimates of the species composition, average size and age of the trees, and the density and site quality of timber stands. In addition, of particular importance to management planning are the rate of growth of timber and the rate of loss through natural mortality, insects, disease, fire, weather, and harvesting.

Figure 12.18 Sample tree measurements are entered directly into this small, battery-operated computer, which is taken into the forest. The computer weighs less than a pound and is capable of performing all the statistical calculations necessary to prepare a stand and stock table (Table 12.5).

Table 12.5 Stand and Stock Table for a Red Oak Stand in the American Legion State Forest, Oneida County, Wisconsin[a]

Diameter at Breast Height (in.)	Red Oak		White Birch		Sugar Maple		Red Maple		Total	
	Trees	Cords	Trees	Cords	Trees	Cords	Trees	Cords	Trees	Cords
6			76.5	2.2	76.5	2.1			153.0	4.3
8	14.3	1.2	14.3	1.5					28.6	2.7
10	82.5	12.0	18.3	2.2					100.8	14.2
12							6.4	1.3	6.4	1.3
14	4.7	1.3							4.7	1.3
Total	101.5	14.5	109.1	5.9	76.5	2.1	6.4	1.3	293.5	23.8

[a]Values are averages per acre.

Forest Growth and Yield

The volume of timber in a forest at a specific point in time is called *forest yield,* and the change in volume that occurs over an interval of time is called *forest growth.* The forests of North America and particularly those of Europe have been surveyed a number of times. Repeated surveys provide data for assessing the growth of a forest, changes in species composition, and the effectiveness of past management. Such surveys are the basis for regulating forests to provide a sustained, even flow of timber over long time periods.

In order to reduce the effects of sampling errors on growth estimates, repeated surveys often rely on permanent sample plots that are carefully monumented so they can be found and remeasured at subsequent points in time, usually at intervals of five to ten years. Permanent sample plots also allow the growth of a forest to be assessed in terms of its basic components.

Components of Forest Growth When a permanent sample plot is remeasured, several distinct components of growth can be observed. There may be new trees on the plot that were not present, or were too small to be tallied, at the previous measurement. The present volume of these new trees is called *ingrowth.* Trees that are alive and tallied at both measurements are called *survivor trees,* and the

difference in the volume of these trees at the two measurements is called *survivor growth.* The volume of trees that were alive at the first measurement but died during the growth period is called *mortality* and is usually classified according to the cause of death. Finally, any trees that were harvested during the period can be identified by their stumps. The volume of harvested trees is called *cut.*

The net change in the volume of a forest is equal to ingrowth, plus survivor growth, minus mortality, minus cut. Important factors that affect the rate of forest growth include site quality, stocking, and density.

Site Quality Forest stands are commonly classified according to *site quality,* which indicates the productive capacity of a specific area of forestland for a particular species. Although many species may grow on the same site, they may not grow equally well. The site productivity measure most commonly used is *site index,* the average height of dominant and codominant trees at a specified index age, usually 50 years. Sometimes an index age of 100 years is used for the longer-lived West Coast species and 25 years for southern plantations.

When height and age have been measured, they are used as coordinates for determining site index from a set of curves (Figure 12.19). Site index curves and tables have been developed for most commer-

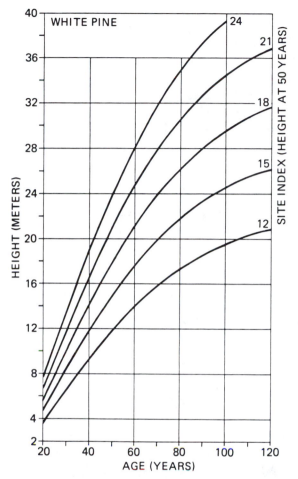

Figure 12.19 White pine site index curves. (From P. R. Laidly, "Metric site index curves for aspen, birch and conifers in the Lake States," U.S.D.A. For. Serv., Gen. Tech. Rept. NC-54, North Cent. For. Expt. Sta., St. Paul, Minn., 1979.)

For example, when there is no forest stand, the site index can sometimes be predicted from such factors as the depth of surface soil, stone, silt and clay content, and slope steepness. However, the concept of site index is not well suited to uneven-aged stands and areas taken over by mixed species.

Stocking and Density The terms forest stocking and density are often used interchangeably, but Avery and Burkhart (2) do not consider them to be synonymous. *Stand density* is a quantitative term indicating the degree of stem crowding within a stand, and *stocking* refers to the adequacy of a given stand density to meet some management objective, for example, maximizing the production of sawtimber. Stands may be referred to as understocked, fully stocked, or overstocked.

Stand basal area is often used as a measure of stand density, and stocking charts (Figure 12.20) have been prepared for different species that show acceptable ranges of basal area for stands of different average diameters. To use a stocking chart, the forester must first determine the average basal area and number of trees per acre in the stand, by using one of the forest-sampling procedures previously described. These values are used as coordinates to locate a point in the stocking chart. If this point falls between the curves labeled *A* and *B*, the stand is fully stocked. If the point falls below the *B* curve or above the *A* curve, the stand is understocked or over-stocked, respectively. For example, a red pine stand with 500 trees per acre and a basal area of 200 square feet per acre would be overstocked (Figure 12.20), whereas another red pine stand with the same basal area but only 150 trees per acre would be fully stocked.

It has been shown that height growth is not greatly affected by stand density. It has also been determined in recent years that there is not as strong a relationship as originally supposed between basal area and site quality. The main reason for the differences in volume on good sites as against poor sites is height. For many practical purposes, therefore, we can assume that basal area varies little with site quality except at the extremes.

cial species. Suppose a white pine stand has an average total height of 20 meters at an age of 70 years. Figure 12.19 shows that this point lies on site index curve 15. This means that the expected dominant tree height for this site is 15 meters at the index age of 50 years.

Site index has been found to be correlated with soil factors and topography related to tree growth.

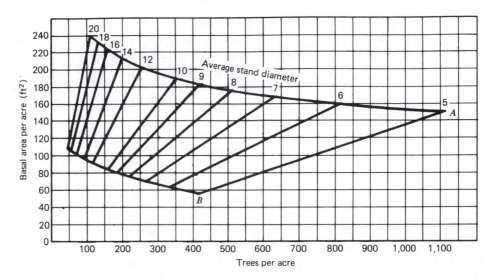

Figure 12.20 Stocking chart for managed red pine stands. (From J. W. Benzie, "Manager's handbook for red pine in the North Central States," U.S.D.A. For. Serv., Gen. Tech. Rept. NC-33, North Cent. For. Expt. Sta., St. Paul, Minn., 1977.)

Growth and Yield Projection Repeated surveys together with site index assessments provide a basis for projecting future stand conditions and associated yields. Growth projection models may also be used to predict stand yield for specific management practices. Table 12.6 illustrates a yield table constructed for pine stands under a particular set of management alternatives—in this instance stand density alternatives. Notice that the model on which this table is based provides estimates of both growth and future product yields. It is important to stress that the growth and yield information for this particular forest type represents estimates based on a sample of observations from various study plots. Many other types of yield tables are available.

A variety of individual tree growth models have been developed to characterize stand growth and dynamics at the individual-tree level. It is possible with some of these models to determine optimal stand treatments through simulation or mathematical programming techniques. Examples of such treatments include planting and thinning to produce optimal tree-size class distributions and stand densi-

ties, optimal fertilization treatments, and harvesting at optimal rotation ages.

Measurement of Nontimber Resources

Measurements are also made on many other resources for multiple-use management of forests. It is not possible in an introductory text to cover all the details for measurement of these resources. However, very brief descriptions of the rationale and the types of measurements obtained for water, wildlife and recreational resources, and urban forests are given in this section. Additional information is provided in separate chapters devoted to the specific resources. .

With *water resources* we are primarily interested in measuring quantity, quality, and timing of the water resource for particular locations. Forest characteristics affect water yield in terms of these variables. Timber harvest operations are one example of

Table 12.6 Variable-Density Growth and Yield Table for Managed Stands of Natural Slash Pine[a]

Initial Basal Area (m²)	Age (years) From	To	Site Index (m)[b] 20	25 Projected Yield (m³/ha)	30	Projected Basal Area (m²/ha)
16	20	20	73	106	136	16
		30	134	194	248	22
		40	181	262	336	25
		50	217	315	403	28
	30	30	102	147	189	16
		40	147	213	273	20
		50	184	267	341	23
	40	40	120	174	222	16
		50	156	226	289	19
20	20	20	89	129	166	20
		30	153	222	284	25
		40	200	290	371	28
		50	235	341	436	30
	30	30	124	180	230	20
		40	171	248	318	24
		50	207	301	385	26
	40	40	146	212	272	20
		50	183	265	340	23
24	20	20	105	152	195	24
		30	171	247	316	28
		40	217	315	403	31
		50	251	364	466	33
	30	30	146	212	271	24
		40	193	280	359	27
		50	229	332	425	29
	40	40	172	250	320	24
		50	209	302	387	27

Source: Adapted from equations given by F. A. Bennett, "Variable-density yield tables for managed stands of natural slash pine," U.S.D.A. For. Serv., Res. Note SE-141, 1970.

[a]Cubic-meter yields and basal area as projected from various initial ages and basal areas.

[b]Base age of 50 years.

a use that could increase water yield. There is also interest in nonpoint pollution[3]and how it might be controlled by forest management practices. In this area we may be concerned with sampling and characterizing the forest resource in much the same way as we do the timber resource inventory, or sampling and measuring streamflow characteristics from a particular watershed. The statistical aspects of this sampling and measurement process are fundamentally like those used for the timber resource. Computer modeling of watersheds in forest ecosystems was discussed in Chapter 6, and a further discussion of watershed management is given in Chapter 19.

For measuring *wildlife resources,* management surveys usually employ census techniques to determine animal population levels or to develop indexes to indicate relative population levels. Examples of such indexes are pellet counts or flush counts for deer and birds, respectively. There is also increasing interest in relating the forest habitat conditions, often described by the timber inventory, to the population numbers and the health of the herds inhabiting or potentially inhabiting the area. A further discussion of the interactions of the forest with wildlife is given in Chapter 17.

Management of *recreation* areas requires surveys that are primarily concerned with the numbers of users and the physical impact they have on particular sites. Thus we may be sampling a population of users or a population of sites used by people engaged in outdoor recreation. In sampling the resource users, we frequently use questionnaires intended to get at their attitudes and likely responses to various kinds

of recreation resource management. Such surveys may consider the forest as a visual resource to be experienced by the visitor. With such concepts it is possible to characterize and subsequently manage the forest environment to give it scenic forest types that contribute to user pleasure. A further discussion of forest recreation management is given in Chapter 20.

Urban forests are receiving much more attention, and many cities now have a forester assigned specifically to this resource. Inventories of the forest resource in small communities frequently take the form of a complete census of all trees. Typical information collected for each tree includes species, diameter, location (perhaps by block or lot), position (such as boulevard or interior lot), ownership, and condition—in terms of vigor and presence of insects, diseases, and hazards. For larger cities, a 5 to 10 percent systematic sample of trees or city blocks may be used. This is sometimes combined with classifications of blocks into two or three tree density classes based on aerial photos. Because of the diversity of species in urban areas, the field crews need considerable background in dendrology.

Given all this information, the urban forest manager is in a good position to estimate future needs for tree removal and replacement and to develop plans for these activities.

References

1. B. Husch, C. I. Miller, and T. W. Beers, *Forest Mensuration,* Third Edition, John Wiley & Sons, New York, 1982.

2. T. E. Avery and H. E. Burkhart, *Forest Measurements,* Third Edition, McGraw–Hill, New York, 1983.

3. E. D. Rast, D. L. Sonderman, and G. L. Gammon, "A guide to hardwood log grading," U.S.D.A. For. Serv., Gen. Tech. Rept. NE-1, Upper Darby, Pa., 1973.

---

[3]*Nonpoint pollution* derives from a dispersed source such as agricultural activity, as compared with *point pollution,* for which a single pollution source can be identified (e.g., a factory drainspout).

CHAPTER 13

Remote Sensing and Geographic Information Systems

Thomas M. Lillesand

Broadly defined, remote sensing refers to any methodology employed to study the characteristics of objects from a distance. Human sight, smell, and hearing are examples of rudimentary forms of remote sensing. The type of sensing systems we treat in this chapter operate on the principle of recording electromagnetic energy over a broad range of the electromagnetic spectrum, from ultraviolet to radio wavelengths. These systems take on various forms and can be operated from aircraft or from space.

Historically, the most important form of remote sensing used in forestry has been *aerial photography*. For example, aerial photographs have been used for decades to aid in the forest-sampling and forest mensuration processes. Aerial photographs provide an efficient means of obtaining a detailed "bird's-eye" view of forest conditions on even the most extensive, remote, and treacherous of terrains.

As valuable as aerial-photographic techniques have become in forest management, these procedures are limited to the study of images recorded on photographic emulsions. These materials are sensitive only to energy that is either in, or near, the visible portion of the electromagnetic energy spectrum. Sensors such as thermal scanners, multispectral scanners, and side-looking radar employ wavelengths expanded beyond the photographic range; in addition, these nonphotographic sensors typically record image data in a *digital* format so they can be analyzed by computer-processing techniques (1, 4, 5).

Today's forest manager has ready access to a broad array of remote-sensing data products—ranging from 35-mm photography to high-resolution digital satellite data collected on a global basis. The objective of this chapter is to describe briefly the major types of remote sensing techniques available. We begin with an overview of the basic nature of electromagnetic energy and then discuss both photographic and nonphotographic sensing systems. We first treat aerial sensing systems, and then we discuss earth resource satellites. We conclude this chapter with a brief description of computer-based geographic information systems—the means through which remote sensing data can be readily merged with other types of spatially related resource information.

Given the scope of this chapter, our discussion is, of necessity, very general. Additional details on the topics covered may be obtained from the various remote sensing texts, manuals, and proceedings volumes listed at the end of this chapter (1–8). Much of the material in this chapter has been extracted directly from the book by Lillesand and Kiefer (1).

Electromagnetic Energy and Spectral Response Patterns

The sun and various artificial sources radiate electromagnetic energy over a broad range of wavelengths. Light is a particular type of electromagnetic radiation that can be seen or sensed by the human eye. All electromagnetic energy, whether visible or invisible, travels in the form of sinusoidal waves at the speed of light. Wavelength ranges of special interest in remote sensing are shown in Table 13.1. The most common unit used to express wavelengths

Table 13.1 Primary Wavelength Ranges Used in Remote Sensing

Wavelength	Spectral Region
0.3 to 0.4 μm	Ultraviolet
0.4 to 0.7 μm	Visible
0.7 to 0.9 μm	Photographic infrared (near-infrared)
0.9 to 1.3 μm	Near-infrared
1.3 to 3.0 μm	Mid-infrared
3 to 14 μm	Thermal infrared
1 mm to 1 m	Radar

in remote sensing is the micrometer or micron (μm) (1 micrometer = 1×10^{-6} meter).

When electromagnetic energy is incident upon an object on the earth's surface, it can interact with the object in any or all of three ways: it can be *reflected, transmitted,* or *absorbed.* The absorbed component normally goes into heating the body and is subsequently reemitted from the object. The particular mix of these three possible interactions depends on the physical nature of objects. For example, healthy vegetation normally appears green because the blue and red components of the incident light are absorbed by chlorophyll present in the leaves. In contrast, concrete surfaces reflect blue, green, and red wavelengths equally and thus appear white. Remote sensors record such variations in energy interaction (both in visible and invisible wavelengths) in order to discriminate between earth surface features and to assist in quantifying their condition.

The amount of energy at various wavelengths that is returned to a sensor from a given object defines a *spectral-response pattern.* Figure 13.1 shows typical spectral-response envelopes (range of values) for deciduous trees and coniferous trees based on their reflection of sunlight over the visible and near-infrared portions of the spectrum. The configuration of these curves gives us insight into the spectral characteristics of an object and has a strong influence on the choice of wavelength region(s) in which remote sensing data are acquired for a particular application.

In Figure 13.1, assume that you are given the task of selecting an airborne sensor system to assist in preparing a type map of a forested area that differentiates deciduous from coniferous trees. One choice of sensor might be the human eye. However, there is a potential problem with this choice. Because the spectral-reflectance curves for each tree type overlap in most of the visible portion of the spectrum and are very close where they do not overlap, the eye might see both tree types as being essentially the same shade of "green." Certainly it would improve things to use spatial clues to each tree type's identity, such as size, shape, and site. However, this is often difficult to do from the air, particularly when tree types are intermixed. How

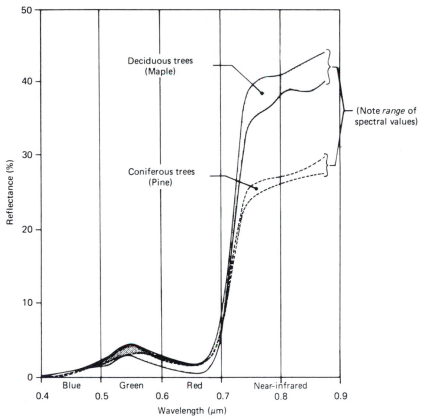

Figure 13.1 Generalized spectral-reflectance envelopes for deciduous and coniferous trees. [From Lillesand and Kiefer (1); adapted from Kalensky and Wilson (9).]

might we discriminate the two types on the basis of their spectral characteristics alone? We could do this by using a sensor system that records near-infrared energy. A camera loaded with black and white infrared film is just such a system. On black-and-white infrared photographs, deciduous trees, having higher infrared reflectance than conifers, generally appear much lighter in tone than do conifers. This is illustrated in Figure 13.2, which shows stands of coniferous trees surrounded by deciduous trees. In Figure 13.2a (visible spectrum) it is virtually impossible to distinguish between tree types, even though the conifers have a distinctive conical shape and the deciduous trees have rounded crowns. In Figure 13.2b (near-infrared) the conifers have a distinctly darker tone. On such an image, distinguishing deciduous from coniferous trees is no task at all. In fact,

if we could somehow electronically scan this type of image and feed the results to a computer in terms of image tone, we might automate our entire mapping task. Many remote-sensing data analysis schemes attempt to do just this. For these schemes to be successful, the cover types to be differentiated must be spectrally separable in the wavelengths used to collect the data.

Spectral Reflectance of Vegetation, Soil, and Water

Figure 13.3 shows typical spectral-reflectance curves for three basic types of earth features: healthy green vegetation, dry bare soil (gray–brown loam), and clear lake water. The lines in this figure represent average reflectance curves compiled by measuring a

Figure 13.2 Low-altitude oblique aerial photographs illustrating deciduous versus coniferous trees. (*a*) Panchromatic photograph recording reflected sunlight over a wavelength band of 0.4 to 0.7 micrometers. (*b*) Black-and-white infrared photograph recording reflected sunlight over a wavelength band of 0.7 to 0.9 micrometers [From Lillesand and Kiefer (1).]

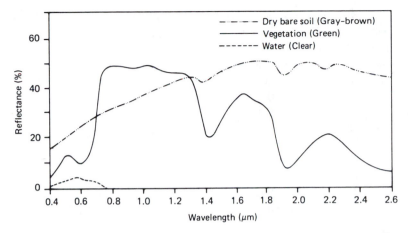

Figure 13.3 Typical spectral-reflectance curves for vegetation, soil, and water. [From Lillesand and Kiefer (1); adapted from Swain and Davis (4)].

large sample of features. Notice how distinctive the curves are for each feature. For example, the curve for green vegetation manifests a "peak-and-valley" configuration. The valleys in the visible portion of the spectrum are due to chlorophyll, which strongly absorbs energy in the wavelength bands centered at about 0.45 and 0.65 micrometer. Hence, our eyes perceive healthy vegetation as green in color because of the very high absorption of blue and red energy by plant leaves and the very high reflection of green energy. If a plant is subject to some form of stress, it may decrease or cease chlorophyll production. This results in less chlorophyll absorption in the blue and red bands, and the red reflectance often increases to the point that the plant turns yellow (combination of green and red).

As we go from the visible to the near-infrared portion of the spectrum at about 0.7 micrometer, the reflectance of healthy vegetation increases dramatically. Plant reflectance in the range of 0.7 to 1.3 micrometers is primarily from the internal structure of plant leaves. Because this structure is highly variable in plant species, reflectance measurements in this range often permit us to discriminate between species, even if they look the same in visible wavelengths. Similarly, many plant stresses alter the reflectance in this region, and sensors operating in this range are often used to detect vegetation stress.

Throughout the wavelength range beyond 1.3 micrometers, leaf reflectance is approximately inversely related to the total water present in a leaf. This total is a function of both the moisture content and the thickness of a leaf (4).

The soil curve in Figure 13.3 shows considerably less peak-and-valley variation in reflectance. Some of the factors affecting soil reflectance are moisture content, soil texture, surface roughness, the presence of iron oxide, and the amount of organic matter.

Probably the most distinctive characteristic of the spectral-reflectance curve for water is the absorption of energy at near-infrared wavelengths (beyond 0.7 micrometer). Water absorbs energy in these wavelengths whether we consider water features per se, such as lakes and streams, or water contained in vegetation or soil. Locating and delineating water bodies with remote sensing data is done most easily in near-infrared wavelengths because of this absorption property.

Atmospheric Effects

Because the atmosphere contains a wide variety of suspended particles, it offers electromagnetic energy interaction, just as "ground" objects do. In fact, in meteorological applications of remote sensing the atmosphere is the object of primary interest. For most forestry applications, however, it is desirable to look through, not at, the atmosphere. The extent to which the atmosphere transmits electromagnetic energy depends on wavelength. Energy in the ultraviolet wavelengths is greatly scattered, and this limits the use of these wavelengths from aerial platforms. The atmosphere is transparent enough in the visible and photographic infrared wavelengths to permit aerial photography. In this region the blue wavelengths are scattered the most, and the infrared wavelengths are scattered the least. Two "windows" exist in the thermal-infrared region where the atmosphere is relatively transparent: the 3- to 5-micrometer wavelengths and the 8- to 14-micrometer wavelengths. Most aerial thermal scanning is done in the 8- to 14-micrometer band. At radar wavelengths the atmosphere is extremely transparent; even clouds and fog are readily penetrable.

Aerial Photography

Aerial Cameras and Photographic Coverage

Aerial photographs can be made with virtually any type of camera. Many successful ones have been made from light aircraft with hand-held 35-mm cameras (10). For example, the photographs in Figure 13.2 were made in this manner. The simplicity and low cost of 35-mm cameras make them ideal sensors for small-area analysis. (The true size of images taken with a 35-mm system is 24 × 36 mm; the width of the film is 35 mm.) Another type of "small-format" camera used frequently in forest management is the 70-mm camera. (The true size of images made with these systems is 55 × 55 mm). In most aerial remote sensing endeavors, however, photographers use precision-built aerial-mapping cameras. These cameras are specifically designed to expose a large number of photographs in rapid succession with the ultimate in geometric fidelity. The film format size of aerial-mapping cameras is typically 230 × 230 mm. Hence, photographs taken with this type of camera are often referred to as "9 × 9 inch" photography. The nominal focal length of the lens used to obtain such photography is typically 152 mm or 6 inches.

Foresters are most often interested in obtaining *vertical* aerial photographs. These are made with the camera axis directed beneath the aircraft as vertically as possible. As Figure 13.4 shows, photographic coverage is normally obtained along flight lines. Successive photographs along a flight line are generally taken with some degree of endlap. This lapping serves two important functions: it ensures total coverage along a flight line, and an endlap of at least 50 percent affords *stereoscopic coverage* of a project area. Stereoscopic coverage consists of adjacent pairs of overlapping vertical photographs called stereopairs. Stereopairs provide two different perspectives of the ground in their region of endlap. When a person views images forming a stereopair through a stereoscope (see Figure 12.4), each eye psychologically occupies the vantage point from which the respective image of the stereopair was taken in flight. The person perceives a three-dimensional stereomodel. Most forestry interpretations of aerial photographs entail the use of stereoscopic coverage and stereoviewing.

Special-purpose photographic coverage of large forested areas has sometimes been obtained with a *panoramic camera*. Instead of taking a frame of photography instantaneously, these systems incorporate rotating optics that scan the terrain from side to side, transverse to the direction of flight. The angular coverage of these systems can extend from horizon to horizon. Because of their extensive coverage and high-resolution optics, such systems have been used over large areas to detect damage from forest pests and for planning the associated timber salvage operations (11).

Film–Filter Combinations

Although several types and brands of film can be used to take aerial photographs, they can all be classified into one of the following four categories: black-and-white panchromatic, black-and-white infrared, color, and color infrared. *Black-and-white*

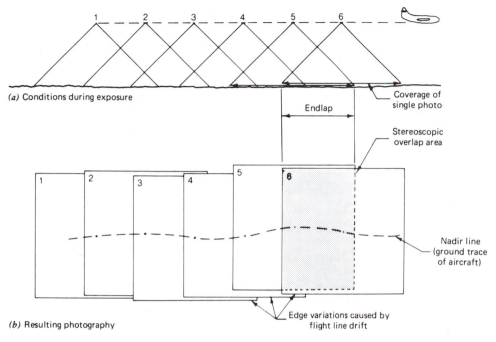

Figure 13.4 Photographic coverage along a flight strip. [From Lillesand and Kiefer (1).]

panchromatic films are sensitive to approximately the same wavelengths as the human eye (0.4 to 0.7 micrometer). *Black-and-white infrared* films are sensitive to both the visible portion of the spectrum and the near-infrared wavelengths from 0.7 to 0.9 micrometer. It is important to note that infrared energy of these wavelengths *does not represent heat* emitted from objects, but simply reflected energy to which the human eye is insensitive.

Normal *color* film is sensitive to essentially the same wavelengths as black-and-white panchromatic film (0.4 to 0.7 micrometer). Color film contains more information, however, because it has three separate emulsion layers sensitive to blue, green, and red wavelengths, respectively. *Color infrared* films have three similar dye layers, but they are sensitive to green, red, and near-infrared wavelengths. Blue light is absorbed by a yellow filter used in combination with the film. The effective spectral sensitivity of this film–filter combination extends from 0.5 to 0.9 micrometer. Again, it is reflected sunlight, not emitted thermal energy, that is photographed with color infrared film.

Color infrared film is frequently called "false color" film because the colors in the final image do not match those of the original objects photographed. That is, blue images result from objects reflecting primarily green energy, green images result from objects reflecting primarily red energy, and red images result from objects reflecting primarily in the photographic infrared portion of the spectrum (0.7 to 0.9 micrometer).

Color infrared film was developed during World War II to detect painted targets that were camouflaged to look like vegetation. Because healthy vegetation reflects infrared energy much more strongly than it does green energy, it generally appears in various tones of red on color infrared film. However, objects painted green generally have low infrared reflectance. Thus they appear blue on the film and can be readily discriminated from healthy green vegetation. Because of its genesis, color infrared film has often been referred to as "camouflage detection (CD) film." With its vivid color portrayal of near-infrared energy, color infrared film has become extremely useful for analyses of forest resources. Its principal advantages include good differentiation of tree species and good detection of vegetation stress and damage (12).

Scale of Aerial Photographs

The amount of detail shown in an aerial photograph is dependent, among other things, on the scale of the photograph. A photographic scale, like a map scale, is an expression stating that one unit (any unit) of distance on a photograph represents a specific number of units of actual ground distance. Scales may be expressed as unit equivalents, representative fractions, or ratios. For example, if 1 millimeter on a photograph represents 25 meters on the ground, the scale of the photograph can be expressed as 1 millimeter = 25 meters (unit equivalents), or 1/25,000 (representative fraction), or 1 : 25,000 (ratio). All three expressions are identical in meaning.

The most straightforward method for determining photo scale is to measure the corresponding photograph and ground distances between any two points mutually identifiable on both the photograph and a map. The scale is then computed as the ratio of the photo distance to the ground distance. For a vertical photograph taken over flat terrain, scale is a function of the focal length of the camera used to acquire the image, and the flying height above the ground from which the image was taken. In general,

$$\text{photo scale} = \frac{\text{camera focal length}}{\text{flying height above terrain}}$$

This equation expresses an important principle: the photo scale for any given point on the terrain is a function of the vertical distance between the camera and the terrain point. If a photograph is taken over flat terrain, it has a constant scale at all points. However, photographs taken over terrain of varying elevation will exhibit a continuous range of scales associated with the variations in terrain elevation.

Photo scale variation causes geometric distortion. Whereas all objects on a map are depicted in their true relative sizes and horizontal positions, points on a photograph taken over varying terrain are displaced from their true map positions. A map is an undistorted *orthographic projection* of the ground surface, but a photograph is a distorted *perspective projection* (see Figure 13.5). On a photograph areas of terrain at the higher elevations lie closer to the camera at the time of exposure and therefore appear larger than corresponding areas lying at lower elevations. Furthermore, the tops of objects are always displaced from their bases (Figure 13.5). This distortion is called *relief displacement* and causes any object standing above the terrain to "lean" away radially from the center or principal point of a photograph.

Photogrammetry

By now the student should see that the inherent geometry of aerial photographs precludes their direct use as maps. However, reliable ground measurements and maps can be obtained from aerial photographs if precise photo measurements are analyzed with due regard for the various geometric distortions present. The technology through which reliable ground measurements are made from aerial photographs is called photogrammetry. The practice of photogrammetry is highly developed, to the extent that virtually all large-area topographic mapping is performed photogrammetrically. Field foresters typically perform many types of operations photogrammetrically. By this means they obtain horizontal ground distances, bearings, and azimuths; measure areas; and calculate heights of objects, terrain elevations, and slopes (13, 14).

Topographic maps are produced photogrammetrically in instruments called *stereoplotters*. These devices accommodate stereopairs mounted in special projectors that can be mutually oriented to correspond precisely to the angular orientations in which the photographs were originally taken. Once oriented properly, the projectors re-create an accurate model of the terrain; when viewed stereoscopically, the model can be used to plot maps without the distortions inherent in individual photographs.

Whereas stereoplotters are designed for distortion-free transfer of *map* information from stereopairs (using lines and symbols to represent fea-

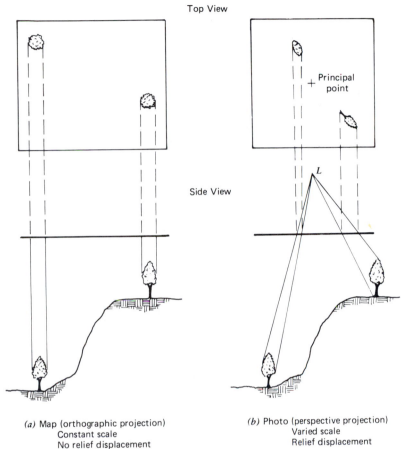

Top View

Side View

(a) Map (orthographic projection)
Constant scale
No relief displacement

(b) Photo (perspective projection)
Varied scale
Relief displacement

Figure 13.5 Comparative projective geometry of (a) a map and (b) a vertical aerial photograph. All rays for the photograph pass through a common point L. Notice the differences in size, shape, and location of the two trees. [From Lillesand and Kiefer (1).]

tures), a similar device can be used to transfer distortion-free *image* information. The resulting undistorted image is called an *orthophotograph*. Orthophotographs combine the geometric usefulness of a map with the interpretive information provided by a photograph. Normally, orthophotographs are produced by scanning across a stereomodel on a line-by-line basis, recording digitally the elevation of terrain points at a systematic grid spacing along each scan line. The resulting terrain profiles are then used to produce the orthophotograph in a computer-driven projection device. This device compensates, grid cell by grid cell, for the geometric distor-

tions in the original photographs as it reexposes one of the original images onto a new negative.

The matrix of elevation data resulting from systematically scanning a stereomodel can also be used to form a *digital elevation model* (DEM) of the terrain. Typically, DEMs constitute one of the basic layers of information in a geographic information system (GIS, described later). Furthermore, DEMs can be manipulated through computer graphics procedures in numerous ways. For example, three-dimensional perspective views of the terrain from arbitrarily defined vantage points can be generated (see Figure 13.6). Similarly, DEMs can be used to

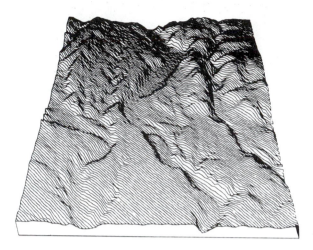

Figure 13.6 Three-dimensional perspective view generated from a photogrammetrically derived digital elevation model. [From Lillesand and Kiefer (1). Courtesy of Riverside County Flood Control and Water Conservation District, Riverside, California.]

produce slope maps to aid in such activities as planning harvesting and assessing soil erosion. Historically, such operations were premised on laborious physical manipulation of maps and aerial photographs in precise optical–mechanical photogrammetric equipment. In contrast, modern photogrammetry depends much more extensively on computers and mathematical modeling to solve photogrammetric problems. These computer–mathematical procedures constitute the field of analytical photogrammetry (15, 16).

Photographic Interpretation

Fundamentals of the Interpretation Process

Aerial photographs contain a detailed record of features on the ground at the time of exposure. However, this record merely contains raw photographic *data*. Only after these data have been "read" and synthesized by the image analyst do they become *information*. In order to accomplish the interpretation, the forester must systematically examine the photographs, normally relying on "ground truth" in the form of supporting maps, data, and field observation to aid in the information extraction process (17).

A systematic study of an aerial photograph usually looks for basic characteristics of the features shown on a photograph. The exact ones useful for any specific task, and the manner in which they are considered, depend on the particular problem at hand. However, most applications consider the following basic characteristics of individual features: shape, size, pattern, tone (or hue), texture, shadows, site, and association.

Shape refers to the general form, configuration, or outline of individual objects. In stereoscopic photographs the object's height also defines its shape.

Size of objects on photographs must be considered in the context of the photo scale. Relative sizes of objects on photographs of the same scale must also be considered.

Pattern relates to the spatial arrangement of objects. The repetition of certain general forms or relationships is characteristic of many objects, both natural and constructed, and gives objects a pattern that helps the photograph interpreter in recognizing them. For example, the ordered spatial arrangement of trees in a seed orchard or nursery is in distinct contrast to that of a natural stand.

Tone (or hue) refers to the relative brightness (or color) of objects on photographs. Figure 13.2 shows how relative tones in black-and-white infrared photographs can be used to distinguish between deciduous and coniferous trees. Without tonal differences, the shapes, patterns, and texture of objects could not be discerned.

Texture, the frequency of tonal change on the photographic image, is produced by an aggregation of unit features that may be too small to be discerned individually, such as tree leaves and leaf shadows. A product of their individual shapes, sizes, patterns, shadows, and tones, texture determines the overall visual "smoothness" or "coarseness" of image features. As we illustrate later, an interpreter can often distinguish between species with similar reflectances based on their texture differences.

Shadows are important to interpreters in two opposing respects. Whereas the shape or outline of a shadow affords an impression of the profile view of objects and thus aids interpretation, objects within shadows reflect little light and are difficult to discern on photographs—hindering their interpretation. The shadows cast by various tree species in open areas can often aid in their identification on aerial photographs.

Site refers to topographic or geographic location and is a particularly important aid in the identification of tree types. For example, certain species would be expected to occur on well-drained upland sites, whereas other species would be expected to occur on poorly drained lowland sites. Furthermore, various species appear only in certain geographic areas (e.g., redwoods occur in California, but not Indiana).

Association refers to the occurrence of certain features in relation to others. For example, haul roads are easily identified in association with clearcuts.

Tree Species Identification

Tree species can be identified on aerial photographs through the process of elimination. The first step is to eliminate species that are unlikely to be present in an area because of location, physiography, or climate. The second step is to establish which groups of species do occur in the area, based on a knowledge of the common species associations and their requirements. The final stage is to identify individual tree species using the basic image characteristics previously described.

Figures 12.5 and 13.7 are panchromatic stereograms that illustrate some of the principles of spe-

Figure 13.7 Black spruce (outlined areas) surrounded by aspen in Ontario, Canada. Scale 1 : 15,840. Stereogram. [From Zsilinszky (18). Courtesy of Victor G. Zsilinszky, Ontario Centre for Remote Sensing.]

cies identification on aerial photographs. A pure stand of black spruce (outlined areas) surrounded by aspen is shown in Figure 13.7. Black spruces are conifers with very slender crowns and pointed tops. In pure stands the canopy is normally regular in pattern, and the tree height is either even or changes gradually with the quality of the site. The crown texture of dense black spruce stands is carpetlike in appearance. In contrast, aspens are deciduous trees with rounded crowns that are more widely spaced than those of the black spruce. The striking difference in photographic texture between black spruce and aspen is shown in Figure 13.7.

Stands of balsam fir and black spruce are shown in Figure 12.5. Balsam fir are conifers that are typically symmetrical with sharply pointed tops. Since the crown widens rapidly toward the base with dense branching, balsam fir appears to be a thicker tree than the slender black spruce. Area 2 is a pure stand of black spruce. Area 1 is a mixed stand containing 60 percent balsam fir and 40 percent black spruce. Balsam fir stands often have erratic changes in size, forming an uneven stand profile and an irregular stand pattern. Notice the contrast in Figure 12.5 between the smooth, fine-textured pattern of the black spruce and the coarser-textured, more erratic pattern of the balsam fir (18).

The extent to which tree species can be recognized on aerial photographs is largely determined by the scale, type, quality, and season of the photographs (19, 20). The format most widely used is panchromatic paper prints at a scale of 1 : 15,840 to 1 : 24,000. Black-and-white infrared films are often used for stands in which a mixture of coniferous and deciduous types is common. Color and color infrared films are also being used with increasing frequency, particularly at small scales.

Changes in the appearance of trees in the different seasons of the year sometimes enable discrimination of species that are indistinguishable on single dates. The most obvious example is the separation of deciduous and coniferous trees, easily made on photographs taken when the deciduous foliage has fallen. This distinction can also be made on spring photographs taken shortly after the flushing of leaves or on fall photographs taken after the trees have changed color.

Photo Mensuration

In addition to identifying species, several other characteristics about individual trees and stands can be extracted from aerial photographs to aid in forest measurement. For example, *stand areas* can be readily measured. Similarly, *stand density* or *degree of stocking* can be measured by estimating the percentage of crown cover in a given stand. A number of visual-density grids have been developed to assist in this process. These typically contain square or circular plots with black dots representing trees of varying percentages of crown density. Or interpreters simply make ocular estimates without referring to guides. Density estimates are also sometimes made by counting the number of trees per unit area.

Species, density, and area estimates are the photograph-derived variables used most extensively in forest surveys. Depending on the particular situation, two other photographic measurements may be used in the mensuration process: *tree (or stand) height* and *crown diameter*.

Heights are calculated either by measuring the relief displacement on single photographs or by measuring the *parallax* on stereopairs of photographs. Parallax is the change in position of an image point from one photograph to the next in a stereopair. That is, the forward motion of the aircraft between exposures causes the images of points on the ground to move laterally across the camera focal plane parallel to the line of flight. The tops of taller objects, being closer to the camera, manifest more displacement (parallax) than do those of shorter objects. Several interpretive aids such as parallax bars (Figure 12.4) and parallax wedges have been developed to aid in the height measurement process based on the principle of parallax.

The task of measuring tree crown diameters is no different from that of measuring other distances on photographs via the photo scale relationship. Again, special-purpose overlays have been developed to expedite crown diameter measurements (21, 22).

Photograph-derived height, diameter, and crown closure data can sometimes be used to prepare *photo volume tables*. These tables are developed by relating the various photographic measurements with field-measured individual tree or stand volumes using statistical regression techniques. The volume of *individual* trees is normally determined as a function of species, crown diameter, and height; it is assumed that there is a strong statistical relation between dbh and *total* height as measured on the photograph. *Stand* volume tables typically express volume per unit area as a function of species, average stand height, and crown closure (21, 22).

Forest Damage Assessment

Aerial photographs have been interpreted extensively to survey forest and urban shade tree damage from disease and insect infestations, as well as from other causes (23). A variety of types of films and scales have been utilized for damage surveys. Although panchromatic photographs have often been used, the most successful surveys have typically used medium-scale or large-scale color and color infrared photographs. Some types of tree damage caused by bacteria, fungi, viruses, and other agents that have been detected by interpreting aerial photographs are ash dieback, beech bark disease, Douglas-fir root rot, Dutch elm disease, maple dieback, oak wilt, and white pine blister rust.

Some types of insect damage that have been detected are those caused by the balsam woolly aphid, black-headed budworm, Black Hills bark beetle, Douglas-fir beetle, gypsy moth larva, pine butterfly, mountain pine beetle, southern pine beetle, spruce budworm, western hemlock looper, western pine beetle, and white pine weevil. Other types of forest damage that have been detected include those resulting from air pollution (e.g., ozone, sulfur dioxide, "smog"), animals (e.g., beaver, deer, porcupine), fire, frost, moisture stress, soil salinity, nutrient imbalance, and storms (6–8, 11, 12, 17, 21–23).

Additional Applications

We have highlighted here the application of aerial-photographic interpretation to tree species identification, forest mensuration, and damage assessment, but its uses extend far beyond the scope of these three activities. Additional applications include tasks as varied as appraising forestland, planning for timber harvest, monitoring of logging and reforesta-tion, planning and assessing applications of herbicide and fertilizer in forest stands, assessing plant vigor and health in tree nurseries, mapping "forest fuels" to assess fire potential, planning fire suppression activities, assessing potential slope failures and soil erosion, planning forest roads, inventorying forest recreation resources, performing censuses of wildlife and assessing their habitats, and monitoring vegetation regrowth in fire lanes and power line rights-of-way (6–8, 12, 17, 21–23).

Nonphotographic Remote Sensing Systems

In this section we discuss various remote sensing systems that use some means other than film to detect electromagnetic energy. These include solid-state array and video cameras, thermal and multi-spectral scanners, and side-looking radar systems. These systems are not currently applied nearly as extensively in forest management as aerial photography, mostly because they are typically less available, have lower geometric integrity, and are more expensive to operate. However, the operating principles of many of these systems are being implemented in various sensors on board present and future earth resource satellites. Accordingly, the application of data collected by nonphotographic systems to forest management is likely to increase substantially in the fairly near future.

Solid-State Array and Video Cameras

Solid-state array cameras use detector arrays of charge-coupled devices (CCDs) to acquire image data. A CCD is a microelectronic silicon chip, a solid-state sensor that detects light. When light strikes the silicon surface of the CCD, an electronic charge is produced, the magnitude of which is proportional to the light intensity and exposure time. Charge-coupled devices are capable of recording a wider range of light intensities than photographic film, and their output can be stored and processed digitally.

Video cameras are electronic systems that generate standard television signals. The type of video camera used for aerial sensing can be black and white, color, or color infrared. Data from these systems can be stored using standard video recorders. This mode of data collection and storage has a number of advantages over conventional photography. The image can be viewed in the aircraft at the time it is acquired. In addition, the resulting videotape cassettes are available for detailed analysis immediately after a flight. Hence, there is no need to wait for processing, nor is any special handling required. The resulting imagery is also inexpensive: material costs are typically lower than for 35-mm photography for the same area of coverage. Another advantage is that video cassettes have an audio track, which means that verbal comments about specific features or locations can be recorded in synchronization with the imagery (24). The principal disadvantages of video recording are the lower spatial resolution and slower "shutter speeds." Similarly, image measurement and image-to-map transfer of information often require specialized equipment, as does the production of prints for use in the field.

Thermal and Multispectral Scanners

Aerial thermal scanners sense in either the 3- to 5-micrometer or the 8- to 14-micrometer region of the spectrum. Thermal scanners provide images that indicate ground areas of different radiant temperatures as varying shades of gray. Thermal scanners typically collect data along a continuous strip of terrain beneath an aircraft (a forward-looking orientation can also be used). The strip is composed of contiguous scan lines repeatedly taken perpendicular to the direction of flight, as illustrated in Figure 13.8.

Multispectral scanners collect data in essentially the same fashion as thermal scanners. However, multispectral scanners use multiple detectors to record image data in several spectral bands or "channels" simultaneously. This means that these

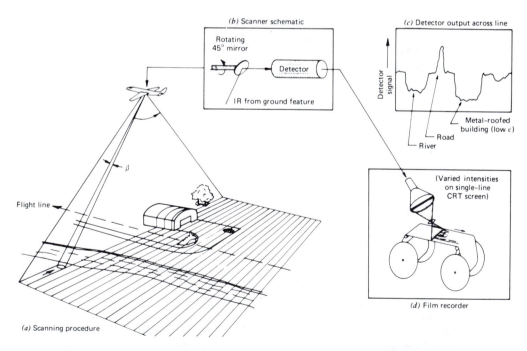

Figure 13.8 Thermal scanner system operation. [From Lillesand and Kiefer (1).]

systems can collect data in the visible, near-infrared, mid-infrared, and thermal-infrared portions of the spectrum at the same time. The signal from each detector is sampled along each scan line and recorded digitally. This forms a digital image of each band of data; a matrix of contiguous picture elements, called *pixels,* makes up the band. The numerical response recorded by each detector within each pixel is then available for use in digital image-processing systems designed for automated interpretation of the image data (1, 4, 5). (We illustrate multispectral scanner data in our discussion of earth resource satellites.)

Side-Looking Radar

The word radar is an acronym for *RAdio Detection And Ranging*. As its name implies, radar was developed as a means of using radio waves to detect the presence of objects and determine their range (position). The process entails transmitting short bursts, or pulses, of microwave energy in the direction of interest and recording the strength and origin of "echoes" or "reflections" received from objects within the system's field of view. Because radar systems supply their own source of energy, they are termed "active" remote sensing systems. (All the other systems we have discussed are considered as being "passive.") Microwaves are capable of penetrating the atmosphere under virtually all conditions. Depending on the specific wavelengths involved, microwave energy can penetrate haze, light rain and snow, smoke, and clouds.

Side-looking airborne radar uses an antenna fixed below the aircraft and pointed to the side. Because the sensor is mounted on a moving platform, it is able to produce continuous strips of imagery depicting very large ground areas located adjacent to the aircraft flight line.

Microwave reflections from earth materials bear no direct relationship to their counterparts in the visible and thermal portions of the spectrum. For example, many surfaces that appear rough in the visible portion of the spectrum may appear smooth as seen by microwaves. In general, microwave responses afford a markedly different view of the

Figure 13.9 Side-looking radar image, Appalachian Mountains, Pennsylvania, imaged from Seasat-1 satellite. (Courtesy of NASA–JPL.)

environment. Figure 13.9 shows a side-looking radar image of a portion of the Appalachian Mountains in Pennsylvania, as imaged from the Seasat satellite. This image was taken from an altitude of 800 kilometers above the earth's surface. Because the spacecraft was oriented beyond the top of this image, illuminating the terrain from top to bottom, there is a "side-lighting" effect; the upper side of the folded ridges of sedimentary rock appears quite light in tone and the lower side of the ridges appears much darker. This image shows an area about 55 by 80 kilometers. Because radar covers very large areas and penetrates clouds, several countries with heretofore incomplete aerial-photographic coverage (e.g., Brazil, Panama, Nigeria, and Venezuela) have been able to obtain radar images of much of their unplotted land areas.

Radar data can be collected in stereo, in multiple planes of electrical signal polarity, and at multiple scene incidence angles. The incidence angle is the angle at which the radar beam is directed toward the ground. Preliminary research with radar data collected from the space shuttle suggests that incidence angle has a strong influence on the appearance of forest vegetation and that multiple incidence angles can be used to discriminate among forest types (25).

Earth Resource Satellites

The use of satellites as sensor platforms has allowed us to acquire repetitive multispectral data of the earth's surface on a global basis. The principal earth resource satellites to date have been the five U.S. Landsat satellites and the first French SPOT satellite. We briefly describe each of these systems here.

Landsat

The Landsat satellite currently crosses each spot on the earth's surface once each 16 days, providing frequent, synoptic, repetitive, global coverage. Each Landsat scene covers an area 185 × 185 kilometers (115 × 115 miles). Three different types of sensors in various combinations have been flown on the five Landsat missions to date. These are the Return Beam Vidicon (RBV) camera systems, the Multispectral Scanner (MSS) systems, and the Thematic Mapper (TM). The MSS was the principal sensor on the first three Landsat satellites (launched between 1972 and 1978). It returned multispectral data with a ground pixel dimension of about 80 meters in four broad spectral bands (green, red, and two near-infrared bands). With this relatively coarse resolution, the application of MSS data to forestry has basically been limited to large-area, generalized land cover mapping and analysis. However, more site-specific information has been made available by the TM. To date, this instrument has been carried on Landsat-4 and Landsat-5 (launched in 1982 and 1984, respectively).

The TM is a second-generation multispectral scanner incorporating several improvements in relation to the MSS. Most importantly, the ground resolution of the system has been improved from 80 meters to 30 meters. The TM also acquires data in seven spectral bands instead of four, with new bands in the blue visible, mid-infrared, and thermal portions of the spectrum.

Figure 13.10 shows all seven TM bands for a portion of a summertime image of an urban fringe area near Madison, Wisconsin. This figure illustrates the resolution of the system with the distinct depiction of urban areas and field patterns. The characteristic appearance of the various bands is also illustrated. For example, the blue–green water of the lake, river, and ponds in the scene has moderate reflection in bands 1 and 2 (blue and green), a small amount of reflection in band 3 (red), and virtually no reflection in bands 4, 5, and 7 (near-infrared and mid-infrared); reflection from roads and urban streets is least in band 4. Notice that overall reflection from agricultural crops is highest in band 4. Notice also the high band 4 reflectance of the golf courses appearing to the right-center of the river and to the right-center of the lake. (The thermal band, band 6, has a less distinct appearance than the other bands because the resolution of this band is 120 meters.)

Thematic Mapper data are available in many different formats. Photographic products include single-band black-and-white images and "color composites" of any three bands. A color composite is produced by combining any three bands through blue, green, and red filters. If bands 1 through 3 are used, the result is a "normal" color composite. The combination of bands 2 through 4 gives a "false" color composite very similar in appearance to an ordinary color infrared photograph. Other band combinations can be chosen for specific tasks. If the data are obtained in a digital format, numerous band combinations may be evaluated interactively using a computer graphics display. Furthermore, the data can be computer-enhanced to aid in visual interpretation, or the data can be automatically classified according to cover type using various *spectral-pattern recognition* algorithms designed for this purpose (1, 4, 5).

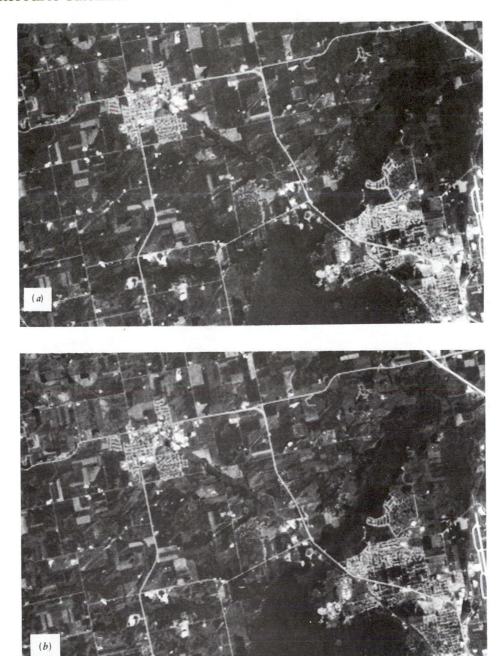

Figure 13.10 Individual Landsat Thematic Mapper bands, suburban Madison, Wisconsin. Scale 1 : 115,000. (*a*) Band 1, blue (0.45–0.52 μm); (*b*) band 2, green (0.52–0.60 μm); (*c*) band 3, red (0.63–0.69 μm); (*d*) band 4, near-infrared (0.76–0.90 μm); (*e*) band 5, mid-infrared (1.55–1.75 μm); (*f*) band 7, mid-infrared (2.08–2.35 μm); (*g*) band 6, thermal infrared (10.4–12.5 μm). [From Lillesand and Kiefer (1).]

Figure 13.10 *(Continued)*

Figure 13.10 *(Continued)*

(g)

Figure 13.10 *(Continued)*

SPOT

With the participation of Sweden and Belgium, France launched SPOT-1 in 1986 to begin the SPOT satellite program. This satellite heralded a new era in space remote sensing, for it is the first satellite system to use a solid-state array of CCDs for image recording, and it is the first system to have pointable optics. The system employs a linear array of CCDs arranged side-by-side along a line perpendicular to the satellite orbit track. A line of image data is obtained by sampling the response of each CCD along the array, and successive lines of coverage are obtained by repeated sampling along the array as the satellite moves over the earth. This "pushbroom-scanning" procedure requires no moving parts, improves the geometric integrity of the sensor data, and increases the signal level recorded over any given ground area per unit time.

Figure 13.11 is a SPOT-1 panchromatic image showing an area located in northwest Wisconsin near the border between the states of Wisconsin and Minnesota. The two light-toned triangular features appearing in this image are fire scars. Roads, lakes, rivers, recent cuts, agricultural fields, and several other features are visible in this 10-meter resolution image. At this resolution, when satellite imagery is further enlarged, it begins to look very much like small-scale to medium-scale black-and-white aerial photography. Data recorded in the multispectral mode appear similar to those recorded by color infrared photography.

SPOT-1 carries two identical sensors employing the operation just described. They are referred to as high-resolution visible (HRV) imaging systems. Each HRV has a pointable optical system operated through a plane mirror that can be rotated by ground command. This allows each instrument to image any point within a strip extending 475 kilometers to either side of the satellite ground track. Among other things, this means that any given area can be repeatedly viewed during satellite passes separated alternately by one and four days (occasionally five days, depending on latitude). This "revisit" capability is important in three respects. First, it is able to provide stereoscopic data on an area obtained from coverage of two separated orbit

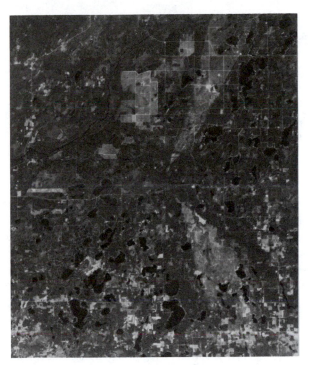

Figure 13.11 SPOT-1 panchromatic image, northwest of Spooner, Wisconsin. Scale 1 : 250,000. (Copyright © 1986 CNES. Courtesy of SPOT Image Corporation.)

Advanced Very High Resolution Radiometer (AVHRR) on board the National Oceanic and Atmospheric Administration (NOAA) series of weather satellites has been extensively used in large-area analyses not requiring fine spatial resolution. These satellites cover the globe twice daily at 1.1-kilometer resolution. They have been used for such applications as wildfire fuel mapping, snow mapping, fire detection, flood assessment, and tropical deforestation monitoring (26).

Several sensors that have utility in forest management have been operated from the space shuttle. Among these are the Large Format Camera, which provides 240 × 480-mm (9 × 18-inch) photographs from orbital altitudes with a photographic resolution of 15 meters or better (depending on film type and altitude) (27). Similarly, the Shuttle Imaging Radar Systems have paved the way for collecting more radar data from space (25).

Finally, we wish to point out that numerous countries throughout the world have earth resource satellites in the planning stage with potential for future applications in forest management. The need for brevity precludes our treating these systems in this discussion.

tracks. Second, it allows more frequent coverage of areas where cloud cover is a problem. Third, it provides an opportunity for viewing a given area at frequencies ranging from successive days, to several days, to a few weeks.

In short, the SPOT system's combination of multispectral sensing with excellent spatial resolution, geometric fidelity, and the provision for multidate and stereo imaging makes its data very valuable for various interpretive purposes. Like Landsat data, SPOT data are available in numerous photographic and digital formats.

Other Space Systems

Before leaving the topic of space remote sensing systems, we wish to point out that numerous other present and planned systems have substantial potential for application in forestry. For example, the

Geographic Information Systems

Rarely, if ever, are forest management decisions based solely on information extracted from remote sensing data. Normally, remote sensing data represent only one of many sources of information that must be analyzed in concert. A *geographic information system* (GIS) is a computer-based system providing for the storage, manipulation, analysis, and display of multiple "layers" of information in a spatial context. These systems represent the merger of computer mapping and data base management technologies; they are becoming increasingly important forest management tools.

The layers in a GIS are typically encoded in the form of either grid cells or polygons. Figure 13.12

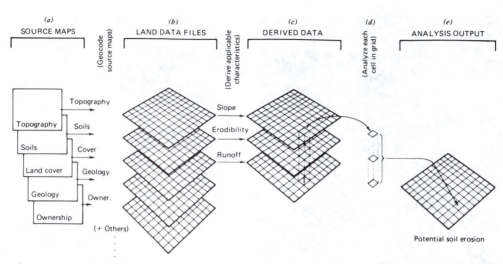

Figure 13.12 Cell-based geographic information system. [From Lillesand and Kiefer (1).]

shows a cell-based GIS containing a series of source maps that have been encoded by recording the information category most dominant in each cell in the grid. That is, each cell is assigned an average elevation in the topographic file, a dominant soil type in the soils file, a dominant cover type in the land cover file, and so on. Once stored in this manner, these data can be easily manipulated and integrated. For example, a forest hydrologist interested in modeling the potential soil erosion in a watershed could use the system to derive a *slope* map based on the original topographic file. He or she could also assign a *soil erodability* value to each cell in the watershed based on the soil type present. Similarly, the *runoff* characteristic of each cell could be estimated on the basis of the cover type present. The resulting slope, erodability, and runoff data could then be composited spatially and used in a hydrologic model to predict the potential soil erosion in each cell. The results from the model could then be displayed or recorded, using any one of a number of computer graphics displays and storage devices.

The number, form, and complexity of data analyses possible within a modern GIS are virtually limitless. For example, a forester could use such a system to characterize spatially both the major physical *and* economic factors affecting timber accessi-

bility. A timber-harvesting plan could be developed by integrating mapped data on topography, road infrastructure, and land cover with economic harvesting considerations. The effective distance from a unit to be harvested to the nearest haul road could be computed, based on such factors as avoiding intervening open water, sensitive soils, and steep slopes Areas of accessible timber could thus be grouped into spatial "timbershed" units that have optimal economic access to particular road segments. Hauling costs from various roadside positions to a mill could also be made a part of the analysis, by considering the relative ease of travel along the various types of roads within a working unit. Finally, the harvesting and hauling factors could be combined with the forest cover information (derived from remote-sensing data) to develop maps of the relative economic accessibility of various timber types (28).

The examples given are intended to illustrate the basic function and flexibility of geographic information systems. These systems provide an efficient way for the forester to merge remote sensing data with the broad array of other information sources that he or she must consider in effective forest management. The future for applications of both remote sensing and GIS technology in forestry is extremely bright.

References

1. T. M. Lillesand and R. W. Kiefer, *Remote Sensing and Image Interpretation,* Second Edition, John Wiley & Sons, New York, 1987.

2. F. F. Sabins, Jr., *Remote Sensing: Principles and Interpretation,* Second Edition, Freeman, San Francisco, 1986.

3. P. N. Slater, *Remote Sensing: Optics and Optical Systems,* Addison–Wesley, Reading, Mass., 1980.

4. P. H. Swain and S. M. Davis, eds., *Remote Sensing: The Quantitative Approach,* McGraw–Hill, New York, 1978.

5. R. A. Schowengerdt, *Techniques for Image Processing and Classification in Remote Sensing,* Academic Press, New York, 1983.

6. *Manual of Remote Sensing,* Second Edition, American Society of Photogrammetry, Falls Church, Va., 1983.

7. *Renewable Resources Management—Applications of Remote Sensing,* American Society of Photogrammetry, Proc.: RNRF Symposium on the Application of Remote Sensing to Resource Management, Seattle, Wash., 1983.

8. *Proc.: 10th William T. Pecora Memorial Remote Sensing Symposium,* American Society for Photogrammetry and Remote Sensing, Ft. Collins, Colo., 1985.

9. Z. Kalensky and D. A. Wilson, "Spectral signatures of forest trees," *Proc.: Third Canadian Symposium on Remote Sensing,* 1975, pp. 155–171.

10. M. P. Meyer, *J. For.,* 80(1) 15–17 (1982).

11. "Panoramic photography and forest remote sensing," American Society of Photogrammetry, *Photogrammetric Engineering and Remote Sensing,* (special issue), 48(5), May 1982.

12. Committee on Remote Sensing for Agricultural Purposes, *Remote Sensing; with Special Reference to Agriculture and Forestry,* National Academy of Science, National Research Council, Washington, D.C., 1970.

13. F. H. Moffitt and E. M. Mikhail, *Photogrammetry,* Third Edition, Harper & Row, New York, 1980.

14. P. R. Wolf, *Elements of Photogrammetry,* Second Edition, McGraw–Hill, New York, 1983.

15. S. K. Ghosh, *Analytical Photogrammetry,* Pergamon Press, New York, 1979.

16. *Manual of Photogrammetry,* Fourth Edition, American Society of Photogrammetry, Falls Church, Va., 1980.

17. *Manual of Photographic Interpretation,* American Society of Photogrammetry, Falls Church, Va., 1960.

18. V. G. Zsilinszky, *Photographic Interpretation of Tree Species in Ontario,* Ontario Dept. of Lands and Forests, 1966.

19. *Forester's Guide to Aerial Photo Interpretation,* U.S.D.A. Agr. Handbook 308, U.S. Govt. Printing Office, Washington, D.C., 1978.

20. L. Sayn-Wittgenstein, *Recognition of Tree Species on Aerial Photographs,* Forest Management Institute, Rept. FMR-X-118, Ottawa, Ontario, 1978.

21. T. E. Avery and G. L. Berlin, *Interpretation of Aerial Photographs,* Fourth Edition, Burgess, Minneapolis, Minn., 1985.

22. D. P. Paine, *Aerial Photography and Image Interpretation for Resource Management,* John Wiley & Sons, New York, 1981.

23. P. A. Murtha, *A Guide to Air Photo Interpretation of Forest Damage in Canada,* Can. For. Serv., Publ. 1292, Ottawa, Ontario, 1977.

24. D. E. Meisner, *Remote Sensing of Environment,* 19(1), 63–70 (1986).

25. R. M. Hoffer, P. W. Mueller, and D. F. Lozano-Garcia, "Multiple-incidence angle shuttle imaging radar data for discriminating forest cover types," *Technical Papers of the American Society for Photogrammetry and Remote Sensing,* ACSM-ASPRS Fall Technical Meeting, September 1985, pp. 476–485.

26. W. A. Miller and D. G. Moore, "Time-series vegetation monitoring with NOAA satellite data," *Proc.: International Conference on Renewable Resource Inventories for Monitoring Changes and Trends,* 1983, pp. 86–89.

27. F. J. Doyle, *Photogrammetric Engineering and Remote Sensing,* 51(2), 200–203 (1985).

28. J. K. Berry and K. L. Reed, "Using a microcomputer system to spatially characterize effective timber accessibility," *Proc.: Geographic Information System Workshop,* U.S. For. Serv., South. Reg., 1986.

CHAPTER 14

Silviculture

Craig G. Lorimer

Under strictly natural conditions a forest is generally a self-perpetuating system that does not require management, even though cyclical changes may occur. Similarly, under certain conditions even cutting operations may require little skill or planning to maintain a vigorous, productive forest. Historically, however, human beings have attempted to favor those species having desirable commercial characteristics, and this has usually not proved to be an easy task. For example, harvesting operations frequently induce a major change in species composition that more often than not is considered undesirable. As early as 1863, Thoreau noted that pure stands of eastern white pine, which were the principal source of construction lumber at the time, were replaced by oak species after logging. Regeneration of white pine was found to be difficult even with human intervention, and the obvious solution of planting pine seedlings was rarely successful except on abandoned fields. Problems with regeneration and insect damage, along with the dwindling supply of mature trees, were enough to cause a regional decline in the lumber industry in New England, and the industry began to migrate south and west.

Such problems in the regulation of forest regeneration, species composition, and growth fall within the realm of silviculture, a specialty within the field of forestry that deals with the biological aspects of forest management, subject to economic and environmental constraints. The purposes of silvicultural manipulation may be to enhance timber production, wildlife habitat, streamflow, and the aesthetic qualities of the forest. A broad definition of silviculture might therefore be stated as the manipulation of forest stands to accomplish a specified set of objectives.

It was not merely the desire to regenerate certain valuable species that spurred the study of silviculture. Many developing regions, such as the eastern United States during the nineteenth century and the tropics at the present time, pass through a exploitive stage of resource use during which forests are cut heavily at a pace that far exceeds the rate of regrowth. There is a concern that regional timber shortages may develop, as well as a concern over how to regenerate many areas that seem destined to be occupied by brush for several decades. The restocking of cutover sites may be especially difficult in areas where repeated fires have followed the initial harvest.

Much effort in silviculture has also been devoted to increasing the growth rates of forest stands. This has long been a concern of European foresters striving to meet the high demand for forest products from a comparatively limited forest area. In North America the vastness of the forests and the relatively low value of individual trees traditionally rendered stand improvement practices impractical on a large scale. But the increasing worldwide demand for forest products in recent decades has altered this situation. It is now the rule, rather than the exception, for forest industries routinely to conduct timber inventories of their holdings, classify the productivity of various sites, make estimates of future growth, and carry on silvicultural practices such as thinning of forest stands.

Silvicultural practices can be used strictly to enhance nontimber values. Prescribed burning, for example, is often used solely to improve wildlife habitat. Owners of small private woodlands make up a major class of landowners whose principal management goal is often recreation, aesthetics, or wildlife. Whatever silvicultural practices are applied to these lands may be designed to enhance these values, and timber might be produced only periodically as a secondary benefit.

Growth and Development of Forest Stands

Silvicultural practices are frequently designed to mimic natural processes in forest development, but in a way that hastens the final outcome. An understanding of the development of natural stands is therefore considered fundamental to the practice of silviculture.

Even-Aged Stands

Major disturbances of human or natural origin tend to set in motion predictable patterns of forest growth and development. Sudden removal of the tree canopy by clearcutting or fire usually improves the chances that seedlings will successfully establish themselves; these sites are often quickly colonized or dominated by a new wave of tree seedlings. By the time these trees have reached the age of 10 or 20 years, their crowns have usually expanded to the extent that a closed canopy of foliage has developed, creating the appearance and environment of a young forest. Forests of this type in which most canopy trees are approximately the same age are said to be *even-aged*. The existence of even-aged stands always indicates that the previous stand was removed over a fairly short period of time, regardless of whether the cause was a harvest cut or a natural disturbance. Ages of the canopy trees, however, will rarely be exactly the same except in plantations, because the initial establishment of seedlings generally stretches over more than a decade. The actual range of ages is frequently 20 to 30 years in natural even-aged stands. When even-aged stands are young, the trees often appear remarkably similar in size (Figure 14.1a). Variation in tree size increases over time, however, and in older even-aged stands the range of tree size is wide because of differences in the growth rates of individual trees.

Figure 14.1 Two even-aged hardwood stands showing the reduction in stem density and increase in average tree size over time, accomplished by the natural competitive process. (*a*) A dense 40-year-old stand of oak, birch, and maple. (*b*) A spacious 250-year-old stand of yellow birch. [(*a*) Courtesy of Harvard Forest, Harvard University.]

Even-aged stands are commonly classified by their stage of development, as reflected by the average size or age of the trees. As arranged by increasing size, these categories are seedling, sapling, pole, mature, and overmature. *Seedling* stands are recently disturbed stands in which the regeneration is less than 1 meter (3.3 feet) tall. *Sapling* stands have trees taller than 1 meter and may range in stem diameter up to about 10 centimeters (4 inches). *Pole* stands are made up mostly of trees between 10 and 25 centimeters (4 to 10 inches) in diameter. The size range of *mature* stands varies greatly according to species and location. In many temperate regions a stand would be considered mature if most of the trees are between 25 and 60 centimeters (10 to 24 inches) in diameter. *Overma-* ture stands, from a commercial point of view, are even-aged stands in which a large proportion of the trees are becoming senescent. Losses from mortality often exceed additions in volume from growth, and a sizable proportion of the total wood volume may show signs of decay and other defects. In managed forests final harvest cuts are generally carried out many years prior to this stage. The age of the stand at which a harvest is planned is known as the *rotation age.*

As individual trees in a young even-aged stand become larger and older, competition becomes more severe. A young stand may have thousands of small trees on a hectare (2.47 acres) of land, but at stand maturity there will be space on the area for only a few hundred trees. As a result of competition, crowns of the slower-growing trees become increasingly crowded and may finally be overtopped completely by adjacent, faster-growing trees. The stands therefore tend to show a certain amount of vertical stratification, and individual trees in even-aged stands are often classified by their relative position in the canopy. These *crown classes* (Figure 14.2) are defined as follows.

Dominant. Trees that project somewhat above the general level of the canopy, having crowns that receive direct sunlight from above and some from the side.

Codominant. Canopy trees of average size that receive direct sunlight from above but relatively little light from the sides.

Intermediate. Trees with crowns extending into the canopy layer but crowded on all sides, so that only the top of the crown receives direct sunlight.

Suppressed. Trees with crowns completely overtopped by surrounding trees so that they receive no direct sunlight except from occasional "sunflecks" penetrating small gaps in the foliage above.

Once a tree has become suppressed, its chances of regaining a dominant position in the stand are relatively meager, and the probability of imminent death is greatly increased. High mortality rates of trees in the lower crown classes progressively decrease the number of trees per unit area until the

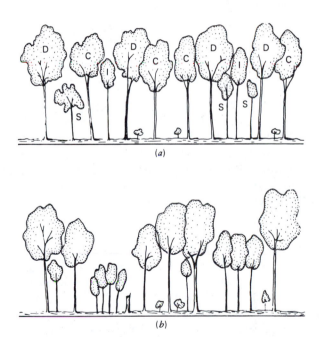

(a)

(b)

Figure 14.2 Diagrammatic profiles of an even-aged and an uneven-aged stand. (*a*) Even-aged stand after crown closure, showing the various crown classes. (D = dominant; C = codominant; I = intermediate; S = suppressed.) (*b*) Mature uneven-aged stand. Notice the irregular profile and small openings.

stand matures. In forty years the number of trees may be reduced by 50 to 60 percent or more. This natural decrease in numbers of trees in even-aged stands because of competition is known as the *self-thinning* process. Older stands tend to be more open and spacious as a result of the natural self-thinning process.

From these principles it follows that a small tree growing beneath the main canopy may not always be younger than the larger trees above it. In addition, the crown class of many trees will be subject to progressive change. Most suppressed trees in even-aged stands were once in a dominant position, and trees in the intermediate crown class are almost certain to become suppressed in the near future if the stand is still growing rapidly.

Uneven-Aged Stands

Unless some catastrophe intervenes, even-aged stands tend to give way gradually to *uneven-aged* stands in which three or more age classes are intermixed. Understories of shrubs and tree seedlings begin to develop in even-aged stands, usually by the time the pole stage is reached. Understory development accelerates as the stand matures, and when canopy trees become senescent and begin to die singly or in groups, the resulting gaps in the canopy are filled by the saplings and seedlings in the understory. The broad age range of uneven-aged stands is a result of the fact that understory trees germinate and then fill gaps over a long period of time. In contrast to even-aged stands, the suppressed trees in uneven-aged stands are often younger than the larger overstory trees, and some of them may eventually attain canopy status. Because uneven-aged stands are more characteristic of the later stages of succession, and because the trees often grow under shade and in small gaps, these stands are frequently dominated by shade-tolerant species. However, uneven-aged stands of intolerant species like ponderosa pine may occur on sites that are too dry to permit the invasion of more shade-tolerant trees. Differences in the structure and appearance of even-aged and uneven-aged stands are shown diagrammatically in Figure 14.2, and actual examples are shown in Figures 14.1 and 14.9.

Pure versus Mixed Stands

Under natural conditions, trees may occur in nearly pure stands of a single species or in mixtures. Pure stands on productive sites are often even-aged, having developed following some natural catastrophe such as intense fire. Examples are the extensive, nearly pure stands of Douglas-fir or lodgepole pine that often spring up following extensive wildfires. When pure stands are established artificially by planting, they are sometimes referred to as *monocultures*.

The relative merits of pure versus mixed stands have long been a subject of controversy. Those who favor pure stands stress the administrative ease in managing pure stands as well as the lower costs of cultural treatments and harvesting. If a site is planted with the most valuable species suited to local conditions, the value of the plantation will often exceed that of a stand containing a mixture of various species. On the other hand, mixed-species forests may be more aesthetically pleasing and may have a greater carrying capacity for wildlife (see Chapter 17). There is good evidence that mixed stands are usually more resistant to insect and disease outbreaks than pure stands. Nevertheless, it is difficult to make valid generalizations, and exceptions can be found. For example, mixed stands of spruce and balsam fir are more susceptible to budworm attack than pure stands of spruce, and mixed conifer–hardwood forests are more susceptible to fire than pure stands of most hardwood species. Clearly the characteristics of the individual species in each case determine the relative susceptibility (1).

Treatments to Improve Existing Stands

In the early years of American forest management, most forest stands received little or no treatment between the time of establishment and the time of harvest. But the benefits of such manipulation in terms of improved species composition, growth rate, and wood quality can be substantial in some cases. Silvicultural treatments applied between the time of establishment and time of harvest are called *intermediate treatments*. Objectives of intermediate treatments may include favoring certain species over others, regulating spacing and stand density, removing poorly formed or diseased trees, improving the wood quality of the remaining trees by pruning branches, salvaging dead or dying trees, and fertilizing the soil to increase growth rates. In the following discussion the most common intermediate treatments are grouped into two categories according to the primary objective. There is no rigid distinction between these groups, however, because a given treatment may have more than one objective or result; for example, improving species composition may also improve stand growth.

Treatments to Improve Species Composition

Manipulating the species composition of a forest is frequently a challenging task. Usually each site in temperate regions has one or two species that are very well adapted to the site and therefore quite aggressive. If these species are capable of resprouting vigorously when cut, as is often the case, then attempts to favor other species may not be feasible without some kind of soil disturbance at the time of stand establishment plus the application of herbicides at one or more times during the first few years of stand development.

Treatments to improve species composition in mixed stands are best done when the trees to be favored are still fairly young (not beyond the pole stage) and still capable of responding to release from competition. *Release cuttings* are performed to free desirable seedlings or saplings from trees of competing species that have already suppressed the crop trees or are likely to do so in the near future.

Release cuttings are often necessary in young coniferous stands that are intermixed with aggressive hardwood species.

Improvement cuts are treatments in pole or mature stands that remove diseased or poorly formed trees in addition to trees of undesirable species. Improvement cuts are especially important in stands that have had a long history of "high grading"—the selective removal of only the best-quality trees. There is really no need to remove all poor trees from a stand, however. Economically, it makes sense to remove only the undesirable trees that are clearly interfering with a promising "crop tree," one which will be carried to the end of a rotation. If the crop tree is already a dominant canopy tree, it is unlikely that the tree would either require release or benefit from it.

Treatments to Increase Growth Rates

Stand density and tree growth are regulated primarily by *thinning* (Figure 14.3). The purpose of thinning is to reduce the stand density so that the growth of the remaining trees is accelerated. Trees to be removed are typically of the same species and age class as those that remain. Thinning does not usually increase the total amount of wood produced by a forest; in fact the amount usually remains about the same and may even sometimes decrease. But since the available light, water, and nutrients are being used by fewer trees, the remaining trees become larger than they would have otherwise. This is the principal benefit of thinning, for large trees are more valuable than an equal volume of small trees. At the same time, less vigorous trees that would probably die anyway from competition can be salvaged for usable material. The eventual result of thinning is a more open, spacious stand of larger trees. Thus thinning basically hastens the natural outcome of competition in forest stands and is a good example of how some silvicultural techniques have natural counterparts.

Figure 14.3 (*a*) Before and (*b*) two years after moderately heavy low thinning and pruning in a twenty-five-year-old pine plantation. Nearly all the suppressed and intermediate trees were removed, as well as about 40 percent of the codominants. About 35 percent of the stand basal area was cut. Tops and branches of the felled trees, which were somewhat unsightly in the first year, have mostly decomposed after only two years.

Several different methods of thinning are possible, but it is useful to recognize three basic approaches. In *low thinning* or "thinning from below," the trees to be cut are mostly from the lower crown classes. A light low thinning would remove only suppressed and intermediate trees, whereas a heavier low thinning would remove some codominants as well (Figure 14.3). A heavier low thinning is usually more desirable because dominant crop trees often do not show any measurable growth response to the removal of suppressed trees. Generally their rate of growth will increase only if gaps are made in the canopy so that they can expand their crowns and increase their total exposed leaf surface area.

In *high thinning* or "thinning from above," the primary objective is to create sufficient numbers of small gaps in the canopy to stimulate the growth of the better crop trees. In most forests this will involve removing intermediate and codominant trees of smaller size or poorer quality to favor the growth of the better dominant and codominant trees. Note that a high thinning may resemble a heavy low thinning in certain respects, but the difference is that suppressed trees are not ordinarily removed in a high thinning. For this reason a high-thinned stand may not have as much of a spacious, parklike appearance as a stand that has had a heavy low thinning.

In the third basic approach, *mechanical thinning,* all trees are removed in rows or strips without regard to crown class. The greatest response therefore comes from trees whose crowns are adjacent to the cleared strip. This method is relatively quick and inexpensive, and it can be easily done in plantations by mechanical tree fellers. In plantations mechanical thinning is often accomplished simply by removing every third row of trees.

Although a single thinning will usually increase growth rates and upgrade the overall stand quality, such improvements are likely to be short-lived, since continued growth and competition will again render the stand crowded, usually within a decade or two. For this reason, intensively managed stands are usually thinned at periodic intervals such as once every ten years. The first thinning can be done even before crown closure of the stand, although the first thinning is often delayed until the trees are pole-sized and the logs removed in thinning are marketable as pulpwood or fuelwood.

Thinning can also be a valuable management tool

for forests in which recreation or fostering wildlife is the principal goal. Young even-aged stands are often unattractive for both people and wildlife because of the extremely high density of stems, poor visibility, profusion of dead lower limbs, and paucity of undergrowth. A moderately heavy thinning can immediately improve the appearance and wildlife habitat of such stands. Private landowners who value their forests primarily for recreation or wildlife are often understandably reluctant to have any cutting done on their property, but judicious light thinning can actually hasten the development of a forest of large stately trees, such as shown in Figure 14.1*b*.

A common method of increasing growth rate that does not involve cutting trees is *fertilization* of the soil. Fertilization is likely to be most successful in areas where the soils are known to contain specific nutrient deficiencies. In North America, for example, nitrogen deficiencies are common in the Douglas-fir region and in boreal spruce–fir forests, and phosphorus is in short supply in many southeastern soils. Standard fertilizer applications may bring 20 to 100 percent increases in growth rate. But a decision to fertilize should be weighed carefully. Fertilizers are energy-expensive to produce, and some of the raw materials are in limited supply. The use of fertilizers for food crops will generally be of higher priority than the application to forest stands (2). Furthermore, some forest types show little or no response to fertilization (3, 4).

Regeneration of Forest Stands

The degree of success in forest regeneration depends in part on the manner in which the stand is harvested. When the goal is to obtain a well-stocked stand of young trees of desirable species and form, the cut should be designed to take into account the biological requirements for germination and growth of seedlings of the favored species. For example, the inability of aspen to tolerate shade generally rules out light, partial cutting as a feasible option if aspen is to be maintained. Paper birch is also intolerant of dense shade, but in addition it requires exposed soil for good seedling establishment; therefore, both heavy cutting and scarification of the ground surface would ordinarily be a prerequisite for good regeneration. The young stand should also meet a certain minimum standard of density of trees or stocking. Moderate competition among trees in young stands is actually beneficial by hastening the self-pruning process and, in the case of hardwoods, by discouraging the development of low forks. Finally, if any kind of partial harvest is made, it is important to remove some lower-quality trees along with the good trees. The operation then combines a harvest cut and an improvement cut.

The consequences of not following such recommendations can often be seen in unmanaged forests that have undergone heavy partial cuttings in which only the larger and better-quality trees have been removed. This may seem to be a reasonable action by private landowners because it appears to give small trees a chance to grow and maintains some of the aesthetic qualities of a forest. However, this practice of high grading may eventually deteriorate the stand, especially when several such cuts are made over a protracted period of time. In addition to the genetically undesirable effects of removing the better trees and allowing many defective trees to repopulate the stand, the quality of the remaining trees is likely to decline over time. Trees that are defective now will generally only become worse, and even smaller trees of good quality may become unacceptably branchy or knotty in response to an overabundance of growing space (Figure 14.4). A further problem with high grading is that usually no thought has been given to whether there are enough young trees of desirable species to restock the stand; often there are not. The long-term economic impact of high grading may be difficult to measure accurately, but there is little question that, especially in the eastern hardwood forest, millions of hectares of forest have been degraded. Private landowners can avoid high grading by having a forester develop a management plan, a service that is provided free of charge in many states and provinces. The forester

Figure 14.4 The result of high grading in an oak stand. Although the stand retains some visual appeal, the residual trees have little present or future value, and the saplings present are not of the desirable species. (Courtesy of U.S.D.A. Forest Service.)

will mark trees to be cut with paint, specifying in a contract with the timber buyer or logger that only the marked trees can be cut.

After a harvest cut the forester can either accom-plish regeneration by artificial means, such as plant-ing, or rely on natural regeneration processes. A comparison of the two approaches is contained in the following sections.

Natural Regeneration

In some areas of the world, natural regeneration after cutting is very dependable. One source of natural regeneration, of course, is seeds carried by wind or animals into the cut area from adjacent standing trees. But careful observations will often reveal that many of the seedlings present on a recently cut area were already present under the forest stand prior to harvest and are in effect unob-trusive survivors of the harvest operation. Such seedlings or saplings are referred to collectively as *advance regeneration* (see Figure 14.9). In addition, many hardwood species sprout from the stump after cutting, and such sprouts constitute an important source of regeneration in hardwood forests (Figure 14.5). A few species of trees may regenerate from seeds stored in the litter.

Natural regeneration is usually more dependable in humid climates than in semiarid climates, but success in favoring a particular species is likely to be

Figure 14.5 Dense regeneration from aspen sprouts one year after clearcutting, northern Wisconsin.

variable in almost any region for the following reasons.

1. Adequate seed production in some species may occur almost every year and in other species only at long or irregular intervals. Good seed crops of red pine, for example, occur only once in seven years on the average. For this reason natural regeneration of red pine is unpredictable and planting is ordinarily recommended.

2. Seedling germination and survival in some species is greatly influenced by the weather. As a result, regeneration may be inadequate even in years of good seed production.

3. The *microclimate* of the stand must be favorable if regeneration is to be satisfactory. Some species require open, sunny conditions for germination, whereas seedlings of other species require partial shade and may be killed by high soil temperatures.

4. The condition of the ground surface or *seedbed* is of prime importance. The forest floor under most stands is covered with a thick mat of leaves and partially decomposed organic matter or *duff*. Seedling germination and survival may be adequate when the duff is kept shaded and moist. When exposed to the sun as after a heavy cutting, however, duff dries out readily and becomes a formidable barrier to seeding establishment. Sometimes removing the duff by burning or mechanical scarification may be necessary (Figure 14.6). Since this procedure also kills most of the advance regeneration, the forester must then rely on seed dissemination or planting.

5. If the advance regeneration, shrub layer, and sprout layer are dense, as they often are, they may largely or entirely preclude the establishment of other, perhaps more desirable species.

6. Seed and seedling predators are sometimes partly or largely responsible for regeneration failures. Insect larvae may infest the seeds before or after they have fallen from the tree, and mammals such as mice and deer can cause almost complete mortality of established seed-

Figure 14.6 Mechanical site preparation reduces competition from advance regeneration and shrubs, and it provides a seedbed more favorable for establishing seedlings naturally. The rolling brush cutter shown here can achieve these results without scraping away or displacing topsoil and nutrients.

lings. This has been convincingly demonstrated in areas fenced or screened to exclude mammals.

Artificial Regeneration

Although natural regeneration is often a dependable means of establishing stands, artificial regeneration may be preferable in certain situations, especially those in which forests are intensively managed and harvested at short intervals. Artificial regeneration can be accomplished either by directly applying seeds to a harvested site or by planting nursery-grown seedlings. Planting gives the forester greater control over stand establishment and growth than artificial dispersal of seeds, but both methods have the following advantages over natural regeneration.

1. Stand establishment may be more reliable because it does not depend on the occurrence of a good seed year or the distance to which seeds are dispersed by wind. On large clearcuts artificial regeneration is often necessary to ensure adequate regeneration on the central portion.

2. Artificial regeneration increases the chances of prompt reforestation.

3. The timing of artificial regeneration can be planned to coincide with favorable weather conditions and to avoid drought.

4. There is greater control over species composition. It permits the option of growing pure stands or stands of nonnative or uncommon species in areas where the expected result of natural regeneration would be highly mixed stands of lower-value species.

5. There is greater control over tree spacing and subsequent growth. Plantations are often established in rows at a predetermined spacing to optimize stand growth, reduce variability in growth rates, and allow easier access for mechanized equipment.

6. Seeds or seedlings can be derived from genetically superior trees.

Direct Seeding Artificial dispersal of tree seed is known as *direct seeding*. It may be accomplished on the ground by hand or machine, or from the air by helicopter or fixed-wing aircraft. Direct seeding is usually cheaper than planting, but it offers less control over spacing and usually has a lower success rate. As a minimal precaution, seeds may be treated with chemical repellents to reduce pilferage by rodents and birds. Germination and survival of seedlings tend to be considerably better on sites with some exposed mineral soil than on sites with a thick covering of litter or logging debris. Maximum success with direct seeding is probably achieved by sowing seeds on the ground in such a way that seeds are covered with soil.

Despite its limitations, direct seeding from the air can be very useful when extensive areas must be reforested quickly, as would be the case following a large forest fire. Direct seeding is also useful on steep, irregular terrain where planting by machine would be impossible and hand planting would be difficult.

Planting The fairly high survival rate of planted seedlings and the convenience of managing row plantations has encouraged the establishment of many plantations in recent years, particularly by paper companies. Most seedlings intended for outplanting in harvested areas are grown either in large outdoor nurseries (see Figure 5.6) or in greenhouses. Seedlings may be lifted from the beds and packaged in a bare-root condition, or they may be grown in individual containers with a specially prepared potting medium. These *containerized seedlings* are more expensive to grow than bare-root stock, but the root systems are less likely to be damaged during the lifting and transporting process, and sometimes the planted seedlings have better rates of survival. Planting is often done in the spring season when soils are moist and root growth is most active, but it is possible at other times, depending on geographic location. If the site to be planted is extensive, fairly level, and not excessively rocky, planting can be done quickly with mechanized equipment. Otherwise the traditional method of hand-planting crews can be used.

Prior site preparation is as important in planting operations as it is for natural regeneration. Equipment such as the rolling brush cutter breaks up residual wood debris, making the site easier to plant, and tears up roots of shrubs and hardwood saplings, which might otherwise overtop the planted seedlings. Other equipment such as the Bracke scarifier scalps small patches of ground to provide a suitable microsite for planting. Although mechanical site preparation is expensive, it is often considered essential to ensure a well-stocked stand of rapidly growing trees. On moderately or steeply sloping sites, where use of heavy equipment would be impractical and the erosion hazard would be too great, prescribed burning of the cutover site is a less expensive and environmentally sound alternative (see Chapter 21).

Despite the higher success rate of plantations compared to direct seeding, failures and losses sometimes do occur. Mice and other rodents may cause the loss of many seedlings, especially in grassy areas, and browsing by deer and other large herbivores can be a problem. Planted seedlings may face stiff competition from shrubs and stump sprouts of other trees, which may necessitate application of herbicides. Furthermore, harsh microclimates on some sites may cause planting failures, particularly on steep slopes facing south.

Planting often represents a sizable proportion of the total cash investment in a forest stand. The cost of the seedlings reflects the expense of establishing and maintaining nurseries. The planting operation itself is fairly labor-intensive, and to this must be added the costs of site preparation and other measures taken to enhance planting success. For these reasons planting is likely to be done only when the increased cost can be justified economically by increased returns, and when the funds for investing in plantations are available.

Silvicultural Systems

From the preceding sections it should be evident that often the conditions necessary for regeneration of a species, and not mere economics, are what dictate the method and intensity of harvest cutting. Certain methods of harvesting to achieve adequate regeneration have found favor in silvicultural practice. Although they have become stylized in concept, they can be adapted to the requirements of each species. These *silvicultural systems* are long-range harvest and management schemes designed to optimize the growth, regeneration, and administrative management of particular forest types, usually with the goal of obtaining a perpetual and steady supply of timber. The total forest property is then said to be managed on a *sustained-yield* basis.

The use of silvicultural systems requires prescribing comprehensive treatments throughout the life of the stand, including the method of harvest, an evaluation of whether or not site preparation is necessary, the use of seeding, planting, or natural regeneration, and a schedule of intermediate stand treatments. Silvicultural systems are generally classified by the method used to harvest and regenerate the stand. These methods vary in cutting intensity, but they may readily be grouped under the categories of even-aged or uneven-aged methods.

Even-Aged Methods   In even-aged management the trees are removed over a relatively short period of time, creating open, sunny conditions, and lead-

ing to the development of even-aged stands. Many species can be managed by even-aged methods, and for certain species intolerant of shade the even-aged methods may be almost mandatory, since regeneration under lightly cut stands would not be adequate. The even-aged methods are *clearcutting, seed tree,* and *shelterwood.* Only in the clearcutting method are all trees removed at once. In the other methods trees are removed over a longer period of time.

Clearcutting method   In the clearcutting method regeneration is accomplished by natural seeding, direct seeding, or planting. If natural seeding is relied on, the effective dispersal distance of seeds may limit the width of the clearcut. Even with species that have light seeds, such as western larch and the spruces, most of the seeds fall within three or four tree heights of the windward edge of the clearcut, and the amount of seeds that fall 300 to 400 meters (1000 to 1300 feet) from the stand margin may be too small for adequate regeneration.

Clearcutting with natural regeneration can work well if size restrictions are followed, but a distinction should probably be made between situations in which seedlings have developed from seed dispersed into the clearcut and those in which most of the new stand saplings developed from advance regeneration and stump sprouts. If desirable advance regeneration is dense and well established, clearcutting simply releases these seedlings and saplings, and the procedure will give a well-stocked stand. If advance regeneration is sparse or absent, however, as is often the case in semiarid regions, even small clearcuts may result in marginal or inadequate stocking (5).

A forest of shade-intolerant trees with a dense understory of more shade-tolerant species is another common problem. Southern pines with a hardwood understory are an example. Clearcutting will release the understory, but this time there is an abrupt shift in species composition toward the more shade-tolerant species. Thus, contrary to common belief, clearcutting by itself on many sites is more likely to hasten succession than to set it back to an earlier stage.

Most regeneration problems of this type—stemming from clearcutting on average or good sites —can be resolved by site preparation and planting. Thus when the clearcutting method is used, artificial regeneration is often preferred over natural regeneration if the funds are available. With artificial regeneration there is also no biological restriction on the maximum width of the clearcut. Nevertheless, large clearcuts will probably be less common in the future than in the past because of their unfavorable aesthetic impact, the limited value of large clearcuts to many wildlife species, and possible erosion hazards. Political opposition has also limited clearcutting practices, as discussed in Chapter 1.

Seed tree method Other even-aged methods are designed to overcome some of the problems inherent in clearcutting with natural regeneration. In the seed tree method, scattered mature trees are left on the site to serve as a seed source for the new stand and to provide a more uniform dispersal of seed. Although this may seem like a good solution to the problem of seed dispersal, experience has shown that the seed tree method may be unsuccessful in many situations. The most serious difficulty is that the presence of seed trees frequently does not result in the establishment of an adequate number of seedlings. Seedlings may not survive on sites that have not been prepared and on sites susceptible to rapid invasion by shrubs. In some stands, such as the eastern oaks, whatever seedlings do become established may not be sufficiently vigorous to compete with advance regeneration and sprouts of other species. Furthermore, the seed tree method does not work well with shallow-rooted species, since many of the seed trees will be blown down by wind. The seed tree method is best suited to situations in which intensive site preparation is feasible and the species are reasonably wind-firm. Western larch and the southern pines are examples of species well suited to the seed tree method.

Shelterwood method Seed trees are also left standing in the shelterwood method, but in sufficient numbers to provide some shade and protection for the new seedlings (Figure 14.7). In the most common variant of the shelterwood method, the

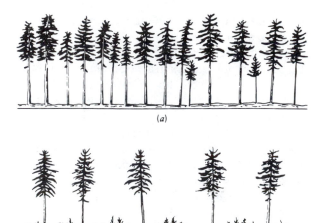

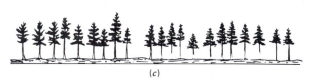

Figure 14.7 An illustration of the shelterwood method to regenerate an even-aged forest. (*a*) This is the mature stand before treatment. (*b*) The first major cut leaves a temporary shelterwood overstory having in this stand about 40 percent crown cover. (*c*) After saplings of the desired species have become well established, the shelterwood is removed to release the even-aged sapling stand.

first major cut leaves a temporary partial overstory in which the percentage of ground surface shaded by tree crowns may vary from 30 to 80 percent, depending on species and local conditions (Figure 14.7*b*). After the seedlings have become firmly established, usually after several years, the residual trees are completely removed so that they do not retard the growth of the new saplings (Figure 14.7*c*).

The shelterwood method is ideal for any species whose seedlings are not expected to germinate well under open conditions. Even some of the more intolerant species may benefit from the protection of a shelterwood overstory during the first few years, when seedlings are vulnerable to desiccation; this is especially true on harsh sites. For example, the shelterwood method has been applied successfully on sites in California and Oregon where clearcutting has failed (6, 7). The shelterwood method also has the least visual impact of any even-aged method, since by the time the last of the residual overstory trees are removed, the new stand is already sapling-sized. It therefore bypasses the typically devastated look of recent clearcuts. In many situations the shelterwood method probably reduces the erosion hazard as well.

Although the shelterwood method bears a superficial resemblance to heavy partial cutting in an unmanaged forest (Figure 14.4), there are important differences. In the establishment phase of a shelterwood cut (Figure 14.7b), the trees retained are among the larger and better-quality trees in the stand, so that they can serve as a good seed source. The overtopped, intermediate, and smaller codominants are usually removed completely. A heavy partial cutting, on the other hand, will generally accomplish just the opposite by removing many of the larger and better trees and releasing the smaller trees, which may not be of desirable species or quality. A second major difference is that after the removal cut in a shelterwood, the resulting stand is young and even-aged and composed entirely of saplings (Figure 14.7c). Such a stand will in fact differ little from a sapling stand that might have developed after a successful clearcut. If this transition to a sapling stand is considered too abrupt, the shelterwood can be modified in visually sensitive areas by accomplishing the removal phase in several steps over a period of several decades. During this time a two-aged stand is created. All other variants of the shelterwood system, however, can be considered strictly even-aged methods rather than some form of partial cutting that is intermediate between even-aged and uneven-aged approaches.

Coppice method   In the coppice method the forester depends on vegetative regeneration by stump sprouts instead of on stands developing from seed, which makes it different from all other reproduction methods. However, since coppice stands are usually harvested by clearcutting, it may be conveniently

discussed with other even-aged methods. The coppice method is restricted to species that typically sprout vigorously and have sprouts capable of attaining commercial size. Good examples of such species are aspen (Figure 14.5) and oak. Coppice stands are usually managed on short rotations, and the products may be fuelwood or pulpwood. Use of the coppice method declined in the mid-twentieth century as oil and gas became cheap and abundant fuels, but price increases of fossil fuels have revived some interest in coppice systems. Forest plantations for energy are discussed further in Chapter 23.

Provision for sustained yield   In all forms of even-aged management, the yield is sustained by successively cutting parts of the total property holding at regular intervals, so that when the cycle is completed, trees on the first tract in the sequence are old enough to be cut again. For example, if trees are being grown on a 100-year cycle or *rotation,* we could divide the property into 100 units and cut a different one each year. Or the tract could be divided into 20 units and a cut made every five years (Figure 14.8). Such a scheme provides a convenient starting point for management, although biological and economic uncertainties often demand that managers be much more flexible than this. Damage from windstorms, fire, or insects may require prompt salvage over areas much larger than originally scheduled. It also makes more economic sense to cut more heavily in years of high demand for timber and less heavily in years of low demand. A more complete discussion of the development of forest management schemes is given in Chapter 15.

Uneven-Aged Methods   Uneven-aged management is accomplished by the *selection method,* in which scattered trees or small groups of trees are cut. This diffuse pattern of timber removal ensures that all ages of trees will be intermixed (Figure 14.9). The selection method has some unique advantages. There is usually no need for expensive site preparation or planting. Regeneration tends to be reliable and more or less automatic, for new trees are simply recruited from the reservoir of saplings in the forest understory. Selection cutting is the only silvicultural

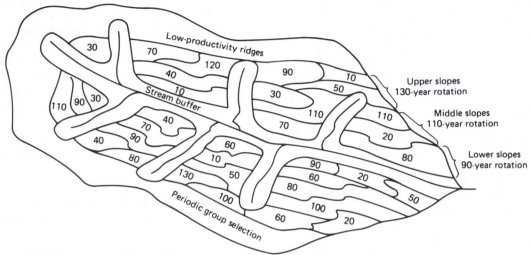

Figure 14.8 Compartment map of a hypothetical watershed managed by the clearcutting system for sustained yield of timber. The number of each compartment indicates the order and year in which it is harvested. Every ten years three compartments are cut, one each at lower, middle, and upper elevations. Cuts are made in irregular strips parallel to the contour to minimize erosion and provide the best wildlife habitat possible. A permanent buffer strip is left around streams to protect water quality. The ridgetop lands are of marginal productivity and are managed by periodic group selection cuts. The most productive lower slopes are managed on shorter rotation than the middle and upper slopes.

system in which sustained yield can be obtained from a single stand of trees. Provided that cutting is not too intense, trees can be harvested in perpetuity, and the forest canopy will remain largely intact with little evidence of manipulation. Erosion and disturbance to the site are minimal. Fire is not much of a hazard because there are no extensive piles of logging debris. For these reasons the selection method is highly attractive to owners of small wood-lots and to managers of multiple-use recreation areas.

Together with the benefits of the selection system are some limitations. Generally only the more shade-tolerant species will prosper under such a scheme. The opening created by the removal of a single mature tree does not usually allow enough light for the adequate survival and growth of shade-intolerant and intermediate species. The list of such species is considerable and includes most of the pines, larches, oaks, birches, and aspens (see Table 6.1). Light cutting in stands of these species not only

will fail to regenerate the species in most situations but will also actually tend to hasten the conversion to whatever tolerant species happen to be in the under-story. Therefore, the selection system is most appropriate for tolerant species such as the maples, hemlocks, cedars, spruces, and true firs. The lack of sizable openings may also be unfavorable for certain species of wildlife, including some of the popular game species. A disadvantage that is more or less inherent in the method and difficult to avoid is injury to some of the standing trees during felling and hauling operations.

Some of the disadvantages of the selection system can be lessened by modifying the method of harvest. Cutting small groups of trees instead of scattered individuals increases the amount of direct sunlight to the extent that some of the shade-intolerant species can regenerate. This *group selection* method will also improve the wildlife habitat for many game species, while still retaining the more or less closed-canopy appearance of the forest as a whole (Figure

Figure 14.9 With the individual-tree selection method of harvest, disturbance is often hardly noticeable, as in this uneven-aged forest of spruce along the coast of Maine. Notice the dense advance regeneration of the same species.

14.10). In many stands the problems that might result from applying the individual-tree selection method can be circumvented by partial or complete substitution of the group selection method.

In actual application, the selection method is somewhat more involved than simply cutting scattered trees or small groups of trees (8). If too many trees are cut at one time, and if the cut is concentrated among the better trees, the operation will differ little from highgrading. Both mistakes are frequently made. Some poorly formed or defective trees should be removed along with good mature trees in each harvest, but some dead or dying trees should always remain as cavities for wildlife (Chapter 17). If there are concentrations of pole-

sized trees in the stand, they should be thinned to promote better growth. This means that the typical selection harvest should include small trees as well as large. And as a general rule, not more than about 30 percent of the timber volume should be removed in a single harvest operation in order to maintain good stand growth and to avoid excessive branchiness.

Choice of Even-Aged or Uneven-Aged Management The choice between growing trees in even-aged stands and growing them in uneven-aged stands will ordinarily depend on particular management goals and constraints. On sites where the tolerant species are valuable and in demand (e.g., maples, spruces, western redcedar, redwood, western hemlock), the selection system can be used to considerable advantage for private landholdings, public forests, and industrial forests alike (Table 14.1). Sugar maple, for example, is a very tolerant species from which fine furniture and flooring can be made, and it is estimated that 90 percent of the managed sugar maple forests in the midwestern United States are under the selection system, whatever the type of ownership (9). In other forests uneven-aged management may not be as attractive economically as an even-aged system for several reasons. Sometimes the more shade-tolerant species on a site are not in much economic demand, as is true of beech and hemlock in eastern North America and of the hickories and sugarberry in the South. Of particular concern to some forest industries is the fact that many species in highest demand for pulp and lumber are shade-intolerant and not readily managed by the selection system unless special measures are taken. The economic gap is widened by the fact that most shade-tolerant species are inherently slow-growing and hence may not be as good an investment as the faster-growing intolerant species. There are some exceptions to these generalizations, however. For example, the shade-tolerant spruces of the Northeast are more valuable for pulp, despite their slow growth, than the intolerant, fast-growing paper birch and aspen. Moreover, if the owner is willing to control a tolerant understory by the application of herbicides or prescribed

Figure 14.10 Group selection cuts near a major road on national forestland. (Courtesy of U.S.D.A. Forest Service.)

burning, even species as intolerant as the southern pines can be feasibly managed under the selection system with comparatively small openings (10).

Logistics and logging costs must also be considered. Clearcutting is administratively easier than other methods when areas are large, and this is undoubtedly a major reason for its popularity with industrial firms. For logging heavy stands of old timber in the Pacific Northwest, which entails the use of expensive cable systems (see Chapter 16), the selection method may not always be economically feasible. In other forest types, however, selection cutting is not necessarily more expensive or less time-efficient—an objection frequently leveled against the system—when costs are expressed per unit of timber volume harvested (11, 12).

In the final analysis, each landholding must be considered individually. But there may be no need to decide exclusively on one system; a sizable landholding could easily accommodate even-aged and uneven-aged systems. It is also probable that most intolerant species could successfully be managed by small patch cuts of one hectare (2.5 acres) or less, a management strategy that falls between the realms of group selection and regular clearcutting.

Forecasting the Results of Silvicultural Treatments

One of the hindrances to studying the effects of silvicultural practices is that trees grow so slowly it takes years or decades to monitor the effects of a treatment. The technique of computer simulation, mentioned in Chapter 6, is therefore a potentially helpful way of circumventing these time constraints. Instead of waiting twenty years to see the results of a thinning or harvest cut, a forester could use a growth model to test a variety of options and predict the outcome in a matter of minutes.

The first step in constructing a forest growth model is usually to define the basic variables and interactions that are believed to exist. For example, we know that the growth rate of a tree depends on its age or current size, as well as on the inherent productivity of the site and competition induced by

neighboring trees. Such a relationship can be expressed by a "word equation" as follows,

$$\text{growth} = f(\text{age, site quality, competition})$$

where f indicates that growth is a function of the variables in parentheses. Such an expression illustrates the important point that biological processes can generally be approximated by equations, which form the heart of most forest growth models. Equations are frequently superior to our intuitive understandings of forest growth, because they can be used systematically to obtain predictions when, as is usually the case in nature, the interactions of variables are exceedingly complex. Of course, the preceding

Table 14.1 Silvicultural Information for Some Major Forest Types of North America

Forest Type	Tolerance[a] (Major Species)	Successional Status	Growth Rate	Current Commercial Value	Methods of Regeneration[b]	Ease of Regeneration[c]
Western						
Douglas-fir	Inter	Variable (site-dependent)[d]	Rapid	High	C, SH (SP, P)	M
Hemlock–Sitka spruce	Tol	Climax	Mod–rapid	High	SH, GS, S, C	E
Coast redwood	Tol	Climax	Rapid	High	GS, C, SH, S	E
Ponderosa pine	Intol	Variable[d]	Mod	Mod–high	SH, GS, S, ST, C (SP, P)	M–D
Western larch	Intol	Successional	Rapid	Mod	ST, C, SH (SP)	E–M
Engelmann spruce-fir	Tol	Climax	Slow–mod	Mod	GS, S, SH, C	M
Lodgepole pine	Intol	Successional	Mod	Low	C, SH	E
Eastern						
Spruce-fir	Tol	Climax	Slow–mod	Mod	GS, S, SH, C	E–M
White pine	Inter	Successional	Rapid	Mod	SH, GS	M
Jack pine	Intol	Successional	Rapid	Mod	C, ST, SH (SP)	M
Red pine	Intol	Successional	Rapid	Mod	C, SH (SP, P)	D (Nat), M (Art)
Northern hardwoods	Tol	Climax	Slow	Mod	S, GS, SH	E
Aspen-birch	Intol	Successional	Rapid	Low–mod	C (SP)	E
Oak-hickory	Inter–Intol	Variable[d]	Rapid	Mod–high	SH, GS, C (SP, P)	M–D
Southern pines	Intol	Successional	Rapid	High	C, ST, GS (SP, P)	M

Principal Sources: "Silvicultural systems for the major forest types in the U.S.," U.S.D.A. For. Serv., Agr. Handbook 445, 1973; R. B. Phelps, "The demand and price situation for forest products," U.S.D.A. For. Serv., Misc. Publ. 1357, 1977; and R. D. Forbes and A. B. Meyer, *Forestry Handbook*, Ronald Press, New York, 1955.

[a]Abbreviations: Tol = tolerant; Inter = intermediate; intol = intolerant.

[b]Abbreviations: C = clearcutting; SH = shelterwood; ST = seed tree; GS = group selection; S = individual-tree selection; (SP, P) = site preparation and planting may be necessary.

[c]Abbreviations: E = easy; M = moderate; D = difficult; Nat = natural; Art = artificial.

[d]Forest types with a "variable" successional status are generally successional on moist or average sites and climax on dry sites.

equation does not show how the variables interact and therefore cannot be used to obtain predictions. An example of an actual diameter growth model with these variables (13) is

$$\Delta D = 0.0716 + 0.0129D + 0.0157S$$
$$+ 2.03 \frac{1}{1 + BA} - 0.0117BA$$

This equation states that diameter growth of a tree (ΔD) is proportional to its current diameter (D) and site productivity (S). In other words, growth rates will be highest for large trees on good sites.

Growth is also shown to be inversely proportional to the degree of competition, which in this model is approximated by the stand basal area (BA). Growth rate of an individual tree will therefore decrease as the sum of the basal areas of competing trees increases. As an actual example, suppose we have a tree 15 centimeters in diameter growing in a stand with 35 square meters per hectare of basal area on a good site with a site index of 22 meters. (See Chapter 12 for an explanation of these terms.) The predicted growth of this tree is then

$$\Delta D = 0.0716 + 0.0129(15) + 0.0157(22)$$
$$+ 2.03 \frac{1}{1 + 35} - 0.0117(35)$$

$$\Delta D = 0.26$$

The tree is therefore expected to grow 0.26 centimeters in diameter in the next year. If we reduce the stand basal area by conducting a thinning, we could recompute the predicted growth with the new reduced basal area in order to estimate how much the tree might respond to thinning.

How accurate are these forest models? Recent studies have shown that very good predictions of forest growth and future yields are possible. Figure 14.11 shows close agreement between the predicted and observed basal-area growth of a forest that had received periodic light harvest cuts over a span of twenty-six years. This particular model demonstrated that good predictions were possible for mixed-species stands regardless of the relative proportions of species, the history of silvicultural treatments, and the age structure of the forest.

However, because models usually have numer-

ous simplifying assumptions (as in the examples just reviewed), there are limitations to what can be concluded from models even when the data base is very good. Accurate long-range forecasts, for longer than forty years, are particularly difficult. Moreover, most available models project only the growth of existing stands over time but do not attempt to predict the regeneration phase in response to a harvest cut. Given that forest simulation is still a relatively young science, perhaps future refinements and improvements can be anticipated.

Environmental Effects of Silvicultural Practices

Many people envision a "natural" forest environment as one consisting of an unbroken canopy of trees with a rich and diverse understory of shrubs and herbs. The contrast with a recently harvested area can be striking, especially after clearcutting. The general public may consider clearcutting and other even-aged harvesting methods to be the exploitive use of a resource in the manner of strip mining. Concern will often be expressed over the possibility of accelerated soil erosion, site degradation, and loss of wildlife habitat. It is therefore important for the forest manager to be well informed on such issues and to be prepared to arrive at balanced, impartial conclusions. Well-informed opinion is possible only after review of careful experiments designed to measure the environmental effects of silvicultural practices.

Soil Erosion

Many early small-scale experiments suggested that a necessary condition for soil erosion is the exposure of bare soil to the impact of rain. This finding has interesting implications for forest management. What would happen if trees are cut and no soil is exposed? The experimental clearcuts shown in Figure 14.12 were designed partly to answer this question. In both clearcuts the boundaries conform to natural watershed boundaries, so that streamwater draining the clearcut area can be monitored at the stream outlet (see Chapter 6). In the North Carolina

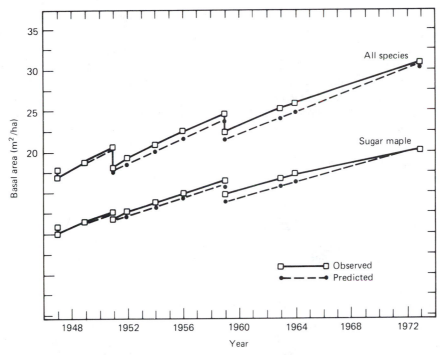

Figure 14.11 Gradual changes in the basal area of this mixed-species hardwood forest, brought about through growth and timber harvest, were accurately predicted by a growth model called FOREST. The long-term increase in basal area shows that there has been net growth in this even-aged stand. The sharp decreases in 1951 and 1959 reflect light timber harvests in those years (14). (Courtesy of R. A. Monserud.)

Figure 14.12 Experimental clearcuts on which erosion levels have been monitored for a number of years. (*a*) In a North Carolina clearcut, erosion over a fifteen-year period was not appreciably higher than in uncut areas. (*b*) In a western Oregon clearcut, located on inherently unstable slopes, erosion was about three times normal levels. Logging roads were not constructed in either forest. (Courtesy of U.S.D.A. Forest Service.)

watershed shown in Figure 14.12*a*, all the trees were cut and left where they fell. No roads were constructed and no timber was removed. Increases in soil erosion were negligible, even though the brush was mowed annually for fifteen years (15). These results are typical of many regions and indicate that protection of the soil by leaf litter and ground vegetation is usually sufficient to prevent erosion on most sites. Some exceptions can be expected on steep slopes and in areas of unstable soils. Thus, in a similar experiment in Oregon, shown in Figure 14.12*b*, erosion rates were about three times the normal rate for undisturbed watersheds, although the actual magnitude of the increase was still small (16).

Most timber-harvesting operations, however, require the construction of roads, and roads often represent a significant area of bare soil susceptible to erosion. The litter may be scraped away and bare soil exposed as logs are dragged or "skidded" to a central loading deck (see Figure 4.5). Skid trails are formed even in the selection methods of harvesting. Roads are also required, of course, for transportation of logs out of the forest by trucks. Erosion may occur from water running along the surface of the road or skid trail, from steep surfaces of the road "cut" and "fill" areas, and from the slumping of slopes into streams where the slope has been weakened by a road cut. In most parts of the country, proper road design can keep soil loss to very low levels. In the more erosion-prone areas such as the Pacific Northwest, the risk can be greatly reduced by using logging methods that minimize the formation of skid trails. With balloon and skyline logging (see Chapter 16), logs can be transported to a loading deck without dragging them along the ground. Restricting the intensity, frequency, and extent of cutting is also recommended on unstable sites.

Nutrient Loss

The generally minor impact of timber harvests on erosion rates does not entirely rule out the possibility of site deterioration. Another problem to consider is the loss of mineral nutrients from the site. Typical harvesting operations remove from the site certain quantities of nutrients that are contained in

the logs and other usable woody material. These nutrients are not lost permanently from the site, because they are gradually replaced by natural sources such as precipitation and the weathering of rock. As long as the rotations are reasonably long, no net loss will occur. But in recent years there has been a trend toward shorter rotations—for example, forty years or fewer in the South—and this clearly accelerates the rate of nutrient withdrawals. In some regions nutrient loss is not merely confined to whatever is removed in the form of wood products. Experimental cuttings in New Hampshire have shown that through an accelerated decomposition of organic matter and the subsequent release of stored nutrients, substantial amounts of nutrients can be leached from the site and flushed into streams (see Chapter 6) (17). Furthermore, the practice of whole-tree harvesting, in which even the branches and leaves are utilized (Figure 14.13), can be expected to increase nutrient loss. The added impact of whole-tree harvesting is more than what a simple tally of additional harvested material might suggest, for branches have higher concentrations of nutrients than stemwood (18).

It is not certain, however, whether even whole-tree harvesting on rotations of twenty or thirty years will necessarily cause a decline in fertility. We do not really know how much of the total soil nutrient reserves are available to plants. Certainly the amount of nutrients stored in plant biomass is small compared to the total quantity stored in the soil, but additional research will be necessary to resolve questions about the impact of short-rotation forestry. It also appears that major nutrient losses from leaching may not be common outside the northern hardwoods region of the Northeast (19). Some specialists feel that, in general, whole-tree harvesting and regular clearcutting are not likely to cause major problems in soil fertility (19, 20), but others foresee such problems with intensive, short-rotation forestry (17, 18, 21).

Use of Chemicals

Silvicultural practices do not necessarily depend on the use of chemicals, but herbicides and chemical fertilizers are frequently applied in certain situations. Of the two, herbicides are probably of greater importance to silvicultural practice, because many conifer species are difficult to regenerate if there is substantial competition from hardwoods and shrubs. Recent concerns about environmental hazards from the use of these chemicals have prompted evaluations of possible harmful effects.

The greatest demonstrated impact of both herbicides and fertilizers is probably on water quality. A few species of fish and other aquatic animals have low tolerance levels to herbicide applications, and concentrations as low as 1 to 10 parts per million can cause high mortality (22). Nitrogen and phosphorus fertilizers can stimulate algal growth in streams and lakes, which in turn reduces the oxygen supply to aquatic animals. However, monitoring of watersheds after typical herbicide and fertilizer applications has shown that concentrations of these chemi-

cals are generally well within safe limits, provided care is taken that the chemicals are not applied directly to bodies of water. For example, peak concentrations of herbicides in streams flowing through treated areas seldom exceed 0.1 parts per million, and concentrations rapidly decline over time (23).

Tolerance levels of mammals to herbicides are much higher than those of fish, and the common herbicides persist for very short periods in the bodies of mammals. High rates of ingestion are unlikely, because herbicides rapidly break down naturally. Thus typical herbicide applications are believed to have little effect on wildlife populations. However, much concern was raised over possible hazards to human health of two herbicides, 2,4,5-T and Silvex, which contain trace amounts of a highly toxic contaminant known as dioxin. In 1979 the Environmental Protection Agency issued an emer-

Figure 14.13 Mechanized whole-tree harvesting. (Courtesy of U.S.D.A. Forest Service.)

gency suspension order prohibiting the use of these herbicides, based on evidence of a statistically higher rate of miscarriages of women living in an area where the use of 2,4,5-T was common. Since that time, 2,4,5-T has been replaced in forestry applications by an array of other herbicides that do not contain the dioxin contaminant.

Aesthetic Considerations

Silvicultural treatments can be designed to harmonize well with landscape features, but unfortunately this has not been common historically. Often in the past stark geometric shapes were used for western clearcuts. This practice understandably caused adverse public reaction, and the tendency of some foresters to appear unconcerned about landscape aesthetics only compounded the problem. It may be true that once a clearcut site has become reoccupied by dense green vegetation, it ceases to be objectionable to many people. But when a clearcut is being made somewhere in the area every few years, the promise of regeneration will not necessarily cause objections to subside.

What is needed is a more imaginative approach to silviculture and a willingness to search for acceptable alternatives to clearcut-and-burn prescriptions. Coupled with this must be a recognition that the visual quality of a forest landscape is in itself a resource that can and should be managed. In recent years foresters and landscape architects have collaborated fruitfully in developing principles and guidelines for landscape management on national forests. When a management plan is made for an administrative unit of national forestland, visual considerations are incorporated directly into the plan. The plan may identify certain zones in which aesthetics will be given major consideration. These zones may lie along major roads, near recreation areas or campsites, or in highly scenic areas. Selection cutting may be feasible in many of these areas. If even-aged management is desired, the shelterwood method is often a highly acceptable substitute for clearcutting. In stands where clearcutting is necessary, many techniques can soften the blow to the visual appearance of the area. Narrow cuts with curved contours

can be shaped to blend in with natural terrain, and islands of uncut vegetation can be left to break up the view and add visual diversity. Logging debris can be lopped and scattered on the clearcut so that the waste is not as visible and will decay more quickly.

Natural Precedents for Harvest Methods

It was previously pointed out that thinning imitates the natural process of mortality that occurs in all even-aged stands. Can natural precedents also be found for harvest cutting? If they can, they clearly have bearing on whether or not silvicultural systems create an unacceptable environmental strain on forest ecosystems.

It is easy to find natural precedents for the selection method in the death of mature trees from old age or disease. It might seem more difficult to find natural precedents to the seemingly drastic methods of harvest such as clearcutting or seed tree cutting. Yet the evidence of natural counterparts to heavy cutting could hardly be more convincing. Land surveyors traveling through extensive tracts of primeval forest in the mid-1800s often reported large windfalls in which all the trees had been blown down in a tangled mass. In Maine, for example, one group of surveyors laying out a township line reported that in some areas the trees were "broken and blown in every direction" and that "half of the first six miles was of the very worst kind of windfalls, so very bad that we couldn't get more than a mile into Vaughanstown." Storms in recent times have caused similar damage. Large tracts were blown down on the Olympic Peninsula in Washington in a storm of 1921, and the 1938 hurricane in central New England caused heavy damage over 243,000 hectares (600,000 acres). In 1977 strong winds generated by a thunderstorm cut a 300-kilometer (160-mile) swath through the forests of northern Wisconsin (Figure 14.14). The extensive forest devastation (230 square miles) caused by the eruption of Mount Saint Helens in the state of Washington is another recent example (see Figure P2.3). In certain regions insect epidemics and forest fires caused by lightning

Figure 14.14 Aftermath of a 1977 windstorm in an old-growth forest in Wisconsin. Strong downdrafts from a summer thunderstorm reached wind speeds of up to 157 miles per hour (290 kilometers per hour) and caused damage on 850,000 acres (340,000 hectares).

periodically destroy forest canopies over thousands of hectares (see Chapter 21).

The philosophical issue is therefore not whether clearcutting is "unnatural" but whether or not natural catastrophes are so common that most stands would be even-aged anyway in the absence of humankind.

In the early part of the century, when the theory of forest succession was being developed, much emphasis was placed on the classification and study of climax forests. Although these pioneer workers were clearly aware of the occurrence of natural disturbances, it appears that catastrophes were viewed as rare or aberrant events. Yet subsequent workers, in the process of studying remnants of primeval forest, often found them to be even-aged with evidence of catastrophic disturbance in the past (24, 25), and for this reason much skepticism developed regarding the validity of the climax concept. This view was well expressed by Cline and Spurr (24) in 1942.

> **The primeval forests, then, did not consist of stagnant stands of immense trees stretching with little change in composition over vast areas. Large trees were common, it is true,**

and limited areas did support climax stands, but the majority of the stands undoubtedly were in a state of flux resulting from the dynamic action of wind, fire, and other forces of nature.

In writing of the forests of northern Minnesota, one investigator has carried this conclusion a step further and considers the local climax type to be "largely unknown to science" (26). For any such forest region the implication is clear: of the various harvesting methods used, the types of heavy cutting applied in even-aged management would most closely mimic the predominant process of tree mortality that occurs in nature.

Nevertheless, disturbance regimes vary considerably in different parts of the world, and in some areas, such as the northern hardwoods region of eastern North America, relatively stable climax forests may have been common. The early government land surveys show that before settlement there were few areas of windfalls and burned lands, and that forests of early-successional species occupied only a small fraction of the landscape in this region (27–29). Studies of primeval forest remnants of shade-tolerant species have also revealed them to be uneven-aged more often than not (30–32). Such evidence suggests that natural catastrophes may indeed be infrequent in some regions.

A Management Overview

It seems reasonable to conclude that natural parallels can be found for virtually every silvicultural system. Selection cutting imitates the death of scattered individual trees from old age or disease. Parallels to shelterwood and seed tree cutting are found in stands partially damaged by wind. The effect of clearcutting is not unlike that of the occasional natural catastrophe. Clearcutting will generally have the highest environmental impact of the four systems and selection cutting the least, but in many regions the impact of clearcutting itself appears to be small provided it is not done repeatedly on the same site at short intervals. It also has certain benefits, such as the perpetuation of intolerant tree species and the creation of favorable wildlife habitats for certain species. For these reasons clearcutting cannot be categorically condemned. It is possible that some optimal level of environmental quality can be achieved by a diversity of management systems that create a landscape with a variety of forest types and age classes. Such a mosaic appears to provide near-optimal habitat for many wildlife species (33), and quite possibly it was the condition of the North American forest when Europeans arrived.

References

1. D. M. SMITH, *The Practice of Silviculture,* Eighth Edition, John Wiley & Sons, New York, 1986.

2. D. M. SMITH AND E. W. JOHNSON, *J. For., 75,* 208 (1977).

3. D. S DEBELL, "Fertilize western hemlock—yes or no?" In *Global Forestry and the Western Role,* Western Forestry and Conservation Assoc., Portland, Ore., 1975.

4. D. M. STONE, "Fertilizing and thinning northern hardwoods in the Lake States," U.S.D.A. For. Serv., Res. Pap. NC-141, 1977.

5. P. M. McDONALD, "Clearcutting and natural regeneration—management implications for the northern Sierra Nevada," U.S.D.A. For. Serv., Gen. Tech. Rept. PSW-70, 1983.

6. R. L. WILLIAMSON, "Results of shelterwood harvesting of Douglas-fir in the Cascades of western Oregon," U.S.D.A. For. Serv., Res. Pap. PNW-161, 1973.

7. P. M. McDONALD, "Shelterwood cutting in a young-growth, mixed-conifer stand in north central California," U.S.D.A. For. Serv., Res. Pap. PSW-117, 1976.

8. D. A. MARQUIS, "Application of uneven-aged silviculture and management on public and private lands." In *Uneven-Aged Silviculture & Management in the United States,* U.S.D.A. For. Serv., Timber Management Research, Washington, D. C., 1978.

9. R. D. JACOBS, "Silvicultural systems for nothern hardwoods in the Mid-west and Lake States." In *Managing Northern Hardwoods: Proc. of a Silvicultural Symposium.* Faculty of Forestry, Misc. Publ. 13, College of Environmental Science and Forestry, State University of New York, Syracuse, 1987.

10. R. R. REYNOLDS, J. B. BAKER, AND T. T. KU, "Four decades of selection management on the Crossett Farm Forestry Forties," Univ. of Ark. Agr. Expt., Sta. Bull. 872, 1984.

11. S. M. FILIP, "Harvesting costs and returns under 4 cutting methods in mature beech-birch-maple stands in New England," U.S.D.A. For. Serv., Res. Pap. NE-87, 1967.

12. R. D. NYLAND, ET AL., "Logging and its effects in northern hardwoods," Appl. For. Res. Inst., Res. Rept. 31, College of Environmental Sciences and Forestry, State University of New York, Syracuse, 1976.

13. G. L. MARTIN AND A. R. EK, *For. Sci., 30,* 731 (1984).

14. R. A. MONSERUD, "Methodology for simulating Wisconsin northern hardwood stand dynamics," Ph.D. thesis, University of Wisconsin, Madison, 1975.

15. J. N. KOCHENDERFER, "Erosion control on logging roads in the Appalachians," U.S.D.A. For. Serv., Res. Pap. NE-158, 1970.

16. R. L. FREDRIKSEN, "Erosion and sedimentation following road construction and timber harvest on unstable soils in three small western Oregon watersheds," U.S.D.A. For. Serv., Res. Pap. PNW-104, 1970.

17. G. E. LIKENS, F. H. BORMANN, R. S. PIERCE, AND W. A. REINERS, *Science, 199,* 492 (1978).

18. J. P. KIMMINS, *For. Ecol. Manag., 1,* 169 (1977).

19. E. STONE, "The impact of timber harvest on soils and water," In *Report of the President's Advisory Panel on Timber and the Environment,* Washington, D.C., 1973, pp. 427–467.

20. J. R. BOYLE, J. J. PHILIPS, AND A. R. EK, *J. For., 71,* 760 (1973).

21. J. B. WAIDE AND W. T. SWANK, "Simulation of potential effects of forest utilization on the nitrogen cycle in different southeastern ecosystems." In *Watershed Research in Eastern North America,* Smithsonian Institution, Washington, D.C., 1977.

22. ANON., "Vegetation management with herbicides in the Eastern Region," Final environmental statement, U.S.D.A. For. Serv., 1978.

23. W. L. PRITCHETT, *Properties and Management of Forest Soils,* John Wiley & Sons, New York, 1979.

24. A. C. CLINE AND S. H. SPURR, *Harvard For. Bull.,* 21 (1942).

25. D. K. MAISSUROW, *J. For., 33,* 373 (1935).

26. M. L. HEINSELMAN, "The natural role of fire in northern conifer forests." In *Fire in the Northern Environment:*

A Symposium, U.S.D.A. For. Serv., Pac. Northwest For. Range Expt. Sta., Portland, Ore., 1971.

27. T. G. Siccama, *Am. Midl. Nat. 85,* 153 (1971).

28. C. G. Lorimer, *Ecology, 58,* 139 (1977).

29. C. D. Canham and O. L. Loucks, *Ecology, 65,* 803 (1984).

30. F. C. Gates and G. E. Nichols, *J. For., 28,* 395 (1930).

31. W. B. Leak, *Ecology, 56,* 1451 (1975).

32. C. G. Lorimer and L. E. Frelich, *Bull. Torrey Bot. Club, 111,* 193 (1984).

33. R. C. Biesterfeldt and S. G. Boyce, *J. For., 76,* 342 (1978).

CHAPTER 15

Timber Management

WILLIAM A. LEUSCHNER
HAROLD W. WISDOM
W. DAVID KLEMPERER

The forest is a living system with many species of flora and fauna interacting together. These flora and fauna form the forest ecosystem and provide forest products desired by society. The trees provide not only timber for paper, lumber, or plywood, but also food and shelter for game and nongame wildlife species. The combined ecosystem can provide recreational and aesthetic experiences also valued by society (Figure 15.1). These can range from activities in high-density areas, such as organized campgrounds and picnic sites, through dispersed-use and wilderness activities, such as backcountry hiking and camping.

The products obtained from the forest ecosystem are too numerous to mention. However, the entire ecosystem is needed to produce them because they are jointly produced. For example, growing oak–hickory forests automatically produces habitat for squirrels (Figure 15.2), and clearcutting timber automatically produces forest openings that provide habitat for deer and some songbirds. This joint production means that the forest must be managed as a system if all products are desired. It also sometimes causes hard decisions or conflict when the production of one product causes the destruction of another. An extreme example is clearcutting in a campground.

Society is interested in the forest because it produces desired forest products. Society begins to manage the forest when there are insufficient products to meet desires or when it becomes too costly to obtain the products. For example, suppose a society harvests raspberries from forest openings created by lightning fires. These people are using forest products but not managing the forest because they simply gather the fruits. Suppose that the forest openings grow over and there are too few raspberries, so that people must now walk a day to reach them. The people may then decide to start their own fires to create openings so that raspberries will grow in the desired location and quantity. This society is now *managing* the forest for its products.

This example shows the historical biological meaning of forest management. Forest management formerly meant only the biological manipulation of trees and forest stands, primarily for timber. Biological manipulation still provides many forest management alternatives, but it is now usually taught in silviculture and forest ecology courses. Forest management now has a broader meaning.

The forest manager is constrained in manipulating the forest by the external and internal variables present. Internal variables include such things as temperature, rainfall, soil type, and species in a forest stand. These variables determine the produc-

tion possibilities for any forest. External influences include federal and state legislation, taxation, and the market for forest products. These external variables will be discussed in more detail in a later section.

The external and internal variables do not always absolutely prohibit or automatically produce the maximum of any one forest product. However, some sites are better suited to producing one forest product than another. For example, some sites produce greater yields from conifers than hardwoods for the same amount of resources used; moreover, different products often have different relative values to society. On most forest acres lumber for housing is relatively more important than wild raspberries for jam. Balancing the relative productivity of a forest site with the relative net value of the product determines which forest management alternative is chosen. Modern forest management has come to mean the application of analytical techniques to aid in choosing the management alternatives that con-

Figure 15.1 Uneven-aged stand of ponderosa pine in central Oregon. Notice the thicket of pine seedlings in the left foreground and the older group of pine saplings in the right background. (Courtesy of U.S.D.A. Forest Service.)

Figure 15.2 A chestnut oak stand, with some black oak, on a ridge in West Virginia. (Courtesy of U.S.D.A. Forest Service.)

tribute most to society's (or an organization's) objectives. This is the context within which we will discuss timber management (1–5).

Basic Management Concepts

Forest management concepts should encompass the multiple uses made of the forest as discussed in Chapter 9. Timber is only one of the multiple uses, and this chapter focuses on its management. However, the reader should remember that it is not managed in isolation because of the joint production process just mentioned. Timber management decisions must consider impacts on other products desired from the forest.

The Regulated Forest

Timber products are usually desired over a continuous time period and in about the same or increasing amounts if a population is stable or increasing. However, the distribution of trees by age and size may not be such that trees will be ready for harvest throughout that period. For example, some trees may be too small to saw into lumber, and there may be some years when no trees are really suitable for cutting.

In these situations the forest owner or society may decide to change the forest structure to meet their needs. The forest may be manipulated in such a way that trees of all ages are present for continuous harvesting. A forest that produces a continuous flow of products of about the same size, quality, and quantity over time is called a *regulated forest*.

Sustained Yield

For what is called a *sustained yield,* the flow of timber products over multiple-year periods must be more or less continuous. Regulated forests, by definition, provide a sustained yield. However, sustained yield becomes problematic during the period when an unregulated forest is in transition to a regulated forest. Imagine that a forest has trees all the same age (Figure 15.3). This means that the trees will be more or less ready for harvest at the same time. However, no timber will be available between the time the trees are harvested and the time new ones grow to maturity. Forest managers may thus begin to convert the forest to one that has all ages present. They will want a sustained yield during the time they are converting to a regulated forest, but they will have to cut fewer trees per year to change the forest. Thus attaining sustained yield, or maintaining the volume of sustained yield, can be difficult during the conversion period.

A sustained yield may come from a forest owned by one person or from a broad geographical area, such as a county, state, or even the nation. A sustained yield is difficult for small landowners to achieve unless they use uneven-aged management, discussed later. The larger the ownership, the more

Figure 15.3 A stand of longleaf pine about 125 years old in Mississippi. (Courtesy of U.S.D.A. Forest Service.)

easily a sustained yield can be managed because there is more flexibility in timing timber harvests. The larger area offers greater variation in age classes for a variety of reasons, including past management activities as well as natural disasters. The tree crops that make up a sustained yield may come from the forests of an individual owner or those of all owners in a multicounty area or in the state, even though, as an extreme, no one owner may have a sustained yield. For example, during a 30-year period all timber may come from federal forests during the first 10 years, from industrial forests during the second 10, and from small private forests during the third 10-year period.

Conceptually, yield need not come from a particular forest or ownership each and every year to be "sustained." A forest could be harvested every two, three, or five years and be both regulated and have sustained yield. However, as a practical matter, there

must be a continuous daily yield over a wide geographic area. Industrial mills must have raw material daily or they cannot operate economically, and people in less developed nations need daily supplies of firewood for cooking and heating.

Even-Aged and Uneven-Aged Management

The forest may be regulated by using either even-aged or uneven-aged management, or a combination of the two. The concept of even-aged and uneven-aged forest stands was discussed in Chapter 14. In an oversimplified example of *even-aged management,* suppose trees take 25 years to mature in a 25-acre forest. Then the even-aged regulated forest would have 25 timber stands of equal productivity, each one acre and each one year older than the next (Figure 15.4).

The acre with the 25-year-old stand is harvested each year and immediately regenerated. For example, the acre in the far lower right of Figure 15.4a is cut in 1990, the acre to its left in 1991, and so on in perpetuity. Each year an acre is harvested, and each year the yield is the same because we have assumed equal productivity. The conversion to even-aged management from, for example, a 25-acre forest with trees all the same age would take 25 years; this is the conversion period discussed previously.

Even-aged management in practice is seldom so simple. The first problem is deciding on the desired age structure. Then the forest manager must decide on how to manipulate the existing forest to obtain it. In addition, the existing tree species may not be those desired, and so the forest manager must decide whether the site can biologically and economically support conversion to the desired species. Or if conversion is unfeasible, the manager must decide how to work with the undesired species so as to obtain the maximum return.

An *uneven-aged* stand is one where "Trees differ markedly in age . . . . By convention, a minimum of 10 to 20 years is generally accepted" (6). Suppose a stand had sufficient age classes that some trees were mature every four years. Then the stand could be

1990

1	2	3	4	5
6	7	8	9	10
11	12	13	14	15
16	17	18	19	20
21	22	23	24	25

(a)

1991

2	3	4	5	6
7	8	9	10	11
12	13	14	15	16
17	18	19	20	21
22	23	24	25	1

(b)

1992

3	4	5	6	7
8	9	10	11	12
13	14	15	16	17
18	19	20	21	22
23	24	25	1	2

(c)

2014

25	1	2	3	4
5	6	7	8	9
10	11	12	13	14
15	16	17	18	19
20	21	22	23	24

(d)

Figure 15.4 Map of a simplified, even-aged, regulated forest over time. Each cell is a separate stand, and the numbers in the cells are stand age.

harvested every four years, and only four different stands would be needed to obtain regulation. One of these stands would be cut each year and each stand would be cut every four years, thus producing a regulated forest and a sustained yield (Figure 15.5).

Rotation age and cutting cycle are terms used to designate when stands are cut. *Rotation age* is the length of time from final harvest cut to final harvest cut in even-aged management. The rotation age in the preceding example is 25 years. Rotation age applies only to even-aged management because there is no *final* harvest cut in uneven-aged management. With the second method a stand always exists

and is only partially harvested each time the stand is cut. The length of time between these major cuts is called the *cutting cycle*. This term applies only to uneven-aged stands. The cutting cycle in the preceding example is four years. Analytical forest management techniques are often used to determine rotation age and cutting cycle.

The Normal Forest

Perhaps the earliest concept of the ideal, regulated, even-aged forest was the "normal forest," developed in Germany and Austria in the mid-nineteenth cen-

Stand 1 Cut in: 1990 1994 1998 . . .	Stand 2 Cut in: 1991 1995 1999 . . .
Stand 3 Cut in: 1992 1996 2000 . . .	Stand 4 Cut in: 1993 1997 2001 . . .

Figure 15.5 Map of a simplified, uneven-aged, regulated forest.

tury. The model was predicated on cutting fairly small, uniform blocks of even-aged timber, and had three requirements. These were that the forest have (1) normal increment (growth), (2) normal age-class distribution, and (3) normal growing-stock levels.

Increment was considered normal if it was the maximum attainable for a particular species on the site. The normal age-class distribution consisted of a series of equally productive stands that varied in age, with the oldest age class equal to the rotation age. These stands were not necessarily the same size because of differences in site productivity. Figure 15.4 is a diagram of a normal age-class distribution if all sites are equally productive, the stands are square, and the rotation is 25 years. Normal growing stock is automatically obtained when the increment and age-class distribution are normal.

The normal forest does not exist in the field but has influenced the thinking of forest managers for many generations. It is the *conceptual model* on which many even-aged forests are based, and it contains several ideas that are prevalent in modern forest management—for example, manipulating the stand's age distribution to obtain an equal annual yield of timber, maximum increment or growth, and uniform rotation age.

Allowable Cut

The *allowable cut* is the amount of timber considered available for cutting during a specified time period, usually one year. It is based on the biological possibilities of the existing stands and the alternatives chosen to obtain a regulated forest. The allowable cut is the amount and species of timber the forest manager would like harvested, but there are many reasons why the cut is not attained. These include fluctuations in the demand for forest products (discussed further later), weather conditions that prevent access to the timber or require cutting timber prematurely to replace inaccessible timber, availability of labor, and so on. The real goal is to achieve the allowable cut over multiple-year periods—for example, a five-year average, which allows for natural fluctuations. Undercutting one year is thus balanced by overcutting in other years.

How Forests Are Managed

Forests are usually managed either by even-aged or uneven-aged systems, although sometimes the two forms are combined in the same forest. Chapter 14, "Silviculture," contains a detailed discussion of these management forms and of *clearcutting*, which is the predominant way even-aged stands are obtained. Briefly, *even-aged management* is the most common management form because

Commercially desirable species are often shade-intolerant or susceptible to windthrow and so grow best in even-aged stands.

There is less expense per unit of volume harvested when clearcutting.

There is less expense to regenerate artificially a clearcut stand, using, for example, site preparation and planting.[1]

Wildlife habitats are encouraged by creating forest openings.

There are, of course, several reasons why *uneven-aged management* may be preferred, as long as the tree species can tolerate the shade generated by this management system. First, small landowners may desire as much of a sustained yield as possible to generate cash more frequently. This is better accomplished with uneven-aged management on small individual holdings. Second, other forest products, such as aesthetic and recreational values, may require continuous forest cover. Finally, diversity of tree species may be enhanced and wildlife habitats improved by providing both food and shelter.

The choice of even-aged or uneven-aged management depends, in the final analysis, on the *landowner's objectives.* Another of the forest manager's jobs is to assist the landowner in analyzing which management form would best suit the owner's objectives. We will emphasize even-aged management because it is the most prevalent and because the concepts are best developed.

Even-Aged Management

Even-aged management conceptually begins with determining *rotation age.* A forest stand grows first at an increasing rate and then at a decreasing rate until it finally levels off and begins to lose volume because of mortality exceeding growth (Figure 15.6). The rotation age must be chosen to accommodate both the landowner's objectives and this growth curve.

Rotation age is determined by first identifying the landowner's objective. The value of this objective is then calculated at each year of a stand's life; the year that produces the *maximum value*[2] is the rotation age. The two most common single objectives are maximizing wood cut and net cash flows, including imputed interest charges.

Maximum wood flow is obtained by maximizing the average annual yield, called *mean annual increment* (MAI) by foresters. The MAI is simply the total volume available for harvest in a particular year divided by the number of years since the stand was established. It would be, for example, the volume found at point V_2 divided by the stand age found at point R_2 in Figure 15.6. The MAI is calculated for all stand ages, and the age at which it is greatest is chosen as the rotation age.

Maximum cash flow is obtained by maximizing the discounted value of expected future cash flows. Cash flows are discounted to allow for the income forgone by investing funds in timber instead of in some other alternative. Discounting also accounts for delaying costs. Many forest economists believe that maximizing *land expectation values* (LEV) is the correct rotation age criterion for both public and private forests (7). The LEV is the residual value of a perpetual forestry investment at a stated interest rate after accounting for all operating and holding costs, other than land value. It is the value remaining after all discounted costs except land have been subtracted from all discounted incomes. Therefore, it sets the maximum price an investor could pay for the bare land and still earn the stated interest rate. The LEV is a more complex criterion than MAI because it includes costs and revenues from perpetual forestry activities, all of which are discounted to allow for the time value of money.

More precisely, if yield (Y) is a function (F) of time (T), then

$$Y = F(T)$$

and

$$\begin{aligned} \text{MAI} &= F(T)/T \\ &= Y/T \end{aligned}$$

---

[1]Artificial regeneration is often preferred to natural reforestation because it usually provides fuller stocking on the site and establishes the new stand more rapidly. On the other hand, it requires a large capital investment that is usually not returned until the end of the rotation. Many small landowners are not willing to bear this cost.

[2]There are various measures of maximum value—for example, maximum average annual value, maximum periodic value, maximum absolute value.

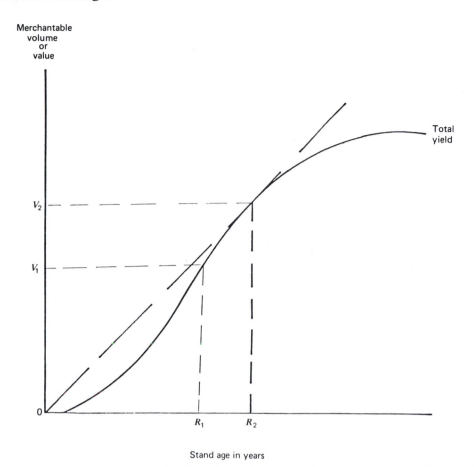

Figure 15.6 Total volume or value growth of merchantable aspen timber on one hectare of land in the Great Lakes states.

A simplified LEV formulation, in which only harvest income and regeneration costs are considered, is

$$LEV = \frac{H - C(1 + i)^r}{(1 + i)^r - 1}$$

where H is harvesting income at rotation age r, C is the regeneration cost to establish the harvested stand, and i is the discount rate. The multiplier $1/(1 + i)^r - 1$ calculates the present value of a perpetual periodic payment occurring r years in the future and every r years thereafter. Notice that the land is assumed bare, and that the same costs and revenues are assumed to occur throughout perpetual rotations.

Rotation age is, again, the stand age when LEV is the greatest. A further discussion of rotation age in which interest rates are taken into account is given in the section on "Timber Culture" in Chapter 24, "The Forest Products Economy."

Rotation ages are for individual stands, but forests are made up of many stands; moreover, it is usually preferable to regulate the entire forest, whether the objective is maximizing the volume of wood harvested, the cash flows, or some other goal. The optimal forest structure for age classes, species, and stocking may be identified in advance. This in itself can be a difficult task. In addition, the manipulation of the forest during the conversion period, when it is being brought to the regulated state, must also be specified. In fact, a forest may never be fully regulated because of additions and subtractions of acreage, changes in owner objectives, changes in technology and utilization standards, and other considerations.

Harvest scheduling specifies the year, or multiple-year period, in which specific stands will be cut. The sum of the cut from all the stands during any time period is the allowable cut for that time period. There are several different ways to determine the harvest schedule and allowable cut. One way is to use *area control,* in which cutting is controlled by specifying the number of acres to cut. The basic idea can be expressed using an oversimplified case with the same rotation age for all stands in the forest. In this case, the total acres in the forest are divided by the rotation age to determine the number of acres per year to be cut. In the preceding example of a 25-acre forest with a 25-year rotation, one acre is cut each year. However, this still does not tell us which stand to cut. Usually, the oldest stand is cut first, but this can be modified by the various factors previously discussed.

Another way to determine the harvest schedule is to use *volume control,* where cutting is controlled by specifying the volume of timber to cut. There are many different formulas to calculate the volume to cut (for example, see reference 8). Most formulas calculate the cut as the sum of the net annual growth on the forest plus or minus an adjustment to increase or decrease the growing stock. Cutting growth and manipulating growing stock seem more in concert with uneven-aged management, discussed later, although volume control can also be used for even-aged management. In any case, the individual stands must again be identified in the forest and scheduled for cutting.

In practice, and particularly for privately owned forests, a combination of area and volume control is used. As mentioned, private owners are often interested in the continuous flow of wood or dollars from their land. They may therefore specify a minimum acceptable level of annual cut with which to modify the acreage cut under an area control scheme. Strict area control may not provide the desired volumes because of understocking or overstocking, differences in site quality and hence yield, and other reasons.

A management plan may be written for all or part of the land owned, depending on the size of ownership. The management plan contains the harvest schedule but is usually broader than a harvesting plan. Its contents will vary by organization, management objectives, and the size of ownership. In fact, some large landowners may have no formal management plan but simply have an idea of which stands will be cut next. Other owners may depend on market demand to determine when they will cut.

The breadth of management plans is indicated by the following outline of major sections (8).

1. Management objectives and policies.

2. Forest description including organization and subdivision, inventory data, growth and yield functions, maps, and narrative descriptions.

3. Economic expectations, including demand for the multiple forest products and supply of productive inputs.

4. Other external factors such as legal restrictions and public policy.

5. Analysis and synthesis of silviculture, regulation and cutting, and multiple-use products.

6. Protection against fire, insects, and disease.

Some sections of the management plan are updated continuously, such as records of cutting and land acquisitions. The entire plan is usually updated on a three- to five-year cycle, generally following the latest continuous forest inventory.

Uneven-Aged Management

The scheme behind uneven-aged management is to determine the desirable level of growing stock for an uneven-aged stand, allow it to grow for a relatively short time (say, 5 or 10 years), and then cut a volume of timber equal to the growth. The forest is regulated by manipulating the stands so that an equal volume of timber is due for cutting each year.

These ideas are expressed in Figure 15.7a, which shows a hypothetical stand with a five-year cutting

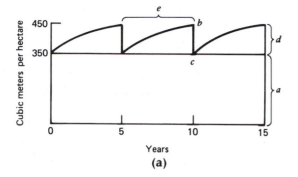

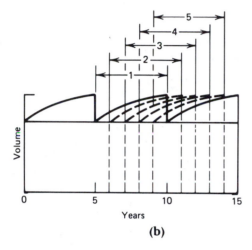

Figure 15.7 (*a*) The cutting cycle for a single stand. (*b*) The cutting cycle for a regulated, uneven-aged forest.

cycle. The *reserve growing stock* is that part of the growing stock reserved (uncut) to produce growth for future cuts, distance *a*. It is 350 cubic meters per hectare in our example. The stand grows to 450 cubic meters during the five years (point *b*) and then is cut back to 350 cubic meters (point *c*). The harvest is $100(450 - 350)$ cubic meters (distance *d*) and the cutting cycle is five years (distance *e*). The cycle continues for as long as the stand is being managed.

The graph for a regulated forest in Figure 15.7*b* is just a series of the individual stands overlaid on each other. In this example, the graphs for five individual stands are overlaid, one stand being cut each year. In

practice, 10, 20, or 100 stands might be cut in any one year.

The concept of uneven-aged management is simple, just like living off the interest from money in the bank. The implementation is far more difficult. Hann and Bare's list of "major decisions" the forest manager must make indicates the complexity (9). These are

1. The optimal, sustainable diameter distribution for a given stand, expressed as number of trees in each diameter class.
2. The optimal species mix for a stand.
3. The optimal cutting cycle length for each stand.
4. The optimal conversion strategy and conversion period length for each stand.
5. The optimal scheduling of compartment treatments and the date of entry for each compartment.

Mathematical Harvest Scheduling

Computers, quantitative analyses, and mathematical planning techniques are firmly a part of both public and industrial forest management. Financial analyses, often in the form of benefit–cost analyses in the public sector, are frequently made to assess investment possibilities ranging from equipment purchases through cultural practices (such as thinning) to land acquisition. We will limit discussion in this section to harvest scheduling and simply mention some applications to multiple-use planning.

Mathematical harvest scheduling has been most widely adopted in even-aged management, although developmental work continues in uneven-aged management (see reference 9 for a discussion). The different stands, or classes of stands, must first be identified for use in even-aged management. Then, all likely management regimes for each stand or stand class are identified. The management regimes detail thinnings, rotation ages, or any other cultural practices that may be performed on the stand. The practices are usually detailed for multiple-year periods so that, for example, period 1 is the first five

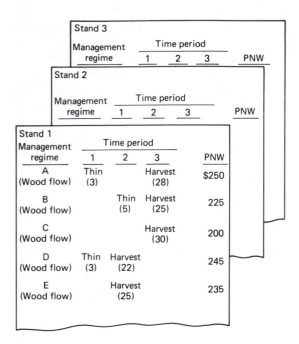

Figure 15.8 Specification of alternative management regimes and objectives values for each stand.

years of a stand's life, period 2 the second five years, and so on. The next step is to calculate the values of the *management objectives* for each management regime for each stand. These objectives might be, for example, wood flow and present net worth (PNW). Thus the forest manager has specified the most likely alternatives for managing the individual stand and has done this for each stand in the forest (Figure 15.8).

These data are then entered into a mathematical program that optimizes an objective or variable. *Linear programs* are most often used because they can efficiently calculate answers for large data sets, are readily available on most computer systems, and are well documented and understood.[3] The linear

program will then either maximize or minimize an objective, such as maximizing present net worth or minimizing cost. The linear programs are also constrained to obtain other management objectives, such as a sustained yield or a fairly constant number of hectares harvested per time period. The answer will tell the forest manager the proportion of each stand to cut by each management regime during each time period to optimize that objective. This becomes a harvest schedule for the forest. The harvest schedule is then checked and modified by the field forester to allow for conditions in the forest that could not be included in the mathematical programming solution.

Several computer programs and algorithms are available for mathematical harvest scheduling. Both optimization and binary-search procedures are available. Optimization procedures *optimize an objective function.* Binary-search procedures *iteratively search* for a solution that will achieve a prespecified set of ending conditions. Optimization procedures include MAX MILLION II (10), Timber RAM (11), and Model I and II (12). Binary-search procedures include TREES (13), ECHO (14), SORAC (15), and SIMAC (16). Harvest-scheduling programs make it less important to establish a rotation schedule (discussed earlier), for many of the procedures choose among several different rotation ages for each stand of trees and pick the combination that optimizes the objective for the whole forest.

External Influences on Timber Management

So far we have been discussing timber management and management objectives as though they were determined solely by either the landowner's personal objectives or the biological and physical limitations of the forest. Another set of factors external to the forest must be considered by forest managers in making decisions. These external influences include the market for forest products, federal and state legislation, and taxation.

---

[3]Linear programming is a mathematical programming technique that either maximizes or minimizes a single, linear objective function. The objective function may be subjected to sets of linear equalities or inequalities, called constraints.

The Market

A major stimulus for private production of salable forest products is their current and prospective price. Just as we see farmers raising more cattle when beef prices are high, forest owners have begun to manage timber more intensively as wood prices have increased.

Some timber output responses to price are very slow because trees take a long time to mature (see Chapter 24, "The Forest Products Economy"). However, many firms and public agencies base their investments in current reforestation and timber stand improvement on projections that real wood prices will be significantly higher in several decades.

In addition, there can be immediate output responses to increased wood prices. For example, in the Northwest red alder was once considered a useless "weed tree." When the furniture industry began using alder, prices rose, and a new resource was available immediately. Similarly, the cut-and-haul cost of some material was more than the selling price, so this material was left in the woods. Much of this material is now harvested because rising wood prices exceed costs. Small trees, thinnings, treetops, and sometimes even branches used in whole-tree chippers are harvested. When wood prices are low, such material is best left in the forest. For example, society is poorly served if $200 is spent on labor, fuel, and equipment to remove and process wood products for which consumers would pay only $150.

Market factors also apply to the resources needed to grow trees. We see less hand planting of trees and more machine planting when labor prices rise relative to equipment prices.

Demand affects whether certain nontimber products are offered. An increased willingness to pay for forest-based recreation has stimulated the sale of hunting permits and leases on private forestlands and more management to improve wildlife. Some landowners have sold or leased forestlands for recreation cabins and campsites.

Certain conditions such as clean air and water, scenic beauty, and dispersed recreation are not so easily sold in the market and are thus not likely to be supplied in optimal quantities from private forests. Thus public agencies tend to concentrate on pro-ducing many of these so-called nonmarket goods. But we also have laws to increase the production of such goods on private lands.

Legislation

One of the most fundamental ways in which the public influences and provides direction to forest management is through legislation. In a broad sense, all of society's laws affect forest management; however, it is possible to identify at least four classes of legislation that have a direct and profound impact on forest management: (1) environmental legislation, (2) health and safety legislation, (3) federal forest management legislation, and (4) state forestry legislation.

Environmental Legislation As discussed in Chapters 1 and 10, the impact of environmental legislation on public forest management has been profound. The National Environmental Policy Act (NEPA) of 1969, which requires environmental impact statements (EIS) for federal lands, is perhaps the most far-reaching single piece of environmental legislation. Legislation to control water and air pollution eliminates some kinds of forestry activities and restricts others.

Safety and Health Legislation Timber management activities characteristically are labor-intensive. All the laws concerning the safety, health, and working conditions of workers apply to timber management activities as well. One of the most important labor laws affecting timber management practices is the Occupational Safety and Health Act of 1970 (OSHA). Perhaps the most important aspect of OSHA for timber management is the health and safety operating standards it imposed on crews engaged in planting, stand improvements, and timber-harvesting activities.

Federal Forest Management Legislation Broad direction and goals for managing public forests are provided by specific legislation at the federal level for federal forestlands and the state level for state lands. Three federal laws are particularly important in the management of the national forests: the Multiple Use–Sustained Yield (MU–SY) Act of 1960, the Forest and Rangeland Renewable Resources Planning Act (RPA) of 1974, and the National Forest Management Act (NFMA) of 1976. A detailed description of the effect of these acts on forest management is given in Chapters 1 and 10.

State Forestry Laws A number of states have laws regulating forestry practices on private forestlands. The scope of these laws ranges from the very broad forest practices laws of California, Oregon, and Washington—which regulate forestry practices from the harvesting and regeneration of timber to environmental protection—to laws for achieving a specific, limited goal, such as the reforestation of forestlands. Thus differences in state forestry laws cause variation in timber management practices across the states.

Taxation

Taxes yield revenues for governments to supply goods and services that citizens feel are best provided by the public sector. Forest owners share in this responsibility by paying local property taxes on their land, state and federal income taxes on forest revenues, and death taxes on inherited forests.

Some foresters have long sought the ideal combination of tax incentives to stimulate "needed" timber production. However, others have pointed out that the same argument can be made for stimulating production of all "needed" products. The difficulty is in identifying how badly a product is needed in relation to other products. Consumer needs are usually expressed through higher product prices, which in turn stimulate production. Many economists have suggested neutral taxes that do not favor one industry over another for the price mechanism to work most efficiently.

Local Government Taxes The *property tax* levied annually on real estate values is a major source of local government revenue. In principle such values include timber, but in practice much timber value has escaped property taxation. Taxing authorities

often have problems in determining and keeping pace with constantly changing timber values. Forest owners have sometimes harvested timber prematurely to reduce taxes in areas where full timber values have been taxed annually.

Practical experience and theoretical studies have demonstrated that an annual property tax on full timber value is usually more discouraging to forestry than to other land uses with annual incomes. Thus the property tax on forests is almost always reduced, modified, or supplemented by another form of tax. One modification of the property tax is to allow forestland to be taxed at *forestry values* instead of at higher development values. This is often done to encourage open-space land use.

Another modification is the *yield tax* levied in several states in place of the timber property tax. This tax is levied as a percentage of harvest value when timber is cut. Yield taxes are often advocated because they do not stimulate premature timber cutting.

Another alternative is the *productivity tax*. This tax is paid annually at a different level for each productivity class of forestland; the greater the land productivity, the higher the tax. In theory, this tax does not penalize good management because the tax is always the same for any given site, no matter how much timber is grown or harvested. Proponents therefore claim it is an incentive for good forest management.

Income Taxes Before January 1987, income from the sale of assets held longer than six months—most timber income—was taxed at federal rates lower than those for other "ordinary income." However, since January 1987, federal income tax rates have been the same for long-term and short-term gains. The new tax rates as of July 1987 are 34 percent for corporations, and 15, 28, or 33 percent for individuals, depending on income levels. Most states also levy taxes on timber harvest income, with maximum rates usually in the 5 to 10 percent range.

Death Taxes A federal estate tax is paid on a decedent's forest property. Starting January 1988, a tax of 37 percent will be paid on estates over

$600,000, rising to 50 percent of estates over $2.5 million. Up to certain limits, federal estate taxes are reduced by the amount of state death taxes. However, several states levy taxes beyond these limits.

References

1. J. Buongiorno and J. K. Gilless, *Forest Management and Economics: A Primer in Quantitative Methods,* Macmillan, New York, 1987.

2. J. L. Clutter, J. C. Fortson, L. V. Pienaar, G. H. Brister, and R. L. Bailey, *Timber Management: A Quantitative Approach,* John Wiley & Sons, New York, 1983.

3. L. S. Davis and K. N. Johnson, *Forest Management,* Third Edition, McGraw–Hill, New York, 1984.

4. D. R. Dykstra, *Mathematical Programming for Natural Resource Management,* McGraw–Hill, New York, 1984.

5. W. A. Leuschner, *Introduction to Forest Resource Analysis,* John Wiley & Sons, New York, 1984.

6. F. C. Ford-Robertson, ed., *Terminology of Forest Science, Technology, Practice and Products,* Soc. Am. Foresters, Washington, D.C., 1983.

7. W. Linnard and M. Gane, "Martin Faustmann and the evolution of discounted cash flow: Two articles from the original German of 1849," Commonwealth Forestry Institute, University of Oxford, Oxford, 1968.

8. K. P. Davis, *Forest Management: Regulation and Valuation,* Second Edition, McGraw–Hill, New York, 1966.

9. D. W. Hann and B. B. Bare, "Uneven-aged forest management: State of the art (or science?)," U.S.D.A. For. Serv., Gen. Tech. Rept. INT-50, Intermountain For. Range Expt. Sta., Ogden, Utah, 1979.

10. J. L. Clutter, J. C. Fortson, and L. V. Pienaar, "A computerized forest management planning system, user's manual," University of Georgia, Athens, 1978.

11. D. I. Navon, "Timber RAM: A long-range planning method for commercial timber lands under multiple-use management," U.S.D.A. For. Serv. Res. Pap. PSW-70, Berkeley, Calif., 1971.

12. K. N. Johnson and H. L. Scheurman, "Techniques for prescribing optimal timber harvest and investment under different objectives—discussion and synthesis," *For. Sci. Monogr., 18,* 1–31, 1977.

13. P. L. Tedder, J. S. Schmidt, and J. Gourley, "TREES: Timber resource economic estimation system," Vol. 1, "A user's manual for forest management and harvest scheduling," Res. Bull. 31a, School of Forestry, Oregon State University, Corvallis, 1980.

14. J. L. Walker, "ECHO: Solution technique for a nonlinear economic harvest optimization model." In *Systems Analysis and Forest Resource Management,* J. C. Meadows, B. B. Bare, K. Ware, and C. Row, eds., Soc. Am. Foresters, Bethesda, Md., 1975.

15. D. E. Chappelle, "A computer program for scheduling allowable cut using either area or volume regulation during sequential planning periods," U.S.D.A. For. Serv., Res. Pap. PNW-33, Portland, Ore., 1966.

16. R. W. Sassaman, W. E. Holt, and K. Bergsvick, "User's manual for a computer program for simulating intensively managed allowable cut," U.S.D.A. For. Serv., Gen. Tech. Rept. PNW-1, Portland, Ore., 1972.

CHAPTER 16

Harvesting

THOMAS A. WALBRIDGE, JR.
ROBERT M. SHAFFER

Harvesting Systems

Tree Processing

Skidding, Forwarding, and Yarding

Loading

Hauling

Reference

Harvesting timber from a forest site, or "logging," is a critical step in the management of many forests (1). It marks the transition from forestry to forest products. A timber harvest is the primary tool forest landowners can employ to attain many of their timber management objectives. This important process is necessary to

Supply raw material to the forest industry.

Provide landowners with a financial return from their timber investment.

Perform certain silvicultural functions such as controlling species composition and stocking levels or regenerating a new timber stand.

Salvage usable wood fiber from trees killed by fire, insects, or disease.

In the eastern United States the actual cutting, processing, and removing of trees from the forest, along with their transport to a delivery point, are usually performed by independent logging contractors. These small business operators play a vital role in the overall wood supply system throughout this region. Typically, procurement foresters, or timber buyers, employed in large numbers by the forest industry, purchase standing timber, or stumpage, from many small private forest landowners. These foresters then negotiate timber harvesting or "cut

and haul" contracts with independent logging contractors who provide timber harvesting services for the forest industry firms. A few large forest products firms employ company-owned logging operations to supplement their force of independent contractors, to test new harvesting equipment or systems, or to carry out specific or unique harvest objectives.

In the West, where public timber ownership prevails, a combination of independent logging contractors and company-owned crews is the norm. As in the East, timberland owners or their agents are generally responsible for specifying harvesting contract provisions, designating timber sale boundaries, and monitoring contract compliance.

To remain in business, logging contractors must be profit-oriented. However, they must do so while complying with a host of federal, state, and local regulations covering nearly every phase of their operation. The public is placing more and more emphasis on loggers' adhering to "best management practices" to minimize the soil erosion and site degradation resulting from the construction of logging roads, skid trails, and loading areas. Principles of engineering, economics, and operations research are used to design machines and systems that can harvest timber efficiently over a wide range of sites and conditions, while limiting soil and site disturbance, minimizing damage to residual timber stands, and fully utilizing the forest resource.

Harvesting Systems

The harvesting of forest products consists of four major phases: (1) processing the tree, (2) moving the tree or its segments to a concentration point, (3) loading the tree or its segments for final transport, and (4) hauling the tree or its segments to a delivery point. Each phase generally consists of one or more functions. For example, processing the tree includes the functions of felling, limbing, and bucking it with a chainsaw or felling and bunching it with a machine (Table 16.1).

Harvesting functions are combined to form the harvesting systems that best fit the timber, terrain, harvesting conditions, and market demands in a given forest region. The resulting systems are usually identified by their delivered product (Table 16.2).

Shortwood, pulpwood bolts ranging from 60 to 100 inches (150 to 250 centimeters) in length.

Longwood, random-length pulpwood of 10 to 20 feet (3 to 6 meters) or measured sawlog lengths.

Tree length, entire delimbed tree bole.

Whole-tree chips, chips produced by feeding large portions of trees into chippers brought to the woods.

In addition, a few experimental operations in the South are currently delivering whole trees, including limbs and foliage, to mills to assess the potential of this method of complete utilization.

Tree Processing

The tree-processing phase of harvesting usually includes severing the tree from its stump, or *felling* it, and removing its limbs, *delimbing;* it may include segmenting the bole to various product lengths, called *bucking,* or processing the tree into chips, called *whole-tree chipping.*

Large-diameter timber is usually felled with chainsaws. Where terrain permits, smaller trees—up to 24 inches (61 centimeters) in diameter at groundline—are felled with hydraulic shears or

Table 16.1 Phases and Functions of Harvesting Operations

Phase	Function	Description
Preparing tree	Felling	Sever tree from its stump.
	Limbing	Remove limbs and top from felled tree.
	Bucking	Cut tree into segments.
	Debarking	Remove bark from tree.
	Chipping	Make chips from tree or segments.
Moving tree to concentration point	Piling	Pile tree segments for in-woods loading.
	Bunching	Put trees or segments in bunches before skidding, prehauling, or yarding.
	Skidding	Move tree or segment, dragging all or part of load on ground.
	Prehauling	Move tree or segment, with whole load off ground.
	Yarding	Move tree or segment using wire rope and stationary machine.
Loading tree for hauling	Sorting	Divided trees or segments into products before loading.
	In-woods loading	Load tree or segment on prehauler in woods.
	Unload at landing	Remove trees or segments from prehauler at landing. A landing is a concentration point where trees are loaded for hauling.
Hauling tree to market	Load for haul	Place trees or tree segments on trucks for haul to market point.
	Hauling	Drive truck from landing to market point.
	Unloading	Remove tree or segments from haul truck at market point.
	Scaling	Measure or weigh tree or segments to determine volume of wood delivered.

Table 16.2 Harvesting Systems Classified by Product Form

Function Performed	Shortwood		Longwood		Full Tree	
	Woods Bucking	Landing Bucking	Random or Multiple Length	Tree Length	Partial-Tree Chipping	Total-Tree Chipping
In woods	Fell, limb, buck	Fell, limb	Fell, limb	Fell, limb	Fell	Fell
	Load, prehaul, or yard	Skid or yard	Skid, prehaul, or yard	Skid, prehaul, or yard	Skid, prehaul, or yard	Skid or yard
At landing	Unload, load, haul	Buck, load, haul	Buck, load, haul	Load, haul	Limb, debark, chip, load, haul	Chip, load, haul

sawheads mounted on rubber-tired or excavator-based carriers (Figure 16.1). Most felling machines are capable of bunching the sheared trees to facilitate in-woods transport. Concern that the sheared ends of sawlogs will be damaged by compression has led to the recent development of alternative sawheads of various designs for *feller-bunchers*.

Most delimbing is done manually with chainsaws, but the frequency of injuries from this dangerous process has led to the development of mechanical

Figure 16.1 Mechanized felling with hydraulic shears transported on a rubber-tired carrier.

Figure 16.2 A stroke delimber removes limbs with a telescoping boom.

devices. A common method in southern pine operations is to use the skidder to push trees backward through a steel gate or grid (delimbing gate), which effectively breaks the branches from the bole. One of the newest machines is the stroke delimber, which uses a telescoping boom with delimbing knives to remove the limbs from the tree (Figure 16.2).

Manual *bucking* with chainsaws is still widespread, but as in limbing, the desire to reduce injuries has led to alternative methods. In one of the most common methods of mechanical bucking, or *slashing,* the material to be bucked is placed in a frame by the grapple loader (Figure 16.3). The hydraulic power from the loader drives the bucking saw.

Whole-tree, or in-woods chipping, is an extremely efficient and effective method of biomass recovery and greatly facilitates site preparation. Boles, limbs, tops, and foliage or any portion thereof are fed into the chipper at the landing, and the chips are blown directly into vans for transport (Figure 16.4). Whole-tree chips may be used as the raw material for pulp mills at some locations, but the predominant use is as fuel for producing energy (see Chapter 23). High-quality sawlog material is removed before the remainder of the tree is chipped.

Skidding, Forwarding, and Yarding

In tree length operations the delimbed bole or the whole tree is usually moved to a concentration point or landing by rubber-tired or tracked machines called *skidders* (Figure 16.5). Skidding is defined as the movement of material when all or part of the load is in contact with the ground. For logging in the United States, skidding is the predominant method of ground-based in-woods transport.

In some instances trees are bucked to shortwood or longwood at or near the stump and are trans-

Figure 16.3 Grapple loader and bucking operation.

ported to the landing by rubber-tired or tracked *prehaulers* or *forwarders*. These machines are usually equipped with a loading device for in-woods loading at the stump and off-loading at the landing (Figure 16.6). Prehauling or forwarding is defined as a movement of material in which all the load is carried clear of the ground. Forwarding is quite common in Europe.

When the terrain is too steep or the soils are too fragile to accommodate ground machines, material may be moved in complete suspension by cable systems, balloons, or helicopters (Figure 16.7). These methods are usually more expensive than

skidding or forwarding and may be uneconomical for certain low-value timber stands.

Cable yarding systems employ rotating drums of wire rope mounted on stationary power units. The logs are brought to these machines, called yarders, rather than the machines moving to the logs. In one basic cable logging configuration the choker, the noose of wire rope for hauling the log, is attached to another wire rope that runs through an elevated pulley or *block*. This arrangement is called a *high-lead system*. In the *skyline system* the choker is attached to a carriage supported by a wire rope suspended between two points of elevation. Both

Figure 16.4 A whole-tree chipper converts the entire tree into chips, which are blown into a van for transport.

systems are depicted schematically in Figure 16.8. The logs are transported to the landing by reeling in the wire ropes with the large stationary yarders. Elevation for the systems is provided either by large, standing spar trees or by portable steel towers (Figure 16.9). There are many variations of cable yarding systems. Cable yarding is a widely used logging technique in the steep, mountainous forests of the Pacific Northwest.

Loading

Except for a very small amount of hand-loaded shortwood pulpwood and firewood, forest products are loaded mechanically onto haul trucks by cable or

Figure 16.5 Skidders are used to transport felled trees to the landing.

Figure 16.6 A prehauler or forwarder is used to transport bucked logs from the stump to the landing.

hydraulic devices. Smaller hydraulic loaders are usually mounted on trucks and run off the truck's power takeoff. Machines used to load longwood and tree-length material are generally independently mounted and hydraulically powered (Figure 16.3). The largest knuckleboom or hydraulic loader models are often mounted on self-powered carriers, making them highly mobile.

Prehaulers and forwarders are usually equipped with knuckleboom loaders for loading material processed at or near the stump (in-woods loading) and for off-loading material onto pallets or trucks at the landing.

Modern knuckleboom loaders are highly efficient and productive. As such, they are often the most underutilized piece of equipment on a mechanized logging job. Some models can now be equipped with weighing devices that will accumulate the net weight on the truck or trailer as it is loaded. Each truck can carry its maximum payload and yet avoid being overloaded, and the logger will not be confronted with overweight fines.

Figure 16.7 Harvesting is sometimes done by helicopter in inaccessible areas and for steep terrains. (Courtesy of U.S.D.A. Forest Service.)

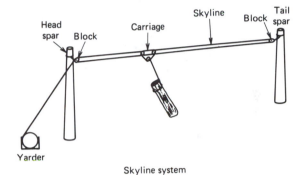

Figure 16.8 Schematic diagrams of the basic high-lead and skyline yarding systems.

Hauling

Trucking is one of the most visible and highly regulated phases of harvesting. As such, it can be a very expensive operation and often represents 50 percent or more of the delivered cost of the raw material. Many high-production logging contractors hire trucking subcontractors to haul their wood. Medium-sized to small-sized contractors usually do their own hauling.

Selection of the proper truck to fit the products hauled, distances covered, road conditions, and loading and unloading facilities is critical for hauling

Figure 16.9 High-lead logging uses a spar tree to support cables and pulleys for moving logs from the stump to the central deck. This cable logging system is powered by a stationary diesel unit and winches. (Courtesy of American Forest Institute.)

Figure 16.10 A tractor-trailer for the transportation of tree length material.

efficiency. Common vehicles for trucking are a tractor with a rigid frame or pole trailer (Figure 16.10), a rigid-frame tandem log truck, or a tractor equipped with a self-loading pole trailer.

The forest industry of the United States is dependent on a healthy and efficient logging force. The men and women who make their living daily in this difficult and dangerous work deserve the respect and admiration of the entire forestry community. They are the Paul Bunyans of the twentieth century.

Reference

1. C. STENZEL, T. A. WALBRIDGE, JR., AND J. K. PEARCE, *Logging and Pulpwood Production,* Second Edition, John Wiley & Sons, New York, 1985.

CHAPTER 17

Forest—Wildlife Interactions

GORDON W. GULLION

Forests provide the basic habitat for a large proportion of the world's wildlife. Trees are important as a source of food and protection from the weather and other animals. Forests also have a stabilizing effect on the streamflow that provides habitats for fish. Dead fallen leaves, branches, and trunks provide crucial habitats or resources for many animals, in addition to being favorable sites for seedling growth, soil stabilization, and nutrient recycling. Taken together these elements constitute *wildlife habitat,* which may be a specific forest type such as a beech–maple forest, or a mixed forest such as a spruce–fir stand intermixed with pine and aspen-–birch. Within each habitat each species of wildlife uses a particular portion, or its niche. The *ecological niche* of an organism depends not only on where it lives but also on what it does.

Some forms of wildlife need the stems and leaves of woody plants growing in full sunlight within a meter or two of the forest floor. Young trees are especially important as food for deer, wapiti (or elk), and moose. These *primary consumers* or *herbivores* feed on the succulent stems and leaves of the growing shoots in summer and on the dormant stems in winter. Predators are *secondary consumers* or *carnivores* that consume little plant material but use trees as cover for their hunting, and for nests or dens while feeding on the herbivores or other carnivores.

Introduction

The relationship between forest and wildlife is so intertwined and complex that little can be done to a forest that does not have an impact on some form of wildlife. One obvious impact is the effect of clearcutting or burning a forest. The habitat of some animals is lost; cover and nesting or denning sites are removed, and seed-producing or fruit-producing trees are destroyed. But clearcutting also creates essential habitats for other species.

There is also an impact on wildlife populations when a forest is allowed to proceed toward climax through normal succession (see Chapter 6). The larger herbivorous species dependent on low-growing plant forms diminish and are replaced by a greater diversity of small carnivorous animals feeding mostly on other animals.

Thus the concept of what is "good" or "bad" forest management for wildlife may vary according to the outlook or preferences of the individual viewing the situation. A practice bad for one group of species may be good for others. The forest management scheme favorable for ruffed grouse, woodcock, and white-tailed deer in the Great Lakes states, for exam-ple, would be detrimental to wood ducks, bald eagles, and Kirtland's warblers.

Wildlife Values

Animals are an integral part of the forest scene, but it is difficult to assign a monetary value to a bald eagle, a flying squirrel, or a chorus of howling timber wolves. Yet several hundred forms of American wildlife are so valued that millions of hectares of commercial timberland are reserved from harvesting in the United States, partly to preserve wildlife habitats.

A national survey of participants in wildlife-associated recreation showed that about 24 million Americans hunted big and small game in 1980 (1). Expenditures for equipment, lodging, food, and transportation in pursuit of forest-associated game exceeded $4.5 billion in 1980. This same study showed that 36 million Americans spent $7.8 billion during 711 million days of freshwater fishing.

A 1971 study in the southeastern United States showed that 11 million out of 16 million households received enjoyment from 472 million days of fishing, hunting, bird watching, and other wildlife-related activities (2). A similar analysis on the Bridger–Teton National Forest in Wyoming indicated that 188,700 recreation days of hunting had a value of $9.3 million during the fall 1977 season. This compares with an estimated timber harvest value from Wyoming of about $14 million statewide in 1975 (personal communication from J. J. Harju).

In addition to the value generated by hunting game animals, the nonconsumptive use of wildlife has become increasingly important. The 1980 national survey showed that more than 93 million Americans participated in wildlife-associated recreation (1). An estimated $14.7 billion were spent in 1980 by persons engaged in "nonconsumptive wildlife-associated recreational activities." Part of that was an estimated $636 million spent for field guides, bird feeders and nest boxes, and birdseed.

Although it is difficult to place a dollar value on finding an osprey nest, hearing a pileated woodpecker call, or hunting an elusive white-tailed deer, these intangible values have a very real influence on how forest managers treat woodlands.

Characteristics of Wildlife

The primary drive for each animal is to survive long enough to *perpetuate its kind.* The animal must consume sufficient nutritious food to sustain it in a thrifty condition until that goal is accomplished. Every animal requires some form of protection from the physical environment or from other animals, and usually from both. Few animals smaller than adult grizzly bears, bald eagles, horned owls, wolves, and mountain lions terminate their existence with a quiet, painless death. Most animals die violent deaths to provide nourishment for other animals (Figure 17.1).

One important difference between plants and animals is the mobility of animals, which allows them to move about seeking food, shelter, and a mate. A concept underlying the discussion throughout this chapter is that the less an individual animal has to move to meet its basic needs, the longer it is likely to survive, and the greater the opportunity to pass its genetic constitution on to a succeeding generation.

Figure 17.1 The site of energy transfer from a primary consumer to a secondary consumer. A ruffed grouse was killed and eaten here by a great horned owl. The owl did not waste much of the grouse.

Population Dynamics Wildlife has annual *cycles of abundance* much like those of annual plants. Numbers are greatest following the hatching of eggs or the birth of young, usually in late spring or early summer. Then numbers decline, the rates varying from species to species and from year to year.

If a population is to remain static, there must be as many alive to produce young the next season as were alive the preceding year. This means that from the parents and fourteen eggs in a wood duck nest, only two need be alive the following spring—a 12 percent survival. Among ruffed grouse two of ten must survive, a 20 percent survival; but for bluebirds two of seven need to survive, a 28 percent survival.

In addition to the annual population cycle, there are longer-term *cyclic fluctuations* among some wildlife populations. In North America the best known of these is the *ten-year cycle,* most evident among snowshoe hares and ruffed grouse (3). Longer-term population fluctuations are most dramatic in regions where environmental stresses are most severe, such as cold northern or arid western regions. Lynx and other predators feeding largely on the hares or grouse also fluctuate in numbers, usually lagging a year or two behind the population changes in the prey species.

The regularity of these cycles is shown by the history of ruffed grouse in Minnesota. During the past half century, numbers of these birds peaked in 1923, 1933, 1941–1942, 1951, 1960–1961, 1971–1972, and in 1980–1981. Populations of these grouse are usually lowest about three to four years after the peaks.

Although much attention has been given to these periodic fluctuations for many years, the basic causes are still uncertain. Wildlife cycles were formerly believed to be the result of overhunting or disease epidemics; as wildlife research expanded, however, it became evident that hunting is extremely unlikely to be a factor, and disease is seldom implicated.

These so-called cycles of animal populations have been associated with a number of different influences, including sunspot activity and lunar cycles, variations in the nutrient quality of the primary forage plants, and the genetic constitution of the animals. A number of other possibilities include predator–prey interaction, fire and forest succession, and climate and weather factors (4).

Although the causes for these periodic changes in animal abundance may be beyond our control, it is important to be aware that they occur. The best-planned habitat management scheme can appear to fail if timing coincides with a regionwide cyclic decline of the target species.

Interactions among Forest Wildlife

Just as trees compete with one another for space, food, water, and sunlight, wildlife living in the forest interact with one another. These interactions occur at two levels, *intraspecifically* and *interspecifically*, and may be expressed as either *competitive* or *consumptive* interaction. At both levels the character of the forest habitat has an influence on how well wildlife maintains viable population levels.

Most wildlife requires certain amounts of space or *territory* to meet its needs. Animals usually have to maintain an aggressive stance to defend territories. This is the purpose of most birdsong in the spring. Many mammals, as well as some reptiles and amphibians, maintain scent posts or other signs to mark territorial boundaries.

The territory may be that of a single individual, a pair, or even a flock or pack, depending on the species. This behavior can serve to isolate a pair to allow undisturbed reproductive activity or to reserve sufficient food and cover resources to allow an individual, a pair, or a pack to survive the winter. Thus territorial behavior often limits animal abundance and density. Mountain lions in Idaho may need from 200 to 400 square kilometers for their territory (5), whereas a red squirrel in Alaska may need only 0.65 hectares (6). Territorial behavior usually represents intraspecific interaction, but interspecific competition also occurs. As timber wolves have expanded their range in northern Minnesota, coyotes have disappeared from those areas.

Consumptive interaction is predation and most often is interspecific. However, most predators occasionally kill and eat their own kind. Cannibalism among siblings appears to be frequent in the nests of hawks and owls when the parents are unable to find enough prey to feed the nestlings.

The effect of predation on wildlife populations has long been controversial. For many years it was felt that all predators (anything that killed other animals) were "bad." Then various studies, especially those of Errington (7), began to suggest that predation was less important than some other factors in limiting wildlife abundance. These studies reinforced the concept of *carrying capacity* put forward in 1933 by Aldo Leopold, widely considered the founder of modern game management in the United States (8).

Basically, carrying capacity is the number of individuals of a species that can survive in a given unit of habitat secure from predation. It is a measure of the adequacy of food and other resources in relation to secure cover. Once a prey species has been reduced to carrying capacity, it is no longer profitable for predators to continue hunting these animals. But rather than being a fixed entity, carrying capacity varies from site to site; on the same site it may vary from year to year depending on the food available, the quality of the cover, and even snow conditions and depth.

Predators enforce carrying capacity, and in the absence of predators some wildlife may become abundant in habitats that otherwise would be marginal. In the Cloquet Research Forest in northern Minnesota, ruffed grouse reached a greater abundance in an aspen–pine forest when goshawks were not nesting in that forest but then declined sharply when these raptors returned. At the same time, grouse living in sapling aspen stands distant from coniferous cover remained relatively secure from raptor predation (9).

Recently Keith and Rusch (10) have developed an impressive argument suggesting that predation by goshawks and other boreal raptors plays a significant role in the cyclic fluctuations of snowshoe hares and ruffed grouse in central Canada and the north-central United States, seemingly independent of the carrying capacity of the habitat.

When big-game animals are living in the absence of their normal predators, the quantity of adequate forage resources needed to maintain the animals in a thrifty, productive condition determines the carrying capacity. In the absence of effective predation among small-game species, territorial behavior supplants carrying capacity as a factor limiting population size. Under these conditions the food and cover resources may have the capacity to support a considerably higher population of a species than intraspecific aggression will permit.

Predation is largely *opportunistic;* that is, it most often occurs when the predator has an advantage. Predation is markedly heavier along the edges between forests and openings, and especially along trails and roadways. Young animals are usually much more vulnerable than adults to predators (and hunters). Minnesota studies have shown that the percentage loss among young ruffed grouse over a seven-month period from the middle of September to the middle of April is as great as the loss among adult grouse over a twelve-month period, and numerically is about 3.4-fold greater on a monthly basis (11).

Wildlife Use of Forests

Dependency on Forests

Use of a forest by an animal may be *obligatory,* meaning that the animal cannot exist in its wild form without trees; or use may be *facultative* or *discretionary,* implying that the animal may use trees if they are available, but can survive without them.

Obligatory Use Among North American terrestrial wildlife about one-half the birds and several mammals have an obligatory relationship to trees or forest cover. Of some 567 species of birds on the continent, at least 272 can be considered to have an obligatory relationship with trees. Similarly, of the 348 species of mammals in North America north of Mexico, about 49 have an obligatory relationship to trees (Table 17.1).

Trees provide all the needs of many birds and some mammals. Most woodpeckers nest in holes excavated in trees, and usually their food consists of insects collected on or in trees. But the common flicker, a type of woodpecker, does much of its feeding on the ground, while depending on trees for nesting. Chickadees and nuthatches also nest in tree

Table 17.1 Numbers of Species of North American Warm-Blooded Vertebrates Dependent on Trees[a]

Normal Habitat		Birds Considered Tree Obligates			Mammals Considered Tree Obligates	
	Total	Food	Nest	Total	Food	Nest
Aquatic	82	0	13	4	1	0
Shoreline	65	0	11	5	0	0
Marshes	19	0	0	37	0	0
Grasslands and tundra	83	0	27	184	0	0
Brush	91	0	14	42	0	0
Trees						
Single or groups[b]	0	0	41	6	6	0
Forests	178	159	160	34	27	23
Aerial foragers	49	0	29	39	1	6

[a]This table differs from Yeager (12) primarily in the separation of brush-inhabiting species from tree-associated species.
[b]These are primarily animals depending on grasslands or brush for their food resources and using trees for nesting.

cavities, and their food consists largely of eggs, larvae, pupae, and adult insects taken from the bark, branches, and foliage of trees. Two species of swallows, purple martins, and swifts use cavities in trees for nesting, but all their feeding is on insects in flight. Gray, flying, red, and pine squirrels depend on trees for their nests as well as for most of their food. Raccoons commonly use tree cavities for their dens but do most of their foraging on the ground.

Facultative or Discretionary Use Several animals utilize trees when use is convenient, but they can survive quite well in the absence of a forest. Ravens will nest in heavy forest cover or on cliffs and rock outcrops, and both black ducks and mallards occasionally use trees for nesting but normally nest on the ground.

Some other species use isolated trees or small groves but avoid a forest consisting of more than a few dozen trees. Examples are mourning doves and magpies.

Some species of wildlife have aversions to trees, or some types of trees. The Midwest's sharp-tailed grouse will abandon long-used, traditional dancing grounds or "leks" if conifer growth exceeds 6 meters within 400 meters of such a site. Still, the catkins and buds of several deciduous trees are important sources of winter food for these birds.

Nutritional Needs Supplied to Wildlife by the Forest

Plant Materials Consumed by Wildlife Probably few trees are not used as food by some form of wildlife at one time or another. Among 224 herbivores (birds and mammals) examined in the most comprehensive wildlife study of food habits made in North America, resources provided by trees constituted an important part of the diet of 89 species, or 40 percent of the total (13).

This study found that oak acorns were used most often and occurred in the diet of at least ninety-six species of wildlife. Other trees used as food by more than twenty-five species of animals include pines, cherries, hackberries, junipers, mulberries, maples, blackgum, beech, and aspen. The fruit or seeds of these trees are the parts usually used as food by wildlife (except for aspen). Collectively these are called *mast,* and for many species of wildlife the annual mast crop is a major determinant of their abundance from year to year.

A reduction in the mast crop can result in a scarcity of the less mobile squirrels, and in some regions deer may suffer. Several species of birds are nomadic, and their wanderings and even breeding activities depend on the regional vagaries of mast production. Most notable among these are the crossbills, pine siskins, evening grosbeaks, and the West's pinyon jay.

Where snow is an important part of the winter environment, resident wildlife depends on other parts of plants for sustenance. The herbivorous mammals such as hares, deer, and moose depend on shrubby plants or the young growth of trees for their food resource, and they take the stems and twigs of these throughout the winter. Beaver and porcupines feed mostly on the bark and cambium layer of various trees.

Because the seeds of most northern deciduous trees are shed when mature and are buried under the snow, only birds such as siskins, redpolls and crossbills, which extract seeds from cones, can survive as seed consumers. A few other birds survive in snow country by feeding on other plant materials. Two North American grouse, the western blue and the boreal forest's spruce grouse, feed throughout the winter on the needles of various firs, spruces, and pines. The ruffed and sharp-tailed grouse survive the winter feeding on flower buds or aments of a few deciduous trees and shrubs, especially those of the aspens, birches, and cherries and of the filbert and hophornbeam (Figure 17.2). One songbird, the western Cassin finch, is dependent on aspen flower buds in some areas, and evening grosbeaks and purple finches also feed on these buds. Pine grosbeaks feed on the vegetative buds of jack pine. The other birds permanently resident in these regions are the insectivorous chickadees, nuthatches, and woodpeckers, the scavenging jays and ravens, and the predatory hawks and owls.

Figure 17.2 Three important winter food resources for wildlife in northern regions. *Top:* The staminate flower buds of trembling aspen are an important food for ruffed and sharp-tailed grouse and are used by blue grouse as well. In some regions these buds are important to Cassin finches, and elsewhere they are used by evening grosbeaks and purple finches. In spring the extending catkins are often consumed by black bears fresh out of hibernation. *Center:* The staminate catkins of paper birch are used mostly by ruffed and sharp-tailed grouse. The seed-laden female cones are often torn apart by feeding pine siskins and redpolls. *Bottom:* The staminate catkins of the beaked filbert are heavily used by ruffed grouse when aspen flower buds are not available.

Food Provided by Forest Litter and Debris

Dead portions of the forest provide important or even critical resources for many species of wildlife. Decaying litter on the forest floor provides the organic material to nourish many invertebrate animals, ranging from microscopic nematodes to quite large insects. In addition, many saprophitic plants ranging from bacteria to the various fungi, and even a group of higher ericaceous or heath plants, utilize these nutrient resources. These are also primary consumers, at the base of a *food chain* that supports a pyramid of secondary consumers.

Although ruffed grouse and the other forest grouse are normally herbivores, their newly hatched chicks are wholly dependent on the invertebrate fauna on the forest floor for their first five or six weeks of life; lacking this resource, the chicks will perish.

But all types of forest litter are not equally valuable as a nutrient base for the primary consumers and their predators. An important portion of the summer diet of young and adult woodcock consists of a few species of earthworms that live in the forest litter atop the mineral soil. The concentration of earthworms in the rich litter under aspen gives woodcocks a marked summer preference for aspen stands. Most amphibians (salamanders, frogs, and toads) as well as several species of snakes, lizards, and small rodents and shrews also depend on the invertebrate animals living among decaying forest debris.

Cover Provided by the Forest

Protection from Environmental Factors The protection from weather that trees provide, shade on a hot summer day or shelter from a heavy rainstorm, is important. Forest cover also provides less obvious but more important benefits.

A large part of North America's forestland lies in cold regions where snow usually covers the ground for three to six months each winter, so it is appropriate to examine how animals dependent on the forest survive this season. Many birds and bats simply migrate to warmer climates, some going as far as South America. In mountain areas this migration may be no more than moving downslope a few kilometers to snow-free lower elevations.

The cold-blooded amphibians and reptiles and

Figure 17.3 A jack pine cone cache made by a red squirrel in the fall. This and other caches will provide food through the winter for the squirrel, which will vigorously defend a territory to protect its stored food supply.

many mice, chipmunks, ground squirrels, raccoons, and bears hibernate for the winter. These animals accummulate fat in the fall, enter a burrow, cave, or den, and reduce body functions (including heart-beat, respiration, and temperature) to such a level that stored fat will meet their energy needs all winter. Although they remain relatively alert and active through the winter, white-tailed deer enter a state of semihibernation, with a marked reduction in the pace of body function.

Animals that are active all winter rely on other means of coping with low temperatures and scarce food resources. Tree squirrels store supplies of cones, acorns, or nuts (Figure 17.3); beaver store a

winter's food supply in the mud on the bottom of their pond. Ruffed grouse cope with winter cold by spending as much time as possible in a snow burrow made by plunging headlong into the snow from full flight (Figure 17.4). Voles, pocket gophers, and other rodents remain active all winter, creating a labyrinth of tunnels on the surface of the ground under the snow and feeding on dried vegetation, seeds, and the bark of shrubs and small trees.

The forest environment must meet two energy-related needs to maintain wildlife in winter. It must provide *adequate energy resources* for species that remain active, and it must provide protection against *excessive energy dissipation*. An adequate energy resource means sufficient mast, woody stems, twigs, or flower buds to meet the needs of the animals living there. This supply may be some 18 kilograms of acorns from sixteen 36-centimeter dbh white oaks to feed one gray squirrel in the southeast, or about 1100 kilograms of balsam fir and hardwood twigs per square kilometer to meet the winter-long needs of a moose in Quebec, or about 9 kilograms of aspen flower buds per hectare to maintain a ruffed grouse population at a breeding density of fifty birds per 100 hectares in Minnesota.

Although conifer cover tends to be detrimental to ruffed and sharp-tailed grouse in mid-continent forests, it is essential for larger animals such as deer and moose. The evergreen canopy provides *thermal cover* by acting as a barrier to the loss of body heat to the night sky.

Protection from Predation Forest growth can be divided into two categories of wildlife cover. One is *vertical cover,* the other *horizontal cover.* The category identifies the physical characteristics of the vegetation; the species of plants or trees is usually unimportant, except to the extent that a certain species most readily develops as one or the other of these categories of cover.

Ideal vertical cover consists of small-diameter stems of sapling trees or shrubs evenly spaced and growing straight from the ground to form a closed canopy 3 to 10 meters overhead (Figure 17.5). This cover must be open enough to allow the desired wildlife to move about easily, without providing concealment for mammalian predators, and too

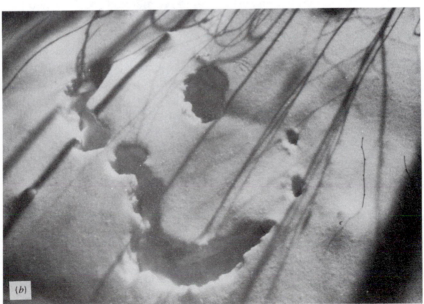

Figure 17.4 Snow burrow roosting by ruffed grouse. (a) The bird plunged into the snow in the foreground and moved about 1 meter in the snow to its overnight roosting position. The bird flew from the burrow when it was disturbed. (b) The bird dived into the snow (20 centimeters depth) at the upper left, and as it moved through the snow for a distance of about 2 meters, the burrow collapsed behind it. Wing marks on the snow show that this bird flew from its overnight roost.

Figure 17.5 Good vertical cover around a ruffed grouse drumming log on a hillside in eastern Tennessee. This sapling stand is composed of sugar maple, sourwood, and yellow-poplar.

dense for raptors (hawks and owls) to fly through. Vertical cover provides protection for ground-dwelling forest wildlife such as woodcock, ruffed grouse, and snowshoe hares.

Horizontal cover favors the predators by providing them a concealed site from which they can ambush prey moving across the forest floor or in flight (Figure 17.6). The branches of evergreens, especially large pines, provide this sort of cover. Fallen logs, brush piles, and logging debris on the ground constitute a hazardous horizontal cover for some species, but a necessary habitat niche for other wildlife.

Nesting Sites

Among the 567 species of birds in North America, at least 254 use trees for nesting. A recent Forest Service publication lists eighty-five species of birds from seventeen families that use tree cavities (14), including as diverse forms as pileated woodpeckers, saw-whet owls, hooded mergansers, purple martins, kestrels, bluebirds, and chickadees. Orioles weave pendulant nests on the tips of limber branches, and many birds build nests in the forks of branches. The tree creeper usually nests behind a piece of loose bark; wrens sometimes use a similar site, although they prefer cavities.

The larger hawks, eagles, owls, ravens, and herons require large trees to support their heavy nests. For example, bald eagles living around the lakes in the level country of northern Minnesota must have tall, sturdy trees with strong branches so arranged that the adult eagles, having wingspans exceeding one meter, can enter and leave the nests without damaging their wing feathers. This means that the nesting tree must have some special attributes, most often provided by the large, mature red and white pines in this region (Figure 17.7).

Use of Forest Ecosystems by Wildlife

Forests are dynamic ecosystems, seldom remaining static. There has probably been more stability in North American forests in the current century than at

Figure 17.6 Mature conifers provide optimum hunting cover for the hawks and owls, which are major predators on grouse, hares, and other small animals.

Figure 17.7 A bald eagle's nest in a large white pine in the Superior National Forest, Minnesota. A large tree is required to support the massive nests of these raptors.

any other time in their recent history. With this stability we have become accustomed to extensive areas of what should properly be considered "unnatural" forest. Much of the information about forest–wildlife interactions obtained during the past half century has dealt with wildlife populations living in these "unnatural" and often "old-growth" forests.

In the primeval forest, periodic catastrophic ecological change was quite frequent in some forest types. The giant sequoia stands in California were subject to occasional fire and depend on the ashes for a seedbed (15). Few Douglas-fir forests in western Oregon and Washington escaped fire for more than 500 years. Forest wildlife has evolved over thousands of centuries to survive in this system of changing forest habitats (Figure 17.8). Regardless of the stage of forest development, some form of wildlife has adapted to utilizing the resources provided.

Wildlife in Changing Forests

Hardwoods Succession A hardwoods forest developing through primary succession is usually invading an area dominated by grass, forbs, and shrubs, as described in Chapter 6. Early in succession there is a considerable mixture of habitat niches, including grassy openings, dense thickets of berry bushes, and low trees. This provides a wide assortment of seeds and browse, and the animals using this stage are largely primary consumers feeding on plant materials. The *granivorous* (seed-eating) sparrows and finches, and various small mammals such as deer mice, chipmunks, and ground squirrels are a part of this early seral stage. This is also a productive habitat for deer, rabbits, and hares, since the shrubs and young trees provide leafy browse in summer and small-diameter twigs within reach of these browsers in winter. Bears also benefit from the abundance of berries produced in the ample sunlight of an early succession.

The young-forest stage is the least diverse in wildlife species of any stage of forest development, but there is usually a great number of individuals of

Figure 17.8 (*a*) This photograph taken in early July, six weeks after a wildfire burned this mixed aspen–balsam fir forest, shows how quickly and densely aspen regenerates when sunlight reaches the forest floor. (*b*) The same site thirteen years later shows the development of an optimum-density vertical cover for wildlife.

the species present, and their biomass is large. This is the stage of forest succession supporting the species having the periodic cycles discussed earlier.

Primary forest succession can require several decades between the initial establishment of tree seedlings and the full development of a closed-canopy forest, providing a habitat for stenotopic wildlife for a comparatively long time. By contrast, the development of secondary succession proceeds quite rapidly, and the niches satisfactory for these species may persist only a few years.

If the preceding secondary succession was a northern hardwoods forest with aspen prominent in the canopy, development will proceed as illustrated in Figure 17.9. For the first several years the site will be dominated by a high density of rapidly growing aspen root sprouts, together with stump sprouts from the birches, maples, oaks, and other hard-

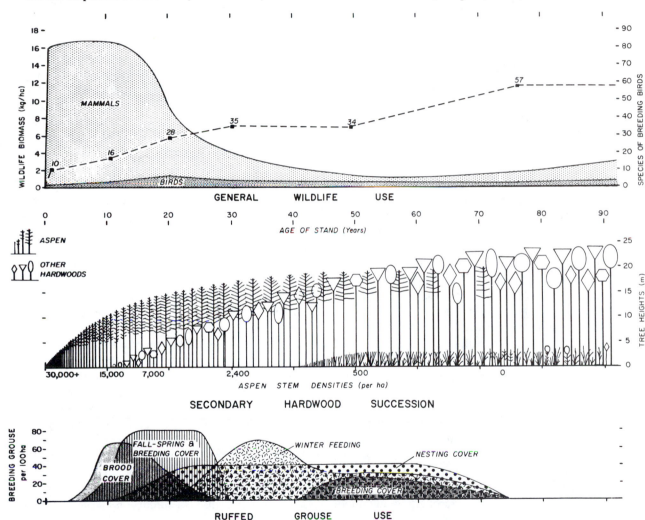

Figure 17.9 The secondary succession in a Great Lakes northern hardwoods forest, showing the sequence of dominant vegetation and the response of ruffed grouse as the forest composition changes. Also shown is the change in animal biomass and bird species diversity associated with this succession.

woods. Stem densities on a site such as this commonly exceed 75,000 per hectare. A hectare of aspen regeneration having 49,000 stems may provide more than 2170 kilograms of highly nutritious food for browsing animals (16).

In high-density stands the less vigorous stems of intolerant species such as aspen lose in the race to maintain access to sunlight, and natural thinning reduces the density of the stand. After about ten years the site becomes more open under a tight canopy 8 to 10 meters overhead. Now the stand, having a density of about 19,000 stems per hectare, becomes an acceptable covert for breeding and wintering ruffed grouse (Figure 17.10). It is also suitable as a summer habitat for red-eyed vireos, catbirds, and several species of thrushes, and as a nesting and brood habitat for woodcock. It is less useful for hares, deer, and moose, however, because the foliage has grown out of reach. Beaver prefer such a stand, and a beaver colony can consume about 0.2 to 0.4 hectare of aspen of this age in a year.

After about a quarter century the aspen thins to the density of a mature stand. The trees are 12 to 19 meters tall and there may be fewer than 4000 stems per hectare, but the other tolerant hardwoods continue to grow and begin to overtop the aspen. Canopy closure limits sunlight penetration to the forest floor, so the intolerant berry and browse plants die. Low shrub cover deteriorates, increasing the risk of predation for wildlife on the forest floor. This forest has lost its value as cover for ruffed grouse and as forage for deer, moose, and other browsers, and even as a source of berries for bears.

The aspen is now becoming important as food for ruffed grouse, and the litter continues to provide food for woodcock. Ovenbirds become common on the forest floor; sapsuckers and downy and hairy woodpeckers begin to use this type of forest. Several species of warblers and vireos live in the canopy, and least flycatchers, goshawks, broad-winged hawks, and barred owls can hunt efficiently under this parklike forest canopy. The composition of the wildlife population has changed from a concentration of biomass in a few species of larger primary foragers to a spread of the biomass among many smaller species, which are mostly secondary foragers preying on other animals.

Depending on the site, the aspens begin deteriorating at 40 to 60 years of age. Heartrot and other types of decay become frequent in the decadent aspen and provide opportunities for the excavation of nesting cavities. The larger woodpeckers such as the pileated and flickers take advantage of this opportunity to develop nesting cavities. Thus nesting sites are provided for the many cavity nesters discussed earlier.

As this northern hardwoods succession proceeds toward climax, changes in the composition of the wildlife continue. Big-game mammals appear only rarely, and as the last aspens disappear, ruffed grouse persist at low densities on the edges or around scattered holes in the forest canopy. Woodcock make little use of this older forest. But gray squirrels increase in numbers, and if winter snow is not too deep turkeys should reach maximum abundance. Many of the longer-lived hardwoods produce the mast critical as a food resource for turkeys, the largest of our native forest game birds. Thrushes become less common with the more open understory, but an abundance of insectivorous warblers and vireos feed among the leaves of the forest canopy, and trunk foragers include black-and-white warblers and white-breasted nuthatches. The size and strength of the trees in the mature forest provide solid support for the heavy nests of larger birds such as the hawks, owls, eagles, ravens, and herons.

As decadence increases, trees die, and the forest canopy begins to open, some of the aerial foragers such as swallows, swifts, martins, and kingbirds find the proper combination of nesting sites, perches, and space in which to forage. More sunlight reaches the forest floor, and intolerant berry and browse shrubs reappear. The wildlife biomass gradually shifts from many individuals of many species of small secondary consumers back to fewer forms of the larger primary consumers associated with a young forest.

Conifer Succession Succession in a coniferous forest goes through the same stages as those in a

Figure 17.10 Four stages in the secondary succession of a Great Lakes northern hardwoods forest. (*a*) A recent clearcut, which was made to harvest pulpwood and create a wildlife habitat, as it looked in late April. (*b*) The same site in early August shows first-season aspen sucker growth.

Figure 17.10 *(Continued)* *(c)* This site seven years later provides an excellent habitat for at least seventeen species of songbirds, woodcock, and ruffed grouse, as well as summer loafing and fawning cover for white-tailed deer. *(d)* This type of forest near the end of the cycle at 60 to 70 years, with one of the last two trees in an aspen clone on the ground and the other in a weakened, senescent state. If the last aspen is allowed to die before it is cut, there will be a loss of the clonal root system and it will be difficult to regenerate highly productive cover for wildlife on this site.

hardwood forest, and wildlife responds in a similar manner. Blue grouse on Vancouver Island, British Columbia, require various ages of coniferous forest in much the same manner as ruffed grouse require different ages in an aspen–hardwood forest. Blue grouse begin using a logged and burned Douglas-fir forest for breeding soon after the forest has been destroyed (17). This use continues for about eight years, until the canopy begins to close in and the forest loses its value as a breeding habitat. Each fall during this period these grouse move up into the mountains to spend the winter feeding on the needles of mature firs. Blue grouse require an early seral stage for breeding and a mature forest for a winter-long food resource.

The Kirtland's warbler is a stenotopic species dependent on a specific stage of succession in a jack pine forest. The birds are found only in 30-hectare or larger homogeneous blocks of dense pines that are 2 to 5 meters tall and have a patchy arrangement with nearly as much area in small openings. This niche exists while the pine stand is between 5 and 20 years old and fades when the lower branches begin to die at 15 to 20 years of age (18).

In a study of the avifauna associated with the successional development of a Douglas-fir forest, Meslow (19) found that only thirty-eight of the eighty-four species in western Oregon's coniferous forests use the earliest (grass–forbs) seral stage, with six nesting (Figure 17.11). But as the succession proceeds into the shrub–sapling stage at 8 to 15 years, bird use increases markedly, with seventy-three (87 percent) of the species present. At least forty are nesting in this seral stage. In the next stage, at an age of 16 to 40 years, the number of species declines to sixty-one, but several efficient predators become part of the nesting component. As the firs grow larger the avifaunal composition changes little, but in the older forest at least thirty bird species find suitable nesting sites lacking in forests less than 40 years old. A similar pattern of animal use was found in a different conifer succession in the Blue Mountains in Oregon and Washington (20) (Figure 17.11).

Wildlife Associated with Interspersed Age Classes or Composition

Forest succession does not always proceed as simply as has just been described. Coniferous forests in the Pacific Northwest remain coniferous as they move toward climax, but in the Southeast coniferous forests represent a *subclimax stage* and are eventually replaced by hardwoods. Aspen forests at higher elevations in the central and southern Rocky Mountains succeed to spruce–fir forests, and aspen–birch stands in boreal forests have the same fate. In eastern deciduous forests succession proceeds from a forest of intolerant hardwoods to one of longer-lived, tolerant hardwoods.

Forests succeeding from hardwoods to conifers or vice versa have more wildlife than either the hardwoods or the coniferous forests alone (21). This mixture in the transitional area, the ecotone, between the northern hardwoods and the boreal coniferous forest in the Great Lakes–St. Lawrence region produces an avifaunal diversity ranging from 129 to 142 species. The only region north of Mexico having greater avifaunal diversity is the coniferous forest zone of western Oregon and Washington, where the habitat variety of the region from Missouri to Hudson's Bay (2100 km) is compressed into a belt about 190 kilometers wide and at a height of 1500 meters.

Some forms of wildlife require an interspersion of trees of different ages or of different species. Primary consumers or *herbivores* are the most dependent on interspersion of forest resources because they use forest vegetation in several ways. Conditions favorable for the production of food resources usually differ from those providing secure cover. Additionally, the forest-dwelling herbivores tend to be nonmigratory and therefore require year-round food and cover from the habitats they occupy. Some herbivores in the Great Lakes region forests such as hares, grouse, and deer require this diversity within comparatively small areas. But deer and wapiti in western mountainous regions find needed forest diversity by being migratory, often

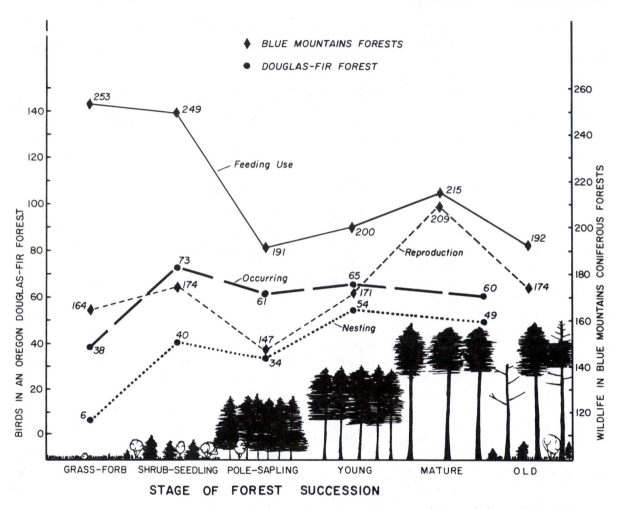

Figure 17.11 Wildlife use of western coniferous forests in two regions. Songbird use of an Oregon Douglas-fir forest shows the increasing species diversity as succession proceeds toward climax. [After Meslow (19).] In the Blue Mountains all species of wildlife use an intermountain pine forest. [Reproduced with permission from Thomas et al. (20).]

moving many kilometers from summer to winter ranges.

Moose require an interspersion of forest types, with the addition of streams, ponds, or lakes to provide aquatic vegetation for their summer diet. In Minnesota the proper mixture for moose on an area of 9300 hectares is given as 40 to 50 percent open land less than 20 years old, 5 to 15 percent in spruce–fir, and 35 to 55 percent aspen–birch stands over 20 years old, and ponds, lakes, or streams (22).

The larger the herbivore and the more severe the climate, the greater the diversity needed in the habitat resources provided by the forest. The same general rule applies for predators as well, except that the secondary consumers have larger foraging ranges, and many are migratory. Goshawks, for example, prefer to nest and hunt in relatively mature forests having an open understory. But the bulk of their prey consists of the medium-sized herbivores (squirrels, hares, and grouse), which require a mixed-age forest for their livelihood.

Wildlife in Old-Growth Forests

In the West the old-growth forests are 250 to 750 years old, and a single Douglas-fir can persist as an ecological entity for as long as 1000 years—600 years as a living tree and 200 to 400 more as a dead snag and fallen log (23).

An old-growth forest is the obligate habitat for a few species of wildlife. Perhaps the spotted owl has attracted the most attention and created the most controversy (24). This bird ranges from northwestern California to British Columbia and needs at least 400 hectares of old-growth Douglas-fir forest for a secure home range (25).

Harris (26) notes that forty species of wildlife living in western mature or old-growth Douglas-fir forests cannot find a satisfactory habitat in younger forests. In eastern forests the woodland caribou requires coniferous forests long protected from disturbance. The lichens growing in old-growth forests are important as a winter food for this ungulate.

Cutting of southern old-growth forests apparently led to the extinction of the ivory-billed woodpecker, and the demise of the passenger pigeon was largely due to the destruction of midwestern old-growth hardwood forests.

Wildlife Associated with Forest Edges

At various times this discussion of forest–wildlife interactions has referred to "properly interspersed" habitat conditions. This term is applied to two different types of forest or to two seral stages of the same forest type that abut each other in a manner best meeting the needs of wildlife. The place where these differing types come together is called an *edge,* and

edges have had a special significance in wildlife management for the past half century.

Aldo Leopold first emphasized this relationship in 1933 when he wrote that

> **Game is a phenomenon of edges. It occurs where the types of food and cover which it needs come together, i.e., where their edges meet. . . . We do not understand the reason for all of these edge effects, but in those cases where we can guess the reason, it usually harks back to the desirability of simultaneous access to more than one environmental type, or [to] the greater richness of border vegetation, or [to] both (8).**

Much effort has been directed toward understanding this *edge effect* since 1933, and it is therefore quite well understood today. Most forest wildlife management plans emphasize maintaining edge, but they may instead use terms such as "habitat diversity," "interspersion," or "a mosaic of types."

Edges are placed in two categories (27).

1. *Inherent edges,* which are relatively permanent, are the coming together of different physical features, such as an upland forest against a sphagnum bog, or a pine stand on a dry, south-facing slope, abutting a mixed Douglas-fir–spruce stand on a more moist, north-facing slope.

2. *Induced edges* are made by the relatively temporary break between two seral stages of one forest type or between two forest types. Such breaks are caused by fire, windstorm, avalanche, or timber harvesting (Figure 17.12). Induced edges could persist for several centuries, but there is no physical reason why the forests on the two sides of an induced edge should not eventually be the same.

For some animals edges are important as the places where they are most likely to find a meal; for others edges are where they are most likely to die. An edge is a critical part of the habitat for species that have to cross it frequently when moving from secure cover to food or water, and thus may lose their lives there.

When resources essential to a herbivorous prey

Figure 17.12 (*a*) Inherent edge, between a forest and a grassy "park" in northern Colorado. Here edaphic factors are probably limiting the expansion of the forest into the opening. Another visible inherent edge, at tree line on the distant peak, is due to climatic factors. (*b*) Induced edge, between an aspen forest and a hay meadow in central Minnesota. If the hay field is not mowed annually, the aspen will rapidly expand vegetatively into the meadow and eventually obliterate this edge.

species are concentrated along an edge, the predators know where they may find a meal when hungry. But if essential resources are well scattered over a broad area, giving the prey species a choice of sites providing food and cover, the "cost" of hunting becomes excessive, and predators can seldom "afford," in terms of energy expenditure, to hunt that prey.

Riparian Forest Habitats

Forest growth along stream courses, or the *riparian forest,* is an especially important wildlife habitat. In the conifer-dominated western mountains the deciduous riparian forests have the highest diversity of wildlife species (26,27). The arid southwestern riparian forests are fragile and require special attention. They frequently consist of a vegetation type unique for this region and extend no more than 200 to 300 meters wide, but many kilometers in length. The forest along the 1300-kilometer length of the Colorado River from western Colorado to the Mexican border is one good example.

Although riparian habitats in eastern forests lack the unique character they have in the West, they still receive special recognition for their importance as wildlife habitat, for their maintenance of the stream bank, and particularly for their protection of fisheries resources.

Figure 17.13 Seeds of mountain ash germinating in the droppings of a ruffed grouse. Seeds of fruits are not crushed by many of the birds that feed on them and can germinate after passing through a bird's gut.

Wildlife Impacts on Forests

Beneficial Influences

Seed Dispersal and Planting Wildlife plays an important role in the distribution of seeds of many trees. Very few of the birds that feed on the fruits of cherries, mountain ash, junipers, and others crush or damage the seeds. The seeds pass through the birds' digestive systems intact and ready to germinate wherever they are dropped (Figure 17.13). The frequent growths of fruit-producing shrubs and

trees along fences and under telephone wires or power lines attests to this function. If the fruits have been taken by a bird in migration, the seeds may be deposited many kilometers from where they were consumed.

Birds commonly carry seeds for some time in a storage pouch, or crop, before the food passes into the stomach or gizzard to be ground and digested. Predators feeding on a bird usually consume the fleshy part of the crop and leave the contents scattered at the site.

Turtles, tortoises, lizards, and fish also transport seeds from one site to another, and if one of these animals happens to be preyed on by a bird, seeds may be moved a considerable distance. Even seeds taken by granivorous mammals may become scattered some distance from the point of origin when they are the victims of predation.

The complexity of forest—wildlife relationships is demonstrated by recent studies concerning the *mycophagous* or fungus-eating habits of some mice in western forests. These rodents act as vectors in the transmission of fungal spores from one site to another and may promote the establishment of conifer plantations by distributing the mycorrhizae important to nutrient absorption by tree roots (see Chapters 4 and 8).

Pest Control There can be little question that the consumption of insects, their eggs, larvae, and nymphs by insectivorous birds and small mammals represents some control over insect abundance, but this feeding seems to be more a matter of cropping the insecure surplus than reducing populations. Insectivorous birds in the Great Lakes states have had little impact on the growth and spread of tent caterpillar infestations when environmental conditions are satisfactory for the caterpillars; nor did the bark foragers and hole-drillers halt the spread of the spruce beetle, which destroyed more than 9.43 million cubic meters of spruce in Colorado forests from 1942 to 1948.

Another indication of the negligible influence birds have in controlling insect epidemics is given by studies that find no response on the part of bird populations to insecticide applications (28). These studies suggest that insect numbers so far exceed the consumptive capacity of birds that the loss of a major portion of an insect population to insecticides has little effect on the food resources of the insectivores.

On the other hand, because of the conflict with human values, we have reduced to ineffective levels some of the predators that at one time were probably fairly effective in controlling other potential forest "pests." Our reduction of the larger predators such as wolves, bears, mountain lions, wolverines, and fishers had favored an increased abundance of deer, wapiti, moose, porcupines, and beaver, all of

which can have serious impact on forest development. But increases in the numbers of these herbivores were not due solely to reduction of predators, for human-induced changes in forest structure and composition also had a profound effect.

Detrimental Influences

Browsing Wildlife use of trees can be detrimental to the forest in several ways. Most prominent among these is browsing on seedlings, sprouts, and saplings by deer, moose, wapiti, snowshoe hares, and various rodents. In some regions the trees that should develop into a new forest are the primary forage for wildlife. This happens in all parts of the continent and is often a major hindrance to forest regeneration.

Destructive use of tree regeneration by wildlife may be quite selective, virtually destroying the new growth of one species while allowing unimpeded regeneration of another nearby species. This is illustrated by the differential browsing pressure exerted by white-tailed deer on aspen regeneration on an experimental ruffed grouse management area in Vermont's Green Mountains in 1977. As shown in Figure 17.14, summer use by deer kept bigtooth aspen regeneration browsed to ground level, while on a similar site only 500 meters distant, root sprouts of quaking aspen grew unimpeded. Even within the block severely browsed by deer, quaking aspen was much less heavily used than bigtooth aspen. However, by 1979 the aspen browsed so heavily in 1977 had recovered and quickly grew out of reach of browsing deer.

Trees and other plants are not defenseless against the feeding activities of animals. Entomologists have long recognized that various plants produce chemical defenses or *allelochemicals* that protect the plant against insect attack. Recently wildlife biologists have begun to realize that plants also mount defenses against herbivory by birds and mammals (29). Shade-intolerant plants that dominate early seral stages of forest succession cannot afford to lose the terminal growing tip to a browsing animal. Produc-

Figure 17.14 An example of the different effects of browsing by deer on aspen regeneration in Vermont. These two sites were both clearcut in the winter of 1976–1977, and the photographs were taken in September 1977. (*a*) This site was dominated by a clone of bigtooth aspen, but in the background area deer browsed the root sprouts almost to the ground. Only a few quaking aspen sprouts in the foreground were allowed to reach a height of about 45 centimeters. (*b*) Quaking aspen (500 meters distant) unaffected by deer browse, with a high density of aspen root sprouts reaching heights of 1.5 to 1.8 meters during the first growing season.

Figure 17.14 *(Continued)* *(c)* The same site in 1979, which shows how the aspen resisted deer browsing and quickly grew out of reach. Although some of the growth is within a deer proof exclosure, the exclosure is almost hidden by the density of growth available to deer outside the fence.

ing chemicals, or *secondary metabolites,* that make the growing tip unpalatable or toxic to browsing animals, is a useful strategy for remaining competitive. An apparent example of this effect is shown in Figure 17.14. There is also mounting evidence indicating that changes in the allelochemical content of aspen flower buds figures in the cyclic fluctuations of ruffed grouse (30).

Feeding on Bark Porcupines most often damage bark, for the cambium layer of trees provide much of their winter-long food resource. The amount of damage done to a forest by porcupines varies depending on the region and the value of the tree species preferred for feeding. In a Maine forest, losses were estimated to be about 0.5 percent of the total volume in a mixed forest of merchantable red spruce, balsam fir, and red and white pines, but in a nonmerchantable black spruce bog, damage represented 2.4 percent of the stand (31). Porcupines were responsible for widespread destruction of merchantable aspen in a Michigan forest in the early 1950s (16).

Rodents and rabbits also do a great deal of damage to forest regeneration by feeding on the tender bark of young trees. During periods when mice populations are large, stands of seedlings or sprouts may be almost completely destroyed by rodent girdling.

Seed Destruction Earlier the importance of seeds to wildlife was discussed, and the dependence of some wildlife on seeds, or the mast crop, was emphasized. Wildlife destruction of seeds scattered for reforestation has been so serious that considerable effort has gone into developing methods for protecting seeds from consumption. This includes dyeing seeds to make them look unacceptable to color-sensitive birds, treating seeds with chemicals to make them unattractive to taste-sensitive mammals, or enclosing seeds in pellets of clay or other materials to make the seeds inaccessible until they germinate.

Felling The impact of beaver is very severe in forests where aspen is an important forest resource.

In the northeastern Minnesota lake country, beaver have nearly eliminated aspen as a part of the forest composition for a distance of 100 to 150 meters from the shorelines, most often leaving a residual hardwoods forest dominated by paper birch and red maple. In a study of aspen in Michigan in the 1950s, it was found that beaver had so depleted aspen stands near waterways that researchers could not study the effects of beaver on aspen (16).

Beaver not only fell any size of aspen they encounter but also feed on sprouts that develop from the roots of the felled trees. This type of utilization soon eliminates aspen from the forest stand. In addition, aspen stands often do not regenerate as readily following cutting by beaver as they do following destruction by fire or logging. Once the beaver have felled all the aspen, they may turn to other trees. But more often when the aspen stand has been destroyed, these rodents will abandon the site.

In regions where aspen does not live, beaver may fell a variety of trees such as cottonwoods, alders, and willows. In Louisiana, for example, beaver feed on loblolly and spruce pine, sweet gum, southern sweetbay, tupelo gum, bald cypress, and blue beech and also make some use of fifteen other hardwoods, including four species of oaks (32).

The role of beaver in the forest–wildlife picture is more complex than simply being a feller and consumer of trees (Figure 17.15). Their damming of streams and the subsequent development of impoundments affect the welfare of a number of other forms of fish and wildlife. In eastern Canada beaver ponds were found to be very important for black duck broods, with ponds larger than 2 hectares being most important (33). Beaver ponds also provide habitat for various fish, turtles, frogs, and other amphibians and for other prized fur-bearers such as mink and otter. Many of the aquatic plants favored by moose in the summer thrive in beaver ponds. The flooding of woodlands frequently kills many trees in addition to these felled by the beaver. This mortality provides snags for cavity-nesting wildlife and openings in extensive forest tracts that favor flycatching swallows, kingbirds, and waxwings.

Miscellaneous Damage Although most of the deleterious impact on the forest is the result of wildlife feeding on trees or their seeds, a certain amount of other damage is related to the behavioral traits of different wildlife species. For example, on sites where deer or wapiti concentrate, trampling of small trees can be extensive (34).

In late summer, as male deer, wapiti, and moose complete their antler growth, the "velvet," which contains the blood vessels providing nutrition to the developing antlers, withers and begins to shed. Then these animals rub the dead velvet off and "polish" their antlers on small-diameter trees or large shrubs. A study in New England forests showed that most of the damage by white-tailed deer was to trees that were 1.2 to 12 centimeters in diameter and extended from about 30 to 80 centimeters above the ground (35).

The damage often affects only one side of the tree, but an occasional tree will be girdled. Sometimes small red pines (up to 3 meters tall) are torn from the ground by especially vigorous buck deer. In northern Minnesota the most severely damaged trees are those that have been pruned or otherwise lost their lower branches while still smaller than 10 to 15 centimeters in diameter.

Impacts of Forest Management on Wildlife

Fire Management

Fire Suppression The place of fire in the forest ecosystem is a controversial subject. There is little argument concerning the place of wildfire in an accessible, commercially valuable timber stand, but the issue becomes clouded when a forest has little commercial value, such as in a wilderness setting where a forest's value as wildlife habitat is greater than its timber value. A large proportion of forest wildlife depends on the *periodic destruction and renewal* of the forest for survival. We have already discussed some species that require young forests or two or more stages in the seral development of a

Figure 17.15 (*a*) Beaver destruction of an aspen stand along a small stream in the Toquima Range in central Nevada. (*b*) Beaver dams often provide stable ponds for fish and other wildlife, as well as slowing streamflow.

forest stand. Stoddard recognized that bobwhite quail living in southeastern Georgia forests 40 years ago needed two seral stages (36), and later the same belief was expressed about wildlife in northern forests.

Successful prevention and suppression of fire have had a profound effect on forest wildlife resources. The most obvious effect is allowing millions of hectares of forestland to proceed toward climax, usually with the loss of the intolerant plants that provide the bulk of the wildlife habitat resources.

Prescribed Burning Depending on the goal, prescribed burning may be either beneficial or destructive to wildlife resources. If the goal of burning is to set back succession to an earlier seral stage, it will probably be of considerable value to wildlife. For the past half century prescribed fire has been used routinely in pine forests of the southeastern United States to maintain bobwhite and deer habitats.

Another outstanding example of the use of prescribed fire to maintain a wildlife population has been the restoration of a prairie from an aspen–jack pine forest on the Crex Meadows Wildlife Area in northwestern Wisconsin. By using fire on a regular basis, wildlife managers have converted some 4800 hectares of scrub forest back to a prairie habitat favored by cranes, geese, ducks, pinnated and sharp-tailed grouse, and a number of other grassland species.

Prescribed fire can also be detrimental to wildlife resources. Summer burning of young aspen regeneration when preparing sites for planting eliminates an important wildlife habitat in Great Lakes states forests. In southeastern pine forests burning may also have a detrimental impact on wildlife. Wood and Niles (37), assessing the effects of longleaf and slash pine management on the habitats of nongame birds, conclude that

> **Prescribed burning is a necessary practice in longleaf–slash pine management, but when carried out with the objective of eradicating understory rather than controlling it, the practice has a highly detrimental effect on nongame bird habitat.**

Effects on Wildlife Food The most obvious impacts of fire on forest wildlife are the changes wrought in the structure or composition of the forest. If a fire destroys a mature pine forest, and it is replaced by a vigorous growth of early seral deciduous browse species, a dramatic change will occur in the wildlife population. One such fire in northern Minnesota in 1971 increased fivefold the moose abundance on the burned area within two years (38), as well as markedly changing the composition of the songbird population.

But there are also less obvious effects. For example, within a month a fourfold increase was recorded in deer mouse abundance on a burned area as compared to their abundance an uncut jack pine forest (39). Seeds had been exposed by the fire and thus became more available. A prompt, marked increase in herbivorous wildlife on burned areas seems to be the general pattern of response, usually accompanied by a decline in species diversity. Of more importance are the longer-duration changes that occur in the nutrient values of browse. Generally the forage quality and quantity of both woody browse and grasses increase markedly after burning.

Timber Cutting

Any discussion of the impact of timber cutting on wildlife is complex and somewhat tentative for several reasons. Not the least of these is the scarcity of long-term research to evaluate the impact of various treatments on wildlife. Only a small number of studies have lasted more than a few years, yet in the Great Lakes states it takes eight to twelve years after logging or fire before a regenerating aspen forest becomes truly valuable as ruffed grouse cover, and a quarter century before the stand begins to be truly useful as a food resource for these grouse. Most studies have looked at wildlife use of existing habitats during a brief time span without considering change or the possibility that animals might be using the best habitats currently available and not necessarily their preferred habitats.

Silviculturists classify the various types of timber cutting as thinnings, release cuttings, clearcutting, seed tree cuttings, shelterwood cuttings, and selec-

Figure 17.16 Disturbances of the soil remaining after areas have been used for skid trails and log landings, when these areas are not replanted, often bring important variety to the wildlife habitat. This site has been used for several years as a singing ground for woodcock and provides important early spring forage for deer.

tion cuttings (see Chapter 14). For wildlife purposes all the cutting schemes are best lumped into two categories: *clearcutting,* with less than about 5 to 10 percent of the canopy trees remaining, and *partial cutting,* with more than 5 to 10 percent of the canopy remaining intact. The amount of sunlight that reaches the forest floor following silvicultural treatment is very important for most species of herbivorous wildlife (Figure 17.16).

Clearcutting When we examine the impact of clearcutting on wildlife, we must take into consideration that the term has several connotations. A commercial "clearcut" having certain diameter limits, or limited to certain species, may really be a partial cut from an ecological standpoint, having either little effect on the faunal composition or a very profound effect, depending on the trees cut. A complete clearcut in which all trees are removed will always have a marked impact on wildlife populations.

Depending on the scale, shape, and dispersion of cutting, the result may be either clearly detrimental or highly beneficial, but *seldom neutral.* Cutting ten dispersed 10-hectare blocks from a 1000-hectare

compartment will affect wildlife differently than would cutting the same amount of forest in one 100-hectare block. If the 10-hectare blocks are rectangular strips, their value to wildlife may be quite different from what it would be were they square or circular in shape.

The farther an animal is forced to range from cover to feed, the less likely it is to escape an encounter with a predator. Ruffed grouse are unlikely to make much use of winter cover in the central part of a 10-hectare clearcut block because of the 150-meter distance to the food resource in the surrounding uncut forest. If the clearing is 50 meters wide by 200 meters long, however, all the 10 hectares would be used, probably by 20 percent more grouse than would be associated with the same size block in a square shape (40) (Figure 17.17).

Deer feeding on new growth in a cutover area dislike ranging too far from the cover of an older forest, and wapiti concentrate their activity in a clearcut within 300 meters of the uncut forest. Obviously, *configuration* of a clearcut is as important as size in determining its value to wildlife.

Although forest clearcutting has been much maligned by some segments of the American public, it is the most satisfactory method for maintaining an abundance of many forest wildlife species. The other management alternative is fire, which is usually less acceptable and often means wastage of woodland resources. In the absence of properly dispersed and timed periodic destruction of forest stands, by either logging or fire, the existence of many forest wildlife species is threatened.

Widespread clearcutting in the past brought virtual explosions of some wildlife species. After the extensive logging of Great Lakes forests in the late nineteenth century, pinnated and sharp-tailed grouse extended their ranges from prairie grasslands northeastward across Minnesota, Wisconsin, and Michigan. Now, as forests have recovered in these regions, these grouse have been reduced to remnant populations in all three states. White-tailed deer numbers are now at what is probably an all-time high abundance over much of their range as a result of widespread forest clearcutting and regeneration.

Figure 17.17 (*a*) Timber harvesting designed to benefit ruffed grouse in central Minnesota. Logging for pulpwood and hardwood sawtimber was done in 10-acre strips with the first two harvests of a four-stage harvest rotated at ten-year intervals. (*b*) Small (0.4 hectare) firewood cuttings on a 15-hectare private woodland. Cutting one block annually will provide firewood to the homeowner and diversification in forest composition for wildlife for 37 years.

Partial Cutting When compared to properly executed clearcutting, partial cutting, which maintains an uneven-aged forest, is less likely to be *beneficial* to wildlife, and conversely will seldom be as damaging to wildlife as improper clearcutting.

Each of the several types of partial cutting may have a different impact on wildlife. A *thinning operation* could be undesirable if the trees removed were primary mast producers supporting a squirrel, turkey, and deer population in the Ozarks. Removal of large overstory trees may also destroy the potential snags or decadent trees most likely to provide the cavities essential to much wildlife. A study of wildlife and cattle use of aspen groves in the Southwest has shown that thinned stands, even though they produced more forage, were less used by deer and wapiti than nearby unthinned aspen stands.

A partial cut may be a *selection cut* in which trees of selected species or certain diameter limits are harvested. A study of the effects of four levels of partial cutting in an Adirondack hardwoods forest in New York provides a good indication of the effect of this type of logging on a songbird population (41). The logging removed 25, 50, 75, and 100 percent of the merchantable trees 30 to 36 centimeters dbh or larger. The residual timber volume on the 100 percent removal area was about one-half that of the stand in the 25 percent removal area. All four logged areas had *greater bird species diversity* than the unlogged control area, with the most heavily cut blocks showing the greatest increase in diversity.

Some stenotopic species dependent on closed-canopy or high-density mature forests were adversely affected by the disturbance of the forest canopy. Removal of only 25 percent of the hardwoods forest in this New York study discouraged continued use by blackburnian warblers and least flycatchers. Five other species of songbirds disappeared as the logging intensity increased toward 100 percent of the merchantable stand.

Group selection cutting, which opens a hole in the forest canopy, is the partial-cutting method most likely to be generally beneficial to wildlife. This procedure may open the forest canopy sufficiently to stimulate dense young growth on the forest floor and improve both food and cover. However, caution must be exercised with this type of cutting. If the clearings are in locations with large big-game populations, excessive browsing may destroy the regeneration and create a fairly permanent opening in the forest. It may be necessary to make a considerable number of these cuttings to provide sufficient browse to satisfy the herbivores and still allow regeneration to occur. In a Michigan aspen forest having a density of ten deer per square kilometer, about 6 hectares of aspen per square kilometer would have to be cut at one time to ensure that enough of the aspen regeneration survived browsing by deer to stock the stand adequately (16).

The size of the group selection clearing may be critical as well. Recent studies in Minnesota have shown that clearings less than about 0.4 hectare in size provide too little cover to be acceptable for year-round occupancy by ruffed grouse. In an Alaskan white spruce forest a shelterwood harvest had detrimental impact on a red squirrel population, reducing numbers 66 percent in two seasons (6).

Usually foresters should expect a favorable response by most wildlife to *shelterwood* or *seed tree* cuttings, for not only are mature trees left as habitats for trunk and aerial foragers, but sunlight reaches the forest floor to stimulate increased growth of the understory vegetation. More browse of higher quality becomes available, and various fruit-producing plants are stimulated to provide the food resource important to many rodents, foxes, raccoons, bears, and birds. Dead or decadent trees left standing as sites for cavity users make the forest more valuable to wildlife than if dead and defective stems are felled.

Forest Fragmentation

Fragmentation of forest stands is creating concern among persons involved with wildlife. Agricultural and urban developments have sometimes disrupted contiguous stands of forest into isolated, ecological "islands." Some forest birds require minimal areas of unbroken forest cover as habitat. The red-shouldered hawk, for example, does not use woodlots smaller than about 10 hectares.

On the other hand, many other species are probably more abundant now than ever before as a result of forest fragmentation and the interspersion of woodlands and openings with extensive edges.

One of the problems with fragmentation is increased parasitism by cowbirds. These nest parasites may penetrate more than 300 meters into a forest, and as the size of a wooded area diminishes, an increasing percentage of the cover becomes accessible to cowbirds. Cowbird parasitism has deterred efforts to recover Kirtland's warbler almost as much as loss of habitats.

Where forests have become fragmented from clearcutting followed by secondary forest succession of the cutover lands, there has been less detrimental impact and more often an increase in wildlife diversity. In a northern hardwood forest in central Minnesota where one-quarter of the stand had been logged in 4-hectare or smaller blocks, habitats were created for seventeen species of birds that did not occur in the uncut forest (42). A similar study in Pennsylvania, where half of a similar forest was clearcut in one-hectare blocks, has shown an increase both in species richness and in numbers of individuals, without loss of any species from the uncut forest through fragmentation (43).

The destruction and fragmentation of forests in Central and South America may be having more impact on the abundance of many migratory birds now than what is happening in North American forests.

Chemical Treatments

Effects of Herbicides Much controversy has revolved around the effects of herbicides on wildlife. It has mostly considered whether or not various species of wildlife are harmed directly or genetically by herbicide applications. Generally the conclusion has been that there is *seldom direct* damage to wildlife from herbicide applications (44). Still, many forms of wildlife suffer *eventual losses* when herbicides are used, for the same reason that some wildlife suffers when a forest moves toward climax. Very often herbicides are used to release conifers from the competition of deciduous vegetation.

The wildlife most vulnerable to the impact of herbicides are the *larger herbivores*. But ruffed grouse, woodcock, and other animals dependent on brush, deciduous vegetation, or mast crops also lose their resources.

Effects of Pesticides The destruction of wildlife resulting from the use of pesticides is well documented (44). Use of the persistent pesticides is banned or sharply curtailed in the United States, and use has shifted to pesticides that degrade rapidly. But when we recognize that nearly every bird in the forest (except for the hawks and owls) and many mammals depend on insects as a food resource at some time in their lives, we would suspect that an insecticide application effective in reducing insect populations would have an adverse impact on wildlife.

Several studies have shown, however, that pesticides do not necessarily affect wildlife adversely. Giles (28), for example, found little change in wildlife populations following aerial application of malathion to an Ohio forest. As noted earlier, in these situations it appears that insect populations were so far in excess of the consumptive abilities of the insectivorous wildlife that a marked reduction in insect abundance had no effect on bird numbers.

On the other hand, Moulding (45) studying the effects of Sevin spraying in a New Jersey forest, found a significant 55 percent decline among birds over an eight-week period in the sprayed forest, but no change in the unsprayed forest. Here the insect numbers before treatment may have been closer to the abundance necessary to sustain the songbird population.

Strategies for Integrating Wildlife and Forestry Management Practices

At the beginning of this chapter we pointed out that any management action in a forest will have an impact on the wildlife inhabitants. It is seldom economically feasible to alter much forestland to benefit wildlife, especially when we are talking about affecting hundreds of thousands of hectares to have a significant effect in regional abundance. Most of this alteration must be achieved through commercial timber management. Thus it is necessary to integrate wildlife and forest management practices.

The U.S. Forest Service currently has two approaches to the integration of forestry and wildlife management. In the southern region the *featured-species* concept has been adopted (46). In this approach a certain wildlife species is selected for featuring on each unit of forestland, and the forest is managed in such a manner that the year-long food and cover needs are provided within the normal foraging range of this species. The objective of the management plan has been reached when "food and cover support the population without waste, without unduly suppressing other necessary habitat features, or without sacrifice of other multiple-use objectives."

Turkeys may be the featured species in one compartment or district, with the management goal directed toward maintaining mature stands of mixed hardwoods, scattered groups of conifers, relatively open understories, and scattered clearings. Water must be available, and the area should be remote from areas of human activity.

This management is directed toward optimizing benefits for the featured species and incidentally the other forms of wildlife that have similar needs. This scheme should produce relatively large populations of the featured species at some cost to a diversity of other wildlife.

The eastern region's plan stresses *species diversity* in contrast to the southern region's goals. Species richness in the ecosystem is sought rather than richness in individual species (47). Management under this concept recognizes wildlife on a community basis, not the needs of individual species.

This concept is being applied in the Ozark Mountains (48). The forests there are divided into compartments of about 400 hectares each, and desired diversity is developed for each compartment. The management guides call for establishing short-range and long-range cover objectives for oak, oak–pine, and pine types, balancing size classes of oak and oak–pine, and of pine stands if they exceed 10 percent of each compartment.

To develop diversity the guides call for 20 percent of each compartment to be in a productive forage condition. In oak and cedar–hardwood compartments 40 percent should be mast-producing, or 30 percent if the compartment is predominantly pine; and 10 percent of each compartment should be in old growth. The plan also calls for one permanent water source on each 260 hectares of habitat.

A variation is the management guideline developed for the Blue Mountains of Oregon and Washington (49). This variation sets as a minimum goal "that habitat for all existing species of wildlife be retained in quantity and quality sufficient to maintain at least *self-sustaining population* of each existing species." This plan differs from the other two programs by indicating the *general abundance* of wildlife to be maintained in a certain-sized area (about 2000 to 2400 hectares), and then tailoring habitat management objectives to create the diversity necessary to attain the goal. This approach addresses the problem of how much wildlife is to be sustained by forest management. This plan is unique in emphasizing the preservation of logs and debris on the ground as a vital habitat for a number of small mammals, lizards, and amphibians.

A new (1986) management plan developed by the 851,000-hectare Superior National Forest in northeastern Minnesota provides a compromise between the "maximum diversity" and the "featured-species" concept (50). This plan identifies and provides priority attention for endangered species such as bald eagles, gray wolves, and peregrine falcons, and for ten "sensitive" species and thirty-three "species of concern." In addition it specifies that "Timber sales will be designed to improve habitat for management indicator species emphasizing habitat for moose, deer, grouse, and threatened or endangered species." Moose management is to be emphasized on the more remote eastern portion of the forest, and deer and ruffed grouse on the western portion in closer proximity to the centers of demand. But ruffed grouse habitat will be enhanced across the forest. Altogether 14,330 hectares will be managed for these grouse (Figure 17.18). Minimum-sized and maximum-sized clearcuts will be 4 and 16 hectares (or as large as 80 hectares in moose management

Figure 17.18 To benefit ruffed grouse, Superior National Forest timber-harvesting specifications stipulate that "When the harvest area is greater than 20 acres and mature aspen is not within 10 chains (660 feet) of the periphery of the stand, one clone of mature male aspen should be left standing." (*a*) Three clones of male aspen left standing on a 10.5-hectare mixed jack pine–aspen clearcut on the Cloquet Forestry Center in northeastern Minnesota. After four years of strong summer thunderstorms and winter blizzards, losses have been negligible. (*b*) Patches of mature forest left for the benefit of wildlife on industrial forestland in northern Minnesota. They will provide an intermixture with dense young forest regeneration.

areas), with fifteen to thirty snags left per hectare (except in grouse management areas, where they would provide raptor perches).

In all regions more specific guides apply to certain endangered species. In the Great Lakes states forests, bald eagle nesting sites and Kirtland's warbler habitats receive special attention; in southern forests habitats for the red-cockaded woodpecker are featured wherever they exist. The preservation of snags is becoming an important consideration in most forest areas, and in western forests the preservation of riparian habitat is given special attention.

References

1. ANON., "1980 National survey of fishing, hunting and wildlife-associated recreation," U.S.D.I. Fish and Wildl. Serv., Washington, D.C., 1982.

2. J. C. HORVATH, "Economic survey of southeastern wildlife and wildlife-oriented recreation," *Trans. 39th N. A. Wildl. Nat. Res. Conf.,* Wildl. Manag. Inst., Washington, D.C., 1974.

3. L. B. KEITH, *Wildlife's Ten-Year Cycle,* Univ. of Wisconsin Press, Madison, 1963.

4. G. W. Gullion, *Ecology, 41,* 518 (1960).

5. J. C. SEIDENSTICKER IV, M. G. HORNOCKER, W. V. WILES, AND J. P. MESSICK, "Mountain lion social organization in the Idaho primitive area," *Wildl. Monogr. 35,* Wildl. Soc., Washington, D.C., 1973.

6. J. O. WOLF AND J. C. ZASADA, "Red squirrel response to clearcut and shelterwood systems in interior Alaska," U.S.D.A. For. Serv., Res. Note PNW-255, Portland, Ore., 1975.

7. P. L. ERRINGTON, *Of Predation and Life,* Iowa State Univ. Press, Ames, 1967.

8. A. LEOPOLD, *Game Management,* Scribners, New York, 1933.

9. G. W. GULLION AND A. A. ALM, *J. For., 81,* 528–532, 536 (1983).

10. L. B. KEITH AND D. H. RUSCH, "Predation's role in the cyclic fluctuations of ruffed grouse." *Proc. 19th Int. Ornithol. Congr.,* Ottawa, Ont., 1986.

11. G. W. GULLION AND W. H. MARSHALL, *The Living Bird, 7,* 117–167 (1968).

12. L. E. YEAGER, *J. For., 59,* 671 (1961).

13. A. C. MARTIN, H. S. ZIM, AND A. L. NELSON, *American Wildlife and Plants, A Guide to Wildlife Food Habits,* McGraw–Hill, New York, 1951.

14. V. E. SCOTT, K. E. EVANS, D. R. PATTON, AND C. P. STONE, "Cavity-nesting birds of North American forests," U.S.D.A. For. Serv., Agr. Handbook 511, Washington, D.C., 1977.

15. B. M. KILGORE, *Quart. Res., 3,* 496–513 (1973).

16. S. A. GRAHAM, R. P. HARRISON, JR., AND C. E. WESTELL, JR., *Aspens: Phoenix Trees of the Great Lakes Region,* Univ. of Michigan Press, Ann Arbor, 1963.

17. J. F. BENDELL AND P. W. ELLIOT, *Condor, 68,* 442 (1966).

18. R. RADTKE AND J. BYELICH, *Wilson Bull., 75,* 208 (1963).

19. E. C. MESLOW, "The relationship of birds to habitat structure—plant community and successional states," U.S.D.A. For. Serv., Gen. Tech. Rept. PNW-64, Portland, Ore., 1978.

20. J. W. THOMAS, R. MILLER, C. MASER, AND R. ANDERSON, "The relationship of terrestrial vertebrates to plant communities and their successional stages," *Proc. Symp. Classification, Inventory, and Analysis of Fish and Wildlife Habitat,* U.S.D.I. Fish and Wildl. Serv., Off. Biol. Serv., Washington, D.C., 1977.

21. D. W. JOHNSTON AND E. P. ODUM, *Ecology, 37,* 50 (1956).

22. J. M. PEEK, D. L. URICH, AND R. J. MACKIE, "Moose habitat selection and relationships to forest management in northeastern Minnesota," *Wildl. Monogr. 48,* Wildl. Soc., Washington, D.C., 1976.

23. C. MASER AND J. M. TRAPPE, "The fallen tree—a source of diversity." In *New Forests for a Changing World,* Soc. Am. Foresters, Washington, D.C., 1984.

24. J. HEINRICHS, *J. For., 81,* 212–215 (1983).

25. R. J. GUTIERREZ, D. M. SOLIS, AND C. SISCO, "Habitat ecology of the spotted owl in northwestern California." In *New Forests for a Changing World,* Soc. Am. Foresters, Washington, D.C., 1984.

26. L. D. HARRIS, *The Fragmented Forest: Island Biogeography Theory and the Preservation of Biotic Diversity,* Univ. of Chicago Press, Chicago, 1984.

27. J. W. THOMAS, C. MASER, AND J. E. RODIEK, "Edges." In *Wildlife Habitats in Managed Forests, the Blue Mountains of Oregon and Washington,* U.S.D.A. For. Serv., Agr. Handbook 553, Washington, D.C., 1979.

28. R. H. GILES, JR., "The ecology of a small forested

watershed treated with the insecticide malathion-S35," *Wildl. Monogr. 24,* Wildl. Soc., Washington, D.C., 1970.

29. G. A. Rosenthal and D. H. Janzen, *Herbivores: Their Interaction with Secondary Plant Metabolites,* Academic Press, New York, 1979.

30. G. W. Gullion and T. Martinson, *Grouse of the North Shore,* Willow Creek Press, Oshkosh, Wis., 1984.

31. J. D. Curtis, *J. Wildl. Manag., 8,* 90 (1944).

32. R. H. Chabreck, *J. Wildl. Manag., 22,* 181 (1958).

33. R. N. Renouf, *J. Wildl. Manag., 36, 740 (1972).*

34. N. V. DeByle, "Animal impacts." In *Aspen: Ecology and Management in the Western United States,* U.S.D.A. For. Serv., Gen. Tech. Rept. RM-119, Fort Collins, Colo., 1985.

35. H. J. Lutz and H. H. Chapman, *J. Wildl. Manag., 8,* 80 (1944).

36. H. L. Stoddard, *The Bobwhite Quail, Its Habits, Preservation and Increase,* Scribners, New York, 1950.

37. G. W. Wood and L. J. Niles, "Effects of management practices on nongame bird habitat in longleaf–slash pine forests," U.S.D.A. For. Serv., Gen. Tech. Rept. SE-14, Asheville, N.C., 1978.

38. L. L. Irwin, *J. Wildl. Manag., 39,* 653 (1975).

39. C. E. Ahlgren, *J. For., 64,* 614 (1966).

40. G. W. Gullion, *Managing Northern Forests for Wildlife,* Ruffed Grouse Society, Coraopolis, Pa., 1984.

41. W. L. Webb, D. E. Behrend, and B. Saisorn, "Effects of

logging on songbird populations in a northern hardwood forest," *Wildl. Mongr. 55,* Wildl. Soc., Washington, D.C., 1977.

42. G. N. Back, "Impacts of management for ruffed grouse and pulpwood on nongame birds," Ph.D. thesis, University of Minnesota, Minneapolis, 1982.

43. R. H. Yahner, *Am. Midl. Nat., 111,* 410 (1984).

44. A. W. A. Brown, *Ecology of Pesticides,* John Wiley & Sons, New York, 1978.

45. J. D. Moulding, *Auk, 93,* 692 (1976).

46. W. D. Zeedyk and R. B. Hazel, "The southeastern featured species plan," *Proc. Timber-Wildl. Manag.,* Occas. Pap. 3, Missouri Academy of Science, Columbia, 1974.

47. K. Siderits and R. E. Radtke, "Enhancing forest wildlife habitat through diversity," *Trans. 42nd N. A. Wildl. Nat. Res. Conf.,* Wildl. Manag. Inst., Washington, D.C., 1977.

48. R. D. Evans, "Wildlife habitat management program: A concept of diversity for the public forests of Missouri," *Proc. Timber–Wildl. Manag.,* Occas. Pap. 3, Missouri Academy of Science, Columbia, 1974.

49. R. W. Miller, "Guidelines for wildlife management in western coniferous forest," U.S.D.A. For. Serv., Gen. Tech. Rept. PNW-64, Portland, Ore., 1978.

50. Anon., "Superior national forest land and resource management plan," U.S.D.A. For. Serv., Eastern Region, Milwaukee, Wis., 1986.

CHAPTER 18

Rangeland Management

Wayne C. Leininger
John D. Stednick

Rangeland Grazing Management
Forested Rangelands
Nonforested Rangelands
Rangeland Water Quality

Hydrologic Evaluation of Grazing Systems
References

Rangelands are areas of the world that, by reasons of physical limitations—low and erratic precipitation, rough topography, poor drainage, and cold temperatures—are unsuitable for cultivation. They remain a source of forage for free-ranging native and domestic animals, as well as a source of wood products, water, and wildlife (1). Approximately 47 percent of the earth's land surface is classified as rangeland, and of the estimated 385 million hectares of rangeland in the United States, a little over one-third is forested range (2, 3). The distribution of rangelands in the United States is given in Table 18.1

Rangeland Grazing Management

Typically, a ranch operation in the western United States is made up of deeded land where hay is produced and cattle are "wintered," and in addition leased land where the livestock graze in the summer. Summer grazing on federal land is regulated by a permit system. The grazing permit entitles the user to a grazing area, a decreed number of stock, and entrance and exit dates during the summer demarking the period when the animals can be present on the range.

Many livestock operations in the western United States depend heavily on forage produced in the forest for part of the grazing year (Figure 18.1). In Colorado, for example, approximately 45 and 50 percent of the summer forage utilized by cattle and sheep, respectively, comes from national forests (4). The number of livestock grazing in the National Forests increased steadily until about 1915. By 1918 the rising number of livestock, the long season of use, and the huge increase during the war caused most of the forest range to decline in productivity. This deterioration in the range prompted both a reduction in the number of livestock grazing in the forest and a change in the manner in which livestock were grazed. Specialized grazing systems that pro-

Table 18.1 Distribution of Rangeland in the United States

Region	Percentage
Rocky Mountains and Great Plains	50
Pacific Region (including Alaska and Hawaii)	37
South Central	12
Other	1

Source: U.S.D.A. Forest Service data.

384

vided recurring systematic periods of grazing and deferment from grazing were adopted.

Deferred-rotation and *rest-rotation* grazing are two common grazing systems used in forested rangelands. Under deferred rotation, grazing on a portion of the range is delayed until after the most important range plants have set seed. Then, by rotation of the deferment over a period of years, other pastures are successively given the benefit of deferment until all pastures have been deferred (1). When this has been accomplished, the grazing cycle is repeated. In rest-rotation grazing a portion of the range is rested for a full year. Deferring other pastures from grazing is also a part of rest-rotation grazing systems. The deferment and rest periods are designed to allow plants to increase in vigor, produce seeds, and establish new seedlings. The design and advantages of grazing systems have been extensively reviewed (5).

A third grazing system, *short-duration grazing,* is gaining popularity in many regions of the United States. This system employs a large number of pastures, frequently twelve or more, and short periods of grazing in each pasture, generally two days to two weeks. Intensive livestock management is required with this system, because of its high stocking density, that is, the large number of animals per area of land.

Major types of forests in which livestock graze in the United States include ponderosa pine, pinon–juniper, aspen, transitory, mountain meadows, and riparian zones.

Forested Rangelands

The *ponderosa pine range* is the most extensive forested range in the western United States. It occurs at middle elevations between the pinon–juniper range or various types of brush for example, sagebrush, and the Douglas-fir and true fir zones at higher elevations. This type is associated with an understory of bunchgrasses and shrubs. Its value as rangeland is the highest of any of the forested range types.

About 560 to 675 kilograms per hectare (dry-weight basis) of understory herbage is produced in open stands of mature pine with 500 saplings per hectare (6). As the density of pines increases, there is generally a curvilinear decrease in understory pro-

Figure 18.1 Sheep grazing in Midway Valley, Dixie National Forest, Utah. (Courtesy of U.S.D.A. Forest Service.)

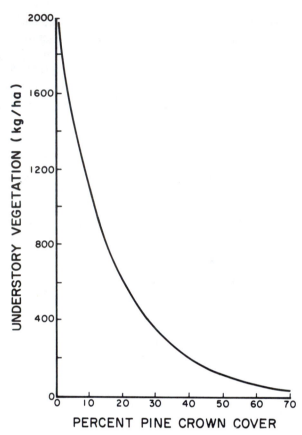

Figure 18.2 Production of understory herbage as related to the density of a ponderosa pine canopy. [After Pase (8).]

story productivity ranges from near zero on poorly developed soils to 900 kilograms per hectare on favorable sites (6, 8). Cattle and sheep frequently graze this range in spring before moving to higher-elevation summer ranges, and again in fall as they return to their wintering areas. The pinon–juniper type is also very important as the seasonal habitat for migratory deer.

Fire suppression and overgrazing by livestock have allowed woodland to expand both upslope and downslope over the past 100 years. Prescribed burns and mechanical removal of pinon and juniper trees by chaining—large tractors pulling anchor chains or cables over the land—are frequently used to reduce the invasion of this type. Desirable grasses are also commonly seeded into recently treated areas to increase forage for livestock and wildlife.

The *aspen range* has long been recognized for its importance to livestock and wildlife because it creates diversity in otherwise homogeneous conifer stands. The aspen range is valued for the variety and productivity of its understory vegetation. This type is the most productive of the forested ranges and often produces more than 2000 kilograms per hectare of understory vegetation. This amount is similar to that of many grasslands. Frequently the aspen range produces more than ten times the amount of understory that associated conifer stands do (9).

Aspen is one of the most common trees in the interior West and grows along moist stream bottoms, as well as on dry ridges and southerly exposures (Figure 18.3), on sloping embankments, and on shallow to deep soils of varied origin. The aspen range extends from Alaska to northern Mexico.

Grazing by cattle and sheep has been the primary consumptive use of the aspen range in the West (10). Livestock grazing usually occurs during summer and early autumn. Overgrazing by livestock during the first half of the twentieth century caused deleterious, long-term changes in much of this ecosystem. Excessive grazing generally changes the composition of understory species and frequently reduces productivity.

Proper management of both the aspen trees and the understory forage resource requires careful planning. Timber management should produce a

duction (Figure 18.2). This range commonly serves as summer range for cattle and spring and fall range for sheep that move to higher elevation rangeland during summer. Both rest-rotation and deferred-rotation grazing systems, under proper stocking, have been reported to benefit these forested ranges (7).

The *pinon–juniper range* is a woodland composed of small trees, generally less than 4.5 meters in height, growing in either open or dense stands. This range is located between the ponderosa pine forest and desert shrub or grassland. The pinon–juniper range generally occurs on rocky, poorly developed soils, and in many locations it alternates with big sagebrush, which occupies deeper soils. Under-

variety of several aspen stages to maximize quantity and quality of the forage and to produce the diversity that is apparently necessary for uses of this type. Grazing guidelines have recently been summarized for this range (10).

Transitory ranges are forested areas that are suitable for grazing for only a temporary number of years following complete or partial forest removal. After that the overstory closes in and intercepts the light needed to produce understory forage. Major areas of transitory range in the United States are found in the South and Northwest. These regions have ample precipitation and long growing seasons. Forage yields in these regions commonly exceed 2000 kilograms per hectare in cutover forests or under sparse tree canopies (11).

Tree overstory is the most influential factor determining forage yields in transitory ranges. For example, in the *southern pine–hardwood range,* forage yield in most clearcuts exceed preharvesting yields by six to twenty times (12). This substantial increase in forage can in turn be allocated to livestock and wildlife populations.

In the past foresters had no desire to integrate livestock with timber production. Their concern was that livestock would damage seedling regeneration through trampling and browsing and therefore reduce timber production. It has been well docu-

mented that when livestock numbers, distribution, or season of grazing have not been controlled, damage to timber reproduction has frequently been unacceptable (13).

In contrast, when livestock numbers and period of grazing have been appropriate, damage to conifer regeneration has been negligible (11). Although cattle may browse or debark trees, the majority of damage to regeneration done by cattle is from trampling and rubbing. Sheep, on the other hand, primarily damage seedlings by browsing their foliage. Browsing of regeneration by livestock is normally confined to current annual growth and generally the early succulent growth. Recommendations for the management of livestock grazing in young timber plantations generally call for the exclusion of livestock either until seedlings are well established (two to three years) or until the terminal leaders of the seedlings are out of reach of grazing livestock.

Controlled livestock grazing can potentially benefit timber regeneration in several ways. These include reducing competition, decreasing the fire hazard, preventing the suppression of seedlings, and decreasing the habitat of rodents, which damage seedlings. Another important advantage of integrated timber and livestock management, called *agroforestry,* is that profits can be higher than with single-resource management. Changing markets encourage flexibility in the overall operation because diversification provides a means of surviving poor markets.

Nonforested Rangelands

The *mountain meadows range ecosystem* consists of wet to intermittently wet sites in the forest zone of the western United States. Typically, this range occurs on nearly flat to gently sloping topography where surface or subsurface water accumulates in the rooting zone for at least a portion of the year (6). Grasses and grasslike plants are generally the dominant vegetation in this type of range (Figure 18.4).

Mountain meadows are extremely productive and often yield ten to twenty times more forage than surrounding uplands (14). These meadows produce

Figure 18.3 Summer grazing on an open mountain meadow range with aspen stands in the background. (Photograph by J. D. Stednick.)

Figure 18.4 Cattle grazing on a meadow in Saint Joe National Forest, Idaho. (Photograph by W. W. Dresskell, U.S.D.A. Forest Service.)

very high-quality forage which remains green and nutritious late into the summer. Mountain meadows support more livestock per hectare than any other type of range in the United States. Because of these advantages, mountain meadows are a very important link in year-round livestock production.

In addition to their great value for the production of livestock, mountain meadows are important for the maintenance of wildlife populations, and many act as a filter to catch sediments from water flowing from surrounding slopes. Mountain meadows also provide scenic vistas and are often preferred by recreationists.

Favorable grazing conditions, coupled with proximity to water and the steepness of slopes in adjacent range types, often encourage high concentrations of livestock and wildlife in the meadows. This uneven distribution of grazing animals can result in overgrazing and deterioration of mountain meadows.

Because mountain meadows already have a great potential for productivity, improving them is frequently cost-effective. Effective range management practices designed to improve livestock distribution include the development of water, placing salt licks in upland ranges, and herding (drifting) stock away from meadows. Where meadows are sufficiently

large to be fenced separately from upland ranges, it may be economical to separate the two to protect the meadows from constant use and to ensure utilization of the upland forage (14). Grazing systems that have been developed for upland ranges have generally been ineffective in improving the condition of overgrazed mountain meadows, largely because they have failed to reduce livestock concentrations in the meadow (15).

Riparian zones, areas near streams, lakes, and wet areas whose plant communities are predominantly influenced by their association with water (16), have been estimated to occupy between 1 and 2 percent of western rangelands. Although these zones constitute a relatively minor proportion of any watershed area, their importance in providing places for livestock to graze, fish and wildlife habitats, and recreational opportunities is disproportionately high.

Healthy riparian ecosystems have become a vanishing resource in the West, particularly in arid and semiarid regions. Estimates are that America has lost between 70 and 90 percent of her indigenous riparian resources and badly damaged much of the rest (17). In 1977 the U.S.D.I. Bureau of Land Management concluded that 83 percent of the riparian systems under their control were in unsatisfactory condition and in need of improved management, largely because of destruction caused by excessive livestock and grazing, road construction, and other damaging human activities. Many riparian zones have been ignored in the planning process because their limited extent made them "sacrifice areas."

Cattle often concentrate in riparian zones and utilize the vegetation much more intensively than that in adjacent areas. This heavy livestock grazing has frequently decreased plant vigor and production, changed the composition of plant species, and altered the streambank channel (15). Numerous studies have reported the deleterious effects of heavy livestock grazing on the regeneration of woody vegetation and the subsequent damage to the fisheries resource.

Riparian ecosystems are the most critical zones for multiple-use planning and offer the greatest challenge to proper management (15). Techniques of *riparian zone management* include

1. Improving livestock distribution, which increases animal use of upland range and decreases stock concentration in riparian zones.

2. Implementing a specialized grazing system to provide deferment and rest from grazing.

3. Changing the kind or class of animals grazing riparian zones. Sheep are generally less damaging than cattle to riparian zones because they are more easily controlled and can be herded away from riparian zones.

4. Managing riparian zones as "special-use" pastures. This increases the flexibility of the operation in regulating the level of grazing in riparian zones and allows grazing during the least damaging period (Figure 18.5).

5. Excluding the zones from livestock grazing. Riparian zones are generally very resilient and often improve in condition within five to seven years after livestock have been removed.

6. Constructing in-stream structures. These are expensive but have generally been successful in improving the condition of riparian zones when coupled with a change in grazing management (15).

Rangeland Water Quality

The most important deleterious effect of range management on water quality is *soil erosion* and the subsequent suspended sediment. Vegetative cover and soil properties determine the infiltration rates of precipitation water and the amount of streamflow that occurs on grazed lands.

Vegetative cover is the dominant factor in controlling runoff and water erosion from agricultural lands and rangelands (18). Livestock grazing may

Figure 18.5 Fenceline contrast between a riparian pasture that has been lightly grazed for twenty-five years (left of fence) and an adjacent heavily grazed area. Notice the willow regeneration in the lightly grazed pasture. (Photograph by W. C. Leininger.)

Figure 18.6 Counting cattle on the Bull Mountain Allotment, Deerlodge National Forest, Montana. (Photograph by G. R. Walstad, U.S.D.A. Forest Service.)

alter the natural infiltration–runoff relationships by reducing the vegetative cover, by reducing and scattering the litter, and by compacting the soil through trampling (Figure 18.6). The magnitude of these changes is determined by the physiography, climate, vegetation, stocking, and animal species.

Raindrops striking bare soil may dislodge soil particles and increase soil erosion. Dislodged soil particles may block soil pores, further reducing infiltration rates, while other dislodged particles may remain suspended and leave the site in overland flow. However, water yield from overland flow may be increased by the decreased infiltration rates and capacities and the soil compaction (also see Chapter 19 on "Watershed Management").

Soil compaction is the packing together of soil particles, thus increasing the soil bulk density (measured in grams per cubic centimeter). As use of an area increases, the probability of soil compaction also increases. Animal bedding grounds, stock trails, watering locations, and salt licks are areas of greatest compaction. Soil texture, moisture, and the amount of organic matter influence the degree of compaction (see Chapter 4). Soil compaction may also reduce plant growth or range productivity through changes in soil aeration and soil moisture. This

reduction in vegetative cover may in turn increase the occurrence of overland flow and contribute to the desertification of marginal rangelands.

Land uses that increase water yield by reducing infiltration may also increase soil erosion and the subsequent amount of suspended sediment. Vegetative cover is important in minimizing overland flow. Land uses that increase infiltration rates help to establish desired plant species and to increase the biomass.

Range management practices designed to increase the growth of desired plants and increase water infiltration include vegetation conversion by chaining, trenching, or root plowing. Land treatment by plowing and seeding generally lowers water infiltration rates at first and increases erosion. However, after two years less soil is usually lost because vegetative cover is greater. Treatment by spraying and seeding has given similar results of lower magnitude. Treatment by burning and seeding may create hydrophobic soils, reduce water infiltration, and increase soil loss. The impact of erosion on site productivity has not been quantified for any rangeland plant–soil complex in the western United States.

Moderate continuous-grazing or specialized-grazing systems that improve the production of vegetation or herbage should reduce sediment yield. If a watershed has been overgrazed, though, institution of a grazing system will not necessarily reduce sediment.

Riparian-grazing systems may alter the morphology of stream channels and cause associated changes in channel hydraulics, water quality, and the accumulation of sediment. Livestock grazed along Meadow Creek in northern Oregon did not accelerate the degradation of the streambank. In this study most streambank erosion occurred during winter periods and was independent of activity during the grazing season (19). In another study in northwestern Oregon, streambank erosion and disturbance were significantly greater in areas grazed by cattle in late summer than in adjacent ungrazed enclosures (20).

Animal activity along stream channels or other open waters may change the chemical and bacterial quality of water. Specifically, animal feces may contaminate waters with bacteria or act as sources of nitrate and phosphate. Studies of two adjacent pastures along Trout Creek in central Colorado indicated only minor chemical effects of cattle grazing on water quality. The bacterial contamination of the water by fecal matter, however, increased significantly. After the cattle were removed, bacterial counts quickly dropped to levels similar to those in the ungrazed pasture (21).

Changes in the chemical quality of water through grazing activities are generally not significant or long-lasting, unless animals and their waste products are concentrated in one area. Specifically, nitrate–nitrogen concentrations may increase and change water quality, since the nitrate–nitrogen is a mobile anion (see Chapters 4 and 19). High nitrate–nitrogen concentrations in groundwaters below feedlots are well known.

Hydrologic Evaluation of Grazing Systems

Most watershed studies have evaluated the impact of livestock grazing on hydrologic variables after grazing treatments have been in effect for several years. Treatment plots, areas, or watersheds are then compared to a nongrazed counterpart and differences are attributed to grazing. The grazing is varied in both duration and intensity. Few studies have assessed seasonal or long-term hydraulic impacts of grazing systems, and additional studies, both intensive and extensive, are needed (22).

In general, the removal of plant cover by grazing may increase the impact of raindrops, decrease the amount of organic matter in the soil, increase surface crusting (puddling), decrease infiltration rates, and increase erosion. Increased overland flow, reduced soil moisture, and increased erosion translate into greater concentrations of suspended sediment. A further discussion of the hydrologic cycle is given in the following chapter. Other water quality impacts such as increased bacterial and nutrient concentrations do not appear to be a problem with grazing systems, except perhaps in riparian zones.

The impact of livestock grazing on watersheds has recently become a resource management issue of national proportions. Research project data have often been evaluated emotionally or according to the political advantages offered rather than by scientific and objective thinking.

The advantages between light and moderate grazing intensities for watershed protection are often not significantly different. Recent interest in federal grazing practices, particularly allotment leases, may bring a reevaluation of the environmental and economic implications of grazing systems on watershed resources.

References

1. L. A. STODDART, A. D. SMITH, AND T. W. BOX, *Range Management,* Third Edition, McGraw–Hill, New York, 1975.

2. R. E. WILLIAMS, B. W. ALLRED, R. M. DeNIO, AND H. E. PAULSEN, JR., *J. Range Manag., 21,* 355 (1968).

3. W. L. DUTTON, *J. For., 51,* 248 (1953).

4. R. G. TAYLOR, E. T. BARTLETT, AND K. D. LAIR, *J. Range Manag., 358,* 634 (1982).

5. H. F. HEADY, *Rangeland Management,* McGraw–Hill, New York, 1975.

6. G. A. GARRISON, A. J. BJUGSTAD, D. A. DUNCAN, M. E. LEWIS, AND D. R. SMITH, "Vegetation and environmental features of forest and range ecosystems," U.S.D.A. For. Serv., Agr. Handbook 475, 1977.

7. W. P. CLARY, "Range management and its ecological basis in the ponderosa pine type in Arizona: The status of our knowledge," U.S.D.A. For. Serv., Res. Pap. RM-158, 1975.

8. C. P. PASE, *J. Range Manag., 11,* 238 (1958).

9. W. R. HOUSTON, "A condition guide for aspen ranges of Utah, Nevada, southern Idaho, and western Wyoming," U.S.D.A. For. Serv., Intermountain For. Range Expt. Sta. Pap. 32, 1954.

10. N. V. DeBYLE AND R. P. WINOKUR, EDS., "Aspen: Ecology and management in the western United States," U.S.D.A. For. Serv., Gen. Tech. Rep. RM-119, 1985.

11. W. C. LEININGER, "Silvicultural impacts of sheep grazing in Oregon's coast range," Ph.D. Dissertation, Oregon State Univ., Corvallis, 1984.

12. P. N. SPREITZER, *Rangelands, 7,* 33 (1985).

13. K. E. SEVERSON, *J. Range Manag., 35,* 786 (1982).

14. J. M. SKOVLIN, "Impacts of grazing on wetlands and riparian habitat: A review of our knowledge." In *Developing Strategies for Rangeland Management,* Nat. Res. Council/Nat. Academy of Sciences, Westview Press, Boulder, Colo., 1984.

15. W. S. PLATTS, "Livestock grazing and riparian stream ecosystems." In *Proc. Forum—Grazing and Riparian/Stream Ecosystem,* Trout Unlimited, Inc., 1979.

16. L. R. ROATH AND W. C. KRUEGER, *J. Range Manag., 35,* 100 (1982).

17. ANON., *The Ninth Annual Report of the Council on Environmental Quality,* U.S. Council on Environmental Quality, U.S. Govt. Printing Office, Washington, D.C., 1978.

18. W. H. WISCHMEIER AND D. D. SMITH, "Predicting rainfall erosion losses from cropland east of the Rocky Mountains," U.S.D.A. Agr. Res. Serv., Agr. Handbook 282, Washington, D.C., 1965.

19. J. C. BUCKHOUSE, J. M. SKOVLIN, AND R. W. KNIGHT, *J. Range Manag., 34,* 339 (1981).

20. J. B. KAUFFMAN AND W. C. KRUEGER, *J. Range Manag., 37,* 430 (1984).

21. S. R. JOHNSON, H. L. GARY, AND S. L. PONCE, "Range cattle impacts on stream water quality in the Colorado front range," U.S.D.A. For. Serv., Res. Note RM 359, 1978.

22. W. H. BLACKBURN, "Impacts of grazing intensity and specialized grazing systems on watershed characteristics and responses." In *Developing Strategies for Rangeland Management.* Nat. Res. Council/Nat. Academy of Sciences, Westview Press, Boulder, Colo., 1984.

CHAPTER 19

Watershed Management

JOHN D. STEDNICK

Recognition of the interrelationship of land and water dates from the ancient Chinese, with their proverb, "Rule the mountain and you rule the river." Early Greeks, Egyptians, and Romans all recognized the importance of water but were often ignorant of the consequences of land use activities on water resources.

Watershed management is a fairly new discipline, defined as the analysis, protection, repair, utilization, and maintenance of drainage basins for optimum control and conservation of water in relation to other resources (1). A *watershed* is any sloping surface that sheds water into a stream or river (i.e., see Figure 6.10), whereas a *drainage basin* is a watershed that collects and discharges streamflow through an outlet or stream mouth (2). Drainage basin areas may range in size from a few hectares for a small creek to thousands of square kilometers for a large river draining several states. The source of all streamflow is precipitation, but precipitation water may be involved in other storage or movement processes.

The Hydrologic Cycle

The hydrologic cycle (Figure 19.1) describes the various paths water may take during its continuous circulation from ocean to atmosphere to earth and back to ocean. Water is only temporarily stored in streams, in lakes, in the soil, and as groundwater.

The water balance equation is

$$P - I - F - E - T - Q \pm S = 0$$

where P is precipitation, I is interception, F is infiltration, E is evaporation, T is plant transpiration, and Q is runoff, and S is storage.

Atmospheric moisture is one of the smallest storage volumes of the earth's water; yet it is the most vital source of fresh water for humankind. The distribution and amount of precipitation (P) depends on air mass circulation patterns, distance and direction from large water bodies, and local topography. Thus the United States has a wide range of annual precipitation values. If surface temperatures are cold enough, snow will be stored on the ground surface until enough energy is available for melting. The meltwater will follow the same pathways as rainwater thereafter. Precipitation may be described in terms of kind, as rain, snow, sleet, or fog; and of amount, by storm intensity, storm duration, and depth of precipitation.

Precipitation may be intercepted or captured by leaves, twigs, stems, and soil surface organic matter and returned to the atmosphere as water vapor. This process, known as *interception* (I), does not help to

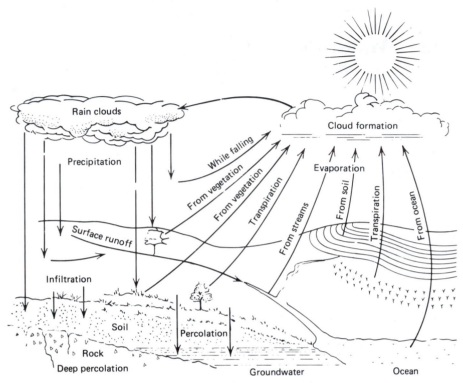

Figure 19.1 The hydrologic cycle. (Courtesy of U.S. Department of Agriculture.)

recharge soil moisture or generate streamflow. Interception by the vegetative cover may dissipate a large portion of the raindrop energy, as can accumulated litter and plant residues on the soil surface. The decreased energy of the raindrop lessens its impact on the soil surface and thus the danger of soil erosion.

Once the interception capacity of a plant has been exceeded, subsequent precipitation may follow the plant stem to the soil surface, by *stemflow,* or drip from the foliage to the soil surface called *throughfall.* These processes are also subject to evaporative losses, but they may help to recharge soil moisture once the interception capacity is exceeded. Total interception loss for a storm is a function of the interception storage capacity and the number of showers per storm.

When the water reaches the ground surface, a portion of it is absorbed by the soil. *Infiltration (F)* is

the process of water seeping into the soil and is controlled by surface soil conditions, such as soil texture, vegetation type, and land use. Table 19.1 shows the high rates of infiltration of various forest floors compared to the infiltration rates of pastures.

Table 19.1 Infiltration Rates of Forests and Pastures

Habitat	Capacity (mm/hr)
Undisturbed forest floor	60
Forest floor without litter and humus layers	49
Forest floor burned annually	40
Pasture, unimproved	24
Old pasture	43

Source: H. W. Lull. In *Handbook of Applied Hydrology,* V. T. Chow, ed., McGraw–Hill, New York, 1964.

Movement of waters through soil, referred to as *percolation,* is largely independent of factors controlling infiltration (cf. Chapter 4).

During an individual precipitation event or storm, changes at the soil surface progressively lower infiltration rates. Raindrop impact may compact or puddle the soil surface. Soil colloids may swell upon wetting and reduce soil pore size and volume. When muddy waters enter the soil, suspended sediments may further reduce soil pore size. Once the precipitation intensity exceeds the infiltration rate, precipitation can no longer completely enter the soil. This excess precipitation becomes surface runoff, which is sometimes called *sheet flow* or *overland flow.*

Water stored in the soil may be returned to the atmosphere by evaporation or transpiration, or may be stored for various periods of time, and may eventually become streamflow. Water losses by *evaporation* (E) and *transpiration* (T) are often combined in the single term *evapotranspiration* (ET). The amount of precipitation returned to the atmosphere as vapor depends on the energy available to evaporate the water. The primary source of this energy is solar radiation, but additional energy may be advective heat transferred from a warmer to a cooler air mass.

High potential evapotranspiration rates are due to warm air temperatures, and these rates tend to decrease from south to north and with increased elevation in North America. The data in Table 19.2 demonstrate that a forest can transpire nearly as much water as an open body of water can evaporate. If soil water is not available, the actual evapotranspiration is less than potential evapotranspiration. The seasonal occurrence of precipitation and the existing (antecedent) soil moisture influence the type of vegetation present on any specific site. *Watershed storage* (S) is the temporary detention of water in a drainage basin. Water may be stored in permanent snowfields, surface depressions, and as soil moisture or groundwater. The most important storage component is soil moisture.

The storage changes of any particular drainage basin are considered to equal zero over a period of five to ten years, depending on the water-holding

Table 19.2 Annual Evapotranspiration Rates for Different Covers in Central Wisconsin

Vegetation	Annual Evapotranspiration (cm)
Water (open)	75–80
Forest	65–75
Alfalfa-brome	55–65
Corn	45–55
Bluegrass	30–45
Bare soil	40–50

Source: C. B. Tanner, University of Wisconsin, Madison, unpublished data.

capacities of the soil. The soil moisture utilized by the vegetation is not available for streamflow generation or watershed storage. If sufficient soil moisture is removed, streamflow will also be decreased.

Soil texture, soil depth, organic matter content, soil structure, and rock content determine pore size, pore volume, and distribution of pore spaces. The pore volume determines how much soil moisture is retained in the soil profile. Soil moisture storage also determines how a drainage basin will respond to a storm.

Streamflow or *runoff* (Q) is the portion of water that is left over after evapotranspirational needs are met, given no change in storage. Runoff is not just a function of precipitation but rather the amount of precipitation that exceeds evaporative losses. Runoff is the collective result of the different hydrologic routes taken by precipitation water.

As stated earlier, rain or snowmelt water not infiltrated may eventually run downslope as surface runoff or overland flow. If soil moisture is increased sufficiently by infiltrated water, subsurface stormflow will result. *Subsurface stormflow* is the part of streamflow derived from subsurface sources that arrives quickly and contributes to stormflow generation. This water has infiltrated and moves laterally through the soil profile because water in the soil is beyond *field moisture capacity.* Soil may retain water up to field moisture capacity, this water is available for evaporation and transpiration. Subsurface flow can become streamflow within minutes to days. The timing of subsurface stormflow is a function of proximity to the stream channel or slope position, soil depth, and soil moisture-holding capacity.

Base flow is the portion of precipitation that percolates through the soil and is released slowly, thereby sustaining streamflow during periods without precipitation. Base flow often cannot be separated from the subsurface stormflow and may occur within minutes to several months following a given storm. The short lives of *ephemeral streams,* are attributable to insufficient moisture retention by the basin soils or to precipitation that is insufficient to generate streamflow year round.

Streamflow is a temporal and spatial integration of the hydrologic cycle processes and represents the volume of water passing a given point in the watershed over a specific time. It is usually represented as Q, with units of cubic meters per second.

A graphical representation of changes in stream discharge with time is called a *hydrograph*. The length of time for a given hydrograph may vary from several days (to represent a given storm) to an entire water year. The hydrograph is commonly used to determine total water yield, that is, the volume of stream discharge distributed over the watershed area.

Management Approaches

All land use activities require evaluation of the land and existing resources. Watershed management often depends on the management of other resources, because any land use within a watershed may affect water resources. Good land management is good watershed management. Land uses and their effects on water resources may change water yield or water quality (Figure 19.2).

Water Yield

As the human population and associated consumer needs increase, so do the demands for water resources. Water rights become more complicated,

Figure 19.2 A fast-moving stream carries water through the Adirondack Mountains, New York. (Photograph by R. A. Young.)

and unclaimed waters are often not located close to areas of urban growth. Water resources are limited, and sources of new water are continually pursued. Therefore, land management techniques designed to increase water yield are becoming more important. These techniques include *weather modification, vegetation manipulation,* and *water harvesting.*

Cloud seeding to increase precipitation has demonstrated a good potential for augmenting winter snowpack accumulations. Effectiveness in other regions and situations is still questionable, however, as is the problem of water rights. Regardless of its success, weather modification is a highly specialized science and is not considered a major factor in land use planning.

Water yield management by *vegetation manipulation* is an important consideration in many areas. Ever since the early watershed studies at Wagon Wheel Gap, Colorado, demonstrated an increased streamflow after removing the forest cover, research has been directed toward the relation between forests and water yields (3). The removal of forest cover, thus reducing transpiration losses and increasing snowpack accumulation, will effectively increase water yield (also see Chapter 6). Other vegetation manipulation techniques include conversion of deep-rooted brush species to shallow-rooted grasses and shrubs, and removal of plants that use large amounts of water (i.e., phreatophytes) from along watercourses and floodplains (4).

The potential for augmenting water yield by manipulating vegetation within a basin has been demonstrated repeatedly. Vegetation manipulation may significantly increase water yield for certain types of vegetation, and it is the most common means of increasing streamflow (Figure 19.3). At present a landowner has little incentive to manage for increased water yield, until it becomes clear that the additional water belongs to the landowner and may be sold as a resource.

Another approach is to reduce water infiltration by soils. Methods of sealing the soil surface include paving the watershed with asphalt, lining catchment areas with plastic or neoprene covers, and using chemical sprays and soil sealants (5). Water falling as

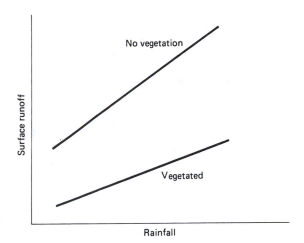

Figure 19.3 Average annual surface runoff from bare and a vegetated area.

rain is not able to enter the soil and runs off as surface runoff (overland flow) to the stream channel or storage reservoir. These techniques of water harvesting have been used to fill stock tanks.

Water Quality

Water from undisturbed forested watersheds is often considered by the public to have excellent quality, whereas water from watersheds with various land uses is often perceived as having less desirable quality; yet the opposite might well be true. The definition of water quality depends on the use for which the water is intended. Water quality may be "good" for irrigating corn, but the same water may not be acceptable for human consumption. Water quality, like streamflow, represents a temporal and spatial integration of hydrologic processes (Figure 19.4). We will examine three factors influencing water quality, namely suspended sediment, dissolved nutrients, and chemical applications.

Suspended Sediment The sediment load of streams, both suspended and bedload, is determined by such characteristics of the drainage basin as geology, vegetation, precipitation, topography, and land use. Sediment enters the stream system through erosion. The sediment source may be from

Figure 19.4 Maintaining high-quality water for fish and wildlife is an important aspect of watershed management. A technician measures dissolved oxygen and temperature in an experimental impoundment. (Courtesy of U.S.D.A. Forest Service.)

within the stream or from off-stream soil erosion. Different erosion processes occur at different rates at different times and places, and the subsequent sediments may have diffuse origins or be nonpoint in origin.

To achieve stream stability, the stream must sustain an equilibrium between sediments entering it and sediments transported through the channel. Because land uses may alter the physical characteristics of the watershed, they have the potential to add to the amount of sediment. Any land use that significantly changes the sediment load can upset a stream's balance and cause physical and biological changes in the stream system (6).

Water-generated erosion is the greatest source of sediment and may be evident as rain splash, sheet, rill, or gully erosion (7–10) (Figure 19.5). *Rain splash* results when soil particles are displaced by the energy of raindrops; the soil particles are often sorted by size. *Sheet erosion* is the removal of thin layers of soil by sheet flow across a uniform slope. *Rill erosion* is the formation of small channels

through concentrated or repeated runoffs. The continued enlargement and deepening of rills will eventually form *gullies*.

Erosion and subsequent sediment movement into lakes, streams, and reservoirs can adversely affect water quality, fish and wildlife habitat, downstream property, road maintenance and safety, and the aesthetics of the area. Sediment suspended in streamflow can disrupt aquatic ecosystems in several ways. Light penetration is reduced in turbid[1] waters, inhibiting photosynthetic plant growth and hindering the efforts of sight-feeding organisms to locate food sources.

Most fish have a temporary response mechanism that flushes sediment from their gills. However, fish subjected to sudden and prolonged increases in sediment levels may be killed. Fish and inverte-

---

[1]Turbidity is a measurement of the light scattered by particles in suspension and may be used to approximate the amount of suspended sediment.

brates may also suffer from habitat damage as coarse bed material is covered with finer sediment. Sediment-laden runoff can pick up and transport other potential pollutants from road or construction activity, including pesticides, petrochemicals, construction chemicals, and fertilizers. The degree to which water quality diminishes depends on the quantity of sediment and other pollutants reaching bodies of water and the existing quality of the receiving water (11).

Maintaining the transport of stream sediments

Figure 19.5 A tributary to Cedar Creek on the Siuslaw National Forest near Mapleton, Oregon, underwent a debris flow in a clearcut logged area that scoured the channel to bedrock. (Courtesy of U.S.D.A. Forest Service.)

and minimizing vegetation growth within the channel should help the channel to retain its ability to pass flood flow discharges (12). The existing form and characteristics of stream channels have developed in a natural, predictable manner as a result of the water and sediment load from upstream. Both water and sediment yields may change depending on how land upstream is used. Increases in water and sediment yields should be evaluated in terms of potential effects on channel stability.

Sediment routing and storage are particularly important components in the transport of sediment loads through the stream system. They are critical to short-term and long-term impacts of land uses on stream channels. However, the storage and routing processes are highly variable and exhibit non-steady-state behavior. Therefore, the continuously evolving relations between sediment supply and the energy available are used to estimate how much sediment discharge will be changed by activities using the land.

Clearly, the land should be used in a manner that minimizes soil disturbance and erosion. If soil disturbances are unavoidable, appropriate "buffer areas" or undisturbed and vegetated areas need to be maintained between the land use and surface waters. Timing of activities is often an appropriate method of minimizing impacts on soil resources, specifically when soils are dry and no major precipitations or snowmelts are forecast. Exposed subsoils are often more susceptible to water erosion; thus the disturbance of sites and their restoration and reclamation should be done in a timely fashion.

Dissolved Nutrients The mechanisms by which nutrients are cycled in the ecosystem were described in Chapters 4 and 6. Outputs of the nutrient cycle have the most influence on water quality. The pool of mobile anions determines water quality. Mobile anions may not be retained in the nutrient system, either because they are not essential to plants or because their supply is in excess of plant requirements and storage (see Table 3.2).

Any activity on the land that interrupts the nutrient cycle, such as crop harvesting or fire, may affect water quality. The quick decrease in nutrient uptake

Table 19.3 The Most Common Ions and Compounds in Surface Waters of North America as a Percentage of Dissolved Solids[a]

Ion or Compound	Average Percentage of Total
CO_3^{2-}	33.4
Ca^{2+}	19.4
SO_4	15.3
SiO_4^{2-}	8.6
Na^+	7.5
Cl^-	7.4
Mg^{2+}	4.9
K^+	1.8
NO_3^-	1.2
Fe_2O_3, Al_2O_3	0.5
PO_4^{3-}	<0.01
Total solute	100%

Source: J. D. Hewlett, *Principles of Forest Hydrology,* Univ. of Georgia Press, Athens, 1982.

[a]The anions (negative charge) occur in combination with cations (positive charge) to form salts. Carbonates (i.e., $CaCO_3$) are the most abundant salts because of the availability and solubility of carbon dioxide.

after vegetation is removed leaves nutrients in solution and susceptible to movement by soil waters (Table 19.3). The nutrient movement decreases as vegetation becomes reestablished and nutrient uptake increases (see Figure 6.13).

Biomass production often may be increased by additions of nitrogen or other fertilizers, as discussed in Chapter 14. Adding too much fertilizer supplies more nutrients than can be taken up, and again nutrients may be subject to movement. The effect of such chemicals on water quality is described in the next section.

Chemical Applications   Three general groups of chemicals are used in land management activities: *fertilizers,* to increase biomass or fiber production; *herbicides,* for species selectivity; and *insecticides* and *rodenticides,* for pest control. Proper application rates and techniques are essential to maintain water quality. The most common concern is chemical spraying directly or by drift into surface waters.

Aerial application, by airplane or helicopter, is the dominant method of chemical application. *Ground application* has traditionally been in small amounts of chemical at such distances from open water that the possible detrimental impacts on streams are less than those of aerial application.

Many of the chemicals have toxic properties even at low concentrations. The minimum dose necessary to produce a measurable effect in an organism, the threshold dosage, will vary considerably from chemical to chemical. The *toxic hazard* of a chemical depends not only on dosage but also on level of exposure, duration of exposure, route of contact, and absolute toxicity of the compound (13, 14). The toxicant concentration has a direct effect on aquatic organisms only in relation to the amount absorbed and the period of retention.

For fertilizers to have a toxic impact, they must be applied in large quantities. The primary concern about improper use of these chemicals is that they will cause excess nutrient enrichment of surface waters. Excess nutrient enrichment in turn causes eutrophication or excess growth of aquatic organisms. Eutrophic waters have often depleted oxygen levels, which may kill fish.

In managing the use of chemicals on land, workers must consider several climate and physical characteristics at the point of application. These include the following.

1. **Precipitation.** The precipitation intensity and form will determine how much water infiltrates into the soil and how much washes the chemical off the aboveground surfaces.

2. **Land Surface.** The land surface characteristics that influence infiltration are surface roughness, surface organic matter, slope, slope length, soil depth, soil texture, and antecedent moisture content. The potential for overland flow will also determine the potential for chemical impacts to surface waters.

3. **Water Resources.** Most important is the distance from surface water to the closest point of chemical application. The extent of streamside cover vegetation, water depth, streambed characteristics, stream velocity, water temperature, suspended sediment, sensitivity of aquatic commu-

nity to the chemicals, and availability of dilution water determine the relative impact of chemical applications.

4. Soils. Chemicals washed from vegetation and through the forest floor may be absorbed by soil particles, where microorganisms are capable of decomposing them. If groundwaters are not near the soil surface and the soil has a suitable texture and microbial population, chemical degradation may occur, leaving little opportunity for the chemicals to affect the environment.

Operational considerations include controlling the proximity of the application to the stream, or the use of streamside buffer strips to isolate the treatment area. The probability that a chemical will impact on a water resource is often related to the rate of chemical application; thus consideration must be given to other chemicals or alternative treatments. Dispersion from aerial application is evaluated by wind speed and direction, the direction of spraying, and the chemical's susceptibility to drift,

that is, its droplet size, and its wettability once in contact with vegetation surfaces.

Water Quality Standards

The Federal Water Pollution Control Act amendments of 1972 (PL 92-500), Section 208, established a legislative framework by which the sources and extent of nonpoint pollution could be assessed and guidelines and procedures to control nonpoint pollution could be developed. Nonpoint water pollution can only be controlled by managing the type of activity that takes place on a watershed. Many nonpoint sources of pollution are present naturally in varying quantities. In the enactment of this legislation, Congress did not intend that water in any given stream be of a quality suitable for a specific downstream use but rather Congress was aiming to ensure that streams maintain or progress toward the state in which they existed when the ecosystems were in their pristine state (15) (Figure 19.6). Water

Figure 19.6 Watershed management seeks to maintain water quantity and quality for many purposes, including fish and recreational use, shown here near Indian Lake, Adirondack Mountains, New York. (Photograph by R. A. Young.)

quality standards are numeric values that are promulgated to maintain wildland water quality and represent an antidegradation philosophy. At present no single index for water quality has found general acceptance because workers do not agree on the definition of water quality and the interpretation of index values. Moreover, there is no method for assessing and comparing the performance of indexes (16).

The most effective unit available for prevention and control of nonpoint source pollution constitutes what is known as a *best management practice* (BMP). This is an administrative creation and initially consists of a combination of practices determined after problem assessment. Practices are examined, with appropriate public participation, for practicality and effectiveness in preventing or reducing the amount of pollution generated from nonpoint sources to a level compatible with water quality goals (16, 17, 18).

The Water Quality Act of 1987, Section 319, requires that each state prepare an assessment report and a management program for nonpoint source pollution. The assessment report will identify (1) the waters that are unlikely to comply with water quality standards without additional controls on nonpoint sources of pollution, and (2) the nonpoint sources causing the problem.

Potential changes in water quality through land uses may be assessed by measuring the expected quality for compliance with water quality standards or by defining cumulative watershed effects. The impact of the action, added to the impacts of other past, present, and reasonably foreseeable future actions, will have a cumulative effect, regardless of what agency or person undertakes such other actions. Actions taking place over a period of time may be individually minor but collectively significant (6).

Cumulative impacts to a stream transcend ownership boundaries. This is of particular concern in mixed-ownership watersheds (checkerboard lands), where no single agency or owner has total regulatory authority. The federal regulatory authorities have approached cumulative impacts from two different directions to date. The first approach is to develop alternative regulatory perspectives that will define cumulative watershed effects more accurately. The second is to determine an allowable impact akin to performance standards. However, the water quality standards give a simple positive–negative answer; yes, water quality standards were exceeded or no, water quality standards were not exceeded. The regulatory approach is institutional and can only be evaluated after implementation.

Summary

Any land use is a form of watershed management, and any change in the hydrologic cycle will affect the immediate area and the remainder of the drainage basin. Population increases put increased demands on natural resources. Land management plans for grazing, mining, timber harvesting, recreation, and, recently, water yield, are opportunities for watershed management.

Land restoration and revegetation efforts have attempted to improve conditions of eroding soils and sediment-related water quality problems. The costs of such restoration efforts are high and further support the idea that preventative costs such as BMPs and other site-specific and land-use-specific activities are environmentally and economically preferred to corrective measures.

References

1. B. Frank, "New concepts in watershed management," *Am. Soc. Agron. Spec. Publ.,* Ser. 4, Soil Sci. Soc. Am., Madison, Wis., 1969.

2. J. D. Hewlett, *Principles of Forest Hydrology,* Univ. of Georgia Press, Athens, 1982.

3. C. G. Bates and A. J. Henry, "Forest and streamflow experiments at Wagon Wheel Gap, Colorado," *U.S. Weather Bureau Monthly Weather Rev.,* Suppl. 30, Washington, D.C., 1928.

4. P. F. Folliott and D. B. Thorud, "Vegetation management for increased water yield in Arizona," *Agr. Expt. Sta. Tech. Bull. 215,* Univ. of Arizona, Tucson, 1974.

5. J. MEDINA, "Harvesting surface runoff and ephemeral streamflow in arid zones." In *Conservation in Arid and Semi-Arid Zones,* FAO Conserv. Guide 3, Rome, Italy, 1976.

6. ANON., "State of Idaho Forest Practices Water Quality Management Plan," *Water Quality Bureau Rept.,* Department of Health and Welfare, State of Idaho, Boise, 1987.

7. H. W. ANDERSON, "Relative contributions of sediment from source areas and transport processes." In *Present and Prospective Technology for Predicting Sediment Yields and Sources,* U.S.D.A. Agr. Res. Serv. Rept. ARS-5-40, Washington, D.C., 1975.

8. W. H. WISCHMEIER AND D. D. SMITH, "Predicting rainfall erosion losses—A guide for conservation planning," U.S.D.A. Agric. Handbook 537, Washington, D.C., 1978.

9. W. H. WISCHMEIER, "Upslope erosion analysis." In *Environmental Impact on Rivers,* H. W. Shen, ed. and pub. P.O. Box 606, Fort Collins, Colo., 1973.

10. L. D. MEYER, "Soil erosion by water or upland areas." In *River Mechanics,* Vol. 2, H. W. Shen, ed. and pub. P.O. Box 606, Fort Collins, Colo., 1970.

11. C. L. LEVINSKI, "Best management practices for road activities," Department of Health and Welfare, State of Idaho, Boise, 1982.

12. ANON., "Procedure for quantifying channel maintenance flows." In *Water Information Systems Handbook,* Chap. 30, Draft FSH 2509.17, U.S.D.A. For. Serv., Washington, D.C., 1985.

13. ANON., *Forest Chemicals and Water Quality, Region X,* EPA 625/5-78-015, Enviromental Protection Agency, Seattle, Wash., 1977.

14. ANON., *Silvicultural Chemicals and Protection of Water Quality,* EPA 910/9-77-036, Environmental Protection Agency, Cincinnati, Ohio, 1977.

15. M. C. MEIER, "Research needs in erosion and sediment control. In *Soil Erosion: Prediction and Control,* Soil Conserv. Soc. Am., Spec. Publ. 21, 1976.

16. J. D. STEDNICK, "Alaska water quality standards and BMPS." In *Proc. Watershed Management Symp.,* Am. Soc. Civil Eng., Boise, Idaho, 1980.

17. R. J. McCLIMANS, J. T. GEBHARDT, AND S. P. ROY, "Perspectives for Silvicultural Best Management Practices," *Appl. For. Res. Inst.,* Res. Rep. 42, SUNY-ESF, Syracuse, N.Y., 1979.

18. M. C. MEIER, "Watershed management—or regulation." In *Watershed Management, Proc. Am. Soc. Civil Eng.,* Logan, Utah, 1975.

CHAPTER 20

Forest Recreation Management

ROBERT H. BECKER
ALAN JUBENVILLE

To the casual observer outdoor recreation appears deceptively easy to understand. To hunt you need an area with game, to boat you need access to water, and to camp you need a site in a natural area. Too simplistic? Absolutely. Think of an outdoor recreational activity and the forms it can take. Camping, for example, includes use of both large motor-home recreation vehicles and featherweight tents. Fishing can take the form of dry-fly-fishing in mountain streams and pan-fishing with several rods on a reservoir or in surf. No matter what form a recreational activity may take, there is a common element among participants—a search for quality.

Introduction

Quality as applied to outdoor recreation is difficult to define and to measure; yet everyone with any experience, as consumer or as manager of a recreation area, will agree that it exists (Figure 20.1). Some outdoor experiences are inspirational, educational, or simply enjoyable. Others are mediocre in

one or more respects, and still others are inferior— some to the point of negative value or dissatisfaction (1).

The extent to which a person achieves *satisfaction* from an activity depends on expectations brought to the activity, and the degree to which these expectations are met. A person who goes fly-fishing expecting to be alone in the stream may seek areas that are known for isolation instead of for an abundance of fish. The person camping who enjoys meeting other campers and making new acquaintances may feel uneasy and even dissatisfied in an empty campground. Conversely, the camper preferring to be with just a group of friends would relish that same empty campground.

Thus the qualities, values, and desired attributes of any outdoor recreation site are perceived differently by various user groups in society. As beauty is in the eye of the beholder, the quality of the recreational experience is in the mind of the user.

Managers of forests, rivers, and parks are faced with a complex set of conditions. Managing agencies must consider a wide range of activities that frequently compete for use of the same parcel of land and are in conflict with one another. They must also provide for a variety of users—old, young, active, passive, among others—and provide opportunities for expression of a wide range of values, many of which are incompatible. To offer varied recreational experiences, managing agencies must have a commitment to provide and continue to improve the full spectrum of outdoor recreation: resources, experience opportunities, and activities that now exist or may exist in the future.

Recreation

The recreational experience is often considered to be actual participation in an activity. The experience is much broader than this and can be separated into four categories (2).

1. **Anticipation.** The period of foreseeing and awaiting a trip or occasion engages the imagination and develops enthusiasm. Events may never occur but still contribute to a person's happiness through anticipation.

2. **Planning.** Actual preparation for the event includes gathering equipment and supplies, packing, and preparing other logistics. Sometimes it involves physical training.

3. **Participation.** The activity and the events surrounding it extend from departure to return. It is the heart of the experience, the time of encounter with the resource and activity opportunities.

4. **Recollection.** After participation, an experience is not usually over. Participation is relived through pictures, stories, and memories. At times, the experience develops new significance and gains embellishments during the recollection phase.

Figure 20.2 is a diagram of an individual's decision to participate in a specific recreational activity (3). Three factors are associated with that decision: individual characteristics, social relationships and societal influences, and available opportunities for recreation. The outcome of the process is an individual's participation in a specific activity at a specific time and place.

Figure 20.1 A "quality" recreational experience may be in many varied forms—such as here on the Lower Saint Croix River along the Wisconsin–Minnesota border.

INDIVIDUAL RECREATION CHOICE

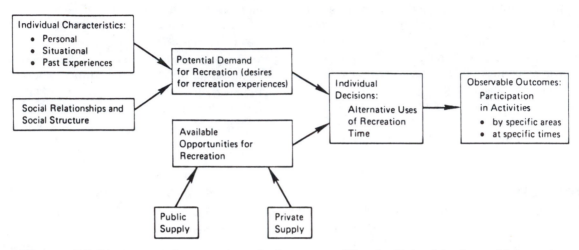

Figure 20.2 Inputs into the recreation selection process. (After the National Academy of Sciences.)

Every person has *goals* for the use of leisure time. Clearly, the ordering and importance of values—such as physical fitness, family togetherness, solitude, achievement, teammate camaraderie—vary among individual groups (3). Specific recreational activities may be viewed as tools or a means by which an individual's goals or motivations can be fulfilled. Very little is known, however, about how an individual's goals are formed.

Five postulates have been presented to explain a *behavioral approach* to recreation (4).

1. Recreation is an experience that results from recreational engagements.

2. Recreational engagements require commitment by the recreationist.

3. Recreational engagements are self-rewarding: the engagement is pleasant in and of itself, and recreation is the experience.

4. Recreational engagements require personal and free choice on the part of the recreationist.

5. Recreational engagements occur during non-obligated time.

The first postulate states what recreation is. The remaining four serve as descriptors to separate recreation from other forms of human behavior.

The key words are *nonobligated time, personal choice,* and *rewarding* (not negative) *engagements.* The word *engagement* is used instead of *activity* to incorporate the psychological dimension; we might be mentally engaged and not physically engaged. Recall that anticipation and recollection were previously identified as part of the recreational experience.

We can observe a person's behavior but experiences are personal. A Scottish psychiatrist, Ronald Laing, has said that

> **Experience is man's invisibility to man; [however,] we must not be content with observation [of behavior] alone. Observations of behavior must be extended by inference to attributions about experience. . . . In a science of persons, I shall state as axiomatic that: behavior is a function of experience (5).**

For a growing number of persons, the quality of a recreational experience is linked to the use and enjoyment of forests, lakes, rivers, and coastlines. The popularity of resource-based recreation has made it necessary for area managers to be as capable of managing the *social use* of the resource as they are capable of managing aspects of the *physical site*—an interesting challenge.

Forest Recreation Management

Forest recreation management is a phase of resource management aimed at providing recreational opportunities in the nonurban setting. Thus its applicability extends from small public-resource areas near urban centers, through large, commercial forestlands, to even larger public lands managed by such agencies as the Bureau of Land Management, the Forest Service, and the National Park Service. The emphasis is on the resource base as the primary planning element, with sufficient development and special services to provide or enhance the particular recreational opportunities. Since many resource uses may be accommodated by a single management agency or a mosaic of land ownerships, any management planning must stress *coordination* of programs. There is one additional ingredient or philosophy that any good land manager must strive to attain: creativity in meeting the expanding needs of the public on a stable to shrinking resource base. In recreation management, we need to search for ways of making heretofore-incompatible uses compatible. We need to handle large numbers of people on a smaller resource base without altering the experience, and to maintain these experience opportunities over extended periods of time. Direct management control should be the minimum necessary to accommodate lower budgets and the participants' preferences. Although this is certainly the direction in which management should be moving, this chapter does not profess to have the answers to achieving such ambitious goals. With these goals as targets, however, the remainder of this chapter will focus on a management framework that we hope will move us in their direction.

Recreation in a Multiple-Use Framework

Recreation competes with and complements other forest products; thus it must relate to these other uses. Planning and management of forest recreation is as important as managing timber, wildlife, or watersheds. Yet wildlife managers know more about their subjects than is currently known about recreation users (Chapter 17). Similarly, timber management has well-established objectives and practices (Chapter 15). Recreation management is often a reaction to a problem instead of an attempt at systematic planning. The recreation component in the total resource management concept, however, may be the most visible and the one to which most people relate. After all, the product of forest recreation is not the placement of picnic tables or the number of campsites; the product of forest recreation is the *satisfaction* of individual visitors. Figure 20.3 places recreation in the context of other forest products. The outline assumes that for all forest-related products, two production stages can be identified: the first converting the raw, basic forest resource into intermediate goods (forest product resources), and the second converting these intermediate goods into final goods that can be utilized directly by the consumer. In actual practice, more than one intermediate good may be produced, requiring more than two production stages, before a final commodity emerges; however, the simple structure described is sufficient to illustrate product relationship. It is also important to note that in the case of a recreational experience, the consumer is actually performing a production role in converting the recreation resource into a directly consumable commodity. The soundest justification for this assumed structure is that no recreation can generally take place at a given site without the other factors—travel, equipment, scheduling—and that these factors are clearly combined and employed to create recreation for and by the consumer, and no one else (6).

Basic Management

As mentioned earlier, the resource base is a primary element; the other two elements are the visitor or user of this resource base and the development of services to offer or enhance the particular pattern of recreational use. These three elements are combined to define the forest recreation management subsystem (Figure 20.4). It is called a subsystem

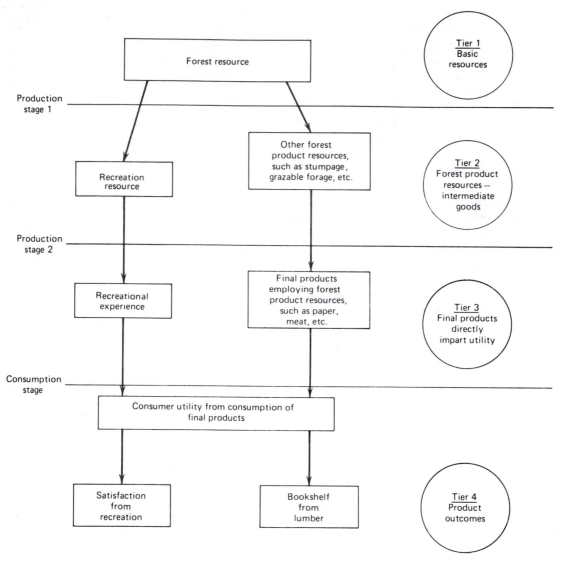

Figure 20.3 The recreational experience placed in an outline structure with other forest products. [After Hof (6).]

because it would typically fit into a larger system of land management that may also include timber, water, wildlife, range, and natural areas.

The manager must then choose options that will, through the manipulation of the resource—improved road access, forest campground development, building a winter sports site complex—provide or enhance the recreational opportunity. The manager must also protect the resource by keeping people away from sensitive areas, by zoning, and by site hardening.[1] Although these principles may be

---

[1]Site hardening consists of any planned modifications to the site undertaken to mitigate the damage that would accompany high levels of visitor use.

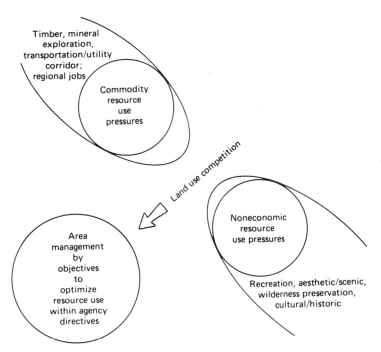

Figure 20.4 Amelioration and mitigation of land use competition through management by objectives.

those of a classic forest recreation management system, how does one apply such principles to the typical dispersed types of recreational opportunities available on public-domain lands? The answer is not simple, but it is not nearly so complex as one would think.

First, recreation area managers are not going to spend much staff time and budget dollars in continually manipulating the resource base, such as fertilizing to increase the vigor of overstory and understory vegetation so it can sustain a higher level of use, even though this may be necessary on a few intensively used sites.

Second, managers are not going to spend similar kinds of efforts for the direct manipulation of the visitor, even though this may be done on a few specific sites. There will be a need for enforcement of rules and regulations, for dispersal of concentrated use, and for dissemination of information through environmental interpretation; but even with all the possible programs available to the manager, the dispersed nature of most forest recre-

ation would preclude the use of such rules and regulations, except at the more heavily used locations, where the use is causing resource or social conflicts, or both. The goal is therefore the periodic manipulation of the resource base to achieve certain recreation program objectives, commonly called recreation area or unit planning, or *master planning.* Manipulation of the resource is in the form of access, such as the development, improvement, or maintenance of the transportation system (roads, trails, airstrips, etc.) and of sites and facilities for the transportation system. The recreational experience can be enhanced by proper location of the transportation system so that the high-quality landscape features are readily seen. The same transportation system can also be used to avoid areas that may be socially congested or environmentally sensitive, have negative visual impacts, or are possibly hazardous to the participant. The location of specific sites and facilities along the transportation system— whether it be a visitors' center or a campground— can enhance the experience. In sum, the process described is called *management by design,* and it is basically accomplished through the planning process.

Area Master Planning

Area master planning is a process of allocating space for specific recreational opportunities or programs based on *program objectives*. The process involves land use zoning for specific recreational opportunities and the careful development of the access transportation system and specific sites to encourage the type and level of recreational use specified in program objectives. Rarely would a manager plan an area today that did not already have an existing access transportation system and some site development; consequently there will always be some level of recreational use of the area. This is particularly true on multiple-use lands where much of the access and developments have been established for the management of all land resource uses. Planning should therefore address the fact that although some changes may be possible, the existing situation is primarily a given in the equation. Furthermore, planning should proceed only if there is need; that is, a problem exists and we need to solve it. We do not need to implement some change just because we were hired as a planner. At the same time, planning is a continuous process, and any actions taken should be based on program objectives. Thus any changes that take place over time should be based on changes in objectives. Even if we decide not to do something in an area, we should develop program objectives to maintain the status quo; otherwise, causal encroachment may change the access, the development, or both. This in turn changes the recreational opportunity offered, or may cause some social or resource conflict that must be resolved through active "hands-on" management. Four concepts related to area planning will be discussed: the Recreation Opportunity Spectrum (ROS, of the Forest Service), visitor norms, management by objectives, and social succession. From the perspective of the total mission of an agency, there should be a district or forestwide plan that coordi-

nates specific land uses to ensure a balance of resource products and services from the land, within the goals of the agency, and that considers the capability of the land to provide and sustain the products and services over time.

Plan for District or Forest

Before plans for an area can be made, we must have an *umbrella plan* or *coordinating document* that establishes targets for the district or forest to meet in supplying identified products and services. Depending on the agency, the district plan attempts to establish an overall mix of products and services and assigns targets to individual areas within the district. Under a typical multiple-use framework, each land area is evaluated based on a resource inventory of its potential for providing specific products and services. Then the areas with the highest potential for a specific product or service would be targeted to provide that product or service. This type of planning would make efficient allocation of resources and theoretically would provide a maximum available supply of the products or services. In terms of recreation, the district plan would also coordinate the continuity of recreational experiences sited in two or more adjacent land areas, such as a hiking trail, a river corridor, or a main travel route (Figure 20.5).

With an expanding demand for various products and services and a diminishing resource base, simple allocation of the resource to any and all uses is not possible. Certain *trade-offs* will have to be made. If you increase recreational use, you may have to modify timber production; if you increase developed recreation, you may have to forgo some dispersed recreational opportunities. Within this framework, it behooves the manager to seek new, creative ways of making incompatible land uses functionally compatible so that the trade-offs can be reduced to a minimum level.

One such response was in the Warm Springs–Crazy Creek unit of the Bitterroot National Forest, Idaho, where hiking, timber management, and watershed protection were all accommodated in a single small watershed. The more productive tim-

Figure 20.5 Hiking in the Cascade Mountains near Mount Shuksan in northwest Washington State. (Photograph by R. A. Young.)

berlands were in the lower watershed, but they were too steep for conventional logging. They were designated for helicopter logging to protect the soil and watershed, and the lands between the road and logging area were left intact to protect visual qualities and preclude off-road vehicle use. The daytime hiking trail started at the end of the road and provided a variety of viewing experiences for the participant. Where the trail passed near the logging, it was directed into the buffer zone along the stream, to keep hikers removed from the visual effects of logging and to focus their attention on the details of the stream environment. It was then directed out of the canyon onto the gentler slopes for a more distant viewing of the upper watershed. The trail for day use looped back, and the wilderness trail angled off the loop and into the more scenic but more environmentally sensitive upper canyon. The upper canyon, though relatively small, was suitable for wilderness designation because it was adjacent to the already-

designated Selway–Bitterroot Wilderness. Furthermore, the upper canyon was deemed to be suitable for grizzly bear habitat, and the primitive trail and limited use were compatible with that habitat.

Spectrum of Recreation Opportunities

Many people have suggested a need for providing a *spectrum* of recreational opportunities. Some experts have offered refinements in the concept by suggesting a *total continuum* from the heavily developed landscape to the totally undeveloped (7). Along this continuum would be identified anchor points with specific qualifying descriptors to distinguish them from one another. These descriptors would distinguish differences in characteristics of the physical settings, the likely experiences visitors could expect, and the types of activities available to the visitor.

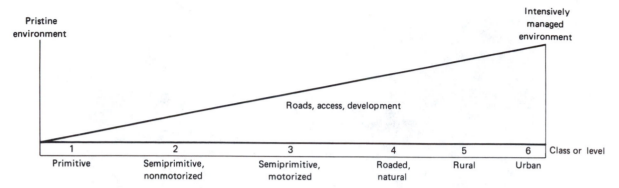

Figure 20.6 The Recreation Opportunity Spectrum (ROS), using the Forest Service terminology

to describe specific opportunities. See Table 20.1 for a detailed discussion of each class or level of opportunity.

Thus the opportunity spectrum would span all activities and would specify the norms of participation for each anchor point. The Forest Service's 1986 Recreation Opportunity Spectrum (ROS) handbook gives descriptions of these anchor points, more aptly termed *segments of the continuum*. The total spectrum is shown in Figure 20.6 (8).

The experience offered by the totally pristine environment with no development is the antithesis of the experience offered by the urban environment. The norms of the experience change as we move from a class 1 experience to a class 6. These norms are described in the next section. For the resource manager, the most interesting and challenging opportunity is in the intermediate or class 3 and 4 experiences. They would occur on the most intensive-use zones under multiple-use management. Several resource uses may be accommodated, including recreation; there is also sufficient flexibility within this segment of the continuum for the manager to respond to both roaded and roadless recreational opportunities.

Participation or Experience Norms

Norms are defined as standards or patterns of participation and preferences of participants that would distinguish one group from another. Three clusters

of norms define the experience along the ROS, so that:

$$\text{Recreational experience} = \begin{cases} \text{Social norms} \\ \text{Development norms} \\ \text{Management control} \\ \quad \text{norms} \end{cases}$$

A description for six experience levels is given in Table 20.1 (9). An example of how the ROS concept is translated into forest recreation management and visitor information is given in Figure 20.7.

On many multiple-use lands, we have typically viewed management controls as a means of achieving social norms; yet, as shown in the equation, they are part of the experience, not a means of achieving the experience. On these same lands, it is essential that we plan the experience opportunities so that we can, to the maximum degree possible, practice *management by design*—a concept described earlier in the chapter. When this concept is used, the integration of the three clusters of norms would take on the following configuration:

The norms of development would establish the social norms and the need for certain management controls. For example, if we develop a typical forest campground with a minimum 100-foot spacing be-

Table 20.1 Recreation Opportunity Spectrum Activities, Setting Characteristics, and Probable Experiences

	ROS Experience Level				
	Semiprimitive		Roaded		
Primitive	Nonmotorized	Motorized	Natural	Rural	Urban

ROS Activity Characterizations[a]

Primitive	Semiprimitive Nonmotorized	Roaded Natural	Roaded Rural
Land-Based	*Land-Based*	*Land-Based*	*Land-Based*
Viewing scenery	Viewing scenery	Viewing scenery	Viewing scenery
Hiking and walking	Automobile (off-road use)	Viewing activities	Viewing activities
Horseback riding	Motorcycle and scooter use	Viewing works of humanity	Viewing works of humanity
Tent camping	Specialized landcraft use	Automobile (includes off-road use)	Automobile (includes off-road use)
Hunting	Aircraft use	Motorcycle and scooter use	Motorcycle and scooter use
Nature study	Hiking and walking	Specialized landcraft use	Train and bus touring
Mountain climbing	Horseback riding	Train and bus touring	Aircraft use
	Camping	Aircraft use	Aerial trams and lifts use
Water-Based	Hunting	Aerial trams and lifts use	Hiking and walking
Canoeing	Nature study	Hiking and walking	Bicycling
Other watercraft (non-motorized use)	Mountain climbing	Bicycling	Horseback riding
Swimming		Horseback riding	Camping
Fishing	*Water-Based*	Camping	Picnicking
	Boating (powered)	Picnicking	Resort and commercial services use
Snow- and Ice-Based	Canoeing	Resort and commercial services use	Resort lodging
Snowplay	Sailing	Resort lodging	Recreational cabin use
Cross-country skiing and snowshoeing	Other boating	Recreational cabin use	Hunting
	Swimming	Hunting	Nature studies
	Diving (skin or scuba)	Nature studies	Gathering forest products
	Fishing	Mountain climbing	Interpretive services
		Gathering forest products	Team sports participation
	Snow- and Ice-Based	Interpretive services	Individual sports participation
	Ice and snowcraft use		Games and play participation
	Skiing, downhill	*Water-Based*	
	Snowplay	Tour boat and ferry use	*Water-Based*
	Cross-country skiing and snowshoeing	Boat (powered)	Tour boat and ferry use
		Canoeing	Boat (powered)
		Sailing	Canoeing
		Other watercraft use	Sailing
		Swimming and waterplay	Other watercraft use
		Diving (skin and scuba)	Swimming and waterplay
		Waterskiing and water sports	Diving (skin and scuba)
		Fishing	Waterskiing and water sports
			Fishing
		Snow- and Ice-Based	
		Ice and snowcraft use	
		Ice skating	

Table 20.1 (Continued)

	ROS Experience Level				
	Semiprimitive		Roaded		
Primitive	Nonmotorized	Motorized	Natural	Rural	Urban
			Sledding and tobogganing Downhill skiing Snowplay Cross-country skiing and snowshoeing	*Snow- and Ice-Based* Ice and snowcraft use Ice skating Sledding and tobogganing Downhill skiing Snowplay Cross-country skiing and snowshoeing	

ROS Setting Characterizations[b]

Primitive	Nonmotorized	Motorized	Natural	Rural	Urban
Area consists of an essentially unmodified natural environment of fairly large size. Interactions between users are very infrequent, and evidence of other users is minimal. The area is managed to be essentially free from evidence of human-induced restrictions and controls. Motorized use within the area is not permitted.	Area consists of a predominantly natural or natural-appearing environment of moderate-to-large size. Interactions between users are infrequent, but there is often evidence of other users. The area is managed in such a way that minimum on-site controls and restrictions may be present but are subtle.	Area consists of a predominantly natural appearing environment of moderate-to-large size. Concentration of users is low, but there is often evidence of other users. The area is managed in such a way that minimum on-site controls and restrictions may be present but are subtle. Motorized use is permitted.	Area consists of a predominantly natural-appearing environment with moderate evidences of human sights and sounds. Such evidences usually harmonize with the natural environment. Interactions between users may be low to moderate in number, but there is considerable evidence of other users. Resources are modified and utilized in a way that harmonizes with the natural environment. Conventional motorized use is provided for in construction standards and design of facilities.	Area consists of a substantially modified natural environment. Resources are modified and utilized to enhance specific recreational activities and to maintain vegetative cover and soil. Sights and sounds of human beings are readily evident, and the interactions between users are often frequent to very frequent. A considerable number of facilities are designed for use by a large number of people. Facilities are often provided for special activities. Moderate densities are provided far away from developed	Area consists of a substantially urbanized environment, although the background may have natural-appearing elements. Renewable resources are modified and utilized to enhance specific recreational activities. Vegetative cover is often exotic and manicured. Sights and sounds of human beings are predominant on the site. Large numbers of users can be expected, both on-site and in nearby areas. Facilities for highly intensified motorized use and parking are available. Forms of mass transit are often available to carry

Table 20.1 (Continued)

	ROS Experience Level				
	Semiprimitive		Roaded		
Primitive	Nonmotorized	Motorized	Natural	Rural	Urban
			sites. Facilities for intensified motorized use and parking are available.	people throughout the site.	

ROS Experience Characterizations[c]

Primitive	Nonmotorized	Motorized	Natural	Rural	Urban
Extremely high probability of experiencing independence, closeness to nature, tranquility, a sense of isolation from the sights and sounds of human beings; and of feeling self-reliant through the application of woodsman and outdoor skills in an environment that offers a high degree of challenge and risk.	High, but not extremely high, probability of experiencing independence, closeness to nature, tranquility, a sense of isolation from the sights and sounds of human beings; and of feeling self-reliant through the application of woodsman and outdoor skills in an environment that offers challenge and risk.	Moderate probability of experiencing independence, closeness to nature, tranquility, a sense of isolation from the sights and sounds of human beings; and of feeling self-reliant through the application of woodsman and outdoor skills in an environment that offers challenge and risk. Opportunity to have a high degree of interaction with the natural environment. Opportunity to use motorized equipment while in the area.	About equal probabilities of experiencing affiliation with other user groups and a sense of isolation from the sights and sounds of human beings. Opportunity to have a high degree of interaction with the natural environment. Few opportunities for meeting the challenge and risk associated with more primitive types of recreation. Practice and testing of outdoor skills may be enjoyed. Opportunities for both motorized and nonmotorized forms of recreation.	Probability for experiencing affiliation with individuals and groups is prevalent, as is the convenience of sites and opportunities. These factors are generally more important than the setting of the physical environment. Opportunities for meeting wildland challenges, for risk-taking, and for testing outdoor skills are generally few, except for specific activities like downhill skiing, in which challenge and risk-taking are important elements.	Probability for experiencing affiliation with individuals and groups is prevalent, as is the convenience of sites and opportunities. Experiencing natural environments, having challenges and risks afforded by the natural environment, and the use of outdoor skills are relatively unimportant. Opportunities for competitive and spectator sports and for passive uses of highly populated and manicured parks and open spaces.

Source: *R.O.S. Users Guide,* U.S.D.A. Forest Service, 1982.
[a]These activities are illustrative only. There may be specific additions or exceptions to activities within a ROS class, depending on local forest situations.
[b]This section is for descriptive purposes only.
[c]These experiences are highly probable outcomes of participating in recreational activities in specific recreational settings.

415

ROS Descriptions

Many believe that the Pacific Crest National Scenic Trail (PCNST) passes for the most part through wild and beautiful country. In fact, it passes through a wide variety of environments offering a range of recreational experiences. The kinds of surroundings and experiences can be viewed as a spectrum of recreational opportunities, from urban, highly developed and used by many people; to primitive, undeveloped and used by very few people. Recreation managers use this Recreation Opportunity Spectrum (ROS) to judge the appropriateness of public facilities, roads, trails, sanitation, and so forth, within particular settings, and to gauge the appropriate design for roads and timber harvest operations in areas where they are allowed. Hikers can also use the ROS to find areas that offer the hiking environment they seek.

 *Urban* The urban setting may be where you live! There are many buildings, paved roads, and a great many people. You will not experience the urban setting along the PCNST in Oregon. Hiking and biking trails through city parks and residential areas would provide an urban recreation experience.

 *Rural* The land between the cities and the forest provides a rural setting. It includes pastoral farmland, small communities, and commercial facilities, or large campgrounds and trailheads along paved highways in the forest. Expect to find many other people along these parts of the trail. These areas offer convenient day hikes and sites for off-road vehicle travel throughout the year.

 *Roaded Natural* Along or near main forest roads and highways, you will find subtle modifications of the natural environment. Improvements are limited to roads, trails, and a few scattered structures. The natural environment still dominates, but timber harvest and preparations for the next generation of trees are visible. Posted regulations as well as contacts with others are likely. In fact, there are limited opportunities to get away from others. You are farther from towns and their conveniences, so you must be self-reliant in supplying your personal needs. Substantial day hikes and opportunities for more relaxed biking and camping prevail. The PCNST trail traverses such areas as it passes near many trailheads and road crossings.

 *Roaded Modified* Along less-used forest roads you will likely find large clearcuts, skid roads, and landings dominant to the view. You will encounter more chances to get away from other recreationists, but logging operations may be dominant. No facilities are provided. You are on your own.

 *Semiprimitive* Leaving roads behind you, you become more isolated from the sights and sounds of human activity. The degree of risk and isolation increases, and recreational activities become dependent on the natural scene. No picnic tables and other improvements are provided; human comfort and satisfactions will be gained through your personal initiatives.

 *Primitive* Primitive settings are the most remote parts of the forest and are little influenced by the works of people. The natural environment dominates the setting and dictates the kinds of recreational challenges: beauty, isolation, uncertainty, risk, and discovery. Woodsmanship skills are important in providing safety and comfort.

Figure 20.7 Recreation Opportunity Spectrum: An example.
Source: From the southern Oregon portion of the Pacific Crest National Scenic Trail map.

tween units and rustic, centralized facilities, such as a vault toilet and water point; and if we use native materials such as wood and stone, the design itself, in terms of social norms, emphasizes natural aesthetics, privacy for the camper, and a sense of being close to nature. At the same time the camper has the opportunity for informal socialization and feels secure because of the limited development and the presence of other people (10). Socially it is the type of camping in which the automobile-oriented person interfaces more directly with nature because development is limited. Therefore, the access transportation system and the facility development tend to attract a person having a certain social norm. The rustic design subtly directs use—where the camper should walk, pitch a tent, and park his or her automobile. Areas of the site have been *hardened* to sustain particular uses. Thus if the use is directed so that the social norms are maintained and the resource is basically protected from unacceptable change, there is very little need for hands-on management. Limitations on the length of stay, to ensure reasonable availability of this particular type of camping opportunity, may be the only necessary direct management control. Such limitations are typical in a forest campground and can be carried out very subtly through simple monitoring to ensure compliance. The arrangement is usually acceptable to forest campers because they usually stay only a few days and move on, or they use sites close to home primarily on the weekend.

Limits of Acceptable Change (LAC)

From this brief discussion of the ROS concept, it becomes obvious that no area is managed rigidly for a specific opportunity. Rather, the notion of ROS is more a guide, an index of the relationships between site constraints and visitor options. The ROS concept has been complemented with the idea that within the continuum of potential uses of a resource, certain changes or alterations would not inflict irreparable harm to the opportunity being provided. Limits of Acceptable Change (LAC) is a planning procedure that enumerates changes to the physical

environment that will cause little harm to the recreational visitor's experience opportunities. An integrative procedure, LAC brings together the work of researchers on visitor expectations and the efforts of managers to understand site resource constraints. It assists managers in arriving at site management judgments by specifying the products and recreational opportunities that a specific resource will provide and by clarifying what changes to the setting would threaten their quality. But, to be successful, the process depends on a clear enunciation of management objectives.

Management by Objectives

Management by objectives (MBO) is important in administering outdoor recreation if we are to maintain a specific identifiable recreational opportunity on the basis of resource capabilities. Simply put, management by objectives means establishing goals or outputs that are agreed on by the members of an organization. It is a focusing effort. An MBO exercise helps participants first to sort out a desired option from among the often wide range of alternatives, and then to direct their energies at providing the desired objective or product. A modification of the MBO model has the following inputs for recreation program objectives (11):

Resource capability
Institutional constraints
Existing situation   } = Recreation program
User preferences   objectives
Coordination

The relationships between these five inputs are described graphically in Figure 20.8 to show the actual band of operation within which the particular program objectives are made.

Usually the *resource capability* will describe the overall limitations on programs, but typically agencies are more constrained by laws, regulations, or policies that effectively reduce the typical band of operation for the particular agency. If the recreation pattern on a specific path has never been managed using program objectives, a certain clientele has usually developed over time. The *existing situation*

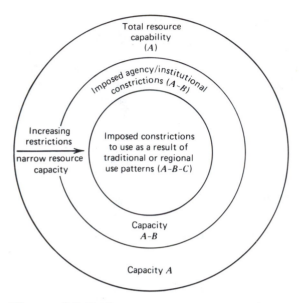

Figure 20.8 Elements constraining use and capabilities of a specific resource. Rarely does the capacity of the resource shape the type or intensity of the area's recreational use. Agencies are often limited by their organic legislation. Similarly, the traditional expectations of visitors often constrict the recreational use of the area even beyond the limitations imposed by the agency.

experience—that is, that they operate in the same band. Negotiation may be necessary to ensure that they operate as nearly as possible within the same band.

Social Succession

According to the axiom presented earlier, that the development norms (expressed in the particular development, either access or facilities) dictate the social and management control norms, any change in development may, and often does, cause a shift in the social and management control norms. This shift in norms, if too great, usually causes a *social succession* to take place, as shown in Figure 20.9 (12).

The net effect of succession is a *displacement* of one group of users by another and is usually caused by a failure to manage by objectives (13). If the primary objective is to maintain a particular experience, the manager may simply not understand the effects of widening the road, improving the trail, or putting in a footbridge. Often these minor modifications of existing development are sufficient (particularly their cumulative effect) to shift the norms to

(the norms of the existing clientele) will probably dictate the direction of the initial management planning, further constricting the operating bands within which the program objectives will be developed. Beyond this, if other *user preferences* can be accommodated within this narrow band, it is appropriate to include them. Or if the area is geographically large or diverse enough to accommodate preferences outside this band, but within the *institutional-constraints* band, it would also be appropriate to include these additional preferences. Occasionally it may be necessary to make plans for an area that has had little past use, and consequently user preferences may play a greater role in determining the actual band of operation. The coordination comes when an opportunity setting overlaps two or more landownerships, requiring that the agencies coordinate with one another to ensure continuity of the

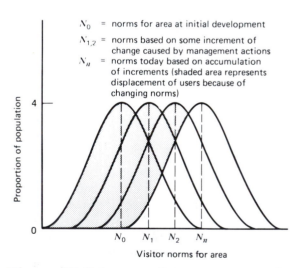

Figure 20.9 Incrementalism in management. The graph records incremental change without regard to objectives and the ultimate effect on the recreational experience. [Modified from Jubenville (12).]

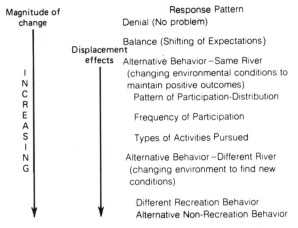

Figure 20.10 Potential levels of adaptation by the recreationist to changes in the recreation environment. [Modified from Schreyer (14); U.S.D.A. Forest Service.]

the point that the experience is no longer attractive to the present group of users, and they are displaced by a new group whose norms more closely fit the new situation. The total process of succession is shown in Figure 20.10 (14).

Displacement is a move away from an *unacceptable situation,* not a move toward a desired one. This distinction is useful in differentiating displacement, a form of reactive movement, from other forms of movement. Among the other forms of movement are the following.

1. **Active Migration.** People seek a suitable destination according to their values—for example, white-water canoeists seek a variety of risk and skill testing.

2. **Passive Migration.** People select a location because it is convenient, such as visiting areas to meet friends for picnics, or because other members of the participation group desire that location.

3. **Movements for Diurnal Requirements of an Activity.** People move to different locations on a lake to fish at various times of day.

Movement is then a general term, whereas displacement is a negative reactive movement (15).

The Area-Planning Process

The preceding processes should then logically be a product of the following underlying actions.

1. **Inventory the Area.** The area should have a complete inventory of the social subsystem: recreational use, history and archeology, nonrecreational use, economics, and legal and political inputs; biological subsystem: flora and fauna, levels and location of sensitive sites and hazards; and the physical subsystem: natural factors such as water and physiography, and artificial developments such as roads and buildings. This information will help in determining significant values that should be maintained or enhanced and the appropriate band of operation.

2. **Determine the Band of Operation.** Use the approach described in the section on management by objectives.

3. **Establish Program Objectives.** State the program objectives within the band of operation and the actual clientele groups whose norms will be adopted in planning the area. While responding to a particular set of norms, also account for specific management concerns in planning the programs, including the access transportation system and specific site developments and their locations. The program objectives should incorporate the experiences to be provided, where they will be provided, and related management concerns such as potential hazards, public safety, and environmental impact (Table 20.1).

4. **Develop and Evaluate Concept Plans.** Concept plans are simply attempts to manipulate the area graphically, based on the detailed inventory, and to test alternative courses of action to meet the program objectives. The following is an example of a concept plan that was considered, though not completed, for Rattlesnake Drainage, a 20,000-hectare area in the Lolo National Forest, Montana (Figure 20.11).

The following is a brief summary of the area.

1. There are five alpine lakes; lakes 1, 2, and 3 are used extensively by hikers, usually from the Divide Trail.

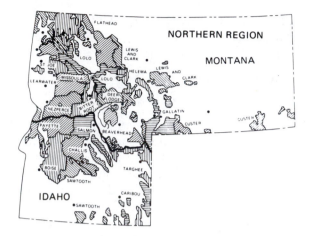

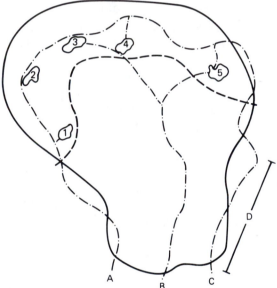

1-5   Alpine lakes
A   Divide Trail entry point
B   Canyon Trail
C   Divide Trail
D   Entry zone

Figure 20.11 Rattlesnake Drainage of the Lolo National Forest, Montana, abstracted for an area management plan.

2. Lakes 3, 4, and 5 are also used by horseback riders. Some conflicts have occurred between hikers and riders centering around the amount of horse manure and the deterioration of the meadows around the alpine lakes. Lakes 4 and 5

are showing severe loss of vegetation around the lakes and problems of erosion.

3. The Canyon Trail is an old four-wheel-drive road that has been closed for nearly a decade so no vehicles are allowed in the area. It is used during the summer by the horseback riders.

4. Summer and fall trail use is concentrated in the alpine zone. Fall hunting is mainly dispersed throughout the forest zone. Winter use is primarily by cross-country skiers along the Canyon Trail.

A quick review indicates that problems are focused on summer use in the alpine zone, primarily lakes 4 and 5. The objectives for the area, assuming such planning should be problem-oriented, should therefore focus on summer use, primarily use of the alpine zone by the horseback riders. The specific objectives are

1. To offer a class 2 summer opportunity in the alpine zone, including access to the zone.

2. To maintain, as closely as possible, the existing patterns of use in the alpine zone and the travel patterns to the zone.

3. To locate minimum horse facilities below the alpine zone that would basically allow the horseback rider to continue to use the lakes, particularly lakes 4 and 5.

4. To allow no camping or fires within 400 meters (one-quarter mile) of any lake.

5. To maintain current pack-in, pack-out policy.

Note that the program objectives included maintaining use by horseback riders, even though a simpler response would have been to zone the area for hiking only.

Both concept plans (Figure 20.12a and b) meet the objectives. Plan A places the horse facilities in relatively stable areas near lakes 4 and 5. The centralized facility in plan B was deemed too far from the lakes for typical day use. However, the bypass concept was initiated in plan B; the Divide Trail was rerouted to give a greater view experience to the hiker and to make the lakes visually available. Lakes 1, 2, and 3 were made accessible via spur trails for people who wanted to spend some time around the

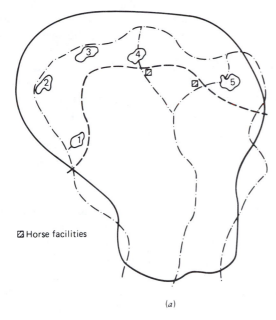

(a)

☑ Horse facilities

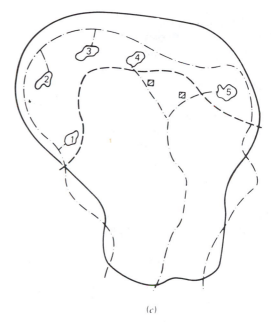

(c)

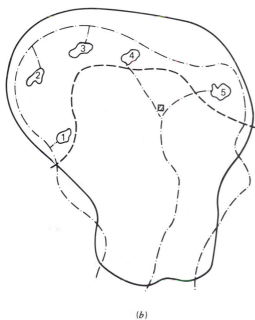

(b)

Figure 20.12 (*a, b*) Concept plans A and B and (*c*) final management plan C for Rattlesnake Drainage, Lolo National Forest, Montana.

lakes. Spur trails from the divide to lakes 4 and 5 were obliterated, and the lakes were made visually accessible at points where steep terrain would effectively eliminate casual use. Where easy access may have been available, the Divide Trail was rerouted to

the opposite side of the divide. The actual placement of the dual horse facilities was adjusted to take advantage of well-drained, stable soil locations. Thus the final plan, plan C, is a mixture of the two concept plans (Figure 20.12*c*).

Although trade-offs are usually necessary in any planning effort to solve a problem, ideally we should strive to *maximize the benefits* to the user at minimum cost either in adjustment of the experience or in loss of environmental amenities. However, any decision we reach today should maintain the maximum possible future management options. Too often we seem to relish the idea of planning every hectare when every hectare is not needed. The same philosophy generally pervades other areas of planning as well; we have the technology to do it, so let's do it. We do not seem to evaluate the appropriateness of the technology in relation to the situation. In forest recreation, planners do not create the experience through technology. They simply use the technology to make available, to protect, or to enhance the opportunity within the limits described in Table

20.1. With some creative planning they can provide the desired types of experiences for larger numbers of people on smaller areas.

Another objective for the Rattlesnake Drainage area is to *establish priorities*. It is not feasible to expect any area plan to be immediately funded in its entirety. The planner must establish priorities of programs and capital improvements within those programs. These priorites should be listed as immediate, short-run, and long-run. Immediate items would be implemented immediately within the existing operating budget. Short-run items would be the sites and facilities needed to implement the basic part for the priority programs. Long-run items would be those needed to finish the higher-priority programs and, as funds permit, to complete some of the lower-priority programs.

Management Issues

Most issues of recreation management involve some of the concepts introduced earlier: defined recreational experiences, management by objectives, and the recreational opportunity spectrum. But they tend to focus on some activity.

Recreational Experiences

Most of the controversy surrounding recreation planning points to one single issue: the failure to define recreational experiences. We can neither plan nor manage specific programs to provide specific recreational experiences unless we have well-defined social, development, and management control norms; this chapter has tried to address that void in forest recreation planning.

To be completely responsive, the planner needs to recognize the total spectrum of recreational opportunities and the discrete segments of the spectrum that constitute the particular experience. The planner must then incorporate the recreational experience into the management objectives and be willing to take the necessary steps to ensure implementation of the program. *Administrative zoning* may be one of the controversial actions the planner

needs to implement to maintain the status quo of the particular experience. To change the status quo would be to change the experience; such change would be acceptable only if it were based on a change in objectives. For example, if an area was established for a class 2 hiking experience, yet it was little used by hikers, the planner might be inclined simply to accommodate off-road vehicle use. As use increased, more hikers would be displaced elsewhere, to the point that the area might be primarily used by recreational-vehicle drivers. Typically, as use builds up, the more modern forms of recreational travel will invade and displace the more primitive forms. Many public-land managers feel that zoning is inappropriate because it tends to discriminate against specific segments of the user population. Yet, as shown in the Rattlesnake Drainage example, the failure to zone constitutes tacit zoning—favoring one user group over another. In this same example, the one we end up favoring because we did not zone is not the one we chose to favor in our objectives. In sum, management by objectives is only as good as the actions taken to implement those objectives.

Wilderness use is one of the activities that the manager has failed to recognize by its unique location on the spectrum—and the associated norms of the experience. Wilderness is not only a class 1 experience; it occupies a unique niche within the class 1 zone. It defines the extremity of the roadless portion of the spectrum. There are only two well-defined points on the continuum, and these are the extremities: wilderness and the inner city.

The typical scenario in *wilderness* has been incremental development such as external road improvement, internal travel access, facilities at trailheads, bridges across streams, toilets near lakes, and the like. With the increase in development, the norms of the experience have changed, causing in many areas a series of visitor displacements (Figure 20.9). The end result is that, although we think we are offering a class 1 experience, we are in fact offering at best a class 2 experience. Unfortunately, many managers have not recognized this and are continuing to erode the experience by more incremental development. The standard argument is that there is more and more "demand" for wilderness, so "we have got to do something." First, people's initial response is an attraction to the word *wilderness,* but thereafter they are responding to the norms of the experience we have designed into the system. Thus the "demand" (consumption) is really based on the norms we develop through the area-planning process. We have typically used the term wilderness as a catchall for most *roadless experiences.* What is needed now is the development of a variety of roadless recreation experiences; ideally many of them would be located nearer to the participant and on lands that could sustain higher levels of use. It appears that most people would prefer a class 2 or 3 roadless experience to a class 1 wilderness. If we refuse to clear downed timber from trails, there is a good probability that the "demand" for wilderness would suddenly drop. The people displaced would be responding to an increment of reverse development—decreased access.

Carrying-Capacity Syndrome

Recreational carrying capacity is a management concept that places recreation into the context of *site capabilities.* There are two reasons why carrying capacity has surfaced as a managerial issue.

1. The growing demand for recreational (particularly outdoor) space is, in some areas, fast outstripping not only the existing and proposed facilities but even the resource. For example, it has been estimated that in New York State the demand for recreational land is growing at a rate four times that of the population.

2. Heavily used, depleted, and deteriorating recreational sites already constitute a serious problem in certain areas (Figure 20.13) and have focused attention on the management of recreational land to its carrying capacity (16).

Because the issue concerns escalating demand for a finite resource base, management models that associate demand for recreation with the capacity and limitation of the resource base have become popular. These methods assume a wide variety of ap-

proaches and the concept applied is generically known as recreational carrying capacity.

Recreational carrying capacity has been defined as the type of use that can be supported over a specific period of time by an area developed at a certain level without causing excessive damage to either the physical environment or the experience for the visitor (17). Carrying capacity has also been used to express architectural or design limits. A parking lot may have a designed capacity of sixty cars. That parking lot's carrying capacity is the sixty spaces multiplied by an automobile turnover rate.

In outdoor recreational settings, capacity may be expressed in design units such as camping spaces or picnic tables. When the recreational experience is separated from designed limitation, application of a design capacity concept becomes less precise. Is the carrying capacity of a beach area the number of towels that can be placed next to each other? Probably not; very few people would tolerate such use levels.

The concept of carrying capacity is not new (18–24). It has been implicit, if not always explicitly defined, in many aspects of land use. Carrying capacity developed as a range management concept, for example, refers to the negative consequences to a population of overusing its feeding range (18). If an elk herd exceeds the capability of its feeding range to regenerate, elements of the herd die—a definite negative impact on the elk. Impacts of recreation overuse do not have similar consequences. In this search for consequences of recreational use, the focus centers on the principal product of recreation: user satisfaction.

Much of the early social carrying-capacity work was based on the assumption that increasing numbers reduced the satisfaction of the visitor. Under this model, average individual satisfaction is reduced with the inclusion of each new user. For a while total satisfaction increases but later begins to level off and soon declines (25). The use level before the leveling off was considered to be the social carrying capacity. By periodically measuring satisfaction in the field, researchers and managers hoped to find the carrying capacity for specific sites. Studies (26, 27), however, indicate that the simple satisfac-

Figure 20.13 Heavily utilized campgrounds, (*a*) A campground managed to sustain a great amount of use; (*b*) a campground with little management. Both are in the Savage River State Forest, Maryland. (Photograph by R. H. Becker.)

tion model based on density of use is not valid, and a more complex, multidimensional model has been suggested. Becker (28) provided an empirical basis by observing user densities as a means of separating users into homogeneous subsets and then statistically testing the perceptions of the desired experiences. His conclusion was that "satisfaction would appear strongly linked with the nature of the experience and is independent of use density levels."

There has been heavy emphasis on studying recreational carrying capacity; this obsession with carrying capacity has tended to oversimplify the role of the manager. Many land managers have already spent a large amount of money on research and gathering other data. At Grand Canyon, during a four-year period, about $500,000 was spent on such studies (29). Grand Canyon personnel spent a considerable amount of time and effort gathering public input through meetings at various major western cities and such things as questionnaires and workbook response to management proposals. Most of the managers generally looked at the research and study programs in combination with public involvement and legislative authority as a means to a "final management plan."

As Grand Canyon managers began their efforts, it became evident that they would *never* reach a final management plan because public demand for river trips is dynamic. As new information becomes available and public demands change, managers have to respond with dynamic plans that adapt to changing conditions and pressure. No management plan can be of value if it is "set in concrete." Grand Canyon is currently involved in a court suit because demands have apparently changed and management has not kept up with that change.

Thus success as a manager should not be measured in numbers of people or capacity but in *how well the participants match with the experiences*. The manager should steer away from capacity—a search for a magic number—and develop recreational opportunities based on *management by objectives*. The primary objective should focus on the type of experience to be offered.

References

1. M. CLAWSON AND J. L. KNETSCH, *Economics of Outdoor Recreation,* Johns Hopkins Press, Baltimore, 1966.

2. D. M. KNUDSON, *Outdoor Recreation,* Macmillan, New York, 1980.

3. ANON., "Assessing demand for outdoor recreation," Nat. Acad. Sci. Rept., U.S.D.I., Bur. Outdoor Rec., Washington, D.C., 1975.

4. J. HUIZINGA, *Homoludens: A Study of the Plan Element of Culture,* Beacon, Boston, 1966.

5. R. D. LAING, *The Politics of Experience,* Ballantine Books, New York, 1967.

6. J. G. HOF, "Problems in projecting recreation resources used through supply and demand analysis." In *Proc. I.U.F.R.O. Meeting on Economics of Outdoor Recreation,* Washington, D.C., 1979.

7. P. J. BROWN, B. L. DRIVER, AND C. McCONNELL, "The opportunity spectrum concept and behavioral information in outdoor recreation resource supply inventories: Background and application." In *Proc. National Workshop on Integrated Inventories of Renewable Natural Resources.* Tucson, Ariz., 1978.

8. ANON., *1986 R.O.S. Book,* U.S.D.A. For. Serv., Washington, D.C., 1986.

9. ANON., *R.O.S. Users Guide,* U.S.D.A. For. Serv., Washington, D.C., 1982.

10. J. A. WAGAR, "Campgrounds for many tastes," U.S.D.A. For. Serv., Intermountain For. Range Expt. Sta., Res. Paper INT-6, Ogden, Utah, 1963.

11. P. J. BROWN, "Information needs for river recreation planning and management," in *Proc. River Management and Research Symp.,* D. Lime, ed., U.S.D.A. For. Serv., St. Paul, Minn., 1977.

12. A. JUBENVILLE, "River recreation research needs for the 1980's: Role segregation/allocation." In *Proc. Symp. on Applied Research in the 1980's for Parks and Outdoor Recreation,* Victoria, B.C., 1980.

13. R. SCHREYER AND J. W. ROGGENBUCK, *Leisure Sci., 1,* 373 (1978).

14. R. SCHREYER, "Succession and displacement in river recreation, Part I, Problem definition and analysis," River Recreation Project Rept., U.S.D.A. For. Serv., North Cent. For. Expt. Sta., St. Paul, Minn., 1979.

15. R. H. BECKER, B. J. NIEMANN, AND W. A. GATES, "Displace-

ment of users within a river system: Social and environmental trade-offs," paper presented at *Second Conf. on Scientific Research in the National Parks,* San Francisco, U.S. Park Service, 1979.

16. J. Tivy, *The Concept and Determination of Carrying Capacity of Recreational Land in the USA,* The Countryside Commission, Perth, Scotland, 1972.

17. D. W. Lime and G. H. Stankey, "Carrying capacity: Maintaining outdoor recreation quality." In *Recreation Symp. Proc.,* U.S.D.A. For. Serv., Syracuse, N.Y., 1971.

18. H. T. Heady, *Rangeland Management,* McGraw–Hill, New York, 1975.

19. R. C. Lucas, "The recreational capacity of the Quetico–Superior area," U.S.D.A. For. Serv., Res. Pap. LS-15, 1964.

20. J. A. Wagar, *The Carrying Capacity of Wildlands for Recreation,* For. Sci. Monogr. 7, Soc. Am. Foresters, Washington, D.C., 1964.

21. M. Chubb, "Outdoor recreation land capacity: Concepts, usage, and definitions," M.S. thesis, Michigan State University, East Lansing, 1964.

22. M. Chubb and P. Ashton, "Park and recreation standards research: The Creation of Environmental Quality Controls for recreation," Recreation Research and Planning Unit, Tech. Rept. 5, Michigan State Univ., East Lansing, 1969.

23. G. H. Stankey, "Visitor perception of wilderness recreation carrying capacity," U.S.D.A. For. Serv., Res. Rept. INT-142, Ogden, Utah, 1973.

24. G. H. Stankey and J. Baden, "Rationing wilderness use: Methods, problems, and guidelines," U.S.D.A. For. Serv., Res. Pap. INT-192, Ogden, Utah, 1977.

25. C. J. Cecchetti and U. K. Smith, *Soc. Sci. Res., 2,* 15 (1973).

26. B. Shelby, "Motors and oars in the Grand Canyon: River contact study," National Park Service, Washington, D.C., 1976.

27. T. A. Heberlein, "Density, crowding, and satisfaction: Sociological studies for determining carrying capacity," in *Proc. River Management and Research Symp.,* D. Lime, ed., U.S.D.A. For. Serv., St. Paul, Minn., 1977.

28. R. H. Becker, *Leisure Sci., 1,* 241 (1978).

29. K. R. Mak, M. O. Jensen, and T. L. Hartman, "Management response to growing pressures in western whitewater rivers—the art of the possible." In *Proc. River Management and Research Symp.,* D. Lime, ed., U.S.D.A. For. Serv., St. Paul, Minn., 1977.

CHAPTER 21

Behavior and Management of Forest Fires

CRAIG G. LORIMER

In many areas of the world, human beings have historically been the principal cause of forest fires, both in the actual number of fires and in the total area burned. Yet lightning fires have probably occurred for as long as there have been regions of dense vegetation and occasional periods of dry weather (Figure 21.1). In some regions, bits of charcoal embedded in lake sediments testify to the periodic occurrence of fires over thousands of years (1), and it is likely that at least some of these were caused by lightning. Evidence of fires in the distant past can also sometimes be found on the forest site itself. Long-lived and relatively fire-resistant trees such as coast redwood and ponderosa pine often bear visible external wounds caused by fire (Figure 21.2). When the trunks of such trees are examined in cross section, scars of fires that occurred centuries ago may be evident (2). Even in forests that show no obvious indication of recent fire, careful examina- tion of the lower layers of the forest floor will often reveal fragments of charcoal from fires that occurred hundreds of years ago.

We need not appeal to historical evidence, how- ever, to establish the importance of fire in natural communities. On a worldwide basis, it is estimated that approximately 500,000 cloud-to-ground light- ning discharges occur in forested regions each day (3). Most of these discharges probably strike trees, although only about 10 percent of them actually result in fires (4). Hardly a year goes by when foresters in western North America are not busy locating and suppressing lightning fires.

Natural Fire Regimes

The frequency of lightning fires is highly variable in different parts of the world, even over relatively

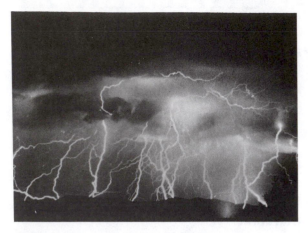

Figure 21.1 Several minutes of lightning during a thunderstorm in the Rocky Mountains. In this region lightning causes 60 percent of all fires. (Courtesy of U.S.D.A. Forest Service.)

Figure 21.2 Multiple fire scars visible on a cross section of this old ponderosa pine tree (inset) in the Bitterroot National Forest, in western Montana, reveal that twenty-one fires occurred on this site between 1659 and 1915. [From Arno (2); courtesy of U.S.D.A. Forest Service.]

short distances. Lightning fires are infrequent in tropical rain forests, and they are relatively uncommon in moist temperate areas such as western Europe and much of eastern North America. The range in natural fire frequency is evident by comparing wildfire statistics for the eastern and western United States. In the eastern forests, lightning causes 2 percent or less of all forest fires. The incidence of lightning fires in the western conifer forests, on the other hand, is probably the highest of any region in the world (3). In the Rocky Mountain region, for instance, lightning causes no less than 60 percent of all fires. It is not unusual for a single storm to ignite more than thirty fires in the region over which it passes.

Much of this variability can be attributed to *climate* and *topography*. Lightning fires are obviously more common in regions with a pronounced dry season and in mountainous country that is subject to more thunderstorms. But the nature of the vegetation seems to exert considerable influence as well. Fires are much more common in conifer forests than in stands of broad-leaved deciduous trees. The reason for this is not entirely clear, but it is possibly explained by the chemical makeup of the foliage and wood. According to one hypothesis, conifers have larger quantities of flammable chemical compounds which, after the impact of a lightning bolt, are easily vaporized and ignited (4, 5).

Relatively few lightning fires reach catastrophic proportions. Lightning strikes often occur during periods of high humidity or rain, whereas fires of human origin are actually more likely to occur in fair weather. For this reason lightning fires are often less intense and more easily suppressed than those caused by human beings. Of the 63,050 lightning fires suppressed on U.S. national forests between 1960 and 1969, 97 percent were kept to a size of 4 hectares (10 acres) or less.

It is clear, however, that under certain weather and fuel conditions, lightning fires can be as large and intense as any other type of fire. "Dry" lightning strikes in the absence of rain are common events, and even under damp conditions, a fire can smolder in leaf litter or a dead tree for days or even weeks until dry conditions return. For example, the light-

Figure 21.3 Surface fire. (Courtesy of U.S.D.A. Forest Service.)

Figure 21.4 Crown fire. (Courtesy of U.S.D.A. Forest Service.)

ning-caused Sundance Fire of 1967 in Idaho burned 23,000 hectares (56,000 acres), and the Great Idaho Fire of 1910, set mostly by multiple lightning strikes, engulfed an area of not less than 1 million hectares (almost 3 million acres). Assessment of the possibilities of lightning fires reaching a large size has become increasingly important in recent years as greater attention has been given to restoration of natural fire regimes in parks and wilderness.

Influence on the Landscape

The frequency and intensity of fires in a particular region may have an important role in shaping the forest landscape. Fire frequency and intensity partly determine whether most forest stands will be young or old, even-aged or all-aged, early-successional or climax. These characteristics, in turn, affect wildlife

populations, forest growth, and insect and disease conditions.

Parts of western North America have a natural fire regime whereby frequent light *surface fires* burn much of the litter layer and may kill some of the understory vegetation, but have little effect on the mature trees (Figure 21.3). Evidence from fire scars on old living trees indicates that frequency of fires in a given stand of trees, known as the *recurrence interval* or *mean fire interval,* was often as short as nine to twelve years (Figure 21.2). Since only the more intense surface fires cause scars, this represents a conservative estimate of fire frequency. The more destructive *crown fires* that sweep through the forest canopy were much less frequent, but extensive even-aged stands of "pioneer" species such as lodgepole pine testify that crown fires must have occurred at periodic intervals as well (Figure 21.4).

Northern Minnesota is an example of an area in which crown fires and intense surface fires are fairly common. As a result, the primeval forest landscape was dominated by early-successional species such as aspen, jack pine, and red pine, and climax forests were rare. The recurrence interval is estimated to have been approximately 50 to 100 years, which is shorter than the maximum life span of the trees.

There is, however, great variability in the frequency of natural fires in different regions. Fires were much less common in the northern hardwoods region stretching from Wisconsin to Maine. Climax forests dominated the landscape of this region in presettlement times (7, 8), and uneven-aged stands were common (9, 10). Intervals between severe fires in a given stand may have been 1000 years or more based on both historical records and field evidence (9, 11).

The Natural Role of Fire

Given that lightning fires are common events in some regions, it is not surprising that a number of species show evidence of adaptations to periodic fire. Although the nature of this adaptation varies among species, most fire-adapted species possess characteristics that enable them to colonize rapidly and dominate severely burned areas. Some of the birches and aspens have light seeds that can be transported considerable distances by wind, thus increasing the chances that seeds will reach a burned area. Other species, such as jack pine, lodge-pole pine, and pitch pine, have seeds that are held in tightly closed *serotinous* cones. Unlike the cones of most gymnosperms, serotinous cones are sealed by resin, and seeds are not released until high temperatures melt the resin and allow the cones to open. The seeds of fire-adapted species germinate rapidly on charred surfaces or exposed soil, and the seedlings tend to be tolerant of the dry surface conditions and extremes of temperature common to exposed sites. As is typical of shade-intolerant species, they grow rapidly, particularly in the early years, and hence usually outcompete other species that may arrive on the site. In areas prone to repeated surface fires, trees of certain species, such as ponderosa

pine and longleaf pine, develop thick bark at maturity that makes them fairly resistant to injury from light fires. Frequent fires may be beneficial to such species by retarding the invasion of these stands by species of later successional stages. Thus in the South, fires in the longleaf pine forests hamper the development of a dense understory of climax hardwood species. The beneficial effects of fire on certain species of trees are paralleled by beneficial effects on the habitat of many wildlife species (see Chapter 17).

Fire may have more subtle beneficial functions as well. In cold, dry climates, forest litter and woody debris have a tendency to build up faster than they can be decomposed. Occasional light surface fires can reduce this accumulation of hazardous fuels, which otherwise might build up to a point that catastrophic fires would become more likely. Burning of this debris may release into the soil and make available to plants some of the nutrients previously locked up in organic matter.

Human Influence

Human modification of the natural fire regime is not a recent development. It is well documented that primitive societies commonly used fire to improve hunting and overland travel, to aid in land clearance, and to reduce insect and snake populations. The shifting pattern of slash-and-burn agriculture has long been widely practiced by native peoples of the tropics. Intentional burning was also a common practice among North American Indians, and although most of these fires were probably light surface fires, we can only guess what proportion of the even-aged postfire forests at this time were the result of Indian activity. In Massachusetts in 1632, a colonist named Thomas Morton wrote the following.

> **The Salvages are accustomed, to set fire of the Country in all places where they come; and to burne it, twize a yeare. . . . And this custome of firing the Country is the meanes to make it passable, and by that meanes the trees grow here, and there as in our parks, and makes the Country very beautifull, and commodius.**

The number of large and destructive fires dramatically increased with the arrival of European settlers. Relatively few of the trees cut down for land clearance were used for lumber or fuel, because settlers had much more timber than they could possibly use themselves, and there was little demand for wood elsewhere on the open market. So the settlers developed a quick method of disposing of the trees: setting them ablaze. Early historians reported that the usual approach was either to fell the trees and wait until the fuels dried sufficiently to burn, or else to save some effort by cutting the trees halfway through and letting the wind do the rest of the work. In either case the resulting fires were clearly risky no matter the precautions taken. Seldom have so many large and disastrous fires occurred over such a short period of time. Some of the worst fires occurred in the northern forests, where large accumulations of slash, an abundance of coniferous trees, and extensive land-clearing operations utilizing fire created especially hazardous conditions. In early October 1825 a series of fires raged over 1.2 million hectares (3 million acres) in Maine and New Brunswick. An equally large area was burned in 1871 and 1881 in Michigan and Wisconsin. In fact, so many large fires occurred during this time that occasionally the amount of smoke and particulates in the atmosphere was sufficient to cast semidarkness over the land. One such "dark day" in 1780, caused by fires raging in Vermont and New York, was described as follows:

> **The legislature of Connecticut was in session at Hartford on that day. The deepening gloom enwrapped the city, and the rooms of the state house grew dark. The journal of the house of representatives reads "None could see to read or write in the house, or even at a window, or distinguish persons at a small distance" (12).**

This scenario set the stage for a policy of vigorous *fire suppression*. Not only did fire frequently destroy a valuable timber resource, but even small smoldering surface fires represented a constant threat to human life and property should weather conditions suddenly create more severe burning conditions. There were too many disastrous fires to allow room for the thought that some fires might have beneficial effects. It is therefore not surprising that one of the top priorities of the American Forestry Association when it convened in 1875 was the "protection of the existing forests of the country from unnecessary waste," of which fire was the leading cause. The fruits of these labors became evident in the Weeks Law of 1911 and the Clarke–McNary Act of 1924, which for the first time provided federal funding to assist the states in developing a cooperative forest fire control program (see Chapters 1, 10, and 11). Although the actual amount of money provided was small at first, it did allow the construction of fire towers and the hiring of fire wardens and equipment.

Fire control on publicly owned lands has undergone several changes in the current century (13). In the 1920s and 1930s by a policy of attempted fire exclusion, all wildfires were suppressed as quickly as possible. In 1935 the "10 A.M. *fire-control policy*" was formulated, setting the objective of rapid and thorough suppression of all fires during potentially dangerous fire weather by ten o'clock the next morning. The planned use of fire under carefully specified conditions, known as *prescribed burning*, was nevertheless soon acknowledged to be useful in achieving certain objectives such as reducing the amount of litter and fallen branches, which act as fuel, and preparing the forest floor as a seedbed.

Some modification of the 10 A.M. policy was required in certain areas. In parts of the western United States, labor and equipment were not always sufficient to suppress all fires, and it was recognized that such attempts had probably passed a point of diminishing returns in terms of costs and benefits. Fire suppression was therefore handled on a priority basis from about 1940 to 1960. On federal lands, fires burning in areas of highest resource values were attacked first. Remote areas of noncommercial forest with low-hazard fuels were attended to last.

The current widely accepted policy on forest fires is that of *fire management,* not simply fire control. This policy takes advantage of the beneficial effects of some forest fires while still carrying on suppression of fires expected to have undesirable effects. Several features of this policy represent a bold departure from previous policies. *First,* it is recognized that the decision on how to handle a particular fire on federal lands should be based not only on the anticipated behavior of the fire, but also on the long-range management objectives for each unit of land. In some national forests, foresters write a management plan for each homogeneous unit of vegetation and fuels, and the degree to which fire is necessary to accomplish the objectives of the plan is clearly stated. *Second,* there is a provision for allowing certain fires to burn under supervision if the predictions of fire behavior indicate that the fire will help achieve the management objectives. For example, a lightning fire or other unplanned ignition may be allowed to burn under surveillance if fuel reduction is needed on that unit of land, and the fire is predicted to burn as a light or moderate surface fire. *Finally,* fire is acknowledged to be more than simply a management tool. It is considered to be an environmental factor that may serve a necessary function not easily accomplished by other methods. Thus, although understory hardwoods in southern pine forests can be controlled by cutting down the hardwood stems and applying herbicides to the stumps, it is recognized that other beneficial effects of fire cannot feasibly be duplicated by mechanical means (13).

Fire Behavior

Anticipating the behavior of a fire is one of the most critical aspects of fire management. The choice of strategy in suppressing wildfires and carrying out prescribed burning depends largely on how the fire is expected to behave—its rate of spread, direction of travel, and intensity. These aspects of fire behavior are regulated by a number of interacting factors. The prerequisites for the start and spread of a forest fire are (1) flammable fuels, (2) sufficient heat energy to bring the fuels to the ignition temperature, and (3) adequate oxygen. Virtually all the phenomena influencing the behavior of a fire, including those related to weather and topography, can ultimately be attributed to one or more of these three factors. Thus the size, total weight, and moisture content of fuel elements partly determine the amount of heat required for ignition and the heat released by combus-

tion. Their spatial arrangement influences the availability of oxygen. Variations in these factors are ultimately reflected in the rate at which the fire spreads and its intensity. Grass fires, for example, spread rapidly but are of relatively low intensity, whereas fires in heavy logging debris spread slowly but burn intensely.

Fuel Conditions and Fire Types

Fuels are often classified in a general manner by their spatial location in the forest. *Surface fuels* constitute a large, heterogeneous group of fuels found on or close to the surface of the ground. Included are undecomposed leaf litter, fallen twigs and branches, logs, grass, herbs, tree seedlings, and low shrubs. *Ground fuels* are found beneath the loose layer of surface litter. They include partly decomposed organic matter or duff, roots, and muck or peat in wet areas. *Aerial fuels* include all flammable material in the subcanopy layers of the forest and in the tree crowns. Fuels are classified in this manner partly because of the three distinctive types of fires associated with them: surface fires, ground fires, and crown fires.

Surface Fires   The most readily available fuels for a forest fire are the dry surface layer of litter on the forest floor, interspersed small dead branchwood, and the cured grass in some forests. This is the material consumed in most *surface fires.* Green herbs and understory vegetation are usually a deterrent to the spread of fire in the spring because of the high moisture content of the foliage, but they may contribute significantly to fire intensity and rate of spread when in a cured condition. Although the larger fuels, such as fallen logs, may be partly or wholly consumed by the time a surface fire has died out, such material is too large and often too damp to influence the forward momentum of the fire. Thus research seems to indicate that the effect of fuels on the forward rate of spread of a surface fire is largely determined by the amount, arrangement, and moisture content of the fine fuels. The effect of larger surface fuels, such as fallen logs, is to cause a more intense fire. For this reason the most intense fires are usually those that start in logging slash or other areas of heavy fuel accumulations. In general, the higher the total weight of fuels, the more difficult the fire will be to control.

Ground Fires In finely divided ground fuels such as peat or duff, oxygen is often limiting to the point that only glowing combustion is possible. As a result, *ground fires* are often of low intensity and spread slowly. They are, however, remarkably persistent, often smoldering for days or weeks. For this reason they present an especially serious problem, and it is often difficult to judge whether suppression activities have been successful in completely extinguishing the fire. Ironically, extinguishing ground fires that burn in bogs may require great quantities of water, much more than might be required on upland sites. One peat fire in Michigan took 36 days for "containment" at a size of 80 hectares, but attempts to extinguish it were not successful until a small river was diverted by bulldozers 20 days later to drown the fire completely (14).

Crown Fires The susceptibility of tree crowns to ignition varies somewhat among species. Especially pronounced is the difference between coniferous and broad-leaved deciduous species. *Crown fires* are fairly common in coniferous forests but rare in hardwoods, probably because of differences in chemical makeup and the average amount of moisture contained in the foliage. Yet even in conifer forests, the probability of a crown fire is low if the understory is sparse and the trees are mature.

Most crown fires start as surface fires, but the reasons why a fire may make the transition in particular cases are still not well known. The surface fire must reach a rather high intensity in order to desiccate and consume live foliage in the crown, especially in mature forests where the lowest limbs are high above the ground. The role of a stratified understory is uncertain. As previously mentioned, green herbaceous and other broad-leaved plants ordinarily act as a fire deterrent. Traditionally, however, a coniferous understory has been thought to serve as a "bridge" to the crowns; by first consuming the foliage of understory conifers, the fire can then climb to the crowns of the mature trees. Although this idea may have some validity, some observations suggest that a dense coniferous understory in a closed stand may actually lessen the chance of crown fire by reducing wind speeds within the forest (15).

Weather Conditions

Within a given fuel type, fire behavior is regulated largely by the state of the weather. Particularly important are the effects of *atmospheric moisture* and *wind*. Fuel moisture is determined not only by the amount and duration of precipitation, but also by relative humidity during rainless periods. As humidity increases, fuels absorb moisture from the air, and more of the fire's energy is used to drive off this moisture prior to combustion. Evaporation of water vapor from the surface of the fuel also has a smothering effect by limiting the amount of oxygen available for combustion. As humidity decreases, fuels give off moisture to the air. The rapidity of response to humidity depends on the size of the fuel elements. The "flashy" fine fuels respond quickly to changes in relative humidity, but the larger fuels respond much more slowly. The rapidity with which fine fuels respond to atmospheric moisture is evident in the diurnal variations in fire intensity, which are caused largely by normal fluctuations in relative humidity. Thus it is common for a large fire alternately to flare up during the day and to die down at night. Fire intensity and the probability of ignition are closely related to relative humidity and fuel moisture (Table 21.1).

Fire behavior is also affected by atmospheric stability, which is defined as the resistance of the atmosphere to vertical motion. In a stable atmosphere winds are steady and horizontal, visibility is relatively poor, and clouds are the layered stratus type. In an unstable atmosphere gusty, turbulent winds, vertical air motion, and cumulus clouds prevail. Crowning and erratic fires are more likely when the atmosphere is unstable, for the vertical air movement encourages the development of a strong convection column of smoke and burning debris fragments. However, if fuel moisture is at a moder-

Table 21.1 Effect of Relative Humidity and Fuel Moisture on Fire Behavior

Relative Humidity (percent)	Moisture Content (percent)		Fire Behavior
	Forest Litter	Small Branchwood	
>95	>25		Little or no ignition.
>60	>20	>15	Very little ignition; fire smolders and spreads slowly.
45–60	15–19	12–15	Low ignition hazard, but campfires become dangerous; glowing brands cause ignition when relative humidity <50%. Fire spreads slowly but readily; prescribed burning may be feasible.
35–45	11–14	10–12	Medium ignitibility; matches become dangerous, "easy" burning conditions. Many prescribed burns are conducted in this range.
25–35	8–10	7–10	High ignition hazard; matches always dangerous. Occasional crowning, spotting caused by gusty winds. "Moderate" burning conditions.
15–25	5–7	5–7	Quick ignition, rapid buildup, extensive crowning; any increase in wind causes increased spotting, crowning, loss of control. Fire moves up bark of trees igniting aerial fuels; long-distance spotting in pine stands. Dangerous burning conditions.
<15	<5	<5	All sources of ignition dangerous. Aggressive burning; spot fires occur often and spread rapidly, and extreme five behavior is probable. Critical burning conditions.

Source: Adapted from reference 35.

ate level, indicating little potential for severe fires, days with an unstable atmosphere may be preferable for prescribed burning because smoke disperses better.

Wind has a dramatic effect on the rate of fire spread and intensity. It has long been a rule of thumb among fire control officials that the rate of spread is approximately proportional to the square of the wind speed; hence, a doubling of wind speed will quadruple the rate of spread.

The effect of wind on the pattern or shape of fires is illustrated in Figure 21.5. Under conditions of moderate or strong winds, fires tend to burn in elliptical patterns with the long axis in the direction of the wind. The strategy of fire suppression is partly based on estimates of the increase in perimeter of this elliptical zone of flames per unit time. The pattern of spread, however, can be greatly changed by abrupt wind shifts, which can turn the flank of a

fire into a much expanded burning head. This greatly increases the area burned by the fire. It is not uncommon for fires to undergo one or more moderate shifts in direction.

Topography

Fires burn more quickly up steep slopes, largely because heat generated by the fire front is directed more closely to the surface of the ground, thereby decreasing the moisture and increasing the temperature of the fuels ahead of the fire. Topography also has many effects on the microclimate of a particular site. Slopes facing toward the south and southwest, for example, tend to be the warmest and driest slopes because they are exposed to the direct rays of the sun during the hottest part of the day. As a result fires are more frequent and spread more quickly on south slopes. Topography also modifies and chan-

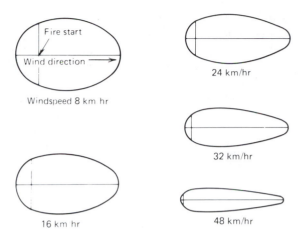

Figure 21.5 The approximate fire shapes created by winds blowing in a constant direction at different velocities. The various fire shapes are drawn to different scales. [From Albini (20).]

nels airflow patterns. In the absence of strong prevailing winds, fires are most likely to be driven by upslope winds during the day and downslope winds at night. Rugged, mountainous topography often induces turbulent winds that increase fire intensity and the possibility of erratic behavior.

Erratic Behavior

It is not uncommon for crown fires at some point in their development to suddenly increase in intensity, which may be visibly apparent from the development of a powerful convection column of rapidly rising smoke and hot gases. Such fires are often called *blowup fires* and represent an unfavorable turn of events for fire fighters because they are often uncontrollable by conventional fire-fighting techniques (Figure 21.6). For a dynamic convection

Figure 21.6 Aftermath of a blowup fire, showing numerous snags which act as a major source of fuel for subsequent intense fires. (Courtesy of U.S.D.A. Forest Service.)

column to develop, the fire must exceed a certain threshold of intensity, the initiating factor for which may be a sudden increase in wind speed or the start of crowning (16). The convection column tends to create its own "draft," which helps maintain fire intensity at a high level. The behavior of blowup fires is frequently erratic. They may generate high winds in excess of 350 kilometers per hour, further increasing fire intensity, as well as whirlwinds of hot air and flames that may hurl burning debris far ahead of the main fire front. Such behavior, known as *spotting,* can start many new fires.

Prediction of Fire Behavior

A fire researcher named H. T. Gisborne remarked at a conference in the 1940s, "I doubt that anyone will ever be able to sit down to a machine, punch a key for every factor of the situation, and have the machine tell him what to do" (17). Be that as it may, the advent of *computer simulation techniques* in recent years has proved to be very useful to fire managers. Clearly it would be desirable to have an estimate at least of the rate of spread and intensity of a fire given certain weather and fuel conditions.

The quantitative study of fire behavior and prediction has been intensively carried out at the U.S. Forest Service's Northern Forest Fire Lab in Missoula, Montana, for the past two decades. One of the basic aims of this research has been to use physical laws, such as the law of conservation of energy, to describe the process of combustion and fire spread in mathematical terms (18, 19). The use of basic principles of physics to predict fire behavior has some advantages over statistical correlations between past fire behavior and various independent variables, because the first approach is more universal in its applicability; that is, it can be used to predict fire behavior in a wide variety of forest types, shrublands, and even grasslands. Developing these equations required much elaborate experimentation with fire behavior in a laboratory environment, because some of the mechanisms of heat transfer and combustion were not known, and carefully controlled experiments were the only way to determine empirically the required factors.

This type of research has had handsome payoffs in practical application, one of the most useful of which has been the development of a revised *National Fire-Danger Rating System* (21). Various systems for rating fire danger had long been used to indicate the relative severity of fire-weather conditions, probable suppression forces needed, and other information. With the new system much more specific and accurate predictions are possible. Included are predictions of the number of fires expected per unit area, ease of ignition, rate of spread, and burning intensity. Using a computer program known as BEHAVE, fire fighters have been able to forecast the perimeter location of individual fires at various intervals of time (22). A current limitation of the system is that it applies only to surface fires; however, it is possible to infer the likelihood of crown fire and spotting from the surface fire ratings. As with all theoretical models of natural phenomena, these predictions must be compared with the observed behavior of many fires before proper interpretation can be made.

Ratings of fire danger are computed daily by utilizing measurements of such variables as wind speed, fuel moisture, amount and duration of precipitation, lightning activity, and the condition of the herbaceous vegetation. Although some of the needed measurements can be obtained from stations maintained by the Weather Service, the stations do not ordinarily make measurements of such important fire variables as fuel moisture or vegetative conditions, and the locations of ordinary weather stations (usually in valleys) are often not representative of vast tracts of forestland. A network of fire-weather stations in forested areas has been established in recent years to meet these needs. Once the necessary data have been obtained, tables or graphs based on the fire-spread equations are used to obtain predictions for various aspects of fire behavior.

The adoption of a standardized National Fire-Danger Rating System has simplified administrative procedures and improved communication among government agencies. In 1954 eight different systems were in use; by 1977 the new national system had been adopted by all federal agencies and by thirty-eight state agencies.

Fire Prevention

Because human beings are the leading cause of forest fires in most areas, fire prevention campaigns have been vigorously promoted to reduce the number of these fires. The most visible efforts are public-education campaigns via conventional media—radio messages, signs, magazine articles, news releases, and so on. Such efforts as the Smokey the Bear and Keep America Green programs have relied heavily on public education. The estimated annual timber loss caused by fires is given in Table 7.1.

In order for fire prevention programs to be highly effective, the relative importance of specific causes needs to be known. This information is usually collected from standard fire reports prepared for each fire by state forestry departments. A fifty-year statistical compilation of these reports (16) indicates that in the United States, the leading cause has been incendiarism, which has accounted for 26 percent of all fires. Other major causes have been smoking, 19 percent; debris burning, 18 percent; lightning, 9 percent; machine use, 8 percent; and campfires, 6 percent. Regional variations are pronounced. Incendiary fires are much less important in the North and West than in the South. Smoking is the leading cause in the northeastern states, with debris burning most important in the north-central states.

This information about specific causes helps indicate where the thrust of prevention campaigns should be directed. The high frequency of fires caused by smoking, for example, has led to regular appeals to crush cigarettes and use ashtrays, especially along highways where most cigarette fires occur. A high frequency of fires attributable to escaped campfires in some localities may indicate the need to install outdoor fireplaces in popular but undeveloped recreation areas. *Incendiarism* is a

more difficult problem to tackle, although it is probable that education has some effect. But particularly in the South, annual or periodic burning has long been a deeply ingrained custom among rural people; it is intended to improve cattle forage, to kill ticks, chiggers, and snakes, and to improve wildlife habitat and hunting prospects. Whatever positive results such fires may have, the fact remains that they are unsupervised wildfires, usually initiated without adequate knowledge of fuel and weather conditions. For this reason they often cause substantial damage to living trees and always have the potential for becoming uncontrollable. They are usually set without the landowners' knowledge or consent. In the late 1920s the American Forestry Association obtained funds for a traveling road show known as the "Dixie Crusaders" to educate rural southern residents about fire protection. Although such programs have achieved positive results, incendiarism is still the principal cause of wildfires in the South, accounting for 39 percent of all fires in the region.

In some areas the appropriate contact is not with individuals but with organizations. To combat the high frequency of railroad fires and those caused by power lines, foresters negotiate with the appropriate agencies to remedy the situation. Fires caused by sparks from mechanized equipment can be reduced by strict enforcement of regulations pertaining to the installation of spark arresters.

Fire prevention can also be accomplished by *hazard reduction,* commonly by reducing accumulations of particularly hazardous fuels or by constructing barriers to the spread of fire. Controlled burning in areas of heavy logging slash, along railroad tracks, and even in some forests can reduce particularly serious accumulations of fuel. The blackened remnants of trees left in the wake of a crown fire constitute one of the most hazardous types of fuel (Figure 21.6). These snags are highly susceptible to further ignition, especially by lightning. Ironically, burned-over areas are actually among the areas most susceptible to fire. Brown and Davis (16) report that examples of repeated fires in the same location "can be cited almost endlessly." Where felling of snags is economically justifiable, as on highly productive timberlands, fire damage can be reduced because fallen snags decay more quickly and have a higher moisture content than those left standing. Even in these areas, however, some snags should be left standing to provide habitat for cavity-nesting birds and mammals.

Fire Control

Wildland fire control in the United States is administered as a cooperative venture by the Forest Service, the Bureau of Land Management, the National Park Service, and the various state governments. In some areas private owners and industrial firms also participate in the suppression of fires. Fire control activities on large fires are usually very tightly organized, and the suppression activity itself may resemble a military campaign.

Detection

In the early years of the century, lookout towers formed the backbone of the fire detection system. Sufficient numbers of lookouts were placed on higher points of land in the area to provide reasonably thorough coverage of the landscape. Aerial detection of forest fires by systematic airplane flights, however, has gradually overshadowed fixed-point lookouts, partly because it is cheaper and allows for more complete and detailed coverage. Over 5000 lookouts were in use in the United States in 1953, compared to only 3500 in 1968. Most agencies continue to use a skeletal system of lookouts, however, in order to supplement the aerial reconnaissance.

More recent developments in fire detection have included the aerial use of *infrared-sensing equipment* that photographically records the location of heat sources. Although some problems in identifying heat sources remain, the use of infrared sensing equipment in aerial reconnaissance experiments has shown that it is possible to detect the presence of small targets such as glowing buckets of charcoal beneath a forest canopy. This technique has considerable potential for identifying small, smoldering fires that do not produce enough smoke to be detected by the unaided eye.

Suppression of Wildfires

When a fire has been spotted by a lookout or aerial observer, its location is reported by two-way radio to the dispatcher at the fire control headquarters. The dispatcher plots the location of the fire on a map, estimates the probable size of the attack force needed to contain the fire, and sends the needed people and equipment to the fire site.

Fire suppression can be accomplished by removing any one of the three essential "ingredients" of fire: fuel, oxygen, and heat. Fuels are removed by digging, scraping, or plowing a strip of earth known as a *fire line* in advance of the fire to halt its progress (Figure 21.7). The application of dirt, water, or fire-retardant chemicals serves to reduce both the fuel temperature and the supply of oxygen.

If the fire is not too intense, the preferred method of control is *direct attack*. The fire line is constructed near the fire edge and the flames are knocked down by water, dirt, or other means (Figure 21.7). If the fire cannot be safely approached at close range, the fire line must be constructed at a distance. In such cases fires will usually be set just inside the line and allowed to spread toward the wildfire in order to rob the fire of fuel. This is known as *indirect attack*.

Although the suppression of large forest fires generally requires the use of hand tools, bulldozers, and water pumps over a period of many hours or days, significant contributions to the overall suppression effort can be made by aerial techniques. Just as small airplanes can be used to spray insecticides on crops, so too can they be used to apply water or fire-retardant chemicals to active forest fires. The usual effects of water on a fire can be augmented by adding flame-inhibiting chemicals or other additives that enhance the "wettability" of water or increase its smothering effect on the combustion of fuels. Fine clays are often mixed with water to increase the cohesiveness of the mixture and prevent excessive dissipation during its descent. These mixtures of clay and liquids are known as *slurries*. The application of slurries from the air is

Figure 21.7 Construction of a fire line (*a*) by hand tools in a western conifer forest, and (*b*) by a tractor and plow unit in a southern pine forest. (Courtesy of U.S.D.A. Forest Service.)

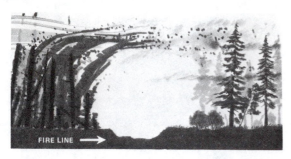

Figure 21.8 Careful surveillance is necessary to control spot fires caused by burning embers hurled across the fire line. (Reproduced with permission of the Robert J. Brady Company from *Wildfires,* 1974.)

particularly helpful as a delaying tactic that allows time for people and equipment to arrive on the scene, especially when the fire occurs in a remote location. However, aerial retardants and slurries are not usually sufficient to extinguish a forest fire, and follow-up work by ground crews is almost always necessary.

The more intense the fire, the more problematic spotting is likely to be for the ground crews. Because spotting may cause the fire to jump the line in many places (Figure 21.8), constant surveillance for spot fires by the suppression crew is necessary. Experienced fire fighters realize that under blowup conditions, the spread of a fire is seldom restricted by the location of firebreaks. Conflagration fires in the north country routinely jump scores of streams, bogs, and even lakes.

When the fire line around the perimeter of the fire has been completed and the fire is no longer spreading, it is said to be *contained.* There remains, however, the often long and tedious process of "mop-up"; all smoldering fires and firebrands near the inside edge of the fire line must be extinguished. Mop-up is necessary to ensure that the fire will not flare up again and cross the line—a quite common occurrence. Fires can even cross a fire line below the ground by burning along root channels. Burned stumps and roots near the line may therefore have to be excavated and soaked with water. Successful mop-up will make the line safe, but the interior

section of a large burned area might not be officially declared extinguished until much later, sometimes not until the arrival of winter rains or snows.

Prescribed Burning

The controlled use of fire to accomplish specific objectives is known as *prescribed burning.* The most common objectives are (1) reduction of logging debris or slash following clearcutting, which typically leaves behind large volumes of mixed fuels; (2) preparation of a seedbed for tree species that require exposed mineral soil; (3) reduction of fuel accumulations in standing forests to lessen the probability of a crown fire; (4) control of understory vegetation in certain forest types, such as hardwood saplings in southern pine stands; (5) improvement of wildlife habitat; and (6) range improvement for livestock grazing in some areas (Figure 21.9) (see Chapter 18).

Prescribed burning requires careful planning to minimize risk and to enhance the likelihood that objectives will be accomplished. Topography and fuel conditions on the treatment area should be assessed in terms of probable effects on fire behavior and desirable location of fuel breaks. It is frequently useful to obtain quantitative estimates of fuel weights and depths by standardized sampling techniques. Samples of woody material and duff can also be transported back to a lab to determine fuel moisture content as a percentage of oven-dry weight. The chances for adequate smoke dispersal must also be evaluated. This information can then be used to write the *fire prescription,* which outlines the desired effects of the burn—the approximate amount of duff and fuels to be removed, the proportion of the area to have exposed mineral soil, the proportion of understory stems to be killed, and so on. The fire prescription will include estimates of the level of fire intensity and spread rate needed to accomplish these objectives and the range of weather conditions under which the burning would be feasible (23). The National Fire-Danger Rating System can provide help in identifying suitable days.

Figure 21.9 (*a*) Before and (*b*) after prescribed burning in a sequoia–mixed-conifer forest in California. In addition to reducing the amount of fuels present as litter and fallen logs, the fire killed most of the pole-sized white fir trees shown in these photographs. [National Park Service photographs (*a*) by Bruce M. Kilgore and (*b*) by Don Taylor.]

Figure 21.10 Prescribed burning with a drip torch to reduce the fuel accumulated on the ground and to prepare the forest floor as a seedbed. (National Park Service photograph by Bruce M. Kilgore.)

Use of available fire behavior models can provide guidance in anticipating probable effects. It is also a good idea to conduct a *test burn* on a small area within plowed lines where there is no chance of escape, in order to see whether the behavior of the fire (flame length, rate of spread, etc.) is similar to what was expected. The final planning steps consist of deciding the method of burning and sequence of ignitions, the placement of fire crews, and the equipment and supplies needed.

Prescribed fires may be set by ground crews using a device such as a drip torch (Figure 21.10), or they may be ignited from the air by delayed-ignition devices ejected from aircraft or by a drip torch attached to a helicopter. Fires are commonly set within preestablished fire lines to minimize the risk of escape. Risk may be further reduced by burning the area in consecutive strips, each delimited by a fire line. Regulation of fire intensity is achieved not only by selecting days with desired weather conditions but also by planning the sequence of ignitions and the direction of spread. Fires allowed to burn in the direction of the wind are known as *head fires* and have relatively fast rates of spread and high temperatures. Fires can be induced to burn against the wind by igniting the fuels on the inside edge of a fire line. Spread in the direction of the wind is therefore prevented by the fire line, and the flames move slowly against the wind. Such *backfires* are somewhat easier to control and may be preferable to head fires on days of relatively high fire hazard.

Although some of the common objectives of prescribed burning can be accomplished by other means—for example, seedbed preparation by mechanical scarification—prescribed burning is often the most economical option available and the one least demanding of petrochemical energy. The principal disadvantages of prescribed burning are the risks involved, the problem of air pollution from the smoke, and the fact that the number of days per year suitable for burning may be few in some regions.

Environmental Impacts of Forest Fires

Early observers of the aftermath of severe forest fires frequently commented on the seemingly destructive effect on the productivity of the site. Land surveyors in 1826 reported that a conflagration in a spruce–northern hardwoods forest in New England had caused the soil to be "burnt off" in places, leaving behind a "bed of stones." Thoreau visited the site of a similar holocaust more than forty years after the fire, and found it to be still "exceedingly wild and desolate, with . . . low poplars springing up" (24). Although these early observations represent a "pre-scientific" assessment of the effects of fire, possible detrimental effects on environmental quality must be considered to understand how fire can best be managed to achieve the beneficial effects discussed earlier.

There seems to be little doubt that massive blowup fires can indeed have detrimental effects on soils. The burning of humus down to bedrock on poor sites, converting stunted forest to bare rock and shrubs, has been observed in recent times (25, 26). Intense fires have also been known to cause erosion on good sites as well. But the effects of fire on site productivity are so variable that generalizations are difficult to make. Some authors have noted that almost any effects of fire—positive, negative, or neutral—can be documented by the results of reputable researchers (27). Clearly the intensity of the fire, characteristics of the site, and weather conditions after the fire have much bearing on the outcome.

Most erosion following fires can be traced to either or both of the following causes: (1) exposure of bare soil through burning of the protective litter layer; (2) reduction of soil porosity (and hence increased runoff of water) through intense heating or clogging of soil pores by fine particles carried in runoff. Light or moderate fires such as most pre-scribed burns do not expose enough soil to cause serious erosion. Rarely do such fires burn down to mineral soil. Similarly, soil temperatures during prescribed burning are rarely hot enough to cause structural changes in the soil.

Crown fires or fires burning in logging slash, on the other hand, may be intense enough to alter soil structure as well as leave bare patches of unprotected soil. Erosion will be more severe on steep slopes than on gently sloping or level sites. Following a severe wildfire in Idaho, about 30 percent of the sample plots on gently sloping sites showed significant erosion, compared to over 80 percent on steep slopes (28). A burned area is usually revegetated by shrubs and tree seedlings within a few years, so the critical period of susceptibility to erosion does not last long.

The influence of fire on soil fertility is also somewhat variable. Even though burning of organic matter theoretically releases nutrients in a form that is more available for plant uptake, very often the addition of ash to the soil does not seem to stimulate the growth of plants, or else the effect is very short-lived (29, 30). For example, twenty years of annual or periodic prescribed burns in South Carolina had little effect on the total amount or availability of nutrients (30). Severe fires can cause some nutrients to be lost by leaching, but the total loss may actually be rather small (31).

Forest fires often have some effects on insect and disease conditions. The susceptibility of trees to insect and disease outbreaks is sometimes increased and sometimes decreased by fire. Injury from fire frequently predisposes trees to insect and disease infestations that might otherwise have been avoided. Coniferous trees weakened by fire, for example, may become more susceptible to bark beetle attack. On the other hand, the mosaic of vegetation types and age classes created by frequent fire may act as a deterrent to the spread of large-scale epidemics. Fire is also known to inhibit certain pathogens directly. In forests of the southern coastal plain, frequent surface fires kill spores that cause brown spot needle blight of longleaf pine.

Smoke from forest fires has come under scrutiny in recent years as a significant contribution to the overall air pollution problem. One ton of burning forest fuel releases approximately 1 ton of CO_2, 25 kilograms of carbon monoxide, 5 kilograms of hydrocarbons, 5 kilograms of particulates, and small amounts of nitrogen oxides. Forest fires are responsible for about 8 percent by weight of all atmospheric pollutants in the United States (32). Although open burning is restricted in many states and counties, exceptions are often granted for prescribed burning, partly because it does not constitute a major source of pollutants. It is probable that prescribed burning will be more closely regulated in the future; even now air quality is often considered in selecting days suitable for burning.

Fire in the Wilderness

In 1968, without much fanfare and on an experimental basis, the National Park Service began to allow certain lightning fires to burn unhindered in parts of Sequoia and Kings Canyon National Parks in California. This marked the beginning of an official policy to restore natural fire to certain wilderness areas.

This alteration of the long-established policy of suppressing all forest fires came about partly in response to the obvious changes that were occurring in the national parks as a result of overprotecting them from fire. For example, in the nineteenth century many forests in the Sierra Nevada were open and parklike with little undergrowth because frequent surface fires burned it away. By 1963 the Leopold Committee, assigned by the Department of the Interior to make recommendations on elk habitat and management in the parks, noted that much of the west slope of the Sierra Nevada was a "dog-hair thicket" of young trees and brush. The committee wondered:

> **Is it possible that the primitive open forest could be restored, at least on a local scale? And if so, how? We cannot offer an answer. But we are posing a question to which there should be an answer of immense concern to the National Park Service.**

Other pressing problems dictated a prompt response. The giant sequoias, whose preservation was

entrusted to the Park Service, were not regenerating because they lacked a suitable seedbed and because of competition with the dense understory of white fir. Moreover, understory fuels were accumulating to the point that conflagrations were likely. In 1965 prescribed burning was initiated in some sequoia groves to remedy this situation.

If the goal of park and wilderness management were merely to maintain certain desirable forest environments, it is likely that the policy of fire suppression would have merely been modified to allow for an active program of prescribed burning. But such action would seem to violate the spirit and intent of wilderness preservation. The congressional act of 1916 that created the National Park Service, to be sure, emphasized mainly protection of parklands in order to leave them "unimpaired" for future generations. But the Wilderness Act of 1964 was much more explicit in defining wilderness to be an area that retains its "primeval character and influence," where "man himself is a visitor who does not remain," and that is managed to preserve natural conditions.

Neither prescribed burning by itself nor total fire suppression seems appropriate under this concept of wilderness—the former because it is manipulative and somewhat arbitrary and the latter because it constitutes major indirect human modification of the vegetation in naturally fire-prone environments.

The Approach

Full restoration of the natural fire regime in wilderness areas is usually not feasible, because some fires would inevitably threaten to burn beyond the park boundaries onto private land, or endanger human life inside or outside the park. The current intent of the natural-fire management policy is to allow fire to "more nearly play its natural role" whenever possible. In most areas several management zones corresponding to different vegetation types and fuel conditions have been established. Each lightning fire is monitored, and a particular fire may be allowed to burn, or its spread may be blocked in one direction, or it may be totally suppressed. The decision will be based on the vegetation types, fuels, projected fire

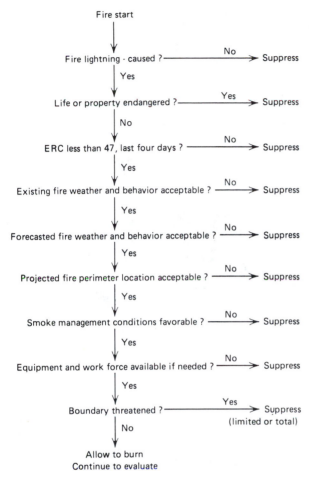

Figure 21.11 Decision flowchart for evaluating fires occurring in high-elevation areas of a wilderness tract in the Kootenai National Forest of Montana. The Energy Release Component (ERC) is an index from the National Fire Danger Rating System that indicates potential fire intensity. [From Fischer (34); courtesy of U.S.D.A. Forest Service.]

weather, and location of the fire in relation to human development or private property (Figure 21.11). Most fires caused by human beings continue to be suppressed. Prescribed burning is sometimes used in zones where management of natural fires is not feasible or where heavy, unnatural accumulations of fuels must be reduced artificially in preparation for natural-fire management.

Twenty Years of Natural Fire Management

Fire restoration programs have been established primarily in the high-elevation zones of some major western wilderness areas, such as Yellowstone, Yosemite, Sequoia, Kings Canyon, and Grand Teton National Parks, and the Selway–Bitterroot Wilderness Area in Idaho. Everglades National Park in Florida is an example of an eastern park firmly committed to natural-fire management, having allowed or conducted over 400 fires by 1981. The more general policy of allowing fires to burn on nonwilderness public lands if the fires meet land management objectives is also in effect in some national forests and national parks (33, 34).

Experience with the policy in a number of different wilderness areas has shown that most lightning fires never burn more than a small area before they die out naturally. In Sequoia and Kings Canyon National Parks, for example, 80 percent of lightning fires allowed to burn never reached more than 0.1 hectare (one-quarter acre) in size, and only 5 percent exceed 120 hectares (300 acres) (33). But some large and dramatic fires have also occurred since 1968. Perhaps the most difficult and controversial aspect of managing natural fires is that in certain forest types, fire cannot be harnessed to burn a small percentage of the forest at regular intervals, analogous to a forest placed under sustained even-aged management. If 1 or 2 percent of a park were to be burned in isolated patches every few years, the policy might not attract more than curiosity from the media and most of the general public. But occasional large and dramatic blazes have a tendency to provoke opposition to the policy from some citizens and government officials, even though most conservationists have accepted the policy allowing natural fires to play their usual role as the best way to maintain biotic diversity and wildlife habitat in wilderness areas.

The first major test of the policy occurred in 1974, when a lightning fire in a dry year burned 1400 hectares (3499 acres) in Grand Teton National Park (Figure 21.12). This event attracted widespread media attention, and for most people it was the first

Figure 21.12 A lightning fire allowed to burn in Grand Teton National Park, Wyoming, as part of a program to restore the natural occurrence and effects of fires in wilderness areas. (*Denver Post* photograph by Bill Wuensch.)

time that they had heard of the policy. The fire, although sizable, was not troublesome to manage and left a desirable mosaic of mature forest and younger vegetation. It also affected only a small percentage of the park. Fires of similar magnitude also occurred in California and Idaho in 1977 and 1979, again without serious problems.

The most difficult test of the natural-fire policy occurred in the summer of 1988 in Yellowstone National Park. A natural-fire policy had already been in effect at Yellowstone for seventeen years, but fires of significant size (greater than 20 hectares) had occurred in only four of these years. Before 1988, none of the fires had ever burned more than a tiny fraction of the park's 890,000 hectares (2.2 million acres). Weather conditions in the late spring of 1988 were fairly close to normal, and a few lightning fires at that time were burning under surveillance. But by midsummer it became apparent that drought conditions were approaching a hazardous level. In mid-July park officials shifted to a policy of vigorous suppression of all fires, regardless of origin. Because of the severe drought and high winds, however, suppression of existing and subsequent fires was virtually impossible.

By the end of the season, eight separate fires had burned about 45 percent of the park, although nearly half of this total area was affected by surface fires that did not kill the trees. Three of the fires, totaling 276,000 hectares (690,000 acres) were started by human beings and had been fought vigorously from the time of their discovery. Two additional fires had burned into the park from adjacent lands. It is evident that even if the natural-fire policy had not been in place, at least 25 to 30 percent of the park would have burned anyway.

There is little doubt that in naturally fire-prone environments—which includes most of the western national parks—occasional large fires are inevitable, even with a policy of total suppression. Conservationists have argued that if fire is allowed a more natural role in wilderness areas, the resulting mosaic of stand ages and fuel types will help reduce the chances of wholesale conflagrations. Thus it would be unfortunate if the Yellowstone conflagrations of 1988 are blamed on the natural-fire policy, when in fact it could be argued that a century of fire suppression had aggravated the situation by encouraging the buildup of vast, uniform expanses of forest fuels.

Nevertheless, the Yellowstone fires put into sharp relief some of the challenges that fire managers face in the coming years. Greater public awareness of the reasons for the policy would be helpful, especially if it does not come at a time when rare "problem fires" are seizing the headlines. Second, models of fire behavior will need to be improved so that the response of fires to incipient drought can be predicted more accurately. Existing models underestimated the impact of a "worst-case scenario" at Yellowstone in 1988. Third, the role of prescribed burning for fuel reduction may have to be increased in places where it might be feasible. And finally, the Yellowstone fires raise the question whether even our largest parks are viable microcosms of wilderness ecosystems. Most ecologists have assumed that in order to sustain viable populations of plants and animals, a park needs to be large enough that individual disturbances cannot alter the balance of the overall park ecosystem. The 1988 fires demonstrated that Yellowstone is probably not an "equilibrium landscape," despite its vast size. Fire managers need to determine whether it is feasible or desirable to reduce the scale of fires proportionally so that the park does incorporate an equilibrium landscape. Thus, although it is unlikely that fire management at Yellowstone or elsewhere will return to the days of permanent and total fire suppression, management of wilderness fires is likely to undergo further modification and refinement.

References

1. A. M. Swain, *Quat. Res., 10,* 55 (1978).
2. S. F. Arno, "The historical role of fire on the Bitterroot National Forest," U.S.D.A. For. Serv., Res. Pap. INT-187, 1976.
3. A. R. Taylor, *J. For., 68,* 476 (1971).
4. A. R. Taylor, "Lightning and trees." In *Lightning,* Vol. 2, *Lightning Protection,* E. A. Golde, ed., Academic Press, London, 1977.
5. R. W. Mutch, *Ecology, 51,* 1046 (1970).
6. M. L. Heinselman, *Quat. Res., 3,* 329 (1973).
7. R. W. Finley, "Original vegetation cover of Wisconsin (map)," U.S.D.A. For. Serv., North Cent. For. Expt. Sta., St. Paul, Minn., 1976.
8. C. G. Lorimer, *Ecology, 58,* 139 (1977).
9. L. E. Frelich, "Natural disturbance frequencies in the hemlock-hardwood forests of the Upper Great Lakes region," Ph.D. Thesis, University of Wisconsin–Madison, 1986.
10. J. M. Hett and O. L. Loucks, *J. Ecol., 64,* 1029 (1976).
11. G. G. Whitney, *Ecology, 67,* 1548 (1986).
12. S. Perley, *Historic Storms of New England,* Salem Press and Printing Co., 1891.
13. W. R. Moore, *West. Wildlands, 1*(3), 11 (1974).
14. R. K. Miller, "The Keetch–Byram Drought Index and three fires in Upper Michigan, 1976." In *Fifth National Conf. on Fire and Forest Meteorology,* Am. Meteorol. Soc., Boston, 1978.
15. C. E. Van Wagner, *Can. J. For. Res., 7,* 23 (1977).
16. A. A. Brown and K. P. Davis, *Forest Fire: Control and Use,* Second Edition, McGraw–Hill, New York, 1973.
17. D. Noble, "An updated national fire-danger rating system." In *Forestry Research: What's New in the West,* U.S.D.A. For. Serv., Fort Collins, Colo., 1978.
18. W. H. Frandsen, *Combust. and Flame, 16,* 9 (1971).
19. R. C. Rothermel, "A mathematical model for predicting fire spread in wildland fuels," U.S.D.A. For. Serv., Res. Pap. INT-115, 1972.
20. F. A. Albini, "Estimating wildfire behavior and effects." U.S.D.A. For. Serv., Gen. Tech. Rept. INT-30, 1976.
21. J. E. Deeming, R. E. Burgen, and J. D. Cohen, "The National Fire-Danger Rating System—1978," U.S.D.A. For. Serv., Gen. Tech. Rept. INT-39, Intermountain For. Range Expt. Sta., Ogden, Utah, 1977.
22. P. L. Andrews and R. E. Burgan, " 'BEHAVE' in the wilderness." In *Proc. Symp. and Workshop on Wilderness Fire,* U.S.D.A. For. Serv., Gen. Tech. Rep. INT-182, 1985.
23. W. C. Fischer, "Planning and evaluating prescribed fires—a standard procedure," U.S.D.A. For. Serv., Gen. Tech. Rept. INT-43, 1978.

24. H. D. Thoreau, *The Maine Woods,* Ticknor and Fields, Boston, 1864.

25. E. H. Bormann and G. E. Likens, *Pattern and Process in a Forested Ecosystem,* Springer-Verlag, New York/Berlin, 1979.

26. S. H. Spurr and B. V. Barnes, *Forest Ecology,* Second Edition, Ronald Press, New York, 1973.

27. C. W. Ralston and G. E. Hatchell, "Effects of prescribed burning on physical properties of soil." In *Prescribed Burning Symp. Proc.,* U.S.D.A. For. Serv., Southeastern For. Expt. Sta., Asheville, N.C., 1971.

28. C. A. Connaughton, *J. For., 33,* 751 (1935).

29. I. F. Ahlgren and C. E. Ahlgren, *Bot. Rev., 26,* 483 (1960).

30. C. G. Wells, "Effects of prescribed burning on soil chemical properties and nutrient availability," In *Prescribed Burning Symp. Proc.,* U.S.D.A. For. Serv., Southeastern For. Expt. Sta., Asheville, N.C., 1971.

31. N. V. DeByle and P. E. Packer, "Plant nutrient and soil losses in overland flow from burned forest clearcuts." In *Watersheds in Transition, Proc. Am. Water Resources Assoc.,* 1972.

32. J. H. Dieterich, "Prescribed burning and air quality." In *Southern Pine Management—Today and Tomorrow,* 20th Annu. For. Symp., Louisiana State University, Division of Continuing Education, Baton Rouge, 1971.

33. B. M. Kilgore, *West. Wildlands, 10(3),* 2 (1984).

34. W. C. Fischer, "Wilderness fire management planning guide," U.S.D.A. For. Serv., Gen. Tech. Rept. INT-171, 1984.

35. F. A. Albini, "Spot fire distance from burning trees—a predictive model," U.S.D.A. For. Serv., Gen. Tech. Rept. INT-56, 1979.

Forest Products

PART 4

In this section the use of wood as a raw material is emphasized. The unique characteristics and comparative abundance of wood have made it a desirable natural material for homes and other structures, furniture, tools, vehicles, and decorative objects. The multitude of uses for wood are summarized in Table P4.1.

Wood is composed for the most part of three polymers namely cellulose, hemicelluloses, and lignin formed into a cellular structure. Variations in the characteristics and volume of the components and in the cellular structure cause differences in wood properties such as hardness, weight, flexibility etc. For a single species, the properties are relatively constant within limits; however, to use wood to its best advantage and most effectively in engineering applications, the effect of specific characteristics or physical properties must be considered (1).

Throughout history different types of wood have served many purposes. The tough, strong, and durable white oak, for example, was well-proven raw material for ships, bridges, cooperage, barn timbers, farm implements, railroad ties, fence posts, flooring, paneling, and other products. In contrast, woods such as black walnut and cherry became primarily cabinet woods. Hickory was manufactured into tough, hard, resilient tool handles. Black locust was used for barn timbers and treenails. What the early artisan learned by trial and error became the basis for intelligent decisions concerning which species was best suited to a given purpose and also what characteristics should be looked for in selecting trees for different applications. It was known that wood from trees grown in certain locations was stronger, more durable, and more easily worked with tools than wood from the same species grown in other locations. Modern wood quality research has substantiated that location and growth conditions significantly affect wood properties (1).

With the decline of the virgin forests in the United States, the available supply of large clear logs free of defects, for lumber and veneer has been reduced. However, the importance of high-quality logs has diminished as new concepts of wood use have been introduced. Second-growth timber, the balance of the old-growth forests, and imports continue to fill the needs for wood in the quality required. Wood is still a very valuable engineering material (1). The inherent factors that keep wood in the forefront of raw materials are many and varied. The structure and chief attributes that give wood these special properties are discussed in Chapter 22, "Properties and Utilization of Wood."

In the United States more than 100 kinds of wood are available to the prospective user, but it is very unlikely that all are available in any one locality. About 60 native woods are of major commercial importance. Another 30 wood types are commonly imported in the form of logs, cants, lumber, and veneer for industrial uses, the building trades, and crafts (1).

An increasing percentage of harvested wood is used for the production of pulp and paper. Thousands of paper supplies are produced every year for household and industrial use. Since smaller-size logs are suitable for pulp production, the second-growth timber in the United States is very suitable for production of these important commodities (Figure P4.1). In addition, many different species of hardwoods are proving suitable for paper manufacture. In Chapter 23, "Wood for Fiber, Energy, and Chemicals," the chemical nature of wood and methods for paper manufacture are described.

The role of wood as a raw material for energy and

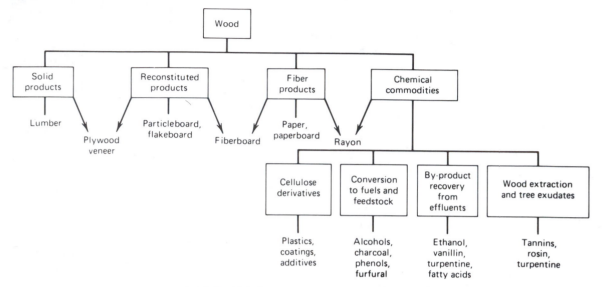

Table P4.1 Summary of Uses for Wood

Figure P4.1 Log drivers wrestling Douglas-fir logs on Oregon's Coos River, using long pike poles and a short peavey. These logs will roar downstream to be processed in a pulpwood mill. (Courtesy of Life Picture Service.)

chemicals is also outlined in Chapter 23. Wood once was a significant primary energy source for the United States but will probably never regain such status. However, up to 15 percent of our energy needs could be potentially derived from biomass, probably through more efficient use of urban, agricultural, and forest residues.

Wood is both imported into and exported from the United States. Thus both the U.S. and the world economies are affected by the marketing of wood and wood products. Chapter 24, "The Forest Products Economy," gives details on the market value of forest products and how their value affects timber management practices.

Reference

1. Anon., *Wood Handbook: Wood as an Engineering Material,* U.S.D.A. For. Serv., Agr. Handbook 72, Washington, D.C., 1974.

CHAPTER 22

Properties and Utilization of Wood

HANS KUBLER

Prehistoric people made their cutting tools from stone, bronze, and iron. Other utensils such as tool handles, spears, and clubs were shaped from wood; wood was also used for shelters, benches, bunks, and fuel. Wood was the most commonly used material by early human beings, and it still serves the same needs, but for many additional purposes. Wood appears in thousands of products that vary in size from toothpicks, pencils, and baseball bats to railroad ties and huge beams. Most North Americans live in frame houses that are constructed of wood, sheathed with wood-based panels, and sided with lumber or lumber imitations. Wood is part of our lives from the cradle to the coffin; in turn, our use of wood has a tremendous impact on forests, which are managed, harvested, and at times destroyed because people want and need wood.

In reality, industrial societies could survive without wood. We could replace this natural material in nearly all categories of use; the options are metals, plastics, concrete, stone, clay, and fossil fuels. For some uses we accept substitutes, but for others we prefer wood, depending on prices and how well the materials suit the purpose.

Wood properties, the demand for wood, and the fate of forests are interrelated. In this chapter we become acquainted with the properties of wood and the major ways it is utilized. To understand wood we should first learn about its function in trees, that is, how the tree utilizes wood for survival. Armed with this knowledge, we can begin to make wise use of this universal material.

Wood as Part of the Tree

Trees are extraordinary living organisms; they live the longest, grow the tallest, and dominate the surrounding vegetation wherever conditions permit rich forest growth. Tree roots, trunks, and branches consist for the most part of wood. Without wood, trees could neither grow tall nor survive the cold winters that wither herbaceous plants to the ground. Wood serves trees; it has adapted and evolved through millions of years in thousands of tree species to aid trees in their struggle for survival. Obviously wood is tailored to the needs of trees; it performs three functions discussed in Chapter 3.

1. Wood carries the tree crown high above ground level.
2. Wood conducts water from the soil to the crown.
3. Wood transports carbohydrates from the bark into wood for storage, until needed for growth.

Function-Related Wood Properties

For carrying the crown, the tree trunk needs strength predominantly in the *longitudinal* direction of the stem axis. Wood is indeed many times stronger longitudinally than *transversely* to the stem axis. The ratio of longitudinal to transverse strength varies with the type of strength measured—bending, compression, and others—and with different tree species. On the average wood resists a tenfold-greater force longitudinally than it does transversely. Therefore, cross-sectional slabs of trees, *tree rounds* (Figure 22.1), break much more easily than do lengthwise sections, or *boards*, of equal thickness. The great longitudinal strength favors many uses of wood. Wall studs in buildings and legs of chairs, for example, need mainly longitudinal strength for carrying the upper parts of buildings and the weight of people sitting, respectively.

The tree trunk has a strength adequate for supporting the crown even when snow and ice add

Figure 22.1 Tree round of bur oak with bark, pale sapwood, and dark-colored heartwood.

several times more weight. Actually, the crown's weight puts less stress on the trunk than do strong winds that bend the stem; the bending is a combination of longitudinal tension on the luff side and longitudinal compression on the lee side. The trunk needs in particular bending strength, which also comes in handy in joists that carry the loads on floors, in beams of bridges, in shovel handles, and in nearly all other wood products (1).

When strength is evaluated in terms of force per unit cross section, no wood species is as strong as steel and other strong metals. On the basis of weight or mass, however, wood outperforms most other materials with the exception of fiberglass and synthetic fibers such as nylon. We can hang more weight on a vertical stick of wood than on a steel rod of the same mass and length (2). The *strength–mass ratio* has great significance. Pole vaulters, for example, want a light but strong pole. This ratio counts also in construction, where most wood is used; the structural members of buildings have to carry the *dead* loads of upper stories and roofs, which typically exceed the *live* loads of inhabitants, furnishings, and equipment. It is the great strength of this light material that permits light construction. The high strength–mass ratio of wood is also crucial for trees, because their trunks must carry not only leaves, snow, and ice but also the entire weight of branches and twigs.

Trees should grow upright for full exposure to light, but they should face strong winds with a low profile. They meet these two conflicting demands with flexibility. Trunks and branches are normally light-oriented and yet yield and bend in the wind, returning to their normal position by virtue of wood's resiliency or elasticity when the wind ceases. Wood yields also to loads in structures as it bends, stretches, distorts, is compressed, and recovers when the deforming forces cease. Floor sheathing and joists yield, softening the impact of our steps. On the other hand, joists and beams need a certain degree of stiffness, a property in which wood again compares favorably, weight for weight, even with steel.

Materials that endure large deformations without rupture are *tough,* in contrast to the *brittle* solids that break without deformation. Wood has substantial toughness, which in combination with its resiliency is crucial for baseball bats and diving boards of hickory, for ax and hammer handles of ash, for railroad ties, guardrails and posts along highways, and for buildings exposed to wind and earthquakes. When the deformation approaches the breaking point, the stressed wood begins to sag, crack, and splinter before there is complete failure, so that mine props and other structural wood products can warn people and give them the opportunity to run away before disaster strikes (2).

Porosity is a vital property of wood in the conduction of water and sugar solutions for the tree. A great deal more water flows longitudinally in the tree trunk than sugar solution flows transversely; thus wood has a much greater longitudinal permeability than transverse permeability. Because of these different degrees of permeability, adhesives, varnish, preservatives, and water soak relatively rapidly into the ends of lumber, and firewood dries through *end surfaces* (cross sections) much faster than through *lateral surfaces* (3).

Wood Structure

Materials whose properties vary according to the direction of measurement are *anisotropic.* The anisotropy of wood is evident in its microanatomy—that is, in the shape and orientation of the billions of tiny wood cells in each tree. The minute structure reflects the functions of wood in the tree—a good example of the law of nature that form rigorously follows function (4).

Engineers conduct water in pipes or hollow cylinders, which in the form of columns lend themselves also to supporting loads. Hence, it should be no surprise that wood tissue consists essentially of pipe-shaped cells or *fibers* that are up to 100 times longer than they are wide (Figure 22.2). In the trunk the fibers run upward, parallel to one another in the *longitudinal* or *fiber direction*. It is the longitudinal alignment of the fibers that makes wood anisotropic. This alignment also explains the tendency of lumber to be much rougher and more difficult to machine on the ends than on the lateral surfaces, as well as the tendency for splits and most other separations, such as drying checks, to run in the longitudinal direction (3).

Approximately 90 percent of the wood tissue of coniferous trees consists of *tracheid* cells (Figure 22.2a), a type of fiber that gives strength and conducts water. Broad-leaved trees evolved after the conifers and specialized their tissue to conduct water in wide cells called *vessels*. Each vessel consists of numerous drum-shaped vessel members with open ends, stacked one above the other to form a continuous vessel pipeline from root tips to the leaves. The width of vessels in oaks and some other broad-leaved trees greatly exceeds that of the species shown in Figure 22.2b (see Figure 22.3a). Indeed, their vessels are sufficiently large to be seen with the unaided eye, that is, as round *pores* at the end surface (Figure 22.4), and as needlelike grooves at the lateral surface (1, 3, 5).

In some woods such as oak (Figures 22.3a and 22.4), the vessels in the *earlywood* (produced early in the growing season) are much wider than those in *latewood* and form the distinct *growth rings* of these *ring-porous* woods. In the *diffuse-porous* maple, birch, and many other genera, the vessels are of the same size throughout the growth ring, the boundary of which is marked only by extremely thin cells (Figure 22.3b). Since coniferous woods lack vessels, they are sometimes designated *nonporous,* in contrast to the *porous* broad-leaved trees, particularly those with relatively wide pores. Coniferous wood

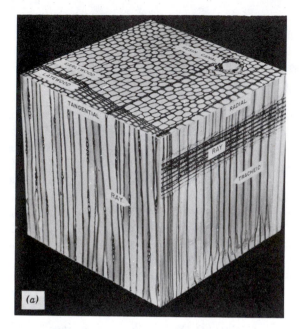 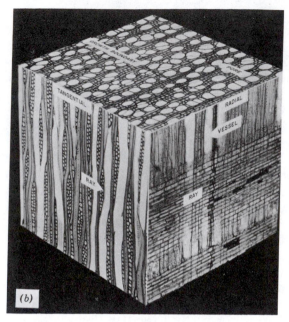

Figure 22.2 Photomicrographic model of (*a*) coniferous wood and (*b*) wood from a broad-leaved tree. [Courtesy of Kollmann and Cote (1968).]

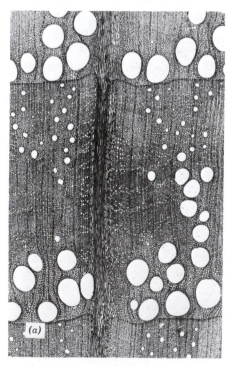 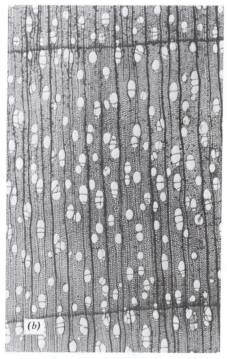

Figure 22.3 Photomicrograph of hardwood cross sections depicting (*a*) ring-porous and (*b*) diffuse-porous wood. (Courtesy of U.S.D.A. Forest Products Laboratory.)

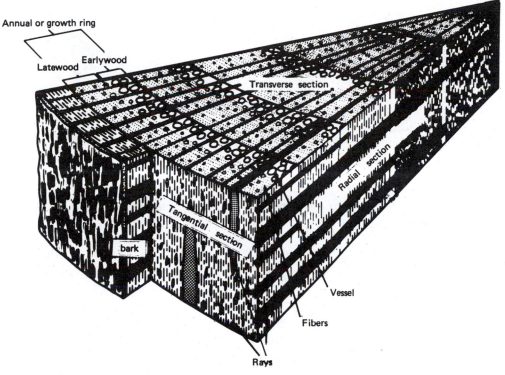

Figure 22.4 Diagrammatic wedge section of a five-year-old oak trunk. The term *transverse section* is synonymous with *end surface* and *cross section*. Both the radial section and the tangential section are *lateral surfaces*.

has growth rings because the earlywood tracheids have wider cavities and thinner cell walls than do the latewood tracheids (Figure 22.2*a*); the earlywood–latewood contrast is especially sharp in southern pines (6).

Sugar solutions flow in *ray* cells from the inner bark across the cambial layer into wood (Figure 22.4). Rays resemble knife blades, stuck horizontally into the vertical trunk between the fibers and tracheids. In many hardwoods the rays have quite a height, about 20 or 30 millimeters (1 inch) in white oak, and are thick enough to be visible on all wood plane surfaces. On tree cross sections, rays resemble spokes of a wheel (Figure 22.4) as they extend from the bark into the wood, in the *radial* direction of the circular growth rings and perpendicular to the tangent of the rings or to the *tangential* direction (Figure 22.5). Radial and tangential are both *trans-*

verse directions, that is, horizontal to the trunk of the standing tree (1).

The rays consist for the most part of thin-walled, brick-shaped *parenchyma* cells, which lack the strength of the fibers (Figure 22.2). Hence, wood splits easily in the planes of the rays (Figure 22.4), and under tangential tension fails within or along the ray tissue. Rays strengthen wood in the radial direction, which explains why most wood species are somewhat stronger radially than tangentially (7).

Fibers and vessels die at an age of a few weeks, after attaining their final shape and chemical composition. Parenchyma cells live much longer, some remaining alive until *sapwood* becomes *heartwood* (Figure 22.1). One of the tasks of parenchyma cells is to convert sugars into storage starch to serve as food reserves for the tree, and to reconvert starch to sugars when needed for growth. The starch and

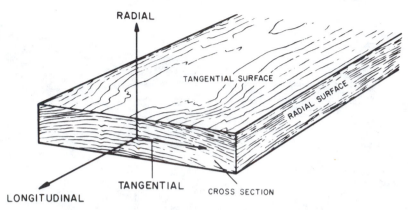

RADIAL

TANGENTIAL SURFACE

RADIAL SURFACE

LONGITUDINAL

TANGENTIAL

CROSS SECTION

Figure 22.5 The three principal axes and surfaces of wood corresponding to the directions of its fibers and growth rings. (Modified from U.S.D.A. Forest Products Laboratory.)

sugar content of sapwood is one reason why most wood-damaging organisms prefer dead sapwood over heartwood, and why sapwood is never quite as durable as heartwood, except in living trees whose still-living sapwood cells fight attacking organisms (4).

Practically all cavities of wood cells are interconnected (Figure 22.2), as mentioned already for the vessel members of broad-leaved trees. Tiny openings in the cell walls of overlapping ends of tracheids provide vertical passageways for water rising from cell to cell in conifers. Thin walls of ray cells are perforated for the radial transport of sugars, and tangential connections provide for growing cells. Hence, wood is permeable in all three of its cardinal directions. The longitudinal orientation of most cells, however, causes liquids and gases to flow and diffuse many times faster in the longitudinal or fiber direction than in the two transverse directions. This explains why stacked firewood dries predominantly at the exposed ends. The radial orientation of rays allows liquids and gases to move radially up to twice as rapidly as tangentially (2).

Wood Density as an Indicator of Wood Quality

As a porous material, wood contains air-filled or water-filled cell cavities surrounded by cell walls (Figure 22.3). The cell wall substance is remarkably uniform; it differs very little even between conifers and broad-leaved trees and has a constant density of around 1.5 grams per cubic centimeter. The density of bulk wood thus depends on the proportion of the cell wall volume to the volume of the bulk wood (2).

The densest commercial North American wood is pignut hickory. With a density of 0.75 gram per cubic centimeter in the ovendry state, the cell walls occupy one-half (0.75/1.5) of the wood volume. Douglas-fir—the most common lumber and plywood species besides southern pine—weighs about 0.5 gram per cubic centimeter, corresponding to a cell wall proportion of 0.5/1.5 or one-third. The density of the lightest wood, balsa from South America, averages 0.17, which means the cell walls make up little more than 10 percent of the volume. Lignumvitae, also a South American wood and known to us in bowling balls, is the densest of all commercial species and weighs around 1.2 grams per cubic centimeter. It is composed of 80 percent cell walls, and sinks rapidly in water, the density of which is unity (1.0) by definition of the mass unit gram (7).

Most wood properties depend on density (7). Relatively dense species are strong, as one might expect from their large cell wall mass. Wood density is *the* indicator of nearly all wood properties and of wood quality. For example, dense woods have relatively little cell cavity space and cannot contain much water, but the water they do contain migrates slowly along the narrow cavities and across the thick cell walls; thus dense wood dries slowly. Wood of high density tends to split when nailed because it lacks cavity space to accommodate the nail shaft; in light woods, by contrast, the nail shaft pushes cell walls aside into wide cell cavities, without separating adjoining cell tissue.

People have always been aware of the relationship between density and wood properties, although they have paid more attention to the related property of *hardness*—that is, the resistance to indentation—which serves as another good indicator of wood properties. Hardness is easy to estimate, for example, by pressing with a fingernail or a small tool into the wood surface. Wood sections of any size, including huge stems too heavy to be weighed, can be given the hardness test, which has the additional advantage of depending very little on the wood's moisture content (2).

In early times in England and other countries, all the conifers harvested were softer than the harvested broad-leaved trees and were therefore called *softwoods,* in contrast with the broad-leaved *hardwoods.* Today we utilize a wider range of tree species, but the terms *softwood* for *conifers* and *hardwood* for *broad-leaved trees* have been retained, even though the wood of broad-leaved species such as balsa and aspen is much softer than the wood of most conifers, and even though some conifers are harder than most broad-leaved species (7).

Wood species also vary in features not related to density, such as color, percentage and arrangement of cell types, and in minor chemical constituents. Therefore, even woods of the same density are likely to differ, with the properties varying more than the densities. People were always aware of these differences and preferred particular woods for certain uses, such as red oak for flooring, light durable redwood and western redcedar for house siding, yew, Osage orange, and lemonwood for bows to shoot arrows, and the bright hard wood of the sugar maple tree for cutting boards and roller skating rinks (8).

Additional Advantageous Properties

Wood features discussed so far affect the tree's life and consequently are advantageous for utilization by people wherever wood has functions similar to those in the tree. This section and the next deal with wood features that have no bearing on the tree's life; therefore they may or may not be advantageous for wood users. Let us consider the advantageous features first.

Availability and Workability

Wood is readily available in most inhabited parts of the world (Chapter 2). In many North American states and provinces most wood on the market comes from the South, Oregon, Washington, and British Columbia, but the industry and consumers have the option to procure it with little effort from local forests (9). In contrast, metals, glass, concrete, and plastics have to be manufactured in elaborate facilities from rare raw materials with great consumption of energy.

Wood is easy to work. People lost in the wilderness without any equipment and tools, in desperate need of protection from adverse elements, can manage to assemble a primitive shelter from stems and branches of trees. Stone Age people shaped wood into special utensils by means of sharp stones, which would be rather useless for working present-day metals. With modern machines and tools, wood is still easier to work than are competing materials (3).

Appearance

All sapwood is pale in color; in some species it is nearly white and in others yellowish. Heartwood color by contrast varies in a wide range from white to red and appears brown in many species (10). People perceive these colors as pleasant and warm, especially when a clear finish enhances the tone. Since some tropical species form heartwood in interesting green and blue shades, wood can be procured in almost any color. In addition, as a porous material it absorbs stain and pigments readily when people want to alter the color.

Some woods such as basswood, sweetgum, and aspen look quite uniform, hardly showing any markings. But most native species feature distinct growth rings and rays that give each piece a particular *figure* or *grain*; in this instance *grain* stands for *growth ring* and not for *fiber* (Figure 22.4). No two pieces of wood look exactly alike because few trees form exactly cylindrical rings, growth rates vary, and the appearance of each surface depends on the cut. Knots add especially conspicuous configurations. This variability appeals to people who perceive wood as a fascinating, intrinsically beautiful natural material with which they feel familiar and comfortable (4). Manufacturers of automobile bodies and plastics imitate wood grain for good reason.

Thermal Insulation

Most frames, sashes, and casements of windows consist of either wood or aluminum. In comparisons of the two, wood has the big advantage because it is a thermal insulator (1, 2, 7). If in winter the window frame faces a low temperature outside and the room temperature inside, aluminum will conduct 1200 times more heat to the outside than Douglas-fir wood of the same size. In reality, the heat losses differ much less because air layers at the surfaces contribute to the insulation and aluminum frames are thinner than wood frames. However, aluminum still drains much more heat than wood.

Thermal insulation also has significance for lumber studs in exterior walls of houses, which unlike studs of steel and aluminum are not heat-conducting bridges between inside and outside. The heat conduction of metal studs is moderated, however, by the fact that they occupy only a small fraction of the wall, with the spaces between the studs filled with rock wool or other insulation.

Low thermal conductivity contributes to the image of wood as a pleasant, warm material. Wood handles of hot coffeepots and frying pans do not feel hot. Similarly, bare feet perceive wood flooring to be less cold than concrete of the same temperature. Wood is always comfortable to the touch, no matter what the real temperature, because wood conducts little heat out of or into the skin, where our temperature-sensing nerves are located.

Fire Performance and Fuel Properties

The combustibility of wood does not make structural lumber a fire hazard (4, 7). First, it should be noted that most fires start on room contents such as beds, papers, furniture, and fabrics, rather than in walls, floors, and ceilings. Second, it is the smoke generated by the combustion of the room contents that usually kills inhabitants. Structural material is barely involved in the early stages of a fire.

In the latter stages of a fire it is crucial that the building retains its integrity and does not collapse. In this regard structural wood outperforms metals, which heat rapidly over their whole thin cross section and become soft enough to bend under the load (Figure 22.6). In contrast, heat penetrates only slowly into the relatively thick structural lumber, and the charred, insulating surface layer conducts little heat to the intact wood underneath (Figure 22.7). Evaporation of wood moisture consumes much of the conducted heat, which is then not available for raising the wood temperature. Furthermore, the high specific heat of wood requires many calories to heat it up. When the core of lumber finally does become hot, it dries out, and the resulting gain in strength mitigates the thermal softening.

High degrees of heat decompose wood into combustible gases and crumbling charcoal (Figure 22.8). Because the decomposition process is controlled by the penetration of heat, it progresses correspondingly slowly from the surface to the core, so that thick timbers in fires continue carrying loads for hours.

Wood was for thousands of years the only fuel available to people. It still serves as the main source of heat in nonindustrialized countries (see Chapter 23). Small pieces of dry wood burn readily to gases that are less noxious than the combustion gases of coal, and minimal solids remain as ashes (11). In fireplaces the ever-changing flames and crackling sounds are always fascinating. One in four house-

Figure 22.6 A burned-out structure showing that structural lumber carries loads long after steel has collapsed. (Courtesy of U.S.D.A. Forest Products Laboratory.)

holds in the United States burns at least some fuelwood. The quantity of wood burned may amount to one-quarter of the consumption of all wood (12). This proportion includes fuelwood harvested or gathered by consumers themselves in urban and in rural areas, and it also includes purchased wood residues. The heat gained, however, equals only a small proportion of the energy gained from other home-heating fuels (see Table 23.6). In furnaces wood can rarely compete with natural gas, oil, and coal or coke, because it is bulky and unsuited for automatic feeding.

It is well known that wood species differ in burning quality. Conifers contain more lignin than hardwoods (see Chapter 23 for a discussion of lignin). Lignin in turn consists of more carbon than the other main constituents of wood and is therefore somewhat higher in heat value. Resin gives about twice the heat of wood, so that the heat value of very resinous conifers such as pines, spruces, and Douglas-fir exceeds that of hardwoods by about 10 percent on a weight basis. The higher heat value of

conifers contradicts the widespread opinion that conifers (in addition to low-density hardwoods) make poor firewood. All species burn very well if they are dry, since all have nearly the same heat

Figure 22.7 Cross section of a post that had been exposed to fire, showing sound wood in the center and charcoal at the surface. Some charcoal broke or burned off. The post had been rectangular before the fire.

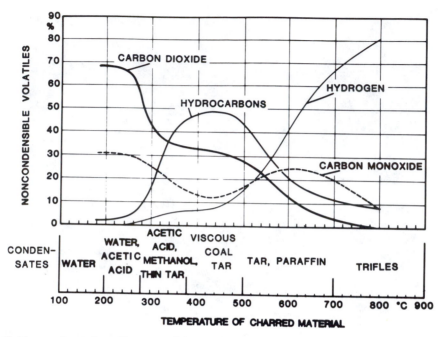

Figure 22.8 The products that effuse out of thermally decomposing wood. The amounts of volatiles are expressed in volumetric proportions.

value per ton (13); this might well be expected, since the species differ little in chemical composition.

The heat value on the basis of volume is another matter, because given volumes of different species contain different masses of wood. One cubic meter of pignut hickory, for example, with a density of 0.75 gram per cubic centimeter, has twice the heat value of a cubic meter of aspen with a density of 0.38. Density is a good indicator of the heat value of a given wood volume (Table 22.1). Dense species not only give more heat but also burn longer than less dense species of the same size. Thick pieces of light wood, however, burn as long as thin pieces of dense wood and release the same amount of heat (1, 7). The combustion of wood is discussed further in Chapter 23.

Electrical Properties

Occasionally people suffer severe and at times lethal electric shocks and burns. Charges of voltage as such do not cause harm; it is the current that hurts. Electricity flows through us if we touch the voltage while in contact with a conducting grounded material, for example, if we hold a defective electrical appliance with one hand and a water faucet with the other. Dry wood does not conduct (2, 7); therefore touching wooden counters, furniture, floors, and paneling cannot contribute to electric shocks. The electrically insulating qualities of wood are similarly an asset in power line poles, although after rain the water at the pole surface can conduct electricity to some extent.

In homes and offices people generate electric charges when brushing along insulating materials, such as carpeting, and receive harmless but annoying shocks from the discharge currents when they touch doorknobs and other conductors. Brushing along wood does not generate charges because the moisture present, even in seemingly dry wood, conducts enough electricity to dissipate the charge. Nor does touching wood with charged fingers cause

Table 22.1 Densities and Heat Values at 12 Percent Moisture Content[a] of Important Woods Grown in the United States

Tree Name	Density (g/cm³)	Heat Value[b] (million kJ/m³)	Heat value[b] (million Btu/cord[c])
Hardwoods			
Live oak	0.99	17.60	40.32
Shagbark hickory	0.81	14.40	32.99
White oak	0.76	13.60	31.16
Honeylocust	0.72	12.80	29.32
American beech	0.72	12.80	29.32
Sugar maple	0.71	12.60	28.86
Northern red oak	0.71	12.60	28.86
Yellow birch	0.69	12.40	28.40
White ash	0.67	12.00	27.49
Black walnut	0.62	11.00	25.20
Sweetgum	0.58	10.40	23.82
Black cherry	0.56	10.00	22.91
American elm	0.56	10.00	22.91
Southern magnolia	0.56	10.00	22.91
Black tupelo	0.56	10.00	22.91
Sycamore	0.55	9.80	22.50
Sassafras	0.52	9.20	21.08
Yellow poplar	0.47	8.40	19.24
Red alder	0.46	8.20	18.79
Eastern cottonwood	0.45	8.00	18.33
Quaking aspen	0.43	7.60	17.41
American basswood	0.41	7.40	16.95
Softwoods			
Longleaf pine	0.66	12.63	28.92
Western larch	0.58	11.13	25.49
Loblolly pine	0.57	10.92	25.00
Shortleaf pine	0.57	10.92	25.00
Douglas-fir	0.54	10.27	23.53
Baldcypress	0.52	9.85	22.55
Western hemlock	0.50	9.00	20.62
Ponderosa pine	0.45	8.56	19.61
White fir	0.44	7.80	17.87
Redwood	0.43	7.60	17.41
Eastern white pine	0.39	7.49	17.16
Engelmann spruce	0.39	7.49	17.16
Western redcedar	0.36	6.40	14.66

Source: Densities from reference 7, heat values from reference 13.

[a]Moisture content based on weight of ovendry wood.

[b]Heat values include heat in fire effluents. Calculated on the basis of 8600 British thermal units (Btu) per pound of ovendry wood, 9200 Btu for resinous-wood species.

[c]One cord equals 128 cubic feet or 3.6246 cubic meters; it is assumed that the pile is two-thirds wood and one-third air (between the pieces); hence one cord contains 2.4164 cubic meters of solid wood.

shocks, because wood is a sufficient insulator. It seems that wood has the ideal electric resistance in these applications.

Disadvantageous Properties

In past decades wood has been replaced in many categories of use, most conspicuously in the manufacture of vehicles. The early carriages, railroad cars, boats, and airplanes consisted solely or mainly of wood. In carriages steel was restricted to wheel rims, axles, and a few bolts, until the turn of the century, whereas today's automobiles retain only an occasional reminder of wood, for example, in the wood grain imitations of the station wagon body. Railroad freight cars are steel throughout; all large boats and airplanes similarly consist of metals and plastics, many containing no wood at all. This mass replacement indicates that wood has some features that are unfavorable for certain purposes. Many people consider swelling and shrinkage as the principal drawback of wood, but in the opinion of the author its insufficient plasticity is a greater drawback.

Lack of Plasticity and Fusibility

Automobile factories mold car bodies in presses by drawing plane sheet metal instantly over a die of the desired shape. Plastics can be similarly molded into spoons and pails, for example, although the raw material might first have to be heated. Wood treated in this fashion breaks before reaching sharp curvatures; it can be press-bent somewhat, but upon removal of pressure it *springs back* because its deformation has been *elastic* and not *plastic*. Paper clips illustrate the difference between elasticity and plasticity very nicely. Normally they bend in an elastic fashion and hold papers together, but when the two loops are bent too far they lose their *spring,* because the deformation has become plastic. Many

materials show elastic behavior in small deformations and plastic behavior in large deformations. Wood has a trace of this characteristic, in that it retains slight curvatures after bending close to the breaking point (1).

Plastic shaping is more efficient. Manufacturers of door casings bend sheet metal into units of U-shaped cross section, whereas in wood the door jamb, two casings, and a stop molding must be nailed together. Steel mills simply *roll* ingots into I-beams, a shape that in structures provides high bending strength and stiffness with a minimum of material. U-shaped wall studs of steel and aluminum sheets use the material equally efficiently. With wood the strong and stiff I- and U-shapes would have to be carved out of solid material or assembled from adhesive-bonded or nailed parts.

Moisture and heat delivered by steam increase the extent to which wood can be bent; cooling and drying in the desired shape sets the bend (3). The technique resembles ironing a crease into cotton pants. But the curvature achievable is limited and the process consumes much time. Curved hardwood strips of chairs (Figure 22.9) as well as some solid hickory and ash skis are still steam-bent. Bending renders stronger products than does shaping through cutting, because bent fibers run parallel to the product's long axis over the entire length, whereas pieces shaped by cutting are inevitably *cross-grained.*

Factories mass-produce many items by casting molten metal, plastic, and glass into a form; examples are motor blocks, packaging foam, and ashtrays. Wood cannot be heat-cast because it would disintegrate before melting; in other words, it lacks *fusibility.*

Wood technologists have developed alternatives to sawing or routing out the desired form from solid wood: the wood is separated into pieces for reassembly, bending, and bonding in the desired form (1). The pieces may be whole boards, as in glued laminated timbers (Figure 22.10), veneer in curved plywood chairs, planer shavings in toilet seats, fibers in imitations of louver doors, delignified fibers in paper cups, or cellulose molecules in viscose rayon (see Chapter 23).

Figure 22.9 Chair with a curving back arch made of solid steam-bent wood.

Figure 22.10 Gymnasium structure of glued laminated timbers, spanning 27 meters, in Lynwood Junior High School near Seattle. As the laminates are bent, they slide along one another; clamps hold the curved shape until the glue bonds prevent sliding back and stabilize the curvature. (Courtesy of American Institute of Timber Construction.)

Shrinkage and Swelling

In wood technology *shrinkage* means *contraction through the loss of moisture,* and *swelling* is *expansion through moisture adsorption* at large internal surfaces of the cell walls. Shrinkage and swelling annoy both the manufacturers and the users of wood products. Green wood when exposed to dry air inevitably loses moisture and shrinks. In dense woods the tangential shrinkage can be several percentage points; light species shrink less but still too much for many purposes. Radial shrinking is about one-half of the tangential, but in the fiber direction the wood shrinks only by negligibly small amounts. The extensive transverse shrinkage opens joints between boards, causes loose drawers and loose tool handles, and opens surface checks in fast-drying lumber. One-sided shrinkage causes warping.

Moisture Equilibrium Many annoying effects of shrinkage can be avoided by drying the wood properly before cutting it to specified sizes and shapes. The moisture content (MC) of dried wood, however, does not remain constant; it responds to varying atmospheres and attains in each different humidity a certain *equilibrium moisture content* (EMC). Wood approaches a MC of 12 percent (based on the weight of ovendry wood) at 65 percent relative humidity (RH), for example, but only 7 percent MC at 35 percent RH. Wood dimensions consequently vary with the humidity, albeit with some delay.

The EMC occurs for two reasons: (1) wood attracts moisture, that is, it is *hygroscopic;* and (2) the water molecules in wood vibrate so vigorously that some escape into the surrounding air. Wood is continually adsorbing and releasing moisture; when wet wood dries in dry air, the release exceeds the adsorption, but in humid air dry wood adsorbs more than it releases, until at the EMC adsorption equals release (2, 7).

Nearly all natural organic substances are hygroscopic and have moisture equilibriums. Dried fruits, seeds, all sorts of plant tissues, and uniform organic compounds such as sugar and honey contain moisture depending on the humidity of the surrounding atmosphere. Their EMCs have the same order of magnitude as that of wood. The interaction of moisture with the cellulose in wood is discussed further in Chapter 23.

Free and Bound Moisture The moisture-attracting forces in wood have a small range and are confined to the cell wall, not reaching out into cell cavities. Hence, we call moisture held inside cell walls *bound* water and water in cell cavities *free* water. The EMC refers only to bound water. Moisture adsorbed by dry wood penetrates the cell walls and forces the cell wall components apart, causing the cell walls and wood as a whole to swell. Bound water impairs the cohesion of cell walls; it weakens and softens wood, and also affects most other wood properties. Free water has no effect on the cell wall components, causes no swelling, and does not affect wood strength. Green wood and wet wood begin shrinking only after all free water has first dried out of the cell cavities; then the bound cell wall moisture begins evaporating. The point at which the wood contains maximum bound water but no free water is termed *fiber saturation* and appears near 30 percent MC.

The MC of dry wood exposed to vapor-saturated air rises to the fiber saturation point and not higher. Wood does reach higher MCs in the range of free water, however, when capillary forces soak liquid *free* water from the outside into the cell cavities. Of course, the *green* wood of living trees contains free water. In fact, water-conducting cells have to be completely filled, for otherwise the tree's leaves could not pull water up from the roots (see Chapter 3).

Real-Dimension Changes in Service Besides swelling and shrinking, wood dimensions also vary through *thermal expansion* when temperature rises (14). Rising temperatures are usually associated with decreasing humidity, however, and the resulting shrinkage opposes the thermal expansion. Wood expands very little thermally in the fiber direction

(less than steel, aluminum, and plastics), about as much as it shrinks, so that in service lumber maintains constant lengths. Consequently, wooden frame houses do not change in height, length, or width, and wooden rulers remain fairly accurate.

In the transverse directions, however, lumber dimensions do change. When the atmosphere in buildings fluctuates between humid extremes in summer and dry extremes at the peak of the heating season, the thickness and width of wood do vary. Since thermal expansion only partly offsets the shrinkage, the actual tangential movements of dense wood can exceed 2 percent. Under outside exposure greater MC fluctuations occur and dimensions vary even more. These movements impose stresses on adhesive joints and impair the durability of paints and other finishes. Finish coats reduce the moisture fluctuations by excluding liquid water; however, these coatings let vapor pass through and therefore do not completely prevent the dimensional changes.

Deterioration

All tissues produced by living organisms serve as food for other living things. Wood nevertheless is in relatively low demand in nature because most animals and plants cannot utilize it as a food source. Human limitations illustrate this fact: we can digest all kinds of vegetables, but our digestive system lacks the ability (i.e., enzymes) to break down wood, even wood powder, and to dissolve the fragments. Some living organisms, however, do have the ability to utilize wood, and thus they, along with fire, impose limits on wood durability (7).

A limit to durability is advantageous in that wood-destroying organisms can live on discarded and unharvested wood, recycling the material by reconverting it to carbon dioxide and water. Most wood fallen to the forest floor fades away within a few years; even the most durable tree trunks last on the forest floor only a few decades. Everlasting wood in forests would accumulate as a mass of decrepit trees, leaving hardly any space for young trees.

Wood-Damaging Fungi Among the organisms that live on wood, fungi are the most destructive, particularly the kinds that cause *wood rot* (described in Chapter 8). Like all plants, wood-inhabiting fungi need moisture and cannot grow on dry wood. But in the presence of moisture it is only a question of time until fungi decompose wood; the rate depends on temperature, availability of oxygen for fungal respiration, wood resistance, and the kinds of fungi.

Some wood-inhabiting fungi cannot decompose the main constituents of wood, but live on parenchyma cells and on food reserves in sapwood. Under favorable conditions these *stain* and *mold* fungi infect and discolor the sapwood of large piles of lumber within a few days. The stainers and molders make the wood more permeable, more absorptive for water, and hence more disposed to decay. For a further discussion of fungal infection of wood see Chapter 8.

Wood-Damaging Insects Carpenter ants and some other insects dig into wood to use it for shelter, but the more destructive species feed on wood. Since the wood feeders digest the material inside their gut and not by external secretion of enzymes, they need less moisture than fungi. Some insects live on dry wood, but most species prefer it damp, for it is then soft and easy to chew, provides a comfortable humid environment for the thin-skinned larvae, and may even have been predigested by wood rot fungi.

By far the most destructive wood-feeding insects are termites. Their colonies are well-organized, efficient societies which can ruin unprotected frame houses made of wood within a few years. Termites prefer warm climates and do the most damage in the southern states, but they occur as far north as Vermont, Ontario, Wisconsin, Colorado, and British Columbia. Other wood-damaging insects are discussed in Chapter 7.

Durability and Preservation Light wood with its abundant space for oxygen and water offers relatively little resistance to damaging organisms; insects find it easy to chew, and fungi rapidly advance across the relatively few or thin cell walls.

Because it contains food reserves, sapwood is never quite as durable as heartwood.

Wood density and food reserves, however, have much less effect on durability than some of the substances that trees deposit when converting sapwood into heartwood. The *heartwood deposits* of many tree species are poisonous to wood-damaging organisms and thus protect the wood to the extent that such heartwood resists decay several times or even many times longer than sapwood. Redwood and western redcedar heartwood fence posts last in most regions of North America for about twenty years, in spite of their low density. It should be emphasized, however, that not all wood species deposit substances in heartwood, not all heartwood deposits are poisonous, and not all deposits change the wood's color. Therefore heartwood, which looks different from sapwood, is in many but not in all tree species more durable than sapwood. The heartwood of a few species has good durability even though its color is the same as that of sapwood.

The preservation industry protects wood from damaging organisms by poisoning it with preservatives such as creosote, a group of coal-tar distillates described further in Chapter 23. Creosote gives utility poles and railroad ties a dark-brown appearance and an obnoxious odor. Interior wood generally needs no protection; where unusual circumstances dictate some protection, odorless preservative salts serve the purpose. The preservatives are brushed onto the surface or applied by soaking, but pressure treatment achieves much deeper penetration and longer-lasting protection. Since 1967 the industry has offered treated studs and plywood for *permanent wood foundations;* these foundations have advantages over concrete foundations and have gradually penetrated the house construction market (Figure 22.11) (1).

Variability

Unfortunately, wood properties vary from tree to tree of each wood species and even within each tree. For example, one unusually heavy Douglas-fir stud may be 20 percent heavier or denser than an unusually light stud of the same size (Figure 22.12). Among

Figure 22.11 Wood foundation for a home. (Courtesy of Osmose Wood Preserving.)

very small, thin pieces of wood the variations are even greater; latewood is three times denser in some species than earlywood (compare Figure 22.4). The thicker and larger the sample, the closer its properties come to the species average (2). Strengths vary more than densities, even in wood free of defects such as knots.

By far the largest variations in strength within each wood are caused by *knots,* the parts of tree branches imbedded in the stem. Knots have the fiber direction of the branches, which is nearly at a right angle to the stem axis and to the normal fiber direction. Knots may therefore reduce the strength of lumber to less than one-tenth. The large fiber deviation of knots affects nearly all wood properties, including workability. Knotty lumber is not service-able for many purposes unless the knotty sections are removed. Structural lumber grades permit

knots, but allowances are made for the lower strengths.

The effect of knots and other growth variations on strength cannot be assessed accurately for each piece without physical testing, particularly when the defect is barely visible. Therefore, structures have to be designed for the potential weakness of each member; more lumber or thicker lumber is re-quired than would be necessary with a uniform material.

Utilization of Solid Wood

The lack of efficient tools compelled prehistoric people to use wood in its natural cylindrical form as *roundwood.* Uses that required noncylindrical shapes were met with forked stems, branch joints,

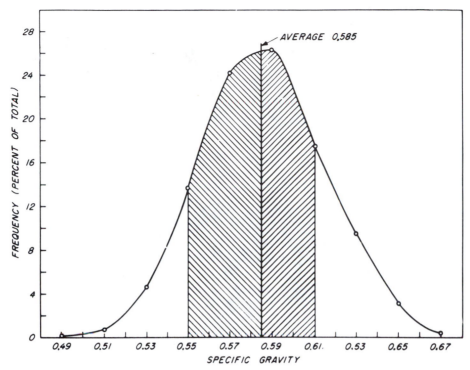

Figure 22.12 Variation in the specific gravity of hard maple, the wood from the sugar maple tree, based on material from twelve stands in eight states. Specific gravity is numerically identical with density expressed in grams per cubic centimeter. (Courtesy of U.S.D.A. Forest Products Laboratory.)

and crooked branches. As people gradually perfected tools and skills for cutting out and shaping the material for diversified needs, the proportion of roundwood used decreased even more. In 1976 only about 7 percent of the timber harvested was for roundwood, of which most (5 percent) served as fuel (9). Roughly 2 percent was industrial roundwood, used as utility poles for carrying electrical power and telephone wires, props in coal mines, piling driven into soft ground to support structures, and posts along highways, for fences and signs, and as logs (long unshaped sections of the tree stem) for log cabins.

Use of Lumber

The rounded profiles of log cabin walls have aesthetic appeal, but plane surfaces are more practical for most purposes, especially where the pieces join

and have to be connected. Early carpenters squared the logs with broadaxes and adzes into *hewn timbers* (Figure 22.13), until sawmill machines were invented to cut smoother planes in less time. Early European sawmills sawed plenty of thick lumber for *timber frame houses* by sawing off or *slabbing* the half-curved *slabs* from the log's four sides. Modern mills produce many additional kinds of lumber, such as planed boards, planks, the well-known *two-by-fours* with 2 × 4-inch cross sections, ten-by-ten-inch posts, and numerous other sizes (Figure 22.14). A great variety of moldings are also produced, especially for the edge trim around door and window openings. *Lumber* is defined as a product of the saw and planing mill, not further manufactured than by sawing, passing lengthwise through a standard planing machine, crosscutting to length, and matching. To give examples, *tongue-and-groove* boards, which form a joint by the projecting rib on the edge

Figure 22.13 A log cabin of hewn timbers, surrounded by a split-rail fence. (Photograph by Gunard Hans.)

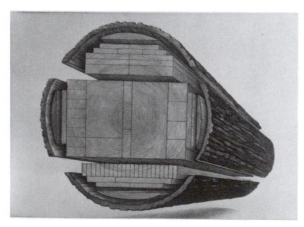

Figure 22.14 How a thick tree trunk is divided up into lumber. The rounded sides (slabs) under the bark serve as raw material for reconstituted wood and paper. (Courtesy of Lignum, Zurich, Switzerland.)

of one board fitting into the groove on the edge of the adjoining board, still belong to the category of *lumber,* whereas stairs, bent barrel staves, and plywood do not. *Ties* for railroads, the rectangular transverse beams that support the rails, may be considered a kind of lumber before the manufacturers drill holes for fastening the rails. Sawmills cut *ties* for retaining walls and other landscaping purposes simply by slabbing the log to obtain two flat surfaces for stacking tie upon tie.

Americans harvest nearly one-half of their timber for lumber (8, 9). In turn, 60 percent of this lumber winds up in residential and nonresidential construction, including upkeep and improvement. Within construction, most lumber goes into skeletons of buildings, namely as floor joists, wall studs, and roof frameworks (Figure 22.15). The load-carrying struc-

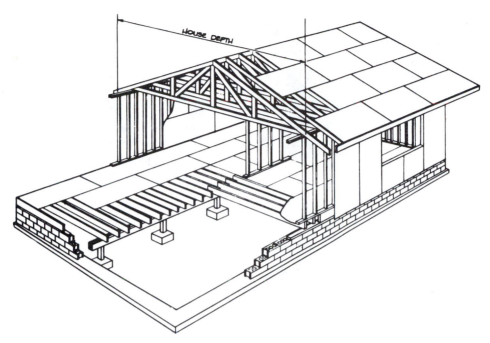

Figure 22.15 Framing of a traditional single-family home with crawl space, showing floor joists, wall studs, and roof trusses, all sheathed with wood-based panels. (Courtesy of National Forest Products Association.)

ture of sloped roofs in earlier times consisted mainly of relatively deep lumber *rafters* (Figure 22.16), until in the 1950s the Americans Carol Sanford and Calvin Jureit invented *nail plates* (Figure 22.17), which—when simply pressed into the sides of adjoining pieces—connect lumber pieces within a rigid *roof truss* (Figure 22.18). Modern roof trusses are designed by computers and assembled in *truss plants* in all sorts of efficient configurations, mainly from two-by-fours. The roof trusses utilize wood more efficiently than do rafters and earlier frameworks. *Parallel-chord trusses* of nail-plate-connected two-by-fours are well on their way to displacing floor joists, at least the deep joists needed for wide spans (Figure 22.18). In buildings, lumber is also needed for doors, windows, and stairs, as trim, for built-ins, and for paneling.

About 20 percent of the lumber winds up in *pallets*—the portable platforms used for handling, storing, and moving goods (Figure 22.19). The remaining 20 percent goes into the manufacture of

Figure 22.16 A carpenter covers the rafter and roof structure of a home with plywood sheathing. (Courtesy of American Plywood Association.)

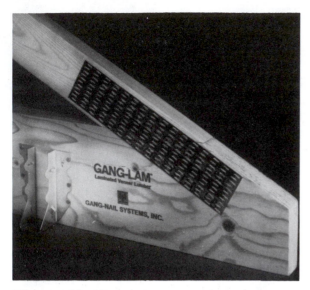

Figure 22.17 A nail plate connecting lumber of a roof truss. (Courtesy of Gang-Nail Systems, Inc.)

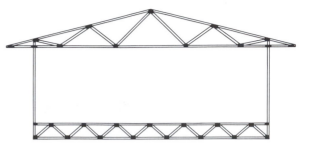

Figure 22.18 Section of a home with parallel-chord floor trusses and roof trusses. All pieces of lumber are connected with nail plates. (Courtesy of U.S.D.A. Forest Products Laboratory.)

Figure 22.19 A pallet designed for entry of a forklift truck from all four sides.

furniture and a great variety of other products such as baseball bats and handles, and for numerous purposes outside manufacturing, including fences and boardwalks (9).

Manufacture of Lumber

In early machine saws, a saw blade was hung in a sash frame, which in turn was driven up and down or back and forth sideways by means of crankshafts and water power. Out of these *sash saws* evolved *gang saws* with several thin, parallel saw blades in the reciprocating sash. The distance from blade to blade within the frame determined the thickness of the lumber. By the early days of this century, gang saws were already converting thick logs in one pass into about twenty boards. Modern gang saws make hundreds of strokes each minute, but the speed of the sawteeth starts at zero in each stroke and does not reach the most efficient magnitude. This is one reason why few North American mills work with gang saws. In the past Europeans preferred the gangs, but the future seems to belong to the continually cutting circular saws and band saws (Figures 22.20 and 22.21). A *band saw* takes the form of a

flexible endless belt of steel with teeth on one edge, running over two vertical pulleys and operating under tension.

On the positive side, circular saws are simpler and cost less than band saws. However, circular saw blades have to be huge for cutting thick logs and must be relatively stiff and thick to prevent deviations from the straight line of cutting; thick blades, in turn, cut wide kerfs and waste too much wood as sawdust. One advantage is that it is possible to assemble several circular blades on one arbor for making more than one cut in one pass. For multiple cuts with band saws, the mills must install several machines along the path of the log. Multiple cuts in

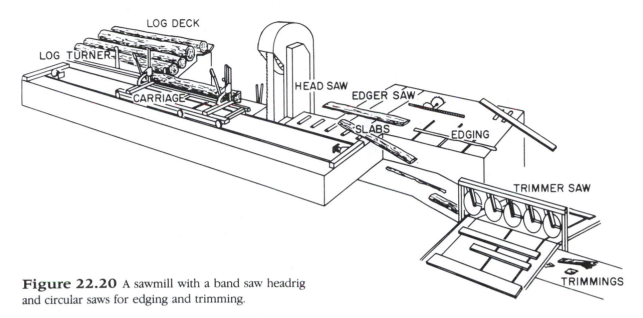

Figure 22.20 A sawmill with a band saw headrig and circular saws for edging and trimming.

Figure 22.21 A slabbed log on a carriage passes along a band saw, which cuts off a plank. (Courtesy of CAE Machinery Ltd.)

one pass are undesirable when the sawyer must adapt each cut to the characteristics of the log; for example, when a log is opened, defects may appear that are acceptable in thick lumber but cannot be tolerated in thin lumber.

In circular-saw and band saw rigs the log is clamped onto a carriage, which is driven back and forth on rails. The carriages are equipped for instantly shifting the log sideways and turning it on another side after each pass, as is required for obtaining the most favorably located cuts. In modern rigs carriages push the log through the running blade within a few seconds.

In addition to the *headrig,* the main saw which breaks the log down, sawmills employ machines for debarking the stems, for *bucking* long stems into logs, and for *resawing* headrig-squared timbers, flitches, and planks into boards; *edger saws* for squaring round edges of lumber; *trimmer saws* for crosscutting the lumber to exact lengths (Figure 22.20); and conveyors for transporting, sorting, and stacking. Many of the operations are computerized. The mills store their stems and logs either in yards or under water in ponds to prevent drying checks and damage by organisms. The lumber products are dry-stacked in the open air (Figure 22.22) or in kilns.

Figure 22.22 The pieces of lumber in these stacked packages are separated by stickers to allow air to circulate over the board surfaces. (Courtesy of U.S.D.A. Forest Products Laboratory.)

Sawmills recover only 40 to 70 percent of the debarked volume of the stem as dry, planed lumber (14). Thick cylindrical logs, rather than odd-shaped thin logs, and relatively thick lumber contribute to high recoveries. High costs for timber—far more than one-half of mill expenditures—force sawmills to minimize the volume of slabs, edgings, sawdust, planer shavings, and trimmings. These *mill residues* are sold, burned, or dumped. Many mills cut slabs, edgings, and trimmings to chips for pulp and reconstituted wood, which is described later. Planer shavings are suited for making particleboard. Sawdust can be used as raw material for pulp and reconstituted wood, but for good paper and panels the sawdust is too fragmented. Most mills burn the sawdust for energy, together with bark. Sorted pieces of bark lend themselves for landscaping and for extraction of tannin (explained in Chapter 23).

Instead of removing slabs from logs and edgings from lumber, some sawmills square the log by converting the sides directly into chips and sawing the cant into lumber in one further step (14). The resulting chips do not have the ideal size and shape for pulp and reconstituted wood, but they are much better suited for this application than sawdust. Sawmills now utilize our valuable timber resources much more efficiently and waste less material than they did before the 1960s. Prior to this time residues were burned only for disposal purposes, and fossil fuels were purchased to obtain the power needed to drive the machines and to heat the dry kilns.

Wood-Based Panel Products

Wood-based panels comprise plywood and the *reconstituted boards,* namely, particleboard, fiberboard, and hardboard, which are defined in the following pages. Early in this century most of the *sheathing* that covered the framework of roofs, exterior walls, and floors of buildings consisted of tongue-and-groove boards. Builders then began using more and more wood-based panels (Figure 22.16) (8). The *siding* that covers the sheathing of exterior walls of houses and contributes most to the outside appearance of homes underwent similar changes, from lumber to other products; however, redwood and western redcedar boards have retained a small share of this market. Most new siding consists of hardboard, followed by plywood, aluminum, and vinyl; all these substitutes are manufactured to look like lumber siding when installed. New paneling in rooms of homes and in commercial buildings is usually thin wood-based board, which again gives the appearance of lumber. Like lumber, about 60 percent of the wood-based panels are used in construction, and the other 40 percent end up in manufactured goods such as furniture and in products for numerous other purposes.

The industry produces all four kinds of wood-based panels principally in the same way, by disintegrating the raw wood into thin or small pieces for reassembly into large boards (8). The four kinds differ mainly in the size of the pieces; accordingly the panels are discussed in the sequence of increasing degree of disintegration, or decreasing size of the pieces.

Plywood

Plywood panels consist of large layers joined with adhesive. Some or all of the layers are thin sheets of wood known as *veneer* (Figures 22.23 and 22.24). Other layers, particularly in the core, may be particleboard, hardboard, lumber strips, and special materials. The fiber direction of each layer is at right angles to that of the adjoining layer. This *crossbanding* makes plywood more uniform and less anisotropic than lumber; its properties in the direction of panel length resemble those in the direction of panel width (7).

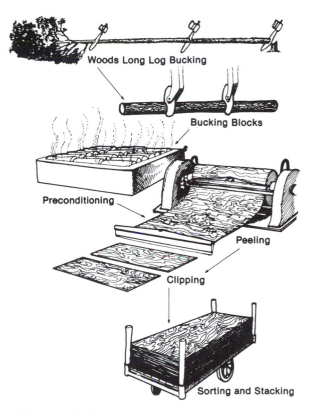

Figure 22.24 Manufacture of veneer. Blocks (logs) are preconditioned for veneer cutting by heating in hot water or steam. Then a lathe peels a continuous veneer ribbon from the block. Next the ribbon is clipped into sheets to be sorted and dried for plywood manufacture. (Courtesy of U.S.D.A. Forest Products Laboratory.)

Figure 22.23 A piece of five-ply plywood opened to show the crossbanding of the layers; black tape indicates the direction of fibers in each layer.

Crossbanding affects strength in a logical way. In both directions of the plane, the panel is as strong as the combined layers. Since in any one of the two directions transverse layers contribute practically no strength, plywood is roughly one-half as strong as lumber is lengthwise. But by the same principle plywood is stronger than lumber in the direction of width and can therefore be thinner. Moreover, it does not split like solid-wood products. Plywood and lumber properties naturally are the same in the thickness direction, provided that the layers are adequately bonded together.

Crossbanding gives plywood dimensional stability. To understand this effect, consider first the fiber direction of the surface veneers in Figure 22.23. Both surface veneers and the core veneer tend to swell and shrink (*move*) very little, whereas the two transverse veneers or *crossbands* have a very strong tendency to move. The adhesive bonds compel all five veneers to move by the same amount, somewhere between the small longitudinal shrinkage and the large transverse shrinkage of lumber. However, since wood is many times stiffer in the fiber direction than in the transverse direction, longitudinal movement dominates and the panel remains fairly stable. Similarly, in the other direction of the plane, the crossbands dominate and restrain the movements. According to a rule of thumb, plywood shrinks and swells in directions of length and width about twice as much as lumber moves lengthwise, which is still very little. For most practical purposes plywood can be considered to be dimensionally stable. Of course, the crossbanding does not affect movements in the direction of the panel thickness, which are large in terms of percentages but small in absolute terms and unimportant.

Many plywood panels are 6 millimeters (¼ inch) thick; the thinnest measure about 1 millimeter, and the thickest several centimeters. In addition to house sheathing (Figure 22.16) and siding, much plywood is used in cabinets, billboards, furniture, bookshelves, concrete forms, skins of flush doors, paneling, boxes, in mobile homes, and for trailers. Americans harvest more than 10 percent of the timber to cut veneer for plywood and for surface layers of the type of panels discussed next.

Particleboard

Particleboard is the youngest of the four kinds of wood-based panels. Developed in timber-short Europe in the 1940s, particleboard penetrated the North American market about 1950 and has realized the highest growth rate of the panel products (see Chapter 24). Particleboard appears in many versions and under various names as *chipboard, chipcore, shavingsboard,* and *splinterboard.*

To understand particleboard, let us engage in an imaginary experiment and make a panel from toothpicks. We spray adhesive on the picks, sprinkle the picks on a steel plate to form a mat, and press the mat under another steel plate until the adhesive has bonded. The picks are oriented at random in the plane of the panel and none points in the direction of thickness. A variable orientation of this kind amounts to crossbanding. Common particleboard, like plywood, has uniform strength and good dimensional stability within the plane (8). Particleboard is somewhat weaker than plywood of the same density and must be thicker or denser when used for the same purpose. The weakness is due to the particles touching one another only at points and not along their entire length. Furthermore, adhesives are too expensive to coat each particle completely and must be applied sparingly.

Many particleboards are 19 millimeters (¾ inch) thick, the minimum being near 3 millimeters (⅛ inch). The industry produces some boards from slivers that resemble toothpicks, but in the past North American factories used mostly crushed planer shavings. Overall the particles vary in size and in form, from wood flour to small pieces of veneer residues up to about 10 centimeters long. Many good boards feature coarse particles in the core, flat flakes under the surface, and *fines* at the very surface. The strongest type consists of thin slices from low-density woods such as aspen, which is marketed as *waferboard.* In another relatively new type of particleboard, the manufacturers align long strands of wood at the surface for increased strength in the direction of panel length (Figure 22.25). This *oriented-strand board* and waferboard replaced a great deal of plywood sheathing in the early 1980s.

Figure 22.25 Two small specimens of oriented-strand board. In the central layer the strands are aligned perpendicularly to the strands in the two surface layers to achieve crossbanding. The numbered scale is in inches. (Courtesy of U.S.D.A. Forest Products Laboratory.)

Fiberboard and Hardboard

Fiberboard and hardboard evolved from paper manufacture and can be considered as extremely thick cardboard (see Chapter 23). Both consist essentially of fibers, fiber bundles, and fiber fragments, which are held together by interfelting, natural bonds, and in some brands by a small percentage of adhesive. Like the particles in particleboard, the fibers from mechanical disintegrated wood lie at random in the plane, crossbanding the panel (1).

Fiberboard factories equalize the mat of loose fibers between screens and rollers, whereas hardboard is press-bonded between hot plates to make it dense and strong. The dividing line between the two types of panels lies at a density of 0.5 gram per cubic centimeter. Both are manufactured for many specific uses and vary accordingly.

Fiberboard is at least 0.16 gram per cubic centimeter dense and typically 13 millimeters (½ inch) thick. *Exterior* fiberboard for wall sheathing looks black because it is impregnated with asphalt for water repellency and durability. *Interior-finish* fiberboard for walls in rooms has a white factory finish. Gray untreated, unfinished *sound-deadening* board inserted within walls reduces sound transmission from room to room. *Acoustical tiles* with numerous holes or fissues for sound absorption represent one of many other versions. Fiberboard was formerly known as *insulating board* until building standards tightened the term *insulation* around 1980. The plastic foam panels, offering superior insulating properties, replaced a great deal of exterior-fiberboard wall sheathing in Canada, in the northern states, and to some extent even in the southern states.

Hardboard densities vary from 0.5 to 1.3 grams per cubic centimeter. Best known under the brand name *Masonite,* hardboard is used for cabinet backs, for drawer bottoms, in visors of automobiles, and in many other hidden parts. Many garage doors have hardboard linings. Hardboard is typically 4 to 5 millimeters (³⁄₁₆ inch) thick. Some panels are smooth on both surfaces, but most have a *screenback* imprint at one side from a wire screen under the fiber mat in the hot press; the screen permits evaporated water to escape. *Pegboard,* with rows of punched holes, holds tools in workshops and articles in hardware stores; it also serves as room dividers and as backings in television and radio cabinets. Hardboard with an imprinted wood grain looks almost like natural wood, but costs much less than plywood paneling. In some brands the surface is molded to imitate a basket weave, weathered lumber for siding, bathroom tiles, or many other patterns. *Medium-density hardboards* are pressed for house siding and marketed either as wide panels or as long, 30-centimeter-wide (1-foot-wide) boards. *Medium-density fiberboard,* known as MDF, is a sort of particleboard consisting of adhesive-bonded fibers. The furniture industry uses MDF as a fine-structured panel or panel core, which can be machined to smooth edges.

Significance of Wood-Based Panels

Wood-based panels have replaced lumber for good reasons. Since they are manufactured in large widths—mostly 122 centimeters (4 feet)—they require little time to install and form large closed surfaces. The few joints between sheets suffice to absorb their relatively small shrinkage and swelling. Since the panels do not split, they can be nailed close to their edges. Because of their thinness, transportation costs are low and they can be handled with ease in spite of their large size.

All four types of panels utilize timber more efficiently than lumber. Most are relatively thin, being roughly one-half and even less than one-fourth as thick as lumber for the same purpose. Thinness is one reason why the total volume of the many panels consumed in the United States makes up only one-third of all lumber consumption. In addition, many reconstituted-wood panels are manufactured from residues with little waste (8).

Summary and Conclusion

Wood has several good and a few disadvantageous properties for human use; it excels in features that play important roles in the life of the tree, but some of the other features are undesirable for utilizing wood. Whenever we wonder about the suitability of wood for a certain category of use, *the importance of the needed property for the tree* serves as a clue.

People appreciate the strength of wood in the fiber direction, as well as its high strength–mass ratio, resiliency, wide variety, availability, ease of working, beauty and warmth, fuel value, and electrical properties. On the negative side, wood cannot be plasticized economically, a property essential for mass production; it lacks dimensional stability, is highly variable, must be kept dry, and should or must be treated with preservatives to prevent destruction by living organisms.

Our early ancestors used mostly roundwood. Later, more and more timber was modified for specific purposes and converted into lumber of numerous sizes and shapes. Increasing proportions of timber are cut into thin or small pieces to be reassembled in the form of plywood and reconstituted-wood panels, which are for many purposes better than lumber and utilize timber more efficiently.

References

1. H. KUBLER, *Wood as Building and Hobby Material,* Wiley–Interscience, New York, 1980.

2. F. F. P. KOLLMANN AND W. A. COTE, *Principles of Wood Science and Technology,* Vol. 1, *Solid Wood,* Springer-Verlag, Berlin/New York, 1968.

3. B. R. HOADLEY, *Understanding Wood: A Craftsman's Guide to Wood Technology,* The Taunton Press, Newton, Conn., 1980.

4. W. M. HARLOW, *Inside Wood—Masterpiece of Nature,* American Forestry Assoc., Washington, D.C., 1970.

5. A. J. PANSHIN AND C. DE ZEEUW, *Textbook of Wood Technology,* Vol. 1, *Structure, Identification, Uses, and Properties of the Commercial Woods of the United States and Canada,* Fourth Edition, McGraw–Hill, New York, 1980.

6. P. KOCH, *Utilization of the Southern Pines,* Vol. 1, U.S.D.A. Agr. Handbook 420, U.S.D.A. For. Serv., South. For. Expt. Sta., U.S. Govt. Printing Office, Washington, D.C., 1972.

7. ANON., *Wood Handbook: Wood as an Engineering Material,* U.S.D.A. Agr. Handbook 72, U.S.D.A. For. Ser., Forest Products Laboratory, U.S. Govt. Printing Office, Washington, D.C., 1987.

8. J. G. HAYGREEN AND J. L. BOWYER, *Forest Products and Wood Science—An Introduction,* Iowa State Univ. Press, Ames, 1982.

9. ANON., "An analysis of the timber situation in the United States 1952–2030," For. Res. Rept. 23, U.S.D.A. For. Ser., U.S. Govt. Printing Office, Washington, D.C., 1982.

10. ANON., *Wood—Colors and Kinds,* U.S.D.A. Agr. Handbook 101, U.S.D.A. For. Ser., Forest Products Labora-

tory, U.S. Govt. Printing Office, Washington, D.C., 1956.

11. J. SHELTON, *The Woodburners Encyclopedia,* Vermont Crossroad Press, Waitsfield, Vt., 1976.

12. K. E. SKOG AND I. A. WATTERSON, *J. For., 82,* 742 (1984).

13. P. J. INCE, "How to estimate recoverable heat energy in wood or bark fuels," U.S.D.A. For. Serv., Gen. Tech. Rept. FPL 29, Forest Products Laboratory, Madison, Wis., 1979.

14. P. KOCH, *Utilization of Hardwoods Growing on Southern Pine Sites,* Vol. 1, U.S.D.A. Agr. Handbook 605, South. For. Expt. Sta., U.S. Govt. Printing Office, Washington, D.C., 1985.

CHAPTER 23

Wood for Fiber, Energy, and Chemicals

RAYMOND A. YOUNG
JOHN N. MCGOVERN
ROGER M. ROWELL

The importance of wood as a raw material supplying fiber, energy, and chemicals is similar in magnitude to its use as a solid material. In 1983 the use of timber for fiber, chemicals, and fuels amounted to about one-half of the total, with fiber accounting for 25 percent. Lumber, plywood, and reconstituted boards consumed the remaining one-half of the timber utilization. In 1986 over 52 million metric tons of pulp fiber for papermaking were derived from the forest (Figure 23.1). Although the relative value of wood as a source of energy and chemicals has varied considerably through the decades, wood continues to be an important source of specialty chemicals and renewable energy, and may be even more important in the future. In this chapter we discuss the chemical nature of wood and provide a description of the technology for conversion of wood to pulp fibers for papermaking, to fuels for energy, and to chemicals for industry and consumers.

Figure 23.1 Unloading at a pulp mill in Kingsport, Tennessee. (Courtesy of U.S.D.A. Forest Service.)

Chemical Nature of Wood

As described in Chapter 3, wood is like all other plant material in that it begins with the basic photo-synthetic equation in which carbon dioxide and water are combined by means of the sun's energy to produce glucose and oxygen:

$$\text{light energy}$$
$$6\ CO_2 + 6\ H_2O \rightarrow C_6H_{12}O_6 + 6\ O_2$$
$$\text{carbon dioxide} + \text{water} \rightarrow \text{sugar} + \text{oxygen}$$

To understand the chemical nature of wood, we need to trace the developments in the plant starting with glucose, a basic sugar.[1]

Glucose, as produced in the equation, is only one of a series of sugars that occur in nature. The sugars are generally classified according to the number of carbon (C) atoms in their structure; thus sugars with six carbons are referred to as hexoses, and those with five carbons are referred to as pentoses. The sugars important in wood structure are the hexoses (glucose, mannose, and galactose) and the pentoses (xylose and arabinose). Because sugars are so important in our lives, a separate field of chemistry termed carbohydrate chemistry, is devoted completely to sugar derivatives.

Sugars generally do not occur as simple compounds in wood but as higher-molecular-weight structures known generally as *polymers*. The concept of a polymer can be visualized by considering one sugar unit as one link, the monomer, in a long chain, the polymer. Thus with each link an identical sugar, a chain of sugar units is formed—a polymer of sugars known commonly as polysaccharides. This linking is depicted schematically as follows.

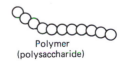

O
Monomer
(sugar)

Polymer
(polysaccharide)

Polysaccharides are characterized by the number of sugars in the chain or the *degree of polymerization* (DP).

---

[1]Sugars such as glucose or dextrose (grape sugar), fructose (fruit sugar), and sucrose (cane sugar) are common sweet-tasting substances and are classed as carbohydrates because of their empirical formula, $C_y(H_2O)_x$.

Because there are many different sugars, many different polysaccharides can be formed. A polysaccharide formed from glucose is a glucan, from xylose a xylan, from mannose a mannan, and so on. If combinations of sugars occur in one polysaccharide, a mixed polymer is formed, usually named for its predominant sugars. Thus if glucose and mannose are present, the polysaccharide is a glucomannan, if arabinose and galactose are present, a arabinogalactan, and so on.

Polysaccharides are of paramount importance in wood and to the uses of chemically processed wood. *Cellulose* is the common term used for the glucan present in wood; it constitutes about 42 percent of wood's dry weight. Cellulose is the primary component of the walls of cells making up wood fibers and is the main structural material of wood and other plants. Paper, paperboard, and other wood fiber products are therefore also composed mostly of cellulose. The chemical structure of the cellulose macromolecule is shown in Figure 23.2. In the plant the DP of cellulose is approximately 14,000.

Closely associated with cellulose in the wood structure and in paper products are other polysaccharides termed *hemicelluloses*. The hemicelluloses have often been labeled as the matrix material of wood. In hardwoods the primary hemicellulose is a xylan (polymer of xylose), whereas in softwoods the primary hemicellulose is a glucomannan, although both of these polysaccharides occur to some extent in both types of wood. The DP of the hemicelluloses is much less than that of cellulose, in the range of 100 to 200.

Table 23.1 gives a comparison of the chemical composition of extractive-free hardwoods and soft-

Table 23.1 Chemical Composition and Fiber Length of Extractive-Free Wood

Component	Hardwood (Red Maple) (percent)	Softwood (Balsam Fir) (percent)
Cellulose	44	42
Hemicelluloses		
Xylan	25	9
Glucomannan	4	18
Lignin	25	29
Pectin, starch	2	2
Average fiber length (mm)	0.8–1.5	2.5–6.0

woods. (The nature of wood extractives is treated in a later section) (1–3). Since cellulose and the hemicelluloses are both polysaccharides, it is obvious that the polysaccharide component of wood is by far the dominant one, making up approximately 70 percent of both hardwoods and softwoods. Additional polysaccharides may occur as extraneous components of wood, components that are not part of the cell wall; for example, the heartwood of species of larch can contain up to 25 percent (dry weight) of arabinogalactan, a water-soluble polysaccharide that occurs only in trace quantities in other wood species.

The third major component of wood shown in Table 23.1 is lignin. Although lignin is also a polymer, it has a definitely different chemical structure compared to that of the polysaccharides. The monomeric units in lignin are phenolic-type compounds. The exact chemical structure of lignin is still not known after 100 years of intensive research. The spaces between fibers in wood are almost pure lignin and are termed the *middle lamella* (3–5). Lignin is also considered the gluing or encrusting substance of wood and adds mechanical strength or stiffness to the tree and to wood. Higher plants are commonly referred to as lignocellulosic because of the typical joint occurrence in them of lignin and cellulose. Figure 23.3 shows the spaces between fibers that are filled with lignin and make up the middle lamella.

Figure 23.2 The chemical structure of cellulose; the cellulose repeat unit is in brackets.

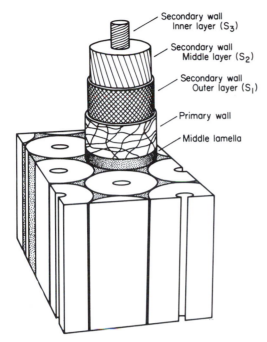

Secondary wall
Inner layer (S₃)

Secondary wall
Middle layer (S₂)

Secondary wall
Outer layer (S₁)

Primary wall

Middle lamella

Figure 23.3 A section of wood made up of fibers and middle lamella. The structure of a fiber is given, showing the microfibrillar orientations in the different layers of the fiber's cell wall. [Adapted from Meier (6).]

A fourth class of wood components is known as *extraneous material* and is present in wood in the amounts of 3 to 10 percent. These materials comprise a vast array of chemical compounds that are not constituents of the cell wall. Most of these compounds, because they can be extracted with water or organic solvents or volatilized with steam, are called *extractives*. They are considered in detail subsequently. A small portion of the extraneous materials—starch, pectins, and inorganic salts—are not extractable.

Structure of Wood and Wood Fibers

In the tree the cellulose polymers are laid down uniformly, the chains paralleling one another, and the long-chain molecules associate strongly through hydrogen bonds that develop between hydroxyl groups. These bonds create very strong associations between the cellulose macromolecules. These associations between the cellulose chains give a very uniform crystalline structure known as *micelles* or *microcrystallites,* shown in Figure 23.4.

The micelles are also associated in the tree to give long threadlike structures termed microfibrils (Figure 23.4). The structure of the microfibrils is not completely uniform in terms of the alignment of the cellulose macromolecules. These regions of non-uniformity between the micelles in the microfibrils are called amorphous regions; the cellulose microfibril therefore has a crystalline–amorphous character (1–5). Water molecules enter the amorphous regions and swell the microfibrils; ultimately this is the mechanism by which fibers and wood swell in moist or wet environments.

The final fiber cell wall structure is essentially layers of the microfibrils or macrofibrils aligned in several different directions, as shown in Figure 23.3. The microfibrils that make up the wood fiber are visible under the scanning electron microscope, which magnifies beyond the light microscope (Figure 23.5).

The entity holding the fibers together, the middle lamella, is almost pure lignin (90 percent), as mentioned earlier. For the cellulose fibers to be separated, the middle lamella lignin must be chemically removed, a process that also removes most of the hemicelluloses, or mechanically degraded to free the fibers for papermaking (Figure 23.6). A paper sheet can then be formed from the separated cellulose fibers by depositing them from a water slurry onto a wire screen. The water drains away and the fibers collapse, leaving a fiber mat that derives its main strength from reassociation of the fibers through many hydrogen bonds—the same type of bond that gives mechanical integrity to the fibers (Figure 23.7).

The long fibers from softwoods (Table 23.1) are usually preferred in papermaking for products that must resist tearing, such as grocery bags, whereas the shorter hardwood fibers give improved opacity, or covering power, and printability to the final paper sheet. The type of pulping process also affects the pulp properties, as described in a later section.

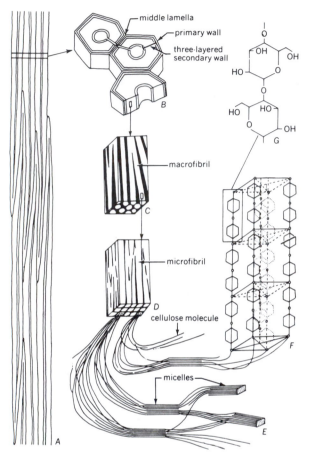

Figure 23.4 Detailed structure of cell walls. *A*, strand of fiber cells. B, cross section of fiber cells showing gross layering: a layer of primary wall and three layers of secondary wall. *C*, fragment from the middle layer of a secondary wall showing macrofibrils (white) of cellulose and interfibrillar spaces (black), which are filled with noncellulosic materials. *D*, fragment of a macrofibril showing microfibrils (white), which may be seen in electron micrographs (Figure 23.5). The spaces among microfibrils (black) are filled with noncellulosic materials. *E*, structure of microfibrils: chainlike molecules of cellulose, which in some parts of microfibrils are orderly arranged. These parts are the micelles. *F*, fragment of a micelle showing parts of chainlike cellulose molecules arranged in a space lattice. G, two glucose residues connected by an oxygen atom—a fragment of a cellulose molecule. (From K. Esau, *Anatomy of Seed Plants,* Second Edition, 1977, courtesy of John Wiley & Sons.)

Figure 23.5 A scanning electron micrograph of a replica of a spruce earlywood tracheid showing the microfibrillar orientation in S_2 and S_3 layers of the secondary wall (see Figure 23.3). (Courtesy of Wilfred Côté and Syracuse University Press.)

History of Papermaking

The concept of making paper from the fibers from lignocellulosic materials—an integrated system of fiber separation (pulping) and re-forming of the fibers into a mat (papermaking)—is attributed to T'sai Lun, a court official in southeast China in 105 A.D. The first fibers were obtained from old hemp rags and ramie fishnets, but shortly thereafter, the inner bark fibers from paper mulberry trees were also utilized for papermaking. Bamboo was used as a

Figure 23.6 Scanning electron micrograph of a cluster of eastern white pine elements after pulping or maceration of a small wood cube. (Courtesy of Wilfred Côté and Syracuse University Press.)

Figure 23.7 Scanning electron micrograph of paper surface showing random arrangement of coniferous tracheid fibers in the sheet. Note the flattened or collapsed nature of the fibers in this cross section cut with a razor blade. (Courtesy of Wilfred Côté and Syracuse University Press.)

source of fiber several centuries later. The rags were macerated into a pulp in water with a mortar and pestle; then, after dilution in a vat, the pulp was formed into a wet mat on a bamboo frame equipped with a cloth screen to drain the free water. The mat was dried in the sun. The invention was based on the need for a writing material to replace the expensive silk and inconvenient bamboo strips. The invention was a closely guarded secret for many centuries but filtered to the West at Samarkand in western China (now in the Soviet Union) early in the eighth century. The chronological journey of papermaking to the United States and its first mill near Philadelphia was as follows.

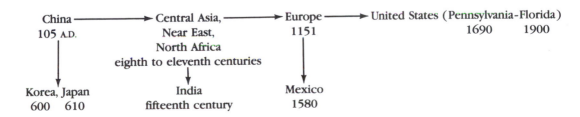

Paper was made by hand essentially as just described, spurred by development of the Gutenberg printing press (1455), until the invention of the long, continuous wire screen machine by Louis Robert in France in 1798. The machine was subsequently developed commercially in England by the Fourdrinier brothers, whose name is associated with it to this day (see Figure 23.11).

Wood became a source of fiber in the mid-1840s when a groundwood pulp grinder was manufactured in Germany. The wood was defibered by pressing against a grindstone. After 1850 several chemical methods were developed to produce chemical pulps, which will be described later. The major sources of fiber in the United States for papermaking in 1985 were pulpwood (roundwood), 40 percent; by-product sawmill chips, 34.5 percent; recycled paper, 25 percent; other (mostly cotton), 0.5 percent.

In 1986, production of paper and paperboard in the United States was 34 percent of the world's total; papermaking in North America and Europe together made up about 73 percent of the world production. The difference in the economies of the developed and less developed countries is shown in the accompanying tabulation by the wide range of per capita consumption of paper and paperboard in 1986.

United States	290 kilograms per capita
West Germany	185
Australia	145
Soviet Union	34
Egypt	9
Indonesia	4.5
Afghanistan	<1

Pulp

The pulping or fiber separation stage of the total papermaking system entails breaking the lignified fiber bonds, in the middle lamella (Figure 23.3), by mechanical or chemical means or a combination of both generally at elevated temperatures and pressures. The historical macerating, stamping, and beating applied to cotton and linen rags and the inner bark of mulberry are inadequate for fiberizing wood. The major processes in use are classified in Table 23.2 and will be described in the section on pulping systems.

Preparing Wood for Pulping

The standing tree in the forest is felled, delimbed, bucked to length, and conveyed to the pulp mill or sawmill (Chapter 16). Small percentages may be debarked and chipped in the woods, or the tree may undergo whole-tree chipping for transport in vans to the pulp mill. At the pulp mills the logs are usually debarked by tumbling against one another in large rotating drums, which removes the bark by impact and abrasion. The debarked logs are next taken to the groundwood mill (5 percent) or to the chipper (95 percent). After chipping, the chips are screened to remove oversize chips and fines. Overlong chips are rechipped and overthick chips are handled in a chip slicer. Optimum dimensions ensure uniform pulp quality (Figure 23.8). Chips are washed before mechanical pulping to avoid damage to equipment.

Pulping Systems

Three major methods are used to pulp wood, namely, *mechanical, semichemical,* and *chemical.* Each process produces pulps with different properties for different applications.

Modern mechanical pulping includes stone groundwood pulping (SGW), in which bolts of wood are pressed against a revolving grindstone, and refiner mechanical pulping (RMP), in which chips are passed between single- or double-rotating plates of a vertical-disk attrition mill (Figure 23.9). Recent developments in stone grinding are applying pressure to the grinder (PGW) and controlling temperature (Table 23.2).

Basic changes in mechanical pulping technology are to pretreat chips with chemicals, steam, or both. These developments started thirty years ago when chips were pretreated with caustic soda, termed chemimechanical pulping (CMP). Presteaming and pressure refining of chips gives a thermomechanical pulp (TMP); and when chemical pretreatment and pressure steaming are combined, the pulp is referred to as chemithermomechanical pulp (CTMP). There are many variations of these processes. These treatments are employed to improve pulp quality. The steam and chemicals aid fiberizing by giving a less-damaged fiber, which makes the final paper stronger.

Figure 23.8 Wood chips of the desired size for pulping of wood. (Photograph by R. A. Young.)

Mechanical pulps are a major component of newsprint. The mechanical pulp imparts valuable properties to the newsprint, all of which are related to printability. These are absorbency, bulk, compressibility, opacity, and uniformity. However, because mechanical pulps are weak, up to 30 percent of a chemical pulp (described later) is blended into the pulp mixture, called a furnish, to provide greater strength. Sufficient strength is required of the newsprint to withstand the tension forces produced by the printing press. Modern mills, however, now use 100 percent TMP to produce newsprint with suffi-

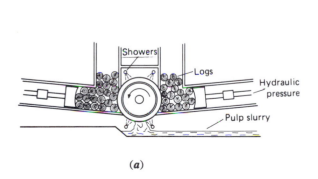

(a)

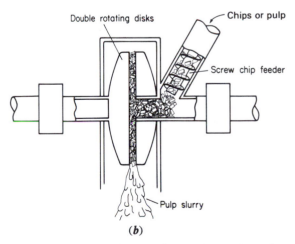

(b)

Figure 23.9 Schematic of (a) a stone grinder which pulverizes wood bolts for groundwood pulp and (b) a disk refiner which grinds wood chips for refiner and thermomechanical (TMP) pulps. Showers provide water for both methods.

Table 23.2 Wood Pulping by Process and Yield

Process	Acronym	Treatment		Pulp Yield (percent)
		Chemical	Mechanical	
Mechanical Processes				
Stone groundwood	SGW	None	Grinder	93–95
Pressure groundwood	PGW	None	Grinder	93–95
Refiner mechanical	RMP	None	Disk refiner (pressure)	93–95
Thermomechanical	TMP	Steam	Disk refiner (pressure)	80–90
Chemithermomechanical	CTMP	Sodium sulfite or sodium hydroxide[a]	Disk refiner (pressure)	80–90
Chemimechanical[b]	CMP	Sodium sulfite or sodium hydroxide	Disk refiner	80–90
Semichemical Processes				
Neutral sulfite	NSSC	Sodium sulfite + sodium carbonate	Disk refiner	70–85
Green liquor	GLSC	Sodium hydroxide + sodium carbonate	Disk refiner	70–85
Nonsulfur	—	Sodium carbonate + sodium hydroxide	Disk refiner	70–85
Chemical Processes				
Kraft	—	Sodium hydroxide + sodium sulfide	None	45–55
Sulfite	—	Calcium bisulfite in sulfurous acid[c,d]	None	40–50
Magnefite	—	Magnesium bisulfite in sulfurous acid[e]	None	45–55
Soda	—	Sodium hydroxide	None	40–50
Soda–oxygen	—	Sodium hydroxide + oxygen	None	45–55
Soda–anthraquinone	SAq	Sodium hydroxide + anthraquinone	None	45–55
Dissolving Processes				
Prehydrolysis kraft	—	Steaming and kraft (two-step process)	None	35
Acid sulfite	—	Acid sulfite (Ca, Na)	None	35

Source: Data taken from references 1 through 5.
[a]Sodium sulfite or sodium hydroxide, 2 to 7 percent of wood.
[b]Also chemical treatment after fiberizing.
[c]Also sodium, magnesium, ammonia.
[d]pH 2.
[e]pH 5.

cient strength. Mechanical pulps are also an important component of publication paper grades, which are generally coated magazine papers. Obviously, printability is important in this application as well.

Semichemical pulping combines a mild chemical treatment with mechanical action for final liberation of the fibers. The major semichemical process is neutral sulfite semichemical (NSSC). The semichemical processes were developed to improve the economic return. These processes give higher yields (75 to 80 percent) than full chemical pulping and better strength than mechanical pulps. The semichemical pulps are very suitable for the stiff corrugating medium in cardboard boxes. The recovery of chemicals and heat value from the semichemical spent liquors is well developed.

Chemical pulping is conducted on wood chips using lignin-dissolving reagents in vessels, called digesters, under elevated temperature and pressure. The major chemical pulping processes were developed about a century ago and are the *soda* (1855 in England), *sulfite* (1867 in the United States), and *kraft* or sulfate (1884 in Germany) processes. The word "kraft" comes from the German word meaning strong. The ability to utilize all wood species, especially pines, and the excellent strength of the resulting pulp have contributed to the growth of the kraft process. Kraft pulping dominated U.S. production at 79 percent in 1986.

The mechanisms for removing lignin and separating fibers in chemical pulping are hydrolysis, which cleaves the lignin bond, and conversion of the lignin to water-soluble fractions through reactions with sulfur compounds. Recovery of spent pulping reagents is economically necessary with the kraft process and involves a series of cyclic steps in which the spent liquors from the pulp washers are evaporated to concentrate the dilute black liquor into a concentrated black liquor for combustion. In the furnace the waste and makeup chemicals are converted (reduced) into a smelt of soda ash and sodium sulfide (Na_2S), which is then converted to a white liquor by the addition of sodium hydroxide. The white liquor is then used for pulping the next batch of chips.

The spent liquor from the sulfite process was traditionally discharged to associated rivers and streams because the base chemicals of sulfur and lime were very cheap, and there were no environmental regulations in effect at the time. Sulfite-spent liquor recovery has never been fully developed except for one process, the magnefite. Around the world many older sulfite mills have closed.

Chemical pulps such as kraft and sulfite, and in particular softwood kraft pulps, are generally used when considerable strength is required. Bags, stationery, and ledger and bond papers contain high percentages of chemical pulp. Sanitary tissues such as facial and toilet tissues also contain large amounts of chemical and recycled pulps. For them a combination of softness and absorbency are sought, along with sufficient strength.

Solvent pulping is another method that has received renewed interest; organic solvents rather than the traditional aqueous sulfur pulping are used for what is called organosolv pulping. Since lignin is an organic polymer, it is naturally soluble in organic solvents once some of the lignin bonds have been broken by an acid, usually, or by a base included with the aqueous organic solvent. Thus a sulfur derivative of lignin is not necessary to solubilize and solvate the lignin, and the severe environmental hazards of sulfur are eliminated from pulping and chemical recovery.

A variety of organic solvents have been evaluated for organosolv pulping. Two systems are alcohol pulping (50 : 50, ethanol/water) and "ester pulping." Ester pulping is based on three chemicals, in roughly equal proportions: acetic acid, ethyl acetate, and water. Energy costs are reduced with the ester pulping process because chemical recovery is based on a liquid–liquid phase separation after pulping. The two liquids do not mix, similar to the way water and gasoline do not mix. Since it is necessary to recover the solvent from all organosolv systems for economic reasons, the pollution hazards are considerably reduced. The first organsolv pulping pilot plant in North America is under construction in Canada and is designed to use alcohol solvents.

Recycled Fiber

Wastepaper fibers can be turned back into paper, depending on the price and supply of new pulp. The amount and share of the total recycled fiber for papermaking in the United States in 1986 was 17 million tons (24 percent). The United States is a major exporter of wastepaper—over 4 million metric tons in 1987.

The majority of the wastepaper exported from the United States goes to "fiber-poor" countries. These countries have much less virgin fiber and therefore recycle much greater quantities of paper. Countries that recycle 40 to 50 percent of their paper include the Netherlands, Japan, Mexico, South Korea, Argentina, Hungary, and Switzerland. A variety of problems are associated with paper recycling, such as collection, distribution, and wild cyclic swings in the market. However, with landfill sites now at a premium and paper representing about 40 percent of municipal solid waste, it makes good sense in the long run to promote paper recycling, which reduces both landfill needs and the consumption of virgin timber.

Pulp is produced from sorted wastepaper (paper stock) by separating the bonded fibers in the recovered paper and paperboard through mechanical action. This is done in water in a hydrapulper, which is a tub equipped with a powerful propeller rotor and auxiliary equipment to separate rags, wire, and other coarse contaminants (Figure 23.10). During the repulping operation sodium hydroxide loosens the ink, called deinking. The coarse contaminants are first removed by screening and cleaning equipment; then the pulp is given an extra fiberizing treatment and finally subjected to fine screening and cleaning (7–9). For use in newsprint, tissue, fine and toweling grades, the deinked pulp requires bleaching in single and multistage processes.

Bleaching and Brightening

Although pulpwood is generally light-colored and can retain its brightness in the acid and neutral sulfite processes, pulps from the dominant alkaline kraft process are dark-colored. This color is evident in unbleached kraft packaging paper and boards.

Figure 23.10 A hydrapulper used for repulping wastepaper. (Courtesy of Black Clawson Co.)

About one-half of chemical pulps are bleached to different degrees of brightness (whiteness). Substantial tonnages of mechanical and chemimechanical pulps are also brightened to intermediate brightness levels. In bleaching the residual colored lignin in pulp is dissolved chemically, whereas in brightening the lignin is altered to a lighter-colored compound without removal (10).

Kraft pulps of high brightness (90 percent) are generally produced in a multistage sequence. In a series of bleaching towers the pulp is treated with chlorine (C), caustic extraction (E), and chlorine dioxide (D), generally in a sequence of CEDED. Multistage bleaching has the serious disadvantage of requiring a considerable capital investment in large, corrosion-resistant equipment with high maintenance costs. In addition, the bleaching process produces chlorinated lignin phenols, which can pose serious toxicity pollution problems. In recent years oxygen bleaching has been substituted for chlorine in the first stage to reduce such hazards.

Paper and Paperboard

The production from pulp of paper and paperboard for the market proceeds in three successive steps: stock preparation, papermaking, and converting to the enormous number of paper products.

Stock Preparation

The separated fibers from the pulping operation, except those in mechanical pulps, are generally not suitable for papermaking. To obtain the optimum paper properties, we must improve fiber bonding by supplemental mechanical treatment of the fiber surface, and by imparting special properties through a blending of additives and other pulps.

Beating or *refining,* a basic step in the transition from pulp to paper, is accomplished by cutting and shortening, rubbing and abrading, and crushing and bruising the pulp fibers as they pass between the rotating and stationary bars of a beater or the disks of a refiner (Figure 23.9b). These actions promote fiber flexibility and the area of contact between the wet fibers by exposing the fibrils and microfibrils on external and internal surfaces. The close contact enables hydrogen bonds to form between the adjacent fibers on drying, as explained earlier in this chapter.

Paper is rarely made from pure fibers: the color is altered by dyes; the writing and printing capacity is improved by internal and surface sizing agents (rosin and starch, respectively); the wet strength is enhanced with resins; required opacity is obtained with pigments such as clay and titanium dioxide, and the pH of the pulp slurry is controlled with alum (aluminum sulfate). These additives can be introduced during the beating operation or in blending chests before the fibers go to the paper machine.

Seldom is paper made from any one kind of fiber. In addition, the pulp can enter the stock preparation system either as a pulp slurry (slush pulp) from an adjoining pulp mill integrated with the paper mill or as bales of dried pulp which need to be repulped in a beater or hydrapulper.

Other functions of the stock preparation stage are control of the fiber length for sheet uniformity, removal of unwanted dirt, specks, and particles, and dispersal of the fibers.

Papermaking

The cleaned and dispersed fibers are formed or combined into a fibrous mat in the papermaking stage of the system by deposition from a dilute headbox suspension (0.5 percent solids) onto the traveling continuous wire screen of the Fourdrinier paper machine mentioned earlier (Figure 23.11). The surplus water is removed by drainage from this wire screen aided by vacuum boxes, foils, and a vacuum "couch" roll, by pressing between rolls, and by drying on steam-heated drums or in a hot-air chamber.

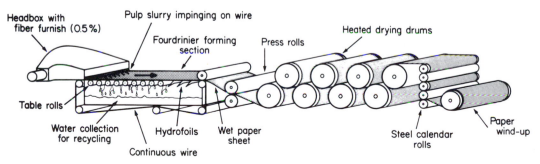

Figure 23.11 Schematic of modern Fourdrinier paper machine.

Other functions of the papermaking stage are to control the sheet density and surface smoothness through application of pressure and some friction in the calender (Figure 23.11). Another function is the application of a surface coating. The solids content of the paper during papermaking progresses from 15 percent after drainage, to 40 percent after presses, to 95 percent after drum dryers.

Finishing and Converting

The objectives in the final stage of the total papermaking system are to improve the paper surface, to reduce rolls and sheets in size, to modify paper for special properties, such as coat or emboss, to convert to finished products, such as bags and corrugated boxes, and to package for shipping. Paper is generally coated to improve printing properties. A surface coating of a pigment, usually kaolin or china clay, calcium carbonate, titanium dioxide; and an adhesive, starch, casein, and others, are applied to the partially dried web by brush, blade, spray, or other method, and dried during the papermaking (on-machine) operation or in a separate operation. The paper surface is brought to a high finish by passing through calenders or supercalenders. Supercalenders are stacks of alternate steel and densified fiber rolls that create a rubbing action on the sheet, imparting an extra gloss to the sheet surface.

Cellulose Derivatives

Although most wood pulp fibers are produced for papermaking as described in the previous section, a small percentage (3 percent) are produced as dissolving pulp for the production of other cellulose-based commodities. As shown in Table 23.2, the yield from dissolving pulp processes is only 35 percent. The percentage is low because all the hemicelluloses, in addition to the lignin (and some low-molecular-weight cellulose), are removed in the pulping process to give an almost pure cellulose fiber pulp. This pulp is then the raw material for the chemical and textile industries (11, 12).

Fibers and Films

Rayon and cellophane are produced from dissolving pulps and cotton linters by modifying the cellulose with carbon disulfide in caustic solution to give a cellulose derivative, namely cellulose xanthate. The cellulose xanthate is then soluble in dilute alkaline solution, and when dissolved, the pulp fiber structure is lost. The resulting viscous solution of cellulose xanthate is termed *viscose*. This viscose can be "spun" into fibers by extrusion of the solution through tiny-holed spinnerets or cast into films by forming a thin sheet of the viscose. The original cellulose is regenerated by contact of the viscose with an aqueous acid bath, which splits off the carbon disulfide to give regenerated rayon fibers or cellophane films. The first textile fibers were produced from cellulose and were termed "artificial silk."

Cellulose acetate is formed from dissolving pulp or cotton linters by reacting the fibers with acetic anhydride using sulfuric acid as a catalyst. The cellulose acetate is then soluble in organic solvents such as acetone and can also be spun into fibers and cast to films. The cellulose is not regenerated but remains as cellulose acetate. The "acetate" fibers are used for textile fabrics and cigarette filters. The films are used in photographic products and as excellent osmotic membranes (11).

Chemical Commodities

Cellulose nitrate is one of the oldest cellulose derivatives and today is most widely used as an explosive (gun cotton) and as an ingredient in "smokeless powder." Alfred Nobel, who bequeathed the Nobel prizes, combined gun cotton with nitroglycerin to form a jellylike substance (blasting jelly) that was more powerful than dynamite.[2] Nitrocellulose is also used as a lacquer coating material.

Carboxymethylcellulose (CMC) is a large commercial-volume cellulose ether. The nontoxic na-

---

[2]Dynamite is nitroglycerin combined with an inert material and patented by Nobel.

ture of CMC makes it very useful in the food, pharmaceutical, and cosmetic industries. It is used as a sizing agent, an emulsion stabilizer, a paint thickener, an oil-well-drilling mud, and a superabsorbent material (in the fibrous form). *Methylcellulose* and *ethylcellulose* are also cellulose ethers but with quite different properties. Ethylcellulose provides exceptionally durable films and is used where extreme stress is encountered, such as in bowling pin coatings. Other uses include paper coatings, lacquers, and adhesives. *Hydroxyethylcellulose* became a commercial product in the 1960s and is chiefly used as a component of latex paints (11).

Environmental Protection

The manufacture of pulp and paper is a chemical-process industry and produces air emissions, effluents, and solid and toxic wastes that are potential hazards. The paper industry uses large volumes of water as a fiber carrier and as a chemical solvent. An increasing volume of water is recycled, but makeup water is still required to cover losses. A bleached-pulp and paper mill may use 100 cubic meters (26,400 gallons) of fresh water per metric ton of product and 50,000 cubic meter (13.2 million gal-

lons) daily for a plant producing 500 metric tons of products. In addition to this aqueous effluent that the mill must clean up, it must also contend with polluted air and solid and toxic wastes. Pulp and paper mills are considered to be minor toxic waste offenders. The nature of these emanations, their sources, and their treatments are summarized in Table 23.3. In this connection the paper industry has generally been in good compliance with governmental environmental regulations, although at considerable nonreimbursed capital expense, which amounts to about 10 percent of the cost of the mill.

Using a revolving cylinder or other equipment (*save-alls*), mills in the 1930s recovered for reuse fibers and clay from the paper machine water (*white water*) system. In the 1970s procedures for removal of the fibers and clay from the paper mill effluent were incorporated through settling or clarification or *primary* effluent treatment. About the same time *secondary effluent treatment* (biochemical treatment) of the pulp mill effluent was necessary to remove pulping residuals. The purpose of this treatment is to reduce the *biological oxygen demand* (*BOD*) of the effluent, which, if untreated, reduces the oxygen content of the stream to a level incapable of supporting aquatic life. The most common method uses microorganisms that react with the

Table 23.3 Summary of Pollution from Pulp and Paper Mill Operations

Type of Pollutant	Mill Operation	Treatment
Effluents		
Suspended solids (SS): fiber fragments, inerts, clay	Papermaking	Primary—clarification
Pulping residuals	Pulping	Secondary—biological treatment and clarification
Air emissions		
Total reduced sulfur (TRS)	Kraft liquor recovery	Oxidation, precipitation, scrubbing, incineration
Sulfur dioxide	Sulfite pulping	
Particulates	Steam generation	Precipitation, scrubbing
Solid wastes	Effluent treatment	Landfill, utilization, incineration
Toxic wastes: chlorinated compounds	Bleaching	Lime pretreatment, oxidation, biological

wood sugars and other oxygen-consuming compounds in the spent liquors; this is called the *activated-sludge* method. The products of primary and secondary treatments are sludges, the handling of which is discussed later under solid wastes.

Two objectionable *air emissions* have characterized pulp mills for years: the sulfur dioxide of the sulfite pulping mill and the malodorous reduced sulfur compounds (TRS) (*mercaptans and hydrogen sulfide*) of the kraft mill. Still another less noxious air emission is the particulate matter from steam boilers. Coal-burning boilers also emit sulfur dioxide, as is well known. The treatments for the particulate emissions are shown in Table 23.3.

Solid wastes represent the ultimate in mill residues and include the accumulated refuse of the mill and the sludges from primary and secondary effluent treatment. There is difficulty in removing water from the secondary sludge; the primary and secondary sludges are often mixed to aid in water removal, which is important if the sludge is to be incinerated for disposal. The sludges from pulp and paper mills are handled mostly as landfill, and sometimes, if not toxic, they are spread for agricultural purposes.

Most mill solids are slightly toxic, predominantly from chlorination compounds in the wash waters from bleaching. This toxicity can be reduced with lime pretreatment and biological treatment. Toxicity has been the main concern of governmental regulating bodies in recent years.

Biotechnology—Biopulping and Biobleaching

The pulping of wood is at present based on either mechanical or chemical methods or combinations thereof, as previously described in this chapter. The interfiber lignin bond is broken down by the mechanical and chemical treatments to free the cellulose fibers for papermaking. In the forest, white rot fungi perform a similar task on wood left behind. The enzymes of the fungi do the work of lignin degradation.

It should be possible to isolate these specific enzymes from the fungus for use in biological pulping or *biopulping*. Indeed, researchers at the U.S.D.A. Forest Products Laboratory in Madison, Wisconsin, recently isolated the first lignin-degrading enzyme (lignase) from the white rot fungus *Phanerochaete chrysosporium*. They are quick to point out, however, that this is only one enzyme in a lignase complex, and they are working to isolate other enzymes in the complex and to produce the enzyme in greater quantities through genetic engineering. Another drawback is the slow rate of reaction.

The initial applications of lignases would be to degrade the lignin partially before mechanical treatment so that the process will require less energy and the pulp will have more strength after this *biomechanical pulping*. *Biobleaching* would also be possible for brightening or whitening pulp fibers in lieu of the toxic chlorine compounds utilized at present by the industry. A particularly exciting application would be to use these types of enzymes for removal of lignin pollutants from waste effluents. Biotechnology should lead to safer and cleaner methods for pulping and bleaching.

Patterns of Energy Usage in the United States

During the past 150 years the patterns of energy consumption have changed dramatically in the United States. Patterns of energy consumption relate to what form the energy takes, who uses it, and for what purposes. The forms of energy are the primary fuels—specifically wood, coal, petroleum, and natural gas—and also electricity, which converts the primary fuels or other inputs, such as hydroelectric, geothermal, and nuclear power, into energy (13).

As shown in Figure 23.12, prior to 1880 wood was the primary energy form but was then gradually replaced by coal. Coal retained one-half of the energy market until after World War II, with the peak period of coal usage around 1920. The petroleum

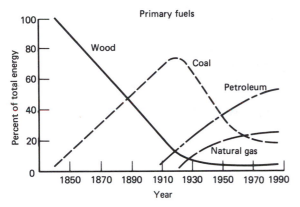

Figure 23.12 Relative usage of primary fuels in the United States from 1850 to the present (1).

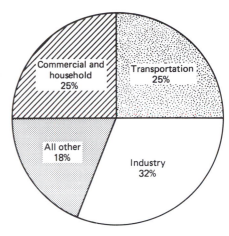

Figure 23.13 Distribution of energy consumption by user.

share of consumption has increased steadily, though at a decreased rate since 1950. Today oil represents close to 50 percent of the share of primary fuels for energy. Natural gas accounted for only 4 percent of the energy usage in 1920, but it jumped markedly in the postwar years to about 25 percent in 1960 and, like oil, has leveled off. The present heavy dependence on the three primary fossil fuels—petroleum, natural gas, and coal—amounts to over 90 percent of the use of all primary fuels. The remaining contribution to the nation's energy supply is 4 percent from nuclear plants, 2 percent from wood, direct and indirect, and 1 percent from a number of other sources such as solar, hydroelectric, and geothermal (13).

The approximate distribution of energy consumption by user is shown in Figure 23.13. The largest sector is the industrial user, which accounts for about 32 percent of the energy consumption. Of this sector, the largest users are the primary metals at 20 percent; chemicals and allied products are at 20 percent, followed by petroleum and related products, 10 percent, and the forest industries, 5 percent. Although the forest industry segment represents only 2 percent of the *total* national energy, it is a major identifiable segment of energy usage (14).

Of the three largest users of purchased energy in the forest industries, the pulp-and-paper sector accounts for 92 percent of the energy purchased.

However, the pulp-and-paper industry, had already achieved 57 percent energy self-sufficiency in 1986, by consuming spent pulping liquors and burning hogged wood and bark. Less detailed information is available from sawmilling operations, but it is estimated that energy self-sufficiency may range from 20 to 40 percent. From these estimates, it may be inferred that the pulp-and-paper segment uses about fifteen times as much energy as sawmills to produce a comparable tonnage of product; hence, the sawmill operations are much less energy-intensive and are much smaller users of total energy. Plywood manufacturing purchases about one-fiftieth as much energy as the pulp-and-paper industry and is about one-third as energy-intensive. At present, it is estimated that plywood manufacturing is approximately 50 percent energy self-sufficient.

Attainment of energy self-sufficiency in the pulp-and-paper industry would have the largest impact on reducing purchased energy within the forest industries. A detailed examination of this segment has shown that it is possible to increase further the present 57 percent self-sufficiency. Most of the additional energy would be supplied through whole-tree chipping (see Chapter 16) and efficient use of residues (14).

The levels of energy consumption for the past 150

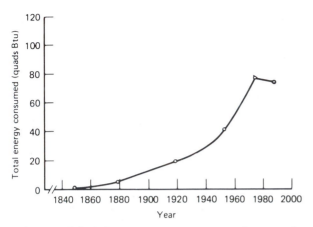

Figure 23.14 Energy consumption in the United States from 1850 to the present.

years are shown in Figure 23.14. In 1880 the nation consumed only about 4 quads of energy.[3] As a result of industrialization and mechanization the energy consumption increased dramatically (13). The rate of energy consumption doubled about every ten years until about 1975, and is now about 75 quads per year.

The reduction in the rate of energy usage since 1975 was due to the "oil crisis," which shocked the industrialized world. Oil exports from the Middle East were severely cut back in 1973, and domestic oil supplies were not sufficient to meet the needs of the nation. This created a near-panic situation, particularly in heavily industrialized areas of the United States, and caused a dramatic shift in the way Americans viewed energy usage. Speed limits on major highways were reduced to 55 miles (90 kilometers) per hour, industry modified processes to reduce energy consumption, new homes were built to optimize energy efficiency, tax breaks were offered to make existing homes more energy-efficient, and Americans generally lowered the thermostat in their homes. These types of energy conservation measures contributed a major share to the reduction in energy consumption in the United States.

[3]A quad is a measure of energy with 1 quad = 1×10^{15} British thermal units (Btu).

The price of oil then plummeted in the 1980s, as shown in Figure 23.15, and again the nation had cheap and abundant oil supplies. With the price of petroleum low, oil exploration and drilling has been reduced, and many oil refineries in the United States have been shut down. Energy conservation measures are slowly being eroded with the changing American attitude.

The United States is becoming more and more dependent on foreign oil imports; current trends indicate that two-thirds of our oil will be imported by the year 2000 (15). Because of the volatile political situation in the Middle East, oil supplies from this region will remain tentative. Therefore it is important not only to remain energy-conscious as a nation but also to continue developing alternate energy sources.

Future Sources of Energy

There are a variety of alternative forms of energy that could be utilized in the future, but to varying degrees of success and expense. The United States has a reasonable supply of *natural gas,* but the dropoff in oil drilling is increasing the vulnerability of the United States through a drop in natural gas reserves. Because there has been little large-scale drilling, reserves of gas are being drawn down twice as fast as they are being replaced. In an abnormally cold winter shortages in deliverability could be a problem (16).

Public pressure will probably limit extensive exploitation of new nuclear facilities. Certainly the near-meltdown at Three Mile Island in Pennsylvania in 1979 and the 1986 nuclear disaster in Chernobyl in the Soviet Union have emphasized the potential for far-reaching disasters in the proliferation of nuclear power plants. *Nuclear fusion* could be an important energy source, but it is only in its infancy of development and will probably not make any energy contribution until well into the next century.

The United States possesses about 31 percent of the world's known *coal* reserves, accounting for about 393 billion metric tons of coal; it is fairly certain that about 225 billion metric tons of this are

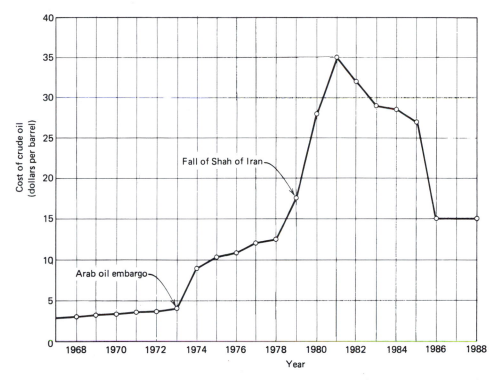

Figure 23.15 Variations in the composite price of crude oil per barrel. (U.S. Department of Energy.)

recoverable. Thus coal is a very important domestic energy resource capable of considerable expansion. Many energy experts feel that the use of coal will enable the United States to bridge the gap between present dependence on foreign oil imports and the development of alternative synthetic fuels (13). The use of coal has a number of negative features such as pollution from burning and unsightly strip mines, if the area is not regraded. New technology, however, permits coal to be burned cleanly in many applications.

Coal can be gasified to form methane and liquefied to yield fuels for transportation. Some progress has been made in both of these options. The Great Plains methane plant in North Dakota, though not a financial success, is a technical success operating at 100 percent of capacity.

For production of liquid fuels the coal must be gasified to carbon monoxide and hydrogen, and then additional energy must be expended to convert these gases to a gasoline-type fuel through a series of complex reactions. This method was discovered sixty years ago by two German scientists, Hans Fischer and Otto Tropsch, and is termed the *Fischer–Tropsch process.*

So far, the Fischer–Tropsch process has been feasible only in a few unusual situations. Near the end of World War II, when Nazi fuel lines broke down, the Germans filled about one-third of their military needs with coal, using the Fischer–Tropsch process. Today South Africa, which is relatively rich in coal but poor in oil, produces most of its gasoline from the Fischer–Tropsch process. The chemical reactors and refineries are put directly on top of the coal mines. For the majority of the world, the cost and supply of petroleum will have to change considerably for the Fischer–Tropsch to be viable.

Solar energy is an environmentally benign source of energy, one which could be exploited to a greater extent. Estimates as high as 20 percent of the nation's energy needs have been suggested as a goal for what could be supplied by solar energy. However, a very large financial investment, on the order of billions of dollars annually, would be necessary to bring solar-generated electricity to a commercial scale. This technology could be very important for regional energy needs if not national.

An important "passive" form of solar energy is the plant biomass produced through the photosynthetic process as described in Chapter 3. The net photosynthetic productivity (NPP) of the earth has been estimated at 140×10^9 metric tons of dry matter per year. Forests account for about 42 percent or 59 billion metric tons of the NPP, which is equivalent to more than the world consumption of fossil fuels (17) (Table 23.4).

In the United States the equivalent of 80 quads of energy is produced each year as total plant biomass; however, much of this is inaccessible, uneconomical to collect, or already utilized for agricultural crops or forest products. It has been estimated that there are approximately 200 quads of standing timber in the nation's forests today. Thus if an attempt were made to have wood as the sole source of energy in the United States, the country would be totally depleted of this reserve in roughly two years. Woody biomass will therefore never be a panacea to an energy crisis, but certainly a greater contribution to the overall energy diet can be supplied by this important resource.

Probably the most significant advantage of biomass is the renewability. The U.S. Department of Energy has estimated that the equivalent of about 8 quads of energy in the form of biomass is produced annually in the nation's forests, but roughly one-half or the equivalent of 4 quads is already harvested annually for timber and paper products. Much of the forest that is not harvested is inaccessible or under harvesting restrictions. Thus the major contribution from woody biomass will probably be in the form of more efficient use of residues and waste.

If all types of waste are included in the scenario of biomass utilization, including urban and agricultural wastes in addition to wood wastes, these wastes and residues represent close to 1 billion metric tons or the equivalent fuel value of approximately 15

percent of the total energy needs of the United States. Wood, in the form of logging and manufacturing residues, accounts for about 25 percent of this figure (18). In addition, roughly 40 percent of most municipal waste is composed of wastepaper, which represents the wood cellulose ultimately derived from the forest. Thus a significant energy contribution could be made by efficient utilization of waste material.

Energy Plantations

Concern over future supplies and cost of fossil fuels has stimulated interest in growing wood for use solely as an energy source. The average yield on commercial forestland is only about 2.3 metric tons per hectare per year. However, the definition of commercial forestland includes, for statistical purposes, much land that is not very productive such as mountain slopes; the national norm might be closer to 3.4 to 6.8 metric tons per hectare if these marginal lands were excluded (14). Advocates of using forest fuels for production of electricity maintain that by short-rotation forestry yields of 7.9 to 33.8 metric tons per hectare can now be achieved, and that through selection and genetic improvement, potential yields can be 45 to 67 metric tons per hectare (Figure 23.16). A further discussion of the applications of forest genetics is given in Chapter 5. Short-rotation forestry has a number of names, including energy plantations, biomass farms, minirotation forestry, puckerbush, sycamore silage, and coppicing.

Management of an energy plantation would more closely resemble a farming operation than conventional forestry. Selected tree species with rapid early-growth characteristics for the climate and soil type would be planted very close together and harvested at appropriate times, perhaps at five- to eight-year intervals. Harvesting would be done mechanically, similar to corn or hay crops; regeneration would be by *vegetative reproduction* such as *coppicing* (see Chapter 14). Thus planting of seedlings need be done only at the start of the operation. For maximum yields of biomass, intensive crop management with fertilization, weed control, and (possibly) irrigation would be necessary.

Table 23.4 Land Area and Net Photosynthetic Production of Dry Matter per Year

Geographic Division	Area (percentage of total rounded)		Net Productivity (percentage of total rounded)	
Forests				
Tropical rain	3.3		21.9	
Raingreen	1.5		7.3	
Summer green	1.4		4.5	
Chaparral	0.3		0.7	
Warm temperate mixed	1.0		3.2	
Boreal (northern)	2.4		3.9	
Subtotal		9.8		41.6
Woodland		1.4		2.7
Dwarf and scrub				
Tundra	1.6		0.7	
Desert scrub	3.5		0.8	
Subtotal		5.1		1.5
Grassland				
Tropical	2.9		6.8	
Temperate	1.8		2.9	
Subtotal		4.7		9.7
Desert (extreme)				
Dry	1.7		0.0	
Ice	3.0		0.0	
Subtotal		4.7		0.0
Cultivated land		2.7		5.9
Fresh water				
Swamp and marsh	0.4		2.6	
Lake and stream	0.4		0.6	
Subtotal		0.8		3.2
Continents total		29.2		64.6
Reefs and estuaries		0.4		2.6
Continental shelf		5.1		6.0
Open ocean		65.1		26.7
Upwelling zones		0.08		0.1
Oceans total		70.8		35.4
Grand total earth		100.0		100.0

Source: J. F. Saeman, ed., *Proc. Institute of Gas Technology Symp. on Clean Fuels from Biomass and Wastes,* Orlando, Fla., 1977.

Selection of tree species for energy plantations differs from that in conventional forestry. Forest species are now selected based on desirable wood properties such as strength, freedom from defects, color, and fiber length. For energy production, the most important factor is the ability to grow rapidly without regard to the strength or shape of the stem. The usual criteria for selecting species for biomass production are rapid juvenile growth, ease of establishment and regeneration, freedom from major insect and fungal pests, and climate and site qualities. Species generally considered as having high

Figure 23.16 This eastern cottonwood grown in Mississippi reached a height of 16 feet in only six months. (Courtesy of U.S.D.A. Forest Service.)

potential for energy plantations are sycamore, hybrid poplars, black cottonwood, red alder, eucalyptus, and loblolly pine (Figure 23.17). Table 23.5 shows yields achieved from experimental work as reported in the literature as well as estimates of yields that can now be achieved by intensive management (19). The national average yield from intensive silviculture can be approximately 17.9 dry metric tons per hectare, and in the near future it could be 33.6 metric tons.

Energy plantations can make a contribution to the nation's energy budget. Major considerations that must be addressed are biomass productivity and land availability. Even in the event that suitable land is available, much research is still needed (1) to optimize productivity through species selection and improvement, (2) to improve silvicultural methods for short-rotation forestry, and (3) to develop equipment for harvesting the crop economically.

Conversion of Wood to Energy, Fuels, and Chemicals

Wood has been a source of energy and chemicals for hundreds of years and continues to be an important raw material for specific chemicals. The use of wood

Figure 23.17 Eight-year-old stand of genetically selected eucalyptus near Aracruz, Brazil. (Photograph by R. A. Young.)

Table 23.5 Annual Productivity, Actual and Estimated, of Short-Rotation Species

Species	Productivity (mt/ha/year)	
	Literature	Projected
Sycamore	2.3–13.3	13.5
Eucalyptus	3.8–8.3	27.0
Hybrid poplar	1.1–11.0	22.5
Black cottonwood	2.3–14.2	13.5
Red alder	2.9–36.0	20.3
Loblolly pine	2.3–6.8	11.3

Sources: Literature, R. S. Evans, "Energy plantations—Should we grow trees for power plant fuels?" Can. For. Serv., Rept. VP-X-129, Western Forest Products Laboratory, Vancouver, B.C., 1974. Projected, R. E. Inman et al., "Silvicultural biomass farms," Vols. 1–6, Mitre Tech. Rept. 7347, The Mitre Corp., McLean, Va., 1977. Forest Products Laboratory data.

as a primary source of industrial chemicals decreased dramatically in the 1940s when oil became the preferred raw material. The term *silvichemicals* is sometimes used to refer to wood-derived chemicals analogous to petrochemicals.

The use of wood for energy, fuels, and chemicals can be conveniently divided into four major categories: direct combustion, saccharification–fermentation (SF), thermal decomposition, and thermochemical liquefaction. Each of these methods is discussed in more detail in the following sections.

Direct Combustion

The concept of using wood as a source of energy through direct combustion dates back to the very beginning of human existence. As soon as early people learned to use fire, wood became the major source of energy. It is important to note that even now approximately one-half of all the wood harvested worldwide is used for fuel by direct combustion. Thus direct combustion is probably the most important method for deriving energy from wood.

Wood has certain advantages over fossil fuels, the most important of which is that it is a renewable resource. In addition, it has a low ash content which is easily and usefully disposed of on land as mineral

constituents essential for plant growth. The sulfur content of wood is low, usually less than 0.1 percent, so that air pollution from this source is negligible, although particulates may cause a serious problem. Generally, wood fuel is used close to where it is grown; thus the need for energy in long-distance transport is reduced. The use of fossil fuels unlocks the carbon that has been stored in them for ages and increases the carbon dioxide content of the atmosphere. In contrast, wood fuel releases the same amount of carbon dioxide that the forest has recently fixed.

Wood does have disadvantages as a fuel. It is a bulky material, and in contrast to other fuels, it has a low heat of combustion, as shown in Table 23.6. The series of gaseous and liquid fuels, from methane to petroleum, evolved in the earth from prehistoric organic material under different conditions than those that produced coal. These hydrocarbons have a higher potential heat content because they do not contain oxygen.

The more recently evolved materials such as lignite and peat have even lower heat contents than coal. Unfortunately, in many regions of the world where wood is in limited supply, materials such as peat and animal dung are used as a fuel, thus

Table 23.6 Heat Contents of Fuels

Fuel	Heat Content (Btu/lb)	Physical State
Hydrogen	61,997	Gas
Methane	23,878	Gas
Natural gas	21,600	Gas
Gasoline	20,750	Liquid
Fuel oil	19,400	Liquid
Petroleum, crude	19,300	Liquid
Coal (anthracite)	14,920	Solid
Coke (high-temperature)	14,030	Solid
Charcoal (wood)	13,780	Solid
Ethanol	12,780	Liquid
Lignite	12,230	Solid
Peat	10,250	Solid
Wood (dry)	8,600	Solid
Wood (50% moisture)	4,210	Solid

Figure 23.18 Peat harvesting in Ireland. (Photograph by R. A. Young.)

robbing the land of a valuable soil and nutrient base (Figure 23.18).

All wood species consist of essentially the same chemical compounds; therefore the various woods differ little in *heat content* per pound. The differences noted in the *fuel value* of different woods when compared by volume are due to differences in *density*. One cord of hickory, a dense commercial wood, for example, gives two times more heat than one cord of low-density species such as aspen or spruce. The heat values and densities of important woods grown in the United States are shown in Table 22.1. An exception to the density rule of thumb are coniferous woods, which contain energy-rich resin. These species can contain up to 12 percent more heat potential.

As shown in Table 23.6, green wood at 50 percent moisture content has only about one-half the fuel value of dry wood. The amount of energy released in a fire depends on the wood moisture content more than on any other factor. Moisture affects the energy release in two ways, by consuming heat for moisture evaporation, and by causing incomplete combustion (21).

Incomplete combustion has several other bad effects in addition to wasting fuel. Gases from burning wood contain formic and acetic acids; these acids, when condensed, corrode stovepipes. The corrosion can be so severe that the pipes may need to be replaced after only one year of operation. Other condensed vapors form *creosote,* a brown or

black stenchy liquid that may leak out of stovepipe joints and cause unsightly stains.

Prolonged exposure to heat converts the creosote to a flaky layer of carbon known as *soot.* Carbon particles in the fire effluents tend to aggregate and adhere to the inside surfaces of stoves, stovepipes, and chimney flues, augmenting the accumulation of soot. These deposits insulate and hinder flow of gases; with unusually hot fires, these deposits can ignite as *chimney fires,* which can crack the chimney and ignite the house. For this reason chimneys should be cleaned periodically depending on the amount of use and completeness of combustion. Hot, oxygen-rich fires reduce chimney deposits, but hot effluents also carry heat out of the chimney (21).

Fireplaces and Wood Burners Wood-burning units have evolved over centuries of use in homes around the world (21). Many old-time stoves in Europe relied on immense heat-storing masses of fireclay, firebrick, and other masonry. Hot, oxygen-rich fires facilitated complete combustion, and the fire effluents passed through a long labyrinth of flues to deliver the heat to the solid mass. The Russian–Ukrainian type of stove, probably still in use today in rural areas, was constructed with a low cooking section containing the combustion chamber, and a much larger (6 to 8 feet) flue section with an immense, flat top surface, which provided warm sleeping quarters for the whole family.

The German *Kachelofen* or tile stove was a showpiece in the living room; many small tile stoves still heat rooms of homes, particularly farmhouses throughout Europe. All stoves store some heat, but modern types lack the storage capacity and versatility of the old brick monsters.

With the escalation of oil prices in the early 1970s, many Americans became more interested in burning wood in their homes to reduce heating costs. Household wood burning varies considerably with the region of the country; roughly 50 percent of the residents of Maine, Vermont, and Oregon burn more than one-third of a cord of wood annually, but fewer than 10 percent of the residents of most southern states burn this much wood.

Many hundreds of different types of stoves, furnaces, fireplaces, and accessories for heating with wood have appeared on the market as a result of the increased interest in wood burning. A few of these are discussed further in the following paragraphs.

Fireplaces The open built-in fireplace is the least efficient heating device. Warm air bypasses the fire, as shown in Figure 23.19a, and escapes through the chimney. This draft pulls equal amounts of cold outside air through joints at doors and other openings into the house so that, in very cold weather, the use of the fireplace may actually cool rather than heat the house. A fireplace door obstructs the bypass of the air and, with the help of a baffle between the grate and door (Figure 23.19b), can eliminate the bypass of air so that the fireplace will heat more efficiently. Whatever the design, watching and hearing a crackling fire has a gratification not to be matched, and people have enjoyed it since the dawn of humanity.

Stoves and furnaces In stoves and furnaces the air takes various paths through the wood fuel. In all of these variations the intent is to have the air pass

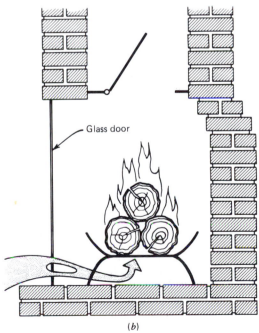

(a)   (b)

Figure 23.19 Movement of air (a) through an open built-in fireplace and (b) through a fireplace with a door to obstruct bypass of air.

through the burning wood pile to promote combustion, heat the air, and then pass to the outlet at the top or back of the stove. There is no intrinsic reason why one type is better than another as long as the air passes through the burning wood in an efficient manner. Hot air streams naturally upward, but the air velocity depends mainly on the chimney draft and can be regulated with vents and dampers. Modern "airtight" stoves provide the best air control and thus more efficient heating.

Recently a completely different heating appliance, the stick wood furnace, was developed at the University of Maine (Figure 23.20). In this stove long sticks or logs stand in a tight jacket. Air enters only at the bottom where burning of the sticks takes place. To confine the burning to just the bottom end of the stove, water cools the jacket and can then be used for hot water in the home. The sticks burn slowly at the bottom and are self-feeding because of their own weight. Theoretically, the stick wood furnace can be used to burn whole-tree stems.

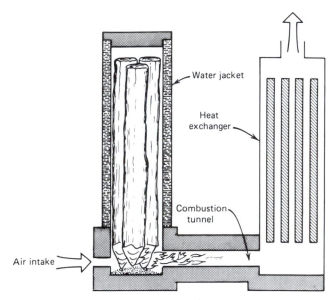

Figure 23.20 "Stick wood" furnace (see text for a description of the operation).

Saccharification–Fermentation

The saccharification–fermentation (SF) method is based on the breakdown or hydrolysis of the polysaccharides in wood to the constituent monomeric sugars. The six-carbon or hexose sugars (glucose, galactose, and mannose) are then fermentable to ethyl alcohol (ethanol or grain alcohol, C_2H_5OH) by yeast fermentation in the same way that ethanol is produced from grains or fruits. Obviously the concept is not a new one; the polysaccharide character of wood has been known for over 100 years. The limitations to the use of wood for ethanol production have been primarily the difficulty in separating and hydrolyzing the crystalline cellulose component in wood. Both acids and enzymes can be used to hydrolyze the cellulose to glucose, but only acids have been utilized commercially for wood hydrolysis to sugars, and only in foreign countries.

In contrast to the western economy, the Soviet Union continued expansion of wood hydrolysis facilities, and about forty such plants are presently in operation. All the Russian plants are based on dilute

sulfuric acid in percolation towers. In the West interest in producing alcohols from wood was revitalized by the dramatic increase in the price of petroleum in the 1970s and the push to decrease oil imports by substituting gasohol, which is one part alcohol in nine parts gasoline, for 100 percent gasoline at gas pumps. Both ethanol and methanol can be used in gasohol blends.

Because of the high oil prices, the country of Brazil took the dramatic step of shifting to much greater use of fuel alcohol. Most of their sugars are produced from sugarcane. One wood hydrolysis plant was constructed, but it was uneconomical to operate and was shut down. However, their experience demonstrates that fermentation ethanol (95 percent ethanol and 5 percent water) is a perfectly satisfactory motor fuel. At least 500,000 Brazilian automobiles operate on undried alcohol continuously, and most of the rest of their fleet operates on this fuel on weekends when only alcohol is available at the gas stations (12). A number of methods can be used for production of ethanol from wood.

Thermal Decomposition

A number of terms are used interchangeably for thermal decomposition of wood and generally refer to similar processing methods: carbonization, pyrolysis, gasification, wood distillation, destructive distillation, and dry distillation. All result in the thermal breakdown of the wood polymers to smaller molecules in the form of char, tar (a condensible liquid), and gaseous products. A liquid fuel derivable from wood by this method is methyl alcohol (methanol or wood alcohol, CH_3OH). A wide variety of other chemicals are also derivable from wood by thermal decomposition, a method with a long history of applications.

During World War II in Germany, automobiles were fueled by the gases produced from thermal decomposition of wood, and research is active today on more efficient gasification of wood. Destructive distillation has been used throughout most of recorded history to obtain turpentine from pinewood; this is discussed further in the section on wood extractives. The range of chemicals derivable from thermal decomposition of wood is summarized in Figure 23.21.

Charcoal and Other Chemicals Production of charcoal and tars by destructive distillation is the oldest of all chemical wood-processing methods. Charcoal was probably first discovered when the black material left over from a previous fire burned with intense heat and little smoke and flame. For centuries, charcoal has been used in braziers for heating purposes. Destructive distillation of hardwoods has been carried out seeking charcoal as the desired product, with volatiles as by-products; for softwoods (pines), volatiles were the principal products (naval stores, discussed later), with charcoal considered a by-product.

In 1812, the additional collection by condensation of the volatile substances from hardwood carbonization began. Products were now charcoal, crude pyroligneous acid, and noncondensible gases. The pyroligneous acid was refined to produce methanol and acetate of lime, which in turn was used to make either acetic acid or acetone and tar. The noncondensible gases in a normal wood distillation consisted of about 50 percent carbon dioxide, 30 percent carbon monoxide, 10 percent methane, 3 percent heavier hydrocarbons, and 3 percent hydrogen (22). The tars and noncondensible gases were usually used as fuel. In the late nineteenth century and until the 1920s, destructive distillation of hardwoods was an important source of industrial acetic acid, methanol, and acetone. This market was lost when these materials began to be made synthetically from petroleum. In 1920 there were approximately 100 plants recovering these products from hardwood distillation; the last of these plants ceased operation in 1969.

Basic techniques for producing charcoal have not changed over the years, although the equipment has. Charcoal is produced when wood is burned under conditions in which the supply of oxygen is severely limited (23). Carbonization is a term that aptly describes the thermal decomposition of wood for this application. Decomposition of carbon compounds takes place as the temperature rises, leading to a solid residue that is richer in carbon than the original material. Wood has a carbon content of about 50 percent, whereas charcoal of a quality suitable for general market acceptance can be analyzed as follows: fixed carbon, 74 to 81 percent; volatiles, 18 to 23 percent; moisture, 2 to 4 percent; ash, 1 to 4 percent. Charcoal with a volatiles content over 24 percent will cause smoking and is undesirable for recreational uses.

Thermochemical Liquefaction

Although a reasonable amount of research effort has been expended on thermochemical liquefaction of wood, extensive commercialization of this process is not anticipated in the near future. The basis of the method is a high-pressure and high-temperature treatment of wood chips in the presence of hydrogen gas or syngas to produce an oil instead of a gas. The low-grade oil produced could potentially be substituted for some present petroleum uses.

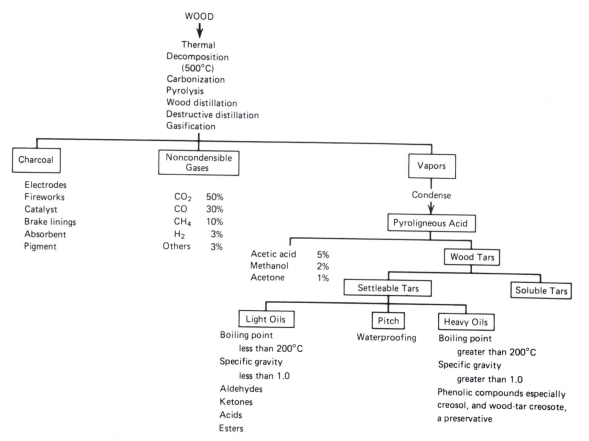

Figure 23.21 Products obtained from the thermal decomposition of wood.

Wood Extractives

All species of wood and other plants contain small (mostly) to large quantities of substances that are not constituents of the cell wall, as pointed out previously. The entire class is called *extraneous components*. Extractives are the largest group by far of this class. The extractives embrace a very large number of individual compounds that often influence the physical properties of wood and play an important role in its utilization. Colored and volatile constituents provide visual and olfactory aesthetic values. Certain phenolic compounds lend resistance to fungal and insect attack with resulting durability, and silica imparts resistance to the wood-destroying marine borers (24).

Extractives can also have a detrimental effect on the use of wood. Alkaloids and some other physiologically active materials may present health hazards. Certain phenols present in pine heartwood inhibit the calcium-based sulfite pulping process and cause pitch problems. The loss of water absorbency properties of wood pulps can also be due to extractives. Extractives from cedarwood and the woods of a number of other species can cause severe corrosion problems in the pulping operation (24). A wide variety of extractives are utilized commercially as will be described.

Two broad classes of extractives occur in wood: (1) those soluble in *organic solvents,* such as wood resins including turpentine, rosin, fat, and fatty acids; and (2) those soluble in water, mostly polyphenolic material including tannins and lignins and the polysaccharide arabinogalactan.

Extractives Soluble in Organic Solvents

The largest aggregate volume and value of industrial extractives are those derived from pinewoods. In 1980 the value of these chemicals was estimated at $612 million and has increased three times since 1963. These materials, which include turpentine, rosin, and fatty acids, are also often referred to as *naval stores.* This term derives from the use of pitch and tars from pine extractives as caulking and water-proofing agents for wooden ships in early American history. The term naval stores has remained in use and now mainly refers to the turpentine and rosin derived from pine trees.

There are three sources of naval stores: gum, wood, and sulfate. *Gum naval stores* are produced by wounding pine trees and collecting the oleoresin. The oleoresin is a sticky substance composed of an essential oil, turpentine, and a resin, rosin. Since turpentine is a low-boiling, volatile material, the two products can be separated by a distillation process (25).

In this country the gum naval stores industry is based on two southern pine species, slash and longleaf, and is centered in the state of Georgia. Though very important in the past, this method today accounts for only a small percentage of U.S. rosin and turpentine production, in fact, less than 2 percent in 1984. Typically the oleoresin is collected in containers by cutting grooves in the tree so that the wound opens the resin ducts (Figure 23.22). Various means have been used to stimulate oleo-resin production such as repeated wounding and spraying with sulfuric acid or the herbicide para-quat. The so-called *light wood,*[4] high-oleo-resin-content wood, then contains up to 40 percent resin (25).

Figure 23.22 Scarification of pine trees for collections of oleoresin. (*a*) View of stand. (*b*) Closeup of tree wound. (Courtesy of University of Georgia, College of Agriculture.)

Wood naval stores are obtained by organic-solvent extraction of chipped or shredded old pine stumps. The old pine stumps have lost most of the outer sapwood through decay and are made up primarily of the oleoresin-rich heartwood where the extractives are mainly deposited. Turpentine and crude resin fractions are obtained by this method.

Sulfate naval stores are derived as by-product streams from the kraft pulping process. As pine chips are treated in the digester to produce pulp, the

---

[4]The term *light wood* relates to the use of the high-oleoresin-content wood as torches in earlier times.

volatilized gases are released and condensed to yield a sulfate turpentine.

Turpentine was used as a solvent in its early history, particularly as a paint solvent. Today this use is small, and turpentine is used for the most part as a feedstock for manufacture of many products, including synthetic pine oil, resins, insecticides, and a variety of flavor and fragrance chemicals. Flavors and fragrances derived from turpentine include lemon, lime, spearmint, peppermint, menthol, and lilac. The synthetic pine oil is further converted to terpin hydrate, a cough expectorant. Obviously, turpentine has become a valuable by-product of the forest and pulp-and-paper industry (25).

Rosins are usually used in a form modified by further chemical reaction. Rosin found considerable use at one time in laundry soap (38 percent in 1938), but this use is negligible today. Rosin soaps are at present important as emulsifying agents in synthetic rubber and chemical manufacture and for paper sizing. The sizing is used to reduce water absorptivity of paper. Rosin is also used in surface coatings, printing oils, and adhesives. Typically pressure-sensitive tapes such as "scotch" tape contain considerable quantities of rosin (25).

Water-Soluble Extractives

The most important group of water-extractable compounds are the polyphenolics. These substances are generally extractable with water at 80 to 120°C from the heartwood and bark of many trees. Of the polyphenolics only the *tannins* have shown commercial value. The traditional source of tannins in the United States was chestnut wood and bark, but this source was removed when the chestnut blight of the 1930s devastated the chestnut tree in North America. The South American tree, quebracho, is now the major source of tannins. Acacia bark extracts, called wattle or mimosa, are also an important source of tannins and together with quebracho extractives amount to a production of 250,000 tons per year (1, 24).

The primary use of tannins is for manufacture of leather from hides. The natural *tanning agents* continue to dominate the market, even though synthetic tanning agents are available. The extractives from each different wood species provide their own unique color and properties to the leather.

Wattle tannins have also been successfully substituted for phenol in phenol-formaldehyde adhesives in South Africa. The phenol-formaldehyde adhesives are used in the production of plywood, particleboard, and laminated beams.

Biotechnology—Chemicals

As with pulping and bleaching, biotechnology could also have a considerable impact on the production of chemicals from wood and other forms of plant biomass. The effects of biotechnology will probably first be noticed in areas of enzymatic hydrolysis of polysaccharides and fermentation technology.

It should be possible to improve the efficiency of the cellulose enzyme complex for hydrolyzing cellulose to glucose. The enzyme complex apparently contains decrystallizing and hydrolysis enzymes that work together to convert cellulose to glucose. Isolation of the specific enzymes and genetic engineering could provide a more efficient complex.

As discussed earlier in this chapter, enzymes are also the basis for yeast conversion of hexose (six-carbon) sugars, such as glucose and mannose, to ethanol. These enzymes could also be genetically engineered to improve the efficiency of alcohol production, and several biotechnology firms are exploring this possibility.

The yeast (*Saccharomyces cerevisiae*) enzymes are specific to six-carbon sugars, but wood and other forms of biomass also contain large quantities of pentose sugars, especially xylose in hardwoods. The pentoses are not fermentable to ethyl alcohol with conventional yeasts. However, researchers at the U.S.D.A. Forest Products Laboratory have discovered a xylose-fermenting yeast (*Candida tropicalis*). Thus it is now possible to convert all wood sugars to ethyl alcohol with a combination of yeasts. Isolation of the specific enzymes and genetically engineering of the enzymes could dramatically improve the efficiency of this conversion.

Many other chemicals can be obtained from both yeast and bacteria fermentation of sugars and pulp mill effluents. Potential fermentation products from wood hydrolysates include acetone, organic acids (acetic, butyric, lactic), glycerol, butanediol, and others (26).

References

1. D. FENGEL AND G. WEGENER, *Wood: Chemistry, Ultrastructure, Reactions,* Walter de Gruyter Publisher, New York, 1984.

2. E. SJOSTROM, *Wood Chemistry Fundamentals and Applications,* Academic Press, New York, 1981.

3. S. A. RYDHOLM, *Pulping Processes,* Wiley–Interscience, New York, 1965.

4. K. KRATZL AND G. BILLEK, EDS., *Biochemistry of Wood,* Pergamon Press, London, 1959.

5. W. A. COTE, ED., *Cellular Ultrastructure of Woody Plants,* Syracuse Univ. Press, Syracuse, N.Y., 1965.

6. H. MEIER, *J. Polymer Sci., 51,* 11 (1961); *Pure and Appl. Chem., 5,* 37 (1962).

7. K. W. BRITT, ED., *Handbook of Pulp and Paper Technology,* Second Edition, Van Nostrand Reinhold, New York, 1970.

8. J. D. CASEY, ED., *Pulp and Paper, Chemistry and Chemical Technology,* Third Edition, Wiley-Interscience, New York, 1980.

9. R. G. MACDONALD, ED., *Pulp and Paper Manufacture,* Vols. 1–3, McGraw–Hill, New York, 1969.

10. K. V. SARKANEN AND C. H. LUDWIG, EDS., *Lignins—Occurrence, Formation, Structure and Reactions,* Wiley–Interscience, New York, 1971.

11. R. M. ROWELL AND R. A. YOUNG, EDS., *Modified Cellulosics,* Academic Press, New York, 1978.

12. R. A. YOUNG AND R. M. ROWELL, EDS., *Cellulose: Structure, Modification and Hydrolysis,* Wiley–Interscience, New York, 1986.

13. M. KRANZBERG, T. A. HALL, AND J. L. SCHEIBER, EDS., *Energy and the Way We Live,* Boyd & Fraser Publishing Co., San Francisco, 1980.

14. ANON., "Feasibility of utilizing forest residues for energy and chemicals," U.S.D.A. For. Serv., NTIS Publ. PB 258-630, 1976.

15. J. H. KRIEGER, "U.S. viewed as unprepared for next energy crisis," *Chem. & Eng. News,* 39 (June 23, 1986).

16. P. H. ABELSON, *Science, 234,* 1169 (1986).

17. J. F. SAEMAN, *Proc. Institute of Gas Technology Symp. on Clean Fuels from Biomass and Wastes,* Orlando, Fla., 1977.

18. K. V. SARKANEN, *Science, 191,* 773 (1976).

19. R. E. INMAN ET AL., "Silvicultural Biomass Farms," Vol. 1–6, Mitre Tech. Rept. 7347, The Mitre Corp., McLean, Va., 1977.

20. R. S. Evans, "Energy plantations—should we grow trees for power plant fuels?" Can. For. Serv., Rept. VP-X-129, Western Forest Products Laboratory, Vancouver, B.C., 1974.

21. H. KUBLER, *Forstarchiv., 55*(6), 230 (1984).

22. A. J. STAMM AND E. E. HARRIS, *Chemical Processing of Wood,* Chemical Publishing Co., New York, 1953.

23. ANON., "Charcoal production, marketing, and use," U.S.D.A. For. Serv., Rept. 2213, Forest Products Laboratory, Madison, Wis., 1961.

24. B. L. BROWNING, ED., *The Chemistry of Wood,* Robert E. Krieger Publishing Co., Huntington, N.Y., 1975.

25. D. F. ZINKEL, *J. Appl. Polymer Symp., 28,* 309 (1975).

26. G. J. HAJNY, "Biological utilization of wood for production of chemicals and foodstuffs," U.S.D.A. For. Serv., Res. Pap. FPL 385, Forest Products Laboratory, Madison, Wis., 1981.

CHAPTER 24

The Forest Products Economy

JEFFREY C. STIER
JOSEPH BUONGIORNO

The early colonists viewed the forests of the new nation almost exclusively as a resource to be exploited for economic development. The first ships returning to England from Jamestown reportedly carried "clapboards and wainscott," and export of lumber was a regular feature of the Plymouth economy by 1621. The very first patent issued in America for a mechanical invention was granted in 1646 for design of an improved sawmill, and sawmills were established in the United States well over a century before their adoption in England. Wood was the principal natural resource of the United States until the middle of the nineteenth century, serving both as fuel and as an industrial raw material. By 1860 the lumber industry was surpassed only by the cotton industry in terms of its contribution to the national economy (1).

At present, the U.S. economy is much less dependent on wood as a raw material, but timber contin-ues to be an important resource. If we examine the composition of domestic timber production since 1900, a somewhat surprising pattern emerges (Figure 24.1). Total production of lumber has varied remarkably little since 1900. Indeed, the volumes for 1900 and 1983 are very similar. However, the same cannot be said for the remaining timber-processing industries. Production of veneer and pulp products was negligible prior to 1900; then fuelwood absorbed fully 40 percent of all timber consumption.

The changing importance of fuelwood over time is a good example of how economic factors help shape the pattern of use of natural resources. As our nation's population and industrial base expanded during the twentieth century, wood was replaced as an energy source by relatively less expensive coal and petroleum resources (Figure 23.12). Petroleum in particular was a cheap source of energy until the advent of the OPEC (Organization of Petroleum-

Exporting Countries) oil cartel in the 1970s (Figure 23.15). When oil prices began to rise, wood once again became cost-competitive for some uses; the switch back to fuelwood is reflected in the dramatic increase in the harvest of timber for fuelwood since 1980 (Figure 24.1).

How is timber used today? The consumption of forest products in 1983 is shown in Table 24.1. Softwoods account for slightly over two-thirds of total consumption, and, lumber is dominant among softwood products, with pulp products second. In contrast, pulp products constitute a slightly greater proportion of the total consumption of hardwoods than does lumber. Fuelwood is of minor importance for softwoods, but makes up about half of the total hardwood harvest.

Employment in the forest products industry was almost 1.2 million persons in 1982, or about 7 percent of all manufacturing employment. Value added amounted to $49 billion, which was approximately 2 percent of the U.S. gross national product (GNP). In the following section we consider industries manufacturing three groups of wood products: lumber, wood-based panels, and paper and allied products. This is followed by a brief examination of the economics of producing the timber on which the wood products industries depend.

A basic understanding of the U.S. forest economy is necessary for the modern forestry professional, but in today's world it is not sufficient. The highly complex structure of interrelationships among the nations of the world makes it equally important to

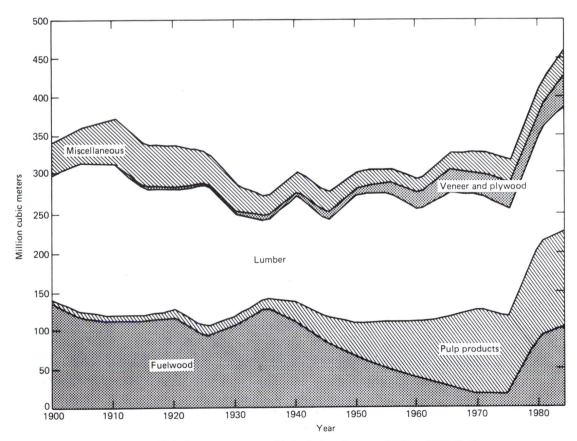

Figure 24.1 Composition of U.S. timber harvest, 1900 to 1983 (2,3).

Table 24.1 Apparent Consumption of Forest Products in the
United States in 1983, by Species Group[a]

Species Group and Product	Apparent Consumption[a]	
	(million m³)[b]	(percentage of total)
Softwoods		
Lumber	203.6	36
Plywood and veneer	38.8	7
Pulp products	106.6	20
Fuelwood	23.2	4
Miscellaneous	7.8	1
Subtotal	380.0	68
Hardwoods		
Lumber	33.8	6
Plywood and veneer	6.1	1
Pulp products	44.6	8
Fuelwood	93.0	16
Miscellaneous	5.1	1
Subtotal	182.6	32
Grand total	562.6	100

Sources: A. Ulrich, "U.S. timber production, trade, consumption, and price statistics 1950–86," U.S.D.A. For. Serv., Misc. Publ. 1460, Washington, D.C., 1988; and Forest Resources Economics Research Staff, U.S. Forest Service, Washington, D.C.
[a]Apparent consumption = domestic production plus net imports.
[b]Roundwood equivalent.

gain an understanding of the world forest economy and how the U.S. situation compares to that of most other nations. This world view is presented in the third section.

American Forest Products Industries and Markets

Lumber

Structure of the Industry The lumber industry is generally considered to be quite competitive. The number of firms is large—about 5800 in 1982—and no one firm or group of firms controls a very large share of the market. More than 75 percent of all mills employ fewer than twenty persons; nevertheless, some are quite large. The twenty largest firms produce about one-third of the total value of all industry shipments (4).

Competition is enhanced when producers are unable to establish consumer loyalty to brand names and when no significant barriers exist to entry of new firms. Product differentiation among lumber producers is difficult; a construction-grade Douglas-fir stud is pretty much the same regardless of which firm produced it. Similarly, entry into the industry is generally easy, in part because of the absence of product differentiation, but also because the capital costs of building and equipping a new sawmill are not prohibitive. However, small mills are likely to be less efficient, and entry into the industry does not ensure economic survival. Records of the U.S. Commerce Department indicate that between 1977 and 1982 exits and mergers accounted for the loss of about 1000 firms from the industry.

The lumber industry is actually composed of two relatively distinct subsectors. The firms in one subsector manufacture hardwood lumber; those in the other produce softwood lumber. The softwood sector is the more important; annual production is four and one-half times that of hardwood lumber.

The location of sawmills is determined primarily by the availability of timber. Hence, the Pacific Coast region—Washington, Oregon, and California—which contains 63 percent of the nation's softwood sawtimber inventory and almost 50 percent of all softwood growing stock, is the center of the softwood lumber industry. Hardwoods are grown primarily in the eastern half of the United States, with hardwood lumber production divided about equally between the North and the South. This unequal distribution is reflected in the disproportionate timber harvest shown by region and species group in Figure 24.2.

Geography is not the only characteristic differentiating the two sectors. Softwood sawmills tend, on average, to be larger than hardwood mills. The largest softwood mills are capable of producing in excess of 2 million cubic meters of sawed lumber

annually, although economic studies have not revealed any significant cost advantages beyond an annual output capacity of about 100,000 cubic meters (5). Many of the larger mills, especially softwood mills, are part of an integrated wood products organization consisting of, for example, a sawmill, a plywood mill, and a pulp or particleboard mill.

Hardwood sawmills frequently have an annual capacity of less than 120,000 cubic meters of sawed lumber. Firms with such a limited capacity are often able to remain viable by supplying local markets that are too small to attract larger competitors and by concentrating on production of specialty items.

Prices, Demand, and Supply Aggregate *price indexes* for "all lumber" and "all commodities" are shown for the years 1950 through 1985 in Figure 24.3. The latter index reflects the general level of prices in the economy; year-to-year changes in it are

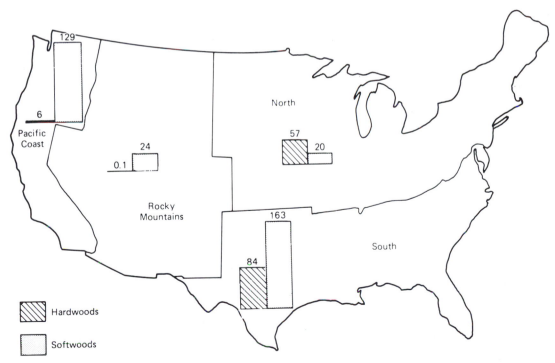

Figure 24.2 U.S. timber harvest in 1986 by region and species group, given in millions of cubic meters of roundwood (6).

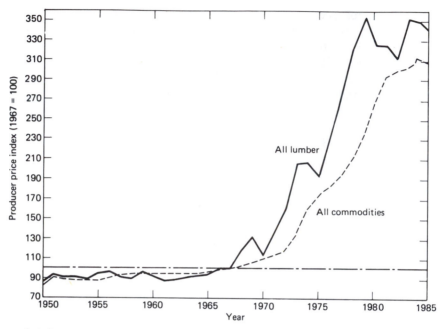

Figure 24.3 Producer price indexes for U.S. lumber and all commodities, 1950 to 1985 (3,7).

a measure of the annual rate of inflation. Several distinct trends in lumber prices are evident in Figure 24.3. From 1950 through 1967 lumber prices were really quite stable; there were even a few years during the late 1950s when prices declined slightly. Although the lumber price index exhibited somewhat greater variation than the general price level, during the period 1950 through 1967 movements in the former largely reflected the general rate of inflation.

Since 1967, however, the picture has changed dramatically. These later years have been characterized by high rates of inflation, as evidenced by the rapid rise of the "all-commodities" price index. But lumber prices have risen even faster; in fact, they more than tripled between 1967 and 1985. This phenomenon—an increase in the price of one commodity relative to the general price level—is what economists refer to as a *real* price increase; it is one signal that a commodity is becoming scarce in an economic sense. The rapid rise of the price of petroleum in past years is another example of such a signal. Note that neither timber nor oil is truly scarce

in an absolute physical sense; yet both have become economically scarce as evidenced by their rising prices.

The "all lumber" price index is constructed as a weighted average of the prices of most of the individual sizes and species of lumber. The volume of softwood lumber consumed is almost seven times that of hardwood lumber, and the "all lumber" price index incorporates this information. The weighting procedure causes the "all lumber" price index in Figure 24.3 to reflect primarily what has happened to softwood lumber prices. Separate price indexes for softwood and hardwood lumber are shown in Figure 24.4.

The indexes in Figure 24.4 are relative price indexes; that is, for each year the producer price index for softwood and hardwood lumber has been divided by the corresponding "all commodities" price index for that year. This adjustment is made to remove the impact of general inflation on price movements. Thus the direction and magnitude of changes in a relative price index indicate price movements that differ from general inflationary

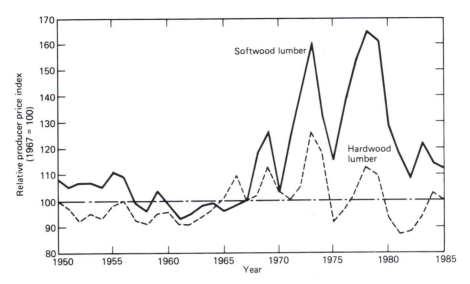

Figure 24.4 Relative producer price indexes for U.S. hardwood and softwood lumber, 1950 to 1985 (3,7).

trends. Note in Figure 24.4 that although the two price indexes generally move in the same direction, softwood lumber prices have exhibited far more variation and in particular have risen much faster than either hardwood prices or the general price level since 1967. Note, also, that in addition to the two longer-term trends in prices that correspond to the periods before and after 1967, several shorter cyclic price movements have occurred, from 1954 to 1958, 1958 to 1961, 1967 to 1970, 1970 to 1975, 1975 to 1982, and 1982 to 1985.

What economic factors account for the price movements evident in Figures 24.3 and 24.4? Prices are determined by the interaction of *demand and supply.* The short-term cyclic swings are caused mainly by variations in demand coupled with a relatively inflexible supply. The demand for lumber, especially softwood lumber, is derived principally from the demand for new construction. Residential construction accounted for 39 percent of the U.S. consumption of softwood lumber in 1984; if nonresidential construction and repairs and remodeling are included, the proportion is increased to almost four-fifths. Thus it is no coincidence that the short-term price cycles shown in Figure 24.4 parallel similar cycles in housing construction.

In economics, as in ecology, diversity enhances stability. It is partly because hardwood lumber enjoys a secondary market for manufacture of furniture that hardwood lumber prices have tended to be less volatile than softwood prices. Dependence on a narrow market, particularly one as notoriously cyclic as the housing industry, results in wide variations in demand.

The economic health of the construction industry is determined primarily by national economic policies, especially *monetary policy,* which largely determines the interest rate buyers must pay for home mortgages. Thus the short-run instability in lumber demand could not be reduced without changing monetary policy, which in turn would have major impacts on the rest of the economy. But demand is only one side of the picture. If supply were very responsive to price, an increase (decrease) in demand would cause price to rise (fall), which would in turn cause supply to increase (decrease). This linkage would tend automatically to dampen the initial price change and restore equilibrium.

Unfortunately, lumber supply responds weakly to price changes, and then only after a certain delay. The sluggish response of supply to price is due to the high cost of maintaining large inventories of lumber, to short-run constraints on mill capacity and the availability of labor and timber, and to the time required to harvest and process additional timber. On balance, supply is not sufficiently flexible to meet the rapid variations in demand brought about by the housing cycle. Historically, when excess U.S. demand for softwood lumber began to cause prices to rise, the volume of lumber imported from Canada also increased. Thus, although imports did help to dampen price increases, they did not constitute a permanent threat to the market share of U.S. producers. However, beginning in 1975 this situation began to change, and by the mid-1980s the volume of softwood lumber imports from Canada had emerged as a major political issue between the two countries.

In 1975 imported softwood lumber from Canada supplied about 19 percent of the total U.S. demand. When the real price of lumber increased dramatically between 1975 and 1978 (see Figure 24.4), so too did the proportion of the U.S. market supplied from Canadian lumber. However, while the real price of lumber declined precipitously from 1978 to 1982, the Canadian share of the U.S. softwood lumber market continued to increase and exceeded one-third by 1985.

Producers in the United States, who saw prices fall and markets shrink, reacted in two ways. First, they shut down older, less efficient mills and laid off workers in an effort to lower their costs of production. Second, they charged their Canadian competitors with unfair trade practices. Specifically, they argued that the Canadian system of pricing standing timber resulted in unreasonably low prices being charged for the timber, and that this underpriced timber in essence represented a subsidy to the lumber industry that allowed it to outcompete U.S. producers.

The Canadians argued that their competitive advantage came principally from the greater efficiency of more modern mills and from the lower value of the Canadian dollar. In addition, they pointed out that the low price charged for timber was economically justified because logging costs were higher in Canada. The U.S. Coalition for Fair Lumber Imports, which sought to obtain a duty on imported Canadian

softwood lumber, was not successful on its first attempt in 1983. However, by mid-1986 the coalition had mobilized a much larger political base and its arguments were receiving a more favorable hearing. On December 30, 1986 Canada agreed to levy a 15 percent countervailing duty on softwood lumber shipped to the United States. This result is at best an uneasy compromise, and the softwood lumber trade issue continues to be a source of political tension between the two countries.

Prospects for the Future　Historically, the average consumption of lumber per person—that is, per capita consumption—has been declining in response to higher real lumber prices. Yet demographic and economic trends suggest that aggregate lumber demand will continue to grow at least through the remainder of the 1980s, by which time the population bulge caused by the World War II baby boom will have passed through the stage of household formation. The supply picture is not likely to improve. Federal timber harvest policies preclude any significant increases in supply from public lands, and additional withdrawals of public land could reduce current harvest levels. Intensified management on private lands is not likely to expand supply fast enough to prevent further price increases. What remains to be seen is the extent to which continued price increases will stimulate further substitution of other wood or nonwood materials for lumber, thus dampening expected increases in the demand for lumber.

Wood-Based Panels

Wood-based panels include the following specific types: (1) plywood, which is further subdivided into softwood and hardwood plywood, (2) particleboard, (3) compressed fiberboard, commonly called hardboard, which has a density of approximately 0.5 grams per cubic centimeter, and (4) noncompressed fiberboard or insulation board, which is less dense than compressed fiberboard. All four types of panels are used in construction, although, as its name implies, insulation board is not used as a structural material (see Chapter 22).

Plywood Large-scale production of plywood was not possible until the development of mechanical veneer-cutting techniques sometime around 1900. However, it was not until the discovery of waterproof glues in the late 1920s that plywood began to gain market acceptance as a construction material. World War II brought increased demand, especially for molded-hardwood plywood products. The market for both softwood and hardwood plywood expanded after the war, but the hardwood plywood industry never experienced the sustained rapid growth of the softwood industry. Between 1945 and 1983, softwood plywood production increased twelvefold. The hardwood plywood industry has suffered greatly from a lack of domestic timber of veneer quality. During the 1950s over one-half of all hardwood plywood was produced from domestic timber: by 1983 the proportion had fallen to one-third.

Structure of the industry The economic characteristics of the plywood industry are very similar to those of the lumber industry. The geographic distribution of plywood mills parallels that of the nation's timber resources, although, somewhat surprisingly, Oregon is the nation's leading producer of both hardwood and softwood plywood.

In the past hardwood mills tended to be smaller and less efficient than softwood mills, but this is no longer true. In 1982 the average increase in the value of the final product was $15.48 per hour worked in a hardwood mill, whereas a softwood mill averaged $13.05 per hour worked (4). In the hardwood industry a substantial number of mills are independently operated. For softwood, however, the number of firms is only about one-half the number of mills. The ownership of two or more mills that engage in the same stage of production is referred to as *horizontal integration*. The softwood plywood industry is integrated to a greater degree than the hardwood industry, although both have remained quite competitive in terms of pricing behavior.

Prices, demand, and supply The uses of plywood are virtually the same as those of lumber; consequently the demands for the two products are determined by the same forces. As a building material, softwood plywood is used mainly for wall sheathing and subflooring; hardwood plywood is used primarily for decorative paneling.

Hardwood lumber and plywood also enjoy a second market, stemming from their use in the manufacture of wood furniture; for softwood products this market is generally insignificant. Since the furniture industry is not subject to the cyclic demand that characterizes the construction industry, demands and prices for hardwood lumber and hardwood plywood tend to be more stable than those for softwood.

Figure 24.5 shows the relative price indexes for softwood and hardwood plywood for the period since 1950. Hardwood plywood prices remained virtually constant until 1973 when strong demand, combined with the removal of national price controls, contributed to a price rise. The relative price index has declined steadily, however, and in fact declined most dramatically in 1974–1975. These trends indicate that hardwood plywood prices have not risen as fast as the general rate of inflation. This outcome is due almost entirely to the flexibility in supply provided by imports. Since 1950 consumption has risen steadily, whereas domestic production has declined by 33 percent. Only by increasing imports has supply been expanded fast enough to meet demand and thereby prevent real price increases.

For softwood plywood the price picture is not so favorable. Prices did decline between 1950 and 1967, but they had tripled by the late 1970s. During the second period the price of softwood plywood increased much faster than the general rate of inflation. Since 1978, however, softwood plywood prices have increased much more slowly than the rate of inflation (see Figure 24.5). Indeed, since 1967 the relative price indexes for softwood lumber (Figure 24.4) and softwood plywood (Figure 24.5) have shown a strikingly similar pattern. This is so because the principal market for the two products is the same, that is, new housing. Thus, in a sense, they are really alternative forms of the same product.

For softwood plywood, imports have not been an effective mechanism for mitigating upward pressure

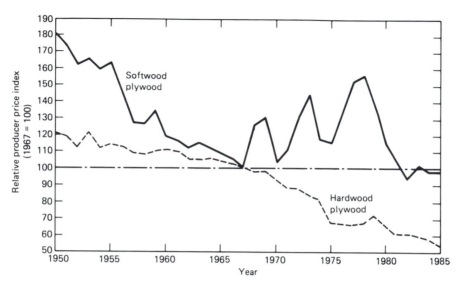

Figure 24.5 Relative producer price indexes for U.S. hardwood and softwood plywood, 1950 to 1985 (3,7).

on prices during periods of strong demand. The United States has been a net exporter of softwood plywood and veneer since 1969, and exports have actually increased substantially during peak demand periods. Hence foreign demand may actually contribute somewhat to price increases in the softwood plywood market.

It was noted earlier that softwood lumber and softwood plywood share the same market and that their prices tend to move in tandem. However, because it is manufactured in large sheets instead of individual boards, plywood has become less expensive to install as the price of labor has risen. This has produced an increase in the per capita consumption of softwood plywood that is in stark contrast to the concomitant decrease in per capita consumption of softwood lumber. Thus even though the prices of both products have risen, the consumption patterns have been quite different over time.

Prospects for the future Currently about 90 percent of all plywood produced in the United States is made from softwoods, and over 60 percent of all softwood plywood is Douglas-fir. The mature stands

of this species in the Pacific Northwest could supply sufficient veneer logs to meet demand for several decades. Large logs are not necessary for production of plywood, however. If public land management policies curtail harvests in the Pacific Northwest, use may veer to southern pines.

On the demand side, the possibilities for substituting plywood for lumber in housing are pretty much exhausted; indeed the current trend is toward increasing use of particleboard and more recently, waferboard, to replace the more expensive plywood. However, Forest Service projections are for plywood consumption to double by the year 2020 (6). This projection is contingent on the relative price of plywood remaining at its 1970 level, but if past trends in prices of plywood and its substitutes continue, the demand for softwood plywood will probably grow at a slower rate than the Forest Service has projected.

Forest Service projections are for consumption of hardwood plywood to grow at about the same rate as consumption of softwoods. The domestic supply of hardwood veneer logs is limited, and the public lands do not contain a reserve inventory. The implication, therefore, is for continued growth of imports, which already account for the bulk of total consumption.

Particleboard Although wood particleboard was patented in the United States as early as 1905, commercial development of the product is usually credited to either Germany or Czechoslovakia in 1941. Production was restricted by a shortage of gluing resins during most of World War II, but in 1945 the first American plant began operation (8). Particleboard did not really begin to gain market acceptance until the 1960s. From 1964 to 1979 consumption increased at an average annual rate of 9.5 percent. In terms of total consumption of wood-based panels, however, particleboard held only about 15 percent of the market in 1984.

Structure of the industry Particleboard is among the *most concentrated* of all the wood products industries. An industry is usually considered concentrated if four firms produce more than 50 percent of the industry's total output. In 1982 four firms accounted for 43 percent of the total production of particleboard. However, the industry appears to remain strongly price-competitive. The product is quite homogeneous, and technological improvements have recently brought down the cost of production. During the early history of the industry, production capacity was divided almost equally between the South and the West, but several very large plants have been built in the West during recent years.

Particleboard plants are frequently integrated with lumber and plywood mills, from which they derive much of their raw material. Approximately 65 percent of all wood used in particleboard manufacture consists of shavings produced when lumber is planed. An additional 10 percent and 9 percent come, respectively, from plywood mill residue and sawdust. Softwood is the preferred species group, making up slightly more than 80 percent of the total raw material output.

Prices, demand, and supply When it was first introduced, particleboard was used as a core material for furniture. Gradually it began to capture from plywood the market for floor underlayment. Recently it has been used as a backing for plastic overlay paneling and for mobile-home decking. In 1979, industrial use and floor underlayment accounted for 83 percent of total output, and mobile-home decking consumed another 9 percent.

Because particleboard is manufactured largely from sawmill residues, it has contributed significantly to the total utilization of timber. Improved bonding techniques and large-scale plants have gradually lowered the cost of production.

Prospects for the future Until recently the most significant limitation on the market for particleboard had been the availability of inexpensive plywood (9). Now plywood is no longer inexpensive relative to particleboard, and this would seem to favor continued growth of the particleboard industry. However, the advent of yet another set of reconstituted-wood panels, waferboard and oriented-strand board or OSB (see Chapter 22), has slowed this growth. These new entrants into the structural-panel market were first manufactured on a large scale in Canada, and much of the Canadian output was initially exported to the United States. Within the last decade, however, U.S. production capacity has increased from 9.8 million to 241 million square meters (9.53-millimeter basis), and there is no indication that this rapid rate of growth will slow in the near future. It appears that waferboard and OSB and several new variants will become the major growth markets among structural panels, and will probably compete most directly with the more expensive softwood plywood. Since these new panels can be manufactured from previously underutilized hardwood species, their development has benefited forest landowners as well as consumers.

Fiberboard In terms of total use, insulation board and hardboard are relatively unimportant. Both products are produced by a small number of firms, but pricing patterns in both industries appear to be competitive.

In 1950 consumption of hardboard was, by weight, roughly 50 percent of insulation board; by 1976 the percentages were almost exactly reversed. This has come about because although total use of insulation board has increased over the past 25 years by 73 percent, per capita consumption has remained constant or even declined, but for hardboard it has doubled (3). These figures indicate the faster growth rate of the hardboard industry, brought about because favorable prices have stimulated substitution of hardboard for plywood and lumber in construction and furniture. About 85 percent of all insulation board is used in construction, but because it is a nonstructural material, it is not readily substituted for either plywood or hardboard.

The demand for hardboard is expected to parallel closely that for plywood, but the demand for insulation board may increase at a faster pace in the future if higher energy costs increase the demand for insulating materials. Roundwood can be expected to assume greater importance as a source of wood fiber for both products as competition for wood residue intensifies. Like particleboard, the fiberboards hold great promise for increasing utilization of wood fiber and for providing markets for low-quality timber.

Paper and Allied Products

Structure of the Industry What is commonly referred to as the pulp-and-paper industry is actually a loose conglomeration of firms that encompasses three stages of production: (1) pulping of wood, wastepaper, and other raw materials, (2) production of paper and paperboard from wood pulp, and (3) manufacturing of paper into final commodities. The science and technology of pulp-and-paper manufacture are discussed in Chapter 23. Only about 12 percent of all wood pulp is marketed without further processing. Many of the largest firms are vertically integrated; that is, they operate at more than one of the three stages of production. Vertically integrated firms frequently grow some or all of their own pulpwood timber, process pulpwood into pulp, and convert the pulp into paper products. The newer mills are also frequently integrated with lumber or plywood mills and are thus able to utilize the residues from those facilities.

The history of the pulp-and-paper industry and the nature of each region's wood resource have produced a *distinct geographic pattern* in the industry. The Northeast contains the oldest, smallest, and

generally least efficient mills. The newest and largest mills are found in the West and the South. Many of the newer installations, especially in the South, utilize the kraft (sulfate) process (see Chapter 23). The characteristics of the industry in the Great Lakes states tend to be intermediate between those of the Northeast and those of the South and West.

The market structure of the pulp-and-paper industry consists of a few very large firms that can to some degree influence the prices of their products, and a much greater number of smaller firms that have little or no control over the prices they receive. Although this description is probably appropriate for the industry as a whole, a wide range of market conditions does exist among the various sectors within the industry. For example, only about a dozen U.S. firms use dissolving processes for producing pulp (see Chapter 23), four of which account for over three-quarters of total output. In contrast, the recycled-paperboard sector contains over 100 firms, and together the four largest control only one-quarter of total production. The combination of a few large firms and many smaller firms often leads to a pricing pattern that is referred to as *price leadership*. The larger firms establish their price, and the remaining smaller firms are more or less forced to adopt if they are to remain economically viable. The steel and automobile industries also have this pricing pattern.

Much of the specialization that has taken place within the industry is regional in nature. For example, in the South and West, where supplies of inexpensive softwoods are readily available, production of kraft paper and paperboard is prominent. Industries in the Northeast, and to a somewhat lesser extent the Great Lakes states, have generally concentrated on the production of high-quality, more valuable papers in which they have a competitive advantage. Thus, although the South dominates the industry in terms of production capacity (Figure 24.6), the northeastern and north-central regions combined greatly outweigh the South in terms of the *value of output*; the leading state on this basis is Wisconsin.

Concentration within the pulp-and-paper industry is likely to increase for several reasons, the most significant of which is probably the cost of entry.

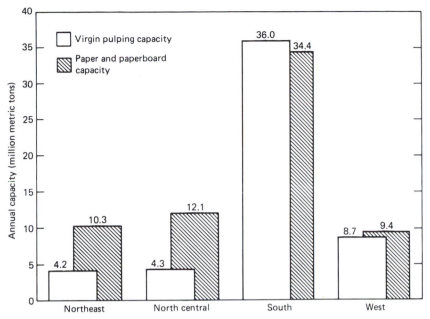

Figure 24.6 U.S. production capacity for virgin pulp and paper and paperboard mills in the year 1984, by region (10). (The West includes the Rocky Mountain states, which have a combined capacity of less than 2 percent of U.S. production capacity.)

Although relatively small scale mills—for example, 100 metric tons per day—may be economically viable for production of some specialty papers, the average daily capacity of unbleached kraft paper mills is approximately 1400 metric tons.

The effect of the large and increasing capital costs for new mills is substantial. For example, a recent study reported that the most economical size for a kraft linerboard mill in 1966 was 630 tons per day (tpd), which could then be constructed for about $40 million. By 1980 the most efficient scale had increased to 1080 tpd, which would cost $308 million in 1980 dollars (11). Small entrepreneurs may still be able to find a niche in the lumber industry, but even established firms sometimes find it difficult to raise the capital needed to finance expansions in the pulp-and-paper industry. Considering the size of the investments required, it is perhaps surprising that the industry is not even more concentrated.

Prices, Demand, and Supply During the 1960s the wholesale price index for paper products remained virtually constant. New production capac-

ity was added at an annual rate of 4 percent, and by the middle of the decade the combination of capacity expansion and increased productivity of existing production facilities began to generate excess capacity. Typically, paper firms have been reluctant to reduce output because the cost per ton of output tends to increase as production is decreased. The industry became fiercely competitive as firms attempted to maintain production levels. This competition held down potential price increases but it also eroded industry profits, a process that was exacerbated by the recession of 1970–1971.

Since 1970 the industry has undergone a major transition. Capacity expansion has slowed to 2.5 percent per year and in some years dropped below 2 percent. The overcapacity problem was further alleviated by the closure of more than 100 mills in the early 1970s. These mills were generally of marginal efficiency and unable to meet the combination of strong price competition and rising costs of pollution control.

When the economy began to strengthen in 1972, the industry was unable to meet the demand. Utilization rates for existing capacity climbed to 97 percent in 1973, well above the 93 percent level at which prices generally begin to rise. And rise they did—by 16 percent per year in 1973 and 1974! However, the price increases were completely in line with the movement of other prices, and the relative producer price index for paper products has remained fairly stable since 1973.

The paper industry learned much about basic economics in the early 1970s. Firms began to employ professional managers in the top executive positions, and profitability replaced volume of production as a management goal. These changes appear to have been effective. Despite a sharp drop in demand during the 1975 recession, the industry was able, by reducing supplies, not only to maintain prices but actually to raise them and thus maintain profitability.

The range of products manufactured by the pulp-and-paper industry is so diverse as to preclude consideration of each product. The two main categories of finished products are (1) *paper,* which includes newsprint, writing and printing papers, packaging papers, and sanitary papers, and (2) *paperboards,* the largest production of which is in the form of corrugated container boards—that is, cardboard boxes. These products are used so pervasively throughout all stages of the economy that aggregate demand for paper products generally parallels movements in *real GNP* at a ratio of about 20,000 tons of paper and paperboard products consumed for every million dollars of GNP. Hence, the industry undergoes periods of alternating strong and weak demand as the nation undergoes economic expansions and recessions. However, since per capita real GNP has increased almost continuously over time, so too has per capita consumption of paper products.

Prospects for the Future The paper industry is a *mature industry;* that is, the majority of products have not changed appreciably in recent years, the production technology is generally available to all firms, and prospects for uncovering large, untapped markets are limited. The long-term growth rate for demand is projected at 3 percent or less per year.

The industry also faces very large capital costs for new investment in mills, land, and pollution control equipment. These characteristics suggest that entry by new firms will be restricted and that consolidation within and competition among firms will increase.

A particular consequence of the new management philosophy brought about by events in the early 1970s is greater scrutiny of land management policies. Instead of owning timberland merely to ensure pulpwood supply, firms are undertaking comprehensive land use plans in an effort to increase returns. On lands that are to remain in timber production, management is continually being intensified, especially in the South where gains in productivity have already been impressive. On the other hand, there has been a movement by a number of companies in the 1980s to divest themselves of their forestland holdings and to rely on timber purchased in the marketplace for their wood supplies.

The future wood supply situation for the pulp-and-paper industry is far more favorable than that for the lumber and plywood industries. Pulp products do not require large or high-quality timber as raw material. Moreover, the industry has been making increasing use of hardwoods, of which there are ample supplies. Since 1950 domestic output of softwood pulp products has doubled, while that from hardwoods has increased fivefold. Should these trends continue, the industry will not face the shortage of timber that might plague the lumber and plywood industries.

The forest products industries have been examined before we discuss the economics of timber production for a very important reason. The demand for timber is a *derived demand;* that is, it is derived from the demand for the final products in which timber is used. Forest economists often make much of the concept of derived demand, perhaps imparting the impression that it is unique to their discipline. Such is not the case, however. Derived demand characterizes primary-commodity industries ranging from milk to iron ore. In all these industries, the demand for the raw product is derived directly from the demand for the end product, be it ice cream or automobiles. Thus it is important to have a firm grasp of the current status and projected changes in the demands for wood products, because they have important implications for how and what types of timber will be grown. We now turn to this second subject.

Timber Production Economics

The timber production process includes all steps necessary to grow trees, from timber culture to harvesting (see Chapters 12–16). Although decisions regarding the culture and harvest of timber are inextricably intertwined, it is convenient to consider the two separately.

Timber Supply

As noted previously, many firms in the timber-processing industries are *integrated backward* into timber production. The extent of this integration can be seen in Figure 24.7 (see also Table 9.2 and Figure 9.6). Industry owns only 14 percent of all commercial forestland, but contributes more than one-third of the total softwood harvest, whereas other private owners, who hold almost 60 percent of the land, supply only 36 percent of the softwood harvest. For hardwoods, the percentage of the total harvest from

industry-owned lands is approximately in line with the percentage for land area ownership, but private owners harvest a disproportionate share of the total. On publicly owned lands softwood and hardwood harvest percentages are roughly the same as those for landholdings.

The disparities between the percentages of land owned and the percentages of timber harvested could be due merely to concentration of holdings in a particular species group. The data on holdings of growing stock (see Figure 9.6) indicate that this is indeed the case among private nonindustrial owners; they own and harvest the greatest proportion of hardwood timber. However, the forest industries own far less softwood growing stock than is suggested by their contribution to the total softwood harvest.

Comparison of Figures 9.6 and 24.7 also reveals that the national forests contain the bulk of the softwood timber inventory, especially for sawtimber, but furnish less than one-quarter of the total softwood harvest.

The forest industries have been able to harvest more softwoods from their lands by liquidating more rapidly their stocks of very old timber in the Pacific Coast region. Harvesting the slow-growing, mature timber and regenerating the areas with fast-growing young stock has increased productivity as measured by net annual growth per unit area. In the Pacific Coast region the current productivity of industry-owned forestland is almost two and one-half times greater than that of the national forests. Potential growth on national forestland is over three times current growth, but still only about 82 percent of that possible from industry lands and about 92 percent of the potential on other privately owned land. The greater potential of industry-owned lands is due primarily to the tendency of forest products firms to purchase the best sites in an effort to increase profitability.

Differences in the amount, inherent productivity, and current timber inventory cannot account for all of the differences in harvest among the various groups of landowners. The decisions on when and how much to harvest are strongly influenced by the objectives of the owner. There is no reason to

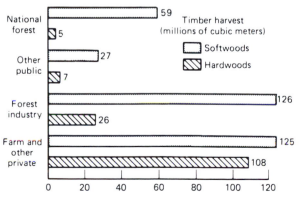

Figure 24.7 Timber harvest in the United States in 1986 by ownership class and species group (6).

suppose that all owners will choose to pursue the same objectives, and indeed they do not. The forest industries expect their forestland to contribute to the overall profitability of the enterprise, either directly if timber production proves to be profitable, or indirectly if such production lowers the cost of timber used and ensures a source of supply. Because profitability is an important objective of industry, timber production decisions depend strongly on prices and costs. For the national forests, the land management objective is sustained production of an array of outputs. Profitability is not the only, or even most important, criterion of timber production decisions. Indeed, some critics contend that economic considerations are ignored almost totally in management decision making for the national forests (12).

The objectives of nonindustrial private forest landowners are diverse and not well understood, as discussed in Chapter 11, but profitability certainly does not appear to be the sole objective of timber production, nor is timber production necessarily the only purpose of landownership. The impact of market conditions on the timber production decisions of this group of forest landowners is therefore very difficult to predict. Suffice it to say, though, that when the profitability of timber production becomes great enough, owners usually do respond to economic incentives.

The aggregate harvest (supply) of timber in any time period will be the sum of the harvests from privately and publicly owned forestland. Because hardwoods are harvested for the most part from private lands, it is reasonable to expect supply to be responsive to price. The same can be said for the supply of both softwood and hardwood timber for pulpwood. However, softwood lumber and softwood plywood and veneer are manufactured primarily from timber grown in the Pacific Coast region, an area in which a large proportion of the forestland is publicly owned.

The national forests of the Pacific Coast region supply 27 percent of the nation's softwood sawtimber. On these forests the timber harvest is governed by the National Forest Management Act of 1976, which limits harvests to "a quantity equal to or less than a quantity which can be removed from such a forest annually in perpetuity on a *sustained-yield basis*" (13). The rationale for sustained yield is the desire to avoid overcutting, similar to that which occurred in the Great Lakes states at the turn of the century. The Forest Service has interpreted the sustained-yield requirement to mean that harvest volumes should be virtually constant from year to year (Figure 24.8). Some critics have argued that this is too rigid an interpretation and that the Forest Service actually has greater discretion than it chooses to exercise in setting harvest volumes. This argument is not likely to be settled for some time. In the meantime, the supply of timber from the national forests remains almost totally unresponsive to price signals; that is, the supply of timber from the national forests is *price-inelastic*. Because the total softwood supply is merely the sum of the harvests from public and private forestland, the aggregate supply is also relatively price-inelastic. This price-inelastic supply of softwood sawtimber, coupled with the wide fluctuations in softwood lumber demand that parallel the peaks and troughs of housing activity, makes timber, lumber, and plywood prices extremely volatile. If harvests from public lands were more responsive to initial price changes, the ultimate variations in prices of timber and derived products could probably be reduced. This potential for dampening price swings lies behind the persistent efforts of the forest products industries to persuade the Forest Service to increase timber harvests. It also prompted President Carter to order a study in 1978 of the potential for dampening inflationary trends in the economy, and in particular in the construction industry, by increasing the harvest from public forestland (see Chapter 10). However, as noted previously, prospects for actual increases in the harvest are remote.

The supply of timber in any time period is a function of existing stocks; in order to harvest more it is necessary to have available timber of merchantable size. Thus supply, as used here, is a short- to medium-run concept. But what of the longer run? Surely prices and costs also affect a landowner's decisions whether and how to grow timber.

Figure 24.8 Reforested area on the Kaniksu National Forest in Idaho. The foreground is stocked with western larch and Douglas-fir, which have reproduced naturally. The central area, edged by mature timber, is a field-planted western white pine plantation. (Courtesy of U.S.D.A. Forest Service.)

Timber Culture

Let us suppose that there is available 1 hectare of forestland from which all timber has just been harvested. The management objective is to maximize the income from this land. We wish to examine how economic factors affect management decisions.

We can begin our examination with a very simple case in which the land is located in the Great Lakes states and previously contained a stand of bigtooth aspen. The site is of slightly better than average productivity, which suggests that pulpwood is the most profitable timber product to grow. Accordingly, the stand is allowed to regenerate itself naturally. Figure 15.6 illustrates the general relationship that might be expected between the volume of harvestable pulpwood and stand age. Notice that the curve does not begin at the origin, because trees must be of some minimum size before they are merchantable. If we assume that the real price of aspen pulpwood stumpage—that is, standing trees—does not vary with time or stand volume, the yield curve can be thought of as representing either physical volume or gross income. To keep this illustration simple we will also assume that gross income and net income are equal—that there are no management costs or taxes of any kind.

The most important management decision for aspen is deciding when to harvest. *Maximization of income* (or harvest volume) per unit of time would lead to harvesting the stand at the age R_2 (as discussed in Chapter 15), defined by the point of tangency of the yield curve with a straight line from the origin. This is the traditional way of determining the *rotation age,* and it is still often advocated. However, the procedure ignores the existence of *interest rates*—that is, the fact that income received at an earlier date than R_2 can be invested in other ventures and generate still more income. Moreover, the interest effect influences not just the first rotation but all future rotations. Taking interest rates into account leads to an economic rotation R_1 that is significantly shorter than R_2. We will ignore details of the procedure by which R_1 is determined, but we note that for aspen growing on moderately good sites in the Great Lakes states, R_2 is about 40 years; even at very low interest rates, R_1 would generally be at least 5 years less (14). The *economic rotation* is especially sensitive to the rate of interest chosen. The higher the interest rate, the shorter the economic rotation, and at very high interest rates timber production may not be profitable at all.

The previous example, though exceedingly simple, is quite representative of aspen management in the Great Lakes states. It demonstrates very well the influence that an important economic variable, the interest rate, has on rotation length. But what about more complex management situations?

Suppose now that our hectare of land is located in Georgia, that the species to be grown is slash pine, and that the stand must be regenerated artificially. The first question to be decided is how much site preparation to undertake prior to planting. Obviously, it is least expensive to do none, but unprepared sites are likely to undergo considerable ingrowth of hardwoods and, consequently, greater mortality among the pine. Intensive site preparation is expensive and can be justified only if timber value will be significantly greater at the time of harvest. A second decision must be made on the spacing between seedlings. Closer spacings produce a greater total wood volume per unit area but it is more expensive to purchase and plant more seedlings for close spacing; the final product also tends to be of smaller diameter and therefore less valuable. In order to determine the most profitable combination of site preparation and spacing, researchers need to compare the present worth of costs and returns that are likely to result from each of a range of alternatives. A study (15) doing just that arrived at the following general conclusions.

1. If it is profitable to plant slash pine on unprepared sites, it is even more profitable to plant on intensively prepared sites.

2. The most profitable tree spacing becomes closer as the site index and the degree of site preparation increase.

3. Optimum spacing is relatively insensitive to the interest rate, but quite sensitive to product values. The optimum spacing increases as the price

of sawtimber rises relative to the price of pulpwood.

Aspen and slash pine are managed as even-aged species. Let us briefly examine how economic factors affect the culture of an all-aged forest of, for example, mixed species of northern hardwoods. As with determination of the rotation, the economic variable most significantly affecting management of uneven-aged stands is the interest rate. The value of the trees in the stand amounts to a capital investment, since the option always exists of harvesting them and putting the income received into some alternative investment. Consequently, the stand should return at least as much as could be earned by investing in the best alternative available; otherwise, it would be more profitable to get out of the timber-growing business.

By what means can the profitability of timber production from an uneven-aged stand be increased? The variables most directly under the control of the forest manager are the *length of cutting cycle* (time interval between harvests), the *stocking level,* the *size (diameter) class distribution* of trees in the stand, and the *species composition*.

Altering the species composition to favor the most valuable species is an obvious management strategy. But what choice of cutting cycle, stocking level, and diameter distribution will contribute most to profitability? The answer is not at all obvious because maximum volume and value productivity are not necessarily identical, and both are jointly dependent on all three variables. For example, volume growth would be greatest if an annual cutting cycle were employed, harvesting each year the annual increase in volume. Such frequent harvests are usually not economical, however, because the volume harvested is quite small. As the cutting cycle is lengthened, maximizing both volume and value productivity calls for a lower stocking level and perhaps also a smaller average tree size. Similarly, a stand that is managed solely for sawtimber and veneer would tend to have a larger average tree diameter than one that is managed for pulpwood, because large trees would be more valuable in the former case.

Each of the three management situations discussed involves slightly different *decision variables.* A number of additional variables could be included: whether and how much to fertilize, to plant genetically superior stock, to thin, to prune, or to control fire, insects, and disease. It is not possible to consider all the many possible management situations. Nor is it necessary to do so. Our three examples illustrate well the general manner in which economic factors affect timber culture.

The variables that a forest manager seeks to control can all be expected to produce the same general effect—to maintain or increase the quantity or quality of timber that is produced. But not all actions that produce this result are profitable. Just which are and which are not is determined by comparing the additional income attributable to a particular practice with the additional cost that is incurred, including the cost of waiting until the income is received. Analysis usually indicates, for example, that pruning is not a profitable cultural practice except for very valuable veneer species. In

contrast, thinning, even when it produces no immediate revenue, frequently increases the rate of value growth of the remaining trees enough to be worthwhile (Figure 24.9).

Forest Products in the World Economy

The previous discussion of forestry and forest product economics dealt exclusively with the situation in the United States. The modern student of forestry would be ill-advised to assume that the U.S. forest economy is representative of the situation in other nations. Forestry problems in industrial countries may be somewhat similar to those of the United States, but they are very different in the rest of the world where at least two-thirds of the human population lives. It is the objective of this section to provide a general overview of the forest economy of several world regions. Particular attention will be

Figure 24.9 A forty-year-old Douglas-fir stand marked prior to thinning, Washington State. (Courtesy of M. Wotton.)

paid to the enormous differences between the rich industrialized countries and those of the Third World.

Forest Resources of the World

Forests cover 30 percent of the world's land area, most of which is closed forest with a small percentage as open woodland. As discussed in Chapter 2, three major types of forest can be distinguished: *coniferous forest* below the Arctic tundra and extending along the major mountain chains, *tropical hardwoods* heavily concentrated in the hot, humid equatorial regions, and the more widely scattered *deciduous types.* The most heavily forested (closed) areas by far are in the Soviet Union, Latin America, and North America, all of which contain more than 2 hectares of forestland per capita. But the numbers can be very misleading. The nature of the resource varies considerably from region to region in terms of timber quality, forest accessibility, and distribution. Coniferous timber found in North America is an all-purpose, homogeneous wood. In contrast, humid tropical forests contain hundreds of species, of which only a few are currently being used. Although the average forest area per capita in Europe (0.3 hectare per capita) is similar to those in Asia (0.2 hectare per capita) and Africa (0.5 hectare per capita), this ignores the fact that 95 percent of all European forests are under some form of use and are geographically well distributed. Vast areas of Africa and Asia are almost bare of trees, and the future of the highly concentrated tropical forests in the Amazon, West Africa, and Southeast Asia is somewhat uncertain.

Data are very scarce and often inaccurate, but it is generally thought that forest area is stable or increasing in the developed world where some balance between agriculture and forestry has been struck. However, tropical forest area appears to be *declining* by about 1.2 percent annually, a figure that corresponds to deforestation of an area the size of Cuba each year.

Some observers claim that at their present rate of decline, the moist tropical forests will be gone in fifty years. It should be recognized that given the pressures of population growth and poverty, some transformation of a forest domain that is currently underused is necessary to generate badly needed capital and agricultural land. On the other hand, the methods used should ensure maintenance of the long-term productivity of the soil. Shifting cultivation, whereby people clear a parcel of forest and cultivate the soil until it is impoverished before moving on to another area, is a frequent practice in developing countries. This problem is particularly serious in the subtropical regions where increasing population density is leading to an overexpansion of agriculture and excessive grazing and fuelwood harvests. Removal of an already light forest cover is accelerating desertification of a naturally fragile environment.

Because about 80 percent of the world's forest area is under some form of public ownership, it may seem that the future of world forests is merely a matter of policy easily settled by rule of law. This is not generally so, however, particularly when the law is not compatible with the immediate needs or longtime traditions of the people. Under these conditions forest laws may be unenforceable, even by a well-trained and well-staffed forestry corps. In India, for example, illegal use of state forests is so great that it almost precludes planned management.

Output, Trade, and Consumption of World Timber Products

As indicated in Table 24.2, the current world harvest (about 3.0 billion cubic meters) is divided evenly between *fuelwood* and *industrial roundwood.* The importance of fuelwood in the world forest economy, to which we will return later, is probably underestimated by official figures. Logs used in the manufacture of lumber and plywood represent 60 percent of industrial wood and production, and the remaining 40 percent consists of pulpwood, the major raw material of the pulp-and-paper industry, and wood for miscellaneous industrial uses, such as poles, pilings, and posts. Pulpwood harvest is growing seven times as fast as log production. Pulp-and-paper manufacturing is rapidly becoming the

Table 24.2 World Wood Production, 1984

Product	Production (million m^3)	Production (percent)	1973–1984 Growth (yearly percent)
Fuelwood	1595[a]	52	2.4
Industrial roundwood	1455	48	0.6
Logs	860	28	0.2
Pulpwood	380	12	1.5
Other	215	7	0.4
Total removals	3050	100	1.5

Source: Anon., *Yearbook of Forest Products 1984,* UN–FAO, Rome, 1986.
[a]Figures may not add up because of rounding.

major user of the world's industrial roundwood harvest. However, fuelwood production is growing even faster than that of pulpwood.

Forest industries are heavily concentrated in the developed nations of the Northern Hemisphere (17). This may seem surprising in view of the somewhat larger volume of timber stock available in developing countries (170 million cubic meters versus 140 million in developed countries). It underlines the fact that many variables affect the growth of timber-based industries. We have already indicated the technological advantages of softwoods, particularly over mixed tropical hardwoods. *Capital* is a factor of production that is relatively scarce in developing countries, as are skilled labor and the general infrastructure needed to support modern industry. Besides adequate supplies of factors of production, a new industry needs sufficient *markets* to be successful. Very often domestic markets are small in developing economies, and international markets are inaccessible because of combinations of high production and transportation costs and import tariffs. For these reasons there is very little pulp-and-paper production in the developing world. Pulp-and-paper manufacturing requires large amounts of capital, technical knowledge, a good economic infrastructure, and large markets. Lumber and plywood industries have been much more successful. They require less capital, use simple skills, and because of the availability of local raw material and cheap labor, have been able to compete on the international market despite heavy import duties levied by importing countries. Nevertheless, the average value of all wood products manufactured in developing countries does not exceed 10 percent of the total value of world output. Furthermore, this share has not increased during the last two decades, an alarming situation given the fact that population growth has increased at least twice as fast in developing countries as in the rest of the world during the same period.

As already suggested, competitiveness in international markets is the acid test of development. There is ample evidence that the lumber and plywood industries of several Third World countries have achieved such competitiveness. Nevertheless, 80 percent of all world forest products trade is between developed countries. Softwood lumber, wood pulp, and newsprint dominate this trade. Developing nations export mostly logs to developed nations and import almost all the paper and paperboard they need, usually with an overall trade deficit. The system of trade preferences is heavily biased against potential exports of manufactured products from developing countries. Whereas logs are usually imported duty-free into industrial countries, heavy tariffs are levied on processed products. For example, the United States imposes a 20 percent duty on hardwood plywood imports, regardless of origin, thereby effectively limiting the ability of Southeast Asian producers to penetrate the American market. Domestic producers are also favored by laws pro-

Table 24.3 World Distribution of Forest Products Consumption, 1980

Market	Population (millions)	Population (percent)	Lumber (million m³)	Lumber (percent)	Paper (million tons)	Paper (percent)
Developed countries	1160	26	351	81	143	84
Developing countries	3270	74	85	19	27	16
World	4430	100	436	100	170	100

Source: Anon., *Regional Tables of Production, Trade and Consumption of Forest Products,* UN–FAO, Rome, 1982.

hibiting export of a large part of the timber harvest in the western United States. Such regulations represent a subsidy to domestic producers and an encouragement to inefficiency relative to foreign competitors who would be willing to pay much higher prices for the raw material involved.

Because of differences in income there are tremendous differences between levels of timber products consumption in the developed and developing world. Developing countries, which make up 75 percent of the world population, consume only 15 to 20 percent of the lumber and paper produced in the world (Table 24.3). Figures for individual country reveal even greater disparities, with consumption of lumber per capita three hundred times higher in Canada than in Mali. Consumption of paper and paperboard is more than sixty times higher in the United States than in the Philippines. Economic studies reveal a systematic relation between the growth of income per capita and the resulting growth in consumption of wood products per capita. These consumption functions allow us to estimate the impact of expected economic and demographic growth on long-term wood requirements. The results tend to indicate that as a whole, the world does not face an immediate wood shortage. In North America, for example, more wood is being grown than harvested. Furthermore, there is ample room for improving productivity in most forests. However, local problems, already serious in parts of the developing world, will increase directly with the growth of population. One problem that is particularly relevant to the world forest economy is the *fuelwood crisis.*

The Fuelwood Crisis

Fuelwood is the basic heating and cooking fuel for at least one-third of the world's people (19). In the Third World, close to 90 percent of the timber harvest is for fuelwood (Figure 24.10). It is the source of up to 66 percent of all energy of the developing world (Table 24.4). In largely rural societies fuelwood does not enter the monetary economy and is therefore taken for granted and ignored in economic calculations. Nevertheless, it has been observed in parts of the Andean Sierra and Africa that fuelwood sold on the market absorbs as much as 25 to 30 percent of the average household income. This high price leads individual households to do their own collection, but this necessarily restricts the land available for collection to a family's immediate vicinity. High population densities, coupled with overgrazing, inevitably lead to deforestation. The Forestry Department of the Food and Agricultural Organization (FAO) estimated in 1980 that more than one billion rural people in the world could not obtain enough fuelwood, or could do so only by cutting wood faster than it is growing. They forecast that this number will double by the year 2000 (20). Deforestation in turn causes increased erosion. In the fragile ecosystem of the Sahel, deforestation is currently leading to rapid desertification. The decrease in the supply of fuelwood requires ever-increasing efforts to collect a minimum amount. It has been observed in Tanzania that fuelwood collection necessitates some 300 days of labor per year for a single household. Fuelwood shortages also cause people to search for substitutes, such as cow dung and crop residues. But this removal of natural ma-

Figure 24.10 Fuelwood supply and collection is a critical problem in developing countries. (UN–FAO photograph.)

nure lowers the productivity of existing arable land. As a result the remaining forest has to be cleared, which inevitably decreases the fuelwood supply even further. This dismal unending circle has spurred fresh thinking in the area of development aid, with ever more emphasis being given to community development.

Forests for People

A large portion of past efforts in forestry development aid centered on the idea that the creation of

Table 24.4 Estimated Use of Wood for Energy as a Percentage of Total Energy (Other Than Animal and Human)

Region	Percent
Asia and Pacific	29
Near East	6
Africa	66
Latin America	20

Source: J. E. M. Arnold and J. Jongma, *Unasylva, 29,* 2 (1978), UN–FAO Publication.

industrial centers, coupled with large-scale national planning, was the key to getting a national forest economy started. This industrial activity would create demand from and supply for other sectors that would have a snowball effect, ever increasing the economic impact of the starting project. Coupled to the large industrial centers were equally large forest estates either publicly or privately owned. Apart from a few success stories, the policy did not work. As indicated previously, the gap between developed and developing countries has not decreased. Perhaps even worse, the differences between rich and poor within developing countries have increased. The domestic urban elites, together with the foreign investors who have participated in the industrial ventures, have reaped considerable benefits, but the fate of the common people has remained unchanged. In fact, the lure of urban industrial jobs that have not materialized has worsened their prospects. It is now recognized that continuous migration to urban slums can only be stopped by improving the quality of life in small rural communities, and that forestry has a key role to play in this venture. It requires a different view of forestry, however—not big forestry, not industrial forestry, not timber forestry but instead small, communal, *multiple-use forestry* (20, 22). In this view the forest would be a source of goods and services for the local community, providing firewood, some grazing, poles, and small construction materials. It would also be used for windbreak and erosion control. To avoid competition between forestry and agricultural use of land, communities should replace traditional stands, when possible, by *agrisilvicultural systems* that integrate trees and other agricultural crops.

Community forestry, as its name implies, requires community acceptance and involvement. Villagers must be convinced that a village woodlot will really serve them; otherwise it is unrealistic to expect them to keep their starving herd from eating the seedlings as soon as they are planted. There is ample evidence from very successful community forestry programs in Korea and China that such community support can be secured. However, it entails a firm commitment by governments to rural development. It may require far-reaching reforms in the land tenure system of a country at the expense of the ruling elite. But a successful program may contribute substantially to a more equitable distribution of social well-being between the urban and rural areas. Only through such redistribution can the massive migration of the rural poor to the slums of most Third World cities be reversed.

This new, grass roots view of development forestry seems to be slowly gaining credibility within the bureaucracies of national and international development agencies. A number of nations are operating *bilateral assistance* in forestry. The United States, particularly through the programs of the Agency for International Development (USAID) and the Peace Corps, is probably the greatest contributor in absolute amount, although other nations such as Canada, Sweden, Great Britain, and France contribute more in proportion to their gross national product. However, these bilateral programs have their usual political biases in favor of the donor country instead of the receiver. *Multilateral aid* is a better approach. International multilateral aid in forestry development is offered by the Food and Agricultural Organization (FAO) of the United Na-

tions, operating from Rome through individual-country projects funded by various agencies including the United Nations Development Program. The field operations of the FAO seem to be at least in part committed to the concept of forestry for community development, but its resources are totally inadequate. The FAO staff of professional foresters, particularly those working in field projects, is ridiculously small compared, for example, to the staff of the U.S. Forest Service. Much larger programs will be required to affect seriously the course of forestry in the developing world. This should not discourage any individual of goodwill from embracing the field of development forestry, for it is by far the most important challenge facing our profession now and in the coming decades.

Summary

The economy of colonial America was marked by a strong dependence on the production, largely for export, of basic food and fiber commodities. Over the years, growth expanded and diversified the American economy; today, the forest-based industries constitute a smaller absolute, but perhaps no less important, segment of the aggregate economy.

Important changes have also taken place within the forest-based sector. With the exception of the Douglas-fir in the Pacific Northwest, the virgin stands of large, high-quality timber have been cut. Technological advances have expanded the timber resource. Lumber and plywood are produced today from smaller logs, though at an increase in cost. The discovery of the kraft pulping process enlarged the pulpwood base to include northern hardwoods and southern pines, and the development of reconstituted-wood products such as the fiberboards has created markets for what were once unutilized residues. Rising stumpage prices permit exploitation of more remote timber stands and make more intensive timber culture profitable.

The "timber resource" is not some fixed inventory but instead a *dynamic concept* defined by the current state of technology and by costs and prices. Given the relatively long time period required to produce timber and the large proportion of commercial forestland that is under public ownership, it is quite possible that the supply and demand for timber will be balanced in the future only if prices increase substantially. Whether such a result will be acceptable to the American people is a question that is sure to spark much debate.

The most striking characteristic of the world forest economy is the staggering difference that exists between industrially advanced countries and the Third World. Either developing countries have little forest, or what they have is difficult to manage. They also have few industries, and those that could compete on international markets face high tariff barriers from importers. Consumption of all forest products in these countries is extremely low. Basic materials such as fuelwood are becoming very scarce in some regions. The view that forestry for community development is more important than industrial forestry is slowly being adopted by development agencies. But to achieve some success in this area, rich countries must give much more consideration to the plight of the Third World than they do at present.

References

1. N. Rosenberg, *Perspectives on Technology,* Cambridge Univ. Press, Cambridge, England, 1976.

2. Anon., "The demand and price situation for forest products, 1964," U.S.D.A. For. Serv., Misc. Publ. 983, Washington, D.C., 1964.

3. A. Ulrich, "U.S. timber production trade, consumption, and price statistics, 1950–84," U.S.D.A. For. Serv., Misc. Publ. 1450, Washington, D.C., 1985.

4. Anon., "1982 census of manufactures," Industry Series MC82-I-24A, U.S. Dept. of Commerce, Bur. of the Census, Washington, D.C., 1985.

5. W. J. Mead, *Competition and Oliogopsony in the Douglas-Fir Lumber Industry,* Univ. of California Press, Berkeley, 1966.

6. Anon., "An Analysis of the timber situation in the United States: 1989–2040. Part I: The current resource and use situation.," U.S.D.A. For. Serv., Washington, D.C., 1988.

7. Anon., *Producer Price Indexes,* U.S. Dept. of Labor, Bur. of Labor Stat., Washington, D.C., (monthly issues, 1985 and 1986).

8. A. A. Moslemi, *Particleboard,* Vol. 1, *Materials,* Southern Illinois Univ. Press, Carbondale, 1974.

9. G. R. Gregory, Resource Economics for Foresters, Wiley & Sons, New York, 1987.

10. Anon., *1985 Statistics of Paper and Paperboard of Wood Pulp,* American Paper Inst., New York, 1985.

11. A. D. Little, "North America in the 80s." In *Pulp, Paper and Paperboard: The Competitive Position and Its Implications,* Cambridge, Mass., 1980.

12. M. Clawson, "The economics of national forest management," RFF Working Paper EN-6, Resources for the Future, Washington, D.C., 1976.

13. PL 94-588, 90 Stat. 2949 (1976), Sec. 13.

14. D. A. Perala, "Manager's handbook for aspen in the north central states," U.S.D.A. For. Serv., Gen. Tech. Rept. NC-36, St. Paul, Minn., 1977.

15. H. D. Smith and G. Anderson, "Economically optimal spacing and site preparation for slash pine plantations," North Carolina State University, School of Forest Resources, Tech. Rept. 59, 1977.

16. Anon., *Yearbook of Forest Products, 1986,* UN–FAO, Rome, 1986.

17. K. F. S. King, "The forestry sector and international relationships," Weyerhaeuser Lecture Series, University of Toronto, 1975.

18. Anon., *Regional Tables of Production, Trade, and Consumption of Forest Products,* UN–FAO, Rome, 1982.

19. E. P. Eckholm, *Ceres* (November–December), 44 (1975).

20. Anon., "Wood for energy," For. Top. Rept. 1, UN–FAO, Rome, 1985.

21. J. E. M. Arnold and J. Jongma, *Unasylva, 29,* 2 (1978).

22. Anon., "Forests, trees and people," For. Top. Rept. 2, UN–FAO, Rome, 1985.

CHAPTER 25

Forestry: The Profession and Career Opportunities

RONALD L. GIESE

Forestry provides a diverse set of opportunities, which can lead to a challenging and fulfilling career. Many people are attracted to forestry by their outdoor orientation or environmental concerns, others by the mathematical and engineering applications so important in modern forestry; still others find the biological aspects of forestry to their liking. Some people find rewarding the elements of social studies in forestry, such as economics, sociology, and political science. Still others are taken with the applications of new technologies such as computers and satellites. Whatever the motivation, a sense of stewardship and an appreciation of natural relationships are common denominators among those who pursue forestry as a professional career.

Events in the last two decades have created momentous changes in the forestry profession. Passage of the National Environmental Policy Act and the establishment of the Environmental Protection Agency, along with various state versions of environmental and forest practices acts, require assessment of the environmental consequences of forest management decisions. The Forest and Rangeland Renewable Resources Planning Act provides new opportunities to set national goals and formulate forest policies. Legal challenges to timber management practices on federal lands, like those arising from the Monongahela clearcutting issue, have led to changes in timber management policies.

The net result of these changes has been to create an institutional setting for forestry that is very different and more complex than ever before. As a society, we are now more concerned with multiple uses, as opposed to single uses like timber management, and resource planning, which must deal with issues relating to biological conservation, wilderness, endangered species, and the right of the people to influence the direction of resource management. Modern foresters are challenged, interested, and motivated by the complexities of their profession in a milieu of biological, quantitative, and social sciences.

During a forestry career, a person usually encounters a progression of duties and expectations (1). Early on, foresters are very dependent on technical field skills. As they move up the career ladder into the broader aspects of land management, economics and decision-making skills become more pertinent to their professional performance. The next stage of the career often places foresters in the role of people managers, who must draw broadly on a background of technology and experience in land management, as well as cope with the challenges generated by people both inside and outside their sphere of control. That such an evolution happens is evidenced by the fact that about half of the active professionals are in management or staff specialist positions. The general direction of a forestry career is therefore from exercising technical forestry skills to employing business and management practices. However, the ability to communicate well and to work effectively on multidisciplinary teams is an asset at all stages of a person's career.

Paths to the Profession

Career Decisions

For students making tentative career choices, forestry is frequently a mystery. Their perception of forestry seems to focus on operating sawmills, cutting trees, and outdoor recreation, according to a recent survey of more than 1000 college-bound seniors (2). Over 30 percent of the sample knew nothing about forestry careers, and only one percent considered themselves well informed. Modern forestry positions emphasize business approaches, computer science, social science, mathematics and engineering skills, as well as the life sciences. Careers in forestry can provide a variety of stimulating challenges in areas that students not primarily interested in biology usually do not consider seriously.

In planning for careers, students must use testing and classification services with caution. To a large extent the counseling services at the high school and college levels are many years out of date with respect to forestry. Vocational tests frequently suffer from biases and outdated bases of information. Recent evidence suggests that current automated testing systems picture a fire fighter wearing a hard hat or a logger with a chainsaw as typifying forestry. These outmoded perceptions fail to do justice to the skills and education of the modern forestry profes-

sional whose background embraces computer science, ecology, operations research, business, policy, resource planning and management, engineering, and communications.

Vocational tests are widely available and generally fall into three categories: aptitude, interests, and personality. The outcomes of some of these tests are clearly wrong (based on outdated information), and others are incomplete. The Holland Classification, for example, takes interests, values, and skills of individuals and combines them into six personality types (3). The types are R (realistic), I (investigative), A (artistic), S (social), E (enterprising), and C (conventional). A combination of R, S, and I types leads to forester in the Holland code of occupations (along with the occupations of podiatrist and boiler inspector). Even if you undergo an analysis under this system using terms such as business management, taking risks, organizing, computing, writing, and decision-making as inputs, you will not be led, for example, to the following important aspects of forestry: planning, trade, paper processing, systems analysis, managerial activities, marketing, technical writing, or administration. Moreover, the concepts of artificial intelligence and expert systems, biotechnology, and geographic information systems—each a component of forestry—have not yet found their way into the repertoire of the occupational codes or counseling services.

Many counselors and their subjects simply place too much credence and emphasis on test results. If taken as an end point rather than a beginning, test results are likely to lead to incorrect conclusions. This is so because the popular *Strong vocational interest* approach incorporates the Holland codes. In turn, the Holland *Occupations Finder* system (4) and *Dictionary of Holland Occupational Codes* (3) provide estimates of the general educational development required. These estimates are based on a U.S. Department of Labor schedule of educational preparation. Aside from the narrow definition of forestry just noted in the discussion of the Holland code, the educational requirements specified do not include advanced mathematics or the ability to read technical literature. (As will be seen in the next section, such a background would not even qualify a forestry program for accreditation.) If you have interests or background in advanced mathematics, computer science, or statistics, an aptitude survey or vocational interest test will erroneously declare that you are overqualified. Because of the interdependency of these counseling tools, incorrect information in one of the components automatically creates flaws in the others.

If you wish to choose career possibilities with an open mind and an eye to future satisfaction, you should use testing information as only one of several sources of input. The informed person will develop a mixed strategy for choosing a career. Testing can provide some direction, but it should also stimulate questions. Interviews with counselors may help interpret the outcome of testing (Figure 25.1). Armed with vocational testing information, you can greatly enhance decisions on careers or academic majors by looking into careers, interviewing professionals engaged in fields that interest you, and taking a summer job to gain firsthand experience.

Forestry Curricula

The Society of American Foresters (SAF) defines forestry as "managing and using for human benefit the forestlands and natural resources that occur on

Figure 25.1 Interactions with knowledgeable counselors can help in career choices. (Courtesy of B. Wolfgang Hoffmann, Department of Agricultural Journalism, University of Wisconsin–Madison.)

and in association with forestlands, including trees, other plants, animals, soil, water, and related air and climate" (5). Within this context the SAF prescribes the curricula upon which professional forestry is built. The general requirements specified by the SAF fall into two categories; a brief description will demonstrate the diversity and strength of a forestry education.

General education

1. **Communications.** Both oral and written communications must be covered.

2. **Science and Mathematics.** Biological and physical sciences, mathematics through calculus, statistics, and computer science are studied.

3. **Social Sciences and Humanities.** Students take courses in economics, other social sciences, the arts, and humanities.

4. **Electives.** Programs reserve space for electives to permit students to broaden their interests and knowledge.

Professional education

1. **Measurement of Forest Resources.** Topics include sampling theory and methods, photogrammetry and remote sensing, land measurement, and assessment of trees, forests, forest products, and other commodities and values of forests.

2. **Forest Biology.** Students take courses in ecology, physiology, genetics, silviculture, entomology, and pathology.

3. **Management of Forest Resources.** Topics covered are systematic approaches to problem solving and decision making, multiple-use principles incorporating management for wood, forage, water, wildlife, fish, recreation, cultural, educational and aesthetic benefits, harvesting, and wood utilization.

4. **Forest Resource Policy and Administration.** Courses on resource policy, administration, land and resource planning, budgeting, and financial and personnel management will provide students with the understanding of the so-

cial, political, legal, economic, institutional, and historical influences on forestry.

An important function of the Society of American Foresters is the study and development of standards in forestry education and accreditation of forestry schools. The SAF is recognized by the federal government as the official accrediting agency for forestry programs in the United States. A listing of forestry schools in the United States is provided in Appendix IV, with those accredited by SAF denoted by an asterisk.

Forestry is atypical among professions (1) because of the high percentage of baccalaureate-trained professionals and the small fraction of self-employed professionals, the highest percentage being employed in the public and private sectors.

Although the majority of students terminate their formal education at the bachelor's level, increasing numbers are proceeding to advanced graduate degree programs, which they enter either from a forestry undergraduate curriculum, or from any number of other undergraduate majors, including mathematics, engineering, botany, and economics or other social sciences. Students who enter from another major or who are new to forestry are eligible to pursue the first professional degree at the master's level. According to the *Occupational Outlook Handbook* (6), the increasingly complex nature of forestry has led some employers to prefer graduates with advanced degrees.

Recent information regarding enrollment and degrees granted indicates that there may be too few foresters in the very near future. In their article, "The Coming Forester Shortage" (7), Christensen and Heinrichs suggest that the demand for well-trained foresters at the entry level will increase at a rate greater than forestry schools can supply. When hiring freezes in industry and government are lifted, and when the large number of foresters who graduated just after World War II retire, opportunities should emerge at an accelerated rate.

Expectations of Employers

An opinion survey of member firms by the American Pulpwood Association recently attempted to identify the desired elements in a candidate for employment

in entry-level industrial forestry (8). The survey included seventy-three companies, which currently employ nearly 2300 foresters. Among human values, over 80 percent of the respondents listed the following as very important attributes: honesty, integrity, ability to get along with people, initiative, commitment, and a good work attitude. Among nonforestry courses deemed very important were communications (writing and speaking), accounting, and principles of supervision.

The balance between technical skills and people skills is important for a career in industrial forestry (9). An executive stated that "The normal course of study in forest management related fields should be augmented with as much math, English, and communication skills as possible." Most forestry positions in industry call for a full range of individual skills and abilities. Other factors cited as important for entrants were participation in internships, the ability to communicate, mobility, willingness to work as a member of a team, and willingness to take reasonable risks (Figure 25.2).

Seeking Employment

Applying for employment is an art, and how to do it most effectively differs by the industry. In the forest

Figure 25.2 The ability to work with others is an important component of a forestry career. (Courtesy of B. Wolfgang Hoffmann, Department of Agricultural Journalism, University of Wisconsin–Madison.)

products industry applicants should develop some knowledge of the company and should not set employment goals that are too narrow. Work experience, a vision of the potential employee's future, and direct contact with the company are desirable (9). All this requires homework. Do not expect most companies to interview on campus; they usually rely on résumés submitted by people seeking employment, and they purposely look for people from various geographic areas, from different universities, and from diverse backgrounds.

Career Opportunities

New careers in forestry continually emerge as general technology advances. Today, computer applications have become important in virtually all aspects of forestry (Figure 25.3). As an example, expert systems based on principles of artificial intelligence promise exciting methods for assessing and diagnosing forestry problems, in much the same way that these systems are used in the medical field. Remote sensing of the environment and geographic information systems are becoming invaluable tools in managing forest resources. Biotechnology and genetic engineering show potential for application to forestry, especially for improving the yield and value of forest products. It is conceivable that scientists can modify species to increase resistance to diseases and herbicides. A greater emphasis on international forestry has become apparent in recent years, and for filling these worldwide positions skills in foreign languages and knowledge of agroforestry practices are especially important. For an expanded discussion on the variety of specialties available in the profession, the interested reader is referred to *Opportunities in Forestry Careers* (10).

Students often fail to realize that a degree in forestry provides an excellent general education, one that can be viewed similarly to the liberal arts bachelor's degree programs offered at many institutions. Students undecided on an academic major should not miss the opportunity to explore forestry, either as a major emphasis or as a minor field to serve as a companion to a degree in statistics, mathematics, engineering, or environmental science. A forestry education provides a background for a broad variety of jobs in management, business, or computer science, and students pursuing forestry degrees should not constrain their job searches just to forest management positions, especially if their interests are broader.

Figure 25.3 Computer technology is utilized in most aspects of forestry. (Courtesy of B. Wolfgang Hoffmann, Department of Agricultural Journalism, University of Wisconsin–Madison.)

Sources of Employment

Public Forestry in Federal Agencies With 6000 foresters, agencies within the federal government constitute a large employment base of professional foresters; 32 percent of the active SAF foresters in the United States fall within this group. The Forest Service (U.S.D.A.) has a total permanent work force of 32,000 people. This department is the largest federal employer of foresters. In 1989 there were nearly 5200 professional foresters working in the Forest Service, with women representing 12 percent of the total. This group of professionals is entrusted with managing large and widely dispersed holdings in 156 national forests. In addition, the Forest Service works cooperatively with state and private enterprises and conducts research at eight forest and range experiment stations, at the Institute of Tropical Forestry, and at the Forest Products Laboratory. Other agencies in the U.S.D.A. that employ forestry graduates include the Soil Conservation Service, Cooperative Agricultural Extension Service, and Agricultural Research Service.

Elsewhere in the federal government, professional foresters are found in the U.S. Department of Interior (Bureaus of Land Management, Outdoor Recreation, and Indian Affairs, as well as the National Park Service and the Fish and Wildlife Service), Tennessee Valley Authority, and an assorted smaller number in the departments of Defense and Commerce, the Office of Management and Budget, and the Environmental Protection Agency. Together these agencies employ 600 to 700 foresters. A more complete description and modes of interaction of the federal agencies is given in Chapter 10, "Forestry at the National Level."

Hirings in federal agencies are made through the U.S. Office of Personnel Management.

Public Forestry in State Settings Most of the states, through their departments of natural resources (or some similar title), maintain a staff of forestry professionals to carry out state policies in managing their forest resources. There are 4400 foresters in the state natural resource departments, and they represent 25 percent of the active practicing foresters who hold membership in the SAF. In addition, the state agencies hire over 6000 seasonal or temporary employees each year. For the most part they are administered by the state forester, usually located in the capital city. Other state agencies employing foresters, though to a lesser extent, include the park services, fish and game divisions, and in some states departments of highways and taxation.

At about 8 million acres nationally, community forests represent an important component of public forests at the state level. Some were established over 100 years ago. Many are owned and managed by municipalities, but others may be operated by counties, schools, or other public institutions largely for multiple use. The school forests often serve an important role in the environmental education programs of local districts.

The increasing importance of forests and trees in the urban setting has given rise to a new emphasis on urban forestry. This emerging field requires integration of traditional forestry and arboriculture.

Forestry in Private Industry By far the largest amount of commercial forest area in the United States is privately owned. An important part of this is held by forest products companies to provide a supply of wood for production of lumber, pulp and paper, and other wood products. Whereas federal and state resource agencies primarily manage forests, industrial firms both produce timber and utilize it to manufacture products. Thus industry also offers a diverse set of opportunities for foresters. Industrial foresters may be involved in wood procurement as well as the management of forests. Private industry also promotes modern forestry practices through formal "tree farm" programs. There are 3500 professional foresters working with large forest products companies. A reasonable estimate of the total number in this category is elusive, however. Wille (10) reports that about 13,000 foresters are employed by private industry.

International Forestry One of the greatest challenges for the forestry profession is the wise use of tropical forests (1). Spurred by population growth and the pressure to gain foreign exchange, developing countries are experiencing depletion of vital forest resources. Nearly half of the world's population depends on wood for fuel; in fact, about 60 percent of the total production of the world's forests is consumed as fuel. An interesting paradox is that in the developed world 80 percent of the wood produced is used for industrial purposes, and in the developing countries 80 percent of the wood produced is used for energy. The Food and Agriculture Organization of the United Nations (FAO) regards the dependence of developing nations on dwindling supplies of fuelwood as a crisis. Over and above the pervasive fuelwood shortage, tropical forests are being whittled away by resettlement programs, development projects, clearing for agricultural purposes and ranching, and logging without attendant forest management. Tropical forests decline each year by an area equivalent to Austria and Switzerland. This rate of destruction is a major social issue of our time—so crucial that every nation has a stake in its solution.

International forestry activities are conducted along three general fronts. *Community forestry* functions in rural development, improving work opportunities and consumable goods and enhancing the environment. With the participation of local people, the community forestry approach takes into consideration the importance of forestry in land use planning and its strong relationship to watershed management, arid-zone reclamation, soil fertility, and integrating forestry and agriculture. Among the techniques available for community approaches are *multiple-product forestry,* the use of forests for wood, edibles, and other products; *small-scale forestry,* cultivating village woodlots for the production of fuelwood (Figure 25.4); *agroforestry,* combining of forest and agricultural crops; and *silvi-pastoral systems,* controlled grazing of forest vegetation. *For-*

est-based industries are being established, but they can benefit the country only if sustainable development of carefully managed forests is achieved. Required are intensified management and reforestation, development of appropriate harvesting, transportation, and marketing systems and intelligent use of residues. The *conservation of forest ecosystems* is recognized as an important emerging effort. Tropical forests help to maintain a stable global environment, provide a major genetic reservoir, and offer a source of new forest products and medicines. Wise use of these ecosystems is a high priority among international strategists.

There are numerous opportunities for contributing to the international forestry effort. The Peace Corps supports forestry projects in many parts of the developing world. Staffed primarily by volunteers, it provides excellent opportunities for professional and personal development. Nongovernmental organizations such as CARE play an important role in international forestry. The Food and Agriculture Organization collects and analyzes information on forestry, serves as a major source of technical assis-

Figure 25.4 Roadside fuelwood plantation in Tanzania. (Courtesy of B. K. Kaale, World Food Program, UN–FAO.)

tance, and helps to identify investment opportunities in the forestry sector. The U.S. Agency for International Development (USAID) promotes sustainable forest production through wise, multiple use of natural resources in Africa, Asia, Latin America, and the Caribbean. In addition to its permanent staff, USAID accomplishes forestry work by employing people for varying periods of time, for short-term consultancies as well as for long-term assignments overseas. To this end the Forestry Support Program of the Forest Service maintains a roster of over 2000 individuals competent in tropical forestry.

Research and Teaching There are about 1500 foresters involved in educational programs at the colleges and universities in the United States (12–14). A major survey (15) showed that the primary functions of faculty positions were distributed as follows: instruction, 46 percent; extension, 10 percent; and research, 44 percent. The largest representation of faculty is in forest management, followed in order by general forestry; forest biology; wood science, technology, and industry; biometry; forest hydrology; forest engineering; and urban forestry. All faculty positions require advanced graduate education and, for the most part, a doctorate. Some of these foresters serve in support staff roles, and others teach instructional programs at community colleges or technical schools.

Some of the larger forest products firms conduct substantial research and development programs, although the number of scientists employed is unknown. The Forest Service plays a major role in research activities, and to a lesser extent some of the major forested states also support research efforts.

Consulting Forestry Some professionals choose a private consulting practice. Two-thirds of the consultants operate as sole proprietors, and except for a small number of partnerships, the rest are organized as consulting firms (16). There are 2000 consulting foresters in the United States. Consultants provide advice and assistance related to forest management, marketing, and sale of forest products. Timber marking and sales, timber inventory and appraisal, timber volume estimates, timber management plans and

harvesting, damage appraisal, and investment advice constitute most of the work collectively conducted by consultants. Sometimes consulting firms deal with large-scale assessments for public agencies and industry.

Other Areas According to the roster of members of the SAF, the remaining foresters are self-employed or employed with trade associations such as the American Forestry Council, National Forest Products Association, or various state forestry associations.

References

1. D. P. THOMAS AND I. G. MORISON, "Future developmental needs of professional foresters." In *The Assessment and Development of Professionals: Theory and Practice,* P. P. LeBreton, ed., Univ. of Washington Press, Seattle, 1976.

2. J. D. WELLMAN, *J. For., 85,* 18 (1987).

3. G. D. GOTTFREDSON, J. L. HOLLAND, AND D. K. OGAWA, COMPILERS, *Dictionary of Holland Occupational Codes,* Consulting Psychologists Press, Palo Alto, Calif., 1982.

4. J. L. HOLLAND, *The Occupations Finder: For Use with the Self-Directed Search,* Psychological Assessment Resources, Odessa, Fla., 1985.

5. ANON., *Accreditation Handbook: Standards, Procedures, and Guidelines for Accrediting Educational Programs in Professional Forestry,* Publ. 86-08, Soc. Am. Foresters, Bethesda, Md., 1986.

6. ANON., *Occupational Outlook Handbook, Bull. 2300,* U.S. Department of Labor, 1988.

7. R. R. CHRISTENSEN AND J. HEINRICHS, *J. For. 83,* 413 (1985).

8. ANON., "The decision to hire: Desired elements in a candidate for industrial forestry employment. A report on an opinion survey of selected American Pulpwood Association members," Rept. 87-A-9, American Pulpwood Assoc., Washington, D.C., 1988.

9. R. S. WALLINGER, *J. For., 86,* 46 (1988).

10. C. M. WILLE, *Opportunities in Forestry Careers,* VGM Career Horizons, Div. National Textbook, Lincolnwood, Ill., 1986.

11. L. STARKE, ED., *State of the World 1988: A Worldwatch Institute Report on Progress Toward a Sustainable Society,* W. W. Norton, New York, 1988.

12. ANON., "Profiles of U.S.A. forestry schools: A report by the forestry support program," U.S.D.A. For. Serv. and Off. Int. Coop. Dev., 1987.

13. ANON, "1986–87 Directory of professional workers in state agricultural experiment stations and other cooperating state institutions," U.S.D.A. Coop. State Res. Serv., Agr. Handbook 305, 1987.

14. ANON., *Peterson's Graduate Programs in the Biological, Agricultural and Health Sciences,* Peterson's Guides, Princeton, N.J., 1989.

15. ANON., "Higher education faculty in the food and agricultural sciences: A national resource," U.S.D.A. Off. of Grants and Program Systems, Higher Education Programs, 1984.

16. D. B. FIELD, *J. For., 84,* 25 (1986).

Common and Scientific Names of Tree Species Mentioned in the Text

Common Names	Scientific Names
Acacia	*Acacia* spp.
Achin	*Pistacia mexicana*
Ailanthus or tree of heaven	*Ailanthus altissima*
Alder, common or European	*Alnus glutinosa*
red	*Alnus rubra*
Aliso	*Alnus jorullensis*
American hornbeam (see Beech)	
Ash, American mountain	*Sorbus americana*
common	*Fraxinus excelsior*
flowering	*Fraxinus ornus*
green or red	*Fraxinus pennsylvanica*
mountain	*Eucalyptus regnans*
Oregon	*Fraxinus latifolia*
white	*Fraxinus americana*
Aspen (European)	*Populus tremula*
largetooth or bigtooth	*Populus grandidentata*
quaking or trembling	*Populus tremuloides*
Baldcypress (see Cypress)	
Balsa	*Ochroma pyramidale*
Bamboo	*Cephalostachyum pergracile*
Basswood, American or American linden	*Tilia americana*
small-leaved linden	*Tilia cordata*
white	*Tilia heterophylla*
Beech, American	*Fagus grandifolia*
blue, or American hornbeam	*Carpinus caroliniana* (*Carpinus betulus virginiana*)
common or European	*Fagus sylvatica*
eastern hornbeam	*Carpinus orientalis*

Common Names	Scientific Names
European hornbeam	*Carpinus betulus*
southern	*Nothofagus* spp.
Bigcone Douglas-fir (see Fir)	
Birch, gray or field	*Betula populifolia*
river	*Betula nigra*
silver	*Betula verrucosa*
sweet or black	*Betula lenta*
white or paper	*Betula papyrifera*
yellow	*Betula alleghaniensis* (*Betula lutea*)
Blackgum (see Gum)	
Blue beech (see Beech)	
Boxelder (see Elder)	
Buckeye, Georgia	*Aesculus georgiana*
yellow	*Aesculus octandra*
Butternut	*Juglans cinerea*
Camaron	*Alvaradoa amorphoides*
Caoba	*Swietenia humilis*
Carob tree	*Ceratonia siliqua*
Castano bellota	*Sterculia mexicana*
Catalpa, northern or hardy	*Catalpa speciosa*
southern	*Catalpa bignonioides*
Cedar, Alaska yellow	*Chamaecyparis nootkatensis*
Atlantic white	*Chamaecyparis thyoides*
eastern redcedar	*Juniperus virginiana*
incense	*Libocedrus decurrens*
Japanese	*Cryptomeria japonica*
northern white, or eastern arborvitae	*Thuja occidentalis*
Port Orford	*Chamaecyparis lawsoniana*
prickly juniper	*Juniperus oxycedrus*

Common Names	Scientific Names
western juniper	*Juniperus occidentalis*
western redcedar	*Thuja plicata*
Cherry, black	*Prunus serotina*
cornelian	*Cornus mas*
pin	*Prunus pensylvanica*
Chestnut, American	*Castanea dentata*
Spanish	*Castanea sativa*
Chinatree or chinaberry	*Melia azedarach*
Chinkapin, golden	*Castanopsis chrysophylla*
Chokeberry	*Aronia* spp.
Coffeetree, Kentucky	*Gymnocladus dioicus*
Cottonwood (see Poplar)	
Crape myrtle	*Lagerstroemia indica*
Cucumbertree or	*Magnolia acuminata*
cucumber magnolia	
Cypress, bald cypress	*Taxodium distichum*
Monterey	*Cupressus macrocarpa*
Montezuma	*Taxodium mucronatum*
Dogwood, flowering	*Cornus florida*
Douglas-fir (see Fir)	
Doveplum	*Coccoloba diversifolia*
Elder, box	*Acer negundo*
Elm, American or white	*Ulmus americana*
English	*Ulmus procera*
Japanese	*Ulmus japonica*
rock or cork	*Ulmus thomasii*
Siberian	*Ulmus pumila*
winged	*Ulmus alata*
Eucalyptus	*Eucalyptus* spp.
False mastic	*Sideroxylon foetidissimum*
Filbert (see Hazel)	
Fir, alpine or subalpine	*Abies lasiocarpa*
balsam	*Abies balsamea*
bigcone Douglas-fir	*Pseudotsuga macrocarpa*
California red	*Abies magnifica*
Douglas-fir	*Pseudotsuga menziesii*
Fraser	*Abies fraseri*
grand or lowland white	*Abies grandis*
noble	*Abies procera (Abies nobilis)*
Pacific silver	*Abies amabilis*
silver	*Abies alba*
white	*Abies concolor*
Fish poison tree, Florida	*Piscidia piscipula*
Ginkgo tree	*Ginkgo biloba*
Gmelina	*Gmelina arborea*
Goldenrain tree	*Koelreuteria paniculata*

Common Names	Scientific Names
Gum, black or black tupelo	*Nyssa sylvatica*
red or sweetgum	*Liquidambar styraciflua*
swamp tupelo	*Nyssa sylvatica biflora*
tupelo or water tupelo	*Nyssa aquatica*
Gumbo-limbo	*Bursera simaruba*
Hackberry	*Celtis occidentalis*
Hazel, European or filbert	*Corylus avellana*
Hemlock, eastern	*Tsuga canadensis*
mountain	*Tsuga mertensiana*
western	*Tsuga heterophylla*
Hickory, bitternut	*Carya cordiformis*
mockernut	*Carya tomentosa*
pignut	*Carya glabra*
shagbark	*Carya ovata*
Holly, American	*Ilex opaca*
Honeylocust	*Gleditsia triacanthos*
Hoja fresca	*Gilbertia arborea*
Hophornbeam, eastern	*Ostrya virginiana*
European	*Ostrya carpinifolia*
Hornbeam (see Beech)	
Horsechestnut (Buckeye)	*Aesculus hippocastanum*
Huisache	*Acacia farnesiana*
Ironwood	*Dialium guianense*
Judas tree	*Cercis siliquastrum*
Juniper (see Cedar)	
Karri	*Eucalyptus diversicolor*
Kentucky coffeetree (see Coffeetree)	
Larch, American, eastern, or Tamarack	*Larix laricina*
European	*Larix decidua (Larix europaca)*
subalpine	*Larix lyallii*
western	*Larix occidentalis*
Laurel, bay	*Laurus nobilis*
California, Oregon-myrtle	*Umbellularia californica*
Leadwood	*Krugiodendron ferreum*
Lemonwood	*Psychotria capensis*
Lignum vitae	*Guaiacum sanctum*
Linden (see Basswood)	
Locust, black or yellow	*Robinia pseudoacacia*
Madrone, Pacific	*Arbutus menziesii*
Magnolia, cucumber (see Cucumbertree)	
southern	*Magnolia grandiflora*

Common Names	Scientific Names
Mahogany, West Indies	*Swietenia mahagoni*
Mangrove, black	*Avicennia nitida*
red	*Rhizophora mangle*
Maple, bigleaf	*Acer macrophyllum*
Norway	*Acer platanoides*
red (including trident)	*Acer rubrum*
silver	*Acer saccharinum*
sugar	*Acer saccharum*
sycamore	*Acer pseudoplatanus*
vine	*Acer circinatum*
Melina	*Gmelina arborea*
Metasequoia	*Metasequoia glyptostroboides*
Monkeypod, monkey puzzle	*Araucaria araucana*
Mulberry, red	*Morus rubra*
white	*Morus alba*
Nettle tree, European	*Celtis australis*
Oak, black	*Quercus velutina*
blackjack	*Quercus marilandica*
bur	*Quercus macrocarpa*
California black	*Quercus kelloggii*
California live	*Quercus agrifolia*
California white	*Quercus lobata*
canyon live	*Quercus chrysolepis*
cherrybark	*Quercus falcata pagodaefolia*
chestnut	*Quercus prinus*
cork	*Quercus suber*
durmast	*Quercus petraea*
English	*Quercus robur*
holm	*Quercus ilex*
Hungarian	*Quercus frainetto*
live	*Quercus virginiana*
northern red or eastern red	*Quercus rubra (Quercus borealis)*
Oregon white	*Quercus garryana*
overcup	*Quercus lyrata*
pin	*Quercus palustris*
post	*Quercus stellata*
pubescent	*Quercus pubescens*
scarlet	*Quercus coccinea*
silky	*Grevillea robusta*
southern red	*Quercus falcata*
swamp chestnut	*Quercus michauxii*
turkey (United States)	*Quercus laevis (Quercus catesbaei)*

Common Names	Scientific Names
turkey (Europe)	*Quercus cerris*
water	*Quercus nigra*
white	*Quercus alba*
willow	*Quercus phellos*
Olive	*Olea europaea*
Oriental plane	*Platanus orientalis*
Osage-orange	*Maclura pomifera*
Oyamel	*Abies religiosa*
Paulownia	*Paulownia tomentosa*
Pecan	*Carya illinoensis*
Persimmon, common	*Diospyros virginiana*
Pine, aleppo	*Pinus halepensis*
apache	*Pinus engelmannii*
bishop	*Pinus muricata*
black or Austrian	*Pinus nigra*
bristlecone	*Pinus aristata*
Caribbean	*Pinus caribaea*
Chihuahua or piño chino	*Pinus leiophylla* var. *chihuahuana*
Coulter	*Pinus coulteri*
Digger	*Pinus sabiniana*
eastern white	*Pinus strobus*
foxtail	*Pinus balfouriana*
jack	*Pinus banksiana*
Jeffrey	*Pinus jeffreyi*
Khasia	*Pinus Kesiya*
knobcone	*Pinus attenuata*
limber	*Pinus flexilis*
loblolly	*Pinus taeda*
lodgepole	*Pinus contorta*
longleaf	*Pinus palustris*
maritime	*Pinus pinaster*
Merkus	*Pinus merkusii*
Mexican weeping	*Pinus patula*
Monterey	*Pinus radiata*
Norfolk Island	*Araucaria heterophylla*
pinabete	*Pinus ayacahuite*
piño colorado	*Pinus teocote*
piño de Montezuma	*Pinus montezumae*
piño prieto	*Pinus oocarpa*
pinyon	*Pinus edulis*
pitch	*Pinus rigida*
pond	*Pinus serotina*
ponderosa or western yellow	*Pinus ponderosa*
(Rocky Mountain form)	*Pinus ponderosa* var. *scopulorum*

Common Names	Scientific Names	Common Names	Scientific Names
red or Norway	*Pinus resinosa*	Sourwood	*Oxydendron arboreum*
sand	*Pinus clausa*	Spruce, black	*Picea mariana*
Scotch or Scots	*Pinus sylvestris*	blue	*Picea pungens*
shortleaf	*Pinus echinata*	Engelmann	*Picea engelmannii*
slash	*Pinus elliotti*	Norway	*Picea abies*
southwestern white	*Pinus strobiformis*	red	*Picea rubens*
spruce	*Pinus glabra*	Sitka	*Picea sitchensis*
stone	*Pinus pinea*	white	*Picea glauca*
sugar	*Pinus lambertiana*	St. Johns bread (see Carob tree)	
Virginia or scrub	*Pinus virginiana*		
western white	*Pinus monticola*	Strangler fig, Florida	*Ficus aurea*
whitebark	*Pinus albicaulis*	Strawberry tree	*Arbutus unedo*
Poplar, California or black cottonwood	*Populus trichocarpa*	Sugarberry	*Celtis laevigata*
		Sugi (see Cedar, Japanese)	
eastern or eastern cottonwood	*Populus deltoides*	Sumac, winged	*Rhus copallina* var. *copallina*
swamp cottonwood	*Populus heterophylla*	Sweetbay, southern	*Magnolia virginiana*
yellow, or tuliptree	*Liriodendron tulipifera*	Sycamore, American	*Platanus occidentalis*
Prickly ash, lime	*Zanthoxylon fagara*	Tamarack (see Larch)	
Quebracho	*Schinopsis* spp.	Tamarind, wild	*Lysiloma bahamensis*
Redberry eugenia	*Eugenia confusa*	Tanoak	*Lithocarpus densiflorus*
Redcedar (see Cedar)		Teak	*Tectona grandis*
Redwood	*Sequoia sempervirens*	Torreya, California	*Torreya californica*
Rompezapato or saffron-plum	*Bumelia celastrina*	Tree of heaven, see Ailanthus	
Rosewood	*Dalbergia* spp.	Trumpet wood	*Cecropia mexicana*
Royal palm, Florida	*Roystonea elata*	Tupelo (see Gum)	
Sassafras	*Sassafras albidum*	Walnut, black	*Juglans nigra*
Sequoia, giant	*Sequoiadendron giganteum*	Willow, black	*Salix nigra*
		Yellow-poplar or tuliptree	*Liriodendron tulipifera*
Silk-cotton tree	*Ceiba pentandra*	Yew, common	*Taxus baccata*
Silktree	*Albizzia julibrissin*	Pacific	*Taxus brevifolia*
Soapberry, wingleaf	*Sapindus saponaria*		

APPENDIX II

Common and Scientific Names of Animal Species Mentioned in the Text

Common Names	Scientific Names
Insectivores	
Mole, eastern	*Scalopus aquaticus*
Shrew	*Sorex* spp.
Hares and Rabbits	
Hare, snowshoe	*Lepus americanus*
Cottontail, eastern	*Sylvilagus floridanus*
Rodents	
Beaver	*Castor canadensis*
Gopher, pocket	*Thomomys* spp.
Mouse, white-footed deer	*Peromyscus maniculatus*
Porcupine	*Erethizon dorsatum*
Squirrel, flying (southern)	*Galucomys volans*
Squirrel, ground	*Spermophilus* spp.
chipmunk least (western)	*Eutamias minimus*
Squirrel, tree	
gray, eastern	*Sciurus carolinensis*
pine or chickaree	*Tamiasciurus douglasi*
red	*Tamiasciurus hudsonicus*
Voles	*Microtus* spp.
Carnivores	
Bear, black	*Ursus americanus*
grizzly	*Ursus horribilis*
Coyote	*Canis latrans*
Fisher	*Martes pennanti*
Fox, gray	*Vulpes fulva*
red	*Urocyon cinereoargenteus*
Lynx	*Lynx canadensis*
Mink	*Mustela vison*
Mountain lion	*Felis concolor*
Otter	*Lutra canadensis*
Raccoon	*Procyon lotor*
Wolf, gray or timber	*Canis lupus*
Wolverine	*Gulo luscus*

Common Names	Scientific Names
Even-Toed Ungulates	
Caribou, woodland	*Rangifer* spp.
Deer, mule	*Odocoileus hemionus*
white-tailed	*Odocoileus virginianus*
Elk (wapiti)	*Cervus canadensis*
Moose	*Alces alces*
Birds	
Bluebird, eastern	*Sialia sialis*
Catbird	*Dumetella carolinensis*
Chickadee, black-capped	*Parus atricapillus*
Cranes	*Grus* spp.
Creeper, brown tree	*Certhia familiaris*
Crossbill	*Loxia* spp.
Dove, mourning	*Zenaida macroura*
Duck, American golden-eye	*Glaucionetta clangula*
Barrow's golden-eye	*Bucephala islandica*
black	*Anas rubripes*
buffle-head	*Bucephala albeola*
hooded merganser	*Lophodytes cucullatus*
mallard, common	*Anas platyrhynchos*
wood	*Aix sponsa*
Eagle, bald	*Haliaeetus leucocephalus*
Falcon, peregrine	*Falco peregrinus*
Finch	*Carpodacus* spp.
Flycatcher, least	*Empidonax minimus*
Grosbeak, evening	*Coccothraustes vespertinus*
Goose, Canada	*Branta canadensis*
Grouse, blue	*Dendragapus obscurus*
prairie chicken or pinnated	*Tympamuchus cupido*
ruffed	*Bonasa umbellus*
sharp-tailed	*Pedioecetes phasianellus*
spruce	*Dendragapus canadensis*

Common Names	Scientific Names
Hawk, broad-winged	*Buteo platypterus*
goshawk	*Accipiter gentilis*
red-shouldered	*Buteo lineatus*
Heron	*Ardea* spp.
Jay, pinyon	*Gymnorhinus cyanocephalus*
Kestrel	*Falco sparverius*
Kingbird	*Tyrannus* spp.
Magpie	*Pica pica*
Martin, purple	*Progne subis*
Merganser, hooded	*Lophodytes cucullatus*
Nuthatch, white-breasted	*Sitta carolinensis*
Oriole, Baltimore	*Icterus galbula*
Osprey	*Pandion haliaetus*
Ovenbird	*Seiurus aurocopillus*
Owl, barred	*Strix varia*
horned	*Bubo virginianus*
saw-whet	*Aegolius acadicus*
Quail, bobwhite	*Colinus virginianus*
Raven	*Corvus corax*
Redpoll	*Carduelis* spp.
Siskin	*Carduelis pinus*
Swallow, tree	*Iridoprocne bicolor*
Swift, chimney	*Chaetura pelagica*
Thrush	*Hylocichla* spp.
Turkey, eastern	*Meleagris gallopavo silvestrii*
Vireo, red-eyed	*Vireo olivaceus*
Warbler, black-and-white	*Mniotilta varia*
blackburnian	*Dendroica fusca*
Kirtland's	*Dendroica kirtlandii*
Waxwing	*Bombycilla* spp.
Woodcock	*Philohela minor*
Woodpecker, downy	*Dendrocopus pubescens*
flicker	*Colaptes auratus*
hairy	*Dendrocopus villosus*
ivory-billed	*Campephilus principalis*
pileated	*Dryocopus pileatus*
red-cockaded	*Dendrocopus borealis*
yellow-bellied sapsucker	*Sphyrapicus varius*
Wren	*Thyrothorus* spp.

Insects

Common Names	Scientific Names
Aphid, balsam woolly	*Adelges piceae*
Beetle, Douglas-fir	*Dendroctonus pseudotsugae*

Common Names	Scientific Names
Japanese	*Popillia japonica*
mountain pine	*Dendroctonus ponderosae*
native elm bark	*Hylurgopinus rufipes*
smaller European elm bark	*Scolytus multistriatus*
southern pine	*Dendroctonus frontalis*
western pine	*Dendroctonus brevicomis*
Borer, bronze birch	*Agrilus anxius*
hemlock	*Melanophila fulvoguttata*
poplar	*Saperda calcarata*
two-lined chestnut	*Agrilus bilineatus*
Budworm, jack pine	*Choristoneura pinus*
spruce	*Choristoneura fumiferana*
Casebearer, larch	*Coleophora laricella*
Engraver, fir	*Scolytus ventralis*
pine	*Ips pini*
Looper, hemlock	*Lambdina fiscellaria*
linden	*Erannis tiliaria*
Moth, gypsy	*Lymantria dispar*
shoot, European pine	*Rhyacionia buoliana*
Douglas-fir tussock	*Orgyia pseudotsugata*
pine tussock	*Dasychira plagiata*
white-marked tussock	*Hemerocampa leucostigma*
Pitch nodule maker	*Petrova albicapitana*
Sawfly, European pine	*Neodiprion sertifer*
European spruce	*Diprion hercyniae*
jack pine	*Neodiprion pratti banksianae*
larch	*Pristiphora erichsonii*
red-headed pine	*Neodiprion lecontei*
red pine	*Neodiprion nanulus nanulus*
Swaine jack pine	*Neodiprion swainei*
Sawyer, southern pine	*Monochamus titillator*
white spotted	*Monochamus scutellatus*
Scale, pine tortoise	*Toumeyella numismatica*
Spanworm, elm	*Ennomos subsignarius*
Spittlebug, pine	*Aphrophora parallela*
Saratoga	*Aphrophora saratogensis*
Tent caterpillar, eastern	*Malacosoma americanum*
forest	*Malacosoma disstria*
Walkingstick	*Diapheromera femorata*
Wasp, wood	*Sirex* spp.
Weevil, pales	*Hylobius pales*
pine root collar	*Hylobius radicis*
white pine	*Pissodes strobi*

APPENDIX III

Unit Conversion Tables

Linear Measure

	cm	m	km	ft	mile	chain	link
1 centimeter	1	0.01	10^{-5}	0.0328	6.214×10^{-6}	4.971×10^{-4}	0.04971
1 meter	100	1	0.001	3.2808	6.214×10^{-4}	0.04971	4.971
1 kilometer	10^5	1000	1	3,280.84	0.6214	49.7097	4970.97
1 foot	30.4801	0.3048	3.048×10^{-4}	1	1.8939×10^{-4}	0.01515	1.5152
1 mile	160934.4	1609.344	1.6093	5,280	1	80	8000
1 chain	2011.68	20.1168	0.02012	66	0.0125	1	100
1 link	20.1168	0.2012	2.0117×10^{-4}	0.66	1.25×10^{-4}	0.01	1

Mass Measure

	kg	m ton	pound	short ton
1 kilogram	1	0.001	2.2046	1.1023×10^{-3}
1 metric ton	1000	1	2204.6226	1.1023
1 pound	0.4536	4.5359×10^{-4}	1	0.0005
1 short ton	907.185	0.9072	2000	1

Area Measure

	m^2	ha	ft^2	$chain^2$	acre	$mile^2$ (section)
1 hectare	10,000	1	107,639.1	24.7105	2.4711	0.0039
1 square meter	1	1×10^{-4}	10.7639	2.4711×10^{-3}	2.4711×10^{-4}	3.8610×10^{-7}
1 acre	4,046.86	0.4047	43560	10	1	1.5625×10^{-3}
1 square mile	2.5910×10^6	258.999	27,878,400	6,400	640	1
1 township	—	9,323.9892	—	—	23,040	36
1 section	2,589,988	258.9997	27,878,400	6,400	640	1
¼ section	647,497	64.7499	6,969,600	1,600	160	0.25
¼–¼ section	161,874	16.1875	1,742,400	400	40	0.0625

Volume Measure

	cm^3 (ml)	m^3	$in.^3$	ft^3	L	qt
1 cubic centimeter	1	1×10^{-6}	6.1024×10^{-2}	3.5315×10^{-5}	0.001	1.0567×10^{-3}
1 cubic meter	10^6	1	6.1024×10^4	35.3147	1,000	1,056.688
1 cubic inch	16.3871	1.6387×10^{-5}	1	5.7870×10^{-4}	1.6387×10^{-2}	1.7316×10^{-2}
1 cubic foot	28,316.85	2.8317×10^{-2}	1,728	1	28.3169	29.9221
1 milliliter	1	1×10^{-6}	6.1024×10^{-2}	3.5315×10^{-5}	0.001	1.0567×10^{-3}
1 liter	1,000	0.001	61.0237	3.5315×10^{-2}	1	1.0567
1 quart	946.3529	9.4635×10^{-4}	57.75	3.3420×10^{-2}	0.9464	1

Forestry Schools in the United States

The following list was prepared from a booklet published by the U.S.D.A. Forest Service (FS-9). Schools currently accredited by the Society of American Foresters are noted by an asterisk.

*School of Forestry
Auburn University
Auburn, Alabama

*School of Forestry
Northern Arizona University
Flagstaff, Arizona

*Department of Forest Resources
University of Arkansas
Monticello, Arkansas

Natural Resources Management
Department
California Polytechnic State
University
San Luis Obispo, California

*Department of Forestry
Humboldt University
Arcata, California

*Department of Forestry and
Resource Management
University of California
Berkeley, California

*College of Forestry and Natural
Resources
Colorado State University
Fort Collins, Colorado

*School of Forestry and
Environmental Studies

Yale University
New Haven, Connecticut

*School of Forest Resources and
Conservation
University of Florida
Gainesville, Florida

*School of Forest Resources
University of Georgia
Athens, Georgia

*College of Forestry, Wildlife, and
Range Sciences
University of Idaho
Moscow, Idaho

*Department of Forestry
Southern Illinois University
Carbondale, Illinois

*Department of Forestry
University of Illinois
Urbana, Illinois

*Department of Forestry and
Natural Resources
Purdue University
West Lafayette, Indiana

*Department of Forestry
Iowa State University
Ames, Iowa

*Department of Forestry
University of Kentucky
Lexington, Kentucky

*School of Forestry
Louisiana State University
Baton Rouge, Louisiana

*School of Forestry
Louisiana Tech University
Ruston, Louisiana

Department of Agriculture
McNeese State University
Lake Charles, Louisiana

*College of Forest Resources
University of Maine
Orono, Maine

*Department of Forestry and
Wildlife Management
University of Massachusetts
Amherst, Massachusetts

*Department of Forestry
Michigan State University
East Lansing, Michigan

* School of Forestry and Wood
Products
Michigan Technological University
Houghton, Michigan

*School of Natural Resources
University of Michigan
Ann Arbor, Michigan

*College of Natural Resources
University of Minnesota
St. Paul, Minnesota

*School of Forest Resources
Mississippi State University
Mississippi State, Mississippi

*School of Forestry, Fisheries, and
Wildlife
University of Missouri
Columbia, Missouri

*School of Forestry
University of Montana
Missoula, Montana

*Department of Forest Resources
University of New Hampshire
Durham, New Hampshire

Forestry Section
Cook College
Rutgers State University
New Brunswick, New Jersey

*College of Environmental Science
and Forestry
State University of New York
Syracuse, New York

Division of Renewable Natural
Resources
University of Nevada
Reno, Nevada

*School of Forestry and
Environmental Studies
Duke University
Durham, North Carolina

*School of Forest Resources
North Carolina State University
Raleigh, North Carolina

*School of Natural Resources
Ohio State University
Columbus, Ohio

*Department of Forestry
Oklahoma State University
Stillwater, Oklahoma

*College of Forestry
Oregon State University
Corvallis, Oregon

*School of Forest Resources
Pennsylvania State University
University Park, Pennsylvania

*College of Forest and Recreation
Resources
Clemson University
Clemson, South Carolina

*Department of Forestry, Wildlife,
and Fisheries
University of Tennessee
Knoxville, Tennessee

*School of Forestry
Stephen F. Austin State University
Nacogdoches, Texas

*Department of Forest Science
Texas A & M University
College Station, Texas

*College of Natural Resources
Utah State University
Logan, Utah

*School of Natural Resources
University of Vermont
Burlington, Vermont

*School of Forestry and Wildlife
Resources
Virginia Polytechnic Institute and
State University
Blacksburg, Virginia

*College of Forest Resources
University of Washington
Seattle, Washington

*Department of Forestry and Range
Management
Washington State University
Pullman, Washington

*Division of Forestry
West Virginia University
Morgantown, West Virginia

*Department of Forestry
University of Wisconsin-Madison
Madison, Wisconsin

*College of Natural Resources
University of Wisconsin-Stevens
Point
Stevens Point, Wisconsin

APPENDIX V

Glossary

A

Abiotic factors. Nonliving elements (factors) of the environment—that is, soil, climate, physiography.

Abscission. Dropping leaves, flowers, fruits, or other plant parts following the formation of a separation zone at the base of the plant part.

Absorbance. A measure of the ability of a surface to absorb incident energy, often at specific wavelengths.

Absorbed light. Light rays which are neither reflected nor transmitted when directed toward opaque or transparent materials.

Absorption. A process of attenuation through which radiant energy is intercepted and converted into other forms of energy as it passes through the atmosphere or other media.

Absorption band. A range of wavelengths over which radiant energy is intercepted by a specific material that may be present on the earth's surface or in the atmosphere.

Adaptation. Genetically determined character or feature of an organism that serves to increase reproductive potential or chance of survival.

Adsorption. Adhesion of the molecules of a gas, liquid, or dissolved substance to a surface, particularly of water molecules to the internal surface within the porous walls of wood and bark cells.

Advance regeneration. Young trees which have become established naturally before a clearcut is made.

Adventitious. Plant part which develops outside of the usual position or time or both.

Aerial film. A specially designed roll film supplied in many lengths and widths to fit aerial cameras. See *Color, Color infrared, Infrared,* and *Panchromatic.*

Aerial photograph, oblique. An aerial photograph taken with the camera axis directed between the horizontal and the vertical.

Aerial photograph, vertical. An aerial photograph made with the optical axis of the camera approximately perpendicular to the earth's surface and with the film as nearly horizontal as is practical.

Aerial photographs, composite. Aerial photographs made with a camera having one principal lens and two or more surrounding and oblique lenses symmetrically placed; the several resulting photographs may be rectified in printing to permit assembly as verticals with the same scale.

Agrisilviculture. System of cultivation combining agriculture and forestry whereby tree plantations are interplanted with agricultural crops (the crops can yield a fast return while trees slowly mature).

Air-dry. Of timber or wood dried to equilibrium with the surrounding atmosphere.

Albuminous cells. Certain ray and axial parenchyma cells in gymnosperm phloem; associated with sieve cells.

Alkaloid. Nitrogen-containing toxins produced by plants that serve as defense compounds.

Allelopathy. Suppression of germination, growth, or the limiting of the occurrence of plants when chemical inhibitors are released by some plants.

Allogenic succession. Ecological succession resulting from factors (such as prolonged drought) that arise external to a natural community and alter its habitat (i.e., changes the vegetation).

Amorphous. Formless.

Analog. A form of data display in which values are shown in graphic form, such as curves. Also, a form of computing in which values are represented by directly measurable quantities, such as voltages or resistances. Analog computing methods contrast with digital methods in which values are treated numerically.

Angiosperm. Vascular flowering plants that produce seeds enclosed in an ovary. Include monocotyledons (grasses and palms) and dicotyledons (herbaceous and woody plants).

Angle of incidence. The angle which a straight line, ray of light, and the like, meeting a surface makes with a normal to the surface at the point of meeting.

Anisotropic. Of a material whose properties vary according to the direction of measurement. The anisotropy of wood corresponds to the main features of wood structure and the marked anisotropy of the cellulose long-chain molecules.

Annual ring. One growth layer as seen in cross section of a woody plant stem. Formed by contrast of springwood and summerwood.

Apical dominance. Influence exerted by a terminal bud in suppressing the growth of the lateral buds.

Apical meristem. Growing point at the tip of the root or stem. Gives rise to primary tissues.

Autecology. Study of the relationship between an individual organism and its environment.

Autogenic. Involving or resulting from a reaction between or in living organisms.

Auxin. A plant growth-regulating substance. Among other effects, it controls cell elongation.

Avifauna. Bird life of a given region.

Axil. Angle between the upper side of a leaf or twig and the supporting stem.

Axis. Longitudinal support on which organs or parts are arranged; the stem and root; the central line of the body. *Axial,* adjective.

Azimuth. The geographic orientation of a line given as an angle measured clockwise from north.

B

Backfire. Fire set along the inner edge of a fire line to consume the fuel in the path of a forest fire, to change the direction of the fire, or both.

Bark. All tissue outside the cambium.

Basal area. Area of the cross section of a tree stem, generally at breast height (1.3 meters or 4.5 feet) and inclusive of bark.

Bast fiber. Any of several strong, ligneous fibers obtained from phloem tissue and used in the manufacture of woven goods and cordage.

Bedrock. Bottom layer, lowest stratum; unbroken solid rock, overlaid in most places by soil or rock fragments.

Bilateral aid. Aid based on a formal agreement between a single donor country and the recipient; in contrast to multilateral aid, which originates from several countries, usually through an international agency.

Biltmore stick. A graduated stick used to estimate tree diameters.

Binder. Extraneous bonding agent, organic or inorganic, used to bind particles together—for example, to produce particleboard.

Biological control. Regulation of pest species through the use of other organisms.

Biomass. Quantity of biological matter of one or more species present on a unit area.

Biosphere. Part of the earth's crust, water, and atmosphere where living organisms can subsist.

Biotic factors. Relation of living organisms to one another from an ecological view (as opposed to abiotic or nonliving elements).

Black liquor. Liquor resulting from the manufacture of pulp by alkaline processes and containing, in a modified form, the greater part of the extracted lignin and sugar degradation products.

Blowup fire. Sudden increase in intensity and rate of flame spread, often accompanied by a violent convection column of smoke and hot gases.

Board foot. Unit of measurement represented by a board 1 foot long, 1 foot wide, and 1 inch thick (144 cubic inches), measured before surfacing or other finishing. Abbreviations: b.f., bd ft, ft.b.m.

Bole. Tree stem of merchantable thickness.

Bolt. Any short log, as a pulpwood or veneer bolt.

Boreal. Of or pertaining to the north.

Brightness. Blue reflectance of a sheet of paper, a measure of the maximum whiteness that can be achieved with proper tinting.

Browse. Leaves, small twigs, and shoots of shrubs, seedling and sapling trees, and vines available for forage for livestock and wildlife.

Buck. To cut a tree into proper lengths after it has been felled.

Bud primordium. Embryonic shoot formed in the axil of a leaf.

C

Calender. Machine in which cloth, paper, or the like is smoothed, glazed, or otherwise manipulated by pressing between revolving cylinders.

Caliper. An instrument for directly measuring tree diameters.

Canopy. More-or-less continuous cover of branches and leaves formed collectively by the crowns of adjacent trees or shrubs. See *Understory*.

Capillary water. Water which fills the smaller pores less than 0.05 millimeter in diameter and which by adhesion to the soil particles can resist the force of gravity and remain suspended in the soil. This water constitutes the major source of water for tree growth, except in soils having a high water table.

Carbonization. Decomposition by heat of organic substances in a limited supply of air accompanied by the formation of carbon. See *Destructive distillation*.

Carnivore. Organism that consumes mostly flesh.

Carrying capacity. Number of organisms of a given species and quality that can survive in a given ecosystem without causing its deterioration.

Cation. Positively charged atom or group of atoms. Cation exchange capacity is the total capacity of soil colloids for holding cations.

Chain. A unit of linear measurement equal to 66 feet.

Chaining. Using a surveyor's chain or tape for linear measurements along the ground.

Charge-coupled device (CCD). A solid-state sensor which detects light; a microelectronic silicon chip.

Chipper. Machine for cutting logs or pieces of logs into chips.

Chlorophyll. The green pigment of plant cells, necessary for photosynthesis.

Chloroplasts. A plastid in algal and green plant cells in which chlorophylls are contained; site of photosynthesis.

Chlorosis. Abnormal yellowing of foliage, often a symptom of mineral deficiency, infection, root or stem girdling, or extremely reduced light.

Chromosome. Body in the cell nucleus containing genes in a linear order.

Clearcutting. Silvicultural system in which the entire timber stand is cut. See *Seed-tree method, Shelterwood method*.

Climatic release. Relaxation of environmental resistance factors and the recurrence of favorable weather for several successive years. Together, these conditions allow a pest species to approach its reproductive potential.

Climax community. Community which has achieved the maximum possible development. The end point of a sere.

Clinal variation. Variation occurring in a continuous fashion along a geographic or environmental gradient.

Clone. All the plants produced by asexual means (e.g., grafting, layering, budding) from a common ancestor and having identical genetic constitutions.

Collenchyma. Supporting tissue containing elongated living cells with irregularly thickened primary cell walls; often found in regions of primary growth in stems and leaves.

Color. The property of an object that is dependent on the wavelength of the light it reflects or, in the case of a luminescent body, the wavelength of light that it emits.

Color-composite image. A color image prepared by projecting individual black-and-white multispectral images in color.

Color infrared film. A color film consisting of three layers in which the red-imaging layer responds to photographic infrared radiation ranging in wavelength from 0.7 to 0.9 micrometer. The green-imaging layer responds to red light and the blue-imaging layer responds to green light.

Combustion. Consumption by oxidation, evolving heat, and generally also flame and incandescence.

Community. Unit of vegetation that is homogeneous with respect to species composition and structure and occupies a unit area of ground.

Companion cell. Specialized parenchyma cell in angiosperm phloem; associated with sieve tube members.

Conifer. Division of gymnosperm; plant producing naked seeds in cones, mostly evergreen, with timber known commercially as softwood.

Coppice system. Silvicultural system in which crops regenerate vegetatively by stump sprouts and the rotation is comparatively short.

Cord. Volume measure of stacked wood. A standard cord is $4 \times 4 \times 8$ feet and contains 128 cubic feet of space. Actual wood volume varies between 70 and 90 cubic feet per cord. A face cord is a short cord in which the length of the pieces is shorter than 8 feet (Figure 12.2).

Cordillera. Entire chain of mountain ranges parallel to the Pacific Coast, extending from Cape Horn to Alaska.

Cork cambium. Lateral meristem that produces cork toward the outside of the plant and phelloderm to the inside.

Cortex. Ground tissue of the shoot or root that is located between the epidermis and the vascular system; a primary-tissue region.

Cotyledon. Embryonic leaf, characteristic of seed plants; generally stores food in dicotyledons and absorbs food in monocotyledons.

Crown fire. Fire which burns the tops of trees and brush.

Cruise (timber). Survey of forestlands to locate and estimate volumes and grades of standing timber.

Cutting cycle. Period of time between major cuts in an uneven-aged stand. See *Rotation age*.

Cytoplasm. Term commonly used to refer to the protoplasm of the cell exclusive of the nucleus.

D

dbh (diameter at breast height). Tree diameter at breast height, 1.3 meters (4.5 feet) above the ground as measured from the uphill side of the tree.

Deciduous. Perennial plants which are normally leafless for some time during the year.

Decurrent. Having a leaf base elongated down the stem. See *Excurrent*.

Deferred-rotation grazing. A system of range management whereby grazing is delayed on a portion of the land until after the most important range plants have gone to seed. Then grazing is deferred on adjacent portions in rotation over a period of years so that all pastures receive the benefit of deferment.

Defoliation. Loss of a plant's leaves or needles.

Deleterious. Harmful, injurious, or destructive.

Dendrology. Branch of botany dealing with classification, nomenclature, and identification of trees and shrubs.

Dendrometer. Instrument for measuring the dimensions of trees or logs.

Denitrification. Process by which nitrogen is released from the soil (as a gas) to the atmosphere by denitrifying bacteria.

Density. Proportion of cell wall volume to total volume of wood. The number of individuals (trees, animals) per unit area at a given time.

Derived demand. Demand for a good coming from its use in the production of some other good; for example, timber is demanded not by consumers but by firms that manufacture wood products.

Desertification. Exhaustion of the soil, often because of removal of vegetative cover in semiarid regions, leading irreversibly to an unproductive desert.

Dessicated. Dehydrated

Destructive distillation. Decomposition of wood by heating out of contact with air, producing primarily charcoal, tarry distillates, and pyroligneous acid.

Diameter tape. A tape measure specially calibrated to convert circumference of the tree to its corresponding diameter, assuming the cross section of the tree to be a perfect circle.

Diapause. State of arrested physiological development of an insect.

Dicotyledons. One of two classes of angiosperms; a plant whose embryo has two seed leaves.

Differentiation. A process by which a relatively unspecialized cell undergoes a progressive change to a more specialized cell; the specialization of cells and tissues for particular functions during development.

Diffuse-porous wood. Wood (xylem) of hardwoods in which the vessels are small in diameter; vessels in springwood do not have much greater diameters than those in summerwood. See *Ring-porous wood*.

Digital computer. A computer which operates on the principle of counting as opposed to measuring. See *Analog*.

Digital elevation model. Model resulting from the matrix of elevation data obtained by systematically scanning a stereomodel.

Digital image. An image having numeric values representing gray tones; each numeric value represents a different gray tone.

Digital image processing. Computer manipulation of the digital values for picture elements of an image.

Digitize. Using numeric values to represent data.

Dioecious. A condition in which staminate and pistillate flowers (or pollen and seed cones of conifers) are borne on different individuals of the same species. See *Monoecious*.

Dominant. Pertaining to trees that project somewhat above the general level of the canopy, having crowns that receive direct sunlight from above and partly from the side. See *Suppressed*.

Dormancy. A special condition of arrested growth in which the plant and such plant parts as buds and seeds do not begin to grow without special environmental cues.

Duff. Organic matter in various stages of decomposition on the forest floor.

E

Ecology. Science which deals with the relation of plants and animals to their environment and to the site factors that operate in controlling their distribution and growth.

Ecosystem. Any complex of living organisms with their environment considered as a unit for purposes of study.

Ecotone. Transition zone between two adjoining communities.

Edaphic. Pertaining to soil conditions that influence plant growth.

Edge. Boundary between two or more elements of the environment, for example, field–woodland.

Elasticity. Relationship, expressed mathematically, between a percentage change in one variable and the resulting percentage change in another variable, when all other things are held constant. The price elasticity of demand (supply) is the percentage change in quantity demanded (supplied) when price changes by 1 percent, with all other variables such as income and population held constant.

Electromagnetic energy. Energy propagated through space or through material media in the form of an advancing interaction between electric and magnetic fields; also more simply termed, radiation.

Electromagnetic spectrum. The ordered array of known electromagnetic radiations, extending from the shortest cosmic rays, through gamma rays, X rays, ultraviolet radiation, visible radiation, infrared radiation, and including microwave and all other wavelengths of radio energy.

Emulsion. A suspension of photosensitive silver halide grains in gelatin that constitutes the image-forming layer on photographic materials.

Endemic population. Natural low population level of most species native to an area.

Energy exchange. Flow of energy through the ecosystem beginning with the capture of radiant solar energy by photosynthesis and ending when the energy is lost back to the environment as heat through metabolism.

Entomology. Study of insects.

Entomophagous. Feeding on insects.

Environmental resistance. Physical and biological factors which inhibit the reproductive potential of a species.

Ephemeral. Short-lived; completing the life cycle within a brief period.

Epicormic growth. Growth of lateral buds after the apical bud is damaged.

Epidermis. Outermost layer(s) of cells on the primary plant body.

Ericaceous. Belonging to the heath family of plants, including the heath, arbutus, azalea, rhododendron, and American laurel.

Ethanol. Ethyl alcohol, C_2H_5OH; a colorless, volatile liquid manufactured from starchy or sugary materials by fermentation; also synthetically produced.

Eutrophication. Aquatic succession characterized by gradual nutrient enrichment and subsequent depletion of dissolved oxygen.

Evapotranspiration. Combined loss of water through evaporation and transpiration, from the soil and vegetal cover on an area of land surface.

Even-aged stand. Stand in which relatively small age differences exist between individual trees, usually a maximum of 10 to 20 years.

Excurrent. Tree with the axis prolonged to form an undivided stem or trunk (as in spruces and other conifers).

Exotic. Not native; foreign; introduced from other climates or countries.

Extractive. In wood, any part which is not an integral part of the cellular structure and can be dissolved out with solvents.

F

False color. See *Color infrared.*

Fecal coliform. Colon bacilli, or forms which resemble or are related to them.

Fermentation. Change brought about by an agent such as yeast enzymes, which convert sugars to ethyl alcohol.

Fiber. Narrow cell of wood (xylem) or bast (phloem), other than vessel elements and parenchyma; includes tracheids. Or a cell material with a length-to-diameter (l/d) ratio greater than 20:1.

Fiberizing. Separation of wood and other plant material into fibers or fiber bundles by mechanical (sometimes assisted by chemical) means.

Field moisture capacity. The greatest amount of water it is possible for a soil to hold in its pore spaces after excess water has drained away.

Filter, optical. A material which, by absorption or reflection, selectively modifies the radiation transmitted through an optical system.

Fines. Pulp fractions having very short or fragmented fibers.

Fire line. Strip of plowed or cleared land made to check the spread of a fire.

Food chain, food web. Chain of organisms existing in any natural community such that each link in the chain feeds in the one below and is eaten by the one above; at the base are autotrophic (green) plants, eaten by heterotrophic organisms including plants (fungi), plant-eating animals (herbivores), plant and animal eaters (omnivores), and animal eaters (carnivores).

Forb. Any herbaceous plant which is not a grass or grasslike—such plants as geranium, buttercup, or sunflower.

Forest yield. The volume of timber in a forest at a specific point in time.

Forties. Term applied to 40-acre parcels of land, equal to one-sixteenth of a township in the standard rectangular survey system.

Fourdrinier. Name associated with the wire-forming section or the entire papermaking machine. Originally developed by the Fourdrinier brothers in England (1804).

Fruit. In angiosperms, a matured, ripened ovary containing the seeds.

Furfural. Oily liquid aldehyde, $C_5H_4O_2$, with an aromatic odor, obtained by distilling wood, corncobs, bran, sugar, and other ingredients with dilute sulfuric acid.

Fusiform initials. The vertically elongated cells in the vascular cambium that give rise to the cells of the axial system in the secondary xylem and secondary phloem.

G

Gall. Pronounced, localized, tumorlike swelling of greatly modified structure; occurs on plants from irritation by a foreign organism.

Gamete. Male pollen cell or a female egg cell, typically the result of meiosis, capable of uniting in the process of fertilization with a reproductive cell of the opposite sex.

Gasification. Conversion of a solid or liquid substance to a gas.

Gene. Unit of heredity; portion of the DNA of a chromosome.

Gene flow. Migration of genes from one population to another via the dispersal of individuals, or of propagules such as seed or pollen.

Gene pool. Sum total of genetic information distributed among the members of an interbreeding population.

Genetic drift. Change in gene frequency in small breeding populations because of chance, in contrast to a similar change under selection.

Genotype. Total amount of genetic information that an individual possesses. See *Phenotype*.

Geographic information system. An information system which can input, manipulate, and analyze geographically referenced data to support the decision-making processes of an organization.

Girdle. To destroy tissue, especially the bark and cambium, in a rough ring around a stem, branch, or root. Girdling often kills the tree.

Globose. Pertaining to a tree having the shape of a globe or globule; approximately spherical.

Grade. Established quality or use classification of trees, timber, and wood products; to classify according to grade.

Gross national product (GNP). Total value at current market prices of all final goods and services produced by a nation's economy, before deduction of depreciation and other allowances for consumption of durable capital goods.

Ground fire. Fire which not only consumes all the organic materials of the forest floor, but also burns into the underlying soil itself—for example, a peat fire. See *Surface fire*.

Ground tissue. Tissues other than the epidermis or periderm and vascular tissue; conjunctive parenchyma, fundamental tissue.

Growth impact. Pervasive, ongoing destruction of forests because of growth loss and mortality. See *Growth loss, Mortality*.

Growth loss. Difference between potential and actual tree growth, caused by destructive agents such as insects, diseases, or weather. See *Growth impact, Mortality*.

Gymnosperm. Vascular plants which produce seeds not enclosed in an ovary.

H

Habitat. Immediate environment occupied by an organism. In forestry, habitat usually refers to animal habitat.

Habitat type. Unit of land capable of supporting a single climax community type.

Hardpan. Indurated (hardened) or cemented soil horizon. The soil may have any texture and is compacted or cemented by iron oxide, organic matter, silica, calcium carbonate, or other substances.

Headbox. Final holding container of pulp slurries for regulation of flow onto the moving papermaking-machine wire.

Head fire. Fire spreading, or set to spread, with the wind.

Heartrot. Decay in the central core of a tree usually caused by fungus.

Heartwood. Inner core of a woody stem, wholly composed of nonliving cells and usually differentiated from the outer enveloping layer (sapwood) by its darker color. See *Sapwood*.

Height poles. Sectioned, telescoping poles used to measure the height of trees.

Hemicellulose. Any of the noncellulosic polysaccharides of the intercellular layer and of the cell wall that can be extracted with aqueous alkaline solutions and are readily hydrolyzable by acids to give sugars.

Hemocoel. General insect body cavity in which blood flows.

Herb. Any seed-producing plant which does not develop persistent woody tissue above ground. Includes both forbs and grasses. May be perennial. *Herbaceous,* adjective.

Herbivore. Organism which consumes living plants or their parts.

Heritability. Proportion of any observed variability that is due to genetic effects, the remainder being attributed to environment.

High grading. Type of exploitation cutting that removes only trees of a certain species, or of high value.

Hogged wood. Wood reduced to coarse chips—for example, for fuel or manufacture of wood pulp or chipboard.

Horizon, soil. Layer of soil roughly parallel to the land surface, distinguished from adjacent layers by different physical, chemical, or biological characteristics.

Hue. The attribute of a color that differentiates it from gray of the same brilliance and that allows it to be classed as blue, green, red, or intermediate shades of these colors.

Humus. Decomposed lower part of the soil organic layer, generally amorphous, colloidal, and dark-colored.

Hydrarch succession. Primary succession beginning on a substrate of water, usually a pond or lake.

Hydration. Chemical combination of water with cellulose or hemicelluloses (usually in fibers) to give a swollen structure; endowing fibers with an increased capacity for water retention through mechanical beating.

Hydrolysis. Conversion, by reaction with water, of a complex substance into two or more smaller molecules.

Hypha. A single tubular filament of fungus; the hyphae together constitute the mycelium.

Hypsometer. Device for measuring tree height.

I

Improvement cutting. Silvicultural treatment in which diseased or poorly formed trees or trees of undesirable species are removed.

Inbreeding depression. Loss of vigor that frequently results from mating closely related individuals.

Incident energy. Electromagnetic radiation impinging on a surface.

Increment. Increase in girth, diameter, basal area, height, volume, quality, or value of individual trees or crops.

Increment borer. Augerlike instrument with a hollow bit, used to extract cores from trees for the determination of growth and age.

Infection court. Site of infection by a pathogen.

Infiltration. The amount of water that penetrates the soil, governed by the texture of the soil, vegetation cover, and the slope of the ground.

Infrared. Energy in the 0.7- to 15-micrometer wavelength region of the electromagnetic spectrum; for remote sensing the infrared wavelengths are often subdivided into near-infrared (0.7 to 1.3 micrometers), middle-infrared (1.3 to 3.0 micrometers), and far-infrared (7.0 to 15.0 micrometers); far-infrared is sometimes referred to as thermal or emissive infrared.

Ingrowth. The increase in timber volume of a given stand owing to new trees that were not measured in previous surveys. See *Survivor growth*.

Inhibition. Prohibition, or checking, of an action or process.

Initial. Undifferentiated cell which remains within the meristem indefinitely and adds cells to the plant body by division.

Initial point. The origin point of the standard rectangular survey system, the intersection of a baseline and a principal meridian.

Inland Empire. Area lying between the crests of the Cascade Mountains and Bitterroot Mountains, and extending from the Okanogan Highlands to the Blue Mountains of northeastern Oregon. Timber production is very important in this region.

Integration (economics). Expansion of a firm into production of other, often closely related, types of products (horizontal integration) or into prior or later stages of the production of a given product (vertical integration).

Intercellular space. Space between the cells of a tissue.

Interception. (1) The process by which rainwater is caught and held on the leaves of trees and vegetation and is returned to the air by evaporation without reaching the ground. (2) The part of precipitation caught by vegetation.

Internode. Portion of a stem or branch that is between two successive nodes.

Intolerance, shade. See *Shade tolerance*.

Ion. Electrically charged atom or group of atoms.

J

Juvenile wood. Wood formed close to the central core of the tree that contains a high percentage of thin-walled cells.

K

Kerf. The narrow slot cut by a saw advancing through the wood.

Kiln-dry. Dried in a kiln to a specified range of moisture content.

Knot. Portion of a branch enclosed in the xylem by the natural growth of the tree.

Kraft pulp. Chemical wood pulp obtained by cooking—that is, digesting wood chips in a solution of sodium hydroxide (caustic soda) and sodium sulfide.

L

Lammas shoot. Abnormal shoot formed late in the summer from expansion of a bud that was not expected to open until the following year.

Landsat. An unmanned, earth-orbiting satellite of the National Aeronautics and Space Administration that transmits images to earth receiving stations; designed primarily for collection of earth resources data.

Larva. Immature, wingless, feeding stage of an insect that undergoes complete metamorphosis.

Lateral meristems. Meristems which give rise to secondary tissue; the vascular cambium and cork cambium.

Lattice. Crossed strips with open spaces between to give the appearance of a screenlike structure.

Leaching. Removal of soluble substances (e.g., from soil or timber) by percolating water.

Leaf primordium. Lateral outgrowth from the apical meristem that will become a leaf.

Lenticel. Small breathing pore in the bark of trees and shrubs; a corky aerating organ that permits gases to diffuse between the plant and the atmosphere.

Lesion. Circumscribed diseased area.

Lignification. Impregnation with lignin, as in secondary walls of xylem cells. See *Lignin.*

Lignin. Noncarbohydrate (phenolic), structural constituent of wood and some other plant tissues; encrusts the cell walls and cements the cells together.

Lignocellulosic. Of materials containing both lignin and cellulose; a characteristic of higher forms of terrestrial plants.

Lignosulfonic acid. Soluble derivative of lignin produced in the sulfite pulping process and present—in the form of salts (lignosulfonates)—in the waste liquor.

Limiting factor. Environmental factor needed by an organism but in shortest supply.

Linear programming. A mathematical programming technique which either maximizes or minimizes a single, linear objective function. The objective function may be subjected to sets of linear equalities or inequalities, called constraints.

Lithosphere. Crust of the earth.

Littoral. Of vegetation growing along a seashore or very large lake. See *Riparian.*

Loam. Rich friable soil containing a relatively equal mixture of sand and silt and somewhat smaller proportion of clay.

Loess. Particles, mostly silt-sized, transported and deposited by wind.

Log rule. Table showing the estimated or calculated amount of lumber that can be sawed from logs of given length and diameter.

Lumen. Cell cavity (often hollow).

M

Macerate. To soften, or separate the parts of a substance by steeping in a liquid, with or without heat.

Mast. Nuts and seeds of trees, serving as food for livestock and wildlife.

Mature. Stage of tree growth when height growth slows and crown expansion and diameter increase and become marked. See *Seedling, Sapling, Pole, Senescent.*

Megasporangium. The ovule-bearing structure in gymnosperms.

Mensuration, forest. Science dealing with the measurement of volume, growth, and development of individual trees and stands and the determination of various products obtainable from them.

Merchantable height. The height above the ground, or in some cases above stump height, to which the tree stem is salable.

Meristem. Undifferentiated plant tissue from which new cells arise. See *Apical meristem, Lateral meristems.*

Mesarch succession. Primary succession beginning on an intermediate substrate that is neither open water nor solid rock, such as a recent mudflow or glacial moraine. See *Hydrarch, Xerarch succession.*

Mesophyll. Parenchyma tissue in a leaf between the upper and lower epidermis.

Methanol. Methyl alcohol, CH_3OH; a colorless, volatile liquid, a product of the destructive distillation of wood, derived mainly from the lignin; also manufactured synthetically.

Microclimate. Climate of small areas, especially insofar as this differs significantly from the general climate of the region.

Microsporangium. The pollen sac of a staminate cone in gymnosperms.

Microwave. A very short electromagnetic radiation wave between 1 meter and 1 millimeter in wavelength or 300 to 0.3 gigahertz in frequency.

Middle lamella. Layer of intercellular material,

rich in lignin and pectic compounds, cementing together the primary walls of adjacent cells.

Mineralization. Breakdown of organic compounds in soil releasing inorganic constituents that can be taken up by plant roots.

Monocotyledones. One of the two classes of angiosperms; a plant whose embryo has one seed leaf.

Monoculture. Crop of a single species, generally even-aged. See *Even-aged stand.*

Monoecious. A condition in which both staminate and pistillate flowers (or pollen and seed cones of conifers) are borne on the same plant. See *Dioecious.*

Monophagous. Feeding on a single host species.

Morphology. Study of form and its development.

Mortality. Volume of trees killed by natural causes in a given time or a given forest, exclusive of catastrophes.

Multispectral scanner. A scanner system which simultaneously acquires images in various wavelength regions of the same scene.

Mutagen. Substance known to induce mutations.

Mutation. Sudden, heritable change in the structure of a gene or chromosome or some set thereof.

Mycelium. The mass of interwoven filaments or hypae making up the vegetative part of a fungus, as distinct from the fruiting body.

Mycoplasmas. Smallest of free-living organisms, lacking a cell wall, but possessing a distinct flexible membrane.

Mycorrhizae. Symbiotic association between non-pathogenic or weakly pathogenic fungi and living cortical cells of a plant root.

N

Naval stores. Historical term for resin products, particularly turpentine and rosin from pine trees; previously also pine tars and pitch.

Nematodes. Parasitic or free-living, elongated smooth worms of cylindrical shape; roundworms.

Niche. Status of a plant or animal in its community—that is, its biotic, trophic, and abiotic relationships. All the components of the environment with which an organism or population interacts, especially those necessary to its existence: its habitat.

Nitrification. Process whereby protein, amino acids, and other nitrogen compounds in the soil are oxidized by microorganisms, with the production of nitrates.

Nitrogen cycle. Worldwide circulation of nitrogen atoms in which certain microorganisms take up atmospheric nitrogen and convert it into other forms that may be assimilated into the bodies of other organisms. Excretion, burning, and bacterial and fungal action in dead organisms return nitrogen atoms to the atmosphere.

Nitrogen fixation. Conversion of elemental nitrogen (N_2) from the atmosphere to organic combinations or to forms readily utilizable in biological processes.

Node. Part of a stem or branch where one or more leaves or branches are attached.

Nodules. Enlargements or swellings on the roots of legumes and certain other plants inhabited by symbiotic nitrogen-fixing bacteria.

O

Oblique photograph. A photograph acquired with the camera axis intentionally directed between the horizontal and vertical orientations.

Oleoresin. Group of "soft" natural resins, consisting of a viscous mixture of essential oil (e.g., turpentine) and nonvolatile solids (e.g., rosin) secreted by the resin-forming cells of the pines and certain other trees.

Optical dendrometer. An instrument for measuring the upper stem diameters of trees to aid in accurate product scaling.

Organ. Structure composed of different tissues, such as root, stem, leaf, or flower.

Organic compounds. The compounds containing carbon that pertain to living organisms in general, and those compounds formed by living organisms.

Orthographic projection. Projection in which the lines are perpendicular to the plane of projection.

Orthophotograph. A photographic copy prepared from a perspective photograph in which the displacements of images caused by a tilt and relief have been removed.

Osmoregulation. Regulation of the osmotic pressure in the body by controlling the amount of water and salts in the body.

Osmosis. The diffusion of water, or any solvent, across a differentially permeable membrane. In the absence of other forces, movement of water during osmosis will always be from a region of greater water potential to one of lesser water potential.

Ovendry. Of wood dried to constant weight in a ventilated oven at a temperature above the boiling point of water.

Overgrazing. Grazing above and beyond the level that a given range can sustain without change.

P

Pacing. A simple method for measuring linear distance for surveys, when great accuracy is not required, whereby a person's individual premeasured pace is used as the measuring tool.

Panchromatic. Pertaining to films which are sensitive to a broad band of electromagnetic radiation, such as the entire visible part of the spectrum, and are used for broadband photographs.

Parallax. The apparent displacement of the position of an observed body with respect to a reference point or system, caused by a shift in point of observation.

Parallax wedge. A simplified stereometer for measuring object heights on stereoscopic pairs of photographs.

Parasite. Organism which lives in or on another living organism of a different kind and derives subsistence from it without returning any benefit. See *Predator, Saprophyte*.

Parenchyma. Tissue composed of living, thin-walled, brick-shaped cells; primarily concerned with the storage and distribution of food materials. Axial parenchyma cells are vertically oriented; ray parenchyma are laterally oriented.

Pathogen. Organism directly capable of causing disease in living material. See *Saprogen*.

Pectin. Complex organic compound (polysaccharide) present in the intercellular layer and primary wall of plant cells; the basis of fruit jellies.

Ped. Visible structural soil aggregate—for example, crumb, block, or prism.

Perforation. Gap in the cell wall lacking a pit membrane; occurs in vessel members of angiosperms.

Pericycle. Root tissue located between the epidermis and phloem.

Periderm. Outer protective tissue that replaces the epidermis; includes cork, cork cambium, and phelloderm.

Perspective projection. Projection in which the lines converge at an arbitrarily chosen station point, to represent on a plane the space relationships of natural objects as they appear to the eye. The perspective projection of the camera lens causes scale variations and displaces image positions.

pH. A measure of acidity; the logarithm of the reciprocal of the hydrogen ion concentration. The value 7 pH is neutral, the values above are alkaline, and the values below are acid.

Phelloderm. Tissue formed toward the inside of the plant by the cork cambium.

Phenol. Hydroxyl derivative of benzene, C_6H_5OH.

Phenology. Study of biological events as related to climate (Figure 7.3).

Phenotype. Outward appearance or physical attributes of an individual. See *Genotype*.

Pheromone. Hormonal substance secreted by an individual and stimulating a physiological or behavioral response from an individual of the same species.

Phloem. Tissue of the inner bark; contains sieve

elements through which carbohydrates are transported.

Photogrammetry. The art or science of obtaining reliable measurements by means of photography.

Photograph. A representation of targets formed by the action of light on silver halide grains of an emulsion.

Photographic scale. An expression or ratio stating that one unit of distance on a photograph represents a specific number of units of actual ground distance.

Photoperiod. Duration of daily exposure to light; length of day favoring optimum functioning of an organism.

Photosynthesis. Synthesis of carbohydrates from carbon dioxide and water by green plant cells in the presence of light, with oxygen as a by-product.

Phototropism. Growth movement in which the direction of the light is the determining factor, as the growth of a plant toward a light source; turning or bending response to light.

Physiography. A general description of nature or natural phenomena; the science of physical geography.

Physiology. Study of the vital functions of living organisms. *Note:* Differences in physiological character may not always be accompanied by morphological differences.

Phytochrome. Chemical compound used by plants to detect daylength.

Piedmont. Plateau between the coastal plain and the Appalachian Mountains.

Pioneer community. First stage in the ecological development of a community.

Pit. Gap or recess in the secondary cell wall that facilitates the interchange of materials between cells.

Pith. Ground tissue occupying the center of the plant stem or root, within the vascular cylinder; usually consists of parenchyma.

Pixel. A picture element or cell within a spatially ordered matrix of numbers.

Planer. Machine for surfacing sawed timber.

Plasmolysis. Contraction of the cytoplasm because of removal of water from the protoplast by osmosis.

Pole. Still-young tree larger than 4 inches (10 centimeters) dbh, up to about 8 inches (20 to 23 centimeters) dbh; during this stage, height growth predominates and economic bole length is attained. See *Seedling, Sapling, Mature, Senescent.*

Polymerization. Transformation of various low-molecular-weight compounds (monomers) into large molecules—that is, polymers.

Polyphagous. Feeding on many different host species.

Predator. Any animal which preys externally on others—that is, hunts, kills, and feeds on a succession of hosts. See *Parasite.*

Prescribed burning. Controlled use of fire to further certain planned objectives of silviculture, wildlife management, fire hazard reduction, and so forth.

Present net worth. Single amount measuring the net current value of a stream of future revenues and costs.

Price index. Price of a good or group of goods in any year divided by the price of the same good or group of goods in a base year. See *Relative price index.*

Price leadership. Determination of prices by one or a few firms, with other producers in the industry tacitly accepting the prices thus determined.

Primary growth. Growth originating in the apical meristem of shoots and roots. See *Secondary growth.*

Primary succession. Succession beginning on a substrate that did not previously support vegetation, such as open water, fresh glacial moraine, or bare rock. See *Secondary succession.*

Primordia. A cell or organ in its earliest stage of differentiation.

Profile, soil. Vertical section of the soil through all

its horizons and extending into the parent material.

Progeny. Offspring produced from any mating.

Progeny test. Evaluation procedure in which parents are rated based on the performance of their offspring.

Protoplasm. Living substance of all cells.

Protoplast. Entire contents of the cell, not including the cell wall.

Provenance. Natural origin of seeds or trees, usually synonymous with "geographic origin," or a plant material having a specific place or origin.

Pulp. Fibers separated by mechanical or chemical means; the primary raw material from which paper is made.

Pupa. Insect in the nonfeeding, usually immobile, transformation stage between larva and the adult. *Pupae* (plural).

Pyroligneous acid. Aqueous portion, after separation of the tar, of the liquor obtained during the destructive distillation of wood; a complex mixture of water (80 to 90 percent) and organic compounds. See *Destructive distillation.*

Pyrolysis. Subjection of wood or organic compounds to very high temperatures and the resulting decomposition. See *Destructive distillation.*

Q

Quad. Unit of energy measure; 1×10^{15} British thermal units (Btu).

R

Radar. Acronym for radio detection and ranging, an active form of remote sensing that operates at wavelengths from 1 millimeter to 1 meter.

Radial increment. The diameter growth over a given period obtained by measuring the length of the last several annual rings in a core sample.

Radiation. The propagation of energy in the form of electromagnetic waves.

Rangeland. Areas unsuitable for cultivation, which are a source of forage for free-ranging native and domestic animals.

Ray. Laterally oriented, ribbon-shaped tissue extending radially in the xylem and phloem; functions in the lateral transport of water and nutrients.

Ray initial. An initial in the vascular cambium that gives rise to the ray cells of secondary xylem and secondary phloem.

Recombination. Formation of new combinations of genes as a result of segregation in crosses between genetically different parents.

Recurrence interval. Frequency of fires in a given stand.

Reflectance. The ratio of the radiant energy reflected by a body to that incident upon it.

Reflectance, spectral. Reflectance measured at a specific wavelength interval.

Regeneration. Renewal of a tree crop, by natural or artificial means.

Regulated forest. Forest which produces a continuous flow of products of about the same size, quality, and quantity over time.

Relative price index. Price index for one good divided by the price index for another good or group of goods. The divisor is usually the wholesale or consumer price index.

Release cutting. Silvicultural treatment in which larger trees of competing species are removed from competition with desired crop trees.

Relief. The vertical irregularities of a surface.

Relief displacement. The geometric distortion on vertical aerial photographs. The tops of objects are located on the photograph radially outward from the base.

Remote sensing. Collection of data by a device that is not in physical contact with the object, area, or phenomenon under investigation—for example, aerial photography or satellite imagery.

Reproductive potential. Ability of a species to multiply in the absence of countervailing forces.

Resin. Pitch; the secretions of certain trees, oxidation or polymerization products of the terpenes, consisting of mixtures of aromatic acids and esters insoluble in water but soluble in organic solvents; often exuding from wounds.

Rest-rotation grazing. A system of range management whereby one portion of the land is left ungrazed (rested) for a full year; the next year another portion is rested.

Rhizome. Horizontal underground stem, usually containing stored food.

Rickettsia. Bacterialike microorganisms of the genus *Rickettsia,* parasitic on arthropods and pathogenic for human beings and animals.

Ring-porous wood. Wood (xylem) of hardwoods in which the earlywood vessels are much larger in diameter than vessels in the latewood; the vessels generally appear as a ring in a stem cross section. See *Diffuse-porous wood.*

Riparian. Of vegetation growing in close proximity to a watercourse, small lake, swamp, or spring. See *Littoral.*

Root cap. Thimble-shaped mass of cells covering and protecting the growing root tip.

Root hairs. Tubular outgrowths of epidermal cells of the young plant.

Rosin. Solid residue after evaporation and distillation of the turpentine from the oleoresin of various pines, consisting mostly of rosin acids.

Rotation age. Period of years required to establish and grow timber crops to a specific condition of maturity. Applies only to even-aged management. See *Cutting cycle.*

Roundwood. Timber or firewood prepared in the round state—from felled trees to material trimmed, barked, and crosscut.

S

Saccharification. Conversion of the polysaccharides in wood or other plant material into sugars by hydrolysis with acids or enzymes.

Sahel. Semiarid region of Africa between the Savannas and the Sahara extending through Senegal, Mauritania, Mali, Niger, Sudan, northern Nigeria, and Ethiopia. Since the late 1960s this region has been afflicted by devastating drought leading to the starvation of hundreds of thousands of people.

Sapling. Young tree at least 1 meter (3 feet) high, but not larger than 10 centimeters (4 inches) dbh; crowns are well elevated and usually many lower branches have started to die. See *Seedling, Pole, Mature, Senescent.*

Saprogen. Organism capable of producing decay in nonliving organic material. See *Pathogen.*

Saprophyte. Plant organism which is incapable of synthesizing its nutrient requirements from purely inorganic sources and feeds on dead organic material. See *Parasite.*

Sapwood. Predominantly living, physiologically active wood; includes the more recent annual layers of xylem that are active in translocation of water and minerals. See *Heartwood.*

Sawlog. A log considered suitable in size and quality for sawn timber.

Scale. Estimated solid (sound) contents of a log or group of logs.

Scanner. An optical–mechanical imaging system in which a rotating or oscillating mirror sweeps the instantaneous field of view of the detector. The two basic types of scanners are airborne and stationary.

Scarification. Wearing down, by abrasion or chemical treatment, of the bark or outer coat.

Scion. Detached living portion of a plant grafted onto another plant.

Sclerenchyma. Supporting tissue composed of cells with thick, often lignified secondary walls; may include fiber cells or sclereid cells.

Sclereid. Sclerenchyma cell with a thick, lignified secondary wall.

Secondary growth. Growth derived from lateral meristem; results in increase in girth. See *Primary growth.*

Secondary succession. Succession starting after the disturbance of a previously existing plant community. See *Primary succession.*

Sedimentation. Deposition or accumulation of mineral or organic matter.

Seedling. Youngest trees from the time of germination until they reach a height of 1 meter (3 feet). See *Sapling, Pole, Mature, Senescent*.

Seed orchard. Plantation of trees established to provide for the production of seeds of improved quality.

Seed tree method. Silvicultural system in which the mature timber is removed in one cut, except for a small number of seed trees left to provide a source of seed for the next crop. See *Clearcutting, Shelterwood method*.

Selection. Any discrimination by natural or artificial means that results in some individuals leaving more offspring than others.

Selection cutting. Silvicultural system in which scattered trees or small groups of trees are cut, providing sustained yield from an uneven-aged stand.

Selection differential. Difference between the value of a selected individual (or mean value of a selected population) and the mean value of the original unselected population.

Senescent. Growing old; aging stands at this stage are overmature; losses from mortality and decay may exceed additions in volume. See *Seedling, Sapling, Pole, Mature*.

Sensor. A device which receives electromagnetic radiation and converts it into a signal that can be displayed as data or an image.

Serotinous cones. Cones of some species of gymnosperms that are sealed by resin, requiring high temperatures to open the cones and release seeds.

Serpentine. Common mineral, hydrous magnesium silicate, $H_2Mg_3Si_2O_2$.

Shade tolerance. Capacity of trees to reproduce and grow in the shade of and in competition with other trees. See Tables 6.1 and 14.1.

Shelterwood method. Silvicultural system in which the mature timber is removed, leaving sufficient numbers of trees standing to provide shade and protection for new seedlings. See *Clearcutting, Seed tree method*.

Shifting cultivation. Itinerant forms of agriculture, common in tropical regions, whereby the farmers clear a parcel of the forest and cultivate the soil until it becomes unproductive, then move onto another area where the process is started anew.

Shoot. Aboveground portion of a vascular plant.

Short-duration grazing. A system of range management employing a large number of separate pastures grazed individually for short periods of time, generally two days to two weeks.

Shrub. Woody perennial plant, seldom exceeding 10 feet in height, usually having several persistent woody stems branching from the ground.

Side-looking radar. An all-weather, day–night remote sensor which is particularly effective in imaging large areas of terrain; it generates energy that is transmitted and received to produce a photolike picture of the ground. Also called side-looking airborne radar.

Sieve element. Cell of the phloem concerned with the long-distance transport of food substances. Classified into sieve cells (gymnosperms) and sieve tube members (angiosperms).

Silvichemicals. Chemicals derived from wood and trees.

Silviculture. Manipulation of forest vegetation to accomplish a specified set of objectives; controlling forest establishment, composition, and growth.

Site index. A particular measure of site quality based on the height of the dominant trees in a stand at an arbitrarily chosen age.

Site quality. A loose term denoting the relative productivity of a site for a particular tree species.

Size, sizing. Additive introduced to modify the surface properties of manufactured board or paper.

Skidding. Loose term for hauling logs by sliding, not on wheels.

Slash. Open area strewn with debris of trees from felling or from wind or fire; the debris itself.

Slurry. Watery suspension of insoluble matter—that is, pulp slurry.

Snag. Standing dead tree from which the leaves and most of the branches have fallen.

Soil–plant–atmosphere continuum. The continuous column of water that begins in the soil, travels across the roots, up the xylem within the roots and stem, through the xylem in leaf vascular bundles, to the wet surfaces of the mesophyll cells, and continues by evaporating into the atmosphere, all of which results in a close coupling of evaporation and uptake of water by a siphonlike action.

Specific gravity. As applied to wood, the ratio of the ovendry weight of a sample to the weight of a volume of water equal to the volume of the sample at some specific moisture content.

Spectral reflectance. The reflectance of electromagnetic energy at specified wavelength intervals.

Spectral-reflectance curve. A plot of the reflectance of electromagnetic energy for a series of wavelengths.

Spectral response. The response of a material as a function of wavelength to incident electromagnetic energy, particularly in terms of the measurable energy reflected from and emitted by the material.

Spectral-response envelope. The range of frequencies in which the spectral response is greatest.

Spectrum. A continuous sequence of energy arranged according to wavelength or frequency.

Sporangium. A hollow unicellular or multicellular structure in which spores are produced.

Spot fire, spotting. Fire set outside the perimeter of the main fire by flying sparks or embers.

Stand density. The average total basal area per acre of a given stand.

Stand table. A table showing the number of trees by species and diameter (or girth) classes, generally per unit area of a stand.

Stenotopic. Organisms limited to a very specific habitat.

Stereogram. A stereopair of photographs or drawings correctly oriented and permanently mounted for stereoscopic examination.

Stereomodel. A three-dimensional mental impression produced by viewing the left and right images of an overlapping pair with the left and right eye, respectively.

Stereopair. A pair of photographs which overlap in area and are suitable for stereoscopic examination.

Stereoplotter. A device which will plot as a contour map data obtained from aerial photographs; operates by means of a stereoscopic instrument.

Stereoscope. A binocular optical device for viewing overlapping images or diagrams to obtain the mental impression of a three-dimensional model.

Stereoscopic image. The mental impression of a three-dimensional object that results from stereoscopic vision.

Stereoscopy. The science or art which deals with three-dimensional effects and the methods by which these effects are produced.

Stomata. Openings in the surface of a leaf through which water vapor, carbon dioxide, and oxygen pass.

Stratification. Placing dormant seeds between layers of moist material, usually a sand and peat mixture, and exposing them to low temperatures to satisfy the pregermination chilling requirements.

Structure, soil. Combination or arrangement of primary soil particles (e.g., sand, silt, clay) into secondary particles called peds. See *Ped.*

Stumpage. Value of timber as it stands uncut, uncut marketable timber.

Suberin. Fatty material in cell walls of corky bark tissue.

Subsoil. Bed or stratum of earth or earthy material immediately under the surface soil.

Substrate. Underlying material; the soil beneath plants or animals; the material on which an enzyme or fermenting agent acts, on which adhesive is spread, or on which a fungus grows or is attached.

Succession. Change in community composition and structure through time.

Sulfite pulp. Chemical wood pulp obtained by cooking—that is, digesting wood chips in a solution of bisulfites and sulfurous acid.

Suppressed. Pertaining to trees with crowns completely overtopped by surrounding trees so that they receive almost no direct sunlight. See *Dominant*.

Surface fire. Fire which burns only surface litter, loose debris of the forest floor, and small vegetation. See *Ground fire*.

Survivor growth. The increase in timber volume of a given stand owing to the continuing growth of previously measured trees. See *Ingrowth*.

Sustained yield. Yield a forest can produce continuously, such as timber.

Sweep. Curve in stem or log as distinct from an abrupt bend, generally as a reaction to environmental conditions.

Symbiosis. Mutually beneficial relationship between two dissimilar living organisms, called symbionts. In some cases, the symbionts form a single body or organ, as in mycorrhizae or lichens.

Synecology. Study of the community and its environment.

Syngas. Synthesis gas; a synthetically produced gas containing two parts hydrogen (H_2) and one part carbon monoxide (CO).

Systemic. Of a pathogen, capable of spreading throughout its host. Of a pesticide, absorbed by a plant so as to be lethal to agents that feed on it.

Systems analysis. Method of analysis which deals with the movement of energy or materials to different parts or components of a complex system.

T

Tall oil. By-product of the kraft pulping of resinous woods (e.g., pine), consisting mainly of resin acids and fatty acids.

Tannins. Complex extracellular water-soluble substances, generally formed from a variety of simpler polyphenols; part of wood extractives.

Terpenes. Class of hydrocarbons, with their derivatives, commonly occurring in many species of wood and generally having a fragrant odor; characteristically noted with pine trees.

Texture, photo image. The frequency of change and arrangement of tones; descriptive adjectives for textures are fine, medium, or coarse, and stippled or mottled.

Texture, soil. Relative proportion of the various mineral particles such as sand, silt, and clay, expressed as a textural class—for example, sandy loam, clay loam.

Thermal band. A general term for middle-infrared wavelengths that are transmitted through the atmosphere window at 8 to 13 micrometers; also used for the windows around 3 to 6 micrometers.

Thermal radiation. The electromagnetic radiation emitted by a hot blackbody, such as the filament of a lamp.

Thermal scanner. A detector which sweeps the instantaneous field of radiant energy across the terrain in either the 3- to 5-micrometer or 8- to 14-micrometer region of the spectrum.

Thermochemical liquefaction. Decomposition of organic compounds to smaller molecules often in the form of an oil. The reaction is usually carried out in the presence of a catalyst and hydrogen or synthesis gas at high pressure and temperature.

Thinning. Silvicultural treatment in which stand density is reduced to accelerate diameter growth in remaining trees.

Threshold dosage. The minimum dose necessary to produce a measurable effect in a given organism.

Throughfall. All the precipitation eventually reaching the forest floor—that is, direct precipitation plus canopy drip.

Tissue. Group of similar cells organized into a structural and functional unit.

Tissue system. Tissue or group of tissues organized into a structural and functional unit in a plant or plant organ.

Tone. Each distinguishable shade of gray from white to black on an image.

Tracheary element. Tracheid or vessel member.

Tracheid. Elongated, thick-walled conducting and supporting cell of xylem. Has tapering ends and pitted walls without perforations. Found in nearly all vascular plants; the main fibrous component of wood. See *Vessel member*.

Tree. Woody perennial plant, typically large and with a single well-defined stem and a more or less definite crown.

Triploid. Individual having one set of chromosomes more than the typical number for the species.

Trophic, -troph, Tropho-. Pertaining to nutrition, feeding.

Trophic levels. Steps in the movement of energy through an ecosystem.

Turgor. Normal distention or rigidity of plant cells, resulting from the pressure exerted from within against the cell walls by the cell contents.

Turpentine. Essential oil which can be obtained by distilling the oleoresin of conifers, particularly pines, consisting of a mixture of terpenes. Most turpentine is now obtained as a by-product of the kraft pulping of pines.

U

Understory. Any plants growing under the canopy formed by others. See *Canopy*.

Uneven-aged stand. Stand in which more than two distinct age classes and a range of size classes (seedling, sapling, pole, etc.) are present.

Ultraviolet radiation. Electromagnetic radiation of shorter wavelength than visible radiation but longer than X rays; roughly, radiation in the wavelength interval between 10 and 4000 angstroms.

Uptake. Amount of water and nutrients absorbed by vegetation.

V

Vascular cambium. Cylindrical sheath of meristematic cells, the division of which produces secondary xylem and secondary phloem.

Vascular tissue. Specialized conducting tissue in plants forming a vascular system—in woody plants making up the whole of the xylem and phloem.

Vector. Any agent capable of transporting a pathogen or saprogen to a host.

Veneer. Thin sheet of wood of uniform thickness, produced by rotary cutting or by slicing.

Vessel member. Elongated cell of the xylem characterized by perforations. Its function is to conduct water and minerals through the plant body. Found in nearly all angiosperms and a few other vascular plants. See *Tracheid*.

Visible radiation. Energy at wavelengths from 0.4 to 0.7 micrometer that is detectable by the eye.

Volatiles. Essential oil distilled from plant tissues, generally characterized by a low boiling point.

Volume table. Table showing the average cubic contents of trees or logs by diameter and merchantable length in a specified unit of volume.

W

Watershed. Total area above a given point on a river, stream, or other waterway, that contributes water to the flow at that point.

Watershed management. The analysis, protection, repair, utilization, and maintenance of drainage basins for optimum control and conservation of water with regard to other resources.

Water stress. Stress or negative pressure exerted on a water column in a plant owing to transpiration.

Water table. Upper surface of the groundwater. A perched water table is one separated by relatively impermeable material from an underlying body of groundwater; may be seasonally impermanent.

Wavelength. The distance between successive wave crests, or other equivalent points, in a harmonic wave. The symbol is λ.

Weathering. The physical and geothermal processes by which rock minerals are broken up and decomposed.

Wholesale price index (WPI). Weighed average of wholesale prices of a representative bundle of goods and services produced by the economy. The rate of increase (decrease) in the WPI is one measure of the rate of inflation (deflation) in the economy.

Wood. Secondary xylem.

Woody plants. Trees or shrubs exhibiting secondary growth.

X

Xerarch succession. Primary succession beginning on a substrate that is solid rock and therefore has minimal water-storing capacity.

Xeric. Of, pertaining to, or adapted to a dry environment.

Xylem. Tissue containing tracheary elements through which water and minerals are transported; wood is secondary xylem.

Y

Yard. To haul logs to a central spot to prepare them for transport.

Index